U MEN

ANNA WENT and TARGET VIBES

DAY THE 13th! 9 o'clock PM
4th APRIL

RAVEN IMAGE 311 S. WASHINGTON ST.

10 MINUTE WARNING

U-MEN
YBGB

NOV. 12 $4

Metropolis 9PM
382-9495 207 Second South — Pioneer Square

DON'T STAY COMMER

MR POP U MEN

4$ DEC. 9

Metropolis
382-9495 207 Second South

MW01194960

Black
ROLAND BARKER
JESSE BERNSTEIN
AT THE GEORGETOWN STEAMPLANT
Big Black is the Best you can get.
MADE IN CHICAGO
SUNDAY AUGUST 9 6 P.M.
CAUTION - LIMITED CAPACITY
TICKETS SOLD IN ADVANCE ONLY
AVAILABLE AT FALLOUT RECORDS AND SKATEBOARDS AND
CELLOPHANE SQUARE
DIRECTIONS TO SHOW AVAILABLE WITH TICKET ONLY.
A BAND THAT YOU WILL NEVER SEE AGAIN IN A PLACE
THAT YOU'VE NEVER SEEN BEFORE

& FALLOUT RECORDS WELCOME

BIG BLACK FROM CHICAGO

AND THE NEW
MEN
WITH
FORMANCE ARTIST
N LANDE
BRUCE "SUBPOP" PAVITT
BY VIDEOALITY

MARCH 28 8PM
E LEGENDARY
OWBOX
EATER

APPEAR IN PERSON AT FALLOUT
3rd E. OLIVE WAY, CALL 233-BOMB
MARCH 15 AT 4 PM

CoCA MEMBERS FREE

EEN PIKE & PINE. ALL AGES. $6 AT THE DOOR
S BENEFIT THE CENTER ON CONTEMPORARY ART

BUTTHOLE SURFERS
GREEN RIVER WICKED ANGEL

DEC. 7 · 8:00

GORILLA GARDENS · 410 5th AVE (JACKSON)

OCTOBER 24 CENTRAL TAVERN
SAT. 9PM 21 AND OVER

KCMU WELCOMES

REDD KROSS
SOUNDGARDEN

$6.5 ADVANCE $8 DOOR

Tickets: FALLOUT, TIME TRAVELLERS, CELLOPHANE SQUARE, & THE CENTRAL

NUTEMEN
AG 13
EN
MELVINS

JULY 5th 8PM

NTAINEERS (NORWAY CENTER)
3rd AVE W. SEATTLE $6 ADV $7.00 AT DOORS
AT: CELLOPHANE, TIME TRAVELERS, ROXY, URBAN
RENEWAL, EASY STREET, KUBATO, DREAMLAND.
BUSSES 1,2,13,15,18,19,24,33!

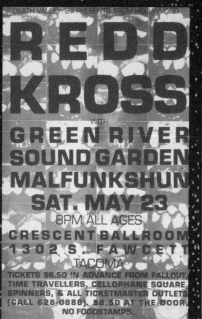

DEATH VALLEY '87 PRESENTS FROM HOLLYWOOD

REDD KROSS
WITH
GREEN RIVER
SOUND GARDEN
MALFUNKSHUN
SAT. MAY 23
8PM ALL AGES
CRESCENT BALLROOM
1302 S. FAWCETT
TACOMA
TICKETS $6.50 IN ADVANCE FROM FALLOUT,
TIME TRAVELLERS, CELLOPHANE SQUARE,
SPINNERS, & ALL TICKETMASTER OUTLETS
(CALL 628-0888). $8.50 AT THE DOOR.
NO FOODSTAMPS.

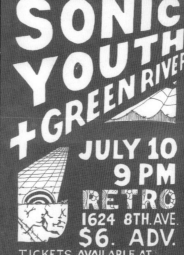

SONIC YOUTH
+ GREEN RIVER

JULY 10
9 PM
RETRO
1624 8TH. AVE.
$6. ADV.
TICKETS AVAILABLE AT
CELLOPHANE
SQUARE   FALL OUT
TIME TRAVELERS

U MEN
HELL COWS
FROM PORTLAND
THROWN UPS

SATURDAY, January 16, 1988

CENTRAL 207 1st Avenue S.

Guest DJ Chili
Bruce Pavitt

SUB POP USA

The Subterranean Pop Music Anthology, 1980–1988

BRUCE PAVITT

Bazillion
Points

Sub Pop USA

The Subterranean Pop Music Anthology, 1980–1988
by Bruce Pavitt

Copyright © 1980–2014 Bruce Pavitt

Second printing, published in 2015 by

Bazillion Points
61 Greenpoint Ave. #504
Brooklyn, New York 11222
United States
www.bazillionpoints.com
www.subpopusa.com

Produced for Bazillion Points by Ian Christe
Cover layout and design by Bazillion Points
Production coordination by Magnus Henriksson

Front and back cover artworks *Sub Pop 5, Sub Pop 7,* and *Sub Pop 9* © Charles Burns
Back cover photo: Sonic Youth, New York City, July 1988, by Michael Lavine.
Photographs © Charles Peterson, Michael Lavine, Bruce Pavitt, David Rauh, Jan Loftness

Bazillion Points thanks Bruce Pavitt, Jon Poneman, Michael Lavine, Charles Burns, Charles
Peterson, Mudhoney, Jad Fair, Dianna Dilworth, Vivienne, Fox, Jules Mayse, and all who made
this book possible. Special thanks to Jacob McMurray, Lauren Holderman, the EMP Archives,
Sub Pop Records, and the independent spirit of regional music uprisings everywhere.

ISBN 978-1-935950-11-0

Printed in China

All rights reserved. No part of this publication may be reproduced or transmitted in any form or by any means, electronic
or mechanical, including photocopy, recording, or any information storage and retrieval system, without prior permission
in writing from the publisher.

Previous overleaf: *Mudhoney, all-ages show with Swallow and Blood Circus, the Boxing Club (Pike and 10th, next to the
Comet Tavern), Seattle, July 8, 1988.* CHARLES PETERSON

Table of Contents

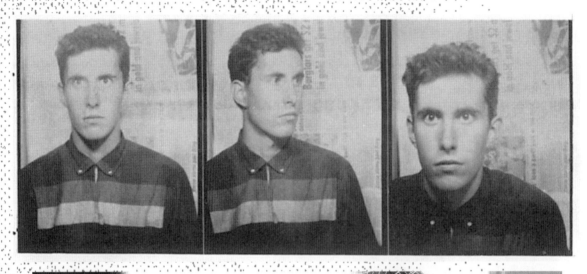

From top: *Bruce Pavitt photo booth strip, Chicago, summer 1980; Checkered shirt projection portrait, Olympia, WA, spring 1981.*

Bruce Pavitt

Welcome to Sub Pop Country

I started Sub Pop because I believe in the localization of culture.

As a teenager growing up in Park Forest, Illinois, an hour south of Chicago, I thankfully discovered the first two Devo singles on Booji Boy Records, which were life changers for me. Realizing that music so bizarre and interesting could happen in Akron, Ohio, reformatted my synapses and became a huge inspiration. Around the same time, I also picked up a regional fanzine called *CLE*, from Cleveland, which featured an index of bands from all around Ohio, most notably Pere Ubu. The idea that an obscure regional location like Ohio could be so abundant in creativity just completely changed my outlook on music. A lightbulb went off in my head; small towns and cities were capable of creating great art, great music. From the summer of 1977 onward, I started to hunt for regional independent records.

Wax Trax!, one of the greatest record stores ever, opened up in Chicago around Thanksgiving of 1978. I spent a lot of time rummaging through their bins. I would also go to the local library every week just to grab the *Village Voice* and see who was playing at CBGB. I was highly aware that there was this key club in New York that featured original music. Indie bands from all around the country wanted to play at that club. Things started to click. I realized the freakiest, most interesting stuff was happening on the fringes, whether that was Devo in Akron or Teenage Jesus and the Jerks in NYC. These regional bands became an obsession of mine.

I managed to make it to New York in the spring of 1978, and I caught the B-52's at Max's Kansas City. Though there were only about twenty people in the room, that show was the most unique musical experience of my life up to that point. Once again, the B-52's were a regional band from the middle of nowhere, Athens, Georgia, coming up with their own unique way of looking at the world. They flipped my switch.

I realized that any scene anywhere could blow up. Olympia, Washington, could blow up. Seattle could blow up. Really, all any scene needs is a modest support system and some media attention. Devo, the B-52's, CBGB, *CLE* magazine, Wax Trax! Records—all these became huge influences. They were all part of an inspired network of enthusiastic amateurs. This is what I was thinking when I ventured west to go to school.

When I enrolled at the Evergreen State College in Olympia, Washington, in 1979, I started hosting a show, *Subterranean Pop*, on KAOS Radio. Through that, I connected with John Foster from *OP* magazine. Both KAOS and *OP* promoted independently released music and furthered my ongoing interest in indie bands and labels. This indie music obsession eventually became an academic focus and pretty much the only thing I thought about for the decade of the '80s, eventually leading up to launching a record label.

•

In May of 1980, I published 500 copies of my first zine, *Subterranean Pop* #1. It was a modest beginning for a project that ultimately morphed into Sub Pop

Records, the Seattle record label that most notably in 1988 signed an unknown local band named Nirvana. Throughout the genesis of Sub Pop, I always maintained that culture starts at home, in local communities, through creative interaction. Revolutions always come up from the grass roots, not top-down through corporate hierarchies.

Initially, there was very little distribution available for indies in the States. The only companies that dealt with small operators were Rough Trade and Systematic in San Francisco, and Jem Imports in New York. I started at ground zero. My thinking was that instead of sending a sample to one of these distributors, I would gamble. I packaged all five hundred copies and sent them directly to Systematic. And so one day they just arrived en masse at the Systematic compound. I made the box look really interesting by covering it in graph paper and putting clear plastic on top of that; it was kind of an art piece. That grand gesture certainly grabbed their attention. Joe Carducci, who ran the company, sold out all of the copies and sent me a check. But he easily could have dumped all my zines in a Dumpster. That was a risk I took. Then again, I was reviewing everything they were distributing, and *Sub Pop* was probably the only zine doing that.

•

The *Sub Pop* zine project (and later, the *Sub Pop* column in the *Rocket*) actively promoted the "decentralization of pop culture" by reviewing independently released recordings, organized by city or region. I wanted to emphasize the tribal energy and flavor of different local, punk-influenced music scenes, as documented by the recordings of the alternative artists from those areas. Non-mediacentric locales that were ignored or deemed insignificant, like Seattle, were especially important to me. Although the punk rock revolution of the late '70s hinted at DIY and regionalism, there was still a long way to go, and I felt that local self-empowerment was absolutely the key to challenging corporate control of youth music. Hence, hundreds and hundreds of indie record reviews appear in this *Sub Pop* compendium.

The reviews and commentary presented in *Sub Pop USA* were all written between 1980 and 1988. Although the writings represent brief, first impressions, there is a depth to the variety of styles and regions represented. As such, I believe this collection serves as a fairly broad index of '80s indie American culture. Some of this music is currently available through digital distribution, or, through the right channels, as collectable vinyl rarities. Much of it is forgotten or lost.

I hope this compilation of writing about independent recordings serves as a unique anthropological guide for those of you who are intrigued by the ancient, pre-Internet, pre-*Nevermind* era of the 1980s.

Clockwise from top: *KAOS Radio DJs* (from left) *Cherri Knight, John Foster, Steve Fisk, Bruce Pavitt, Olympia, WA, summer 1981.*
Graffiti by Stella Marrs. **DAVID RAUH;** *Winter 1980, Olympia, WA; Summer 1981, Olympia, WA.*

ABOVE: *The complete run of Sub Pop zines, #1–#9*

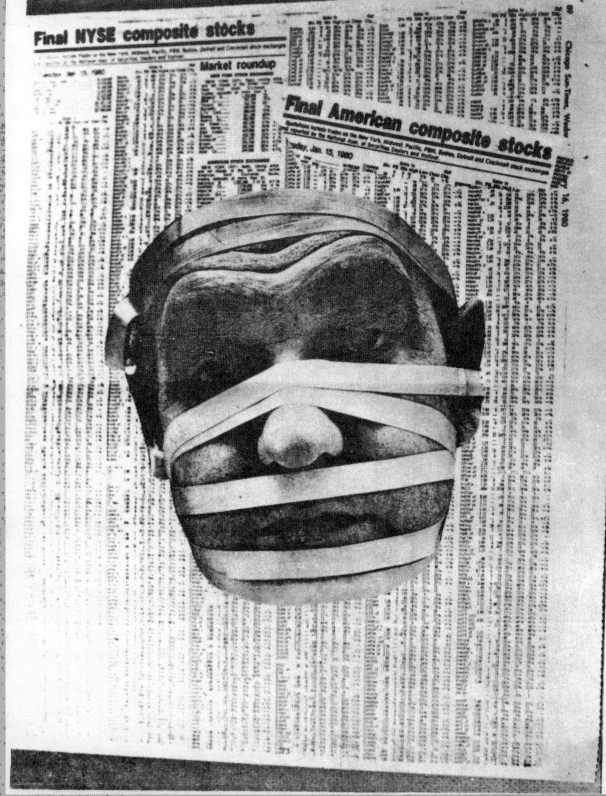

DOUG TAYLOR

EDITING, WRITING, LAYOUT. . . . . BRUCE PAVITT

SUBTERRANEAN POP IS A FANZINE DEDICATED TO IN-
DEPENDENT RECORDINGS FROM THE NORTHWEST AND THE
MIDWEST. ALL RECORD REVIEWS ARE HIGHLY PREJUDIC-
ED AND REFLECT THE PERSONAL TASTES OF THE EDITOR.
ALL PHOTOS WERE USED WITHOUT THE EXPRESS WRITTEN
CONSENT OF THE ARTISTS WHO TOOK THEM. SORRY.
SUBTERRANEAN POP IS PUBLISHED TRI-YEARLY. NEXT
ISSUE IS DUE OCTOBER 1980. PLEASE FEEL FREE TO
SEND ANY PHOTOS, PROMOS, INFO OR AMERICAN CURRENCY
TO SUBTERRANEAN POP C/O radio KAOS, olympia, wa.
98505. . . . .
BECAUSE THIS PUBLICATION CANNOT EXIST WITHOUT FUR-
THER FINANCIAL SUPPORT, ADVERTISEMENTS AND SUBSCRIP-
TIONS WILL NOW BE AVAILABLE. SUBSCRIPTION RATES ARE
$2.00/yr. (INCLUDES POSTAGE). . . ADVERTISING RATES
ARE 5.00/quarter page, 20.00/full page. . . . . . .

SPECIAL THANX TO : LISA GENET, TONI HOLM, DAVE RAUH,

JOHN FOSTER, STEVE PETERS, RUSSEL BATTAGLIA, ANNE AND

DOUG TAYLOR . . . .

NEW POP!! MANIFESTO

As our teen-bongo, Space Age counter-culture becomes infiltrated by wimpoid TV "mop tops" in skinny ties and leather pants, it becomes apparent that the bland sameness of the pop suprastructure is with us once again. Once-adventurous bands who now opt for major label contracts are immediately becoming the robot-slaves of a system that is interested in one thing only -- money. Believe me, wealthy biz-execs who sit in their air-conditioned penthouses are not contemplating anarchy and invention. Likewise, the machine-like organisations they work for could care less about new sounds or new cultural heroes.

We must recognize the fact that BIG BEAT music (next to TV) is the dominant cultural force of our time. When people buy a record, they are not only plugging into the music, but into the values & lifestyles that are implied by that artist. By supporting huge New Hollywood music corporations, you (yes, you) are not only allowing middle-aged capitalists to dictate what goes over the airwaves, but you are giving them the go-ahead to promote macho pig-fuck bands whose entire lifestyle revolves around cocaine, sexism, money and more money. The '80s need new sounds, but just as importantly, they need new cultural heroes.

Only by supporting _new ideas_ by local artists, bands, and record labels
can the U.S. expect any kind of dynamic social/cultural change in the
1980s. This is because the mass _homogenization_ of our culture is due
to the claustrophobic _centralization_ of our culture. We need diverse,
regionalized, _localized_ approaches to all forms of art, music, and
politics. It is important to remember that bands like Pere Ubu, B-52's,
Specials, DEVO, Patti Smith, the Voidoids, the Romantics and Elvis
Costello all started on independent labels; and we all know that fat,
cigar-smoking dough-boys at Warner Bros. didn't give a fuck about these
bands until they realized there was a profit involved.

A few of the aforementioned bands have been able to maintain a sense of
strength and adventurousness since becoming employees of major corporations. Others definately have not (drop dead Patti). The important
thing to remember is this: the most intense music, the most original
ideas... are coming out of scenes you don't even know exist. Tomorrow's
pop is being realized _today_ on small decentralized record labels that
are interested in taking _risks,_ not making money.

2

SEATTLE

Seattle - Seattle has seen a lot of rock'n roll action since the SHOWBOX opened up in '79. Physically, it's a great club -big enough for "name" acts and small enough to make you feel like you're at a Party. Modern Productions, who manage the club, seem to be truly interested in support-ing local bands and opening shows to all age groups. It is not uncommon to see people from 4 to 40 dancing to new music. Modern Productions has also produced some excellent 45's - The Dishrags (Vancouver) and The Blackouts (Seattle). A third release, a 12" Pink Section (San Francisco) E.P., will be released this summer. If you would like to play at the "Showbox" contact Modern Productions (P.O. Box 2305 Seattle, WA 98111).

Other important factors of the Seattle scene include "Roscoe Louie", Lynda Barry, and radio. "Roscoe Louie", an art gallery, has done a force-ful job of supporting a number of abrasive young visionaries. They also hold verycrowded concerts and occasional fashion shows. If you're in the area, be sure to check them out.

Lynda Barry is a Seattle artist that deserves special mention. As a cartoonist, Lynda is probably the most intensely original spokeswoman of the 1980's. She has a precise, lacerating insight into the world of boys, girls, parents and teenagers. Through her work, anxieties and confrontations are examined with compassion and intelligence; she has been a very influential figure in the Northwest.

Another aspect of Seattle is radio; Seattle's KRAB-FM plays independent 45's a few hours each month. In contrast, Olympia's RADIO KAOS has one of the most extensive independent playlists in the U.S.; here one can hear abrasive pop at least 10 hours a week. RADIO KAOS plays any and all independent re-leases, so...send your promos to RADIO KAOS, CAB 305, Olympia, WA. 98505.

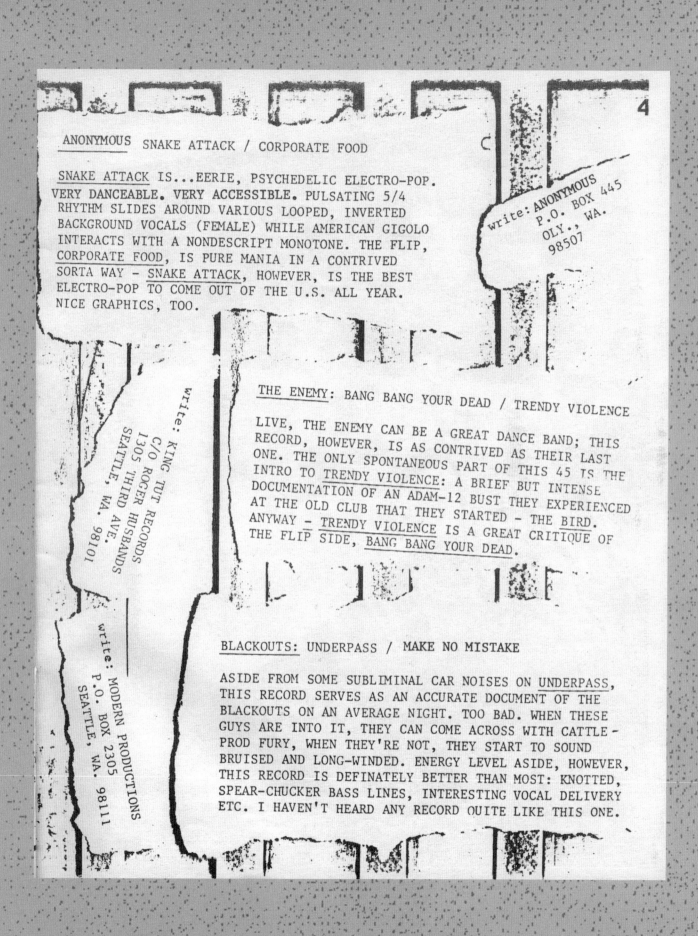

<u>ANONYMOUS</u> SNAKE ATTACK / CORPORATE FOOD

<u>SNAKE ATTACK</u> IS...EERIE, PSYCHEDELIC ELECTRO-POP.
VERY DANCEABLE. VERY ACCESSIBLE. PULSATING 5/4
RHYTHM SLIDES AROUND VARIOUS LOOPED, INVERTED
BACKGROUND VOCALS (FEMALE) WHILE AMERICAN GIGOLO
INTERACTS WITH A NONDESCRIPT MONOTONE. THE FLIP,
<u>CORPORATE FOOD</u>, IS PURE MANIA IN A CONTRIVED
SORTA WAY - <u>SNAKE ATTACK</u>, HOWEVER, IS THE BEST
ELECTRO-POP TO COME OUT OF THE U.S. ALL YEAR.
NICE GRAPHICS, TOO.

write: ANONYMOUS
P.O. BOX 445
OLY., WA.
98507

write: KING TUT RECORDS
C/O ROGER HUSBANDS
1305 THIRD AVE.
SEATTLE, WA. 98101

<u>THE ENEMY</u>: BANG BANG YOUR DEAD / TRENDY VIOLENCE

LIVE, THE ENEMY CAN BE A GREAT DANCE BAND; THIS
RECORD, HOWEVER, IS AS CONTRIVED AS THEIR LAST
ONE. THE ONLY SPONTANEOUS PART OF THIS 45 IS THE
INTRO TO <u>TRENDY VIOLENCE</u>: A BRIEF BUT INTENSE
DOCUMENTATION OF AN ADAM-12 BUST THEY EXPERIENCED
AT THE OLD CLUB THAT THEY STARTED - THE <u>BIRD</u>.
ANYWAY - <u>TRENDY VIOLENCE</u> IS A GREAT CRITIQUE OF
THE FLIP SIDE, <u>BANG BANG YOUR DEAD</u>.

write: MODERN PRODUCTIONS
P.O. BOX 2305
SEATTLE, WA. 98111

<u>BLACKOUTS</u>: UNDERPASS / MAKE NO MISTAKE

ASIDE FROM SOME SUBLIMINAL CAR NOISES ON <u>UNDERPASS</u>,
THIS RECORD SERVES AS AN ACCURATE DOCUMENT OF THE
BLACKOUTS ON AN AVERAGE NIGHT. TOO BAD. WHEN THESE
GUYS ARE INTO IT, THEY CAN COME ACROSS WITH CATTLE-
PROD FURY, WHEN THEY'RE NOT, THEY START TO SOUND
BRUISED AND LONG-WINDED. ENERGY LEVEL ASIDE, HOWEVER,
THIS RECORD IS DEFINATELY BETTER THAN MOST: KNOTTED,
SPEAR-CHUCKER BASS LINES, INTERESTING VOCAL DELIVERY
ETC. I HAVEN'T HEARD ANY RECORD QUITE LIKE THIS ONE.

LIFE ELSEWHERE (E.P.)... THE HOTTEST EXPERIMENTAL-POP TO COME OUT OF THE NORTHWEST WILL BE RELEASED THIS JUNE... FEATURING THE BEAKERS, JOHN FOSTER, AND STEVE FISK (A.K.A. ANONOMOUS), THIS EXPLOSIVE 12" WILL BE RELEASED ON THE VERY DISCREET MR. BROWN LABEL.

LOCAL BANDS:

(1) <u>The Blackouts</u> - A cross between XTC and a razor blade, these guys can be as inventive as any band from the U.S. or the U.K. Although usually long-winded and arrogant, their mix of subtle atonality and rousing pop harmonies can occasionally create a truly fun-filled vortex of modern anxiety.

(2) <u>The Beakers</u> - a new band on the scene, this interesting quartet has been destroying alotta good minds around here. Influences include <u>Talking Heads</u>, <u>Pere Ubu</u>, <u>Contortions</u>. Hyper-abstract sax and a beautiful rhythm section provides the soundtrack for lyrics like,
    "I'm lying on the floor... staring at the spot on the floor"
Fun. I don't know why, but this band <u>is</u> fun.

(3) <u>The Mac's Band</u> - A very distinctive pop trio that seems to be generally looked down upon around here. Maybe their name isn't trendy enough. Anyway- young, teen bass player shares the vocals with one of the most melodic guitarists around.

(4) <u>Psycho Pop</u> - Promising, high-energy teen band. Pass the amphatimines.

(5) <u>Larry & the Mondellos</u> - Very promising, very accesible new pop band. Too bad there's already a band called the Mondellos in Frisco.

(6) <u>FRED</u> : Unconventional new band. Sports the traditional
2 guitars,bass,drums line-up; however, their use of props
and their sense of humour keeps them heads above more "professional" bands.

(7) <u>The Debbies</u>: Conventional new band. An interesting sax, keyboards, bass, drum, guitar line-up does little to make this band sound interesting.

    Other, more success-oriented bands include the <u>Cowboys</u> (G. Parker influence), the <u>Girls</u> (female guitarist), the <u>News</u> etc.,etc.,etc. I should also mention the "new wave" of bar bands - <u>The Heats</u> (British Invasion), the <u>Nu Vitations</u> (good 60's R&B), <u>The Frazz</u> (60's anglo-pop), and the <u>Magnetics</u> (rockabilly). First wave bands like <u>Chinas Comidas</u> and <u>The Enemy</u> seem to be more comfortable in California these days. The Enemy, however, are supposedly collaborating with owner-manager Roger Husbands, to start a club called the "Gorilla Room"- the emphasis will be on video as well as music. As you might remember, these are the people who formed the original Seattle punk environment-"The Bird".

THE DISHRAGS

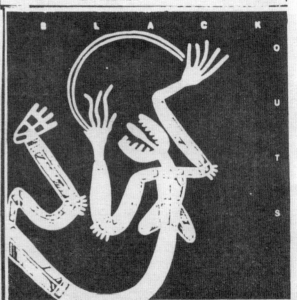

NEW RELEASES NORTHWEST

neo boys
dishrags
anonymous
blackouts

portland
vancouver
olympia
seattle

PORTLAND

local bands:

(1) Wipers- *great rock n' roll trio*
(2) Neo-Boys- *Fantastic all-girl teen-age band*
(3) Malchicks, Styphnoids - *high energy teen bands*
(4) Smegma, Sado-Nation - *local avant-garde*
(5) Odds- *good, new, R&R group*
(6) Bop Zombies- *rockabilly*
also... The Cleavers, The Rats, Johnny & the Distractions, Inputs.

Look out for a possible compilation L.P. of 10 or so local bands. Recorded live at the "Earth", There are tapes waiting to be pressed as soon as financial matters are resolved.

Portland - Portland is an important scene. Lotsa bands, some diverse 45's...more important however, is the sense of control and organization these bands have. First off, the local club, "The Long Goodbye" always has two shows: all ages and over 21. Great!

Secondly... most of these bands work together as a cooperative, and have created a general fund. This fund can be used for (1) helping a band put out a record, (2) helping to aid the influx of major out-of-town acts, -- (3) hiring both a sound and a video technician to record all acts at "The Long Goodbye". Outrageous! Since Portland is currently gaining 26 stations through cable T.V. a lot of these shows will eventually get airtime.

In short, Portland should serve as an excellent model for any scene that is interested in gaining control over its own cultural economy.

8

NEO BOYS: GIVE ME THE MESSAGE / NEVER COMES DOWN /
RICH MAN'S DREAM

ALONG WITH THE DISHRAGS, THE NEO BOYS HAVE CREATED AN ALL-GIRL,
TEEN-PUNK SOUND THAT SEEMS TO BE INDIGENOUS TO THE NORTHWEST.
BOTH BANDS HAVE THE SAME BEAUTIFUL, GIRL-TEEN HARMONIES, BUT
YOUR PARENTS MIGHT LIKE THE NEO BOYS A LITTLE BETTER (I.E. THEY!
DON'T SAY FUCK, THEIR GUITARS DON'T SOUND LIKE THEY WERE PLAYED
WITH BRICKS, ETC.)...VERY GOOD RECORD. PICK IT UP.

NEO BOYS
C/O TRAP RECORDS
P.O. BOX 42465
PORTLAND, OREGON
97242

(L.P.) WIPERS: IS THIS REAL?

ONE OF THE BEST INDEPENDENT L.P.'s TO COME OUT
OF THE U.S. THIS YEAR. WHILE NOT PRESENTING ANY-
THING OUTRAGEOUSLY NEW OR ORIGINAL, THERE IS AN
INCREDIBLE HONESTY CONVEYED BY THESE GUYS. NOT
AS DENSE AS MOST NEW ROCK, THE WIPERS SHOW AN
AMAZING AWARENESS OF EMOTIONAL INTERPLAY, TENSION
AND RELEASE. THEY'LL CONSTANTLY STRIP BACK A LAYER
OF SOUND, LEAVING ONLY THE BASS, DRUMS AND VOCALS;
WHEN THE GUITAR FINALLY RIPS IN, YOU FEEL IT. HAVE
PLAYED THIS RECORD ALOT. BE SURE TO CHECK OUT THE
6-TONE ALBUM JACKET-IMPRESSIVE.

write: PARK AVE. RECORDS
P.O. BOX 14947
PORTLAND, OREGON
97214

P
O
R
T
L
A
N
D

SMEGMA: FLASHCARDS / CAN'T LOOK STRAIGHT

INTERESTING AVANT-PUNK FROM PORTLAND. THE B-SIDE
IS A PAINFULLY RELAXING 3 MINUTES OF BARBITURATE
TAPE LOOPS. THE A-SIDE, FLASHCARDS, IS A DISSONANT
EXCURSION INTO THE WORLD OF SMALL CHILDREN AND THEIR
CLASSROOM ENVIRONMENT. FUN.

write: SYSTEMATIC DISTRIBUTORS
BERKELEY INDUSTRIAL COURT, SPACE 1
729 HEINZ AVE.
BERKELEY, CA. 94710

9

Vancouver - If you know what's happening in
Vancouver, drop me a line.

CANADA —

vanc
ouver

Briefly- Vancouver is home of a very good
indie label- "Quintessence". Local bands
include Pointed Sticks, Dishrags, Subhumans,
Female Hands, and Young Canadians.

QUINTESSENCE RECORDS
1869 W. 4TH AVE.
VANCOUVER, BRITISH COLUMBIA
CANADA

POINTED STICKS: (1) WHAT DO YOU WANT ME TO DO? / SOMEBODY'S MOM
(2) THE REAL THING / OUT OF LUCK
(3) LIES / I'M NUMB

SHARP, DRIVING POP. THE POINTED STICKS HAVE CREATED THE MOST
CONSISTENTLY EXCELLENT SERIES OF INDEPENDENT POP 45'S TO COME
OUT OF NORTH AMERICA. TEARING, HEART-THROB VOCALS, MUSCLE-BEACH
ORGAN HOOKS AND SOME TRULY INSPIRED LYRICS CREATE THE LOVE-POP
SOUND OF THE POINTED STICKS. THE SECOND RECORD, REAL THING/OUT
OF LUCK IS PROBABLY THE STRONGEST. THEIR LATEST IS GREAT BUT
SOUNDS OVERPRODUCED; PROBABLY INDICATIVE OF THEIR UPCOMING L.P.
ON STIFF.

DISHRAGS: PAST IS PAST / LOVE IS SHIT / TORMENTED

dishrags. . .

MODERN PRODUCTIONS
P.O. BOX 2305
SEATTLE, WA. 98111

MORE ABRASIVE THAN THE NEO BOYS OF PORTLAND, THIS
ALL-GIRL TEENAGE-TRIO COMES ACROSS MORE LIKE A
BRILLO PAD THAN A DISHRAG. FEELS GOOD, TOO. THE
B-SIDE HAS TWO SONGS THAT RIP THROUGH LOVE AND
REBELLION WITH RAMONES-LIKE ENERGY; AND THE A-SIDE
PAST IS PAST, IS AN ACHING, LIBERATED SONG ABOUT
NOT NEEDING THAT GUY ANY MORE. GOOD STUFF.

THE REAL THING

I'M NUMB

Pointed sticks. . .

QS104

10

Chicago!

Chicago- Despite being the second largest city
in the U.S., one rarely reads about Chicago in
major underground publications. One reason for
this is a lack of supportive media. <u>Praxis</u>, an
excellent art-pop magazine, displays a strong
interest in local artists, but tends to ignore
local bands; the music they do represent is usually
from N.Y. or the U.K. Likewise with <u>Coolest Retard</u>.

In a way, this attitude is typical of the way
Chicago looks at itself. It is interested in art
(via the Art Institute) and is cool to the latest
trends in Europe; however it is not supportive of
locally produced 45's. This is really depressing
as Chicago is responsible for some of the most
<u>original</u> records to come out of the U.S. Unfortun-
ately, due to lack of organization (and initiative)
most of these 45's have never been distributed
outside of the midwest.

Aside from the fact that Chicago produces a
great artzine, and has created some <u>excellent</u>
singles, what else is it noted for? "New Wave"
discos for one. Ever since "La Mere Vipere"
(now defunct) got people dancin' to records in
'77, several other alternative robot bop-hops
have opened up, including "O'Banions",and "Neo's"
(the best). As for clubs, there has never been a
decent place to play original dance music in Chicago.
You can't dance at "Gaspars";"Huey's", and "Mother's"
have always been interested in nothing but money,
and the "Park West" is the most insipid glitter-
disco environment imaginable. Apparently, "TUTS",
a club that opened last summer (and is now relocated
at the old "Quiet Knight" space) is actively interested
in promoting area bands. Lets hope so. Chances are,
however, that it will be just one more teen-age dance
club that won't let teenagers in without fake ID. For
the most part,in Chicago, the only <u>good</u> shows are at
<u>loft parties</u>. Here, teen rebels don't have to worry
about fake ID's; and better yet, weird art bands and
under 21 teen bands get to play in non-restrictive,
truly <u>supportive</u> environments.

11

LOCAL BANDS!

Dadistics-Developed out of the Art Institute of
Chicago. Although their live performances can be
fairly one-dimensional, their records are fantastic.
Currently signed with BOMP, they are re-releasing
both "Paranoa Perception" and "Modern Girl" on separate 45's.
Currently undergoing personnel changes, maybe their
live shows will become a little more dynamic. As it
stands, the _Dadistics_ will probably be the first
Chicago band to put out a really good album. (Sorry
Wazmo.).

Immune System/Poison Squirrel-Immune System, another
Art Institue band, split up into two bands last year.
Neither one is as good as the original.

Epicycle-Quite possibly the best live band in Chicago,
this mod-pop, teen-age quartet will be releasing their
their third single this summer.

Imports-Another great teen-age band. The 12 year old
drummer had to resign because it interfered with his
homework. Influences include Buzzcocks, Public Image.
Features 15 year old vocalist, 3 string bass player.
Lookout for upcoming record.

Skafish-Jimmy Skafish leads the only Chicago band to
do any extensive touring. Whether his tormented,
lunatic pop will eventually influence large masses
of U.S. citizens remains to be seen.

Wazmo Nariz-Although his early 45's were very interesting, this guy comes across as a stoopid,
suburban, jerk-off on stage

Jim Desmond- cross between David Thomas (Pere Ubu)
and Bruce Springsteen, this guy is a great performer.

Other local bands include: _Special Affects_. _Ferrari's_. _Bohemia-_ _Swingers_

Clox, _Minimal Graphics_,

Phil n' the Blanks,

Tutu and the Pirates- _Boulevard_, etc.,etc.

WAZMO NARIZ

WAZMO NARIZ: (1) TE-TE-TELEPHONE / GADABOUT
(2) THE E.P.

ALTHOUGH SOME FIND HIS QUIRKY CHARM TO BE PHONY
AND REPULSIVE, I HAPPEN TO FIND MR. WAZMO'S
RECORDS TO BE REFRESHINGLY ORIGINAL. CURRENTLY
SIGNED BY I.R.S., WAZMO HAS AN ALBUM OUT THAT
COST ONLY $1500 TO PRODUCE. UNFORTUNATELY, THIS
FINANCIAL FEAT IS A BIT MORE IMPRESSIVE THAN THE
RECORD ITSELF. SO... PICK UP HIS EARLY STUFF.
TE-TE-TELEPHONE IS AN UNDERGROUND POP CLASSIC
AND HIS E.P.'S WORTH PICKING UP ALSO.

                    write: FICTION RECORDS
                           P.O. BOX 375
                           WILMETTE, ILL. 60091

SPECIAL AFFECTS: INNOCENSE / DRESS ME DOLLS
                 IKNOW AH GIRL / VERTIGO FEELING

NO HYPER-NORMAL GUITAR CHORDS FOR THESE GUYS...
SPECIAL AFFECTS HAS CREATED AN E.P. OF VERY ORIGINAL
ROCK N' ROLL. SPIDERY LEAD GUITAR RACES ALONG W/SOME
EXCELLENT DRUMMING...LEAD VOCALIST FRANKIE FUN HAS
A GREAT VOICE, TOO (ALTHOUGH THE RECORDING DOES MAKE
HIM SOUND RATHER PROCESSED). INNOCENSE IS MY FAVE.
CHECK OUT THIS VERY GOOD, VERY OVERLOOKED RECORD.

                    write: SPECIAL AFFECTS
                           701 jefferson
                           CRETE, ILL, 60417

SKAFISH

these records   are not
                     new.

they are good. BUY
               THEM,

SKAFISH: DISGRACING THE FAMILY NAME / WORK SONG

AS PURE STATEMENT, THE COVER OF THIS 45 IS PROBABLY
MORE IMPORTANT THAN THE MUSIC INSIDE. NONE-THE-LESS,
THIS IS A RECORD WITH A DISTINCTIVE MUTANT-POP SOUND:
JIM SKAFISH'S BEAUTIFULLY OBNOXIOS NASAL DRONE, A
LUMBERING 1-4-5 ORGAN RIFF, PLUS AN OCCASIONAL FEMALE
CONTORTIONIST ON BACKGROUND VOCALS MAKES FOR QUITE A
PARTY. THE FLIP IS PURE GARY, INDIANA, "WORKS ALL DAY
IN STEEL MILL" ETC. PRESSED ON ILLEGAL RECORDS IN THE
U.K., FIND THIS ONE IN YOUR LOCAL IMPORT SHOP.

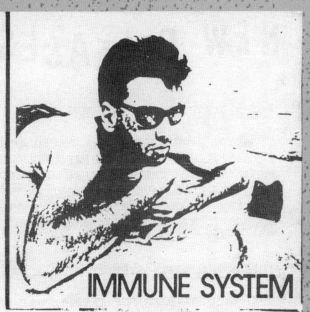

EPICYCLE: UNDERGROUND / DEPEND ON YOU
        IT'S YOU / DANCIN' SHOES

LIVE, THIS YOUNG, TEENAGE BAND PLAYS THE MOST
DYNAMIC SET OF POWER POP IN CHICAGO. THIS RECORD
IS NO EXCEPTION. UNDERGROUND IS PROBABLY THE BEST
TEEN-MALE ANTHEM SINCE THE SIMPLETONES DID
I LIKE DRUGS. FOR SOME HONEST, TEENAGE ROMANCE
CHECK OUT DEPEND ON YOU. THIS IS YET ANOTHER GREAT
RECORD THAT NEVER GOT OUT OF ILLINOISE. BUY IT OR
I'LL KILL YOU.

                write: CIRKLE RECORDS
                       C/O TERRY TURNER
                       657 ASH STREET
                       WINNETKA, ILL.
                       60093

                write: BRAILLE RECORDS
                       C/O SLIMALUNIE STUDIO
                       840 N. HARVEY
                       OAK PARK, ILL.
                       60302

IMMUNE SYSTEM: AMBIVELENCE AND SPARK PLUGS / SUBMERGED

ALTHOUGH A LITTLE TOO CUTE FOR MY TASTES, THIS RECORD
STILL REMAINS ONE OF THE MORE ORIGINAL 45'S TO COME OUT
OF 1979. "AMBIVELENCE..." WAS THE BIG HIT ON WXRT, BUT
MOST PEOPLE I KNOW SEEM TO PREFER THE WEAVING COUNTER -
POINT OF SUBMERGED. "WANNA BE A FROG MAN" THE MAN SINGS.
BASS AND TWO GUITARS SPIT OUT NOTES IN A SEEMINGLY RANDOM
PATTERN OF SONIC POLKA DOTS. AIMLESS...? NO. THIS SONG
IS ONE LONG, DANCABLE GROOVE.

                write: IMMUNE SYSTEM
                       C/O 1657 W. EVERGREEN
                       CHICAGO, ILL. 60622

t o d a y .

DADISTICS: MODERN GIRL / PARANOA PERCEPTION

CULT CLASSIC OF 1979. MODERN GIRL IS CLEVER, CATCHY
AND POWERFUL; THE PRODUCTION IS FULLY THOUGHT OUT
BUT NEVER SOUNDS CONTRIVED. GREAT MUSIC, GREAT PACK-
AGING, THIS RECORD IS AS DYNAMIC AND INVENTIVE AS ANY
POP 45 TO COME OUT OF THE U.S. I'M SERIOUS... THIS
RECORD IS A MUST.   THIS BAND HAS SIGNED
UP WITH BOMP... WATCH FOR UPCOMING RELEASES.)

NEW RELEASES...CHICAGO!

RAY MILLAND: TALK / DISTANT VIEW

TWISTED, AVANT DANCE-POP. NAMED AFTER THE TRASH B-MOVIE ACTOR, RAY MILLAND
IS A ST. LOUIS BAND WHO HAVE RELEASED A RECORD IN CONJUNCTION WITH PRAXIS
MAGAZINE. (BY THE WAY, THIS IS A REAL 45, NOT A FLEXI-DISC.) ANYWAY.......
THIS MUSIC IS HAUNTING, SCARY AND DEEPLY NEUROTIC. HIGHLY RECOMMENDED.....
ISSUES 4 + 5 OF PRAXIS COME ALONG WITH THIS RECORD, SO SEND 5.00 + POSTAGE
TO PRAXIS MAGAZINE, C/O JACKSON GREY GRAPHICS, ROOM 1202-A, 180 W. WASHING-
TON STREET, CHICAGO, IL. 60602

POISEN SQUIRREL: STEP BY STEP / IT'S ALL FIRE

TOXIC, BLUES-RIFF POP THAT SHOULD HAVE BEEN BURIED YEARS AGO...I HOPE WE'RE
NOT SEEING A REVIVAL. ON THE POSITIVE SIDE, THIS RECORD IS DANCEABLE AND IT
FEATURES SOME STRONG VOICE HARMONIES; BEST OF ALL, HOWEVER, IS THE GREAT
PSYCHO-POP BUTTON THAT COMES FREE WITH THE RECORD. SHARP FASHION, DULL MUSIC.
WRITE: ACME RECORDING, 3821 N. SOUTHPORT, CHICAGO, IL. 60613

MENTALLY ILL: GACY'S PLACE /

I HAVE NOT HEARD THIS RECORD. SUPPOSEDLY, IT'S THE FIRST REAL GARAGE-PUNK 45
TO COME OUT OF ILLINOIS. HAS BEEN RECIEVING WEST COAST AIR-PLAY...........
WRITE: AUTISTIC PRODUCTIONS, 26 GREENBRIAR, DEERFIELD, IL., 60015

MAR-VEL' MASTERS VOLUME 3: ROCK AND ROLL, ROCKABILLY, COUNTRY ROCK

SOME OF THE VERY BEST ROCKABILLY RE-ISSUES IN THE U.S. ARE COMING OUT OF
PARK FOREST, IL. ON COWBOY CARL RECORDS. "HOT WAX FOR BOPPIN' CATS".
MY FAVORITE CUTS OFF THIS ISSUE INCLUDE COME ON LET'S GO - CHUCK DALLIS AND
OH RICKY - BEVERLY SISTERS.
WRITE : COWBOY CARL RECORDS, P.O. BOX 116, PARK FOREST, IL. 60466

DADISTICS: PARANOIA PERCEPTION / CRY FOR ME

PARANOIA PERCEPTION, A RE-RELEASE, IS A GOOD POP TONE...SHARP GUITAR RHYTHMS
INTERPLAY WITH DRAMATIC SHIFTS IN MOOD AND TEMPO. CRY FOR ME IS DISAPPOINTING.
DESPITE SOME INTERESTING LYRICS, THIS OVERDRAWN, COMMERCIALLY INSPIRED TEAR-
JERKER IN NO WAY COMPARES WITH THEIR FIRST MASTERPIECE, MODERN GIRL.
WRITE : BOMP/QUARK C/O SLIMALUNIE STUDIOS, 840 N. HARVEY, OAK PARK, IL. 60302

LATE NEWS : BELUGA AND THE HUMAN ASHTRAYS, A COLLABORATION BETWEEN PERFORMANCE
ARTIST BELUGA AND TEEN BAND EPICYCLE HAS RESULTED IN A 45, MARS NEEDS WOMEN.
SPECIAL AFFECTS WILL SOON RELEASE THEIR NEW 45, NUCLEAR GLOOM / HEADACHE.

ed Endlessly !

I Was Tortured Endlessly !

Miracle mom victim of **Modern** Weird **Voodoo** Carnivorous Test-tube savage baby horror...

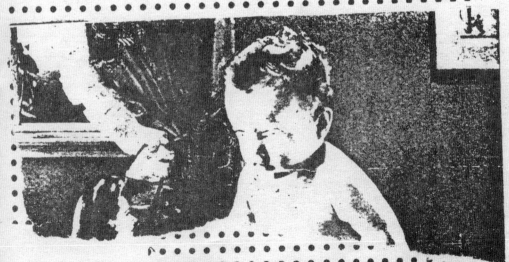

I Was Tortur

Minneapolis - This town is probably most noted for two strong, independent, record labels- "Twin Tone" and "Break'r". Other than that, you can go to the "Longhorn" and watch college kids smoke cigarettes to "New Wave" music... Seriously, we can't forget Marathon '80 - a great attempt at organizing a new-no wave music festival. Contortions, Feelies, Monochrome Set, etc. Nice try.

GREAT HITS OF MID-AMERICA VOL. 3 (DOUBLE L.P.)

TAKING THEIR CUE FROM 2 ANTHOLOGIES RELEASED YEARS AGO, TWIN-TONE HAS DONE AN EXCELLENT JOB W/THIS COMPILATION. TOO BAD EVERY BAND (EXCEPT THE SWINGERS) ARE FROM MINNEAPOLIS.

THE SUBURBS: IN COMBO (L.P.)

IT'S TAKEN ME 3 YEARS TO GET USED TO THE VOCALIST IN THIS BAND, AND IT'S BEEN WORTH THE WAIT. TALKING HEADS INFLUENCE RESULTS IN SHIFTING RHYTHMS AND OFF KEY PHRASING. THIS IS THE BEST INDEPENDENT POP L.P. TO COME OUT OF THE MIDWEST IN YEARS. GREAT PICTURE SLEEVE, TOO.

TWIN/TONE RECORDS
445 OLIVER AVE. SO.
MPLS., MN. 55405

BREAK'R RECORDS
P.O. BOX 20326
MPLS., MN. 55420

MAGNETIC HEAD CLEANERS: I WANT TO FUNCTION WITH YOU / MECHANICAL RIGHTS (SERVICE ME)

SILLY, SELF-INDULGENT, ENO-ESQUE NO-WAVE. I'D LIKE TO SEE SOMEBODY DANCE TO THIS STUFF - THEY'D PROBABLY HAVE TO CRAWL AROUND LIKE A WORM. SERIOUSLY, FOLKS, THIS RECORD CREATES "ATMOSPHERE".

HYPSTRZ (LIVE): HOLD ON / CAN'T STAND THE PAIN
ACTION WOMAN / HEY JOE

RECORDED LIVE AT THE LONGHORN, THE HYPSTRZ RIP THROUGH 60'S
COVERS WITH MANIAC INTENSITY. ONE OF THE BEST LIVE BANDS IN
THE MIDWEST, THESE GUYS HAVE SUCCESSFULLY TRANSLATED THEIR
ENERGY TO VINYL. BE SURE TO CHECK OUT ONE OF THEIR SHOWS.

BOGUS RECORDS
P.O. BOX 2141
LOOP STATION
MPLS., MN. 55402

HYPSTRZ

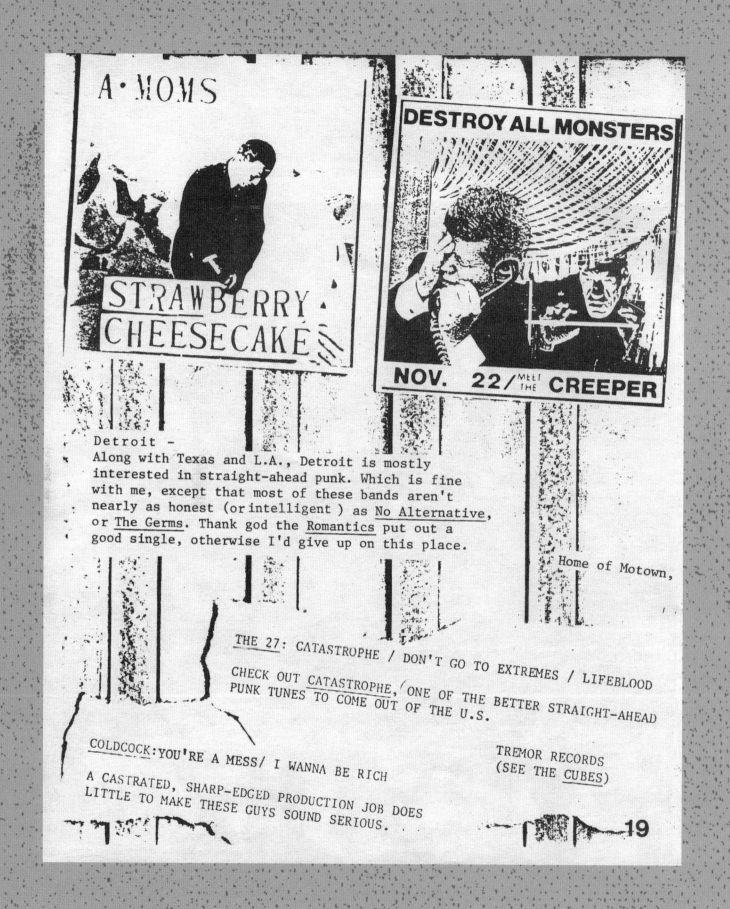

A·MOMS

STRAWBERRY·
CHEESECAKE

DESTROY ALL MONSTERS

NOV. 22/MEET THE CREEPER

Detroit –
Along with Texas and L.A., Detroit is mostly
interested in straight-ahead punk. Which is fine
with me, except that most of these bands aren't
nearly as honest (or intelligent) as No Alternative,
or The Germs. Thank god the Romantics put out a
good single, otherwise I'd give up on this place.

Home of Motown,

THE 27: CATASTROPHE / DON'T GO TO EXTREMES / LIFEBLOOD
CHECK OUT CATASTROPHE, ONE OF THE BETTER STRAIGHT-AHEAD
PUNK TUNES TO COME OUT OF THE U.S.

COLDCOCK: YOU'RE A MESS / I WANNA BE RICH   TREMOR RECORDS
                                                   (SEE THE CUBES)
A CASTRATED, SHARP-EDGED PRODUCTION JOB DOES
LITTLE TO MAKE THESE GUYS SOUND SERIOUS.   19

CULT HEROES: PRINCE AND THE SHOWGIRL / BERLIN WALL

ONE OF THE BEST RECORDS TO COME OUT OF DETROIT. FEATURES DYNAMIC BLACK VOCALIST, "HIAWATHA". SONG TITLES LIKE THE PRINCE AND THE SHOWGIRL DON'T SELL MANY RECORDS THESE DAYS, AND NEITHER DO CARTOONISH PICTURES OF BLACK MEN WEARING LEOPARD SKIN, BUT THIS SONG MARCHES RIGHT THROUGH DOWN-TOWN DETROIT AND THE HOOK PULLS YOU ALONG WITH IT.

write:
TOO BAD RECORDS
P.O. BOX 10008
DETROIT, MI. 48210

e: AFTERTASTE RECORDS
distributed by IBDI
P.O. BOX 1038
SOUTHFIELD, MICH. 48075

ALGEBRA MOTHERS: STRAWBERRY CHEESECAKE / MODERN NOISE

NICE GRAPHICS, THE A-MOMS ARE AN EXPERIMENTAL BAND. WOW. TRANCE-LIKE, REPETITIVE ORGAN RIFFS ARE PLAYED OVER SOME HARSHLY-TEXTURED BASS LINES. THE VOCAL MIX IS VERY UN-DISTINGUISHED; PROBABLY FOR THE BEST - THESE GUYS SHOW ABOUT AS MUCH EMOTION AS A TEXTBOOK. GIMME THE ARCHIES.

DESTROY ALL MONSTERS: NOV. 22 / MEET THE CREEPER

NOV. 22 IS YET ANOTHER SONG ABOUT THE KENNEDY ASSASINATION. AS IT STANDS, BOTH SONGS ARE "ALRIGHT"; FEMALE VOCALIST NIAGARA HAS AN EXPRESSIVE VOICE, BUT IN NO WAY COMPARES WITH PENELOPE OF THE (NOW DEFUNCT) AVENGERS. IF YOU WANNA HEAR FEMALE PUNKS CONTEMPLATE THE FATE OF JACKIE AND JOHNNY, BE SURE TO PICK UP THE NEW AVENGERS E.P. IF YOU WANNA PICK UP A 45 WITH SOME GREAT PACKAGING, BUY THIS...OR, CHECK OUT YOU'RE GONNA DIE, D.A.M.'S FIRST 45 AND THEIR BEST MUSICAL STATEMENT TO DATE.

IBDI RECORDS
P.O. BOX 1038
SOUTHFIELD, MI. 48075

WRITE: TREMOR RECORDS
403 FOREST
ROYAL OAK, MI.
48067

THE CUBES — SPACEHEART / PICK UP ON A LEASH / CHANGING FRACTIONS

SQUARESVILLE. FEMALE-VOCALIST WANTS TO JOIN IN A "ROCK AND ROLL BAND". THROW IN SOME TRENDY SYNTHESIZER AND YOU HAVE THE CUBES. NOT BAD, BUT THAT DON'T MEAN MUCH.

20

PYLON: COOL / DUB

GRIPPING, EMOTIONAL...<u>COOL</u> IS ONE OF THE MOST
ABSORBING INDEPENDENT RELEASES TO COME OUT THIS
YEAR. ALTHOUGH VAGUELY REMINISCENT OF <u>PUBLIC IMAGE</u>,
THIS FEMALE-FRONTED QUARTET HAS CREATED THE MOST IN-
TENSELY ORIGINAL 45 TO COME OUT OF GEORGIA SINCE
<u>ROCK LOBSTER</u> (BOTH RECORDS WERE PRODUCED BY DANNY
BEARD). PICK THIS UP OR DIE.

GEORGIA...

PYLON

> write: CAUTION RECORDS
> 229 BROAD
> ATHENS, GA. 30601

<u>KEVIN DUNN</u>: NADINE / OKTYABRINA

INTERESTING TREATMENT OF THE OLD CHUCK BERRY STANDARD.
I FIND THIS RECORD TO BE ABOUT 30 SECONDS TOO LONG, BUT -
OTHER PEOPLE SEEM TO THINK IT'S PRETTY HOT. YET ANOTHER
RECORD PRODUCED BY DANNY BEARD.

> WRITE: DB RECORDS
> 432 MORELAND AVE. N.E.
> ATLANTA, GA. 30307

B

<u>BRAINS</u>

<u>THE BRAINS</u>: MONEY CHANGES EVERYTHING / QUICK WITH YOUR LIP

FOR SOME REASON, THE <u>VILLAGE VOICE</u> THOUGHT THAT THIS WAS THE
BEST INDIE OF 1979. WELL, FUCK <u>THEM</u>. IT'S AN ALRIGHT TUNE,
BUT C'MON...ANYWAY - THE VOCALIST SOUNDS LIKE HE COULD BE
IGGY'S BROTHER, SINGS ABOUT SOME GIRL WHO'S STOOPID AND DUMPS
HIM FOR SOME GUY WITH MORE MONEY. AGREEABLY, THE ORGAN HOOK
<u>IS</u> CATCHY. BE SURE TO BOYCOTT THEIR NEW ALBUM ON A MAJOR LABEL.

> write: GRAY MATTER
> P.O. BOX 10141
> ATLANTA, GA. 30319

21

huns

THE HUNS: GLAD HE'S DEAD / BUSY KIDS

SICK, PERVERTED...SINISTER. LEAD VOCALIST CRIES
ABOUT LEE HARVEY OSWALD (GLAD HE'S DEAD) WHILE
ANONOMOUS BACKGROUND PERSONALITY GIVES INSIDIOUS
DEADPAN RESPONSE. THE FLIP IS A QUEER, HIGH-PITCHED
BALLAD THAT MAKES YOUR SKIN WANNA SHRIVEL UP AND
DIE. EXCELLENT MINIMAL-STUDIO PRODUCTION.

            write: GOD RECORDS
                   3101 B FUNSTON
                   AUSTIN, TX. 78703

    THE HATES: NO TALK IN THE 80'S / NEW SPARTANS
               ALL THE WHITES ARE GOING NEGRO / LAST HYMN

    DENSE AND CAUSTIC, THIS GARAGE-BAND E.P. SOUNDS LIKE
    PURE CONCRETE. LAST HYMN DEALS WITH GOD, ALL THE WHITES...
    DEALS WITH RACISM. WHAT MORE COULD YOU WANT FROM TEXAS?

            write: FACELESS RECORDS C/O
                   5201 W. 34TH #316
                   HOUSTON, TX. 77092

hates

22

TEXAS...

COOL

PINK SECTION

San Francisco's art-pop dance band PINK SECTION have been extremely popular up here in Olympia. This spring, after playing both the Showbox and the Roscoe Louie Gallery, PINK SECTION started taping their upcoming 12" E.P. for Modern Productions (Seattle). Unfortunately, somebody tried to light a couch with a cigarette and Triangle Studios went up in flames. Oh well, the tapes were completed and the E.P. will be released in June. Songs include: Flat DOG, Wine World, Francie's List + 2 others.

BAND NEWS: PINK SECTION, always a fluid organization, have temporarily mutated into other bands: guitarist Mathew is involved with lounge band NAKED CITY, Carol + Judy are playing with girl-trio INFLATABLE BOY CLAMS, and bass player Pontiac is playing with the interesting synthesizer-bass- film experiment MINIMAL MAN.

23

San Francisco - GREAT SCENE-This place is organized.
Order your NEW YOUTH PRODUCTIONS Underground Directory
today.(Send $1 to New Youth Productions, P.O. Box 6029
San Francisco, CA 94101). If you want to know more about
the local scene write DAMAGE MAGAZINE (678 S. Van Ness Ave
San Francisco, CA 94110).

Some good inventive bands down here; some good 45's
too. *NEWS FLASH:* The Deaf Club compilation L.P. should
be out immediately. ALSO: Subterranean Records is planning
on releasing an L.P. with Nervous Gender (!), Factrix,
ZEV, *and* Flipper.

L.A.- Read more than you'd ever want to know about
L.A. in SLASH magazine (P.O. Box 48888, L.A.,CA 90048).

This place is the "punk rock" capitol of the world.
If you want to be ugly and hate people, go to L.A. Other
than that, buy the Germs L.P. and read the lyric sheet.
Darby Crash is the best songwriter in the American
Underground.

New York - Read all about Hip City in the New
York Rocker (166 5th Ave. NYC 10010).

Most of the more interesting bands-Bush Tetras,
Rae Beats, Lounge Lizards, 8-eyed Spy etc.- can
be directly related to the NO NEW YORK L.P., a brilliantly
pretentious exercise in the art of poetry and self-abuse.
Both The Contortions and Lydia Lunch have stayed alive
long enough to create incredible records.

Another facet of this no, no... no scene are the
Super-8 films by Scott and Beth B.(B-movies) and Vivienne
Dick among others. It's great that films like "The Black
Box" can actually be shown in between bands. If you're
in town be sure to boycott the Mudd Club and drop by
Tier 3. *NEWS FLASH:* DNA will supposedly be in the
Northwest this summer. All right ....!

SANFRANCISCOSANFRANCISCO LOSANGELESLOSANGELESLOSANGELES

NEWYORKNEWYORKNEWYORKNEWYORK

NEWYORKNEWYORK

24

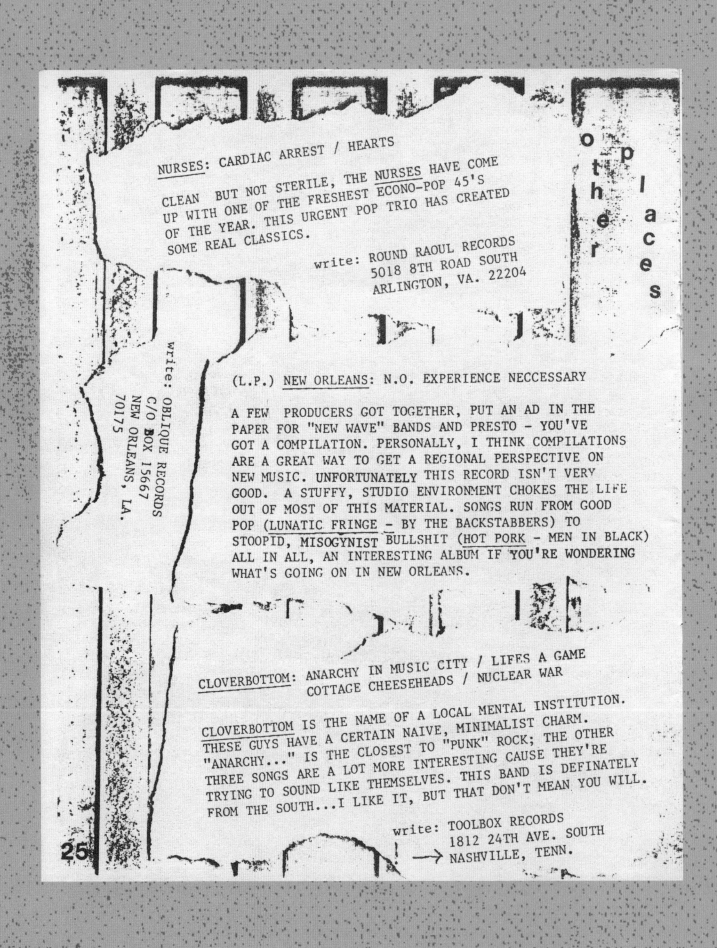

NURSES: CARDIAC ARREST / HEARTS

CLEAN BUT NOT STERILE, THE NURSES HAVE COME
UP WITH ONE OF THE FRESHEST ECONO-POP 45'S
OF THE YEAR. THIS URGENT POP TRIO HAS CREATED
SOME REAL CLASSICS.

write: ROUND RAOUL RECORDS
5018 8TH ROAD SOUTH
ARLINGTON, VA. 22204

write: OBLIQUE RECORDS
C/O BOX 15667
NEW ORLEANS, LA.
70175

(L.P.) NEW ORLEANS: N.O. EXPERIENCE NECCESSARY

A FEW PRODUCERS GOT TOGETHER, PUT AN AD IN THE
PAPER FOR "NEW WAVE" BANDS AND PRESTO - YOU'VE
GOT A COMPILATION. PERSONALLY, I THINK COMPILATIONS
ARE A GREAT WAY TO GET A REGIONAL PERSPECTIVE ON
NEW MUSIC. UNFORTUNATELY THIS RECORD ISN'T VERY
GOOD. A STUFFY, STUDIO ENVIRONMENT CHOKES THE LIFE
OUT OF MOST OF THIS MATERIAL. SONGS RUN FROM GOOD
POP (LUNATIC FRINGE - BY THE BACKSTABBERS) TO
STOOPID, MISOGYNIST BULLSHIT (HOT PORK - MEN IN BLACK)
ALL IN ALL, AN INTERESTING ALBUM IF YOU'RE WONDERING
WHAT'S GOING ON IN NEW ORLEANS.

CLOVERBOTTOM: ANARCHY IN MUSIC CITY / LIFES A GAME
COTTAGE CHEESEHEADS / NUCLEAR WAR

CLOVERBOTTOM IS THE NAME OF A LOCAL MENTAL INSTITUTION.
THESE GUYS HAVE A CERTAIN NAIVE, MINIMALIST CHARM.
"ANARCHY..." IS THE CLOSEST TO "PUNK" ROCK; THE OTHER
THREE SONGS ARE A LOT MORE INTERESTING CAUSE THEY'RE
TRYING TO SOUND LIKE THEMSELVES. THIS BAND IS DEFINATELY
FROM THE SOUTH...I LIKE IT, BUT THAT DON'T MEAN YOU WILL.

write: TOOLBOX RECORDS
1812 24TH AVE. SOUTH
→ NASHVILLE, TENN.

25

Make Your Own Records

MAKING YOUR OWN RECORDS IS ALOT CHEAPER THAN YOU THINK.

WRITE THESE ORGANIZATIONS FOR MORE INFO. . . . .

MANUFACTURORS - HERE ARE THE NAMES OF SOME RECORD FACTORIES.
ASK FOR PRICE ESTIMATES ON LACQUERS, MASTERS,
PRESSINGS, LABELS AND POSSIBLE RECORD SLEEVES.

1) UNITED RECORD PRESSING
   453 CHESTNUT STREET
   NASHVILLE, TENN. 37203

2) H.V. WADDELL CO.
   231 W. OLIVE AVE.
   BURBANK, CALIF. 91502

3) EVA-TONE SOUNDSHEETS, INC. (FLEXI-DISC)
   4801 ULMERTON ROAD, CLEARWATER, FL. 33520

DISTRIBUTORS-- DISTRIBUTORS WILL BUY LARGE UNITS OF YOUR RECORDS
AND GET THEM INTO RECORD STORES ALL AROUND THE
COUNTRY. SYSTEMATIC IS HIGHLY RECOMMENDED AS THEY
ARE INTERESTED IN ART AND POLITICS AS WELL AS MONEY.
THEY PURCHASE IN UNITS OF 50. THEY'RE AVG. PAYMENT IS
$1.00 PER RECORD. DROP THEM A LINE.

1) SYSTEMATIC RECORD DISTRIBUTORS
   BERKELEY INDUSTRIAL CT. SPACE #1
   729 HEINZ AVE. BERKELEY, CA. 94710

2) JEM IMPORT RECORDS
   18615 TOPHAM ST.
   RESEDA, CA. 91335

15 fave 45's

SPRING 1980

1)	NOH MERCY	REVOLUTIONARY SPY (FAST)	SAN FRANCISCO
2)	ANONYMOUS	SNAKE ATTACK (FLAT)	OLYMPIA, WA.
3)	PYLON	COOL (CAUTION)	ATHENS, GA.
4)	RAY MILLAND	DISTANT VIEW (PRAXIS)	ST. LOUIS
5)	AVENGERS	AMERICAN IN ME (WHITE NOISE)	L.A.
6)	POINTED STICKS	I'M NUMB (QUINTESSENCE)	VANCOUVER
7)	VOICE FARM	MODERN THINGS (OPTIONAL)	SAN FRANCISCO
8)	NEO BOYS	THE RICH MAN (TRAP)	PORTLAND
9)	DISHRAGS	PAST IS PAST (MODERN)	VANCOUVER
10)	OFFS	EVERYONE'S A BIGOT (415)	SAN FRANCISCO
11)	DADISTICS	PARANOIA PERCEPTION (BOMP)	CHICAGO
12)	BLACKOUTS	MAKE NO MISTAKE (MODERN)	SEATTLE
13)	NURSES	CARDIAC ARREST (ROUND ROUAL)	ARLINGTON, VA.
14)	HUNS	GLAD HE'S DEAD (GOD)	AUSTIN, TX.
15)	S.F. UNDERGROUND	E.P. (SUBTERRANEAN)	SAN FRANCISCO

(1979)

1)	DADISTICS	MODERN GIRL (BRAILLE)	CHICAGO
2)	POINTED STICKS	OUT OF LUCK (QUINTESSENCE)	VANCOUVER
3)	SUBURBAN LAWNS	GIDGET GOES TO HELL (SUB./INDUSTRIAL)	LONGBEACH,CA.
4)	DEAD KENNEDYS	CALIFORNIA UBER ALLES (ALT. TENTACLES)	S.FRANCISCO
5)	PINK SECTION	TOUR OF CHINA (PINK SECTION)	SAN FRANCISCO
6)	GIRLS	JEFFREY I HEAR U (HEARTHAN)	BOSTON
7)	EPICYCLE	UNDERGROUND (CIRKLE)	CHICAGO
8)	LUXURY	GREEN HEARTS (ANGRY,YOUNG)	DES MOINES
9)	BLACK FLAG	WASTED (SST)	L.A.
10)	SKAFISH	DISGRACING THE FAMILY NAME (ILLEGAL)	CHICAGO
11)	WIPERS	BETTER OFF DEAD (TRAP)	PORTLAND
12)	CULT HEROES	PRINCE & THE SHOWGIRL (TOO BAD)	DETROIT
13)	PRESSLER-MORGAN	HANDPIECE (HEARTHAN)	CLEVELAND
14)	BRAINS	MONEY CHANGES EVERYTHING (GREY MATTER)	ATLANTA, GA.
15)	TEENAGE JESUS	FREUD IN FLOP (MIGRAIN)	NEW YORK

ANONYMOUS

SNAKE / ATTACK
CORPORATE / FOOD

Dana Squires

OLYMPIA, HOME OF "SNAKE ATTACK", RADIO KAOS, SUB POP...AND OP,

THE MOST EXTENSIVE PUBLICATION OF INDEPENDENT RELEASES IN EXISTENCE.

ZIP 98507)   (WRITE: LOST MUSIC NETWORK, OP MAGAZINE, P.O. BOX 2391, OLY., WA.

Calvin Johnson

Emergency Late-Night Peanut Butter Sandwiches

From the beginning, punk was a story told in regional terms. New York City was not a national mass media and entertainment capital; for punks it was just another local scene where weird-outs played the local hangouts. Someone took a photo, and things snowballed from there. As it turned out, weird-outs in Cleveland, Boston, Minneapolis, Houston, San Francisco, and Pittsburgh had the same ideas—or better ones.

Cowboy Carl understood. Right there in Park Forest, Illinois, where our young hero Bruce Pavitt began, Cowboy Carl documented native asseverations all the way from Tennessee to the overlooked Indiana, only ten miles to the east—but who ever noticed or even looked in that direction? Carl's enterprise is not insignificant to our story. During the 1970s, Cowboy Carl Records devoted three quarters of its discography to the criminally overlooked role that Indiana and the Midwest in general played in the development of country and western music in the United States.

Just like the blues, country, and other indigenous musics, local new wave had regional attributes and identifying characteristics. Even if the mainstream music press dismissed regional bands as mere Ramones or Blondie soundalikes, the local weird-outs unerringly staked out their own inimitable styles. Art rock and new wave came alive in the Rust Belt, an industrial dreamscape that tasted like the bleak factory neighborhood in *Eraserhead*. The parents moved to the suburbs, but a disparate population of weird-out kids couldn't wait to get back downtown where everything looked like a street corner on *Sesame Street*, a dirty tableau complicated by overlapping generations of development and neglect. Industry had moved on, leaving behind a wake of warehouses and loft buildings ripe

for occupation. The resulting Petri dish of Midwestern rock 'n roll experimentation bred Oil Tasters in Milwaukee, Wisconsin; Algebra Suicide and Sport of Kings in Chicago; the Embarrassment in Wichita, Kansas; Ray Milland in St. Louis, Missouri; and Los Reactors in Tulsa, Oklahoma.

The always expressive participants of local music scenes undertake the crucial dual tasks of exposing the village to what's going on in the world, while letting the world know about everything happening nearby. Meanwhile, every town is alive with the creative byproducts of nurture in a struggle with nature; regional disdain crossed with regional pride, trapped under glass and buzzing up against the glass ceiling. The participants can see the great beyond, but feel like they cannot reach out and grab it by the throat.

Before heading west to Olympia, where KAOS-FM and *OP* magazine and the legendary John Foster awaited him, young Bruce Pavitt had two important experiences regarding the regional and artistic dimensions of the music underground. First, the band Television, already revered in their adopted home city of New York, returned to its members' Midwestern point of origin to show the hinterlands what the band had achieved. In support of their brand-new album *Marquee Moon*, the band toured in 1977 as opening act for Peter Gabriel, a pillar of progressive rock as a founding member of Genesis. Television was not wild, offensive, or theatrical in any way. Tom Verlaine and the rest of the combo stood defiantly stock-still in their jeans and T-shirts, staring down the crowd while steadily playing their spidery intonations. The Chicagoland audience was confused—to them, a band's "artistic merit" required theatrical amplification. The band radiated a feeling of disdain for what they had left behind in the big city. For Bruce in the audience, a secret communication was received concerning the value of art for art's sake.

Fade soon after to New York, New York, and Bruce's first pilgrimage to acknowledged seat of rock 'n roll bohemia, Max's Kansas City. On this off night, the provinces provided the cultural experience; the B-52's from Athens, Georgia—wherever that is. Almost no one besides Bruce was in the audience, but the band and the lucky few on the dance floor paid no never-mind, and all had too much fun to notice. The city mouse/country mouse fable was turned inside-out. The country mice came to the city, bringing exactly what the cosmopolitan scene desired, yet they went unrecognized because they were wearing the wrong electric-blue socks, so to speak. Thus, another important lesson in overlooked expectations was absorbed.

Olympia, Washington, in the late 1970s was undergoing a transition, as the folks rotating through local community radio station KAOS-FM pursued a chain of thought that inevitably led to *Sub Pop* fanzine. As a *community* radio station, a type of noncommercial radio that makes a point of getting more down and localized in its programming than public radio ever thinks of doing, KAOS prioritized music released via independent and artist-owned record labels, especially local ones. Former KAOS music director John Foster started *OP* magazine to cover all types of music on small labels from all over the planet. The more mainstream-oriented music press on the margins, like *New York Rocker* and *Trouser Press*, had trouble keeping up with the corporate new wave fodder being pumped out by major labels, from the Clash, Talking Heads, XTC, and Bow Wow Wow on down. Those magazines barely acknowledged anything more outré and truly underground, unless it was produced by Brian Eno. KAOS went beyond. Playing the Cars six months before commercial radio made them famous was not enough. KAOS championed Linda Waterfall, Half Japanese, Gary Wilson, Annette Peacock, James Ulmer, and the Crap Detectors—artists who were never going to receive commercial radio play.

In 1979 this independent music focus was still a new idea, barely even accepted in Olympia, when Bruce Pavitt began his Friday night ten-to-midnight program *Subterranean Pop*. Taking *OP* magazine as a starting point, Bruce narrowed his new wave concentration to independently released music from the Midwest and the Pacific Northwest. That was almost unthinkable! Even someone closely following the new wave scene could be forgiven for wondering if there was anything coming out of the Midwest and the Northwest at all, let alone enough to fill two hours of radio programming each week. But taking Vancouver, Seattle, Olympia, and Portland on one end; and Akron, Madison, Detroit, Lincoln, St. Louis, Indianapolis, Cincinnati, Chicago, Des Moines, Wichita, Columbus, Kansas City, and Milwaukee on the other, Bruce found more than enough music—too much, even.

The rest of us wanted more, and Bruce delivered. He extended his radio show into a fanzine that announced a New Pop! Manifesto: "Only by supporting new ideas by local artists, bands and record labels can the US expect any kind of dynamic social/cultural change in the 1980s. This is because the mass homogenization of our culture is due to the claustrophobic centralization of our culture. We need diverse, regionalized, localized approaches to all forms of art, music and politics…the most intense music, the most original ideas are coming out of scenes you don't even know exist. Tomorrow's pop is being realized today on small decentralized record labels that are interested in taking risks, not making money."

•

I met Bruce Pavitt in September 1980, just he was opening his mail from the post office box *Subterranean Pop* shared with *OP* magazine. He was holding a Big Boys 45 in one hand and a Dicks 45 in the other. He greeted me with that wide-eyed look of his, as if always in a constant state of wonder. We hit it off immediately. He invited me to join the *Sub Pop* staff—in what capacity was never clear. In one issue I was credited with "Emergency Late-Night Peanut Butter Sandwiches," a title I still wear with pride. To this day, if anyone asks what I do at the K Records office, the answer is: "Emergency Late Night Peanut Butter Sandwiches."

We knew we had relevant artists in the Pacific Northwest creating seminal work: the Dishrags, the Wipers, the Beakers, Subhumans, Anonymous (actually Steve Fisk, responsible for Olympia's first punk/new wave 45 in 1980), Pell Mell, Pointed Sticks, Blackouts, Fastbacks, Neo Boys, and Jungle Nausea, for starters.

Calvin Johnson and Heather Lewis, Beat Happening, "Jack Yr Body" storefront party, 2323 2nd Ave., Seattle, February 27, 1987. **CHARLES PETERSON**

Bruce brought us knowledge of another world, and bands including Epicycle, the Imports, Ama-Dots, Strike Under, Vague-leys, Fensics, and Duchamp. This was a time in-between times, after the initial propulsive punk burst but before the advent of prolific labels like Homestead, SST, Caroline, and Touch and Go in the '80s, setting a standard for bands producing an album a year. Every startlingly stark 45 was enough to curve our ears outwards. The people making this vital music were everywhere, and almost universally ignored by the rock media. Even fanzines paid them scant attention. The response to *Sub Pop* magazine, as it was known from issue two forward, was profound. We could hear and feel the collective sigh of relief, as these weird-outs finally encountered somebody who got them. *Sub Pop* reviews didn't just compare bands to Patti Smith or Pere Ubu. And "next big thing" status wasn't necessary in order for *Sub Pop* to take an artist seriously.

By 1981, Bruce was living in downtown Olympia, above the Barnes Floral Building, on the one bohemian block of 4th Ave. Across the street from him were a

record store, an art gallery, a jazz restaurant (the Rainbow), and Olympia's first espresso machine at Café Intermezzo. Also living above Barnes Floral were Gary May and Stella Marrs, who were making things happen downtown in their own ways. Gary organized the first new wave shows at the Gnu Deli, a restaurant that hosted all sorts of jazz, bluegrass, and folk music—everything except rock 'n roll. Stella made waves with female-centric art exhibitions that ruffled the feathers of the local bohemian pooh-bahs. Above the Rainbow was the Angelus Hotel, several stories of one-bedroom and studio apartments, most with shared bathrooms. A sizable proportion of the early Olympia punk scene lived there. This burgeoning scene was the perfect spot for Bruce.

Even when I first met Bruce, with those Texas punk 45s in his hands, he was poring over the simple but arresting imagery gracing their sleeves. The visual of the covers had as big an impact on him as the audio content. *Sub Pop*'s exploration of design was a significant aspect of its being. Prior to desktop computers, the tools of the graphic design trade were esoteric and

Tiny Holes: Steve Peters (guitar), Phil Hertz (drums), Bruce Pavitt (guitar), Evergreen State College, Olympia, WA, February 1981. JAN LOFTNESS

specialized: photostat cameras, T-squares, halftone screens, line tape, reduction wheels, wax machines, typesetters, and X-Acto knives. Access to a copy machine required a trip to the library or a print shop; if a particular machine even enlarged or reduced images, it would only be at certain preset sizes. The IBM Selectric typewriters with changeable type elements were golden. Bruce was inspired by underground magazines and comics (*Praxis, No Mag, Cle, Raw*) and a few adventurous fanzines (*Bikini Girl*) to create a striking visual style that pushed the limitations of the inexpensive graphic tools at hand: scissors, Wite-Out, glue sticks, found graphics, tape, and the natural distortion of multigeneration photocopies.

Bruce also experimented with the format of the fanzine. Most fanzines were printed using standard sizes of photocopy paper, either 8 ½" x 11" or legal-size, 8 ½" x 14". The first three issues of *Sub Pop* were printed on legal-size paper, folded in half, and saddle-stitched with a cardstock cover. Issue number four went pocket-size, with plastic comb binding and a color copy cover. Issue number six was a striking throwback to the newsletter format of the earliest sci-fi and rock 'n roll fanzines of the '60s and '70s, 8 ½" x 11" sheets stapled in the upper left-hand corner; no

nonsense, just pure information. With issue number eight, we got real and printed a full "pony tab" on book paper at the *Shelton-Mason County Journal*: twenty-four pages of music and cultural distractions with a cover contrasting the abstract expressionism of Jackson Pollock with the Oklahoma wholesomeness of the American cowboy. The price was eighteen cents.

Bruce was also delving into making music himself. In 1980 he formed Tiny Holes, a band with other KAOS staff, including engineer Steve Fisk and music director Steve Peters. I loved Tiny Holes. After they dissolved, Bruce and Steve Fisk collaborated with local free-jazz saxophonist Jeffrey Morgan as War with Elevators, playing noise improv synth skronk with Bruce vocalizing over top. Michael Huntsburger used his four-track reel-to-reel to record Bruce accompanying himself on drums, bass, and guitar, doing quick free-form auto-biographical sketches, all entirely improvised. One of these pieces, "Debbie," was included on the cassette included with *Sub Pop* number five. Bruce owned a very cool primitive rhythm box that was the size of a small block of cheese. It had two knobs, speed and volume, and two set rhythm patterns. We hatched a plan to start a minimal vocal/drum machine duo and tour England. Somehow this never happened.

SUB POP #2, *November 1980*

32pp, 7" x 8 1/2" format, print run of 500

rock

und

roll

WAX TRAX
RECØRDS

2449 N. LINCOLN AVE. CHICAGO, IL. 60614

(312) 929-0221

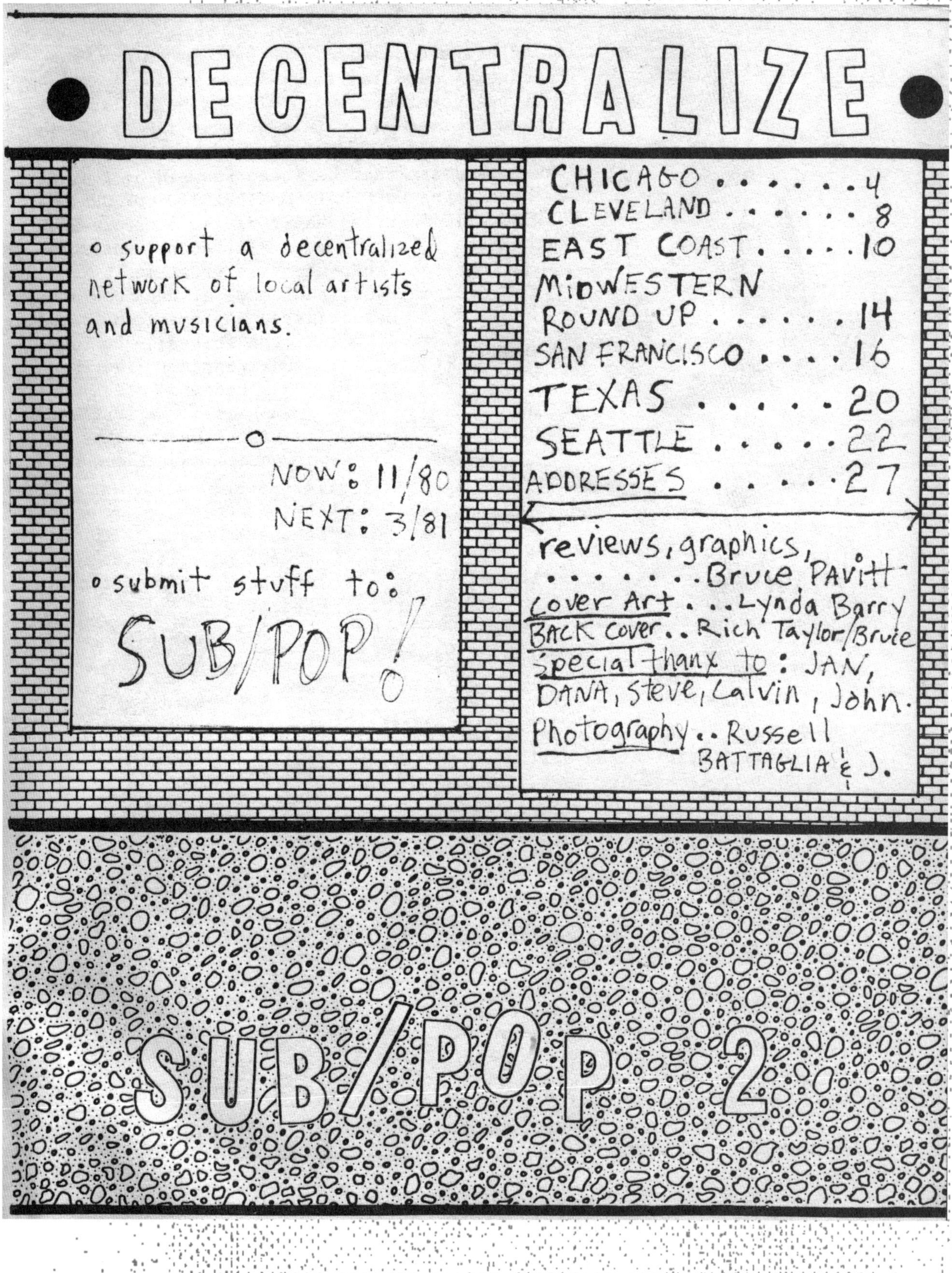

DECENTRALIZE

● support a decentralized network of local artists and musicians.

————————o————————

NOW: 11/80
NEXT: 3/81

● submit stuff to:

SUB/POP!

←——————————————→

reviews, graphics,
. . . . Bruce Pavitt
cover art . . . Lynda Barry
BACK cover . . Rich Taylor/Bruce
special thanx to: JAN,
DANA, Steve, Calvin, John.
Photography . . Russell
          BATTAGLIA & J.

SUB/POP 2

①

Sub/Pop is concerned with U.S. bands and independent record labels. We are trying to perceive a network: a possible series of links between points and points between lines. If we don't maintain the radically localized approach to music and art that has been spawned by the, ahem, "New Wave", the CORPORATE MANIPULATION OF OUR CULTURE will flourish as it did so predominantly in the fab 70's. We must all become energetic about the fact that there is great music in America; and, that some of the most truly avant-garde pop hysteria is coming out of traditionally boring environments (i.e. Ray Milland from St. Louis). emphasis: EXPLOSIVE artistic hanky-panky is everywhere. Sometimes it just needs a little support, so... write these bands, communicate, buy their records, do something insane and send it to 'em in a package... the addresses are here... for a reason. Use them.

What we are all about.

LOST MUSIC NETWORK
(a non-profit enterprise)

LOST MUSIC NETWORK
P.O. Box 2391
Olympia WA 98507

1. Op Magazine - published quarterly. This is the only magazine on earth devoted to independent labels and every form of American music... "pop", jazz, blues, experiemental, country... you name it, it's there. Informative, witty and cool to look at. buy it or I'll kill you.   ○   ○   ○

2. Sub/Pop - published tri-yearly. The editor is close to starvation and deserves you support. Ads are only $20.00 a full page! Send a check for $3.00 and get the next 4 issues for free! All subscribers receive their copies in fully sanitized seal-a-meal plastic! Wow! Next "ish"... N.Y., L.A., Portland, Alaska, Chicago, Minneapolis and more. Gaw-Damn!

independent Music

radio KAOS
89.3 FM
. . . .

OLYMPia, Wa.

. . . .

Fave
Raves

TUESDAY	WEDNESDAY	Thursday	Friday
JOHN: Besides Mr. Brown...	Toni:	DAVE: Low flying aircraft	Russell: girl on the run
tex Rubinowitz	FALL — totally Wired	Pulp Music	Honey BAIN
Hot Rod Man —	Neo Boys gimme tha message	FALL — totally Wired	Twinkeyze Alien in our midst.
Billy Hancock	BEAKERS Red Towel	Orchestral Manoeuvres mess- ages	ROY Orbison only the lonely
Lonely Blue Boy			
Nurses — Hearts —			
JAN:	Steve:	Calvin:	BRUCE:
PINK SECTION	Fred Frith: -Dancing in the street-	PYLON: Cool	YOUNG MARBLE GIANTS Final Day +
PART Time —	Minimal Man She	BAD BRAINS: Pay to cum	Orch. Manoeuvres
Slits — ...rhythm	was a visitor-	Pulp Music Low Flying aircraft	+ messages +
Delta 5	Snakefinger What wilbur?		JOY DIVISION Shes lost control +
—YOU—			

Masquerading as an obese, hillbilly metropolis, "Hick-ago" is actually the home of a very cool and contemporary new/pop underground. Below are some highlights:

3

CLUBS: (a) Tuts - Ultimately the best venue in town. Although they support local acts, their main source of income is based on all those hip young British bands. Comfortably cramped, this is the only place in town for national and international intrigue. Also: good jukebox w/ local 45's. (b) Lucky Number - although it sounds like a hang-out for cowboy homosexuals, the Lucky Number is actually a low-key night club featuring the best of Chicago pop underworld. The subversive potential of this place is doubtful however, as the manager seems to be more interested in fondling his gold medallion than in creating a low-cost, artistic alternative. Should be squaresville by the time you read this. (c) Space Place - great. Located in a sleazy loft in the heart of Grade-B Chicago. The Space Place is the only "club" in town that (1) allows minors, and (2) is open to unestablished pop combos. Subversive and fun.

o

STORES: Wax Trax - the only centralized media hang-out in Chicago. After killing an afternoon flipping through an endless file of inde- pedent records (and publications), chances are good that your fave pop icon will make a dramatic cameo appearance. bring a camera and a credit card.

o

PUBLICATIONS: (a) Praxis - professional and expensive. This glossy textbook showcases the best of the local art scene. As for music, each issue usually contains either a flexi-disc or a real piece o' vinyl (i.e. the brilliant Ray Milland 45). Unfortunately, there's so many arty references to international art-bands that there's hardly room for any mention of local talent. Regional neglect aside, though, this magazine is outstanding. Classy and bourgeois. (b) Fanatic - at long last, a 'zine devoted to Chicago pop ... fun graphics, a zany sense of humor and big, glossy pages make this one of the most distinctive fanzines in the U.S. of A. (c) Coolest Retard - like most of Chicago, this modest publication spends most of its time lusting after the latest corporate import. don't forget the horrible cartoons. An integral part of the local scene... informative and occasionally insightful.

CHICAGOGO

NAVASTRAU: *VERGESS MIR NIT/Navastrau Theme/LOOKING FROM AN AIRPLANE/Continental Welcome*   *** DISTURBED**

A handful of mature, sophisticated intellectuals got together and created some modern pop. <u>Vergess Mir Nit</u> is sung in German and sounds great for something that's basically phony and pretentious. cultural blasphemy aside, however, this record is really very good... a rhythm box keeps the pulse on some contemporary muzak and the result is similar to Tuxedo Moon. The vocals are shared equally between a man and a woman: both of whom sound smart and seductive and are probably holding a cocktail in one hand and a textbook on Nietzche in the other. One of ze year's best records. 4

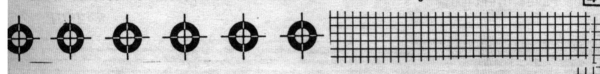

PAINTER BAND: *REACTOR/Sky*   *** DISTURBED RECORDS AND FILMWORKS:**

political consciousness, progressive rock stylings. "well crafted". features some violin a la The Jefferson Airplane. <u>Reactor</u> is a catchy number... low-pitched vocals tell us about "*suburban despair...cancer of the mouth, curlers in your hair*". Another example of the strong musical <u>diversity</u> happening in Chicago.

PHIL 'N THE BLANKS: *AUTOSEX/PRL-853*   *** PINK:**

professional New Wave. suffers from an excess of cuteness. PRL-853 is a bouncy, funny song about a drug that erases your brain. haw haw. Phil knots his throat and sounds like a munchkin; Carol sounds exactly like that girl in <u>Renaissance</u> (medieval hippie-rock, remember them?) <u>Autosex</u> is a buncha trendy garbage that makes me laugh everytime I hear it; I'm sure this band is destined for major-label stardom... If you buy your clothes at Fiorrucci's you'll probably love this record.

IMPORTS: *VISIONS OF REALITY/Darkness of Light*   * CIRKLE:

aggressive hypnotism. deep, throaty vocals fog through a stark, repetitive background. "the zombies are among us". one of them stares blankly as a booming echo leaps from the snare drum. Brilliant 4-track recording - will appeal to anyone interested in Joy Division.

IDENTITY CRISIS: *OVERTIME/Pretty Feet/BORN TO BE A BOZO*

young, teen-age Romeo croons and cries... *"the clock is sounding, my brain is pounding"*. Identity Crisis is a suburban band who have managed to re-synthesize the Ramones, Kiss and Barry Manilow into one of the most original pop 45's of the year. recorded on a 4-track with a final mix-down in a studio, the production of this record achieves just enough basement sparkle for major FM-airplay. pop rave: Overtime.

5   * CIRKLE:

EPICYCLE: *COLLEEN/You're Not Gonna Get It/HARDCORE PUNK*

Just as the Jam and Secret Affair can rip-off the 60's British Invasion (and make it sound exciting), so can Epicycle. A prolific teen-age combo, Epicycle once again displays an intuitive, aggressive understanding of melody and harmony. With their 3rd record, however, these cuddly mop-tops start to sound more derivative than "classic". Their system of sound is slowly being poisoned by a lack of fresh ideas and a tendency towards bigger & "better" production techniques; for a band with a great 60's mod sound, a contemporary studio recording simply destroys both the charm and the mystique. Personally, I favor the timeless quality of It's You from their 1st E.P. (recorded on a 4-track when they were all but 16 years old). Don't listen to me though, 'cause most fans love the big, fat sound of Hardcore Punk (dumb title, great anthem). Colleen is infectious wimpoid pop (piano overdubs etc.). Overall, a good E.P. by a talented young band that has yet to reach their potential.

                                                        * CIRKLE:

OUTLINED A STEP-BY-STEP, INTELLECTUAL ANALYSIS OF THEIR EXCITING DEBUT ALBUM.

NUCLEAR GLOOM: moody masterpiece. melancholy _synthesizer line tugs at your_
heart through-out. radically different from anything else on the record.
judy teen on background vocals: ghostly. will be released as a 45.
HEADACHE: abrasive pop. Al (guitar) dives into a bed of nails while Frankie
meditates on his migraine...a killer. will also be released as a 45.
BLONDES ON THE RUN: great trash-b imagery. more dagger-like _rhythm guitar._
Unfortunately, we have to yawn through an incredibly professional _guitar solo._
NOTHING,NOTHING: suspenseful intro. Frankie sounds like a dismantled
Bette Davis; heavy, textured arrogance. more mood music.
TOO MUCH SOFT LIVING: more haunting atmosphere from judy teen..."hollywood
bed and a hole in her head."...lotsa accelerated pitter-patter on the cymbals.
bulging bass lines. a hit. play this one for your middle-class relatives..

. . . .

WHAT NEXT: embarrassing reference to heavy-metal boogie. catchy as hell.
CLEAN CUT: mongoloid chanting on "clean cut,clean cut"..."so young, so hung".
BRUISER BOY: "there's a snake in your heart, chase the noise out of the dark".
UNBREAKABLE: "she looks so durable and she's only 13". sexist. judy teen
sounds like a martian being stabbed in outer space. nice echo.
KILLJOY INTERFERENCE: loopy, fun-time. features some of the best production
on ze record. vocals sound triumphant: a gang war for squares. another hit.
LET GO: more full-bodied production. it has a beat. 1-2, 1-2.

6.

THE ORIGINAL SOUNDTRACK FROM THE MOTION PICTURE "Too Much Soft Living" **SOON TO BE RELEASED**

SPECIAL AFFECTS   **859 W. FLETCHER**   **CHICAGO, IL 60657**

CLEVELAND

The purpose of this letter is to tell you everything you need to know about ~~about~~ Clevo's modern muzak scene. Anyway, of all places, do you know where I acquired a copy of your mag? Well, since your so interested I'll be more than happy to tell ya. Today I was bored and I decided to see what was going on around Coventry (Coventry is a section of Clevo Hts. that is infested with burn-out hippies). So, I stroll into Record Revolution (Coventry headshop/record store) wearing my infamous "kill hippies" t-shirt. I go downstairs and but to my surprise do I see assorted magazines such as Zigzag, Damage, Slash and something called Subterranean Pop?! Well I looked through all my pockets for cash and all I could find was 80¢...I thought "what the hell, it looks unique, it can't be all that bad!" So I came home and I sat down to the new UBU l.p. The Art of Walking, and the reading of your rag. Well, your magazine is very good and it reminds me of Cle #2. Now for some FACTS: There are two main places to play: Hennessey's and Fitzpatrick's; sometimes Pirates Cove, (used to be great; where UBU started out, also: DEVO, RUBBER CITY REBELS, DEAD BOYS Etc. (first wave bands)). There was also the REAL WORLD (best venue to date), a.k.a. Phantasy Nightclub; it was above where the Drome used to be but closed when the Drome moved downtown...There also used to be free concerts at the Drome which were the best concerts this area has ever seen. The person largely responsible for the whole Cleveland scene is Johnny Dromette. He owns the Drome, he does the artwork for all of Pere Ubu's albums (except Modern Dance); this work is done under the alias of John Thompson. Devo's song "Come Back Jonee" is supposedly about him and was first performed in his store live by DEVO. He organized everything, concerts etc. but now says he's too old. Organized Disastos (which he still does); Disasto is a principle he made up which takes too long to explain. The only way to describe disasto is total chaos and confusion. All the Disastos have been alot of fun...He also has a record label, DROME records of course. There are 3 Pagans singles (a band that has broken up that he managed; Pagans were a great punk band), 1 Lepers e.p., 2 x_____ x singles. Due for release: Tulsa Jacks, Bernie and the Invisibles, Jet Spacely.....................

Other local bands: AK47's, Clam, Decapitators, IUD COYS, Pressler/Morgan, Lepers, Impalers (the punk band of the 80's...Features the reknowned Scruffs Suicide on lead vocals, Charlie on bass, Guy on drums, Wally on electric violin, Richard Richmond - ex of Lepers on guitar...When looking for a drummer and guitar here is what their ad in Mongoloid Mag said: "Wanted: lead guitarist, drummer for wild, insane punk band to bring Clevo to it's knees. Musical ability unimportant...you just gotta be violent, dangerous, insane suicidal and able to take alot of abuse. Sidney's dead now and we want revenge..."

[Z]

                    NUFF SAID,
                    TOMMY COMMANDO, CLEVELAND

<u>PERE UBU</u>: *THE ART OF WALKING* (L.P.)   * ROUGH TRADE:

You're four years old: you're in a day care center. Mr. Thomas, your
big, round schoolmaster is about to read you some stories about ants and
little fishies and God. As he starts his little stories, your vision
begins to wobble and your limbs feel like taffy. You want your mommy
but you know it's too late... you are about to discover <u>The Art of Walking</u>,
the most enlightening children's record ever impregnated within the con-
fines of a classroom. The vocals are friendly, happy - they want to teach
you a lesson, tell you a story. The noise in the background is mean and
scary - oh no, it wants to splinter your memory (with shards of glass),
suffocate your subconscious (with packages of foam). A smiling nightmare,
50% of this material is suitable for naptime; the other half has a big
beat and is great for chasing girls at recess... Another shocker from one
of our most experimental U.S. combos.

<u>FOREIGN BODIES</u>: *THE INCREDIBLE TRUTH/Long Walk Home*   * BIZART:

Shadows; layers of musical notes and rhythms. disco. fast paced mood
music. Occasional squeeky sax solo (yawn). no vocals. Works best as
aimless radio filler. It's got a beat. Wow. "avant garde".   8

<u>PAGANS</u>: *STREET WHERE NOBODY LIVES/What's This Shit Called Love?*
        NOT NOW, NO WAY/I Juvenile
        DEAD END AMERICA/Little Black Egg   * DROME:

In a midwest devoid of punk and politics, it's easy to see the Pagans as
one of the most vital and energetic young bands to come out of garage-
band America. Within their chaotic life span, the Pagans played true rock
'n roll in the classic punk/nihilist format (and even managed to document
a total of 3 45's). Hey, this stuff is angry and compelling and has
definitely stood the test of time. <u>Not Now No Way</u> was produced by David
Thomas (Ubu) and is undoubtedly the catchiest punk anthem to come out of
the midwest ever and the only reason I'm writing this is cuz the guitarist
bought a subscription to my mag. so there. Actually, this stuff's got
about as much gusto as a Schlitz beer commercial...hey, just kiddin'.

SCIENTIFIC AMERICANS: *TAKING TIME/Call Home* (Flexidisc)

Taking Time: brainy, swirling caucasion reggae. time-tunnel echo. whirling into dub city. Call Home: galloping, spatula percussion. self-conscious urban white boys try to sound "heavy". silly, radioactive phase-shifter. College pop.

* TEKNO TUNES:

THE SHAGGS: *PHILOSOPHY OF THE WORLD* (L.P.)

* RED ROOSTER:

naive. stupid. ignorant. beautiful. two disjointed guitars and a minimal drum set create "music" that is wandering and fragmented yet somehow cohesive. Recorded by three teen-age sisters in the late 60's (Betty, Helen, and Dorothy Wiggen), this is, has gotta be, the most bizarre cult record of the decade. Isolated from almost everything in the world except the Beatles, the Shaggs are pure folk art: naive, original. Painfully honest and sincere (they sing about their pet "Foot-Foot"), this raw-folk manifesto will definitely appeal to addicts of Noh Mercy, the Slits.

BONGOS: *TELEPHOTO LENS/Glow in the Dark*

* FETISH:

if the Beatles were beatniks they'd sound like the Bongos. Glow in the Dark: smoky, moog-filled coffeehouse features acoustic guitar, organic percussion. (spotlight: and they're on the stage, the singing Bongos!) cool merseybeat.

BONGO

The BONGOS

Dear Bruce,

I sure am having fun in D.C. this summer. What I like to do most is go to the Club 9:30, pay my money and walk in (no fat bouncer sitting on a stool, checking i.d. like at some of the other "rock 'n roll clubs" around here). 9:30 is great because of the bands that play there: X, James Ulmer, Bad Seeds, Pylon, Insect Surfers, Los Microwaves, Joe King Carrasco all make for frantic teen-age dancing.

Sometimes I hang around a bar called One Flight Up. They have a small dance floor but they play O.K. music. The best live band I have seen there is the Dark. They consist of two males and two females and play groovy rock 'n roll that reminds me of the Animals or the Searchers. I especially like the lead guitarist's shiny red boots.

Two of my fave D.C. Bands, Tru Fax and the Insaniacs and the Insect Surfers, will soon release 12" e.p.s on WASP records. Oh boy.

The most interesting new band I've seen is Anthony Perkins and the Psychotics. An interesting Punk/Funk combo, the lead singer (who looks exactly like the real Anthony Perkins) is carried on stage in a straight jacket. He does a lot of jumping about and crazy dancing and playing of toy instruments. The keyboard player also sings and keeps pens in his breast pocket. I saw them when they opened for the Cramps/ Slickee Boys/ Teen Idols, when they were joined onstage by two Enzymes and Danny Frankel of the Urban Verbs.

I guess that's all I have to tell you right now. Hey, ~~say hello to the wife and kids for me.~~ See you in September.

CALVIN JOHNSON

INSECT SURFERS

INSECT SURFERS: *POD LIFE/ Into the Action*   * WASP:

slick New Wave pop. cute 'n clever. Pod Life is witty vegetable lore
and features some truly obnoxious synthesizer (hey, I think there's
some real inventive lead guitar work in there too, somewhere). Lotsa
potential here but it's definitely marred by a tinny production job.
also: poor, understated mix on the vocals. What a shame, somebody
told me that this was D.C.'s no. 1 band... I hope their new album sounds
better than this.

⑪   **THEIR FIRST SINGLE ON WASP RECORDS**

JAD FAIR: *ZOMBIES OF MORA TAU (7" E.P.)*   * ARMAGEDDON   12

Jad Fair is the most interesting person in the United States.

drawing by   *JAD FAIR*

KANSAS

EMBARRASSMENT: *PATIO SET/Sex Drive*

Fresh, fluid, spontaneous. PiL-inspired guitar, shoe-box drum set.
The Embarrassment have come up with one of the most dynamic sounds I've
heard all year: it's loose, it's comfortable and it's original. However,
though their sound seems partly improvised and open to new boundaries,
their lyrics are about as art-school as you can get (with all of the
negative connotations that that implies)..."*you were my favorite lawn
chair*"? C'mon guys, snap out of it! By the way, this recording has a
lot of presence, really hot. Give these guys a listen. * BIGTIME RECORDS

OKLAHOMA

FENSICS: *FULL TIME JOB/Tornado Warning*

Tornado Warning is macabre rock and roll. A vengeful, slithering tornado siren bends and smears the intro...up in the sky: a stinging guitar
line dives and swarms around our hero (some gagging, half-human hillbilly). "*four o'clock/ in the morning/ television/ tornado warning...
it pushed my baby through a barbed wire fence/ haven't seen that girl
since*". This is hot, weird, demented. Herman Munster even sits in on
some perky organ fills. buy it. The A-side is some contrived dialogue
between mom and her lazy boy who won't get a job. so-so.   * NO SWEAT

MISSOURI

DUCHAMP: *INTIMACY/Energy*

Intimacy starts off with a quick, goose-stepping introduction and is
followed up with an excellent, acoustic folk-pop song. If anyone out
there remembers The 12 Dreams of Dr. Sardonicus by Spirit, then you'll
know exactly how dated this song is. The flip, Energy, is a garbled,
synthetic safari into a land of flesh-eaters; (I think)...barbaric * CHAMP

INDIANA

GIZMOS/DOW JONES AND THE INDUSTRIALS: *HOOSIER HYSTERIA (L.P.)*

Everything by the Gizmos is one-dimensional, poorly recorded rock 'n roll
(punk). Here's what they did: they stuck (one) mike in the middle of the
room THEN THEY BROKE OUT THE BUDWEISER. Whoopee!

Dow Jones and the Industrials: features the same flat cardboard sound as
the aforementioned band. the big difference however, is this: these boys
aren't miming the same worn-out drama. definitely an 80's band. (hide
your children)   * GULCHER

IOWA

LUXURY: *GREEN HEARTS/One In a Million*

Green Hearts is the best wimpoid pop I've ever heard; a masterpiece.
Enough hooks for 5 good singles and enough psychedelic edge to melt
your pacemaker. also available on the Declaration of Independents compilation (Ambition Records). * ANGRY YOUNG RECORDS

Although Kansas might seem to be isolated from the major cultural spots in the world, there are constantly developing scenes. Every town has their own garage bands in various stages of developments. The majority of the current bands are concentrated in the northwest section of the state-- in Topeka, Lawrence and Kansas City. The city of Wichita is also another area producing bands like The Moderns and The Embarrassment, both of whom have recordings out. One of the bigger, more successful groups is Thumbs, who have received extensive coverage from their first debut album. The Blue Riddim Band, a local reggae group, are extremely popular in the midwest. An important club in Kansas City, The Downliner, has weekend shows by area bands and is the spot for premiere appearances. Some bands that play there include The Regular Guys, The Clean, Abuse, The Debs, Hitler Youth, Office Supplies, and The Hodads, to name a few. There is a fast-developing scene emerging from the underground which is bound to have an effect on the midwestern way of life.

Bill Rich   (is the editor of Talk Talk, "the midwest rock and reggae magazine".)

MidWESTERN ROUNDUP!

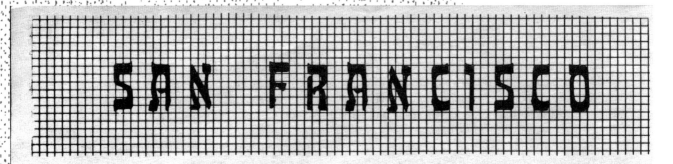

VOICE FARM: *MODERN THINGS/Sleep*   * OPTIONAL:

"...*systems of packaging, product design...*" <u>Modern Things</u> is snappy,
EXUBERANT techno-pop...synthesizers and a rhythm box intersect on rolling
hills, wavy lines. Vocalist Charly Brown is human and avoids the frigid
alienation usually associated with synthetic pop. A dynamic young Sinatra,
he gives us a strong/ yet vulnerable/ statement on global marketing. A
truly great 45. The flip, <u>Sleep</u>, is a beautiful rip-off and shoulda been
on Talking Heads' <u>Fear of Music</u>.

(15)

△ △ △ △ △ △ △ △ △ △ △ △

DEAD KENNEDYS: *HOLIDAY IN CAMBODIA/ police truck*   * OPTIONAL:

Suspence...Drama...Intrigue............ fluttering, accelerated snare drum,
I-spy lead guitar...this is definitely a soundtrack: starving, naked villag-
ers run slip-sliding through the muddy backroads..."you work all day for a
bowl of rice/ then you get your head skewered on a stake". Sweaty, paranoid
Jello Biafra tortures his quavering vocal chords, "...and your never coming
baaaccckkkk!!...". Exciting:: gut-shredded pop; as distinctly original as
their first 45 (and a heck of a lot more convincing, gosh dammit.)
p.s. - the production by Geza X is excellent and sounds alot more mature
than the sped-up, cartoonish version on the import l.p. (Fresh Fruit for
Rotting Vegetables...Cherry Red Records.)

▲ ▲ ▲ ▲ ▲ ▲ ▲ ▲ ▲ ▲ ▲ ▲ ▲ ▲ ▲ ▲

BOB: *THE THINGS THAT YOU DO/Thomas Edison*   * DUMB:

nervous pop. By negating electronics in favor of an xylophone, these
high-strung intellectuals come across as an organic, California Devo.
A distinctive element to, uh, "Bob" is the ping-pong vocal interaction
explored between a member of the male species and a member of the female
species. Ultimately... this record is stiff and predictable; arty, boring:
these bongo-brains just don't know how to have any fun. With a name like
"Bob", I really expected something a little more exciting...a band to
keep an eye on.

TUXEDO MOON: *HALF-MUTE* (L.P.)   * RALPH:

forget the leather studs and butt-fuck doggie collars gang, Tuxedo Moon
is it. definitive West Coast underground. The perfect California answer
to <u>No N.Y.</u>: whereas D.N.A. is sharp as nails, Tuxedo Moon is smooth as
glass, easy listening. Despite their obvious dream-like accessibility
though, Tux/Moon is creating some of the most innovative elevator music
in the world. Unlike the silent ambience of the latest Eno material,
T.M. focuses their meditation with a large electronic beat, suave and
handsome voice control and enough integrated circuits to keep your neurons
dancing for hours....They explore the same "cool" terrain as the Lounge
Lizards, the same moody isolationism of the new (dare we say it?) British
existentialists - Joy Division, The Cure, and so on. On their own turf
they clash with Factrix, who have similar electronic interests but prefer
to remain more abrasive, possibly more challenging. Tuxedo Moon is
cool and accessible (and alien); martini music for martians. However,
for those of you who wish a little poison in your cosmic cocktail (an
invasion from deathly outer-space), you should check out the new <u>Live</u>
<u>At Target</u> L.P.

16

BAY OF PIGS: ADDICTION/Aliens   * SUBTERRANEAN

weird and crazy. Addiction features bloopy, synthesized guitar-mania
(processed through a ring modulator). Aliens is more underground fever:
scratchy abstractions with an occasional limbo beat. It makes me feel
uncomfortable. As for the vocals... I'm sure I've heard this guy on a
cartoon somewhere (you know, the big dumb guy who says "duh, yeah boss"
and then gets punched in the nose?). The Bay of Pigs is a garage band
for the 90's. "smart".

SOCIETY DOG: WORKING CLASS PEOPLE/ Bad Dreams   * SUBTERRANEAN

early Clash. They've got it down. Working Class People is vicious, barking
dogma about your average mindless robot. Jonathan Christ sounds exactly
like Mick Jones. Should appeal to the dog collar crowd (California, Idaho,
etc.).

JARS: START RITE NOW/Psycho/ELECTRIC 3rd RAIL   * SUBTERRANEAN

basement pop. organ. catchy. makes me feel good. Start Rite Now is
the hit. Also: a good, revved-up, raved-up version of Psycho. Will
probably appear on Pebbles vol. 20.

FACTRIX: electronic, hypnotic landscape. lunar intensity.   * SUBTERRANEAN:
         a third world factory in outer space.

NERVOUS GENDER: dangerous. more electronics. chicano homosexuals
torture their instruments: radical politics. devastating.

UNS: sounds like pop after nervous gender. bright, clean production.
basically some local yokel talking over some electronic sandpaper. love it.

FLIPPER: unfortunately, these guys didn't have the money for synthesizers, so they had to create all their grit and asphalt with
ultra-distorted guitar. Whining, hopeless white boys desperately
searching for talent. A joke.

ARTY AND ABRASIVE. KEEP AWAY FROM CHILDREN. PLEASE.

NOH MERCY: *REVOLUTIONARY SPY/Caucasian Guilt*   * FAST:

2 girls play raw folk. <u>Revolutionary Spy</u> features one on maracas, one
on drums; gutsy chanting: earthy, ceremonial. they want to "*sabotage
the brakes of government cars*"....<u>Caucasian Guilt</u> (drums/vocals) is
enough to catapult any armchair liberal into an empty, suburban limbo;
after all, "*I never made no black my slave, I never dug no latino grave*".
Supposedly recorded on a cassette player, this record survives as a document;
Noh Mercy no longer exists... Politically and artistically, this is one
of the most radical statements yet to emerge from the U.S. underground.

OFFS: *EVERYONE'S A BIGOT/O*   * 415:

Whereas the Contortions (and the rest of the funky, N.Y. avant-gardists)
proclaim JAMES BROWN as *god almighty*, these cats seem to be more influenced
by the Stax/Volt sound-Sam and Dave etc. A big beat better than their 1st
45 (Johnny Too Bad), <u>Everyone's a Bigot</u> is the red hottest (white) R & B
to come out of the 1980's. Great dance record...

<u>PINK SECTION</u>: *PARTTIME/Francine's List/CALL HOME/Wine World/*
                   FLAT DOG

Judy plays a perfect glassy-eyed Lucille Ball (stoned on housework) who
lustfully admires her laundry list. "*...push-up bras, ankle-ettes...*"
<u>Francine's List</u> is the hit and picks up right where their first 45
(<u>Shopping</u>) left off. This whole E.P. is experimental and FUN and recommended. Unfortunately, this "West Coast B-52's" has broken up.
see: Naked City, Inflatable Boy Clams, Blackouts.   * MODERN:

TEXAS

houston

CULTURCIDE : CONSIDER MUSEUMS AS CONCENTRATION CAMPS/
Another Miracle

The Throbbing Gristle of Texas. vocalist/poet Perry Webb eats peyote
and strychnine and wakes up on the wrong side of town: moody, primitive
electronics and guitar. Webb's distinctive Southern drawl then proceeds
to compose aimless, neurotic dribble about Ricky Ricardo etc. The perfect
gift for that "special someone"(i.e. your gym coach).

* INFORMATION

REALLY RED: WHITE LIES/Modern Needs   * C.I.A.:

studio punk. occasional, effective use of dub echo. White Lies is about
as Texas as you can get: "Black folks prayin' to a White God". Modern
Needs is more catchy, social dogma (but nowhere near as sick and angry as
the Huns' Glad He's Dead 45). nice cover art.

19

austin

THE JUDYS: THE WONDERFUL WORLD OF APPLIANCES (12" E.P.)

minimalist Archies. doo-wop. Buddy Holly. The Judys are a teen-age
band with some diverse influences and a distinctive sound. Despite
unnecessary lyrics about Gary Gilmore and the Son of Sam (typical, boring),
The Judys prove themselves to be one of the most promising pop combos of
the year. young and talented... The E.P.'s got 6 songs and comes w/ a
bonus 3-track e.p.

D-DAY: TOO YOUNG TO DATE/ Everytime I Ask You Out   * WASTED TALENT

Las Vegas punk; 70's mainstream production. The lyrics are trendy and
simply drip with teen-age sexploitation. Expensive, glossy packaging
aims for a real dick-brained audience. Too Young to Date: some middle-
aged woman says she's 14 yrs. old and wants the boy next door to pop
her cherry. Should appeal to 95% of the male population.

* MOMENT PRODUCTIONS:

DELINQUENTS: ALIEN BEACH-PARTY/Motivation Complex/
DO YOU HAVE A JOB FOR A GIRL LIKE ME?   * LIVE WIRE:
file next to the trash-pop consciousness of Pink Section and the B-52's.
Alien Beach Party has got all the right clichés. fun, garbage pop.

BIG BOYS: FRAT CARS/Heartbeat/MOVIES/Mutant Rock   * BIG BOYS
good garage-band E.P. wham-bam punk (Frat Cars etc.) plus Heartbeat,
which is slower and could almost be called real music (by jocks and
parents at least). loose and sloppy. human touch. I like it, man.

* TEXAS - long regarded
as a mecca for chain-
saw punk bands, the mu-
sic in both Austin and
Houston is starting to
diversify. On a grand-
er scale, Texas is an
outpost for two of
the most exciting
publication sin the
U. S. of A.
read: X L R 8:
(Houston): local
news;great graphics.
SLUGGO: (Austin)
brilliant concept-
ual art. o

Big Boys

20

SUB POP #2 • 69

SEATTLE

Remember that scary article in NYR about "New Wave" being co-opted by Middle-America and all those "New Wave" bands playing "New Wave" covers in "New Wave" bars. Well, Seattle bought it, hook, line, and skinny tie.

And with "New Wave" bars came "New Wave" club owners. These guys can be traced directly down the evolutionary chain to old tire irons and smelly butcher's aprons.

When all you want to do is sell drinks, there is no functional difference between unique, true-blooded visionaries like the Macs and sleazy goons like the Frazz who specialize in ruining sixties classics. "New Wave" club owners wouldn't think twice about booking these diverse bands on the same bill. (is that bad?...ed.)

Another interesting aberration... the club owners and booking agents all despise each other. If a band works "steadily" for one agent or club, it runs the risk of loosing gigs with another because the respective owners despise each other. Most of the clubs are real dives too.

For better or worse, the Showbox (Modern Productions) still books locals to open for touring "big" bands. Also there's this X-leather bar called Wrex's.

Audiences are another problem. Seattle could easily be like Boston or Portland where people actively support local music. Seattle is certainly provincial. They love to emote about local dance, art openings, etc. There's supposed to be a lot of money in Seattle too. But people are too lazy or disinterested to go check out local bands. A friend of mine calls Seattle "a city looking for someplace to plug in the television."

Radio is part of the problem too. There's KZAM-AM's hybrid brand of Corporate Skinny Tie Schlock. How many times can anybody listen to Pat Benetar? Stephen Rabow does do a couple of shows a week which feature independent singles from the U.S. and Europe. That's really good for AM. But aside from that, it's pretty dismal.

LARRY BOURDAINE

21

CORRECTIVE LENSES is sparse, loose, cool but imposing. Sax, guitar, bass, vocals, coffee tin drums and lots of toys. Short songs. Arty with a sense of humor (though they wouldn't admit it).

1. *THE MACS* have just added a keyboard player who's supposed to be very "tasteful".

2. *THE BEAKERS* are rubbing elbows with Warner Brothers though there's nothing definite yet. They have lots of new material, Definitely Seattle's leading edge.

3. *LARRY and the MONDELLOS* have also added a keyboard/synthesizer geek and have really good new material. Upbeat girl/guy songs about heart attacks, fabric and love gone astray.

4. *BLACKOUTS* have recently added Steven Wymore (Pink Section bass player) to the group. This group is really fun these days. They're also playing a lot less which is a very good idea. Great vocal delivery. *(Please don't underestimate this incredible band. The Blackouts have just released some demo tapes, "Deadman's Curve" and "Probabilities", which will probably result in one of the hottest records to come out of the U.S. underground... ed.)*

5. *STUDENT NURSE* is a "multi-media" event with dancers, visual artists and poets- Mommy I'm confused!

7. *VISIBLE TARGETS* is three girls, one guy. Good 60's harmonies over "relentless" rhythm section. A cross between Leslie Gore and MX-80 SOUND.

8. *CUSTOMER SERVICE* is two guys with synthesizers, reeds, guitar and pre-recorded electronic rhythm sections. Disco-flavored dance music. Occasionally they use found films (auto safety/drug abuse). Not a concept but not really a band either. Orchestral Manoeuvres in the centerfuge.

The old Blackouts

LIFE ELSEWHERE 12" E.P.

FOSTER: "awkward, sincere, melodramatic"...ultimately the most original
act on the compilation. minimalist. possible reference point: Young
Marble Giants. short, one-minute songs are sung to a sparse, funky bass
line (synthesizer: played by Fisk). oh yes...an occasional off-balance
organ chord ignites when you least expect it. explosive. "Western Man",
"Cool World", "Junkie Reggae". this music is unlike anything I've heard.
(ever)

,,,,,,,,,,,,,,,,,,,,,,,,,,,,,,,,

FISK: "quirky, unrelenting electro-pop". premier synthesizer-brain
Steven Fisk mutates an avant-disco version of "Woodstock". the only song
i can think of that would sound good next to Donna Summer, Joni Mitchell
and/or Throbbing Gristle. You're Everything is more caffeine-inspired
pop technology. the beatniks never had it so good. Steve Peters steps in
on a wild sax break.

23 >   ,,,,,,,,,,,,,,,,,,,,,,,,,,,,,,,,,,,,,,

BEAKERS: "smart, loud, dissonant". insurging, 4/4 drum attacks. animated
vocals whip around the room like a lasso. static bass and some hot, amateur saxaphone. should be a hit in N.Y. "(I'm crawling) on the Floor" is
catatonic and fun. also: Figure 21. the first recording by Seattle's .
most vile and ugly and disgusting punk band. *I mean fun, funky & bright.*

* MR. BROWN:

BEAKERS: _RED TOWEL/Football Season is in Full Swing_   * MR. BROWN:

Football Season: "_Ed Lake/he has big ears/his lawnmower pulls him/around his yard/He goes step by step by step by step..._" Lyrically, the Talking Heads have had an obvious influence on the Beakers; they both make every-day observations that seem both simple and curious. Unlike the Heads however, the Beakers fuel their curiosity with a saxophone; a horn that is forever getting into trouble and creating tension... On Red Towel, Jim's **saxophone** wakes up disjointed and gives us a brief free-jazz introduction. As the funky march begins, he picks up the pace and bounces along with the rest of the troops... until, the dangerous climax: a chance encounter with what appears to be a giant sponge. The strangled result is a guttural, polluted sound that is about as deep and dirty as anything I've ever heard... With Jim Anderson's evolution as a sax player, the Beakers are quickly becoming one of the nation's most inventive dance bands.   24

THE MACS: _WALKING DOWN THE STREET/Cowboy Song_   * MR. BROWN:

Along with the Bongos and Epicycle, The Macs are undoubtedly one of the strongest students of 60's pop in the U.S. of A. In Walking Down the Street, we see an aching pop vocalist slide down some haunted London back alley: chilling. Cowboy Song is the real sleeper here though: a one-minute guitar intro (!?) proves Colin McDonell to be the most melodic guitarist in the U.S. underground. a classic.

(   ): _FUSCHIA RAYON/Song 4 America_ (tapes)   * MR. BROWN:

(   ) have undergone a number of name changes, from Larry & the Mondellos to the Sinatras to American Neighbor. Like lots of developing bands out there, (   ) spend as much time trying to come up with a name as they do playing music. Not that (   ) don't sound good (even great) 'cause vocalist Judy has got the sexiest, uh strongest, female vocal chords in Seattle. The (   ) pick up some bits and pieces from Pearl Harbor/Explosions and crowd in some squeeky-toy organ (ska beat). Hey, don't forget the drug-altering techno loops... wowsville, I'm not sure if I'm tripping or dancing. PLAY LOUD (Fuschia Rayon)... should be released as soon as a marketable image is "created".

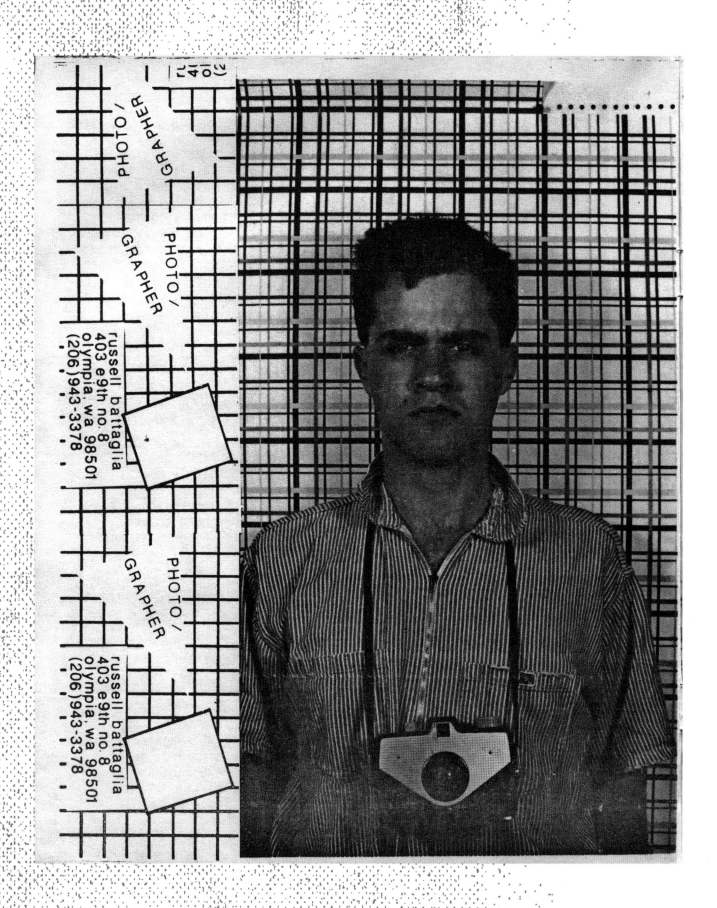

PHOTO/
GRAPHER

PHOTO/
GRAPHER

russell battaglia
403 e9th no. 8
olympia, wa 98501
(206)943-3378

PHOTO/
GRAPHER

russell battaglia
403 e9th no. 8
olympia, wa 98501
(206)943-3378

* ANGRY YOUNG RECORDS: 3701 Carpenter, Des Moines, Ia. 50311
* ARMAGEDDON: import label
* BIGTIME RECORDS: 641 N. Woodlawn #14, Wichita KS. 67208
* BIG BOYS: c/o Beth Kerr 4808 Ave. G, Austin, TX. 78705
* BIZART: 6609 Biddulph Rd., Cleveland, Ohio, 44144
* CHAMP RECORDS: 609 E. Nettleton, Independence, Mo. 64050
* C.I.A.: c/o Real Records, 2009 S. Shepard, Houston, Tx. 77019
* CIRKLE: c/o 657 Ash street, Winnetka, Ill. 60093
* DISTURBED RECORDS AND FILMWORKS: P.O. BOX 11463, Chicago, Il. 60611
* DROME: 11800 Detroit, Cleveland, Ohio 44107
* DUMB: 625 Post Street, Suite 129, San Francisco, CA. 94109
* FAST: import label
* FETISH: import; order through: 1118 Hudson St., Hoboken, N.J. 07030
* 415: P.O. Box 14563, San Francisco, CA. 94114
* GULCHER: (new) P.O. Box 1635, Bloomington, IN.
* INFORMATION: #114 3305 Montrose, Houston, TX. 77006
* LIVE WIRE: 5254 Meadowcreek Dr., Austin, TX. 70745
* MR. BROWN: P.O. Box 445, Olympia, WA. 98507
* MODERN: 1932 First Ave. Suite 1004 Seattle 98101
* MOMENT PRODUCTIONS: 1418 Preston, Austin, TX. 78703
* NO SWEAT: P.O. BOX 2791, Norman, Oklahoma 73069
* OPTIONAL: Berkeley Industrial Ct., Space #1, 729 Heinz Ave., Berkeley, CA.
(94701)
* PINK: c/o Franklin Stark, 1342 West Newport, Chicago, IL. (no zip given)
* RALPH: 444 Grove Street, San Francisco, CA. 94102
* RED ROOSTER: c/o Rounder Records, 1186 Willow Ave., Somerville, MA. 02144
* ROUGH TRADE: 1412 Grant Street, San Francisco CA. 94133
* SUBTERRANEAN: 912 Bancroft Way, Berkely CA. 94710
* TEKNO TUNES: Box 504, Amherst MA 01002
* WASP: 821 N. Taylor, Arlington VA. 22203
* WASTED TALENT: c/o 2111 Cedar, Pearland TX. 77581

(singles)

SEND 'EM $2.50

AMERICAN 45's

(1)	PYLON	COOL/DUB (Caution)	Athens GA
(2)	JAD FAIR	ZOMBIES OF MORA-TAU (Armageddon)	Baltimore MD
(3)	VOICE FARM	MODERN THINGS (Optional)	San Fran CA
(4)	RAY MILLAND	DISTANT VIEW (Praxis)	St. Louis MO
(5)	DEAD KENNEDYS	HOLIDAY IN CAMBODIA (Optional)	San Fran CA
(6)	GO-GO'S	WE'VE GOT THE BEAT (Stiff)	L.A. CA
(7)	PERE UBU	FINAL SOLUTION (Rough Trade)	Cleveland OH
(8)	BEAKERS	RED TOWEL (Mr. Brown)	Seattle WA
(9)	IMPORTS	VISIONS OF REALITY (Cirkle)	Chicago IL
(10)	FENSICS	TORNADO WARNING (No Sweat)	Norman OK
(11)	NOH MERCY	REVOLUTIONARY SPY (Fast)	San Fran CA
(12)	BAY OF PIGS	ADDICTION (Subterranean)	San Fran CA
(13)	MISSION OF BURMA	MAX ERNST (Ace of Hearts)	Boston MA
(14)	ANONYMOUS	SNAKE ATTACK (Flat)	Olympia WA
(15)	NEVASTRAU	LOOKING FROM AN AIRPLANE (Disturbing)	Chicago IL
(16)	HUNS	GLAD HE'S DEAD (God)	Austin TX
(17)	BUSH TETRAS	SNAKES CRAWL (99)	New York NY
(18)	BONGOS	GLOW IN THE DARK (Fetish)	Hoboken NJ
(19)	DILS	SOUND OF THE RAIN (Rogelletti)	San Fran/L.A.
(20)	WIPERS	ALIEN BOY (Trap)	Portland OR

ten 12" timebombs

(1)	TUXEDOMOON	HALF-MUTE (RALPH)	SAN FRANCISCO
(2)	DARK DAY	EXTERMINATING ANGEL (LUST/UNLUST)	NEW YORK
(3)	SHAGGS	PHILOSOPHY OF THE WORLD (RED ROOSTER)	PLUTO
(4)	PERE UBU	THE ART OF WALKING (ROUGH TRADE)	CLEVELAND
(5)	COMPILATION	LIFE ELSEWHERE (MR. BROWN)	OLYMPIA/SEATTLE
(6)	COMPILATION	LIVE AT TARGET (SUBTERRANEAN)	SAN FRANCISCO
(7)	PINK SECTION	12" E.P. (MODERN)	SAN FRANCISCO
(8)	SPECIAL AFFECT	TOO MUCH SOFT LIVING (S/AFFECT)	CHICAGO
(9)	WIPERS	IS THIS REAL? (TRAP)	PORTLAND
(10)	SUBURBS	IN COMBO (TWIN-TONE)	MINNEAPOLIS

"...we were forced to use parrot training records, etc., until a suitable vocalist finally showed up. After two weeks of practice, the complete and current band debuted at a party... 30 songs later, our playlist is no larger-- just enough to put out an album. It will be released around 30 October 1980, with our current rep still being decided by fans and critics, ranging from "Down-South AAnglophilia" to "spare boot-heel funk/rock." (?)"

PYLONFRÖMATHENS

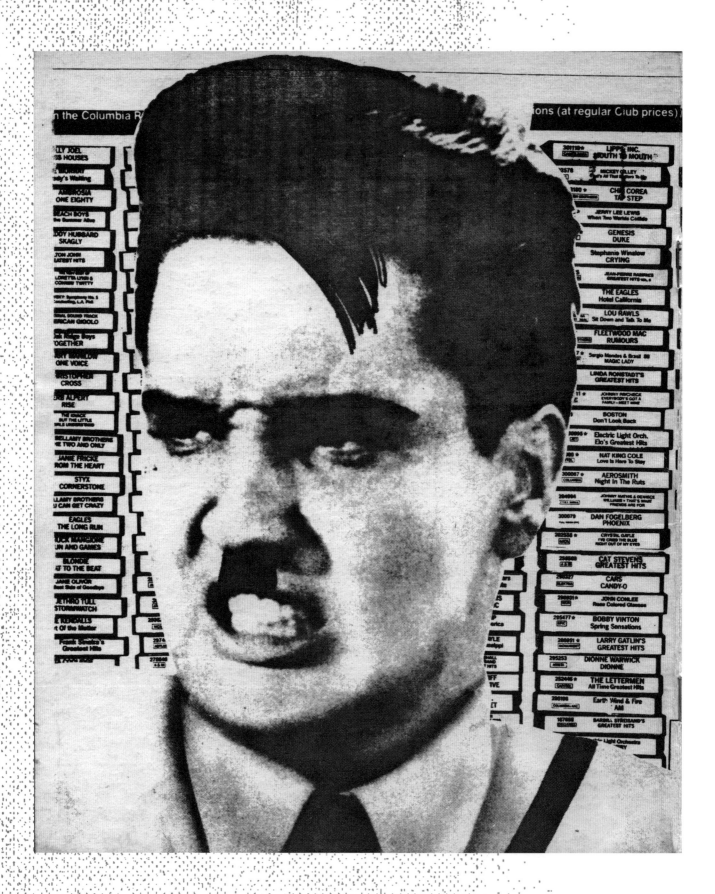

Faculty Review

The Evergreen State College – Olympia, Washington 98505

Faculty Evaluation of Student Achievement: 9/80 – 12/80

Bruce Pavitt produced very satisfactory work this quarter. Most of his time went into Subterranean Pop, a self conceived graphically pleasing national magazine about "de-centralized culture" as it applies to the rock subculture. Pavitt is knowledgeable and excited about independently-produced rock n' roll, and seems to have come up with a formula for the magazine that translates to sales at the marketplace. The issue he produced this quarter sold out its run of 500 immediately, minimizing the role he had to play in marketing it effectively. Of course, this ignores his real accomplishment, that of producing a magazine that fills a need.

Pavitt, like any good publisher, knows his audience. He reads every publication they read, and then some, and then figures out how it could best be examined and how it could best be presented. I was of help in some of the technical aspects of publishing and as an advisor.

Subterranean Pop is a fine magazine, and though location and resources keep it fairly simple, it is more cohesive and effective than any of the other rock n' roll magazines that we poured over. Pavitt has a clear idea of what he is doing, and the intensity he brings to everything he does shows through in the final product. It is a very personal and expressive magazine...

John Foster
Editor, OP magazine
12/29/80

SUB POP #3, *Spring 1981*
32pp, 7" x 8 1/2" format, hand-colored covers, print run of 500

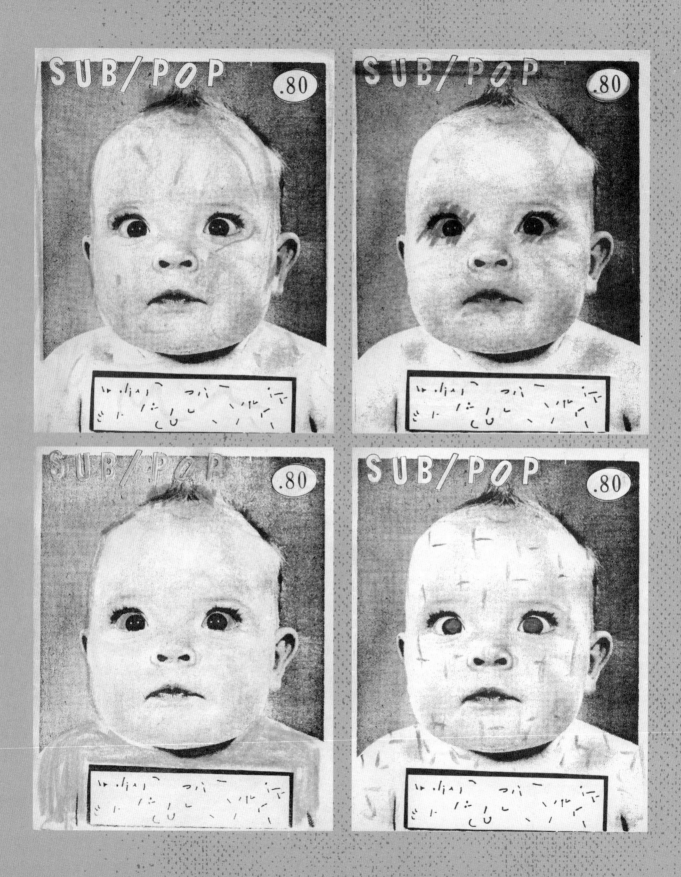

SUB POP #3, *Spring 1981*
32pp, 7" x 8 1/2" format, hand-colored covers, print run of 500

SPRING

1981

s u b · p o p

EDITING, WRITING, GRAPHICS - Bruce Pavitt
BACK COVER - Jad Fair
TYPING - Jan Loftness
SPECIAL THANKS TO: Lisa, Doug, Russell, Calvin,
                    Raliegh, John, Nancy, & Michael

3

SUB/POP IS PUBLISHED QUARTERLY BY THE LOST
MUSIC NETWORK, WHICH ALSO PUBLISHES OP MAGA-
ZINE.   LMN SERVES AS A CLEARING HOUSE FOR
INFORMATION ON INDEPENDENT MUSIC.
Sub/Pop: Ads are $25 a page. Subscriptions are $3/yr.
PLEASE WRITE US AT: LMN Box 2391 Olympia WA 98507

Hi there —

My name is Bruce and we have to decentralize our society and encourage Local art and things and music. SUB/POP can be an outlet for this kind of subversive entertainment perspective but only if you help me by writing local gossip and sending it in right away to me with money and photos of you and your friends playing rock star. Send it in and I will print it. O.K.

x Bruce

*ACE OF HEARTS   Box 579, Kenmore St., Boston MA 02215

*AMBITION   Box 3584, Washington D.C. 20007

*ARMAGEDDON   c/o 2775 E. Bankers Industrial Dr. Atlanta GA 30360

*BAD TRIP   11020 Ventura Blvd. Suite 218 Studio City CA 91604

*DB   432 Moreland Ave. N.E. Atlanta GA 30307

*EAT   400 Essex St. Salem MA 01970

*ENGRAM   P.O. Box 2305 Seattle WA 98101

*FETISH: import

*FRIENDS   319 E. Broadway Vancouver B.C. Canada

*FRONTIER   P.O. Box 22 Sun Valley CA 91352

*HUNKY RECORDS   Box 1287 Milwaukee WI 53201

*HYRAX   P.O. Box 274 Old Chelsea Stn. NY NY 10011

*LAFMS   c/o Box 2853 Pasadena CA 91105

*LUST/UNLUST   P.O. Box 3208 Grand Central Stn. NY NY 10163

*MUTE: import

*MYSTERY TOAST   Box 195 Saratoga Springs NY 12866

*99   99 MacDougal St. NY NY 10012

*OIL TASTERS   Box 92823 Milwaukee WI 53202

*ON/GO-GO   P.O. Box 8333 Philadelphia PA 19101

*PARK AVENUE   P.O. Box 14947 Portland OR 97214

*POSH BOY   P.O. Box 38861 Los Angeles CA 90038

*QUINTESSENCE   1869 W. 4th Ave. Vancouver B.C. Canada

*RED   810 Longfield Rd. Philadelphia PA 19118

*ROLLIN ROCK   6918 Peach Ave. Van Nuys CA 91406

*SHAKE   186 5th Ave. NY NY 10010

*UPSETTER   Box 2511 LA CA 90023

*SST   P.O. Box 1 Lawndale CA 90260

*STIFF: import

*SUBURBAN INDUSTRIAL   1218 Loma Vista Long Beach CA 90813

*TRAP   Box 42465 Portland OR 97242

*TWIN TONE   445 Oliver Ave. So. Minneapolis MN 55405

*UPSETTER   Box 2511 L.A. CA 90023

*WHIZ EAGLE RECORDS   308 S.W. Washington Portland OR 9720?

PYLON
GYRATE

ATHENS

METHOD ACTORS: THE METHOD/Can't Act/BLEEDING   *ARMAGEDDON

Minimalist dance band. 1 guitar, 1 drum. Upbeat rock and roll with
odd guitar tunings and occasionally abstract phrasing. A tearful,
wailing voice comes across as emotional, melancholy even. The A-side
has overdubs and is not minimal. Some songs "go on too long". I like
this 45 a lot but most of you pea-brains out there probably won't
appreciate it.

PYLON: GYRATE (L.P.)   *DB

Like the flourescent orange cones they're named after, Pylon signifies caution.
Too bad. With the dangerous, mid-tempo marching of their debut 45 (Cool/Dub),
Pylon warned the Western world that there was more to Athens, Georgia than a
few boring B-52's. Vanessa, dancing in her pretty dress, showed Mom and Dad
what passion and torment was really all about. ,This woman was <u>possessed</u>
and she had a microphone to prove it. But here it is.... the big time. An
album: slick artwork, expensive studio time, international distribution.
Pylon - "The next big thing". Obviously, we are talking about a band that is
honored by important people with insight and money. After hours of painful
listening however, I've gotta say that this record is disappointing. Sure,
it's "good"; believe me folks, this is a good, good, good record. But it's
not a fucking masterpiece. You know, like I won't be playing this 10 years
from now. This album... is just... a little... too cautious. Pylon, you
people are scared of your own shadow. If you just opened your heart and
ripped into something, you could tear this universe into tiny little pieces.
Instead, you plod through your tunes like a hostage in handcuffs. You're
lazy. This record lacks involvement and it lacks ideas. Fortunately, Vanessa
sinks her teeth into a few minor miracles; for the most part though, she
hesitates   looks both ways before crossing. She sounds unsure
of herself, as does the rest of the band... This is a beautifully packaged
album by one of the best new groups around. Oustanding cuts include: *Danger,
Feast On My Heart.* <u>Be sure to check out their first 45.</u>

Human Body

BOSTON

HUMAN SEXUAL RESPONSE: *FIG. 14 (L.P.)*   *EAT

College pop. Fun, witty and occasionally obscene. Four New Wavy people
open their mouths and sing like the King Family (deep throats make beautiful harmonies). The only problem here is a (yawn) very traditional
back-up band. In fact, there's barely a new musical idea to be found anywhere on this record; lyrics and harmonies are this band's only strong
points... "Jackie Onassis" is funny. "Anne Frank" is tender and poignant
and serious. "Cool Jerk" is a total dud. "Guardian Angel" is another
cover tune and is coated with sticky glucose, layers of rich white icing.
"Dick and Jane" is quoted straight from the textbook. How cute. The
guitar here is very modern and cool (for a change). The obvious anthem
here though is "What Does Sex Mean To Me". This is bound to be a co-ed
slumber party favorite. Dig these words: I touch my finger to my tongue/
I taste vagina/I licked Betty Ford's boots/She wore them all over China.
Ha Ha. squirm. giggle. Yes, this record will appeal to many.

MISSION OF BURMA: *MAX ERNST/Academy Fight Song*   *ACE OF HEARTS

In *Academy Fight Song*, we hear a wired, fragmented tale about love, sex,
and the sound of marching feet. The tone is desperate and the music is
driving. The flip, *Max Ernst*, is more of the same but not quite as powerful.
The in-joke here is the pretentious chanting of Dada, Dada, Dada; a contrived
reference to an art movement based on spontaneous action. Overall though,
this is a literate, compassionate 45 and is definitely recommended.

MISSION of
BURMA.

Los Angeles

Two excellent compilations of stupid L.A. punk rock. After listening
to minutes and hours and days and nights of thrashing, bashing, smashing
Excedrin pogo-pop, *my head is now a purple marshmallow. my intelligence
is obviously bruised beyond recognition.* I can't see and I can't hear but
*I will try and speak openly and frankly about what your son is doing tonight
Mrs. Johnson.* Yes... this is Los Angeles, City of the Dead. The music
here is numb and of course it is exciting. It's manic and it's depressing.
It's angry and it's hostile and it's heavy and it's blistering and it's
dizzy. You bring the leather and I'll bring the beer. We're gonna bust
the cops and dive head first into a bobbing mass of stupid pussies you
dumbfuck. Suck on this. My head fell off louder, faster, bigger.

The Decline of Western Civilization was recorded live and is filled with
sweat, spit, leather, bandanas, mohawks, insults from the crowd, insults
from the band and yes even a few profound interviews with fans and stars.
... All the big names are here: X, Germs, Black Flag, Cirkle Jerks, Alice
Bag Band, Fear, and Catholic Discipline... Catholic Discipline was fronted
by Claude Bessy (ex-editor of SLASH) and sounds cute and weird (confused
French accent with choppy guitar and Doors-type organ)... Out of the most
obvious of the "hard core" bands - Black Flag, Cirkle Jerks and Fear - it
is Fear that gets the green light as they run over their audience with
some of the rudest, ogre-like witticisms I have heard in ages. As a whole,
this sound track L.P. (yeah, I forgot to tell ya SLASH made a movie of
all this) is a - deep breath - MUST for anybody interested in L.A.
Plenty of chaos, comments, insights, and all 'round human degradation.

*SLASH

Rodney On the Roq is the other record you should try and track down.
Rodney is a jerk-off D.J. in love with Brooke Shields (Brooke even
introduces the first song). Rodney has puppy-dog eyes and he loves his
punk rock. He's been playing tapes of obscure young bands on KROQ radio
for a few years and now he's helped get these lost children of paradise
into a good recording studio! Praise God 'cause this record is a smash.
The sound is very produced and the result is more of a punk/pop sound
than pure chainsaw - buzz - orgasm. Most of these tunes are catchy,
accessible and will probably receive the airplay they deserve. Top 40
punk. Some outrageously strong anthems (Cirkle Jerks, Crowd, Agent Orange,
Adolescents, Simpletones, U.X.A., Black Flag) some pure pop (David
Microwave, Nuns) and even some trash avant-garde (New York, Fender Buddies).
Although definitely not as raw and sloppy as Decline..., Rodney on the ROQ
is still a hit. In fact, *this is the most exciting rock 'n roll compilation
to come out of America since the whole scene started.* Turn up **the volume.**

*POSH BOY

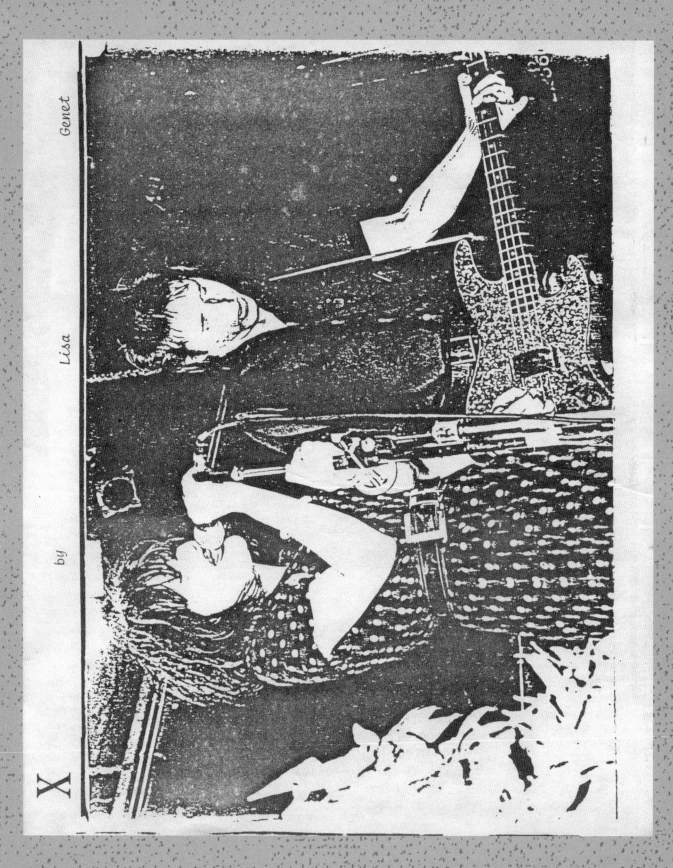

X

by

Lisa

Genet

BLACK FLAG: *JEALOUS AGAIN (12" E.P.)*   *SST

I guess it's unfair to ask for another record on par with "Nervous
Breakdown". They've gone through so much since then/ It really
doesn't matter what I think of this record anyway. Black Flag fans
are legion and militant. - Calvin

FLESH EATERS: *NO QUESTIONS ASKED (LP)*   *UPSETTER

Intense, satan-inspired poetry. The vocalist is a distinctive, wormy
tenor. Creepy punk rock.

UXA :   *ILLUSIONS OF GRANDEUR (L.P.)*   *POSH BOY

One of my top ten albums of 1980. Lots of power and sometimes
scary lyrics. Good females vocals, too. POSH BOY's best album
for sure. - Calvin

GERMS: *G.I. (L.P.)* *SLASH

This album has been out for over a year and by now the Germs have disbanded.
So what. Genius homo Darby Crash has come up with one of the most literate
works of art ever to come out of the U.S. underworld. Like Shakespeare
with a vibrator in his hand, Darby led the Germs into a blur of chaos,
confusion and radical adult entertainment. This band was outlawed from
every club in L.A. Onstage, the Germs inspired everybody to do everything -
riots were mandatory. On this record, our poet laureate snarls and slurs
his sloppy vocal technique all over the bulging microphone. What a record.
Buy this album, read and memorize the lyric sheet - it's incredible.
... By the way, smart genius Darby recently shot heroin into his body and
died.

ANGRY SAMOANS: INSIDE YOUR HEAD (12" E.P.)   *BAD TRIP

Stupid fascist pigs play stupid fascist rock 'n roll. If you like to
kill and maim, well then, I guess this is your kinda dog food. Bow Wow.
Kill 'em Tiger. I think there is a difference between anger and frustration (Black Flag) and ugly, violent neo-fascism. Bad trip indeed.

CIRCLE JERKS GROUP SEX (L.P.) *FRONTIER

Mellow folk rock. Kinda like Jackson Browne.

BLASTERS: AMERICAN MUSIC (L.P.)   *ROLLIN ROCK

The cover is your typical Rollin' Rock ugly graphics type. The music,
according to their liner notes, is "highly influenced by Rhythm and
Blues, New Orleans, Cajun, Blues, Hillbilly, and Rockabilly." O.K.,
I can dig it. My personal faves: "Flat Top Joint", "Barefoot Rock",
"American Music", and "Marie, Marie". - Calvin

NON: (multi-song 7" E.P.)   *MUTE

This record has two holes in it: ~~please~~ play ~~it~~ at any speed.
Literally warped, elliptical and abstract, this is the most con-
ceptually interesting record to come out of the U.S. since the
Archies released "Sugar, Sugar" on the back of a cardboard cereal
package. (Also note: Smegma from Portland is on the flipside).

X: WHITE GIRL/Your Phone's Off the Hook   *SLASH

I predict big success for this single. A commerical record without
losing that distinctive X sound. It will actually remind you of the
Mamas and Papas. The flipside is my fave song from LOS ANGELES (L.P.).
Put toge
Put together, this is a must have for anybody's 45 collection. - Calvin

GO-GO's: *WE GOT THE BEAT/How Much More*   *STIFF

America's premier girl band comes up with an A-plus dance 45.
The Go-Go's mix Motown and traditional rock 'n roll for a classic
60's sound: "We've Got the Beat" works great next to "Dancin' in
the Street" by Martha and the Vandellas. This is a hit.

SUBURBAN LAWNS: JANITOR/Protection *SUBURBAN INDUSTRIAL

Riding high on the success of their distinctive first 45 (Gidget Goes to Hell/
My Boyfriend), *and* a blurb on the corporate Sharp Cuts anthology, this band
seemed obvious candidates for big time subversion. This record is a dud, though
... On *Janitor*, Sue Tissue is still inventive (shades of Lene Lovich) but she
is irritating; about as fun and squeeky as Doris Day in a rubber suit. boring
guitar chords. some interesting reggae inspired drumming, Hmmmmm... Keep an
eye on this band - I know they can do a lot better than this.

DARKER SCRATCHER: (L.P.) *LAFMS

Side One   (Los Angeles Free Music Society L.P. #12)

BOYD RICE, DANIEL MILLER (*Cleanliness and Order*) Robotic female narrative
instructs children on how to keep clean and pick up toys, all in front
of a pleasant, rythm-box beat. JAD FAIR (*XXOO*) Childish, "naive", primitive
instrumentation. "Boys like girls/girls like boys; kiss, kiss, kiss/kiss,
kiss, kiss." 30 seconds of pure genius. Jad is from the state of Maryland.
VETZA (*Stale Puppy Dog Tails*) Vetza is a woman. Zsa Zsa Gabor at midnight
in a see-through plastic nightgown. Seductive and alien. Free-form drums
and tape processing. THE RICK POTTS BAND (*Platform Swimfins*) Very funny
cabaret lounge act. Rick sings about dancing in platform swimfins.
MONITOR (*Guardian*) Zoned-out instrumental. Rhythmic, electronic waves
running backwards and forwards simultaneously. DOODOOETTES (*Pork Had
Better Behave*) Weird noise. 45 GRAVE (*Riboflavin-flavored, Non-carbon-
ated, Polyunsaturated Blood*) A silly and sinister top 40 hit. Stick
between the Munsters and Monster Mash. NON (*Non-Watusi*) Droning tape
loop drags against the inner label. Chew you pencil and drink your coffee
and chew your pencil.

Side Two

FOUNDATION (*Nap*) Hypnotic and accessible. Top 40 mood music. AIRWAY
(*Perpendicular Thrust*) Astronaut feedback with drums. DENNIS DUCK
(*Davey the Worm*) Sax, interesting percussion, tapes and vocals. rhythmic.
LE FORTE FOUR (*The Lowest Form of Music*) Ugly and funky. Back in your cage.
Get back. HUMAN HANDS (*I Got Mad*) gross, intelligent and aggressive. This
tune pulls at your ankles till your lungs full with quicksand. Synthesizer:
sophisticated pogo. BPEOPLE (*The Other Thing*) Notorious art band
rocks out. Outer Limits on wheels. Iggy Pop on Mars. Lots of heavy guitar
chords, man. And best of all: the synthesizer is like that Dick Van Dyke
rerun where Dick dreams about having a green cabbage for a head. Laura
slides out of a closet of walnuts. "I seeee you" get me outta here.

MILWAUKEE

<u>AMA-DOTS</u>: *HIT GIRLS/The Cease is Increase*   *HUNKY RECORDS

Boys and Girls play Modern pop with a garage band sound.

<u>OIL TASTERS</u>: *GET OUT OF THE BATHROOM/What's In Your Mouth?*

Milwaukee's most blabbed about dance band comes up with a real shoe-tapper.
For a rather small combo (sax, bass, drums), these young men certainly
punch with a big fist. "Get Out of the Bathroom" starts off with a bright,
metallic bass guitar. The sax is obese and bouncy and basically takes
over your entire house; very full and very rhythmic - James Brown fans
take note. The flip, "What's In Your Mouth?" is a lazy rubber ball and
is more interested in dribbling on your carpet than in making people
dance. It is definitely O.K. though. The <u>Oil Tasters</u> are one of the
most interesting bands in the U.S. right now. There is only one problem:
a tasteless jr. high sense of humor that tends to fall flat on its
funny little face. If these boys would just *please* stop giggling about
poo-poo and regurgitated pizza, I think we'd have one hell of a brilliant
dance band. *OIL TASTERS

OIL TASTERS by Doug Taylor

MINNEAPOLIS

OVERTONES: *RED CHECKERED WAGON/Surfer's Holiday/CALHOUN SURF*

The term "surf music" means more than nice Beach Boy harmonies and striped shirts. It includes wild surf instrumentals, hot rods, girls, teen-agers and other stuff like that. The Overtones have captured that scene perfectly. "Red Checkered Wagon" is the most danceable hot rod song ever. Don's voice is cool, not high and smooth, more like Ronny and the Daytonas or the Rip Chords. "Surfer's Holiday" is an old Wilson/Usher/Christian tune, and "Calhoun's Surf" is a class A surf instrumental. Yea for American surf (dance) music! - Calvin   *TWIN TONE

CURTISS A: *COURTESY*   *TWIN TONE

Curtiss A is a live performer. I first saw him a year and a half ago at the old Longhorn in Minneapolis. It was a time of immensely high popularity for Curt, a time when the big buzz around town was his debut album, certain to come out at any time. On "Courtesy", it appears he has everything going for him. The first tracks on both A and B sides are interesting, but subsequent tracks are disappointing to say the least. Tempos run astray from any production consistency, material is trite, Curt's vocals become frantic screams, a smell of unevenness abounds (the LP was produced by Paul Stark, SUBURBS). The single taken from the album, "Afraid", is strong material - if it weren't driven into the ground with needless length.

The Twin City music scene has been alive since the inception of the the town square, and live energy has always built up good, even great, reputations. The fledgling recording industry there, on the other hand, lacks good producers, and appears to maintain the feeling of sterile environment for the artists when a recording is made (unless, as in the case of the Lamont Cranston clan, live cuts are incorporated on the disc). Everyone - producer and artist alike - has to relax more at the helm. I think there's a big rush in the Twins right now to try and get as much material out as fast as possible and point out to the world that something's happening there.

- Raleigh Schwenker

Some New Yorkers will tell you that the New York music scene is dead. Others will swear it's at its best ever. While we've got to admit we haven't been around the scene forever, we'd tend to agree with the latter opinion. There are always good bands playing, there is always something to do. There are many, many new bands, there are new clubs opening all the time, and there are always out-of-town bands passing through, playing a few gigs at this club and that club.

Top "modern sound" NY bands right now include the Bongos, Liquid Liquid, the Individuals, ESG, Raybeats, Bush Tetras, Polyrock (just signed to RCA), Nite Caps and the Dance. Two popular hardcore punk bands are the Stimulators and the Bad Brains.

Totally new, unheard of bands and the hardcore punk bands usually play a circuit of CBs and Max's, plus Botany, S.N.A.F.U., the 80's Club and sometimes at a private club called Cartune Alley. Popular out-of-town

bands and bigger New York bands plus some British groups play Hurrah, Peppermint Lounge, Privates, Rock Lounge and Mudd. Bigger, international bands usually play at Club 57/Irving Plaza or the Ritz or Bonds International Casino (formerly Bonds International Disco). There are some ommissions in our listing here, but generally these are the main live-music night spots.

A big news item around town now is that Ron Delsener, dreaded BIG "Rock Promoter" in NY (who owns outright the 3,000 seat Palladium, formerly the Academy of Music), is converting a club he's owned for several years into a "new wave club". This very well-off promoter has so much power and influence that, sadly, his "new wave club" might force the smaller, struggling promoters to fold their operations.

Ruth Polsky, who books band into Hurrah, is setting a gig in London at the Rainbow Theatre in cooperation with a British promoter, featuring 6 New York bands. The following bands will perform in London on February 20th: the Bongos, the Raybeats, the Bush Tetras, the dBs, Polyrock and the Fleshtones. This promises to be a big event, as there has been no all-NY bill like this in London before.

One piece of advice we'd like to slip in here for out-of-town bands trying to get gigs in NY: aside from of course sending your tape to the club, it will be very helpful in getting them to remember you if you have a lot of favorable local press. Try to make yourself sound like a real big deal in your home area. Rather than writing and saying "We are the Neurotic Blobs from San Francisco. Here's our tape," it's much better to write, "We're the Neurotic Blobs from San Francisco. Along with our tape, we've enclosed copies of some of our better write-ups in such important

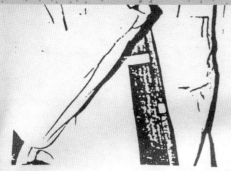

New York

publications as Damage, Boulevards, Slash, Creep, the LA Times, the SF Examiner, Subterranean Pop and Another Room. We've been headlining on weekends at the Mabuhay for several months now, and we'll be making our NYC debut during the first week of April. We were referred to you by our friends the Offs and Factrix, both of which played your club. They told us you have a great sound system (are a great club to play, etc.), so we'd like to get in at least one gig there." Etc, etc.

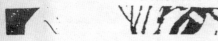

In short, do anything to establish your band in their minds and make them believe they <u>must</u> have you play at their club. Make them want you!

Hope this helps anyone planning an East Coast tour.

Note to fanzine writers: if you want to sell your 'zine in New York, contact Stan at Sohozat, 307 West Broadway, NYC. They sell a lot of mags and 'zines from all over, and Stan is a serious fanzine nut, so he's anxious to here from you all.

Nancy Breslow and Jim Short
Short Newz Fanzine
P.O. Box 1028
Gracie Station NYC 10028

photo by lisa genet

LOUNGE LIZARD

GLEN BRANCA: *LESSON NO. 1 FOR ELECTRIC GUITAR/DISSONANCE* (12" 45)

"New Music". Glenn Branca is the Beethoven of the New York underworld. *99 recommended.

LOVE OF LIFE ORCHESTRA: *GENEVA* (L.P.)   *LUST/UNLUST

Johnny Carson pop. Sappy, commercial and intriguing. Peter Gordon is the Doc Severinsen of the New York underworld.

MATERIAL: *DISCOURSE/Slow Murder*   *RED

Loose and funky combination of jazz "fusion" and dub. Vocalist sounds like xeroxed Stranglers on side 1 and Magazine on side 2. A "progressive" record that comes across as both serious and artificial.

OUR DAUGHTER'S WEDDING: *LAWN CHAIRS/Airline*

More artificial sound from N.Y. This time it's from the barren, frozen wasteland of sythetic pop. "Lawn chairs are everywhere, they're everywhere and my mind describes them to me." This vocalist is some rich, suave kinda guy whose parents decided to buy him a rhythm box so he could be in a band. This is the closest American counterpart to Mr. Gary Numan. Not bad.

BONGOS: *HUNTING/In the Congo/MAMBO SUN*

The latest release from Fetish, a British label that is in love with New York City. The Bongos, along with the d.b.'s, are a "great" New York pop band. They are good at what they do. You will find them pleasant and charming and even lovable (like the Beatles). This record was recorded in an expensive studio. It will receive lots of airplay. "Mambo Sun" is a T. Rex cover.

MECHANICAL SERVANTS: *MIN X MATCH (12" E.P.)*   *MYSTERY TOAST

Synthetic Slits. Two girls and a friend play lush, perky electronic pop.
Very interesting vocal interaction between Pamela and Victoria. fave rave:
"Problem, What Problem?"

BUSH TETRAS: *TOO MANY CREEPS/Snakes Crawl/TASTE LIKE THE TROPICS*

The Bush Tetras are a very popular N.Y. band. Pat Place (ex-Contortion)
plays her famous atonal slide guitar. I am really impressed. Too bad
she hasn't had a new idea in two years. This is funky, experimental
art-school pop. I'm sure everyone in N.Y. just l-o-v-e-s it. You
probably will too. Fave cut: Taste Like the Tropics.   *99

CHANDRA : *(12" E.P.)* *ON/GO-GO

Spooky, spiraling disco sung by a 13 year old girl named Chandra. She is
backed up by the DANCE.   This is a very interesting
record. (I like "Kate" - typist).

JOHN GAVANTI *(L.P.)*   *HYRAX

Former members of no-wave combo Mars, plus Iko (D.N.A.) on drums, strings.
This is "opera", a reinterpreted version of Don Giovanni. Imagaine this:
through some bizzare accident, Captain Beefheart suddenly becomes a total
vegetable. Meanwhile, an amateur jr. high orchestra decides to play the
local looney-bin. The two parties intersect. Beefheart grabs a microphone and starts mumbling and drooling. *(This record is not for the sane
or the insane, it's for the terminally ridiculous.)*

RICHARD HELL/NEON BOYS: *LOVE COMES IN SPURTS/That's All I Know*
              /VOIDOIDS: *TIME/ Don't Die* *SHAKE

Richard Hell. His original, Ork recording of *Blank Generation* defined an
entire decade in 3 minutes. A legend. Then, after a visionary, underrated L.P. on Sire and a one-off single on Stiff, Richard went into hiding.
All right, enough background. This earthy, excellent E.P. includes 2 cuts
by the *historically imperative* Neon Boys of the early 70's (featuring Tom
Verlaine, ex-Television). These are wild, garage band classics. The flip
contains 3rd generation Voidoids doing *Time* and *Don't Die*. *Time* is a ballad
- it's beautiful. *Don't Die* features cha-cha sandblock percussion and a
mysterious Nico-like figure in the foreground. Both tunes are reminiscent of
the Velvet Underground. Buy this record.

DARK DAY: EXTERMINATING ANGEL [L.P.] *LUST/UNLUST

Somber, trance-pop. Hypnotic and very adult. Sacred electronic rituals.
Soothing. Soak it up through your pores. Dark Day. Bewitching Robin
Crutchfield is a modern day warlock reciting deep dark incantations.
"Cats whisper/Cat's whisker/Cat's breath... Cat's paw/Cat's cradle/
Crib death". Alone in his room, Robin is a lonely man. He is brooding
over mystery. He is sacrificing his soul on a marble slab in an empty
room. He is staring at his thoughts. Robin likes to think. He has a
friend who plays drums and a friend who plays guitar and other things.
Dark Day is perfectly suited for a Long Playing record. This music just
goes on and on and I am in a trance.

SNATCH: JOEY/Red Army/SHOPPING FOR CLOTHES   (3-song 12" E.P.)

Patti Smith marries Brian Eno. The mystical, pregnant result is a   *FETISH
female double duo quietly referred to as "Snatch". These girls grew
up very beatnik: a combination of jive talk, tape loops and nightclub
jazz; bongos, German monologues and half-sung pop dialogues. I literally
have to wear a beret every time I listen to this abstract double talk.
Pass the espresso. By the way, this is a 12" import and it's very expensive.
I recommend you borrow a copy and tape it. This music definitely deserves
more than one listen.

photo by Lisa Genet

S
N
A
T
C
H

PORTLAND PUNK - LIVE AT THE EARTH 10-29-79   *TRAP

This record features: Wipers, Neo Boys, Smegma, Lotek, Bop Zombies, Rubbers, Cleavers, Sado-Nation, Styphnoids. Punk Rock Live. Not as sick and danger- ous as ~~the~~ L.A. ~~████████████~~ punk rock ~~████████~~ ~~████████████~~ Of special note: the quasi-mystical girl band NEO BOYS have on this here record possibly the greatest female rock 'n roll tune ever. It is called "Running in the Shadows". This is the Neo Boys at their best.

WIPERS:(4 song 7" E.P.)   *PARK AVENUE

An excellent release by Portland's most popular rock band. The sound here is not modern; it is classic and timeless. "Alien Boy" is from their highly recommended "Is This Real?" L.P. The Wipers will probably appeal to fans of Iggy Pop.

PORTLAND

THE RATS: (L.P.)   * WHIZ EAGLE

Peter, Paul, and Mary play Punk ro

Peter, Paul and Mary play punk rock. Sometimes it works and sometimes it doesn't. I really like the minimal recording;it sounds authentic enough for the Library of Congress.

SADO NATION: (4 song 7" E.P.)   * TRAP

Good punk with female vocals. "Mom and Pop Democracy" is a hit. Nice Nice cover art. recommended.

The A.A.A. is a non-profit organization which promotes alternative music. The A.A.A. (Alternative Arts Association) has been around in one form or another since early 1978, with the idea of opening a club run by the bands and other interested people. We got together and put on some shows downtown at *Revenge*, set up *The New Arts Center* (which died a rapid death), put on shows at halls around the city, and ran all age shows at a number of bars. This group, The A.A.A., now runs *Clockwork Joe's*.

Clockwork Joe's is a club that has shows most weekends, has five practice rooms and also houses the *Friction Art Gallery*. The A.A.A. also distributes Portland records, has one compilation album out and will be releasing another compilation later this year. MICHAEL X. KING

The upcoming A.A.A. sampler L.P. will contain: Sado Nation, The Rats, Bop Zombies, Smegma, Jungle Nausea, The Imperialist Pigs, The Braphsmears, Poisen Idea, The Preps, The Dot, and more. A.A.A. Box 40580 Portland OR 97204

The forthcoming *Pigface* compilation record will feature: Smegma, Spy vs. Spy, Jungle Nausea, and more. Pigface 76 N.E. Thompson Portland OR 97212

The soon to be released *Trap* sampler will include The Wipers, The Untouchables, Bill M., and Pell Mell. Trap Records Box 42465 Portland OR 97242

photo russell battraglia

the rats

National Acts: call Singles Going Steady at (503) 226-7592 for booking info

MORE NOTES ON A.A.A. - All members have equal say about projects that they
are or want to be involved in... for example, show bookings are handled
by the bands themselves, records distribution policies are set by the
groups that have records out to be distributed, the Joe's space downtown
is operated by its working staff, etc. We don't play it up or even
mention it too often, but A.A.A. runs along anarcho-syndicalist lines,
as opposed to capitalist or authoritarian ones. We are a business, and
we deal with money and real-life business problems, but our internal
affairs are determined on a more progressive basis than you'll find at,
say, the Showbox. It works.

Portland in more general terms is harder to condense into, what, three
paragraphs? I would say that Portland has been unusually supportive
of its own local bands since a "scene" first emerged at the beginning
of '78. The new wave bands over the last 3 years are a diverse bunch,
but two features strike me a characterizing Portland punk in general.
1) No pop influence at any point - pop in the sense of Tom Petty/
Beatle rip-offs/safe-for-the-music- industry good time smiling bands
with nice ties. This sort of escapism never took root among any of
the new wave musicians here. 2) Minimalism - this is a bad town for
bands like the Blackouts, who take complication as a value in itself;
there are "modern" bands in Portland, but it is not a false modernity
achieved by tricky, over-intellectualized arrangements of pallid
material. Excess is not a substitute for ideas, and Portand bands
have tended to frame strong ideas against simple backdrops. Portland
is not "stuck in 1977", but neither is it hung on the notion that 80's
new wave must be played by university students with specialized
training in how to be avant-garde.

                                                MARK STEN

ARNI MAY	MIKE SCHENK	BILL OWEN	BOB BEERMAN
GUITAR / SAX	BASS	GUITAR	DRUMS

THIS IS AN ADVERTISEMENT FOR pell mell
a modern dance band from portland..........
if you would like them to play for you, call Bob
at 503-295-1938.................................
PELL MELL will be releasing 2 songs on the upcoming
TRAP SAMPLER L.P. These songs are called Red Rhythm
and Catwalk. This summer, Pell Mell will release
a 12" 45 featuring New Saigon plus 2 other songs.
This record will also be on TRAP Records. PELL MELL
IS A GOOD BAND AND YOU SHOULD LISTEN TO THEM.......

BLACKOUTS: (4 SONG 12" E.P.)   *ENGRAM

A great E.P. by Seattle's legendary Blackouts. Although the frowning,
contemplative sound of this band was usually boring live (no room for
spontaneity), this tightly knit combo is perfect on record. These songs
are thoughtful, controlled compositions - somewhat reminiscent of Ultravox
at their best. Some notes I have jotted down here in my notebook include
pretentious phrases like "clusters of barbed wire guitar/outlined by
fields of open space." Fuck am I clever. I guess I should also mention
that "sax and synthesizer add a rich variety in texture and dynamics".
By the way, the Blackouts spent a hundred million dollars recording these
four songs and it was worth every penny. The sound here is extremely
3-dimensional. Like Einstein after dark, this record *actually walks out
of your living room*, stark and naked. Embarrassingly brilliant, this
E.P. is an epic, a masterpiece and a monument to human civilization.
Highly recommended.

*Briefly - here are some of the big, big changes in the Seattle music scene...
KZAM-AM, which featured the most subversive am show in America (Music For
Moderns), has now changed its format to heavy metal, soft pop, killer tunes
man, and other such garbage. Thanx KZAM, it was fun while it lasted...
Seattle's most culturally redeeming combos - the Beakers, the Blackouts,
and the Macs, have all disbanded. The Blackouts will retain their name
but they've recruited girl bass player Frankie from the Beakers. They are
also without a drummer (he's in Scotland). Drummer George and guitar-
voice Mark from the Beakers have joined up with Colin (guitar, voice) from
the Macs. This is undoubtedly a supergroup on par with Crosby, Stills,
Nash and Young. They are the 3 Swimmers. Sax player Jim (Beakers) will
form a band with Danielle (16 year old drummer) and That Girl from ROSCOE
LOUIE ART GALLERY. Sounds interesting... There's two new club spaces,
both all ages - DANCELAND and PARADISE LOFT. The other good club in town,
WREX's, is actively looking for video... Engram Records, a very strong
new label, will release an E.P. by X-15 in April. Also, be sure to pick
up their compilation L.P. (featuring Beakers, Blackouts, Macs, X-15, Student
Nurse, Refuzors, the Pudz, Jim Basnight, Ace Oom and the Eons, Magnetics,
Phillip Scrooge, Fastbacks, Marc Berrecca and more.*

SEATTLE

flash: Beakers ⟶ dissolve.

<u>D.O.A.</u>: *SOMETHING BETTER CHANGE (L.P.)*   *FRIENDS

Vancouver's most paranoid punk band comes up with some political thrillers.
Dumb and smart, this Clash-rock will undoubtedly sell big to the leather
crowd.

<u>SUBHUMANS</u>: *FIRING SQUAD/No Productivity*   *QUINTESSENCE

"Firing Squad" is excellent punk/pop. Also of note: their first
release was a 12" E.P. and featured mellow classics like "Fuck You"
and "Slave To My Dick". Both records are recommended.

<u>FEMALE HANDS</u>: *(12" E.P. 6 songs)*   *QUINTESSENCE

Quirky rock and roll. Some interesting twists and turns. The vocalist
gets on my nerves. Worth listening to.

<u>UJ3RK5</u>: *(12"E.P. 4 songs)*   *QUINTESSENCE

Frantic art band. Tight and mechanical, excellent recording quality,
features violin, keyboards. Really good.

<u>YOUNG CANADIANS</u>: *THIS IS YOUR LIFE (12" E.P.)*   *QUINTESSENCE

Incredibly boring rock music. Oh, I mean "New Wave". This is their 2nd
release.

<u>MODERNETTES</u>: *TEEN CITY (12" E.P.)*   *QUINTESSENCE

"Confidential" is   classic pop/rock and is worth the price of the record.
Good hook with boy-girl harmonies. The other five songs are rather nondescript. (They should've just put out a single). (I hate this band -
typist).

<u>POINTED STICKS</u>: *PERFECT YOUTH (L.P.)*   *QUINTESSENCE

Good pop album by Canada's catchiest combo. Too bad most of this stuff
was produced to sound like Cheap Trick. This record will appeal to
many though, especially young girls with throbbing hearts.

VANCOUVER

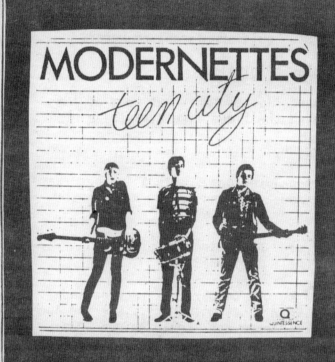

B.C.

Q: So...you guys are from St. Louis, I think that's pretty amazing, reminds me of Pere Ubu and Cleveland. Could you talk about St. Louis? Anything happ

A: There's nothing really going on down there...We don't consider ourselves a St. Louis band. We draw a big crowd when we do play (let's see...last time was over 1/2 a year ago..) but generally, it's a hassle. You have to arrange everything, ther's nowhere to play ...the clubs that have a house P.A. don't want anything to do with you, they want established bands. Occasionally, we'll open for a British band (we've played with Ultravox, Magazine...) but basically, the only groups that come to St. Louis are "arena rockers".

Q: What about the local bands, do they play originals?

A: A few of them do. There are alot of bands in St. Louis but most of 'em are what you would call "bad". Sorta behind the times like everything else.

Q: Your named after a famous movie actor. Why?

A: There's some really uninteresting personal reasons...with all bands there comes a time when the name becomes synonymous with the group. After that, it really doesn't make any difference.

Q: Could you talk about your upcoming record? Also, are you planning on re-releasing Talk/Distant View outside of PRAXIS magazine?

A: Our next record should be a 12". It'll be out on Wax Trax records and will probably feature a remix of Distant View plus two others....As for our first 45, it'll be released with a picture sleeve and should be out soon.

Q: What music have you been listening to lately?

A: It depends...alot of new things tend to sound alike. I've been listening to Cowboys International, the Associates...

Q: If your not playing much in St. Louis, are you restricting yourself to chicago?
A: No, not really. Actually, we're primarily interested in recording that 12" and possibly producing a videotape; so we're more interested in selling ourselves through videotape than touring cause it's far too expensive...
St. Louis is wide open for recording adventures. Everything is extremely inexpensive there...so, whereas we don't have the option of being constantly in touch with the latest sounds, we do have a definite economic advantage.

Q; is there anything you would like to say to St. Louis before you leave?

A: NO.

photo   by   Doug   Taylor

RAY MILLAND

Snippets of this interview were pasted into a conversational montage. This resulted in an economy of space and a slight distortion in character. Over 90% of the answers were given by Rick Buscher (above), vocalist, synth player and obvious leader of Ray Milland. I highly encourage you to listen to their first 45 (Talk/Distant View), recently re-released outside of Praxis Magazine.

SUB/POP TOP TEN
(independent, North American records)

swingin' singles

(1)	JAD FAIR	FRANKENSTEIN	ARMAGEDDON	D.C. Area
(2)	IMPORTS	SIDE 1	CIRKLE	Chicago
(3)	X	WHITE GIRL	SLASH	Los Angeles
(4)	OIL TASTERS	GET OUT OF THE BATHROOM	OIL TASTERS	Milwaukee
(5)	PYLON	COOL	CAUTION	Athens
(6)	VOIDOIDS	DON'T DIE	SHAKE	New York
(7)	VOICE FARM	MODERN THINGS	OPTIONAL	San Francisco
(8)	TUXEDOMOON	WHAT USE?	RALPH	San Francisco
(9)	BEAKERS	RED TOWEL	MR. BROWN	Seattle
(10)	JARS	START RIGHT NOW	SUBTERRANEAN	San Francisco

12" E.P.'s and 45's

(1)	BLACKOUTS	MEN IN MOTION	ENGRAM	Seattle
(2)	BEAKERS/FOSTER/FISK	LIFE ELSEWHERE	MR. BROWN	Olympia/Seattle
(3)	CHANDRA	TRANSPORTATION	ON/GO-GO	New York
(4)	BLACK FLAG	JEALOUS AGAIN	SST	Los Angeles
(5)	MECHANICAL SERVANTS	MIN X MATCH	MYSTERY TOAST	New York
(6)	UJ3RK5	UJ3RK5	QUINTESSENCE	Vancouver B.C.
(7)	BONGOS	MAMBO SUN	FETISH	New York
(8)	THE DANCE	DANCE FOR YOUR DINNER	ON/GO-GO	Philadelphia/N.Y.
(9)	INSECT SURFERS	WAVELENGTH	WASP	D.C.
(10)	PINK SECTION	PINK SECTION	MODERN	San Francisco

L.P.'s

(1)	VARIOUS	RODNEY ON THE ROQ	POSH BOY	Los Angeles
(2)	DARK DAY	EXTERMINATING ANGEL	LUST/UNLUST	New York
(3)	PYLON	GYRATE	DB	Athens
(4)	X	LOS ANGELES	SLASH	Los Angeles
(5)	VARIOUS	DECLINE OF WESTERN CIV.	SLASH	Los Angeles
(6)	TUXEDOMOON	HALF-MUTE	RALPH	San Francisco
(7)	PERE UBU	ART OF WALKING	ROUGH TRADE	Cleveland
(8)	SPECIAL AFFECT	TOO MUCH SOFT LIVING	SPECIAL AFFECT	Chicago
(9)	RESIDENTS	COMMERCIAL ALBUM	RALPH	San Francisco
(10)	VARIOUS	DECLARATION OF INDEPENDENTS	AMBITION	U.S.A.

BaBy Ga's Portraits of the stars

Chuck Dukowski
Black Flag

Richard stotts
Plasmatics

concept ©1981 STIFF DOLLY for CORPORATE RECORDS

Baby Ga knows Corporate Records really caves.
The only record store for miles and miles that really does
specialize in NEW imports, independents, hard to find stuff and
extensive reggae. Mail order service available — write for
catalogue. Plus! ask and Corporate will try to find it.
Give us a call — new number 625 9834

CORPORATE RECORDS

1511 SECOND AVENUE, SEATTLE, WA. 98101   206·624 7806

Larry Reid

Greener Pastures

The somnambulant city of Olympia, Washington, seemed an unlikely locale for the birth of a cultural revolution. Olympia was known primarily as the namesake of a popular, if undistinguished, brand of beer, and as the state capital of a region that was recognized nationally—if it was recognized at all—for natural beauty. That assessment began to change in 1967 with the establishment of the Evergreen State College. With a strict adherence to interdisciplinary independent studies and environmental steward-ship, the experimental curriculum attracted a breed of creative students from across the country, known both affectionately and derisively as "Greeners."

At the dawn of the punk era in 1977, a trio of gifted cartoonists emerged from the Evergreen State College. Matt Groening, Lynda Barry, and Charles Burns gained regional notoriety and earned a modest income by publishing comic strips in small alternative week-lies. Groening did *Life in Hell*, Barry had *Ernie Pook's Comeek*, and Burns made *Big Baby*. While each would eventually escape the area for "greener" pastures, they helped lay the foundation for the pop culture phenom-enon that followed.

Soon after the departure of Groening, Barry, and Burns, the punk ethic arrived at Evergreen, ushered in by a crop of students attracted to the academic and cre-ative freedom promised by the unorthodox institution. Among the incoming class was Chicago transplant Bruce Pavitt. He soon began producing his hand-crafted *Subterranean Pop* fanzine, and he tapped the recent Evergreen alumni to contribute. A Lynda Barry drawing graced the cover of the second issue of *Sub Pop*, and Charles Burns illustrated the back cover of the fourth. At this point, the young editor was anxious

to have the esoteric regional music he was promoting available for readers to experience. The inexpensive cassette format with a mini-zine folded into the case suited the dual-purpose publication ideally. Thus the revolution spread.

Cartoonist and illustrator Charles Burns, himself a Seattle native, soon came to broad national attention through his exposure in Art Spiegelman and Françoise Mouly's avant-garde *Raw* comics magazine. While the story of Burns' introduction to Spiegelman and Mouly varies, there is no doubt that future Pulitzer Prize win-ner Spiegelman was exposed to the work of Burns in *Sub Pop* #5, the first cassette-format issue, released in 1980. In a handwritten 1981 letter to Pavitt, Spiegel-man remarks, "Thanks for keeping us posted w/*Sup Pob* [sic]. Neat stuff. I like the design of the cassette bklet mucho. 'Reagan Speaks for Himself' [a track from the *Sub Pop* cassette] to be a flexidisc insert into *Raw* 4, which will also include a nine-page story by *Sub Pop* cover artist C. Burns."

Spiegelman neglected to mention the controversy sur-rounding the "Reagan Speaks for Himself" flexidisc. The conservative Clearwater, Florida, company Eva-Tone Soundsheets refused to press the provocative track by Evergreen graduate Doug Kahn, which clev-erly rearranged Ronald Reagan's words to make him seem even more incoherent than usual. The publishers of *Raw* were forced to press the record offshore. By the time of publication of this issue of *Raw* in 1982, the influence of Pavitt's fledgling *Sub Pop* enterprise was gaining national currency.

Pavitt continued to enlist Burns to create covers for subsequent issues of the cassette edition of *Sub Pop*. Meanwhile, Pavitt relocated north to nearby Seattle, and was thus able to interact with a larger cultural community. He soon found new homes for Sub Pop as a regular feature in the *Rocket*, a free Seattle music monthly, in addition to a weekly radio show on college station KCMU. At the *Rocket*, Pavitt joined an extended family of talented writers, artists, cartoonists, and graphic designers that would play an important role in the future development of the Sub Pop aesthetic. The second installment of the column, in May 1983, featured an early appearance of what would become Sub Pop's signature logo. The *Rocket* regularly ran comix and illustrations by Lynda Barry, Charles Burns, Matt Groening, Gary Panter, Robert Crumb, Carl Smool, Diane Noomin, Gilbert and Jaime Hernandez, among others, and became widely regarded for accomplished art directors including Helene Silverman, Robert Newman, Dale Yarger, and Art Chantry. The *Rocket* also introduced writers like Ann Powers, Karrie Jacobs, Gillian Gaar, and Charles R. Cross. The substantial infrastructure of support provided by the *Rocket*, the adventurous KCMU radio format, and many lively all-ages music venues in Seattle during this era helped stimulate a creative environment that would later penetrate popular culture worldwide.

In retrospect, one can to equate the seminal counterculture of Seattle in the mid-1980s to what happened in San Francisco some twenty years earlier. Both cities were developing a distinctive style of music, graphic design, and fashion (or anti-fashion) sensibility. Perhaps most importantly, each was home to a wealth of talented young cartoonists who were eager to chronicle their respective scenes in an unfiltered medium.

Among these artists in Seattle, Peter Bagge played a pivotal role in popularizing the regional youth culture of the period. Bagge relocated to Seattle in 1983 from Hoboken, New Jersey, where he was editing R. Crumb's *Weirdo* comics anthology, a West Coast counterpart to Speigelman's *Raw*. Coinciding with Bagge's move to the Northwest, Crumb was immediately drawn to the *Rocket* and began including local cartoon-

ists in the pages of *Weirdo*, gaining national exposure for the region's young artists.

In 1985, Bagge created *Neat Stuff* for comics publisher Fantagraphics Books, then based in Southern California. This title gave birth to many of the memorable characters that would later populate Peter Bagge's *Hate*, the serial that documented the alternative culture rapidly gaining momentum in Seattle. Bagge's fictional crew of lovable losers came to personify Seattle's self-deprecating "grunge" counterculture. Going beyond satire, *Hate* helped define the attitudes and aesthetics of the last significant youth movement of the millennium. In a contemporary review of the comic book series, Bruce Barcott of the *Seattle Weekly* observed, "Twenty years from now, when people want to know what it was like in 1990s Seattle, the only record we'll have is Peter Bagge's *Hate*."

Before the end of the 1980s, Bagge's success in Seattle attracted Fantagraphics Books to the area, beginning a mass migration of aspiring cartoonists to the region. In short order, Seattle's relative low cost of living, appealing urban environment, and emerging high-tech economy combined to draw some of most resourceful and creative minds in the country.

By now, Pavitt's unimposing Sub Pop endeavor was poised to provide the soundtrack to a cultural upheaval with international implications, along with a full complement of ambitious artists, writers, musicians, producers, and cartoonists eager to collaborate.

The rest, as they say, is history.

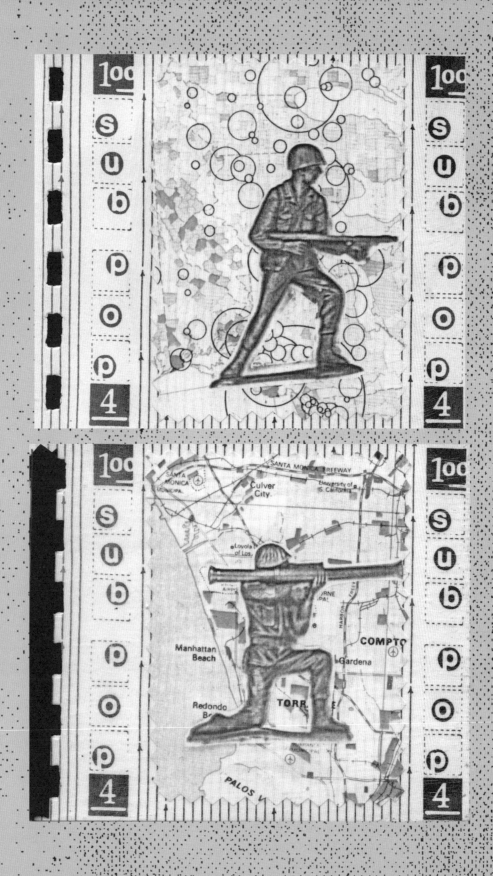

SUB/POP 5 will be released as a **cassette magazine**. We are looking for diverse, modern **American** music. Punk, Folk, Ambient, Trance, Industrial, Funk, Pop...anything goes. Release is scheduled for Sept. 15, 1981. Please write us c/o **LOST MUSIC NETWORK**, Box 2391, Olympia, WA 98507.

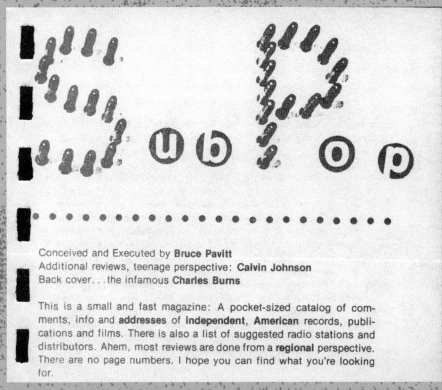

Conceived and Executed by **Bruce Pavitt**
Additional reviews, teenage perspective: **Calvin Johnson**
Back cover...the infamous **Charles Burns**

This is a small and fast magazine: A pocket-sized catalog of comments, info and **addresses** of **independent**, **American** records, publications and films. There is also a list of suggested radio stations and distributors. Ahem, most reviews are done from a **regional** perspective. There are no page numbers. I hope you can find what you're looking for.

Hi Folks—

Send in your tapes, please. SUB/POP will alternate between a C-60 cassette and a magazine. Okeedokee? Narrow-minded bigots need not apply, though; we want to hook up with **open-minded** people who flip on all kindsa music.

Cassettes are the ultimate tool. Unlike records, production and manufacturing can happen—within minutes—in your own living room(!) While we will continue to review **independent** records, we urge everyone to start making and trading cassettes. Our **winter magazine issue** will give addresses of as many **cassettes** as possible (flexi-discs too) ...so please, please, please let us truly sabotage the corporate record industry by ignoring their system completely. Personally, I refuse to allow my thoughts, my values and "our" music to be **controlled** by an **economy based on exploitation and conformity**. Network T.V., shopping malls and major record labels are doing their damnedest to homogenize and white-wash our thinking...In order to mobilize any kind of alternative, we need open minds and open lines of communication. We must maintain the network. Let's decentralize, diversify and keep those local scenes going...O.K.?

X Bruce

Los An·gel·es (lôs an'jə ləs, läs;

FLESH EATERS (A MINUTE TO PRAY, A MINUTE TO DIE) Adult men. L.A. rock 'n roll intelligentsia. Members of **X**, the **Blasters**, plus **Chris Desjardins** on vocals. This guy is the deadliest songwriter since Darby of the Germs. Divine, religious inspiration. Also: sax, tropical marimbas. Unfortunately, the overproduction tends to water down any kind of real aggressions. (Ruby Records: contact through SLASH Box 4888, L.A., CA 90048

ADOLESCENTS (ADOLESCENTS) Teenage anthems. Waves of army ants. Great production. (Frontier Records, Box 22, Sun Valley CA 91352)

POSH BOY RECORDS A bunch of new 12" E.P.'s on this label, 2 good, 2 not so good. **T.S.O.L.** are 4 idealistic young hippies, I mean punks, who preach over a blistering heavy metal assault on the ears. Listen to song like "Property Is Theft" and see the light. **Red Cross** offers 6 songs of lighter content with a more traditional sound. They talk about girls and school and stuff like that. S&M Party is hot... **The Stepmothers** are kind of nothing special. I don't know what David Microwave is trying to do, but it's boring. The only good song on his E.P. "I Don't Want To Hold You" is already available on **Rodney on the Roq** or **Los Microwaves** first single.-Calvin (Posh Boy, Box 38861, L.A. CA 90038)

JOHANNA WENT (SLAVE BEYOND THE GRAVE/NO U NO) Infamous L.A. witch doctor/performance artist gives us abstract vocals, percussion, primitive electronics. Comes with an x-ray insert. (Mail Mart, Box 44241, Panorama City CA 91412)

San Fran·cis·co (san′ frən si

VOICE FARM (ELEVATE/DOUBLE GARAGE) Fun electro-pop. Not as brilliant and catchy as their first release, "Modern Things." (Optional: Berkeley Industrial Court, Space #1, 729 Heinz Ave, Berkeley CA 94701)

NEGATIVELAND (POINTS) Experimental. Random tapes, rhythm box, electronics. For fans of Cabaret Voltairs, Robert Rental, John Cage. (Optional...)

ZRU VOGUE (NAKWEDA DREAM/CUMULONIMBUS) Nakweda Dream: "God is infinitely small/I am infinitely tall/I bought a new revolver/I keep it at my bedside." This typically laid back Adolescent release is my fave American 45 of the year. The whispers of San Francisco are sometimes more haunting than the screams of L.A.... (Adolescent, 1732 Grant Ave., San Francisco CA 94113)

SLEEPERS (MIRROR/THEORY) This typically laid back Adolescent release puts me to sleep real fast. Lots of interesting people rave about this band though, so definitely give it a try. For **Tuxedomoon** addicts. (Adolescent...)

FACTRIX (EMPIRE OF PASSION/SPLICE OF LIFE) "Industrial." Art student sings his poetry over clanking percussion, electronics. Overrated and pretentious. (Adolescent...)

JAMES HIMSELF/FAST FORWARD (CITY OF MERCHANDISE/BYE BYE LOVE) Art and technology: electronic. Noodles of discreet circuitry. Extremely modern mood music. Interesting package design. (Pink Noise, 1411 Center St., Oakland, CA 94607)

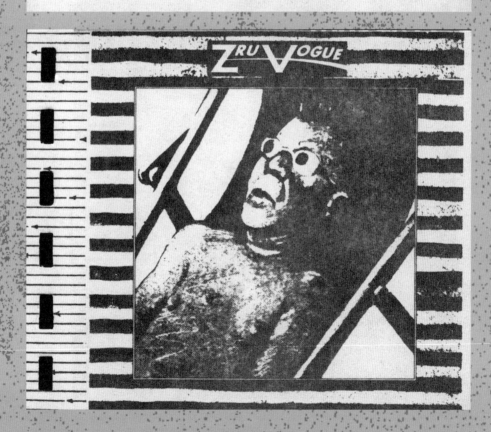

CLUB FOOT (LP) "Jazz." A compilation of four bands: **Longshoremen, Alter-boys, Naked City, Bay of Pigs**, plus the Club Foot orchestra. If you are hep to the **Lounge Lizards**, you might dig this record a lot; these guys are into a big band/Henri Mancini sound, though, as opposed to early fifties "cool" jazz. As a whole, this record is both inventive and humorous, but its cool guy-beatnik self-indulgence can really get on your nerves. Also of note: this is one of the first U.S. independents to be distributed behind the Iron Curtain. I hope Yugoslavia likes this record. (Subterranean Records, 912 Bancroft Way, Berkeley CA 94710).

ULTRA SHEEN (4 SONG 7") Cabaret-rock. Lots of horns. File next to Club Foot. (Subterranean...)

FLIPPER (LOVE CANAL/HA HA HA) Raw, slow, dark psychedelia. Somewhere between the **Sex Pistols** and **Public Image**. Bitter, poisoned lyrics. **Ha Ha Ha** is their best release yet. (Subterranean...)

SAN FRANCISCO UNDERGROUND NO. 2 (4 SONG 7" E.P. FEATURING THE LEWD, UNDEAD, SOCIETY DOG, SPIKES) 4 bands on one 7 inch is a good deal and a great idea. As for the music, this is the kind of lame, anemic punk rock that only San Francisco could come up with. The real high point is when **Sid Terror** of the **Undead** sings, "Be a man, not a nigger, join the Klan, pull the trigger." This is total, absolute garbage. (Subterranean...)

THE JARS (TIME OF THE ASSASINS/JAR WARS) Such a comedown from "Start Rite Now." I'm sad. This pop band had such a promising start. The A-side is a weak attempt at white reggae. What happened? (Universal Records, 2309½ Telegraph Ave, Berkeley, CA 94704)

(PORTLAND)—**NEO BOYS** best girl band in the Northwest. **Classic rock 'n roll**. Album out in fall. **PELL MELL** shimmering instrumentals. Ventures of the Northwest. Very modern. These guys can play. Expect a 12" E.P. on Trap. **JUNGLE NAUSEA**—Weird industrial stuff.

(OLYMPIA)—**JOHN FOSTER'S POP PHILOSOPHERS**: electronic soul. Very original. "Kennedy Saga" is a thirty-minute groove/rap/lecture. **TINY HOLES**—wild electronic combo. Pere Ubu, funk, Steve Reich. Now defunct. I used to sing for 'em. Cassette out soon. Write to Sub/Pop. **MILLIONS OF BUGS**: great pop/rock. **TEST PATTERN**: prolific pop combo, good vocals. **TWIN DIET**: 2 girls, vocals, percussion, dresses. Somewhere between Noh Mercy and the Bobbsy Twins. **POSITRONICS**: noise, Throbbing Gristle. Electric, cello, rhythm boxes, tapes, guitar, texture. **CHERI KNIGHT**: "new music." A genius, I kid you not. Will appear on Olympia soundtext (words as music) compilation (Palace of Lights, P.O. Box 4235, Seattle WA 98104). **CUSTOMER SERVICE**: studio duo. Creepy electronic pop, hypnotic "new music." **BREADWINNERS** cover band. Makes a religion out of the "big beat." **MAN ATTACKS BEER TRUCK** fat hippie goes crazy.

(SEATTLE)—**3 SWIMMERS**: modern. 4 white boys play sparse, minimal funk/pop. Features some ex-Beakers. Will probably release an album on a really BIG label (cough). **X-15**—haven't seen 'em, lots of raves. Aggressive, political. Good lyrics. E.P. out on **Engram**. **BLACKOUTS**—a new line-up and a new sound. Gettin' funky. **VISIBLE TARGETS** three sisters and a boy play driving relentless pop, good harmonies. Party Time. **LITTLE BEARS FROM BANGKOK** —Another band with 3 girls and a guy. 2 bass players. FUN.

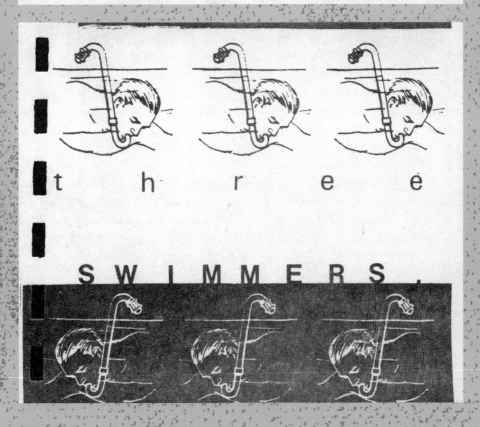

t h r e e

S W I M M E R S.

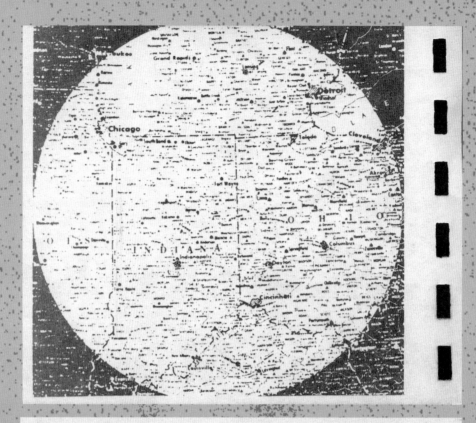

Mid·west (mid′west′) *n.* *same*

INDIANA—Suburban teen-punk band **THE PANICS** come up with a knee-slapper called "I Wanna Kill My Mom"...haw haw. Those darn hillbillies... (Gulcher, Box 1635, Bloomington IN)

ILLINOIS-**VIBRANT FIASCO** (LIZARD LIPS T 2) Rock 'n roll, kind of. Instruments include melodica, pencil sharpener, synthesizers. Incredible Living Room recording; a weird and obscure record. (Disturbed Pyramid, Box 3151 Fox Valley Station, Aurora, IL 60505)

OHIO—Cincinnati has two semi-established independents. (Shake it!) offers us a new release from the **Customs**, a band that plays that boring old rock 'n roll stuff very well. "Long Gone" and "She'll Always Be Mine" are two drivin' originals reminiscent of the Stones, Animals, etc. **Candy Apple** are three women who prove that they can be just as mediocre as any boy group and then some. (Waldo Records Inc.) was started so "emerging talent of the Ohio Valley could bring their musical concepts to the public." Their first release, by **News**, is a pleasant surprise. Post Gang of Four with an American accent. I recommend you pick this one up, easily recognized by the ugly likeness of a stop sign on the cover. -Calvin

*(SHAKE IT! 2530 Luna Ave, Cincinnati OH 45219)
*(WALDO RECORDS, c/o Another Record Store, 5 W. Charlton, Cincinnati OH 45219)

KANSAS—EMBARRASSMENT (5 SONG E.P.) Innovative grass roots rock 'n roll. Locomotive music with voices fading in and out. This is the second release by these suave and handsome country bumpkins. Really good. (c/o Dan Rouser, 4204 E. Douglas, Wichita KA 67208)

IOWA—THE LAW (4 SONG E.P.) Billy Disease, Bold Upright and friends give us Iowa punk rock. Not exactly extremist "hardcore," they still sing lyrics that would make the Reagan administration feel uneasy. "Reason for Treason" is outstanding. (The Law, 2313 33rd, Des Moines IA 50310)

MICHIGAN—ALL NIGHT MOVIES (CASSETTE)... A brainy encyclopedia of new ideas. 3 horns, a synthesizer and a punk band play everything from Steve Reich to Black Flag and actually pull it off! Despite poor sound quality, this basement tape is definitely worth picking up. From the people who do SMARM fanzine (Box 106, Mt. Pleasant, MI 48858)

PENNSYLVANIA—The T.M.I. label has two interesting records out. **Car Sickness** (SHOOTING ABOVE THE GARBAGE L.P.)... Calvin says "B+ effort heavily influenced by such British bands as Wire and early Clash." My fave is the **Cold Warrior and the Mercenary Band** 45. In "Vietnam," a straightfaced, liberal college student says, "We have to spend our funds on education, housing, full employment, a national health insurance program..." Noble causes, I agree. The tone is so serious though, the whole thing comes off as the funniest record of the year. (T.M.I., 4626 Forbes Ave., Pittsburg PA 15213)

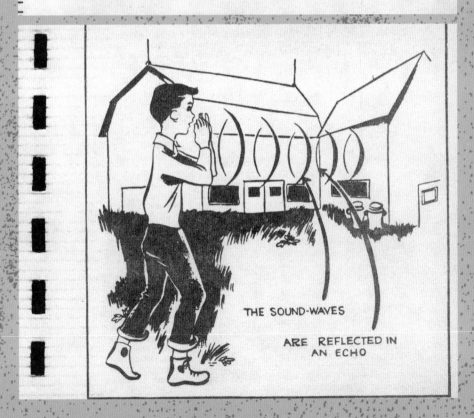

THE SOUND-WAVES

ARE REFLECTED IN AN ECHO

Chi·ca·go (shə kä′gō, -kô′-)

PHIL 'N THE BLANKS (I WANT SOME MORE/I'M LOSING INTEREST) Any band with a manager is going to be marketed like a pack of potato chips. Phil 'n the Blanks is no exception. Clever and catchy pop for hip, suburban adults. (Pink, 1342 Newport, Chicago IL 60657)

SPORT OF KINGS (EVERY NIGHT/THE SAME BREATH) A lonely and existential man sings about "good" and "evil," love and faith. It's all very deep and serious and will obviously appeal to people who only buy records from Britain. Great picture sleeve. (Sport of Kings, Box 11131, Chicago IL 60611)

STRIKE UNDER (IMMEDIATE ACTION E.P.) The first release by Chicago's emerging hardcore. These guys wear Anarchy and Peace T-shirts. Most of this stuff is medium-tempo, melodic and hypnotic, soft around the edges. A distinctive sound, although not very aggressive. Limited edition, silk-screen cover. Looks good. (Wax Trax Records: 2449 N. Lincoln Ave, Chicago IL 60614)

DA! (DARK ROOMS/WHITE CASTLES) 3 girls and a guy mix art with politics. **Dark Rooms** deals with shadows at night, **White Castles** confronts the middle-class and riots in Miami. Great lyrics, great amateur sound. Highly recommended to people who worship Siouxsie and the Banshees. This is the first release by **Autumn** Records, a strong, diverse label who will also be releasing a 12" by the **Effigies**, a single by the **Subverts** and (finally) Chicago's first underground compilation, with: **Naked Raygun**(!), **DA**, **Silver Abuse**, **Subverts**, **Strike Under**, and the **Effigies**. Write these guys. (Autumn Records, 2427 North Janssen, Chicago IL 60614)

D.C. 1. District of Columbia

There are lots of good records by people who just want to rock if you take the time to find them. The **Bad Brains** released the fastest record ever last summer, "Pay to Cum" (Bad Brain), recommended to all. **Slickee Boys** give us wild jungle music on "The Brain that Refused To Die" (Dacoit). **The Dark**, an interesting combo led by two women, offer their electric folk music through a four-song E.P. on Limp. **Martha Hull** delivers a truly wonderful tough girl version of "Feelin' Right Tonight" (Ripshaw) produced by Tex Rubinowitz. And last but whatever, the **Teen Idles** have a brilliant punk rock EP on Dischord. Can't understand a word this guy's singing but he must be saying something right for it to sound this cool. I've heard nothing from my favorite D.C. band, the **Psychotics**. Hope they haven't broken up or anything silly like that. -Calvin

> Bad Brains Records, 2700 Gaither St., Hillcrest Heights MD 20031
> Dacoit Records, 1235 N. Irving St., Arlington VA 22201
> Limp Records, 1327 J Rockville Pile, Rockville MD 20852
> Ripsaw Records, 121 N 4th, Easton PA 18042
> Dischord Records, c/o Limp Records

THE NURSES: (I WILL FOLLOW YOU/LOVE YOU AGAIN) Pop: smart and fun. Buy it, you'll like it. ($2.00 ppd. c/o H.S.M. Weulfing, 5018-8th Rd. S., Arlington VA 22204)

1/2 JAPANESE: (SPY/I KNOW HOW IT FEELS...BAD) The B-side is primitive art, noisy and fun. The A-side is a very, very slow Doors cover complete with thunder sounds. Hide under your covers for this one. (Armageddon: c/o 2775 E. Bankers Industrial Dr., Atlanta, GA 30360)

New York [after the Duke of Y

COOLIES (GOVERNMENT TIME E.P.) Smart white funk. "Great Minds" deals with shallow topics like ecosystems and world government. Highly recommended to fans of Talking Heads, A Certain Ratio. (The Coolies, 2069 W. 8th St., Brooklyn NY 11223, $4.00 ppd.)

Y-PANTS (3-SONG 7" E.P.) If you enjoyed the artsy sophistication of the Bush Tetras, you'll probably kill yourself over the Y-Pants. 3 girls play with bells and toys. "Cute." This outstanding label also has experimental releases out by **E.S.G.** and the infamous **Liquid, Liquid.** Check 'em out. (99 Records: 99 Macdougal Street, NY NY 10012)

ZANTEES (OUT FOR KICKS L.P.) Hep-cat rock 'n roll, man. Couple of good covers, some even better originals. In "Blonde Bombshell" they degenerate into a cramps-like. . . they scream a lot. Good rockin' stuff. Buy it, baby. -Calvin (Bomp Records, Box 7112, Burbank CA 91510).

LAURIE ANDERSON (O SUPERMAN/WALK THE DOG) "New Music" intersects with pop. Although Laurie tries to sound like an android with mucho vocal processing, she can't hide her warm, human personality. 16 minutes of tape loops, sax, farfisa, violin, story line. Very unusual and very fun. Performance artist **Laurie Anderson** is **Johanna Went's** alter-ego. (110 Records, 110 Chambers St., NY NY 10007)

CIRCUS MORT (4 SONG E.P.) Expensively packaged, art-school psychedelia. Pretentious and interesting. Digitally mastered recording. **Labor** Records also release blues and jazz. (P.O. Box 1262 Peter Stuyvesant Station, NY NY 10009)

RE/SEARCH: America's most interesting magazine. Search and Destroy teams up with Rough Trade to produce a post-punk publication concerned with: world culture, modern technology, dreams, performance art, right-wing conspiracy theories, literature, prostitution and even some references to modern music. A serious academic magazine that cannot be ignored. **You've got to read this.** (20 Romolo B, San Fran CA 94133) $2.00

FALLOUT: Political. It's about time a punkoid publication started mumbling furiously about El Salvador, nuclear power, faceless condo reality, **corporate exploitation** of everything... Lot's of 50's photo montage, some comics. Thick newsprint. Recommended. (Box 355, Fairfax CA 94930) $1.50

VACATION: The "new art, performance, and music magazine." Lots of celebrity portraits, token DNA interview, token Factrix interview, etc. A serious and interesting magazine. Very well done. (1071 A Natoma, San Fran CA 94103) $1.25

NO: L.A.'s best underground. Thank God they stopped printing diseased bodies and surgical pornography. Yes, folks, they've cleaned up their act. Features—celebrity portraits, interviews (i.e. lesbian folksinger **Phranc**, **Darby Crash**), some very smart write-ups (i.e. telecommunications), color cover, flexi-disc (i.e. the bizarre **Wild Kingdom**). Highly recommended. (Box 57041, Los Angeles CA 90057) $2.00

FLIPSIDE: America's strongest teenage punkzine. Last issue (24) was as loud and aggressive as ever. Lots of interviews with morons, bigots and visionaries, plus: lyrics to anthems, record reviews, fanzine addresses. Buy or die. (Box 363, Whittier CA 90608) $.75

RIPPER: Hardcore punkzine with a friendly, small-town paper attitude. Interviews are a little long, but they're all there: token Black Flag. Token DOA, etc. -Calvin (1494 Terisita Dr., San Jose CA 95129) $.75

PARANOIA: Teen-punk newsprint from Reno, Nevada. Fun and stupid. (1408 12th St., Sparks NV 89431) $.50

ANOTHER ROOM: Excellent, Bay Area art newsprint. Color, hot graphics, performance art, good art/pop record reviews. Highly recommended. (1640 18th St. Oakland CA 94607) FREE

OP: A bible. **The** independent music magazine. Now published bi-monthly, Op gives addresses and info on all kinds of music...there are no boundaries with this magazine. Absolutely the most up-to-date source of addresses available for independent records and publications. "The true voice of the American underground." (Lost Music Network, Box 2391, Olympia WA 98507) $1.50

PUNK ROOLS OK: Thick xerox hardcore. Stolen essays on anarchism. Record reviews. Lucky enough to have a Boeing xerox card (that's the corporation that makes those big jets)... Soon to be called **Circle A**. (516 E. Union #306, Seattle WA 98122) $.75

TALK TALK: America's most professional fanzine. British and Reggae interviews, record reviews, local Kansas news. Flexi-disc. (Box 36, Lawrence KA 66044) $1.50

SMARM: Three folded sheets in an envelope. Social commentary, record reviews, poetry. A fun basement publication. (Box 106, Mt. Pleasant, MI 48858) $.75

COOLEST RETARD: Chicago's best fanzine. Local news, British raves, etc. (c/o Schmidt, 2042 N. Bissell, Chicago IL 60614) $.80

PRAXIS: Expensive graphics magazine. The design changes with every issue. British interviews, Chicago: art, fashion, poetry. Comes with record or flexi-disc. Tres chic. (180 West Washington, Chicago IL 60602) approx. $4-$5

NEWCOMERS: Distinctive literary magazine. Looks good. Also: British record reviews, some Chicago music news. (Box 6012, Chicago IL 60680) $1.25

RAW: "The graphics magazine for damned intellectuals." Highly creative international comics magazine. **Mark Beyer**, Drew Friedman, **Charles Burns**, Art Spiegelman, **Gary Panter**, etc. Highly recommended. (27 Greene St., NY NY 10013) $4.00 ppd.

SHORT NEWZ: Enthusiastic New York free sheet. Fun and personal. Live music reviews, great source of fanzine addresses. Ahem, could use more visual style. Also: **NOT-AS-SHORT-NEWZ** comes out every few months. (Box 1028 Gracie Station, NYC 10028)

NON LP B SIDE: Red and black ink. Classic design. New York news, British photos. Looks good, reads well. (7 Stuyvesant Place, Lawrence NY 11516) $.25

SMEGMA: Disappointing art-zine. Lots of photo montage, some humorous conceptual art. Slick paper. Open to contributors. (Box 400 Old Chelsea Station, NY NY 10013) $2.50 ppd.

CAPITAL CRISIS: "D.C. hardcore" Reviews too much corporate rock to be considered subversive. (4120 N. 41st St., Arlington VA 22207)

DISCHORDS: Best source of local news in the country. A cheap (10¢) monthly newspaper. Good indie coverage...condensed local reporting will appear in N.Y. Rocker. It's your duty as an American citizen to read this magazine. 5018-8th Road S., Arlington, VA 22204

GAIKOWSKI,

HOPPER,

WHIFFLER

film (film) n. [ME. < OE. filmen, me

ONE WAY FILMS (c/o Richard Gaikowski, 1035 Guerrero, San Fran
CA 94110)

Richard Gaikowski's **DEAF/PUNK**: At San Francisco's legendary Deaf
Club, we see punk poseurs juxtaposed with the animated presence
of deaf/mutes. Hands talk and wave around as we hear the dirty
R & B of the **Offs**. This film basically works because of the **concept
of the environment**. (8 mins.) B/W $15.00 rental.

Marc Huestis' **X-COMMUNICATION**: A lonely man in an elegant room
decides to eat glass and spit blood. Excellent use of black and
white. Music by **Factrix**. So serious it's funny. Order this one. (5
mins.) B/W $10.00 rental.

Scott Ryser's **UNITS TRAINING FILM NO. 1**: Extremely entertaining.
Found footage includes home movies, industrial and medial films,
porno, photos and diagrams. Almost as good as Bruce Conner's
Mongoloid. Music by San Francisco synth band The Units. (12.5
mins.) B/W and color $25.00 rental.

Loren Jones' **THE UFO ABDUCTION**: Low, low budget sci-fi. Hey, it
works. (10 mins.) B/W $20.00 rental.

Mindaugis Bagdon's **LOUDER, FASTER, SHORTER**: The Sleepers,
Mutants, Dils, Avengers, and UXA perform live at the Fab Mab in
San Francisco. High-quality sound and color. Hot graphics inbe-
tween sets. Uninspired camerawork though. Overall, this San Fran
documentary isn't nearly as powerful as or as interesting as L.A.'s
DECLINE OF WESTERN CIVILIZATION. A Search and Destroy production. (20 mins.) color $40.00.

Ian Turner's **NEW AGE SUBWAY**: The psychedelic sound of Chrome serves as a backdrop for these 16mm negatives. Contrived characters in derbies (Clockwork Orange) walk around a subway and rock out on their guitars. Lots of squiggly lines. **Psychedelic**, man. (10 mins.) B/W $20.00 rental.

The Resident's **THIRD REICH AND ROLL**: "The first film performance by the mysterious Residents, featuring Klansmen in newspaper suits and pixillated spaceship shopping carts with a medley of the Resident's demented renditions of "Land of a Thousand Dances" and "Wipeout." Well-done cheap-o set design, overall, very entertaining. Graeme Whiffler has done two films with the Residents: **The Resident's One Minute Movies**, and **Hello Skinny**. Also: Tuxedomoon in **Jinx**, MX-80's **Why Are We Here?** and Snakefinger in **Snakefinger**. These bands are all on the RALPH Label and their films should be interesting and FUN. All films in color. (Approximately 5 min. each.) Package deal fifty bucks.

Don Marino's **ROBOTICS**: Some androids in foil diapers climb into a room and start dancing. This is an "art party"...really stupid. (5 mins.) color $10.00 rental.

Alex DeLazslo's **HUMAN FLY**: The Cramps are the perfect combo for this cheap monster footage...these guys are ugly and creepy. I especially like it when Poison Ivy gets acid thrown in her face. Wow, violence against women is fun. (5 mins.) B/W $10.00 rental.

Phil Hopper's **DECADE**: "**Ground Zero** from Boston performs musically and dramatically in this portrayal of life in the last days of the Industrial Age." Too bad the music sucks and they don't know how to act. Nevertheless, Hopper's **directing** is interesting and **ambitious**. Recommended. (12 mins.) B/W $20 rental.

CHE CHIRD REICH 'N ROLL

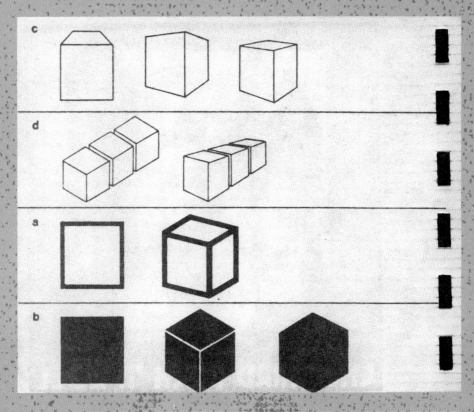

☆ra·di·o (rā′dē ō′) n., pl. -os′ [con

RADIO STATIONS—These stations play independent records.

KAOS c/o Steve Peters, CAB 305, Olympia, WA 98505

KRAB "Life Elsewhere" 2212 So. Jackson, Seattle WA 98144

KMVR Box 328, Nevada City CA 95959

KUSF "Harmful Emissions" c/o Tim Maloney 2130 Fulton, S.F. CA 94117

KUGS c/o Scott Boggan WWU 410 Viking Union, Bellingham WA 98225

KRCC c/o Bennett Colorado College, Colorado Springs CO 80903

KUOI University of Idaho Student Union, Moscow ID 83843

KZSC c/o Rich Wheeler UCSC 117 Communications Bldg., Santa Cruz CA 95064

WCUW 910 Main St., Worcester MA 01610

WBRS c/o Matt Rosenberg 415 South Street, Waltham MD 02154

WMBR "Late Risers Club" 3 Ames Street, Cambridge MA 02141

WKCR c/o Mark Abbott "Transfigured Night" 324 West 101st St #3, NYC 10025

WZIR (100,000 watts) c/o Gary Storm 2692 Staley Rd., Grand Island NY 14072

WRUW c/o Wade Toleson 11220 Bellflower Rd., Cleveland OH 44106

WMSE c/o Paul Host Milwaukee School of Engineering, Box 644, Milwaukee WI 53201

WCMU c/o Joe Brant CMU 155 Anspach Hall, Mt. Pleasant MI 48859

WXYC c/o Ken Friedman "Anarchy in the PM" 311 South LaSalle St. #35-P, Durham NC 27705

dis·trib·u·tor (-tər) *n.* [L.] a perso

ROUGH TRADE (1042 Murray St., Berkeley CA 94710) Rough Trade is a record label, a store, and a distributor. Basically British, this is the address of their American office.

SYSTEMATIC (Berkeley Industrial Ct. Space #1, 729 Heinz Ave, Berkeley CA 94710 (415) 845-3352) Major West Coast distributor, very interested in American records, some fanzines. Like Rough Trade, these guys distribute **only** independents.

AMERICAN INDEPENDENT DISTRIBUTION (37 W. 70th St. NYC 10023 (213) 724-7145) Handles independent video as well as records and publications.

CONSTANT CAUSE (679 Arbor Lane, Warminster PA 18974) Major distributor of independent publications, fanzines, comix,, some records. They are also planning to carry independent cassettes!

RAW (27 Greene St., NY NY 10013) Printers of RAW magazine. Also distribute little booklets, posters, etc.

ONE WAY FILMS Distributor of independent 16mm films. Mostly new wave/punk oriented. (c/o Richard Gaikowski 1035 Guerrero, San Francisco CA 94110)

BETTER BADGES: major distributor of U.K. fanzines and badges. Nancy of **Short Newz** is their American representative. (Box 1028 Gracie St., NY NY 10028)

BOMP (Greg Shaw, Box 7112, Burbank CA 91510) used to be a major fanzine, now they're a record label and a distributor. Very interested in American **rock 'n roll**. American fanzines.

Mark Beyer ©1981 . . . RAW

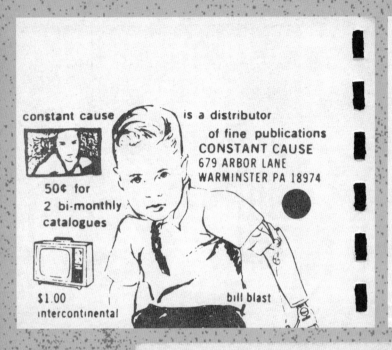

constant cause is a distributor of fine publications
CONSTANT CAUSE
679 ARBOR LANE
WARMINSTER PA 18974

50¢ for 2 bi-monthly catalogues

$1.00 intercontinental

bill blast

RADIO

KAOS-FM
We are interested in all types of independent music, including women's, Native American, SE Asian, folk reggae, classical, experimental, jazz, rock and other music from all over the world. KAOS is run by people, not corporate interests. KAOS-FM, CAB 305, Olympia, WA 98505. 206-866-5267.

Charles Burns

"You're in Charge"

Sub Pop stood out from the crowd, and made readers want to hear the music they were seeing. Unfortunately, that was a real problem. Besides our radio shows on KAOS, we had no way to share the sounds of the underground. We became inspired by Bruce Milne and Andrew Maine from non-commercial radio station 3RRR in Melbourne, Australia, and their cassette fanzine, *Fast Forward*. Essentially a radio show on cassette with impressive packaging, *Fast Forward* was distributed around the world, introducing lucky recipients to unusual Australian artists like the Moodists, Go-Betweens, Pel Mel, M Square, and Laughing Clowns. *Fast Forward* included a booklet with photos and crossword puzzles, and was fun, entertaining, and informative. We wanted to adopt the compilation cassette format without the spoken introductions and interviews found on *Fast Forward*. We would let the music do the talking. We started to alternate between cassette and print issues, the first tape being *Sub Pop* number five.

This was just after the introduction of the Sony Walkman. Cassette tapes had only recently become high fidelity and widely accessible. They were not yet a dominant audio format. The LP was still king, and compact discs were years away. Cassettes were attractive to us, because the blanks were assembled at an audio wholesaler in Olympia. Our print run could be duplicated inexpensively by a local technician in small quantities, allowing us to sell them for $5.00—a price between the common cost of a 45 and that of a full album. Artists were eager to be included on the first cassette, which we roughly divided between "Northwest" and "Midwest" sides. A few East Coast artists were added at the end of side one—how could we not include Jad Fair, from booming Westminster, MD?

"Phenomenal" is the only word to describe the response to the first cassette issue. *Sub Pop* number five sold like hotcakes—first a hundred, then hundreds, then ultimately over fifteen hundred. People were *hungry* for this mess. *Sub Pop* number seven continued in this vein, with important audio contributions from expansive Pacific Northwest artists Pell Mell, Neo Boys, and 54/40; the Midwest's Get Smart!, Sport of King, and Vibrant Fiasco; Texans the Mydolls; and Florida band A New Personality.

•

In the summer of 1982, I moved into a space in the Capitol Theater building next door to where Stella Marrs was surreptitiously living and operating her Girl City studio. Prior to this, I had shared a house with Stella on Legion Way. I figured that for only seventy-eight dollars a month rent, I could get by with a bathroom-down-the-hall situation, too. There were a couple other artists in the building, including Stella's best pal, Kathy Doherty, whose band Havana 3AM held late-night rehearsals in her studio.

We would play music together for hours at Girl City; me on guitar through a Fender Vibro Champ amplifier I purchased from Gary May, and Stella playing one or two random drums with great concentration, using high-heeled shoes as drum sticks. When we performed elsewhere, we never played any of the music or used any of the instruments we played with at Girl City. We would always borrow what we needed from the other bands playing, which worked fine—until Stella pulled out the high heels. Then most drummers would suddenly have a change of heart. Tom Shoblom was the only drummer in town who never flinched. Instead of a set list, I would give Stella brief instructions before each song, like: "play something fast and then slow and fast again." The music was entirely improvised, taking a cue from KAOS and *OP* folks like Steve Peters, Steve Fisk, and Michael Huntsberger—who organized "Olympia Goes to Bellingham" type shows where several Olympia artists played short, improvised sets.

In July 1982, just as we were putting *Sub Pop* number eight to bed, Pell Mell left on a cross-country tour and invited Bruce along. Such a journey was unusual for a Northwest band. Only the Wipers had ventured so far away for so long a time. As he left town, Bruce said, "You're in charge." I wrote "Sub Pop" across my office door in red magic marker, and started making daily trips to the post office. There was a lot of mail. Besides orders for the cassettes, cool records and fanzines just poured out of the mailbox.

During that month, I hosted local underground party dance trio Supreme Cool Beings on my KAOS radio show. Supreme Cool Beings was started by Gary May, along with two denizens of the Olympia's Angelus Hotel, Doug Monahan and Heather Lewis. Doug excelled at what he called "crappy sax." Heather could pound the drums. Gary played either electric bass or electric guitar. Having only one or the other instrument created a unique sound, and Supreme Cool Beings was—in case anyone is keeping track—the original "Olympia band without a bass player," a configuration which has haunted this town ever since. I really dug Supreme Cool Beings. I interviewed them for *Sub Pop* number eight, and I started the K Records label to release their *Survival of the Coolest* cassette. The time had come for me to go beyond writing about obscure local music and start producing it.

There was still no regular venue in downtown Olympia for original music, but epic parties were held that combined the three apartments above Barnes Floral. Apt. #1 would have a DJ. Apt. #3 would be the lounge for refreshments and conversation. Films were shown in the laundry room. Apartment #2 was reserved for local bands to aromatize with their primal scent.

Meanwhile, Bruce started actually going to Milwaukee, Kansas, Cleveland, and Boston, and meeting the people we only knew through the mail. He encountered fanzine writers, label folk, record store proprietors, radio programmers, bands, bands, and more bands, and fans, fans, and even more fans. Upon his return, he was super-charged by the experience of traveling with Pell Mell. He propelled himself into the next issue, *Sub Pop* number nine, the third cassette. He also broke up with his girlfriend, and so needed a new place to live. Fortunately Kathy D. was preparing to share an apartment with Steve Peters, so she let Bruce stay with her cat at her Capitol Theater studio.

This move was great for us, but proved to be too much for some of the commercial artists with offices in the building, who complained to management. One morning at 7:30 a.m., an assistant manager drove out from the head office in Lacey, Washington, to serve eviction notices. Bruce answered the door without a shirt, and the guy said, "Where's Kathy? Doesn't matter—you're out!" Just then, the cat walked by. "The cat, too!" Stella Marrs was more streetwise than us. After some fast-talking on her part, the Girl City studio remained, but we still had to go.

I moved into an uninsulated garage just in time to celebrate my twentieth birthday. Bruce moved to Seattle, taking his *Sub Pop* radio show to KCMU-FM. He opened a record store in Seattle with Olympia artist Russell Bataglia, a one-time Girl City studio mate of Stella's. The store was called Bomb Shelter, and was soon followed by Fallout Records. Eventually, Bruce landed a job duplicating cassettes at Yesco Foreground Music—soon to merge with Muzak—working with Mark Arm of Green River, Tad Doyle, and other rabble of the Seattle underground. Extrapolate the rest.

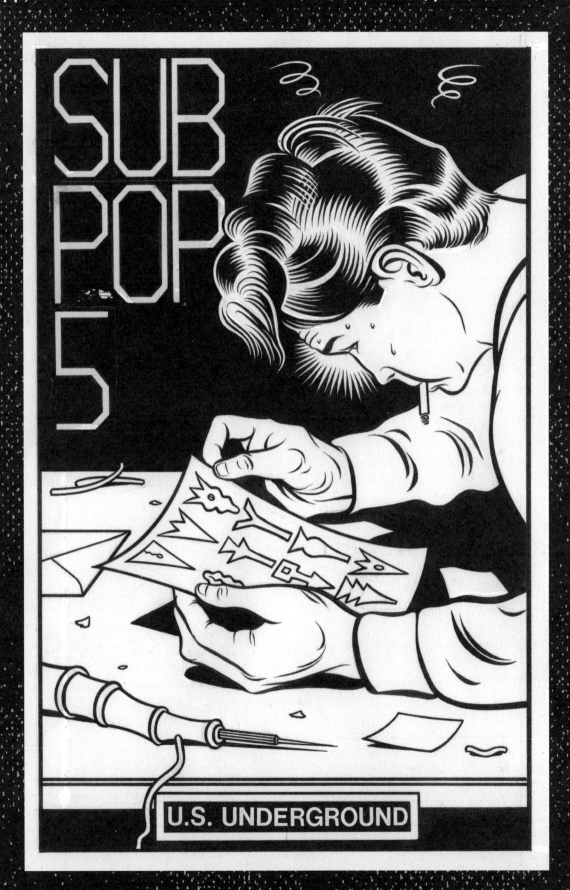

This is an introduction. In the next two minutes, you can read about great **American** bands. Or, you can toss this book and spend big bucks on the latest hype from England. It's your choice. Furthermore, you might be interested to note that none of these modern combos comes from L.A., San Fran or New York city. Not one. Think about it. Then send us **four** U.S. dollars for the other half of this magazine: a 60-minute **cassette**! Write: **SUB/POP, Lost Music Network, Box 2391, Olympia, WA 98507.**

Coordinated by **Bruce Pavitt** and **Calvin Johnson**. Cover art created in a trance by **Charles Burns**. Invaluable technical assistance: **Phil Hertz, Shaun O'neil**

(V) ISIBLE TARGETS: JUST FOR MONEY
Modern Pop. Rebecca, Laura and Pam Johnson are sisters and have been playing together for years; Ron plays drums. A great dance band. The Targets will not give you a headache or push you out the window. Catchy and fun. Write: **Visible Targets, 1922 9th West, Seattle, WA 98119**...

(B) EAKERS: WHAT'S IMPORTANT
It's sort of a tradition when writing about the **BEAKERS** to mention how they were a sloppy dance band, so obviously influenced by Contortions/Talking Heads/Pere Ubu. Oh yeah, they were the Gang of Four's favorite American group. They have a highly recommended single plus two songs on **Life Elsewhere** and one on an anthology of Seattle bands (Engram). Too bad they broke up. They did a **great** version of "Funky Town"...meanwhile, they've splintered into three different groups: Little Bears from Bangkok, Children of Kellogg and 3 Swimmers. Write: **Mr. Brown Records, Box 445, Olympia, WA 98507**...(Calvin)

(K) AHN, DOUG: REAGAN SPEAKS FOR HIMSELF
One of America's best kept secrets, Doug is a genius at tape manipulation. His Reagan interview is absurd, hilarious. A real hit. His latest project will condense two weeks of the Tomorrow show into 12 minutes. Write: **Doug c/o Xchange: Seattle Art & Politics, 911 E. Pine, Seattle, WA 98122**...

(F) ISK, STEVE: DIGITAL ALARM
Steve is my friend and he is a talented person. He lives in a house with Phil and Mike and they have wires and synthesizers and tape decks all over the place. Steve is always busy. He's in lots of bands. He released a great 45 called **SNAKE ATTACK**; the B-side, **CORPORATE Food**, will be on Jello's new compilation album. He's also on a 12" E.P. called **LIFE ELSEWHERE**. Steve plays all the instruments except drums. Phil plays the drums. This music comes from a small town in Washington. Write: **SUB/POP, Box 2391, Olympia, WA 98507**...

C OOL RAYS: DIARY OF YOU
Notorious for not knowing how to play their instruments, the **COOL RAYS** fool everybody in Olympia by coming up with a song that actually has a beat. Kind of. Calvin's sexy voice should drive the women crazy. Their 15-minute cassette is very diverse. Write: **Calvin c/o SUB-POP, Box 2391, Olympia, WA 98507**...

P AVITT, BRUCE: DEBBIE
While on a visit to his analyst, Bruce tries to recount the events in his life that helped shape his bizarre mind. To use both "creative" and "pretentious" in reference to Bruce Pavitt would be redundant. All I can say is, if you like this, there's probably something wrong with you. Write **Bruce c/o SUB/POP, Box 2391, Olympia, WA 98507**...

P ELL MELL: SPY VS. SPY
...ventures of the Northwest. "Spy..." is a blistering instrumental and will appear on **PELL MELL**'s upcoming 12" E.P. (along with their 7-minute, hypno-surf masterpiece, "New Saigon"). They recently lost a guitar player and replaced him with a machine. Expect big changes. Write: **Bob Beerman, 929 S.W. Salmon #201, Portland, OR 97205**...

J UNGLE NAUSEA: JOB CLUB
Your parents will love this one. Real mellow. Portland's top art/damage combo. These folks are subversive so write them c/o **Michael X King, 76 N.E. Thompson, Portland, OR 97212**...

N EO BOYS: DIRTY WHITE LIES
This all-female quartet has been playing in Portland for a couple of years now. It's been said that they used to sneak out to performances through their bedroom windows at night because their parents didn't want them playing in a punk rock band. (Relatively) new guitarist Meg has brought a new dimension that had always eluded their previous recorded efforts. They're so wonderful. It's like poetry, man. I can't wait to hear the album. Write: **NEO BOYS c/o Meg, 0230 S.W. Faines, Apt. #23, Portland OR 97201**...

P RODUCT ONE: IT HURTS ME TO REMEMBER
Pamela (ex of Mechanical Servants) wrote, sang and played all the instruments on this. She is now in London, recording and trying to make the big time, or at least the big small time. I guess most people would call this "electro-pop" but I don't think that sterile, box-like phrase really describes what's going on here. Dig the Mechanical Servants E.P., **MIN X MATCH**, on Mystery Toast records and watch out for **Product One**! Write: **Mystery Toast, Box 195, Saratoga Springs, NY**...

N URSES: RUBBER HEADS
The **NURSES** were an infamous D.C. area band led by Howard Wuelfing (**Dischords** magazine) and Marc Halpern. I always thought of them as an intelligent mixture of hard rock and desperate pop. They have two excellent singles out, "Hearts" and "Love You Again," and will have two songs on the upcoming Third Limp Sampler. Write: **Dischords, 5018-8th Rd. South, Arlington, VA 22204**

F AIR, JAD: IT SAW ME
JAD is possessed by scary forces beyond his control. His **ZOMBIES OF MORA-TAU** E.P. is my favorite record ever. He is also one of the great minds behind **½ Japanese**. Write: **Jad Fair, Box 143, Westminster, Maryland 21157**...

HE BOHEMIANS: SWITZER BOY

(T) A team of professionals relax at a ski lodge and do some outstanding yodeling. Thank you Steve Fisk for discovering this cultural treasure chest. The **BOHEMIANS** were from Portland...

(V) **AGUE-LEYS: SOFA OR A CHAIR?**
My favorite Chicago band, these guys play the kind of moody, post-Joy Division pop that is quickly becoming a Chicago trademark. Sweeping keyboards and lonely lyrics. Live, however, the **VAGUE-LEYS** are crazy and fun. They recently opened for the Lounge Lizards. Write: **Doug Taylor, 2525 N. Clark St., Chicago, IL 60614**...

(S) **PORT OF KINGS: SING, MARY, SING**
SPORT OF KINGS are an intellectual/pop duo whose recent 45 (The Same Breath) is one of the fastest selling independents in Chicago. This new song displays a more psychedelic direction for the group, and will surely not disappoint fans of this very important Chicago combo...They are also working on an E.P. Write: **Sport of Kings, Box 11131, Chicago, IL 60614**...

(T) **HE MEN: MEN AT WORK**
THE MEN are a cultural cooperative. They live in a huge loft. Their sound and their personnel are constantly changing. Video is common. **THE MEN** have a brand-new album out called **HERMENUETICS**. These hipsters enjoy brainy types like Cage, Miles, Einstein, and Sabotnik. **THE MEN** like to experiment and get funky, baby. Write: **Jack Santee, 411 S. Sangamon, Chicago, IL 60607**...

O IL TASTERS: GET OUT OF THE BATHROOM
...bass, drums, sax. The tightest, most original dance band in the Midwest. They've released two nicely packaged 45's on their own label. "Get out..." is from their classic first 45. These guys have a great sound. Write: **Box 92823, Milwaukee, WI 53202**...

A LL NIGHT MOVIES: SLAUGHTERHOUSE
This is weird music. But then again, Lon C. Diehl is a strange guy. He's the editor of **SMARM** (a great art/damage newsletter) and is currently selling hardcore pornography in a small town in Michigan. His new band is called **HEROIC RICE FARMER**. Send him some cash and he'll send you the A.N.M. 45 and a copy of SMARM. Write: **Lon C. Diehl, 720 Lincoln Ave., Port Huron, MI 48060**

G ET SMART!: EAT, SLEEP A-GO-GO
Minimalist rock n' roll. Two guys and a girl. Their skeletal sound is refreshing. Lots of space—you'll rarely hear a guitar chord. "Eat, Sleep A-go-go" is a dance hit and features Lisa on vocals. It is from their upcoming 4-song E.P.; **GET SMART!** also has a flexi-disc release in conjunction with Talk Talk magazine. **GET SMART!** write: **Frank Looge, Box 493, Lawrence, KS 66044**...

E MBARRASSMENT: LIFESPAN
A great rock and roll band: simple, honest, sophisticated. Some of them are visual artists. The **EMBARRASSMENT** are real Americans; they do not wear sashes and make up. They are from Kansas. Lifespan is about vitamins. Their new 12" E.P. is highly recommended. Write: **The Embarrassment, c/o Dan Rouser, 4204 E. Douglas, Wichita, KA 67208**...

ⓇAY MILLAND: TRONADA

A chilling, 8-minute soundtrack. I can see the vampires now. **RAY MILLAND** is definitely the spookiest act in town. Named after an exotic movie star, this band has a synth/sound that will actually inspire you to write to St. Louis and order their classic Talk/Distant View 45. Write: **Rick Buscher, 9825 Luna Ave., St. Louis, MO 63125**...

ⒸHURCH OF THE SUBGENIUS: EXCERPTS

This is propaganda. A huge joke, a big satire. Funny and comprehensive, the subgenius tapes mix drama with found footage to create a disorienting statement on cults, religion and power. Weird but strange. Write for their tapes and pamphlets: **Subgenius Foundation, Box 140306, Dallas, TX 75214**...

Side One		Side Two
Visible Targets		Vague-leys
Beakers		Sport of Kings
Doug Kahn		Men
Steve Fisk		Oil Tasters
Cool Rays		All Night Movies
Bruce Pavitt		Get Smart!
Pell Mell		Embarrassment
Jungle Nausea		Ray Milland
Neo Boys		Church of the Subgenius
Product One		
Nurses		
Jad Fair		

Assembling and packaging Sub Pop 5 cassettes. Olympia, WA, summer 1981.

The Suits Take Notice

COLUMBIA RECORDS

CBS Records
A Division of CBS Inc.
51 West 52 Street
New York, New York 10019
(212) 975-4321

Dear SUBPOP —

Please send 1x SubPop 5 —
Various Artists cassette. Find enclosed $5.00 to cover
the costs.

thanking you in advance,

Howard Thompson

(Dir. talent acquisition — east coast)

really got a kick out of this one.

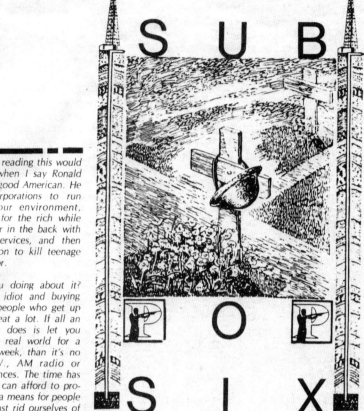

OIL WELL DERRICK

OIL WELL DERRICK

S U B

P O P

S I X

Probably anyone reading this would agree with me when I say Ronald Reagan is not a good American. He allows large corporations to run rampant over our environment, huge tax breaks for the rich while stabbing the poor in the back with cuts in social services, and then spends $55 million to kill teenage girls in El Salvador.

So what are you doing about it? Dressing like an idiot and buying records by four people who get up on stage and sweat a lot. If all an alternative scene does is let you forget about the real world for a couple hours a week, than it's no better than T.V., AM radio or Harlequine romances. The time has passed where we can afford to provide a place and a means for people to forget. We must rid ourselves of the things that hold us back from being truly alternative. One of those things is alcohol. It is provided for us by a leach-like industry that makes a few people (filthy) rich while numbing and anesthetizing the rest. When bands play in bars, not only do they segregate the scene by discriminating against their younger fans, but they teach their younger fans that it is cool to go to bars and get drunk, and thus support Reagan's best friends. Alcohol is just one way they use to oppress the populace, to funnel your hard-earned money back into the hands of the few. What we need is a network of all-ages performance halls where music can be experienced free of all that corporate bullshit, where the audience isn't segregated by age, and where the state liquor board (Police) would have no business interfering.

So. Don't just sit around picking your nose. If you're a musician, when you've got the audience's attention, use it to do something other than getting a hard on. If you edit a fanzine or do a radio show, you have a perfect opportunity to educate people about their government as well as their music. Don't think you can't make a difference, because you do.

CALVIN

Howdy neighbor. Put down that gun and pick up this magazine.

SUB/POP IS AMERICAN. WE ALTERNATE BETWEEN A C-60 CASSETTE AND A PUBLICATION. WE ARE INTERESTED IN A DE-CENTRALIZED NETWORK OF REGIONAL AND LOCAL BUMS WHO REFUSE TO GET AN HONEST JOB. SEND US YOUR INDEPENDENT RECORDS, TAPES AND MAGAZINES. WRITE: SUB/POP C/O LOST MUSIC NET-WORK, BOX 2391, OLYMPIA, WA 98507.

GRAPHICS, COORDINATION.... BRUCE PAVITT FRIENDS AND NEIGHBORS.... CALVIN JOHNSON, JAN LOFT-NESS, TUCKER PETERTIL, GARY MAY FINALLY PRINTED IN FEB. 1982

1981? Simple enough . . . Britain gave us New Romantic white/electro/disco/funk and America gave us . . . what? Hardcore.

While art bands continued to take their orders from the U.K., aggressive muscleheads from around the country formed bands, started labels and bull-dozed an anti-authority network that is digging its way into every suburban high school in the U.S. Punk-thrash is now faster, louder and more American than ever.

Surprise. Today's Hardcore teenage army is the most dominant, the most obvious scene in the American music underground. Hardcore is intense, honest American music; burning red, white and blue images confronting specific American problems. Anthems like "Justice For All," "Six Pack," and "Guns or Ballots," band names like the Dead Kennedys, The Minutemen, and yes, even Jody Foster's Army. Does this sound British? No!

Things are bad. America is falling apart; the economy is collapsing; Reagan is a puppet of the rich and the Pentagon is going to blow life as we know it into fragments. We must react. American culture desperately needs to confront American problems.

Hardcore America is organized. L.A. puts out a new compilation every time I open the mailbox. Posh Boy, Happy Squid, New Alliance, Bemisbrain, SST—all working on organizing teenage revolt. D.C.'s Dischords—savage and defiant. Incredible. Chicago's Autumn records has released the first regional compilation to emerge from Chicago-Hardcore. Touch and Go fanzine just released a compilation of Mich/Ohio bands—more youth riots. Noise fanzine (Ohio) is collaborating with Reno, Nevada, and putting out a great-looking trans-regional cassette. Teenage America in action!

Of course, any strongly defined movement is going to be guilty of bigotry, and Hardcore is no exception. Bands are either Hardcore or they suck. How depressing. Gang mentality is no substitute for independence. Like Black Flag says: "Think for yourself."

I like Hardcore. I like the rush and I like the attitude. Fuck Authority. I hate war and I hate big business and I'm glad that other people feel the same way. Isn't it great that not all teenagers are sucking bongs on the way to play Pac-Man at some sick zoo or a shopping mall? RISE ABOVE.

BRUCE

8 WASHINGTON: (SEATTLE): <u>Seattle Syndrome L.P.</u> - diverse, pop/hardcore/industrial. recommended. (Engram Records, Box 2305, Seattle WA 98101). *Punk Lust: sincere, gothic, totally original.* (5021 43rd Ave S., Seattle WA 98118) *Patio Table: fold-out art mag. social commentary.* (Box 31638, Seattle WA 98103) *Inaudible Noise: last ish featured international hardcore.* (11937 Lakeside N.E. Seattle WA 98125). (OLYMPIA): Absolute Elsewhere: 60 minute cassette, strange pop. (Mr. Brown c/o Lost Music Network Box 2391, Olympia WA 98507). <u>Regional Zeal:</u> excellent new music compilation. lots of sound-text. out in March. (Palace of Lights, Box 4141 Seattle WA 98104). *OP: awesome trans-regional music tabloid. punk, electronic, polka, jazz- everything. 100% independents.* <u>SUB/POP:</u> *trans-regional cassette label/fanzine. You're reading it, buddy. All-American.* (Both magazines available from Lost Music Network, Box 2391 Olympia WA 98507.
OREGON: (PORTLAND): <u>Trap Sampler:</u> 4 bands - Wipers, Napalm Beach, Drumbunny, and (our fave) Pell Mell. (Trap Records, Box 42465, Portland OR 97242). <u>XGNFZSK:</u> *new fanzine. edited by Michael X. King of Jungle Nausea.* (M.X. King, 76 N.E. Thompson, Portland OR 97212).

7 CALIFORNIA: (SAN FRANCISCO/BAY AREA): <u>Red Spot:</u> interesting package design from S.F.'s most prolific and ambitious indie label... experimental. (Subterranean, 912 Bancroft Way, Berkeley CA 94710). <u>Savoy Sound Wave Goodbye:</u> recorded live. diverse, arty. Tux Moon, E-Z Teeth, even some reggae. (753 Lonbard St. S.F. CA 94133). *ANOTHER ROOM: excellent graphics. heavy on the art side. comics by Charles Burns.* (6140 18th St. Oakland CA 94607). RIPPER: *strong hardcore zine. good fanzine and radio directories.* (1494 Teresita Dr., San Jose CA 95129) RE/SEARCH: *will now be released in "perfectbound" book form. still the most interesting mag in the world.* (20 Romolo B, S.F. CA 94133) Special mention: <u>Last Gasp Comics</u> - Anarchy, Young Lust, etc. *great stuff*
(LOS ANGELES): L.A. is the most prolific city in the country. FUTURE LOOKS BRIGHT CASSETTE: Hardcore release of the year. includes: Black Flag, CH3, TSOL, Social Distortion, Descendents Minutemen, Shattered Faith, etc. (Posh Boy...) RODNEY ON THE ROQ VOL. II: side one is more classic hardcore. pure adrenelin. features the hit "Rise Above". Also: Red Rockers from out of town. (Posh Boy, Box 38861, L.A. CA 90038). <u>Hell Comes to Your House:</u> Halloween Hardcore: 45 Grave, plus Modern Warfare, 100 Flowers, Social Distortion, etc. (Bemisbrain: 2738 E. 221 St. Long Beach CA 90810) <u>Chunks:</u> quirky hardcore: Minutemen, Saccharine Trust etc. (New Alliance Box 21 San Pedro CA 90733) <u>Keats Rides a Harley:</u> more aggressive noise, featuring 100 Flowers, Gun Club, and art-thrashers The Meat Puppets (Happy Squid, Box 64184, L.A. CA 90064) <u>L.A.F.M.S. Light Bulb Emergency Cassete Vol. 1 and 2:</u> without a doubt, the top art/damage collection of the year. trans-regional. Jad Fair, The Bachelors Even,... where's Boyd Rice? (L.A. Free Music Society, Box 2853, Pasadena CA 91105) <u>Battle of the Garage Bands:</u> trans-regional collection of 60's inspired garage bands. punkadelic. (Bomp Records, Box 7112, Burbank CA 91510). *Flipside: the nation's no. 1 hardcore zine.* (Box 363 Whittier CA 90608)
Night Voices: Halloween Hardcore (14306 Runnymede St. Van Nuys CA 91405)
(SAN DIEGO) <u>Be My Friend:</u> *great name. covers the local scene* (3636½ University Ave San Diego CA 92104).

DEPARTMENT OF THE ARMY
OFFICE OF THE SECRETARY OF THE ARMY
Office of Civil Defense

Regional Boundaries and Field Installations

REGIONAL compilations and fanzines :CENTRAL intelligence

NEVADA (RENO): "Skeeno" Compilation Cassette features 7 Seconds plus other local thrashers. (Vicious Scam, 2302 Patton Dr. Reno NV 89512). PARANOIA: Hardcore, real "rad". (1408 12th St Sparks NV 89431) Media Massacre and Aggression H.C.: yep, even more hardcore. (both available from 2302 Patton Dr. Reno NV 89512).

6 KANSAS: (LAWRENCE): Really organized scene here. FRESH SOUNDS FROM MIDDLE AMERICA - two beautifully packaged cassettes featuring modern pop bands from all over Kansas. includes S/POP faves Get Smart! and the Embarrassment. released by Bill Rich of the now defunct Talk Talk magazine (Fresh Sounds Box 36 Lawrence KS 66044). Bullet: new mag interested in all kinds of U.S. indies (615½ Mass. Lawrence KS 66044).
IOWA: (DES MOINES): Music for No Man's Land: recorded live. lots of 60's inspired rock 'n pop (Times Up Box 65592, Des Moines IA 50265). Aftertaste: local zine (Box 65592 W. Des Moines IA 50265).
NEBRASKA: (LINCOLN): Capital Punishment: surprisingly good zine. Sept. '81 ish contained features on Get Smart! and DA! (c/o Jim Jones 2128 B. St. Apt B Lincoln NE 68502). (OMAHA): Beef: Large format art-zine. I like it. (Box 3932 Omaha NE 68103)
MISSOURI (ST. LOUIS): Home of Ray Milland... Jet Lag fanzine (Box 7941 St. Louis MO 63106).

5 TEXAS: (HOUSTON): Wild Dog: big zine, lots of interviews (Box 35253, S. Post Oak Station, Houston TX 77035). (AUSTIN): Idle Times: real fun mag (c/o Dixon 1905 Forest Trail, Austin TX 78703).
LOUISIANA: (NEW ORLEANS): No Questions, No Answers L.P.: includes Red Rockers (c/o Final Solution, 4304 James Dr., Metaire LA 70003). Final Solution: this mag has been around a long time. has released the No Questions, No Answers L.P. Public Threat (c/o Leisure Landing 5500 Magazine, New Orleans LA).

4 MICHIGAN: (DETROIT): Detriot On a Platter: hard rock, nu wave (Automotive, 11471 Mitchell, Hamtramck MI 48212). Anonymous: hardcore zine (20107 Mada Ave. Southfield MI 48075). (LANSING, PORT HURON, ETC.): Process of Elimination E.P. a comp of Mich./Ohio Hardcore featuring Detroit's truly aggro Negative Approach this is released in conjunction w/ Touch and Go fanzine, a decadent and perverse mag with great national hardcore coverage (Box 26203 Lansing MI 48909). Smarm: art/damage newsletter. recommended. editor Lon C. Diehl plays with Heroic Rice Farmer and does a radio show called Smarm On the Air. (Box 1282 Port Huron MI 48060).
ILLINIOS: (CHICAGO): Busted at Oz L.P.: recorded live. mostly hardcore. includes Strike Under, Effigies (Autumn Records 2427 N. Janssen Chicago IL 60614). Coolest Retard: local zine (c/o Schmidt, 2042 N. Bissell Chicago IL).
INDIANA: (BLOOMINGTON): Red Snerts L.P.: slick package. features Amoebas In Chaos etc. (Gulcher Box 1635 Bloomington IN 47402).
WISCONSIN: (MILWAUKEE): Skid: is an open-minded mag - pretty rare these days. (J. Hope, 34233 S. Bayview Rd. Oconomowoc WI 53066).
MINNESOTA: (MINNEAPOLIS): Great Hits From Mid-America Vol. 2 is still available. includes Suburbs, Curtiss A. (TwinTone 445 Oliver Ave S. Minneapolis MN 55405).

3 GEORGIA: (ATHENS/ATLANTA): D.B. Records is the center point for the South. Pylon, Method Actors etc. They also work in association with Armageddon U.K. (c/o Danny Beard, Moreland Ave. Atlanta GA 30307).
FLORIDA: The Borington Journal: funny (2421 Nassau Dr., Mirimar FL 33023). Destroy: violent (4546-A N.W. 13th St. Gainesville FL 32601).

OHIO: an incredible state. 10 or more zines here, including The Offense: a huge project, covers just about everything. heavy on the art/Brit side. (c/o Magnolia Thunderpussy Records, 1585 N. High St. Columbus OH 43201) Noise: one of the most informative hardcore zines around. will soon release a transregional cassette (3588 Southbrook Dr., Xenia OH 45385). CLE: mostly history. last ish featured on eclectic 6-song flexi (585 Walnut Dr., Cleveland OH 44132). Bowling Balls From Hell Vol. 2: diverse. includes the waitresses, Bizarros, Tin Huey. (Clone Records Box 6014 Akron OH 44312).

D.C. Area: awesome hardcore scene. a 12" Hardcore Sampler will be out soon, featuring Minor Threat, Youth Brigade, Artificial Peace, etc. (Dischord 3819 Beecher St. N.W. Washington D.C. 20007). Connected: comp. includes the Nurses. diverse. (Limp Records 1327 J. Rockville Pike, Rockville MD 20852). Dischords: trans-regional American news! not affiliated with Dischords records (5018 8th Road S., Arlington VA 22204).
PENNSYLVANIA: (PITTSBURG): Modern Angst (311 Ewing Rd. Coraopolis PA 15108). Made in Pittsburg Vol. 1-3: not very interesting. (Bogus Records 4806 Liberty Ave. Pittsburg PA 15224).
DELAWARE: (WILMINGTON): The Bob: funny. supposedly releasing flexi-discs. (508 Whitby Dr., Wilmington DE 19803).

NEW YORK: Noise Fest Tapes: Mofungo, Y-Pants, Avant-Squares, etc. should be great. (White Columns, 325 Spring Street N.Y., NY 10013). Start Swimming: D.B.'s, Bongos, Raybeats, Tetras, Fleshtones recorded live in (cough) England. on Stiff Records... Volume: 2nd and last book due in spring. Thousands of addresses (110 Chambers St. N.Y. NY 10017). New York Rocker: is definitely more interested in American music these days (166 5th Ave. N.Y. NY 10010). Short Newz: great source of fanzine addresses (Box 1028 N.Y. NY 10028). Non L.P. B Side: is starting to recognize U.S. music (7 Stuyvesant Place, Cedarhurst N.Y. NY 11516). Tribal Noise: (234-5 Ave Apt #2 Brooklyn NY 11215). Decline of Art: too British (351 W. 30th St. N.Y. NY 10001).
MASSACHUSETTS: (BOSTON): A Wicked Good Time Vol. 2: more new wave pop (268 Newbury St. Boston MA 02116). Propeller Product: 60 minute tape (21 Parkvale Ave. No. 1, Allston MA 02134). Take 1t!: large tabloid. new ish includes Dead Kennedys, Flipper flexi-disc. (196 Harvard Ave. Suite 5 Boston MA 02134).
NEW JERSEY: Cold Blood: newsletter (655 E. Passaic Ave. Bloomfield NJ 07003).

SUB/pop 5 update

VISIBLE TARGETS have signed with Park Ave. Records... DOUG KAHN has some new tapes-Rona B. interviewing karate star Chuck Norris. STEVE FISK is working with electronic duo Customer Service....... BRUCE PAVITT is releasing work on Glass Records in the U.K...... PELL MELL's E.P. is doing very well; they are now a trio featuring some really brainy guitar. great...JUNGLE NAUSEA will soon release a 10-inch e.p.; Michael is editing XGNFZSK fanzine... NEO BOYS L.P. out soon...Pamela of PRODUCT ONE is in England recording with former members of Magazine...JAD FAIR is in a new combo called After Dinner, expect a record...THE VAGUE-LEYS will be making their vinyl debut...SPORT OF KINGS new e.p. is excellent; their album will be out this Spring...THE MEN are releasing cassettes in small paint cans,"Men in a Can"...theOILTASTERS are still active...ALL NIGHT MOVIES are now Heroic Rice Farmer...GET SMART! and the EMBARRASSMENT both have strong tracks on the new Fresh cassette compilations from Kansas...RAY MILLAND has lost their guitarist; they'll probably release something on Glass or Situation 2 in the U.K....post-mortem releases: the NURSES have just released a cassette; Howard's Dischord mag has just folded (unfortunately) ...the BEAKERS have an incredible track on the Seattle Syndrome L.P....the COOL RAYS will release material on the upcoming Absolute Elsewhere cassette compilation and maybe even Dub Communique 2!!....Oh yeah, THE CHURCH OF THE SUBGENIUS always has new stuff coming out...

DISTRIBUTED BY ROUGH TRADE, SYSTEMATIC, SKY DISC, SEIDBOARD

SUB/POP 7, trans-regional U.S. cassette compilation, will be released around April or May, 1982. Expect to hear: 3 SWIMMERS,TWIN DIET, FASTBACKS, FAULTY DENIAL MECHANISM, HEROIC RICE FARMER, PELL MELL, ANGST, SPORT OF KINGS, ZYKLON, EMBARRASSMENT AND MORE!!

DEADLINE FOR TAPES: APRIL 1, 1982. TRY AND SEND REEL-TO-REEL, 15 ips, 1/4 TRACK!!!!!!

MODERN LOVERS

Boston **Modern Lovers** L.P.
     Boys Life 45
N.Y. **Liquid Liquid** 12"E.P.
     Individuals 12"E.P.

MINOR THREAT
In My Eyes

D.C. **Minor Threat** 7"E.P.
     Trouble Funk 2-L.P.
     Billy Hancock L.P.
     Youth Brigade 7"E.P.

A New Personality

Florida **A New Personality** 45
Athens **R.E.M.** 45

Chicago **Effigies** 12"E.P.
     Sport of Kings 12"E.P.
     Men L.P.
     Ministry 12"E.P.

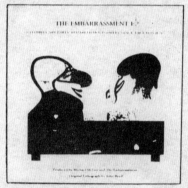

THE EMBARRASSMENT E.P.

Kansas **Embarrassment** 12"E.P.
     Get Smart! 7"E.P.

MEAT PUPPETS

Phoenix **Meat Puppets** 7"E.P.
     Jody Fosters Army 45
Austin **Radio Free Europe** L.P.
Houston **MyDolls** 45

Pell Mell

Portland **Pell Mell** 12"E.P.
     Wipers L.P.
Seattle **3 Swimmers** 12"E.P.
     Fastbacks 45
     Fartz 7"E.P.

MINIMAL MAN

S.F. **Minimal Man** L.P.
     D. Kennedys N/Punks 45
     Flipper S/Bomb 45
     Romeo Void 12"E.P.

45 GRAVE
BLACK CROSS

L.A. **45 Grave** 45
     Black Flag L.P.
     Agent Orange L.P.
     Salvation Army 45
     Descendants 7"E.P.

TOP of the SUB/POP

AS IN ANY DEMOCRATIC SOCIETY, ALL RECORDS ARE EQUALLY RECOMMENDED.

FELLOW AMERICANS, THE ABOVE U.S. RELEASES SHOULD BE AVAILABLE IN YOUR TOWN. IF YOU HAVE TROUBLE FINDING THESE, OR ANY OTHER GREAT NOISE, THRASH AND/OR POP RECORDS, PLEASE WRITE US HERE AT SUB/POP FOR ADDRESSES AND/OR INFO CONCERNING THESE VALUABLE CULTURAL ARTIFACTS.

C O M I X

The most prolific of the underground publishers is: **Last Gasp**, Box 212, Berkeley, CA 94107. Their books are politically motivated and make for great reading. **Young Lust** and **Anarchy**, coordinated by **J. Kinney**, are compilations which feature national and international artists...other highly recommended books from Last Gasp are:

JAY KINNEY ANARCHY 2 ©1979

Weirdo, which looks like the old **Mad** comic and features the best of Crumb's new work.
Zippy & You features **Bill Griffith's** pinheaded anti-hero.
Slow Death, the magazine devoted to modern fatal conditions.
Street Art, a compilation of 140 punk art posters from San Francisco. New!

Krupp or **Kitchen Sink** at Box 7, Princeton, Wisconsin 54968, publishes:
Corporate Crime, an absorbing look at big business' inevitable darker side.
Bunch's Power Pak by **Aline Kominsky**. Her native artwork goes great with her glimpses into her neurotic life.
Mondo Snarfo is stream of consciousness comics from some of the best underground artists.
Bizarre Sex is just that.

Raw, "the graphix magazine for damned intellectuals," is organized by veteran cartoonist **Art Speigelman** of **Arcade** fame. This is the best-looking comics compilation to come out of the U.S. The upcoming fourth issue will feature a cover and 9-page story by **Charles Burns** and will include a flexi-disc of **Doug Kahn's** infamous Reagan interview. Write **Raw Books**, 27 Greene St., NY, NY 10013.

Also there are the individual artist who publish their own comix. Because of a lack of capital, some of these books are the most innovative and interesting. Here are a few of them:

Comical Funnies, my current choice for the funniest comic. It features **John Holmstrom**, who did the art for **Punk** magazine and The Ramones' **Road to Ruin** cover. Write PO Box 711, Old Chelsea Station, NY, NY 10113.

Okupant X by **Gary Panter**, known for his cartoons in **Slash**. He has done album art for Ralph Records and has spawned hundreds of imitators. Available from: Diana's Bimonthly Press, 71 Elmgrove Ave., Providence, RI 02906. (Gary has also released a 45 on Index records, produced by the Residents.)

Beach Lake is **Marc Beyer's** latest; he has appeared in **Raw** and **Arcade** and has published several landmark comix, including: **Death, A Disturbing Evening**. Beyer is yet another cartoonist who has contributed artwork to Ralph Records. Write him at: PO Box 2304, Allentown, PA 18104.

Hunt Emerson is an English fellow who did tons of work for Melody Maker. His book **Thunder Dogs** is available through **Last Gasp**. He's published a lot of his own books in England, the best being **Dogman** and **Street Comix**. Write for his latest at: 86 Church Hill Road, Handsworth, Birmingham, England, 20.

Harvey Pekar's comic **American Splendor** features bleak stories of boredom; they remind me of Andy Warhol's early films. They're illustrated by Robt. Crumb and others. From: Box 18471, Cleveland Heights, Ohio 44118.

CHARLES BURNS RAW 3 ©1981

LYNDA BARRY BOYS AND GIRLS ©1981

Boys and Girls by **Lynda Barry**—short stories of conflict, embarrassment, guilt, even something like love. Highly recommended by the editors. Write: 932 18th Avenue East, Seattle, WA 98112.

David and Jad Fair are brothers. They do primitive art for their band, 1/2 Japanese. Jad has also done artwork for The Residents. David has three books out: **Worms In It**, **Becky the Monkey**, and **I Like Cats**. Get these! Write to them at Box 143, Westminster, MD 21157.

Raymond Pettibone is best known for his cover art on Black Flag's records. His book **Captive Chains** shows us his crude vision of a personal hell. Write: SST Publications, PO Box 1, Lawndale, CA 90260.

Last but not least is **Steve Willis' Cranium Frenzy**, a great example of a labor of love. It's got belly laughs and snappy art and even some quasi-intelligent stuff thrown in for good measure. Write Steve at: 6012 30th NE, Seattle, WA 98115.

Two mail order sources that carry a vast selection of undergrounds are: **Monkey's Retreat**, 2400 N. High Street, Columbus, Ohio 93202, and **Bob Side Bottom**, 73 E. San Fernando, San Jose, CA 95113. Send an SASE and a quarter for catalogs.

I'll be writing about comix from time to time, so if you've done some, send 'em in.

Tucker Petertil has drawn and published several undergrounds. He plays bass in Jumbo Zen and his next project is a mini-mag insert in Jumbo Zen's March cassette release.

Gerard Cosloy

Going Waaaaaay Back

The exchange of information was wildly different back then, almost laughably primitive (other than the content, of course) compared to today. You would wait months for certain zines to emerge, finally reading reviews of like-minded publications; then sending a SASE (I cannot remember the last time I wrote that!) and a nominal sum in the hopes of some great moment of discovery coming back to you, ages later. If you knew where to look, this exercise was usually worth the time and hassle.

Bruce's *Sub Pop* zines and the cassette comps were eye-openers, gateway drugs, and so on, in the best sense possible. His efforts weren't the only examples of the bar being set pretty high (Columbus, Ohio's, amazing *Offense* and subsequent *Offense Newsletter* come to mind), but *Sub Pop* was inspiring stuff.

These days, every schmuck with a "smart" phone is seconds away from a wiki-style summation of any cultural curio. I will not argue that music and art were better in 1982—they weren't! But I'm eternally in debt to those who did the digging, back when the notion of a payoff (or even getting laid) seemed improbable.

Thanks Bruce!

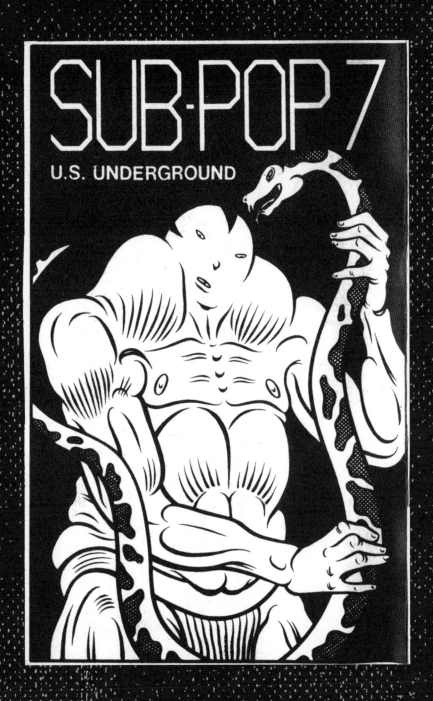

Fellow comrades, I have read your letters and you are right—Nationalism **is** the father of Fascism. So, while we will continue to embrace grass-roots American pop, we will also open our arms to any and all contributions, both national and international. . SUB/POP now alternates, quarterly, between a 60-minute trans-regional cassette and a networking newsletter. Tapes are now TDK normal bias; $5.00 ppd. Write: **Lost Music Network, Box 2391, Olympia, WA 98507**

Information: **Bruce Pavitt.** Spiritual Guidance: **Calvin Johnson.** Cover Art: **Charles Burns.** Invaluable Technical Assistance: **Phil Hertz, Shawn O'Neil**. 1982

CHARLES BURNS (COVER ART)
Other works of art by Mr. Burns can be found in
DEATH RATTLE COMICS ("an 18-page story about sex,
violence, insects and egg incubation"), ANOTHER
ROOM (S.F. music mag) and of course RAW #3 and
#4. For more info, write: **Charles Burns, 6643 8th St.,
Philadelphia, PA 19126.**

SPORT OF KINGS "DARK CLOUDS MOVING"
S.O.K. are refined, tasteful; they prefer beauty over
senseless decadence and nihilism. This epic, 6-minute
pop adventure could've been called the Illiad; a truly
majestic song by one of the most prolific bands
around. Order their 45, their 12" and hold your breath
for their L.P., due out any day. Write: **Box 11131,
Chicago, IL 60611.** "Dark Clouds Moving" © and ℗
1981 Sport of Kings

BONEMEN OF BARUMBA "THICK PROMISE"
The Bonemen hail from Lombard, IL. Their 10" e.p.,
the most interesting package I've seen in awhile, is
doing quite well internationally. This song is taken
from their upcoming 2nd release. Write: **Box 841,
Lombard, IL 60148.** "Thick Promise" © and ℗ 1982
Bonemen of Barumba.

VIBRANT FIASCO "LIZARD LIPS"
Wacky, irreverent pop from Aurora, IL? Talk about nowheresville, man, this is about as obscure as we get. Write and ask about their new record: Box 3151 Fox Valley Station, Aurora, IL 60505. "Lizard Lips" © and ℗ Vibrant Fiasco.

ZYKLON "GARY, IN" (edited version)
An Industrial Report from the Midwest. "We pay $2-3 million a week in pollution fines alone." This is intense, regional music; if you're adventurous, order their 60-minute cassette. Write: **Grim Records, Box 9539, Wyoming, MI 49509.** "Gary, IN" © and ℗ 1981 ZYKLON.

HEROIC RICE FARMER "NUMBER ONE"
HEROIC RICE FARMER obtained their name from an enlightened 5th grader in Lansing, MI. Containing former members of **All Night Movies**, this band is separated by "many miles of pavement." This piece was composed by Rod A. Sanford. Write: **808 S. Washington, Mt. Pleasant, MI 48858.** "Number One" © and ℗ 1982 Heroic Rice Farmer.

GET SMART! "BLACK MIRROR"
GET SMART! is a leader in the Kansas pop explosion. **Black Mirror** is abrasive; reminds me of that Sonics classic, The Witch. "The lyrics are by Vance Lyon, our friend imprisoned in Utah." This trio is on the road a lot, so catch 'em live. Write: **Box 493, Lawrence, KS 66044.** "Black Mirror" © and ℗ 1982 Syntax.

YARD APES "ANOTHER LITTLE MIRACLE"

Percussion and pop dance together in this exotic black magic/white voodoo hoedown. Put on your grass skirt baby, we're goin' to Kansas City. More of the Yard Apes can be heard on the Fresh 101 cassette (as well as Get Smart! and the Embarrassment.) Write: **Chris Ape, 911 W. 44th, Suite 69, Kansas City, MO 64111.** "Another Little Miracle" © and ℗ 1982 YardCo Entertainment.

EMBARRASSMENT "SOUND OF WASPS"

Grass roots pop of the 1st order. Outstanding production. **Wellsville (from their 12")** defines the "small town Midwest" better than anything I've ever heard. The Embarrassment are touring a lot these days, so see 'em in person. Write: **Box 293, Wichita, KS 67201.** "Sound of Wasps" © and ℗ 1981 Embarrassment

JASON and the NASHVILLE SCORCHERS "BROKEN WHISKEY GLASS"

The Scorchers play roots-American music from the heart of C&W territory. Son of a hog farmer, Jason leads the way with a leap and a shout—guitar and vocals. This living room, 4-track recording is taken from their **Wreckless Country Soul E.P.** Look out Blasters, here come the Scorchers! Write: **PRAXIS Records, 152 Kenner, Nashville, TN 37206.** "Broken Whiskey Glass" © and ℗ 1982 Nashville Scorchers

BILL LAGASSE "WORMS IN IT"

BILL LAGASSE, from the DUPLEX NURSING HOME reads "Worms In It," a comic book created by David Fair. Bleeps courtesy of Steve Fisk. Write **Bill, c/o The Duplex Planet Magazine, D.B. Greenberger 16 University Rd., #2, Brookline, MA 02146.** Order the book from **David Fair, Box 143, Westminster, MD**

54/40 "YANKS"
"54/40 or fight" is a regional war cry you might
remember from some dusty history book. Fortunately,
this band is alive and breathing in Vancouver, B.C.
Thank you, Canada. write: **MO-DA-MU Records,
c/o Brad Merritt, 10722 Parton Rd., Surrey, B.C.,
Canada, V3V3T7.** "Yanks" © and Ⓟ 1982 54/40

LITTLE BEARS FROM BANGKOK "CAR BUYING TIME"
2 bass guitars, a new drummer and a girl who speeds
away in her own hot-rod feedback. This anthem is a
beautiful tribute to our blindly consumerist all-
American lifestyle. By the way, bass player Tracy
helps coordinate Roscoe Louie, easily the most radical
art gallery in Seattle. Write: **c/o Roscoe Louie, 87 S.
Washington, Seattle, WA 98104.** "Car Buying Time"
© and Ⓟ 1982 Little Bears from Bangkok

TWIN DIET "COMMUNICATE"
Two girls and a microphone. Very minimal, very
intimate. This is great. Bev is in France right now,
but Jan will forward any fan mail. Write: **c/o 207 W.
4th St. #3, Olympia, WA 98501.** "Communicate" ©
and Ⓟ 1982 Pip McCaslin

SHAWN O'NEIL "GENERATIONS PAST"
60's psychedelia, complete with trash organ solo by
Steve Fisk. A riot. This song is taken from **CAIRO'S
RIDE**—a 30-minute soundtrack to a Biker movie that
will never be made. If you like surf instrumentals, buy
his cassette! (Produced by Peter Randlett). Write: **Dr.
Stimson, 824 S. Decatur, Olympia, WA 98502.** "Generations Past" © and Ⓟ 1982 Shawn O'neil

ROCKING FELLOW "UNDEAD"
The mysterious Rocking Fellow. Who is this masked man? "Undead" is an industrial pop ditty concerning a young corpse who is the "same as you or me." The crooning on the chorus is what knocked me out...
write: **Lost Music Network, Box 2391, Olympia, WA 98507.** "Undead" © and ℗ 1982 Rocking Fellow

PELL MELL "SOME THINGS WE DO FOR FUN"
There's only a few instrumental combos in this country and Pell Mell is my hands-down favorite. This 4-track recording is the first hint of their exciting new sound (they've recently streamlined their outfit from 4 to 3). Pell Mell's 12" E.P. is highly recommended.
Write: **Box 40302, Portland, OR 97240.** "Some Things We Do For Fun" © and ℗ 1982 Pell Mell.

NEO BOYS "UNDER CONTROL"
Another hit from this Northwest girl group. Sparkling guitar, introspective lyrics. A nice light funk sound this time around. Their album should be out any day now...produced by Tom Robinson. Write: **c/o Meg, 0230 S.W. Gaines, Apt. #23, Portland, OR 97201.** "Under Control" © and ℗ 1982 Neo Boys

ANGST "GIVE ALL THE POWER TO THE U.S."
"Give all the power to the U.S./cause we know who to kill and we do it the best." Someday, the U.S. Pentagon is going to self-destruct; hopefully this song will push the button... Little is known about these guys, so write 'em: **c/o J. Pope, 766 Sutter #49, S.F., CA 94109** "Give All the Power to the U.S." © and ℗ 1982 MMM

A NEW PERSONALITY "A FEELING"
Florida, the state that brought you alligators and ruthless Colombian dope smugglers, is now proud to
present **A NEW PERSONALITY**, a heart-warming trio
with modern songs of love and loneliness. Their
3-song 45 is definitely recommended. Send "love
letters" to: **A.N.P., c/o 4216 Harbour House Dr.,
Tampa, FL 33615.** "A Feeling" © and ℗ 1982 A New
Personality.

MYDOLLS "IMPOSTER"
Strike oil? You bet. An intriguing pop hit from
Houston—whirling tom toms, heavy phase on the
bass. These femme fatales are definitely putting Texas
on the map. Check out their 3-song 45 or inquire
about upcoming vinyl. Write: **1231 Ashland, Houston,
TX 77008.** "Imposter" © and ℗ 1982 MyDolls.

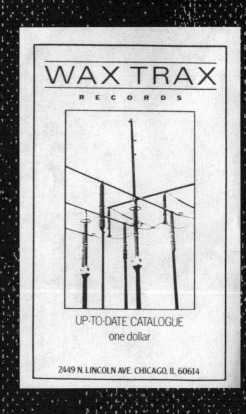

WAX TRAX

R E C O R D S

UP-TO-DATE CATALOGUE
one dollar

2449 N. LINCOLN AVE. CHICAGO, IL 60614

SPORT OF KINGS
BONEMEN OF BARUMBA
VIBRANT FIASCO
ZYKLON
HEROIC RICE FARMER
GET SMART!
YARD APES
EMBARRASSMENT
JASON and the
NASHVILLE SCORCHERS
BILL LAGASSE/DAVID FAIR

54/40
LITTLE BEARS FROM BANGKOK
TWIN DIET
SHAWN O'NEIL
ROCKING FELLOW
PELL MELL
NEO BOYS
ANGST
A NEW PERSONALITY
MYDOLLS

Ann Powers

I Missed Grunge

I missed grunge. Not really. Like virtually everyone who loved rock and roll in the 1990s, I inhaled the brick dust when Nirvana toppled the genre's hierarchies. And since I grew up in Seattle, I could pretty easily read the ethical code by which the scene's main bands lived: laconic sarcasm, the smirk displayed for outsiders, masking fierce loyalty toward the chosen tribe; punk energy for burning through bullshit; behind that, a deep-seated work ethic that didn't diminish the fun, just made it more powerful. These qualities were characteristic of indie rock as a whole, but in the grey-green, gorgeous Pacific Northwest, they went back farther, to fisherman elders and serious Scandinavian founding fathers and mothers. I understood that part of grunge, and also knew why the guys (mostly guys) behind the music hated that term, not only because it was for marketing but because naming something that way—as if it were a novelty, a product that needed a brand—both diminished it and pulled it out of its makers' hands.

So I *got* grunge, but I missed it, because I left Seattle in 1984. I never saw Green River or Mother Love Bone; I didn't hang out in Belltown before sushi was on every corner. At twenty, I fled to San Francisco—a warmer, curvier, more classically bohemian place where I could do things some of my Seattle artist friends thought were silly, like study poetry and drink red wine in cafés, instead of beers in a basement. I stayed there for eight years. By the time Seattle became an infamous musical hot spot, I was in New York, where Pussy Galore epitomized unkempt cool, and the people who wore plaid listened to hip hop.

It was strange to reconnect to my hometown's sound from so far away. I didn't recognize much at first. When I was a kid, immersed in a fugitive all-ages scene dominated by warehouse parties and gigs in old benevolent society buildings, underground Seattle was theatrical and psychedelic. Mushroom tea brewed on the stove in musicians' lofts, and inspiration came from Captain Beefheart and Patti Smith. The bands I loved had new wave-y names like Mental Mannequin, Audio Leter, Red Dress, the Blackouts, and the Macs. Made up of girls with half-shaved heads and boys in neon jackets and eyeliner, these gender-bending anarchist ensembles bore little resemblance to the headbanging hesher punks that, according to the world, expressed the essence of Pacific Northwest rock.

There was one connection, though: *Sub Pop*—the column first and foremost, and also the magazine and the label. I never really knew Bruce Pavitt, though we both worked at the Seattle rock mag the *Rocket*. I was just a girl reporter, my confidence as shaky as the beat of my favorite B-52's songs. I kept to myself in that office of local stars. But Bruce's column, an offshoot of the zine I thumbed through at his tiny record store on Capitol Hill in Seattle, taught me that weirdo scenes like the one I loved were scattered all across the country. He wrote about punk and indie rock, but also funk and early hip hop; whatever was turning on the people who liked to get sweaty in semi-legal spaces. "Hi There. My name is Bruce and we have to decentralize our society and encourage local art and things and music," Pavitt wrote in one of *Sub Pop*'s first issues. That friendly mandate made sense to me, as a kid with a **QUESTION AUTHORITY** button pinned to my Army surplus jacket, hearing the noise of punk saxophones in my head.

Grunge, the pop goldmine, had no saxophones. But Sub Pop survived as a label partly because it never stuck to a narrow idea of what rock should sound like. Oddball artists found a place there from the beginning. Even the breakthrough bands that recorded for the label had a strong eccentric streak. Kurt Cobain didn't just wear dresses; he wore housedresses, the ugliest and silliest and most subversive kind of drag. Mark Arm of Mudhoney maintained the spirit of his youth playing for Mr. Epp and the Calculations, a hardcore band whose sound was constantly unraveling into chaos—a real Bruce Pavitt Sub Pop kind of band.

Today, two decades after the brief period when Seattle rock sold like Twitter stock, Seattle underground music has returned to its raggedy, eclectic, stubbornly utopian roots. Not that it ever really strayed from them. And Sub Pop is still in the alley with the bands. I don't live anywhere near my salty home these days, but I think I still get it. I thank Bruce Pavitt for helping me to understand how wide the net of the weird can be cast.

S U B * P O P 8 $. I 8

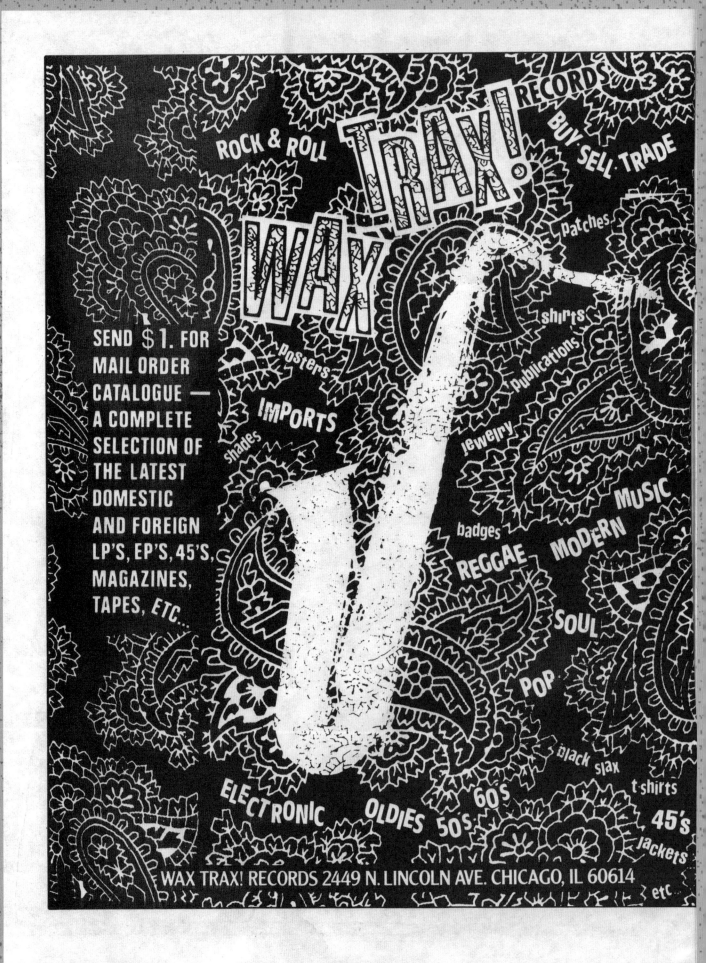

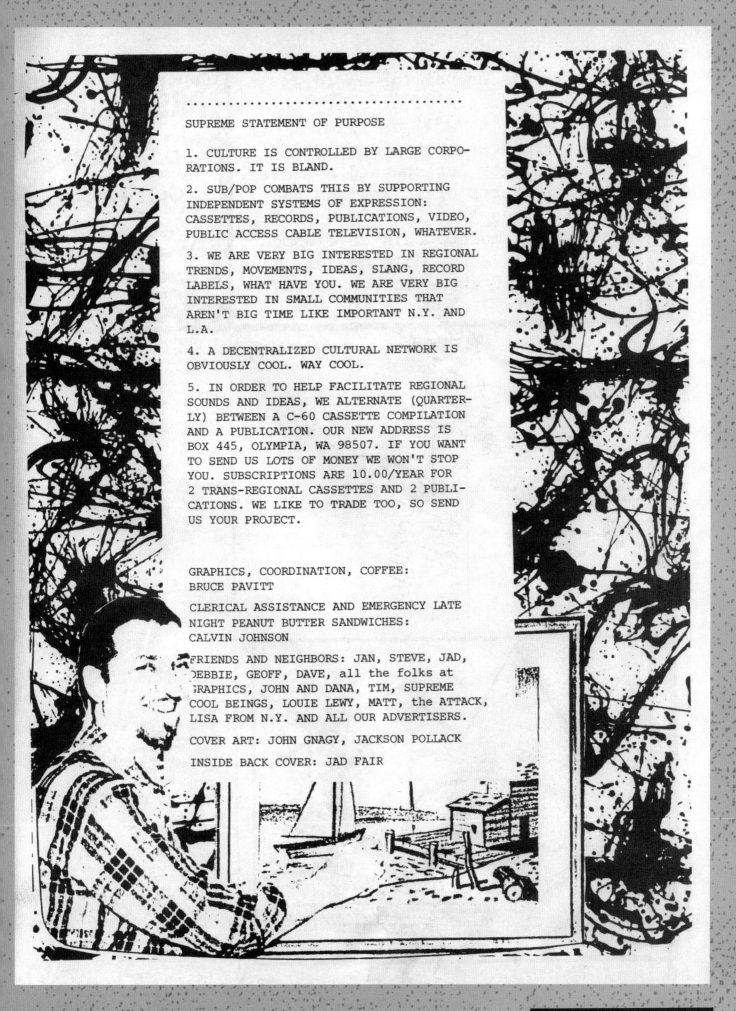

SUPREME STATEMENT OF PURPOSE

1. CULTURE IS CONTROLLED BY LARGE CORPO-
RATIONS. IT IS BLAND.

2. SUB/POP COMBATS THIS BY SUPPORTING
INDEPENDENT SYSTEMS OF EXPRESSION:
CASSETTES, RECORDS, PUBLICATIONS, VIDEO,
PUBLIC ACCESS CABLE TELEVISION, WHATEVER.

3. WE ARE VERY BIG INTERESTED IN REGIONAL
TRENDS, MOVEMENTS, IDEAS, SLANG, RECORD
LABELS, WHAT HAVE YOU. WE ARE VERY BIG
INTERESTED IN SMALL COMMUNITIES THAT
AREN'T BIG TIME LIKE IMPORTANT N.Y. AND
L.A.

4. A DECENTRALIZED CULTURAL NETWORK IS
OBVIOUSLY COOL. WAY COOL.

5. IN ORDER TO HELP FACILITATE REGIONAL
SOUNDS AND IDEAS, WE ALTERNATE (QUARTER-
LY) BETWEEN A C-60 CASSETTE COMPILATION
AND A PUBLICATION. OUR NEW ADDRESS IS
BOX 445, OLYMPIA, WA 98507. IF YOU WANT
TO SEND US LOTS OF MONEY WE WON'T STOP
YOU. SUBSCRIPTIONS ARE 10.00/YEAR FOR
2 TRANS-REGIONAL CASSETTES AND 2 PUBLI-
CATIONS. WE LIKE TO TRADE TOO, SO SEND
US YOUR PROJECT.

GRAPHICS, COORDINATION, COFFEE:
BRUCE PAVITT

CLERICAL ASSISTANCE AND EMERGENCY LATE
NIGHT PEANUT BUTTER SANDWICHES:
CALVIN JOHNSON

FRIENDS AND NEIGHBORS: JAN, STEVE, JAD,
DEBBIE, GEOFF, DAVE, all the folks at
GRAPHICS, JOHN AND DANA, TIM, SUPREME
COOL BEINGS, LOUIE LEWY, MATT, the ATTACK,
LISA FROM N.Y. AND ALL OUR ADVERTISERS.

COVER ART: JOHN GNAGY, JACKSON POLLACK

INSIDE BACK COVER: JAD FAIR

The Northwest is one of the world's most prolific centers of activity in the visual arts, as well as film, video, performance and new music. This wealth of activity has spawned a number of alternative arts organizations and exhibition spaces in order to accomodate this development. This is meant as a run down on some of the more vital of these in the Northwest.

ROSCO LOUIE
PRESENTS:
Sept. 9 – Sept. 28
David Baze
Sept. 30 – Oct. 19
Gale McCall
Oct. 21 – Nov. 9
Joyce Moty
Wendy Brawer
Rosco Louie Gallery
Seattle, WA   206-682-5228

Alternative ART Spaces
by Louie Lewy

UNIT PITT GALLERY

163 W Pender, Vancouver, B.C. V6B 1RS
A highly regarded exhibition space funded by the exhibiting artists. A neo-dada sensibility. Recent shows include an art show and performance by the Braineaters (No Art Now!), and neo expressionist Vicky Marshall.
Contact: Helen Pitt

WESTERN FRONT

303 E 8th Ave, Vancouver, B.C. V5t 1S1
A funded space for visual art, video, performance, new music, etc. A little off the beaten path, but a very active program. Recent performances by Techno Primates, Elenor Antin, and Eric Bogosian, a residence by Anna Banana, and an art show by Buster Simpson.
Contact: Corry Wyngaarden

FRICTION

1637 SW 17th, Portland, Ore. 97205
A co-op gallery run by artist members with lots of open group shows and musical and performance events. Recent shows have included an artists book show, an anti-fascist show, a feminist show, a performance series and a one man show of fave toys by Russ Bataglia.
Contact: X.J. Elliot.

PORTLAND CENTER FOR THE VISUAL ARTS

117 NW 5th, Portland, Ore. 97209
One of the best establishment "Alternative Spaces" in the Northwest, if not the whole country. They alternate shows of local talent, "Blue Chip" artists and U.S. Underground. Recent shows include Vito Acconci, Mike Glier, and performances by people like Michael Smith and Eric Bogosian. Worth cheking out.
Contact: Donna Milrany

NORTHWEST ARTISTS WORKSHOP

522 NW 12th, Portland, Ore. 97205
A terrific, pristine gallery operated by real artists and funded by various grant sources. The workshop has been around for 7 years. Since moving into their new space they have put on a soundworks show, a video show and have regular performances featuring artists like Alan Lande, Little Bears from Bangkok, Ken Butler, Pell Mell, Babylon 2000 and the like.
Contact: Darrell Cleeg.

ROSCO LOUIE GALLERY

87 S Washington St, Seattle, Wa. 98104
"the Only Gallery that Matters". Real good modern art by regional and national artists. Commercially funded. Recent shows include a 4th annual Post Card Competition, artists video games, an Etch-a-Sketch Invatational, and coming up, a show of underground comix artists. Also a showcase for new music, video, poetry, fashion, etc. Bands like: Bush Tetras, DNA, Tuxedomoon, Raybeats, 3 Swimmers, and Sub/Pop-ers Neo Boys and Pell Mell.
Contact: Louie Lewy

GROUND ZERO GALLERY

207 3rd Ave S, Seattle, Wash. 98104
A new co-op gallery run by artists. Nice gallery space with group shows. The quality is mixed, but the attitude is great. Recent shows featured the Fastbacks, Mr. Epp and the Calculations, and a Blackouts/U Men show that was cancelled by the Gestapo. A competition curently underway is "Kopy Katz", open to all xerox artists.
Contact: Adam Lake

THE ANNEX

911 E Pine St., Seattle, Wash. 98122
The remnents of the once esteemed And/Or Gallery. After coming to a pathetic and long overdue demise, And/Or left us with the Annex and Focal Point Media Center. These organizations seem to function as decrepid social service centers for former art students who couldn't cope with the outside world. But there is hope for the future under the new director who comes from the Franklin Furnace in New York.
Contact: Jill Medvedow

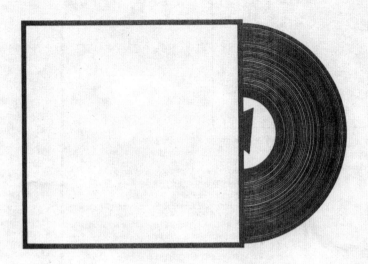

So, you wanna make a record ... but, where you gonna go? Well, lots of people make their records at Triangle Recording. Sure, we've got a 24 track recorder and a 48 input mixing board. Sure, we've got more effects and microphones than you can use in a lifetime. Big Deal. What you need is a studio you can work in. What you need is a studio that can help you make a record that not only sounds good, it looks good too. We've got the best gear. We've got the best prices. Wanna make a record? Call Jack or Bill at 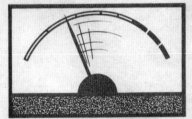 Triangle Recording • 4230 Leary Way NW • Seattle, WA 98107 • 206/783-3869.

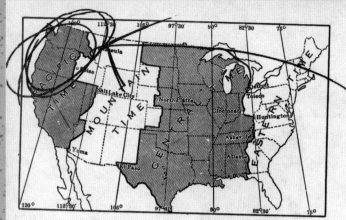

NW UPDATE
x Bruce

LIFE IN GENERAL: 12".

Formerly X-15. These guys have some "heavy" things to say. Check out One Way if your still listening to Ziggy Stardust. (c/o 766 Marine Drive, Bellingham, WA 98225)

3 SWIMMERS: American Technology 12"

Beautiful. Sounds great. As pure Vegas entertainment this is solid gold. Yes, it is a better record than their first. The roto-toms on I'll Make the Tea, Colins distinctive morse-code guitar, kick-ass bass and oh yes a very striking package design will send this to the top of the pops. Compare Technology to American Technology and get a glimpse of the new, keyboard-dominated Swimmers. If you dig the upwardly mobile pop-socialism of the new Gang of Four, then pick up this modern sound 12" today. (ENGRAM: Box 2305, Seattle, WA 98111)

K7SS: A 12 Year Old Boy Could Understand / Phantom Sects Cassettes.

Lets get this straight. 21.252 is a morbidly sinister masterpiece; as discreetly damaging as anything by TG or Caberet Voltaire. It's by K7SS and and it's neatly tucked away on the last groove, side 2, Seattle Syndrome L.P. Once you've checked that out, you might want to hear their two cassettes. The first one, A 12 year Old..., features distorted vocals and tapes; the compositions are long. The newly released Phantom Sects cassette features predominate rhythm box; perky pop muzak. The title track is more relaxed and will melt into your wallpaper; ambient. Along with Portlands Faulty Denial Mechanism

Mechanism and Olympias Steve Fisk, the Northwest is buzzing and beeping rather nicely. (ENGRAM...)

THE ACCUSED: 19 song cassette.

Very loud, fast and obnoxious teenagers from Whidbey Island (!?). Transplanted from L.A. Songs include Wake the Fuck Up, Reagans War Puppets and (smirk) Highway Star. Very raw; well executed. Only 1.00 plus two stamps. Ask for the lyric sheet. (c/o 4251 E. St., HWY 525, Clinton, WA 98236).

REJECTORS: 7' E.P.

Anti-war, anti-establishment. On F@rtz Records. Good hardcore; at least, compared to the rest of the Northwest. (c/o 1112 S. 211th R., Seattle, WA 98148)

PRAVDA: Seattle Compilation Vol. 1 (cassette)

Congradulations. A strong local statement. Hits include: Mohawk Man by Mr. Epp and the Calculations and How the West Was Won by Joe Despair and the Future. Both bands make excellent, raw social commentary without sounding like generic thrash. Too bad they couldn't come up with any band names. The rest of this diverse compilation goes from the folkish Hair Dyed Green by Billy Shaffer to the artful Recht Op Staan by Student Nurse to the modern, processed sounds of Rapid-I. The Spectators feature a reincarnated Jimi Hendrix on guitar. The dude can play. As with a lot of these local compilations, half of the bands are history. Overall, this is entertaining, stimulating and informative. (PRAVDA: Box 9609, Seattle, WA 98109).

VISIBLE TARGETS: 12"

Quirky, catchy, these girls sing about the 'modern world'. This 4 song e.p. is pure pop, pure product and will probably receive heavy college radio airplay. (PARK AVE. RECORDS: Box 19296, Seattle, WA 98109)

ABSOLUTE ELSEWHERE: Olympia/Seattle C-60 compilation.

Lots of interesting, experimental tracks by Olympia's (defunct) Tiny Holes, Pop Philosophers, Steve Fisk, Cool Rays. Don't forget the pop humor of the Westside Lockers. Out of the vaults come brilliant tracks by Seattles Beakers plus early r ecordings of Little Bears From Bangkok. It's all damn good stuff; wonderfully optimistic for the most part. The electrosoul "Candy Store" is heartstopping and without a doubt my favorite song of the year. (MR. BROWN: Box 445, Olympia, WA 98507)

DUB COMMUNIQUE 2: Olympia C-30 cassette compilation.

Wow. This punches hard. highly diverse, ultra highly recommended collection of unusual "pop" sounds from Olympia (cultural mecca of the universe?) It's taken a long time for this town of 35,000 to get a scene together and this is it. Buy or die. The best local compilation I've ever heard. Regional chauvinism is right. This is fantastic. Humor, optimism, imagination, eccentricity. It's all here. I'm not even going to tell you what's on it. Buy this today. (MR. BROWN)

ALLIED BODY: Shelter and Visions C-20.

One man, two tape decks, random chaos.

Beautiful color xerox cover. (Steven Suski, 915 Deschutes Pky S.W., Olympia, WA 98502).

MILLIONS OF BUGS: Bug You 9 song cassette.

Melodic pop. Great vocals, great song-writing. Not as "arty" as the Lost Music Network crowd. Sometimes referred to as 'Billions of Notes'. (c/o Pip McCaslin, 504 E. 4th #5, Olympia, WA 98501).

JUNGLE NAUSEA: 5 song 12".

Silkscreen, spray paint cover. Synthesizer, intense percussion, psychedelic whang-bar guitar, some trombone, female "vocals". Slave Boat To Hell is an instrumental. If you enjoyed the cynical posturing of Teenage Jesus then pick this up for sure. If you want a more positive perspective listen to the new Bailing Man by Pere Ubu. (Inner Mystique c/o Smegma Records, 76 N.E. Thompson, Portland, OR 97212)

RANCID VAT: Stampeding Cattle L.P.

Maximum Damage. Song titles include Hot Cages Rattle in Viet Nam and Puke On My Face. Brigham Young contains the most obscene lyrics in the history of rock and roll. Music ranges from Flipper to Nervous Gender. Another important, disgusting cultural document that will probably gather dust in your closet. (SMEGMA: 76 N.E. Thompson, Portland, OR 97212)

NEO BOYS: Crumbling Myths 12" e.p.

Simple, documentary style production. Meg is a great guitar player, lots of scales, very stylish. Kim reminds me of a young Patti Smith; poetic, dramatic delivery. Rave: Nothing to Fear. (c/o Box 6681, Portland, OR 97228).

THEATER OF SHEEP: 9 song cassette.

A real find. These excellent, early recordings include keyboards, guitar, bass and rhythm box. Nacreous Caberet is a high speed spaghetti-western-in-outer-space instrumental. Fun from Brixton and 1000 Miles Grey are pop classics. this guy's got a great voice. Pill City features drugged out sax...Despite technical problems (music doesn't start for two minutes) this is highly recommended. (Theater of Sheep c/o 2265 N.W. Kearney, Portland, OR 97210)

WIPERS: Romeo / No Solution 45.

Take the best 'garage band' in America. Put them into a studio. Do not overproduce. Create one of the best records of 1982. Include simple boy-desperately-searching-for-girl lyrics.. A dd riveting car screech in middle of song. Produce a romantic, gutter/punk classic. Make Johnny Thunders, the Rats and Sado-Nation look mellow by comparison...Why did Portlands greatest band move to the East coast?? I wonder. (TRAP: Box 42465, Portland, OR 97242).

NATIONALS by Calvin

Seven Inch

Social Unrest have unleashed "Making Room for Youth"(Infra-Red), a rather aggressive teenage anthem that sounds like it was recorded on an Army-base. Over in Kansas a band called Start are beginning to turn some heads with their Tales of Glory E.P.(L-Ert). Real low-key stuff. "Let's Dance" is a an extremely minimal finger-snapper, there's almost no instruments at all. "Tales of Glory is my fave song , a catchy instrumental with a real light feel (only guitar, keyboard and drums, no bass). Hot on the heels of "All Over You in Seconds", the Conn. based Furors dish up "Hey Joni" (Big Plastic), a rockin' pop smash hit that'll knock your socks off. No Kidding. From nearby Patchogue, N.Y.(home of Bill Kern and Barry Knoedl) come the Noogs. Although their pop-rock'n'roll is of a less distinctive style than the Furors, "Everybody Loves You" is pleasant enough and deserves a few listens. The Individuals e.p.(Plexus) isn't nearly as good as N.Y.Rocker led me to expect, but "My World" does warm the heart and I've heard it a couple of times on KAOS. I'm still not sure what to make of the Leopard Society. "Screaming" is totally cool, classic hard rock. The flip is kinda dumb though, so maybe they're just a one-shot band. But "Screaming"'s great. I don't like the 100 Flowers e.p. Presence of Mind(Happy Squid) as much as their stuff on Keats Rides a Harley, but Bruce wanted me to review it anyway. The Insect Surfers have a new single on Wasp, but I think it's only available to radio stations. It's pretty good though, two instrumentals

that twist, turn, stop and glide on through. Oh yeah, there's one more, a guy on Varulven named Ron Scarlett. First he does "Hanging On", some twisted American psycho-dellia, then ol' Ron turns around and plays accoustic guitar for some slow, heartfelt love poetry, "Fire from the Sun" and "Constellation Dance". Really nothing special, but I can't help but liking it.

Twelve Inch

Mandingo Groit Society's Mighty Rhythm(Flying Fish) is cool. They blend African, Carribean and American sounds into some delightful little ditties. Fun for the whole family. Sweet Honey in the Rock have a new one, Good News (Flying Fish) recorded live at a church in Washington, D.C. They're four women who sing in a Gospel style, but instead of always screaming how we should praise God, they take time out to tell us about Stephen Biko, racism, love, parental resposibilities, various martyrs and oppression in Chile and the U.S.A. Some of you revolutionary punk bands running short of material would do well to check this one out. Afterall, creative and inspired blacks have always been a good source for lame and talentless white performers. Regional Zeal:Mouth Music from Olympia Washington(Palace of Lights), a delightful collection of Olympia weirdos; my faves (on this record, not necessarily in person) being Robin James, Cheri Knight and Mark Vale. Steve Fisk's "Donna Summer on the Radio" is a hit and Alex Stahl's "Timbre Management" a pleasent change of pace. Channel 3 have a new album that I really dig, Fear of Life(Posh Boy). Macho

little-boy heavy metal punk. Yeah. The lyrics deal with some interesting topics, especially "Strength in Numbers", about running with the pack, and "Double Standard Boys", about hypocritical male attitudes toward women. It also includes their classics "Manzanar" and "You Lie".

L-Ert 1221 W 19th Terrace, Lawerence
        KS 66044
Big Plastic POB 6069, Hamden CT 06517
Beatbad POB 407, Patchogue NY 11772
Plexus 203 W 25th St, N.Y. N.Y. 10001
Leopard Society Box 7166 Albany NY
                 12224
Happy Squid Box 64184 LA CA 90064
Wasp 821 N Taylor Arlington Va 22203
Varulven 39 Beverly Rd Arlington MA
Flying Fish 1304 W Schubert Chicago
             IL 60614
Posh Boy POB 38861, LA CA 90038
Palace of Lights POB 4141, Seattle WA
                  98104
Fartz 3915 SW Lander, Saettle WA 98116

The Fartz have a new cassette, Live to an Audience of One (Fartz Wreckordz) containing mostly different songs from their Because this Fuckin' World Stinks e.p., plus covers of "In the Year 2525" and Black Sabbath's "Children of the Grave". The songs deal with war, apathy and rights(or a lack thereof). Steve and Loud have a Knack for writing about these subjects, and have come up with some darn good ones. These guys seem a little naive(maybe it's their spelling), but very sincere. It only costs $3.50, "supplies are limited".

You're probably familiar with Flipside, Noise, Touch & Go, NME, the Offense, Take It!, New York Rocker, the Ripper, and some of the more widely distributed long-running fanzines. However, you might not know about Sub-Pop's older cousin Op, which is a shame, because Op has more U.S. independent new rock reviews/contact addresses than any of them, though those publications all have their merits. Op covers independent music of all types - hardcore to Jarrocho, punk to polkas - from all over, with an emphasis on records & cassettes from the good old USA. We don't represent any one style or scene, our commitment is to independent culture. We know that every form of music can inspire greatness and rarely does, recognizing that most vital music today is made in a non-corporate or anti-corporate setting. We feel that if a bunch of people working independently can be supportive and critical of one another that music will improve and be more fun. The most important thing is that we get in touch. Op helps facilitate that. We'll also help you find out about lots of great music no one else is talking about. FIND OUT WHAT YOU'RE MISSING & HOW TO GET IT! ------------------------------✂

Okay Okay, I'm ready for Op. Here's $8 for 6 issues (one year) or $2 for a sample issue.

name_____

address_____

Send to: LOST MUSIC NETWORK, PO Box 2391, Olympia, WA 98507

NOTE TO BANDS, FANZINES, STORES, DJ's, CLUBS: Add us to your mailing list so we can tell everyone what you're doing.

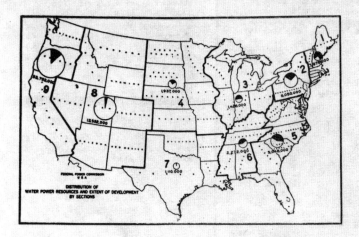

U. S. INDIE REPORT by Bruce P.

L.A.

NEW ALLIANCE: BOX 21, SAN PEDRO, CA 90733

Pick Hit: <u>Feeble Efforts</u> 7" compilation. "Each song produced by it's respective artist on cassette tape recorders." Radical, diverse compilation.Includes various members of the Minutemen, Saccharine Trust, the Plebs and friends doing strange and weird things. Highly recommended.

SST: BOX 1, LAWNDALE, CA 90260

Pick Hit: <u>Saccharine Trust</u> Pagan Icons 12" e.p. "I'll cry wolf when all my sheep are dead". Intense, creative H/core. Scraping guitar; creepy,lonely, vulnerable, "holy" vocalist- sounds like no one else on Earth. Great lyrics, great band, great record.

FRONTIER: BOX 22, SUN VALLEY, CA 91352

Pick Hit: <u>The Salvation Army</u> L.P. Song titles include <u>She Turns to Flowers</u>, <u>While We Were In Your Room Talking to Your Wall</u>, and <u>I Am Your Guru</u>. Melodic, totally hip interpretation of 60's psychedelia - comes complete with tambourine. Includes both sides of the great <u>Mind Gardens</u> 45 (New Alliance). Unfortunately, everythings mixed to sound like a tin can; will probably sound good on a cheap transistor radio.

S.F.

SUBTERRANEAN/THERMIDOR: 912 BANCROFT WAY, S.F., CA 94710

Subterranean is S.F.'s most prolific and uncompromising record label. Thermidor is a trans-regional subsidiary; their catalogue includes bands from Australia, SST, New Alliance and Sub/Pop (Sport of Kings, Oil Tasters).

Subterranean: Pick Hit: <u>Flipper</u> Generic Flipper L.P. These class clowns hit it big with the most obnoxious,the most self-indulgent and possibly the most liberating L.P. of 1982. A bizarre phenomenon.

Thermidor: Pick Hit: <u>Minutemen</u> Bean Spill 7" e.p. This great American band has finally matched thier incredible Paranoid Time e.p. (SST). Sorry guys, the production on the Punchline was uh, anyway... Fragmented, spastic jazz meets H/core. totally

Chicago

AUTUMN: 2427 N. JANSSEN, CHICAGO, IL 60614

Pick Hit: <u>DA</u> Time Will Be Kind 12"e.p. For a city it's size, Chicago sorely lacks consistant record labels. Autumn is the exception. Time Will Be Kind is reminiscent of Sioxsie; lyrics deal with strangers, silence, screams and shadows. Distinctive guitar, excellent production. You might recognize a few of these faces from the infamous Phil Donahue "punk rock" show.

Lansing/Detroit

TOUCH AND GO/SPECIAL FORCES: BOX 26203, LANSING, MI 48909

Touch and Go is a H/core fanzine with its own record label. Special Forces is a subsidiary and was established so that bands like L-7, who don't fit the H/core mold, could see some action.

T and G: Pick Hit: <u>Meatmen</u> Blood Sausage 7" e.p. This record features SEX, "Tooling For Anus" and VIOLENCE, "Snuff 'em". Banned by 4 (?) pressing plants. You decide.

Special Forces: Pick Hit: <u>L-7</u> 3 song 45. This band features Larissa on vocals, whose youthful voice (I <u>know</u> she's not 11) gives this record an eerie edge. All songs deal with creatures and the subconscious. Heavy, studio sound. Interesting.

Kansas

FRESH SOUNDS: BOX 36 LAWRENCE, KS 66044

An outgrowth of the now defunct Talk Talk magazine, Fresh Sounds, along with N,Y,'s ROIR, is a cassette label. Their two previous releases were regional Kansas compilations.

Pick Hit: <u>SPK</u> Last Attempt at Paradise cassette. It's hard to believe that Australia's avant-noise SPK actually played a show in Kansas. Fresh was smart enough to tape the affair. Unfortunately, one does miss out on the slides; however, the cover art is probably all you'll want to see anyway. For extremists only.

Atlanta

DB/PRESS

DB is unquestionably the best indie rock label in the Southeast. Press, formerly Armageddon, is affiliated with DB and releases trans-regional and international artists.

Press: Pick Hit: <u>XXOO</u> 3 song 45. Primitive genius! Forget the Misfits! Forget Flipper! Forget SPK! This is the cult record of the year! This is stripped down 1/2 Japanese! No more saxes, no more s ludge! Jad and David are back in the right groove! 'How Can I' is eloquent, awkward, beautiful. 'How will I know when I'm really in love?...Will I be nervous and stutter when I talk?' The flip con- two covers: Buddy Hollys 'That's What They Say' and a terrifically caustic version of Smokey Robinsons 'Tracks of My Tears'. Don't forget the chimes and woodblock. Shaggs and Modern Lovers fans will pick this up for sure.

DB: Pick Hit: <u>Pylon</u> Crazy/ M-Train 45. America's most unpretentious dance band. Vanessa is the coolest. Pylon would rather hang out in Athens with their friends and neighbors than move to N.Y., wear black make-up and be rock stars.

Pittsburg

TMI 4626 Forbes Ave., Pittsburg, PA 15213.

Pick Hit: <u>Carsickness</u> For You/They Came Crawling 45. Dance clubs would pick up this great Psy Furs ripoff for sure if only it had some decent cover art. Buy.

D.C.

DISCHORDS 3819 Beecher St. NW, Washington, D.C. 20007

I won't bore you with the phenomenal success story of this countrys top teenage hardcore label. For more info, check out their FLEX YOUR HEAD 32 song compilation album.

Pick Hit: <u>Minor Threat</u> 4 song 7" IN MY EYES: 'You think that you wanna be like me, you just hate yourself!' Ian gives a lecture then hits thrash gear. I'm sorry but'awesome' is the only word that comes to mind. Next to Black Flags 'Rise Above' this is <u>the</u> anthem of 1982.

Boston

MODERN METHOD 268 Newbury St., Boston, MA 02116

Modern Method is affiliated with Newbury Comics record store and Boston Rock magazine. They release a wide variety of music.

magazine. They release a variety of local music.

Pick Hit: This Is Boston, Not L.A. compilation L.P. Aside from a few throwaways (Groinoids, Decadence) this is powerful teenage protest music that is sure to put Boston 'on the map'. Gang Green is ultra-fast (big deal). The Freeze come up with some distinctive phrasing (slurring, falsetto); they do tunes like Idiots at Happy Hour and It's Only Alchohol. Jerry's Kids thrash out with Wired, Desperate, Uncontrollable. The Proletariat sing,'Without regard/for loss of life/we infiltrate their countrys/amid chaos and strife'. Real cool.

PROPELLER: 21 PARKVALE AVE., APT. 1, ALLSTON, MA 02134.

Propeller is run as a collective.

Pick Hit: Neats 'Six' (from the Propeller Product 4 song 7" compilation.) Clever lyrics, spiraling Vox organ, this song is one continuous hook. A modern pop classic! Great!

N.Y.

NEUTRAL: 415 Lafayette St., N.Y., N.Y. 10003.

This is a new label coordinated by minimalist, wall of sound composer Glen Branca.

Pick Hit(s): Sonic Youth 12"
           Y Pants Beat It Down L.P.

A real toss up. Y Pants are 3 girls who play drums, keyboards (i.e. toy piano) and ukelele. Cute at times; however, this record has a calming Zen-like quality that is like mellow and uh, refreshing. The ukelele sounds like a Japanese koto. 'That's the Way Boy's Are' is sung acapella and is recieving airplay on KAOS.

Sonic Youth features some interesting guitar - from one chord minimalism to dense whatever. 1/2 the tunes include vocals (male, female). This is bohemian, loft-nik pop and it's really cool. I Dream I Dreamed is great. So check out this hip new label.

REACH OUT INTERNATIONAL RECORDS (ROIR) 611 Broadway, Suite 214, N.Y.,N.Y. 100 12.

ROIR is by far the largest independent casstte label available for modern pop, thrash etc. Most of their releases are of N.Y. bands; music ranges from the ultra-fast Bad Brains to the post-Contortions outfit 8-Eyed Spy.

Pick Hit: Fleshtones cassette. Wow. Early tracks. The Fleshtones were at their peak. Catchy 60's garage rock. Makes ya feel good. C'mon, you've gotta like this!

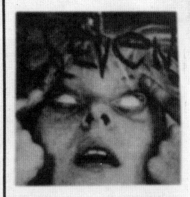

SYSTEMATIC RECORD DISTRIBUTION
Berkeley Industrial Court Space #1
729 Heinz Ave Berkeley, Ca 94710
(415)845-3352
Wholesale
&
Mail Order

FIGHTING FOR INDEPENDENTS !!!

ZICK ZACK
modern method
ace of hearts
Solid Smoke
POSHBOY
crass
SUBTERRANEAN
PALACE OF LIGHTS
touch and go
ROUGH TRADE
new alliance
OPTIONAL
THERMIDOR
SST
Bemisbrain
DISCHORDS
& MANY MORE !

Live Cassette Out Now
Appearing

Minneapolis	8/19
Milwaukee	8/21
Chicago	8/24
Cleveland	8/26
Cincinnati	8/28
Louisville	8/29
Boston	9/2
Boston	9/4
Boston	9/5
Philadelphia	9/7
New York	9/11

PELL MELL

P.O. BOX 40302, PORTLAND, OREGON 97240.

(503) 227-7303

STUDIO SERVICES

2265 NW KEARNEY   PORTLAND, OR 97210

100 C-60 CASSETTES   **$160.**
PRICE INCLUDES:
PLASTIC BOXES WITH HINGED LID.
QUALITY REAL TIME DUPLICATION,
FROM YOUR MASTER TAPE. COPIED
ON CALIBRATED SONY CASSETTE
MACHINES. BLANKS ARE CUSTOM
WOUND TO YOUR EXACT PROGRAM
TIME.

CALL US ABOUT OUR COMPLETE
RANGE OF DUPLICATING SERVICES.
WE SHIP ANYWHERE, FAST SERVICE.

Neo Boys

Crumbling Myths

AVAILABLE IN AUGUST

Neo Boys
PO Box 6681
Portland OR 97228
$5.00 PPD IN US

ROUGH TRADE - SYSTEMATIC

3 SWIMMERS

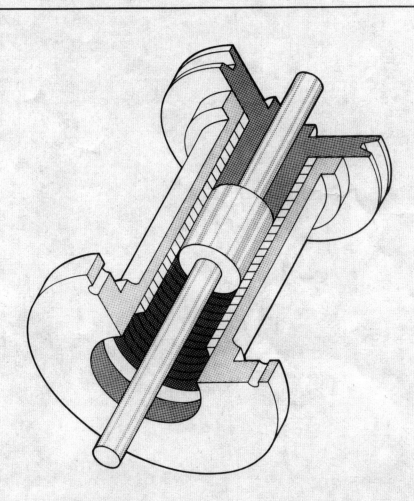

AMERICAN TECHNOLOGY

(ENG 010)

ON ENGRAM RECORDS AND TAPES

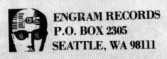

ENGRAM RECORDS
P.O. BOX 2305
SEATTLE, WA 98111

also available
The Worker Works to Live
(ENG 009)

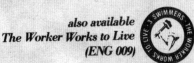

SCOTT Tension in the Cathedral
(Northgate apt 1A6, Rochester, NH 03867)

1. "I Want You Back" Jackson 5
2. "Snob" Gang Green
3. (old)Little House on the Prarie
4. 40 oz. Colt 45's
5. Destruction runs

JIMMY JOHNSON Forced Exposure
(76 Broomfield St, Watertown, MA 02172)

1. the Misfits
2. Touch+Go magazine
3. SS Decontrol The Kids Will Have Their Say
4. Rudimentary Peni
5. Mission of Burma "Trem Two"

DAVID GREENBURGER The Duplex Planet
(16 University Rd. #2, Brookline MA 02146)

EVA
NRBQ
the polar bears at the Providence Zoo
the Incredible Casuals
Hoover the talking seal

ANDY SCHWARTZ New York Rocker
(166 5th Ave, N.Y.,N.Y. 10010)

my girlfriend Lucia Minervini
James Blood Ulmer
"Soup for One" CHIC (12 inch)
Rank and File (the group, from Austin)
Kid Creole "No Fish Today" (from Wise
Guy lp)

NANCY BRESLOW Short Newz
(P.O.B. 1028, Gracie Sta. N.Y.C. 10028)

1. Patsy Clines voice
2. FANZINES
3. the Chrysler Building
4. Motorhead-live only
5. FREEDOM OF CHOICE

DEANNA Schrik
(34 Longford Cres., Agincourt Ont. M1W 1P4)

1. people
2. Youth Youth Youth (great T.O. band)
3. mail
4. etiquette books
5. black licorice

LUKE MCGUFF Proper Gander
(POB 14846 MPLS MN 55414)

1. James "Blood" Ulmer
2. Summer
3. "BUB"
4. Black Uhuru
5. "smokin sinsemilla"

JON HOPE Skid
(34233 S. Bayview Rd, Oconomowoc WI 53066)

1. the Flower Children
2. U2
3. Ama-Dots
4. Minutemen
5. Windsurfing

REV. NORBERT ELMO UGLY Sick Teen
(708 St Joseph St, Green Bay WI 54301)

1. A generic pepperoni pizza and 2 liters
of Tab with the boys after a hard fought
mini golf game in which play was inter-
upted because of forced sexual contact
on the greens by a horde of nubile neo-
groupies w/ their own mini golf clubs
set.
2. Singing "Junior Birdman" at lunch while
creating a massive food sculpture so
nauseating that Eugene threatens to give
me detention and throw me outside "coat
or no coat", even though I'm eating it.
3. Hearing what kids' moms say about me and
Sick Teen.
4. Those little slurpy noises heard during
intense sexual foreplay.
5. Fashion Plates by Mattel

TESCO VEE Touch & Go
(POB 26203 Lansing MI 48909)

1. Negative Approach
2. Lisa De Leleeuw
3. sloe gin enemas
4. Minor Threat
5. my gal's Gazonkas

DAVID GINSBURG Fandomania/Goldmine
(POB 322 Mt Pleasant MI 48858)

1. my girlfriend
2. my cat
3. Noise fanzine
4. Jonathan Richman
5. Human Switchboard

SCOTT SM/Operations (formerly Smarm)
(POB 83 North Street MI 48409)

five favorite ways of killing with a
screwdriver
1. piercing the soft spot just under the
chin at the back of the jaw, thus piercing the soft palet in the mouth and in
the brain.
2. Piercing the inner corner of the eye,
and drive through to the brain.
3. Stab into the kidney.
4. Piercing the base of the throat, where
doctors perform tracheotomies.
5. Listening to TG or SPK while performing
any of the above methods.

JEFF HEARN Psychedelic Boneyard
(POB 2924, Station A Champaign Ill 61820)

the dB's Repercussion
Dave Edmunds, especially early solo work
Pretenders II side 1, tracks 3,4,5,6
U2 Boy
Vertebrats "Left in the Dark" on The
Battle of the Garages (Bomp!)

CRAIG SCHMIDT Coolest Retard
(2042 N Bissell Chicago Ill 60614)

"Why" the Byrds (45 version) great guitar break
'82 Milwaukee Brewers-the Home Run Hit-
tingest Team in Baseball History
Billy McKenzie(Associates) & his helium
Chicago's Naked Raygun
Edwyn Collins(Orange Juice), Gershwin's
successor

TKA The Offense
(1585 N High St Columbus O

1. Joy Division, the only b
any sense of
2. playing the easier video
Jill (You don't have any
3. going through my mail
4. 4AD releases, past presen
simultaneously spinning t
emptying the dance floor

R. MOORE Version Sound (
(POB 174 Xenia OH 45385

100 Flowers "Without
Augustus Pablo "Thu
JFA "Baja"
my new hat (#1)
David Lynch films

JIM THE MAGGOT/BOB DRUG
(206 Westwood Ave Columb

1. Lost Cause. A new band
2. the Crass records label
3. reggae
4. drugs/sex
5. Throbbing Gristle

JIM Capitol Punishment
(1928 E St #6, Lincoln

1. going to see bands
2. the Passage
3. traveling
4. reading
5. Cabaret Voltaire

DIXON Idle Time
(1905 Forest Trail Aus

bagpipe music
dreadlocks
Canadian whiskey
reggae
Tunnel music

HENRY Wild Dog
(11214 Cliffwood, Hou

1. Roky Erickson
2. 45 Grave
3. 100 Flowers (form
4. Chesterfield King
5. Dred Scott

JONE Paranoi
(POB 20391 R

1. all things
2. "Wordy Rapp
3. Red Cross
4. Bored Youth
5. Social Distor

GARY PIG GOLD Pig
(POB 2700 Hunting

1. the Loved Ones
2. Police Squad A
3. Law & Order
4. "Pray for Su
5. The Crazy Pe

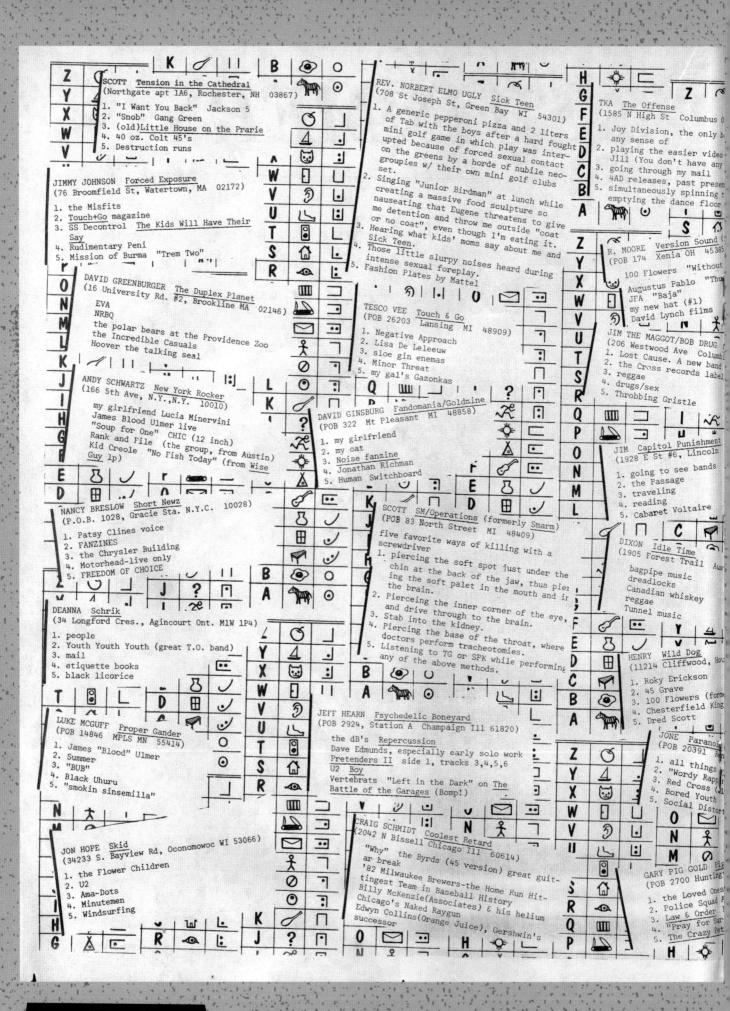

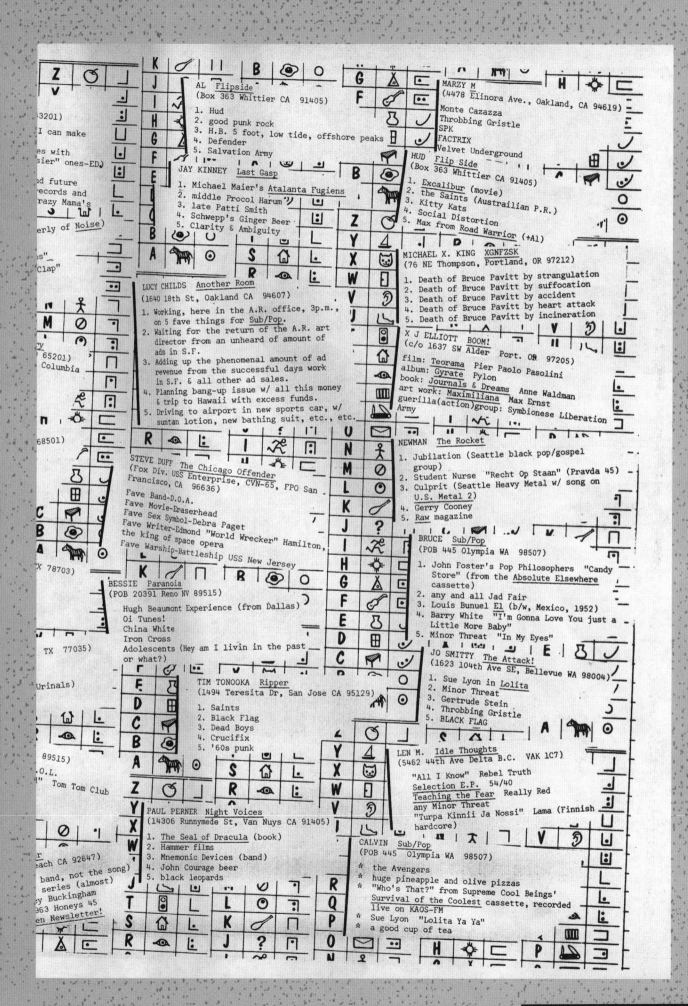

AL Flipside
(Box 363 Whittier CA 91405)

1. Hud
2. good punk rock
3. H.B. 5 foot, low tide, offshore peaks
4. Defender
5. Salvation Army

JAY KINNEY Last Gasp

1. Michael Maier's Atalanta Fugiens
2. middle Procol Harum
3. late Patti Smith
4. Schwepp's Ginger Beer
5. Clarity & Ambiguity

LUCY CHILDS Another Room
(1640 18th St, Oakland CA 94607)

1. Working, here in the A.R. office, 3p.m., on 5 fave things for Sub/Pop.
2. Waiting for the return of the A.R. art director from an unheard of amount of ads in S.F.
3. Adding up the phenomenal amount of ad revenue from the successful days work in S.F. & all other ad sales.
4. Planning bang-up issue w/ all this money & trip to Hawaii with excess funds.
5. Driving to airport in new sports car, w/ suntan lotion, new bathing suit, etc., etc.

STEVE DUFF The Chicago Offender
(Fox Div. USS Enterprise, CVN-65, FPO San Francisco, CA 96636)

Fave Band-D.O.A.
Fave Movie-Eraserhead
Fave Sex Symbol-Debra Paget
Fave Writer-Edmond "World Wrecker" Hamilton, the king of space opera
Fave Warship-Battleship USS New Jersey

BESSIE Paranoia
(POB 20391 Reno NV 89515)

Hugh Beaumont Experience (from Dallas)
Oi Tunes!
China White
Iron Cross
Adolescents (Hey am I livin in the past or what?)

TIM TONOOKA Ripper
(1494 Teresita Dr, San Jose CA 95129)

1. Saints
2. Black Flag
3. Dead Boys
4. Crucifix
5. '60s punk

PAUL PERNER Night Voices
(14306 Runnymede St, Van Nuys CA 91405)

1. The Seal of Dracula (book)
2. Hammer films
3. Mnemonic Devices (band)
4. John Courage beer
5. black leopards

MARZY M
(4478 Elinora Ave., Oakland, CA 94619)

Monte Cazazza
Throbbing Gristle
SPK
FACTRIX
Velvet Underground

HUD Flip Side
(Box 363 Whittier CA 91405)

1. Excalibur (movie)
2. the Saints (Austrailian P.R.)
3. Kitty Kats
4. Social Distortion
5. Max from Road Warrior (+Al)

MICHAEL X. KING XGNFZSK
(76 NE Thompson, Portland, OR 97212)

1. Death of Bruce Pavitt by strangulation
2. Death of Bruce Pavitt by suffocation
3. Death of Bruce Pavitt by accident
4. Death of Bruce Pavitt by heart attack
5. Death of Bruce Pavitt by incineration

X J ELLIOTT BOOM!
(c/o 1637 SW Alder Port. OR 97205)

film: Teorama Pier Paolo Pasolini
album: Gyrate Pylon
book: Journals & Dreams Anne Waldman
art work: Maximiliana Max Ernst
guerilla(action)group: Symbionese Liberation Army

NEWMAN The Rocket

1. Jubilation (Seattle black pop/gospel group)
2. Student Nurse "Recht Op Staan" (Pravda 45)
3. Culprit (Seattle Heavy Metal w/ song on U.S. Metal 2)
4. Gerry Cooney
5. Raw magazine

BRUCE Sub/Pop
(POB 445 Olympia WA 98507)

1. John Foster's Pop Philosophers "Candy Store" (from the Absolute Elsewhere cassette)
2. any and all Jad Fair
3. Louis Bunuel El (b/w, Mexico, 1952)
4. Barry White "I'm Gonna Love You just a Little More Baby"
5. Minor Threat "In My Eyes"

JO SMITTY The Attack!
(1623 104th Ave SE, Bellevue WA 98004)

1. Sue Lyon in Lolita
2. Minor Threat
3. Gertrude Stein
4. Throbbing Gristle
5. BLACK FLAG

LEN M. Idle Thoughts
(5462 44th Ave Delta B.C. VAK 1C7)

"All I Know" Rebel Truth
Selection E.P. 54/40
Teaching the Fear Really Red
any Minor Threat
"Turpa Kinnii Ja Nossi" Lama (Finnish hardcore)

CALVIN Sub/Pop
(POB 445 Olympia WA 98507)

* the Avengers
* huge pineapple and olive pizzas
* "Who's That?" from Supreme Cool Beings' Survival of the Coolest cassette, recorded live on KAOS-FM
* Sue Lyon "Lolita Ya Ya"
* a good cup of tea

Tim Brock plays drums with Havanah 3:00 A.M. Also, check out his solo effort, Now the State Needs Me, available on Dub Communique 2; sung in Russian and simultaneously translated in English.

BRUCE interviews TiM

B: Tell me about your childhood.

T: Well, our house used to get spray painted alot. My father was a bishop and a self proclaimed socialist.

B: What were some of the things you used to see spray painted on your house when you woke up in the morning?

T: 'Commie'. Your typical 'commie-pinko-fag' type of thing. 'Go back to Russia'. 'Get out of the U.S.'

B: You told me your father was black-listed during the McCarthy era. Is this true?

T: Uh, yeah. Well, my father was black-listed during the 50's and 60's, supp-osedly for preaching sermons that were 'left'... He started his own church in Indiana, the Disciples of Christ. It's just a protestant religion, maybe a little more liberal than others. Any-way, the government knew of his reputa-tion and he was constantly being crit-icized by the government and was told to 'watch your step around here', you know, and the sheriff was always talking to him.

B: This wasn't during the McCarthy era.

T: No. This was around 1966. Then he got arrested. We were all sitting around at dinner one night and we were all talking rather loud, you know how kids are, and all of a sudden we heard this large noise and they came rushing in and said ' Robert Clark Brock you have the right to remain silent' and then they were

doing it to my mother too. They hand-cuffed them and took them away. There were four kids at that time and we were all just standing there looking at each other.

B: They left the kids in the house?

T: Right, they didn't take us away or anything. A neighbor came over and took us over to his house... And they were in jail for two days! Supposedly for tamper-ing with the water system of Indiana. They thought my parents were putting some sort of chemicals in the water, some sort of drug.

B: This is totally absurd.

T: Yeah, it's sort of like the McCarthy era lasts a lot longer than everybody thought it did.

B: Isn't that song you did with Jumbo Zen about this event?

T: Yeah, 'Business First, Pleasure Sec-ond', where I'm rapping in Russian in the background.

B: You speak fluent Russian. Could you tell us about this?

T: Well, I learned most of the grammer in high school but I grew up speaking it to relatives. And I spent time at Brighton Beach, a small community of Russian jews, exiles. We were living there for a short period of time. Few people speak English there.

B: You've told me that it's easier for you to read Russian than it is to read English. Why?

T: Well, I'm a dyslexic. It's difficult for me to read English because English uses a part of my brain that is deficient ... I don't want any wisecracks about that!

B: What do you see when you look at an English sentence? How is it interpreted?

T: Some letters look upside down and backwards. Mainly backwards. It's a processing problem... So yeah, I've been reading Russian for a long time, it's easier for me.

B: You used to review films for the Seattle Sun. What's your favorite film?

T: Planet 9 from Outer Space. It's one of the funniest films ever made. Refer-ences to communism, the alien menace.

B: You wrote a symphony that was per-formed by the Seattle Philharmonic.

T: Yes. It was aired on PBS and KING-FM. It's a piano concerto. I started writ-ing it when I was in the 9th grade and finished it when I was a junior in high school.

B: Could you briefly recount what happ-ened the first time you concerto was performed. How old were you?

T: I was a senior in high school. I was drumming with the the F@rtz at that time, then known as the Anti-Toxins. They were neighborhood friends of mine ...We opened for D.O.A. once...Anyway, I was a very short haired idiot with

very dark sunglasses who had a piece being performed by the Seattle Philhar-monic at the Seattle Opera House. I was rehearsing with the Anti-Toxins that afternoon and we were just playing rea-lly hard and fast and sweating and we were all real tired. And I said, 'Oh well, I have to go to the Opera House'. So I went there and there were all these women in fur coats and rhinestones and men in tuxedos and suits and ties. And I'm sitting there in my ripped jeans, just this scrounge-idiot. So I sit down towards the back next to this lady who's sort of a hot head. A fat lady who pro-bably eats a lot of choclates, Whitman Sampler lady. So the performance starts, they play the 1st violin concerto by Tchaikovsky and the Liszt prelude #2, things like that. Then they played my piece! Brock piano concerto #1 (laughs) So the piece is playing, the lady next to me probably thinks I'm on drugs, she's probably on valiums ... They end it on the last C# and everybodies clapping for this Brock guy who's probably some old guy in Illinois somewhere...And then the conduc-tor says ' The composer of that piece is in the crowd with us this evening and we'd like to invite him up'...Everyone starts clapping and then I stood up and the lady next to me says, 'Oh why don't you sit down! That's not funny!' and she was really angry that I was making fun of this composer named Brock. And I walked up there in my leather jacket and jeans and accepted a bouquet of roses and when I came back to my seat I heard that lady say, 'That's really him'. She was pretty shocked.

B: You tell me that the Anti-Toxins thought you were too materialistic or that you worked too much.

T: No. They didn't think I was material-istic because I was really poor. They thought I shouldn't have to work for a living and that I could just 'live'.

B: How are they living?

A: Hand to mouth. They all live in this place called the Gas Chamber. It's in west Seattle. They basically believe that you shouldn't have to get a job to survive, you know, that's just a sucker thing for the world... I had just got a job working in a graveyard for almost 8 hours a day, digging graves, mowing lawns... saw a lot of funerals.

B: That's a rather morbid job.

T: I've had a lot of jobs like that. I was a body bagger at Harbor View Medical. When bodies were mutilated they were shipped into Harbor View Morgue. After they were cleaned up and stuff I would bag them so they could be shipped from the morgue to the funeral home, because if you expose the bodies to the air they'll decompose quickly...Let me see, I worked in a Russian restaurant...I also worked in a factory making cardboard boxes for plants...

B: Do you like living in Olympia?

T: I like Olympia. It's naive, it's human...it's untouched by culture of other cities. It's also a lot more ex-citing; things that happen in small towns really happen. Like last night there was a car wreck, two cars smashed into Ben Moore's restaurant. Now, in a small town that's really exciting where as in N.Y. that's bullshit.

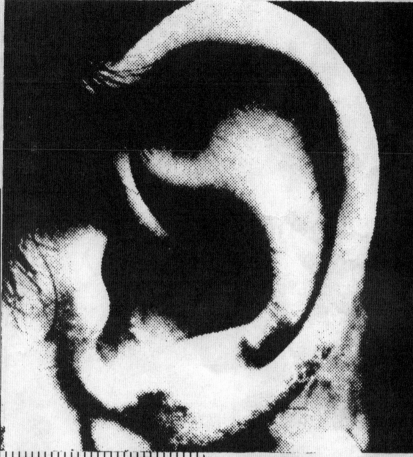

A C M E
RECORDS!

IMPORTS   INDEPENDENTS (206) 624 - 7806
FIFTEEN   ELEVEN   2nd. SEATTLE, WA.   -   98101

Heather

Gary Doug

Supreme

Cool

Beings

This interview with Olympia's Supreme Cool Beings took place at King Solomons in mid-July. Present were Heather (drums)Gary(guitar/bass), Doug(sax), Karen and Calvin.

CALVIN: Tell us how you jumped the gun on the United States of America by getting in on the Beatles on the ground floor.
GARY: Well...uh...gee, you want to talk about me? I could talk all night. I dunno, I just grew up with rock'n'roll I guess. I lived in Germany in the early '60s, heard the Beatles
HEATHER: How old were you?
G: I dunno about 10...and really liked them right away. I remember my mom showed me Newsweek magazine with the Beatles on it when they got big it was "How would you like to have a haircut like that?" I said "No way!". A few years later the only thing I wanted to have was long hair. So I grew up with rock'n'roll but I sort of forgot about it along the way.
C: Why?
G: Um...I became a Jazz Fascist in High School. I listened to nothing but jazz. I used to go to peoples turntables and grab records off them and break them, "What is this shit?". But during this period also rock'n'roll was bad music.
DOUG: Sez who?
G: From 1970-1980 mainstream r'n'r was awful and mainstream r'n'r was all you heard in the early '70s. There was Iggy and Captain Beefheart...and David Bowie maybe...
C: What changed your mind?

G: The Cramps. For sure. Well actually the Cramps didn't change my mind, the Missing Persons(early Oly band infamous for their musical non-ability) changed my mind. That was a live show and I realized nothing could beat live rock'n'roll as soon as I saw them I realized that was the secret of life. And then when I heard the Cramps I realized that I could make music. It's like the stuff they do...

C: Well Heather did you ever get in trouble when you were in high school? For anything?
H: Um...smoking in the girl's room... cutting school. I never got in any big trouble.
C: How about you Doug? Did you ever get in any really big trouble?
  (general laughter)
D: Where shall I begin? I used to get beat up by cops a lot when I was a teenager. But I always noticed that cops will only beat you up if they're completely in the wrong. Like I've been arrested for major stuff where they've been completely in the right, and they're always the sweetest guys, but if they're completely in the wrong, they'll beat you up. Remember that.
G: I'll bet that's true.
D: It's absolutely true. I got proof. Wanna see my scars?
C: You've been arrested for various things...
G: Yeah, big stuff: drunk and disorderly, putting up posters. Once I got a ticket for driving without a license... but I had a license, the ticket was for not having it on me while I was driving. It was a $10 ticket. I didn't pay it. They came and arrested me. Two cops- Boom Boom Boom-"You Gary May?" "Who wants to know?" It was the wrong thing to say. So they searched the house, found drugs and stuff. Then they said, "We'll have to establish ownership for these drugs. We'll have to take your friends in, too" "Oh, oh they're my drugs".
D: (laughs)Oh I would have said,"they were his or that guy's over there or the other guy who just split. You better catch him, he's running down the road".
G: I'm loyal to my friends. I pissed on a cop car one time. Actually, one time I did it on purpose, but this time it was accidental. He was hiding in the bushes waiting for speeders, and it

was in a public park late at night. I go stumbling in the bushes and pissed on his car and got arrested. Spent two weeks in jail.
H: Uh-oh.
G: Wenatchee, Washington. Lovely town. They got great apples, lousy cops.
D: It's a pretty nice place though, Wenatchee is.
G: It's pretty.
D: As a matter of fact, we might as well get this on tape. Washington is the greatest place in the world.
G: I dunno. You ever been to Oregon?
D: Oregon stinks. Ore. is like-
G: You just say that cause you're from Vancouver.
  (Doug giggles...a long pause, and then Calvin burps)
D: When you put that in the interview, say "Heather".
  (general laughter)
H: Excuse me.
G: Parenthesis,"Heather burps".
  (general laughter)
G: Parenthesis, "general laughter".

C: You guys work pretty hard for the local scene, get arrested for it...
D: Yeah, that's true. He gets arrested for it.
G: Yeah, well, I dunno. Seems like the thing to do. Everybody's doing it. It's a new sensation.
C: Local scenes?
G: Yeah.
D: Actually, it's the new-old sensation.
C: What do you think is the next step?
G: The next step is to organize communities and get everybody thinking about how to keep the money they make in their town instead of exporting it through McDonald's amd malls...
C: It's more than rock'n'roll then.
G: Oh, yeah. Rock'n'roll's just...rock-'n'roll's just a religion. It's not anything else, really...it's not an important economic force but it is an important social force...and I don't think you've really changed that much but you can sort of like show people

that (inaudible) play along...

D: It's the reason I like local scenes, cause in high school I listened to a bunch of bands that if I ever went to their concerts I'd be 30 feet away from them, that's if I crawled my way to the front and got mauled doing it...and got bruised around by a bunch of people and these guys are all 10 years older than me and they didn't give a fuck about who was in the audience anyway cause they got their money. With local music, especially local young music, you can spark some creative energy. Instead of just sitting around smoking dope, you can start a band.

G: It's not just consumption; it's process of involvement. We're not just buying somebody's ideas. What do we have in common with somebody that lives in England?

D: Or L.A.?

G: L.A., yeah. Nothing really, we have the chance to vote in the same national elections. The culture's completely different, as different as Italy and France. This is more interesting. We write songs about ourselves, and people who know us have a shot at understanding what we're talking about. Although I don't think we say all that much, really, we just have fun. We have fun with our friends and it doesn't cost that much to do it. You could spend more on a stereo system than we have on this band.

D: It's a stereo system without records.

C: What about these songs here. What's the song you wrote about?

H: "Who's That?"

C: What's it about?

H: It's not really about anything, it's about like—

D: It's a mood piece.

G: It's a great song, man.

C: Is that the only song you've written?

H: Well Gary and Doug and I, one night we were sitting at Doug's table. Debbie had gotten this Mr. Potatohead at some garage sale and it was sitting on the table. We were sitting there drinking vodka and we all wrote this song about how, um, how Mr. Potatohead's—

D: Cause when we were kids, Mr. Potatoheads, they had little spikes on the back and you could stick them in real potatoes.

G: That's the whole point of the toy, in those days. Not anymore though.

H: You could put his ears in his eyes, you could make him all distorted. So we sort of all wrote that song together.

D: And he had a lot more pieces.

C: What song is that?

D: "Modern Home". Our band by the way, is two construction workers and an art student.

G: Yeah, let's get that on the record, please.

H: I'm not a student.

D: You will be.

C: What's the difference, in your eyes, between Olympia a year and a half ago and now? Music wise.

G: About the same. It's a real struggle.

D: But there's even less places to play then a year and a half ago.

G: I'm involved with more musicians, but there's still very little happening.

D: I mean, it's the same people that we see at every show. It's not like were drawing a public crowd.

C: How many people would you say?

D: I dunno, probably a hundred people all n all but it's not very accessible to somebody who happens to be running through town and happens to see a poster or something because it's all word of mouth. And most of the gigs we play are parties and stuff...I'd like to do something to change it. I don't really know what to do. I don't have many resources and that sort of thing.

G: People don't really want to get committed to things. Most music people are young people and they don't want to have responsibilities they can't deal with.

D: Which is understandable.

G: It's a heavy responsibility to get something like a cooperative music club going, which is basically the only why it could happen.

H: And money.

G: Nobody has any money.

H: I know. That's what I meant.

G: We've got a hundred people, right? That's the money right there. But the thing is getting a hundred people organized, and that's pretty fuckin' hard to do.

C: Lotta time. It takes a lot of time.

G: Yeah, and a lot of committment on the part of—

D: A hundred people.

G: Well no, on the part of 2 or 3 people to keep track of the other hundred people.

C: One of you said the school(The Evergreen State College) is a major part of it, but it's becoming more independent of the school all the time.

G: I'm really anti-school scene.

D: I am, too.

G: Everytime something happens at Evergreen, it detracts from what can potenially happen in town. I think it's a great college, I went there, and it's the best thing that's happened to me in a lot of ways. I still think that economiclly it has strangled this town, and culturally, it has totally stifled the town.

C: So hey, what do you think?

KAREN: Oh, I think you guys play really well. I think...I just saw some graffitti about me in the bathroom. It said, "Amy loves Karen, Platonically".

C: where do you go to school?

K: Evergreen.

C: Why?

K: So I can get the extra money left over from my financial aide, basically.

G: Noble aspirations.

D: If you play for Evergreeners they're all smiling at you and clapping and being real nice to you, where as if you play for normal people they come up to the stage and say,"Louie, Louie! Can't you rock'n'roll!?!"

G: "AC/DC!"

D: Yeah, and there's fights and stuff and it's really cool, you know. And it's more real.

G: It's a lot more r'n'r territory then the average Evergreen audience, who'll listen to anything.

D: And they'll dance to anything. You could get up and beat on a garbage can with a dead fish and they'll all dance like maniacs.

G: In fact, I've seen it done.

D: Yeah, really.

Let's talk about the retarded people. Me and Gary, we played with a couple of hippies for these retarded people—

G: The drummer had a beard, man.

H: Oh my God.

D: So did the bass player.

G: You hardly noticed though, I mean, he plays good at least.

D: Yeah... anyway, we played for these retarded people and it was so much fun because these people have no pretentions whatsoever. They jump around and have a good time and you could do anything in front of them. You can go crazy and they eat it up, they love it, they don't think you're posin' they just think you're having fun, which Personally, me, that's what I'm doing.

C: Wait a minute. You just put down Evergreeners for the exact same thing.

G: No, see Evergreeners are like...

. Well, I think they're emotionally retarded, intellectually impaired. Evergreen is like a dumping ground for lost souls. You get all these people that are really smart, really young, have no idea what they want to do. They just know they don't want to go along with what everyone else is doing. So they go to a place like Evergreen, and as soon as they get there they've got it all figured out: they're gonna be a hippie, or they're gonna be a rastafarian, they're gonna be a punk or they're gonna be this, or- or they're gonna be an audio engineer. Very few of them are capable of criticizing anything. They just love to stand there and go along with just about anything anybody does, unless it's dangerous, like good rock'n'roll.

C: Unless it's sexist and racist, as done by a white male.

G: These people I'm talking about have all these virtues that are negative, like all these things they're not. They're not racist, they're not sexist, they're not capitalists—

D: I've found people that go around spouting that they're not sexist, particularly, I don't know—

G: Oh, yaeh. Sure, sure.

D: ...are generally the most sexist people around and it's a defense to cover up for it, cause they know they shouldn't be but they know they just naturally are.

G: Everbody is a sexist and a racist both.

D: That's true.

G: The question is, do you let it motivate you in malicious ways? Well anyway, negative virtues. I mean, everybody thinks they're great because they're not all these things. But being not something is not a virtue as far as I concerned. If you're not a racist that doesn't mean a thing. What are you?

D: Ho-hum. Let's be funny and say something fun. This is too serious and boring.

G: I'm a serious and boring guy.

D: We noticed, Gary.

G: You're out of the band.

D: My next band is going to be Salsa Brava.

C: Tell us about it.

D: It's gonna be 2 saxaphones, one genuine South American on sax. Genuine, no kidding. My ex and Tom of the Pet Products sharing drums.

C: You're going to play Percival Landing.

D: Yeah, we're gonna play when it's busy down in the parks and stuff. We're gonna put a hat out. As a matter of fact, when I mentioned it to Tom I said, "We could put a hat out, maybe we could make some money" and he said "One hat? Let's put three out!!". So that is going to be fun—

(tape ends)

FIG. 48. Specialized training is needed for our police protectors and aids.

DETROIT

Whipping Boy (SF), Negative Approach (Detroit), Necros (Maumee), Minor Threat (DC)

Detroit, industrial midwest, car town, Motown, Ghost town hit hard by the present depression. The Cass Corridor, a bad neighborhood for a generation, it spawned Iggy Pop among others. And next to a trashed old house, the Freezer theater, a hole in the wall with a real meat locker door. Flanked a block down on either side by liquor stores, one conveniently right across from the plasma donation center. Inside, the stores feature bulletproof plastic and beer. Winos, whores, whores, vacant lots, burly blacks with sti sticks on street corners, yes Virginia there is a concrete jungle. From all across the metro Detroit area packed in cars come hardcore youth. No rah-rah skirts or music for 'punk' night at the U.

Some familiar faces from the Black Flag show, the DC van, visitors from Ohio, Necros bumper stickers on legs and backs, all grouped outside the door. Reagan America cruises by in late model cars, staring. Inside are the spray painted walls, a stage, a wall for amps to sit on, and three raised benches at the other end.

Whipping Boy opens, black mohawked singer with stage presence, giant white guitar player in a kilt and a song about video games. Who could ask for more? Keep an eye peeled for 'em and Negative Approach; both are carving distinctive sounds from Hardcore raw materials.

The Necros simply weren't as good as their record. Maybe due to the absence of their guitar player from Ann Arbor.

If the Necros meant sitting and some skanking, then Minor Threat meant standing and six foot amp dives. They sustained the essential edge through intensity and variation, not just speed. A pause, a swig of liquid by drummer Jeff Nelson, and their off again. One second rocking harder than any heavy metal band, then slamming into thrash gear. Nothing to say except, the best. After a frantic "Stepping Stone" it was all over.

Footnotes: During the show I noticed two guys exchanging some hostile words. After the show, there was a riot in which the show there the show, there was a riot in which one of the above mentioned

Footnotes: During the show I noticed two guys exchanging some hostile words. After the show, there was a riot in which one of these gentlemen was chased down the streets by insulted Detroit skinheads wielding skateboards. Good old rivalry between Detroit and Ann Arbor. This was the last hardcore show in the freezer.

The steam still rises from the sewers, whores still walk the streets, and in the suburbs they skateboard.
G. Kirk

Tacoma, Washington by Doug

Recipe for a Hardcore show. Ingredients - Bands (Wad Squad, Hobo Skank, Pet Products, Rejectors, Extreme Hate, F@rtz) - 1 dilapidated building (former Odd Fellows Hall) - 200 bored clones in leather jackets - 1 police dept. (Tacomas) - liberal amounts of beer and amphetamines.

STEP 1 - Take clones, season liberally with beer and speed, add dilapidated building (be sure at least half or more don't pay admission).

STEP 2 - Add first band.

STEP 3 - Let clones start fight. They should fight untill something disgusting happens - a nipple being bitten off will do.

STEP 4 - Add second band. Clones should be slamming by now; make sure nobody says anything friendly or intelligent.

STEP 5 - Clones will trash building and break everything not made of metal; make no move to stop them.

STEP 6 - Cancel third band (no show). Add fourth band; season clones with lots more beer, make sure all bottles get broken on the floor.

STEP 7 - Add fifth band.

STEP 8 - Add sixth band - let play 10 minutes - add police dept., they should be looking for trouble with clubs in hand. Clones should not disperse immediately; cops should hang around and threaten people. At least one clone should be dragged away kicking and screaming.

STEP 9 - Go home disgusted with the whole scene - blame it all on the cops.

ANACORTES JULY 2

The Spoiled are a band of locals who have carved their own little scene in the middle of nowhere. This show was in a Grange hall. Most of the people there(about 40) were under 20 years of age. You've got to hand it to these guys: if nothing else, they are tireless self-promoters, this being one of the last in a long line of similar all-ages shows. They played mostly covers(Iggy, Ramones, Clash, etc.), but everyone was having a good time, dancing and hanging out. The Skagit County Sheriff Dept. busted it, minors in possession of alcohol. It was so blatant, they had to break it up. People have to realize the only way these kind of shows can happen is if alcohol stays outside. It isn't fair to the people who worked hard putting on the show or to the rest of the audience who payed their money.

VANCOUVER JULY 3

We got there just in time. I had a little trouble at the border(forgot my I.D.) but Sam talked them into letting me in ("We're as honest as apple pie" he says). The Wrecks, our buddies from Reno, Nev., opened the show. They sound a lot like their cassette: loud, with lots of presence. "Punk Is an Attitude", that's their motto; punk is also a generic form of muzak nowadays, but the Wrecks don't need silly labels. They were too wild for such societal constraints. They had a banner that said "The Wrecks" with little pictures of a kitty cat and someone's breakfast and I don't know what all else spray-painted

on, it looked cool. I talked to Bessie (bass) and Jone(guitar), real nice people, they took our picture and never once used the word "rad". They didn't have a very successful trip though. Some stuff was stolen, had personal differeces with each other, and have since broken up. You can't even get their tape anymore because the band member in possession of the master doesn't want anymore copies made. So they're gone for good, with a song on the Maximum Rock'n'Roll compilation and (maybe) Sub/Pop 9 as a reminder. Saccharine Trust followed with their own special brand of torture. Wow. A hard band to describe, fun to dance to, even better to listen to, get the album Pagan Icons(SST) now! Next came Vancouver's own Braineaters. These guys have been around the scene in one form or another for years. I'm sure all their friends loved it, but I didn't. Imagine two giant Bam-Bam's dressed in black mini-skirts, with a miserable synth/guitar accompanyment. Ha, ha, ha. Sam thought they should be put to death. Luckily, I missed most of it talking fanzines with Bessie. Anyway, Black Flag finally hit the stage and were worth sitting through six Braineaters shows (what a dreadful thought). Henry was incredible, pacing back and forth, lunging, lurching, growling; it was all real, the most intense emotional experiences I have ever seen. During the two B.F. performances I witnessed, I laughed, cried, danced, screamed, stood in awe and used my brain. Henry has come a long way since I saw SOA 18 months ago. He is at home in front of an audience, that's where he belongs. Never mind that he will have no voice in two years, right now he is Henry and as such should not be missed next time Black Flag stumbles through your town. Most of their songs deal with individuality and independence, leading your own life, no matter what. Although I don't always agree with them, I respect this band more than any other, they've shown us it's not who you know but who you are that is important.

SEATTLE JULY 4

Besides taking 11 hours to get there(10 rides & 2 city buses) we only got 2 1/2 hours of "sleep"(in an alley, I'd thought we'd freeze to death), so you can imagine what kind of emotional state I was in. However, there was only one thing that mattered: Black Flag at Norway Center. A Seattle band opened, the Silly Killers, and were thoroughly dull. It seems like the only thing people in Seattle care about is getting drunk. Ho-hum. About 30 "fans" crashed an exit door without paying the measly 5 bucks. I bet the same people coughed up $9.50 for Killing Joke a week later. Nig-Heist played next. Mainly members of B.F. & S.T. playing slow heavy metal and their roadie singing a dumb song wearing a dumb wig. These guys are going places. Then somebody hit Greg Ginn in the head with a chair and the whole band jumped into the audience to get the guy. Afterwards, the guy in the wig gave a little speech about how Seattle punks are tough and cool and a bunch of pussies. Saccharine Trust, hey, these guys are the final nail in the coffin of the art vs. hardcore argument. They transcend either label and are simply Saccharine Trust. Black Flag were awsome, what else can I say? —Calvin

Report on America's Youth

by Debbie

Photos: Lisa Grenet

WHAT EVER HAPPENED TO JOHNNY QUEST?
by Bill Apgood

The Quests moved to New York in 1967. Johnny's father, Dr. Benton Quest, secured a teaching position at NYU, and the family settled into a brownstone near Washington Square. Although Johnny had grown up in exotic and dangerous places and had always been able to take care of himself, the Greenwich Village scene exacted a heavy toll from him. He became heavily involved with drugs and dropped out of school in the tenth grade. He moved into a SoHo loft with some friends, other young black sheep of notable families, and was arrested there on charges of cocaine possession in 1974 (charges were dropped, it is rumored, because a Kennedy was present).

Johnny was occasionally seen jamming with the New York Dolls during their early saran wrap days, but little else is known of his activities during the mid-seventies. He seemed to lose direction and drifted to Europe. And North Africa.

Johnny ended up in L.A. in the late seventies. He became re-involved in the martial arts and this provided a much needed discipline and direction for him. Johnny now lives in Westwood with a young actress. He teaches in a dojo and attends UCLA at night, majoring in administration.

As for the others: Benton Quest is now tenured at Hunter College and has married a former student. Race Bannon is a de-programmer working for Ted Patrick. Hadji became involved with the Guru Maharaj Ji's following in the early seventies, until the demise of that organization (following a 60 Minutes treatment of the 15-year-old "Perfect Master"). Hadji knew a good thing when he saw it, however, and now runs a New Age human potential resort in Aspen. Bandit, sadly, was run over by a checker cab shortly after the move to New York.

craig(3): yah! he flys! i watch spiderman and iceman and firestarter, that's the one where he's fire.
don(3): i like spiderman, he flys, superman is on t.v., he flys too, i can fly off my couch.
craig(3); we got monsters who bite you, they live outside.
(me): why doesn't superman take care of the monster?
craig(3); he didn't come over. he was asleep.
don(3): superman is a real person. i w-w-watch scooby-doo...they always run into ghosts and monsters, t-t then it ..it chases after them...
(me): does that happen every show?
don: yah...i watch the muppet show sweetums is on the muppet show!
(me): is he funny?
don: no he's real scary!

mary (2): monsters on t.v....scary... clowns on t.v....i don't like clowns... they scary...makes me cry...monsters come in your room at night...
(me): what do you do?
mary: say .."go away monsters!"!

THRIFTstore 1000

MARTINI MUSIC FOR MODERN LOVERS

by Jan Loftness

Adult pop has been with us ever since the advent of rock 'n roll. Not that rock 'n roll is adult pop; precisely the opposite. Before rock, all modern music was pop music, but then came teen pop, so what was left had to become "adult pop". This sound was in no way related to a rockin' beat. What it was related to was the swingin' beat: the jazz influenced, wartime, big-band sound. Even into the 60's, Frank Sinatra, Tony Bennett, Bobby Darin, and even Tom Jones among others, carried on the tradition of belting it out in front of a full-piece orchestra. It didn't sound wartime though. It was swingin'.

But of course, others types of adult music came about: the Latin sounds of Herb Alpert, Sergio Mendes & Brasil '66; the romantic "mood music" of Jackie Gleason's orchestra; the original "Muzak Maestro" Ray Coniff, who started his own revolution in adult listening pleasure; the hip soundtracks of Henry Mancini. The list goes on. It's not all good but when it is it's great! You can get a whole stack of these records at your neighborhood thrift store for the price of the new X album. And if you like 50's and 60's graphics and artwork, it's a goldmine (it seems like the worst records have the best covers). Anyway, go exploring...

BOBBY DARIN: If you're swingin', you'll love Bobby Darin because he's the swingin'-est! This teen idol turned nightclub entertainer and movie star is the essence of early 60's sophistication. He's got a million records out there and my best advice is to buy anything before 1965. "The Bobby Darin Story" includes his big hits like "Mack the Knife" and "Beyond the Sea", and his early teen hits "Splish Splash" and "Queen of the Hop", and the master plates were autographed by Bobby himself (look below the label on side two). Other choices include "Bobby Darin: Love Swings", "Bobby Darin: That's All", "Twist with Bobby Darin", "The Best of Bobby Darin" and "This is Darin". Anyway, you won't forget his name. He's got a great haircut and a great voice. I think he's a dreamy guy.

SERGIO MENDES & BRASIL '66: There's tons of Brasil '66 records in thrift shops and I used to snobbishly overlook them. But I recently picked up a copy of "Look Around" and found some pleasant background music for my many sand, sun, and margarita parties up here in apartment three. Soft female voices overlap soft male voices, built to crescendos, and gently fade away into pink sunsets. That's about the gist of it. But it's so nice. Beatle songs sound good to a Latin beat! These guys were adult swingers and knew what was hip.

GIRL FROM IPANEMA: "Tall and tan and young and lovely the girl from Ipanema goes walking and when she passes, each one she passes goes ahhhh!" Adult pop doesn't get any better. You can see the heat shimmering off the sand from your cool vantage underneath the shady palms (If there are in fact palms in Ipanema). Anyway, this is probably the most covered song in the history of pop, and every one is good. Can't beat the original though, and Stan Getz is the one who did it first: sexy sax, Spanish lyrics. Look in the jazz section.

IMPACT: The cover of this rare and

priceless 1959 record looks much like a hardcore compilation - and I thought it was at first glance. A "glass cracked by bullet hole" motif superimposed over the huge red letters IMPACT. But instead of band names thrown across the front, it was t.v. shows: Naked City, M-Squad, Perry Mason, Highway Patrol, Sea Hunt, Peter Gunn, Racket Squad, and more! "Orchestra under the direction of Buddy Morrow". Here's some excerpts from the liner notes: "Brassy and succinct... has an overweening urgency... replete with agitated adventure... the pulse beat of jazz". Talk about video noir, this is the darkest sultriest, smokiest music around. and listening to it brings back all those great rerun memories: Raymond Burr in the courtroom, Broderick Crawford in the patrol car, Lloyd Bridges in the wetsuit. What a find. I just hope someone else is lucky enough to come across it.

TOM JONES: What does Tom Jones have besides a buldging crotch, lots of chest hair, and a gold cross on a chain? A simply terrific voice! Now this guy knows how to sing! Most people remember him as the guy who's t.v. show their mom used to watch and/or someone rather revolting.

But, times have changed and we've all grown up and can now see and hear past this superficial image. "It's Not Unusual" was THE song of the year for me - I even lip-synched it during the "air guitar" contest at the Xmas party where I work, and won first place (Tom did, not me)! As for his albums, these too abound in thrift store record racks. What to keep an eye out for: the "aTOMic Jones" album cover.

Of course there's things to avoid: 101 Living Strings, Roger Williams, Martin Denney. But it's fun to take risks too. Hope you find some favorites!

FISK'S FAVES

THE IN SOUND FROM WAY OUT!- ELECTRONIC POP MUSIC FROM THE FUTURE: a torturous collection of synthesizer based instrumentals. Very, very old. Maybe 1966. Tape loops of animal sound effects, snare drums and synthesized burps. Devasting kitsch. Includes the original "Spooks in Space", "Barnyard in Orbit", and "Jungle Blues from Jupiter". This music makes me fear for the future

LSD - BATTLE FOR THE MIND: "Why has a United States Senator described LSD as a greater threat to America than the atomic bomb? What is so different about LSD that thousands of college students who use it call it the 'intellectual drug'? Who is sometimes considered to be Mr. LSD?" Noted speaker William Cantelon patiently answers all of the above over the course of the lp's two awesome sides. Of particular interest are: Cantelon's astute connection between LSD and the television experience, his rap on "LSD, the Magnigicent Human Brain, and the Spiritual Nature of Man", and his dramatic interpretation of a young man having a negative LSD experience. Should go over big in D.C.

AFTER SKI AT THE TIMBERLINE LODGE - THE BOHEMIANS: Perhaps you may have heard the speeded up version of "Switzer Boy" at the end of Sub Pop 5. Well, when played at a conventional rpm, the Bohemians are an all male 13 piece vocal extravaganza specializing in German folk music (i.e. yodelling). In fact, when they toured Europe in 1959 at the behest of the Army USO, Germans were saddened and embarassed to learn that they were Americans - not real Germans.

The record was made as a promotional tool for the Timberline Lodge were the Bohemians "after ski" evening concerts were a regular event. I think "The Shining" was filmed there. Half the liner notes are about the Timberline Lodge.

The other half of the back cover is about the Bohemians' day jobs. 6'4" 250 pound lead yodeller Joe Einwaller is a school teacher. Baritone Dale Morgan is a drug salesman. Bass Norm Browning sells steel. There are no bums or goldbricks in the Bohemians. I don't think any of them wear berets and sunglasses either, they just sing.

¡VIVA! LA TROPA LOCA: La Tropa Loca ("The Crazy Group") are a major label Mexican pop group that loves "La onda de los 60's" more than life itself. Originally purchased for 25¢ in Ellensburg, this record has become a real favorite. As well as covering many pop classics ("I Will", "Chewy Chewy", Lady Will Power", "Gotta Get a Message to You"), they also do really striking, idiomatically correct originals featuring San Fran fuzz guitar, Zombies style organ, hand claps, and George Martin sax sections, all with an authentic mariachi sense of intonation. They sing about their favorite bands "Con Los Beatles Via DAYEE, Con Los Monkees Via DAYEE". The back cover's worth quoting too:
¡ Viva la onda de los 60's!
¡ Viva los Beatles!
¡ Viva las melenas largas!
¡ Viva las minifoldas!
¡ Viva los hippies!
¡ Viva Bob Dylan!
¡ Viva Ravi Shankar!
¡ Viva los Love-ins!
¡ Viva las motorcicletas!
¡ Viva Raquel Welch!
¡ Viva Donovan!
¡ Viva la musica de rock 'n roll!
¡ Viva la Tropa Loca!

CAIRO'S RIDE

30 minute Surf Opera

DOCTOR'S DAUGHTER

30 MINUTE AUDIO PSYCHO DRAMA
with music by Judy Buzz - Hunter
and the Chains of Hell Orchestra
produced by Randlett - Fisk - O'Neill
available from Dr. Stimson Tapes
824 S. Decatur, Olympia, Wa 98502

NEW RELEASE

CAIRO'S RIDE/DR.'S DAUGHTER
SPECIAL OFFER send 5 dollars
for 2-30 minute cassettes -10 songs ea.
Hurry offer lasts forever. Send
check or moneyorder to Dr. Stimson
824 S. Decatur, Olympia Wash.
98502

Bill Lagasse
by David Greenburger

TELL ME ABOUT YOURSELF
  Well, I have money.
VERY MUCH?
  Ya, quite a little.
HOW'D YOU GET IT?
  Work for it.
DOING WHAT?
  Worked in post offices and denim shops,
dungarees. And I worked a tomato plant.
That gave me my money
TELL ME MORE.
  Of course, I ain't drunk.
WHAT ELSE?
  I don't know. There ain't no more.(laughs)
WHAT DO YOU READ?
  Not much, the funnies.
WHAT'S YOUR FAVORITE MOVIE?
  I can't tell you right now. I ain't seen
to many.
WHAT'S YOUR FAVORITE SONG?
  Electric Pole.
WHO'S YOUR FAVORITE SINGER?
  Patty Page.
FAVORITE ARTIST?
  Frank Sinatra.
WHAT DO YOU THINK ABOUT THE SPACE SHUTTLE?
  Good for the country. Learnin' about the
earth, how to preserve it.
HOW FAR CAN YOU SWIM?
  A couple of miles.
WHAT'S YOUR FAVORITE SPORT?
  Baseball.
FAVORITE TEAM?
  The Red Sox right now.
DID YOU EVER HAVE A NICKNAME?
  Baldy.
BUT YOU'RE NOT BALD.
  No, but they called me Baldy Two. My broth-
er's Baldy One.
IS HE BALD?
  No.
WHAT'S THE WORST THING GOING ON THESE DAYS?
  Well, You can't even get a decent smoke
for a reasonable price. And well, people
overseas are starvin'. I guess the govern-
ment helps 'em out..That's one of the worst
things I can see.
WHAT'S THE BEST THING GOING ON THESE DAYS?
  Well, the movies I guess. You can go to
the ballgames, that's nice.
WHAT'S YOUR FAVORITE MUSICAL INSTRUMENT?
  Trumpet.
EVER PLAY IT?
  No.
WHAT DID YOU PLAY?
  Nothin'.
EVER?
  Never played a musical instrument in my
life.

TELL ME A JOKE.
  I don't know any jokes.
TELL ME A TRUE STORY.
  I used to read huntin' and fishin' mag-
azines. But I came to find out they're
fiction.
TELL ME A LIE.
  I don't know any lies.
MAKE ONE UP.
  (Laughs)
WHAT'S YOUR FAVORITE KIND OF COOKIE?
  I don't know the name of it. It's a
cookie with two sides and stuff inside.
They're pretty good.
WHAT DO YOU KNOW ABOUT DINOSAURS?
  Not a thing. I'm wonderin' how the
caveman got around 'em.
WHERE ARE YOU FROM?
  Newport, Rhode Island.
WHO ARE YOUR HEROES?
  Superman, that's about all.
DO YOU BELIEVE IN MAGIC?
  No, too tricky.
HOW ABOUT GHOSTS?
  Well, you see 'em once in a while.
WHAT ADVICE CAN YOU GIVE PEOPLE?
  Save your money.
WHAT FOR?
  A rainy day.

S/P7 UP-DATE

SPORT OF KINGS will be releasing a 9
song L.P. on S.F.'s Thermidor label
called Sing Mary Sing...THE BONEMEN OF
BARUMBA tell us that their 5 or 6 song
12" e.p.,Damn Good Pleasure, will be out
tomorrow... VIBRANT FIASCO hopes to have
an L.P. out by the end of the year...
ZYKLON has disbanded due to a lung operation in Germany...HEROIC RICE FARMER
is in flux. Lon is making noise with
Hate/grey in Port Huron...GET SMART!
will have an L.P. out real soon. They
will also be moving to Chicago at the
end of this year...THE YARDAPES have
been playing in St. Louis, Witchita,
Chicago, Boulder and other fine towns.
An e.p. and an east coast tour is in
the works...Hope you caught the big
feature on the EMBARRASSMENT in the
Sept. N.Y. Rocker. These guys just recorded 8 tunes in Dallas and are seeking the help of a larger independent
label. New address is:Box 3643, Wichita, KS 67201...JASON AND THE NASHVILLE
SCORCHERS are blazin' a trail through
the midwest and the east coast. They
just finished a date at N.Y.'s Dance-
teria. BILL LAGASSE is a new cult hero.
We've received lots of enthusiastic
feedback concerning his reading of David
Fair's "Worms in It". Read an interview
with Bill in this very issue of SUB/POP.
...Speaking of DAVID FAIR, he and JAD
have a hit with their new XXOO e.p.
They're also playing in a band called
Sit: Boy, Girl, Boy, Girl. A recent accoustic show at the Duplex Nursing Home
was quite a success...54/40 includes
horns on their Selection e.p....LITTLE
BEARS FROM BANGKOK have officially disbanded. Tracy is in a new outfit called
Pack of Wolves...TWIN DIET does a hot
version of It's Not Unusual on the Dub
Communique 2 cassette. Read Jan's article on Martini Music in this issue of
S/POP...ROCKING FELLOW is now working at
Rough Trade in S.F....PELL MELL will be
touring the midwest and the east coast
this August. They're also releasing a
very hot live cassette; brilliant packaging. They'll also be moving to S.F.
NEO BOYS e.p. is finally out!...ANGST
appears on the awesome Maximum Rock and
Roll compilation...A NEW PERSONALITY will
make a cameo appearence on the Florida
compilation, The Land That Time Forgot.
MYDOLLS should have a record out soon.

KEN'S CORNER

BILL LAGASSE-Worms in It
Where'd you get that weird record?
That's weird. Weird record. No way, I
don't dig that record at all. I just
didn't get it. Snakes, cookies, heehee
hee-ah, no. I don't dig that song at
all. There's nothing there. It has no
feeling-unless you're in a haunted
house. Play something like this, it's
enough to scare the shit out of you.
No, no, no, I wouldn't buy that record
in a million years. It's too weird,
ther's nothing there. Snakes and cookies, that's all that's there. I just
don't get it, it don't make no sense to
me at all. I don't think anybody else
could make that record make sense to
them. Snakes and cookies. Oh man,
that's weird. (ED NOTE: Ken and Bill
both live at the Duplex-apparently Ken
was unfamiliar with Bill's "project")

BONEMEN OF BARUMBA-Thick Promise
Very good, I like it. Oh man, the
drums! Yes, it's very good. I
couldn't make out the name of the song,
but it had a dance beat for me. That
drummer in this here was beautiful.
the beat went very well.

JASON AND THE NASHVILLE SCORCHERS-
Broken Whiskey Glass
Great, it's great! I was digging that
bass, it was great, terrific. The
whole damn record was good. Beat,
drums, everything. It's probably an
old record, but not that old. That
music can't be that old because it's
got that beat.

TWIN DIET-Communicate
That's about sex. The singin' was
weird, I couln't get nothin' there.
It's all about sex. It's weird, very
weird, talkin' to another girl like
that. It's got to be gay people singin' like that, that's the only way I
can figure it. Oh man, sex. That's
got to be about sex, two girls talkin'
like that. That's a very weird record.
A guy with a girl would never listen to
that.

NEO BOYS-Under Control
Crazy! They're goin' crazy, that's
lovely. I like the last part of it,
everyone goin' crazy-the drums are
beatin' like hell, the guitars are goin' - everybody's goin' crazy. That's
the way the world is out there, they're
bangin' whatever they want. You can't
stop 'em. They are tearin' up everything in the music world.

ROUGH TRADE

ROUGH TRADE MAIL-ORDER
326 SIXTH STREET
SAN FRANCISCO, CA. 94103
(415)-621-4160
TOLL FREE # 800-272-8170

LP'S:

POP GROUP	HOW MUCH LONGER DO WE TOLERATE MASS MURDER?	5.75
WANNA BUY A BRIDGE?	ROUGH TRADE SINGLES COMPILATION	5.75
PERE UBU	THE ART OF WALKING	5.75
PERE UBU	SONG OF THE BAILING MAN	5.75
PERE UBU	THE MODERN DANCE	5.75
PERE UBU	390 DEGREES OF SIMULATED STEREO(UBU LIVE, VOL. 1)	4.75
DAVID THOMAS	SOUND OF THE SAND	5.75
STIFF LITTLE FINGERS	INFLAMMABLE MATERIAL	5.75
YOUNG MARBLE GIANTS	COLOSSAL YOUTH	5.75
THE FALL	GROTESQUE(AFTER THE GRAMME)	5.75
THE FALL	SLATES(10")	4.00
CABARET VOLTAIRE	VOICE OF AMERICA	5.75
CABARET VOLTAIRE	RED MECCA	5.75
CABARET VOLTAIRE	LIVE IN JAPAN	5.75
CABARET VOLTAIRE	2x45	9.50
THE RED CRAYOLA	KANGAROO	5.75
THE RAINCOATS	ODYSHAPE	5.75
PANTHER BURNS	BEHIND THE MAGNOLIA CURTAIN	5.75
THROBBING GRISTLE	GREATEST HITS	5.75
MAUREEN TUCKER	PLAYIN' POSSUM	5.75
TOILING MIDGETS	SEA OF UNREST	5.75
THE FIRE ENGINES	AUFGELADEN UND BEREIT	5.75
IKE YARD		5.75
JOY DIVISION	UNKNOWN PLEASURES	5.75
JOY DIVISION	CLOSER	5.75
JOY DIVISION	STILL(DOUBLE LP)	10.75
JOY DIVISION	STILL(DELUXE CLOTH-BOUND EDITION)	18.00
NEW ORDER	MOVEMENT	5.75
FLIPPER	GENERIC FLIPPER	5.75
FLEX YOUR HEAD	32 TRACK HARDCORE COMPILATION FROM D.C.	5.00

12"S:

JOY DIVISION	ATMOSPHERE/SHE'S LOST CONTROL	3.25
NEW ORDER	TEMPTATION/HURT	4.75
SCRITTI POLITTI	FAITHLESS	4.75
A CERTAIN RATIO	SHACK UP/SON & HEIR/DO THE DU(CASSE)/THE FOX	3.25
CABARET VOLTAIRE	SLUGGIN' FOR JESUS	3.25
THE SMASHCORDS		3.25
SCRITTI POLITTI	SWEETEST GIRL/LIONS AFTER SLUMBER	3.25
PAUL HAIG	RUNNIN'AWAY/TIME	3.25

FREE JOY DIVISION FLEXI-DISC: KOMAKINO/INCUBATION, AVAILABLE WITH EACH ORDER. OR SEPERATELY FOR $1.00 POSTAGE & PACKING. POSTAGE RATES: 1 OR 2 DISCS: $2.00; 3 OR 4 DISCS: $2.35; 5 OR 6 DISCS: $2.75; 7, 8, OR 9 DISCS: $3.00; 10, 11, OR 12 DISCS;

$3.50. CATALOGUE AVAILABLE FOR 50¢ POSTAGE.

SECRET CODE: MENTION SUB/POP WITH ANY ORDER AND RECEIVE A SIX SONG ROUGH TRADE CASSETTE FOR FREE.

Calvin Johnson with Mark Smith of the band 3 Swimmers, Evergreen State College, Olympia, WA, February 1981 JAN LOFTNESS

The Evergreen State College

20 February, 1986

Letter of Recommendation
for
BRUCE S. PAVITT

Mr. Pavitt worked with me through the 1981
academic year during the beginnings of his
self-published SUB/POP magazine. Over the
ensuing years I've had the good opportunity
to maintain contact with Bruce through a
variety of pursuits. I think he is a swell
guy.

During the time he worked with me he proved to
be one of the most organized, resourceful and
self-disciplined students I've had. He was
able to make insightful observations on current
design and its' historic roots and synthesize these
into his own work. He pretty much organized his
own curriculum, and studied design history,
theory, production techniques and tackled each
subject with vigor. Bruce also demonstrated
a unique ability to see numerous possibilities
given circumstances that most students would
regard as overwhlemingly impossible. In light
of severe budget and produciton restrictions,
the various SUB/POPs seem to me a catalog of
inventive and appropiate design.

But the main thing I find refreshing about Bruce
is that he is a person who wnats to learn in order
to get things done, not simply to think about
them. That he is resourceful, creative, and fun at the
same time makes him all the more prepared for
future study in design.

Brad Clemmons
Senior Graphic Designer
(206) 866-6000

Olympia, Washington 98505

SUB POP #9, *June 1983*

16pp, 2 1/2" x 4" cassette case format with cassette, print run of 500

DEAR FRIENDS—
After a brief vacation SUB/POP is back in action. New format is international. We're very interested in artists who sing in their **own language**. None of this pandering to other cultures, please. We're discontinuing Sub/Pop magazine; cassettes only from now on! **Sub/Pop U.S.A.** is a column in Seattle's Rocket; it's also a radio show on KCMU. So send in those promos. If you haven't guessed it by now, **Sub/Pop** is now based in Seattle. Remember: buy local, think global, but order it from **SUB/POP**, Box 85136, Seattle, WA 98105. Tapes are $5.00 ppd.

Writing/Graphics: **Bruce Pavitt**. Maximum Coolness: **Calvin Johnson**. Cover Art: **Charles Burns**. Knobs and Wires: **Shawn O'Neill**. Special thanks to: **Mikael Hakanson, Mike Peskura**.

© and ℗ 1983 SUB/POP or artists

RANDOM AMERICAN TELEVISION

VELVET MONKEYS
EVERYTHING IS RIGHT
Wow! Spooky psychedelia from this great up and coming D.C. band. The Monkeys will be releasing a 45 on Version Sound records; they'll also be appearing on a Verson Sound national psychedelic compilation. Write: **Don Fleming, 1619-A Corcoran St. NW, Washington, D.C. 20009.**

EGOSLAVIA
LOST SONG
This song punches hard. Atonal slide, industrial percussion. This dance hit is available on their 12″ EP on 9½ × 16 Records. Hope this team makes it to the west coast soon. Write: **9½ × 16 Records, 1737 DeSales St. NW, 3rd Floor, Washington, D.C. 20036.**

UNDERHEAVEN
TIME DOES NOT CONFINE HER
Beautiful acoustic folk/rock classic from this brand new band. I've been humming this one for days. Vocalist Howard Wuelfing used to be in the Nurses. Write: **c/o Truly Needy fanzine, Box 2271, Rockville, MD 20852.**

DUPLEX PLAYERS/INCREDIBLE CASUALS
PICNIC APE (VERSION)
Members of the Duplex Nursing Home participate in a surreal soundtext experiment; this is an alternate take of the flipside to the Incredible Casuals great "Picnic Ape" 45. To order their record, write: **Eat Records, 400 Essex St., Salem, MA 01970.** For interviews with the Duplex folks, write: **The Duplex Planet c/o David Greenberger, 16 University Road #2, Brookline, MA 02146.**

SIT: BOY, GIRL, BOY, GIRL
ALL SHOOK UP
Mark Jickling, Jad and David Fair give a rare acoustic performance at Boston's Duplex Nursing Home (July 5, 1982). Hope you've seen David's latest book, Wiggly Worms! Write: **Box 143, Westminster, MD 21157.**

FURORS
HEY JONI
Like hey, these cats are crazy in love and they mean it! Awkward, fun and totally rockin'. The Furors have lots of 45's out, including this one. Check 'em out: **Big Plastic Records, Box 6069, Hamden, CT 06517.**

LEOPARD SOCIETY
SCREAMIN'
Two gentlemen from Albany, N.Y. eat raw meat and only go out "when the moon is full." Drums and guitar. This anthem is available as a 45. Write: **Sacred Lance Records, Box 7166, Albany, N.Y. 12224.**

CARSICKNESS
FOR YOU
The steel industry may be falling apart, but Carsickness, Pittsburgh's most prolific combo, keeps right on going. Mood and atmosphere, this song's a hit for sure. Check out their second L.P., "Sharpen Up For Duty." Write: **T.M.I., 6030 Penn Circle S., Pittsburgh, PA 15206.**

AMA-DOTS
SAMIZDAT
Out of all the cool bands that are coming out of Milwaukee (Oil Tasters, Violent Femmes), the Ama-Dots are the most sinister. Vocalist Boola sounds like a witch in need of a throat lozenge. Send fan mail to: **Box 1287, Milwaukee, WI 53201.**

XXX
Two songs brought in from behind the Iron Curtain. Due to diplomatic promises on my part, no address or info can be given.

RANDOM SWEDISH RADIO

STEVE FISK
LOVE IS
Mr. Fisk has recently taken his machines down to S.F., where he'll be performing with Pell Mell. This way-out disco hit features various popular rhythm tracks, looped. Judy (Doctor's Daughter) on vocals. Order Steve's new cassette through: **Pell Mell, Box 1482, El Cerrito, CA 94530.**

PARIS WORKING
SLEEP
Sharply chanted harmonies and strong guitar work make this dance band stand out of the pack. Paris Working's new debut 12″ EP features an outrageous seven minute dub, mixed and produced by Steve Fisk. Check it out: **c/o 1640 18th St., Oakland, CA 94607.**

JOHN FOSTER'S POP PHILOSOPHERS
CHAIN OF ABUSE
OP editor John Foster has come up with a sweet, soulful electronic dub workout. This brief pop masterpiece has appeared previously on the Dub Communique 2 cassette. John also appears on the "Life Elsewhere" 12" and the "Absolute Elsewhere" cassette compilation. For info on John and OP magazine, write: **Lost Music Network, Box 2391, Olympia, WA 98507.**

HEATHER, CALVIN AND LAURA
TO THE BEACH
Intimate beat/folk combo. Tom tom, vocals and maracas. Olympia's coolest band, if not the worlds. Keep your fingers crossed for possible triple live LP. Write: **K, Box 7154, Olympia, WA 98507.**

RICH JENSON
NO CANNIBALS ON THIS CUL-DE-SAC
A truly modern folk fable. Simple, hubcap percussion with occasional electronics. Abusively funny. Write: **Lost Music Network, Box 2391, Olympia, WA 98507.**

LIMP RICHERDS
MY DAD FORGOT HIS RUBBER
Who let these guys out of their cage? Clarinet and feedback. Noisy, funny, intense. "Bob Hope's U.S.O. El Salvador Show, 1983" is featured on the "Public Doesn't Exist" cassette compilation; they're also on the "What Syndrome?" compilation. Write: **c/o Dave Middleton, 29719 34th Ave. S., Auburn, WA 98002.**

SUPERSHAFT
THEME FROM SUPERSHAFT

A commercial, a T.V. theme song or a football chant? Always unpredictable, Supershaft recently open for Savage Republic and encored with a furious Z Z Top cover. This track features stolen "drum drops," prerecorded rhythms by some inportant L.A. session musician. Su-per-shaaaaffttt! Write: **c/o SUB/POP, Box 85136, Seattle, WA 98105.**

WIPERS
NOTHIN' TO PROVE

Scorching live # by one of the toughest bands around. The Wipers have released three 45's and two classic albums; look for their third, "Over the Edge." Maximum tuneage. Write: **Trap Records, Box 42465, Portland, OR 97242.**

ACTUEL
THINGS

Hypnotic vibrato guitar. A very pretty song, kind of shows us the London side of Nashville. Steve Anderson on guitars and vocals, Gary Rabasca on bass, Soren Berleu on drums. "Things" is from the "Actuel" 12" single released in 1982 on Tiki Records. Write: **Actuel c/o 304 W. Bellevue Dr., Nashville, TN 37205.**

MAGNETIQUE BLEU
VIRGIN BOY

Apparently, there's not much of a new music scene in France. That's why SUB/POP is happy to introduce Magnetique Bleu, featuring Christian Dezert and his sexy French accent. This cut was released as a 45; they also appear on the Bain Total International Compilation 2. Write: **Christian Dezert, 12 Rue Rollin, 2100 Dijon, France.**

*S*TART
*S*LIES

Honest, unpretentious pop hit from the great midwest. Their excellent new LP, "Look Around" includes a song/poem by Allen Ginsberg, as well as "Lies." They've also released a 7″ called "Tales of Glory." Contact: **Fresh Sounds, Inc., Box 36, Lawrence, KS 66044.**

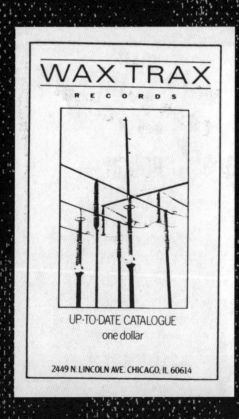

WAX TRAX
R E C O R D S

UP-TO-DATE CATALOGUE
one dollar

2449 N. LINCOLN AVE. CHICAGO, IL 60614

More Fun than goin' back to school!!

ROUGH
TRADE
MAIL ORDER
326 SIXTH Street
SAN FRANCISCO
CA   94103

discs
tapes
'zines

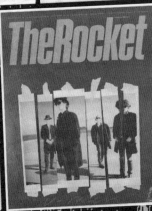

Charles R. Cross

An Entirely Different Seattle

I first met Bruce Pavitt in our offices at the *Rocket* magazine. I started working there as an associate editor in 1982, and Bruce began his *Sub Pop* column the following year. There was so little money in publishing a regional musical magazine; the *Rocket* ran a trade ad for a local restaurant, and our staff could eat there for free, but only after two A.M. Otherwise, we starved.

Bruce wrote record reviews for us during the era when vinyl was king and the cassette was queen. The *Rocket* paid five dollars for a record review, but at least you usually got free records. That was part of my motivation, and, I assume, some of Bruce's as well.

This was an entirely different Seattle than the city that would later become the headquarters of Microsoft and Amazon. The club scene was anything but healthy. Most clubs were taverns, where bands could make their living only by playing covers. A few outlying punk clubs opened up, but they would usually shut down within weeks. The early '80s Seattle clubs had names like the Metropolis, the Gorilla Room, the Gorilla Gardens, and the Graven Image Gallery. None of them stayed in business long, due to inevitable problems with liquor laws, noise ordinances, and fire inspectors. I remember an early show by Hüsker Dü—a band Bruce promoted in his *Sub Pop* column— where the club owner cut an extra fire exit in the wall with a chain saw to stop the gig from being shut down by authorities.

It's important to remember how bad the scene was. When the Seattle music world took off a few years later, many people looked back in retrospect, or from outside our city, and got the idea that Nirvana, Mudhoney, and Soundgarden were typical representatives of a healthy music mecca. They were not. But the scarcity of local options and lack of money to be made doing shows prompted many of those bands to release records. Original bands would often play at community centers, art galleries, old movie theaters, or hip taverns; but they usually performed to crowds that could be counted in the dozens. Given the dead-end prospect of gigging, many groups decided that records were their best possible angle for breaking out. The cry of the DIY Seattle punk rocker was that when you have nothing, you have nothing to lose. That was the situation—the world—that spawned Sub Pop.

Bruce was Seattle's most ardent evangelist, preaching that a band could put out an indie seven-inch single, sell a few copies, and maybe get some press attention; if only in his *Sub Pop* column in the *Rocket*. Making a living as a recording artist was unheard of in the Northwest; other than Heart, no band had ever managed to do that. Bruce worked a day job at Muzak, the company that produced smaltzy instrumental tapes to be played in elevators. Mark Arm of Mudhoney worked there, too. That a company that manufactured background music would serve as the breeding ground for a loud musical revolution is one of the sweetest ironies in history.

Bruce first used the "Sub Pop" name on his fanzine in college. That eventually evolved into cassette compilations, then into his column in the *Rocket*. The

Rocket's circulation was fifty thousand then, the paper was distributed for free throughout the Northwest. In Aberdeen, the local music store charged a quarter for it to pay for shipping, so Kurt Cobain had to pay to read it—and he did. *Sub Pop* was the most closely-read monthly item. I helped paste up the column sometimes. Bruce always stood watch over the production, wanting to make sure everything was perfect. His column was as much a typographic mish-mash as it was a musical one. The design—overseen by such graphic design luminaries as Dale Yarger, Bob Newman, and Art Chantry—was also groundbreaking.

Bruce's column was the first place I heard about the Minutemen, the Butthole Surfers, and Sonic Youth. His musical picks were so varied and diverse that no one other than Bruce could embrace everything he wrote about. Even if you didn't agree with Bruce's taste, you had to admire that every band he covered had a stance, and an attitude. These were not wishy-washy bands, just as Bruce was not a wishy-washy critic. If he liked a band, he loved them. If he didn't like them, and the rest of the world did, he didn't shift his opinion just because of their popularity. He almost exclusively wrote about bands he loved, so in a way his column was less of a critical analysis, and more of a valentine to a certain style and aesthetic of music. (I never liked Sonic Youth as much as Bruce did—I'm not sure Sonic Youth liked themselves as much as Bruce did—but he produced smart writing that sold records. I bought their *Evol* album based on his review, and so did others.)

As far as I could tell, Bruce had no rules about what he might cover. He promoted pop records, punk records, and some spoken-word records which could only be categorized as weird art projects. Everything was an indie release. He championed labels like Homestead, Alternative Tentacles, SST, and Twin/Tone. The stuff major labels were putting out had less edge, that was just a fact. If a Northwest band put out a single, he was sure to mention that. Still, there weren't enough local releases to keep the Sub Pop column strictly regional—although the focus of the column and magazine shifted to the city as the local scene grew.

Eventually, Sub Pop morphed into a record label that reflected the same iconoclasm Bruce had displayed as a columnist. Jonathan Poneman, Bruce's partner, was always more populist in his musical taste; he seemed to even out some of Bruce's edges. Sometimes the story of Sub Pop has been told that Bruce was the music guy, and Jonathan the marketer. From what I observed, there was never a stark contrast of duties. Both had their strengths and weakness. Managing their finances was their weak point, and during many moments it seemed the whole business would fall completely apart.

Everything Sub Pop released had a similar look, though the music in the sleeves varied. Nothing was candy-sounding or over-produced; both the design of their album covers and their sonic production reflected minimalism. Jack Endino became their producer and engineer, and Charles Peterson their central photographer. Overall, the organism felt as if a salon of great thinkers had planned a musical revolution. Nothing was planned, though. All four men would later describe Sub Pop Records as more of an accident; their talents simply ran headlong into a series of bands that were ready to take on the world.

The same pure devotion to substance that Bruce had in picking singles for his *Sub Pop* column was central to the Sub Pop label. Not everything the label put out worked. For every Nirvana's "Love Buzz," there was a Rapeman's "Inki's Butt Crack."

Some records sold like hotcakes, some did not. Like great chefs of the musical sort, everything Bruce and Jonathan put out had taste. It took Sub Pop several years of turmoil before they found commercial success. Whether a Sub Pop release sold a million copies, as Nirvana's *Bleach* eventually did, or only a handful—such as Blood Circus' *Primal Rock Therapy*, an obscure Sub Pop

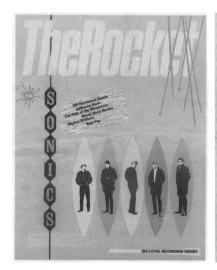  

record that I'll forever argue was more "grunge" than any other—everything had a uniqueness yet felt tied to everything else on the label. Sub Pop didn't just put out bands, they created a label that was more cohesive than any other in the nation, or maybe the world, at the time.

Most bands signed to Sub Pop because they knew that Bruce and Jonathan believed in their vision. You can see that appreciation for vision taking shape in these years of columns, just as you can hear it coalescing in the first few Sub Pop singles. Bands that signed with Sub Pop—which was mostly a matter of a hand-shake—knew that at their record release party there would always be one person in the very front, bopping his head to their music, promoting their strengths to anyone who would listen, and openly enjoying himself all the while.

And that person would be Bruce Pavitt.

Evidence of Life in Portland?

HI THERE

SUB POP USA will be a regular column, focusing on a different American city with each issue. Radio stations, record stores, and publications that support local, independent releases will be featured, as well as clubs that book bands playing original rock, pop, or soul. In the past few years, local labels have developed and expanded—I'd like to emphasize that development by highlighting the labels as well as the artists. Besides local documentation, **SUB POP USA** will also include a **SUB 10** list of local/regional releases from around the country that deserve national/international attention. Please send me free records.

GHOST TOWN?

Portland certainly seems to be in a state of transition. First off, the Metropolis, a great all-ages club that served alcohol and featured a mod, psychedelic dance floor, is dead. The best alternative rock club in the Pacific Northwest will no longer feature original music. Secondly, bands are leaving. After a cassette release and a cross-country tour, **PELL MELL** has moved to San Francisco; electronics whiz Steve Fisk is now a part of their sound. **NAPALM BEACH** will also be releasing a cassette and moving to SF. The **WIPERS** are in town to record their third LP, then it's back to New York and the big time. Right-wing combo **LOCKJAW** will thankfully go to Texas this spring, and **SADO-NATION** will be touring California in May. Also, the infamous **NEO BOYS** have officially dissolved; pick up their EP before it goes out of print!

LABELS/ARTISTS

TRAP RECORDS (Portland, OR) The Trap catalogue includes the **WIPERS**' *Better Off Dead* 45 plus upcoming cassettes by **NAPALM BEACH** and Olympia's **YOUNG PIONEERS**. The **WIPERS** "Romeo"/ "No Solution" 45 is a scorching tribute to love, desperation, and tall dark buildings casting ghostly shadows at night. The **WIPERS** have a raw, classic rock sound that transcends trends or movements. This record is timeless. The *Trap Sampler* LP includes two tracks apiece by the **WIPERS**, **PELL MELL**, **NAPALM BEACH**, and **DRUMBUNNY**. Although the **WIPERS** and **PELL MELL** have released better stuff, this is worth picking up for the **NAPALM BEACH** cuts. Will probably become a collector's item.

SMEGMA/PIGFACE (Portland, OR) One of the most intense "noise" labels in the country. Includes the **SMEGMA** LP *Pigs for Lepers*, the **RANCID VAT** *Stampeding Cattle* LP, plus other pleasantries. **SMEGMA** double cassette: soon-to-be released cassette package includes one studio tape plus a live recording from the Dammasch State Mental Hospital. The *Flies Like Holidays* LP is a noisy, experimental collection includes **SMEGMA**, **RANCID VAT**, **FAULTY DENIAL MECHANISM**, **JUNGLE NAUSEA**, **DICKENSMEGLEE**, **GOURMET DOGS**, and **POSSUM SOCIETY**—for those intimate moments.

INDOOR RECORDS (El Cerrito, CA) The Indoor label is synonymous with **PELL MELL**. Pell Mell *Live* cassette: instrumentalists Pell Mell released a minimal, hypnotic 12-inch EP called *Rhyming Guitars* in the fall

SUB/POP

U. S. A.

By Bruce Pavitt

Evidence of Life in Portland?

Ghost town? Portland certainly seems to be in a state of transition. First off, the Metropolis, a great all ages club that served alcohol and featured a mod, psychedelic dance floor is dead. The best alternative rock club in the Pacific Northwest will no longer feature original music. Secondly, bands are leaving. After a cassette release and a cross country tour, Pell Mell has moved to San Francisco; electronics whiz Steve Fisk is now a part of their sound. Napalm Beach will also be releasing a cassette and moving to SF. The Wipers are in town to record their third LP, then it's back to New York and the big time. Right-wing combo Lockjaw will thankfully go to Texas this spring and Sado-Nation will be touring California in May. Also, the infamous Neo Boys have officially dissolved; pick up their EP before it goes out of print!

Labels/Artists

► **TRAP** (Box 42465, Portland, OR 97242) The Trap catalogue includes the Wipers' "Better Off Dead" 45 plus upcoming cassettes by Napalm Beach and Olympia's Young Pioneers. . . . **WIPERS** *Romeo/No Solution* 45. A scorching tribute to love, desperation and tall dark buildings casting ghostly shadows at night. The Wipers have a raw, classic rock sound that transcends trends or movements. This record is timeless. . . . **TRAP SAMPLER** LP. Includes two tracks apiece by the Wipers, Pell Mell, Napalm Beach and Drumbunny. Although the Wipers and Pell Mell have released better stuff, this is worth picking up for the Napalm Beach cuts. Will probably become a collector's item.
► **SMEGMA/PIGFACE** (76 N.E. Thompson, Portland, OR 97228) One of the most intense "noise" labels in the country. Includes the Smegma LP *Pigs for Lepers*, the Rancid Vat *Stampeding Cattle* LP plus other pleasantries. . . . **SMEGMA** Double cassette. Soon to be released cassette package includes one studio tape plus a live recording from the Dammash State Mental Hospital . . . . **FLIES LIKE HOLIDAYS** LP. Noisy, experimental collection includes Smegma, Rancid Vat, Faulty Denial Mechanism, Jungle Nausea, Dickensmegle, Gourmet Dogs, Possum Society. For those intimate moments.
► **INDOOR** (Box 1482, El Cerrito, CA 94530) The Indoor label is synonymous with Pell Mell. . . . **PELL MELL** Live cassette. Instrumentalists Pell Mell released a minimal, hypnotic 12-inch EP called *Rhyming Guitars* in the fall of '81. A great record. This tape captures them nine months later, stripped to a trio. It's a busier sound, with radical changes in tempo, mood and texture. Although quite unlike the EP, it's every bit as original.
► **BRAINSTEM** (Box 332, Portland, OR 97207) Brainstem will soon be releasing an international hardcore compilation cassette, submissions welcome. . . . **SADO-NATION** *We're Not Equal* LP. Their press release states that "Sado-Nation has been Portland's leading underground band for the past three years." Guitarist Corboy looks like a trucker and could probably kick your ass. He's got presence, and so do Sado-Nation; but the cheap, grungy production on this hardcore release lacks punch. Catch 'em live and loud.
► **LOCKJAW** (Box 8382, Portland, OR 97207) Have also released the Lockjaw *Shock Value* EP. . . . **LOCKJAW** *Dead Friends* 7-inch EP. Songs like "Need a Gun" and "She's a Slut" represent everything that's bad about American hardcore. Socially corrupt bands like Fear, Angry Samoans and Meatmen at least know how to tell a good joke; these guys are just plain sick.
► **FATAL ERECTION** (714 S.E. 148th, Portland, OR 97233). . . . **POISON IDEA** *Pick Your King* 7-inch EP. 13-song hardcore release on clear vinyl. Haven't heard it, but with perceptive phrases like "fatal erection" and "pick your king" it should be interesting.

New Bands

► **DIRGE** (Flipper, etc.) **THEATRE OF SHEEP** (Pop, keyboards), **MIRACLE WORKERS** ('60s garage), **REDHEADS** (female rockabilly), **SQUAD 5, FILM AT 11.**

Station(s)

► **KBOO 90.7 FM** (65 S.W. Yamhill St., Portland, OR 97204) Community station, plays independents.

Store(s)

► **SINGLES GOING STEADY** (949 S.W. Oak, Portland, OR 97205) Excellent selection of US indies, imports, classic pop and reggae.

Club(s)

► **LOUIS LA BAMBAS** (58 S.W. 2nd, Portland, OR 97204). [503] 227-0247.) Over-21 club. Sometimes books bands that play original material.

Fanzine(s)

► **NOT MUCH ACTION** in this dept. The *Willamette Week* is a weekly newspaper with some coverage of local music and indies. (320 S.W. Stark St., Portland, OR 97204).

Hi there.

SUB/POP U.S.A. will be a regular column, focusing on a different American city with each issue. Radio stations, record stores and publications that support local, independent releases will be featured, as well as clubs that book bands playing original rock, pop or soul. In the past few years, local labels have developed and expanded—I'd like to emphasize that development by highlighting the labels as well as the artists. Besides local documentation, SUB/POP U.S.A. will also include a SUB 10 list of local/regional releases from around the country that deserve national/international attention. Please send me free records.

S·U·B·10

► **MISSION OF BURMA** *VS.* LP (Ace of Hearts) Wired, fragmented art/hardcore crossover. Includes the mellow, hypno-pop hit "Trem Two." (Boston)
► **SPORT OF KINGS** *SING MARY SING* LP (Thermidor) Intriguing pop melodrama. Good use of atmosphere. (Chicago)
► **PLANET PATROL** *PLAY AT YOUR OWN RISK* 12-inch single (Tommy Boy) Soulful gospel harmonies, electronic polyrhythms, voice loops. Wow. Techno-funk minus the vocoder. (NY)
► **TROUBLE FUNK** *LET'S GET SMALL* 12-inch single (D.E.T.T.) Party time. Organic percussion, chants, horns, harmonica. A killer. (D.C.)
► **VOID/FAITH** LP (Dischords) The Faith side is standard hardcore. Void shreds to no mercy — uncontrollable. (D.C.)
► **SEATTLE SYNDROME 2** LP (Engram) Face it, few cities could put out a commercial pop compilation this good. Home of "the wave."
► **PELL MELL** *LIVE* Cassette (Indoor) Highbrow instrumentals. Masters of technique. Brilliant package. (SF/Portland)
► **WIPERS** *ROMEO* 45 (Trap) Iggy move over. The Wipers refuse to sound dated or trendy. (NY/Portland)
► **OIL TASTERS** LP (Thermidor) Bass, drums, sax. Unusual pop with a wacky sense of humor. (Milwaukee)
► **DESCENDENTS** *MILO GOES TO COLLEGE* LP (New Alliance) Catchy thrash LP includes songs about love, marriage, jealousy, sex, loneliness. A breakthrough. (LA)

Please send records and tapes to:
SUB/POP U.S.A. c/o The Rocket / 2322 Second Avenue/Seattle, WA 98121

"*Sub Pop USA* will be a regular column, focusing on a different American city with each issue. In the past few years, local labels have developed and expanded— I'd like to emphasize that development by highlighting the labels as well as the artists. Please send me free records."

of '81. A great record. This live tape captures them nine months later, stripped to a trio. It's a busier sound, with radical changes in tempo, mood, and texture. Although quite unlike the EP, it's every bit as original.

BRAINSTEM RECORDS (Portland, OR) Brainstem will soon be releasing an international hardcore compilation cassette, submissions are welcome: **SADO-NATION** *We're Not Equal* LP; Their press release states that "Sado-Nation has been Portland's leading underground band for the past three years." Guitarist Corboy looks like a trucker and could probably kick your ass. He's got presence, and so does Sado-Nation, but the cheap, grungy production on this hardcore release lacks punch. Catch 'em live and loud.

LOCKJAW RECORDS (Portland, OR) Have also released the **LOCKJAW** *Shock Value* EP. On the Lockjaw *Dead Friends* 7-inch, songs like "Need a Gun" and "She's a Slut" represent everything bad about American hardcore. Socially corrupt bands like **FEAR, ANGRY SAMOANS**, and the **MEATMEN** at least know how to tell a good joke; these guys are just plain sick.

FATAL ERECTION (Portland, OR) **POISON IDEA** *Pick Your King* 7-inch EP is a 13-song hardcore release on clear vinyl. I haven't heard it, but with perceptive phrases like "fatal erection" and "pick your king" it should be interesting.

NEW BANDS

DIRGE (Flipper, etc.); **THEATRE OF SHEEP** (Pop, keyboards); **MIRACLE WORKERS** ('60s garage); **REDHEADS** (female rockabilly); **SQUAD 5**; and **FILM AT 11**

STATIONS

KBOO 90.7 FM (Portland, OR) Community station, plays independents.

STORES

SINGLES GOING STEADY (Portland, OR) Excellent selection of US indies, imports, classic pop, and reggae.

CLUBS

LOUIS LA BAMBAS (Portland, OR). Over-21 club. Sometimes books bands that play original material.

FANZINES

Not much action in this dept. The *Willamette Week* is a weekly newspaper with some coverage of local music and indies. (Portland, OR)

SUB 10

MISSION OF BURMA *VS.* LP (Ace of Hearts) Wired, fragmented art/hardcore crossover. Includes the mellow, hypno-pop hit "Trem Two" (Boston)

SPORT OF KINGS *Sing Mary Sing* LP (Thermidor) Intriguing pop melodrama. Good use of atmosphere. (Chicago)

PLANET PATROL *Play at Your Own Risk* 12-inch single (Tommy Boy) Soulful gospel harmonies, electronic polyrhythms, voice loops. Wow. Techno-funk minus the vocoder. (NY)

TROUBLE FUNK *Let's Get Small* 12-inch single (D.E.T.T.) Party time. Organic percussion, chants, horns, harmonica. A killer. (D.C.)

VOID/FAITH split LP (Dischord) The **FAITH** side is standard hardcore. **VOID** shreds to no mercy —uncontrollable. (D.C.)

VARIOUS *Seattle Syndrome 2* LP (Engram) Face it, few cities could put out a commercial pop compilation this good. Home of "the wave." (Seattle)

PELL MELL *Live* cassette (Indoor) Highbrow instrumentals. Masters of technique. Brilliant package. (SF/Portland, OR)

WIPERS *Romeo* 45 (Trap) Iggy move over. The Wipers refuse to sound dated or trendy. (NY/Portland)

OIL TASTERS LP (Thermidor) Bass, drums, sax. Unusual pop with a wacky sense of humor. (Milwaukee)

DESCENDENTS *Milo Goes To College* LP (New Alliance) Catchy thrash LP includes songs about love, marriage, jealousy, sex, loneliness. A breakthrough. (L.A.)

Boston's Got the Best (White) Radio

RADIO. Boston's got the best (white) radio in the country. Because of this exposure, bands flock here from all over the country. Drum roll please. The legendary **BLACKOUTS**, formerly of Seattle, are doing good. They've played all the major clubs, recently played with **BAUHAUS**. They are ready to release a 3-song 12", recorded at the Cars' Synchro Sound Studios. The tape was produced by whiz kid Al Jourgensen of **MINISTRY**. Like the **BLACKOUTS**, **MINISTRY** decided it was better to move to Boston than to stay in their home town, Chicago. Work on developing a local scene, and you won't have to feel the urge to move on. Other major gossip: **MISSION OF BURMA** has stopped playing live shows. Guitarist Roger Miller is suffering from tinnitus, a chronic ringing in the ears. Miller, a classically-trained pianist, will collaborate with Martin Swope on a project called **BIRDSONGS OF THE MESOZOIC**; avant-garde piano and tape loops.

LABELS / ARTISTS

ACE OF HEARTS (Boston, MA) All releases produced by Richard Harte. Excellent label; very high standards. Expect upcoming releases by the **LYRE** and **BIRDSONGS OF THE MESOZOIC. MISSION OF BURMA** VS. LP. Uncompromising. This band is torn apart at the seams, very intense. Amid the chaos you'll find "Trem Two," a tranquil, seductive pop classic. The **NEATS** *The Monkey's Head in the Corner of the Room* 12-inch EP is timeless electric folk/rock. Open, ringing chords. Gruff vocals, no harmonies; **THE BYRDS** meet **CREEDENCE**. Beautiful.

EAT RECORDS (Salem, MA) Eclectic, often eccentric pop label. Upcoming releases include a **RUBBER RODEO** dance EP plus LPs by **MEN AND VOLTS** and **VINNY**. "Modern cowboys find a home on the radar range" on the **RUBBER RODEO** *Eatum* 12-inch EP. Despite a colorful package and an interesting premise—country & western plus electronics—this record fails to deliver. Glossy production is the villain. **THE INCREDIBLE CASUALS/DUPLEX PLAYERS** *Picnic Ape* 45. This totally rockin' number features weird lyrics, radical reverb production, and a great drum sound. Flip side is a dub/soundtext experiment showcasing various members of the Duplex Nursing Home. Double A-side, for sure.

MODERN METHOD RECORDS (Boston, MA) Affiliated with Newbury Comics/Record Store and *Boston Rock* magazine. These guy have a lot of political muscle. Have released two major Boston compilations, *A Wicked Good Time Vols. 1* and *2.* The *This Is Boston Not L.A.* LP is the best document available of Boston's thriving hardcore scene. Includes the **PROLETARIAT**, **GANG GREEN, THE FREEZE, THE F.U.'S**, plus more. Recommended! **NOVEMBER GROUP** 12-inch EP showcases Boston's "next big thing." The November Group is a synth/dance quartet. "We dance... one body, one mind." No substance, totally artificial, very pretentious. Any band that has named themselves after an "early 20th century German art collective" has got to have some brains somewhere. I sincerely hope they start using them.

PROPELLER RECORDS (Boston, MA) Propeller is run as a cooperative and is a good resource for some of the more "alternative" pop bands. **CHRISTMAS**

S›U›B / P›O›P USA

Radio. Boston's got the best (white) radio in the country. Because of this exposure, bands flock here from all over the country. Drum roll please. The legendary Blackouts, formerly of Seattle, are doing good. They've played all the major clubs, recently played with Bauhaus. They are ready to release a 3-song 12'', recorded at the Cars' Synchro Sound Studios. The tape was produced by whiz kid Al Jourgensen of Ministry. Like the Blackouts, Ministry decided it was better to move to Boston than to stay in their home town, Chicago. Work on developing a local scene, and you won't have to feel the urge to move on. . . . Other major gossip: Mission of Burma have stopped playing live shows. Guitarist Roger Miller is suffering from tinnitus, a chronic ringing in the ears. Miller, a classically trained pianist, will collaborate with Martin Swope on a project called Birdsongs of the Mesozoic; avant-garde piano and tape loops.

Boston

Labels/Artists

► **ACE OF HEARTS** (Box 579, Kenmore Station, Boston, MA 02215) All releases produced by Richard Harte. Excellent label; very high standards. Expect upcoming releases by the Lyres and Birdsongs of the Mesozoic. . . . **MISSION OF BURMA** *VS.* LP. Uncompromising. This band is torn apart at the seams, very intense. Amid the chaos you'll find *Trem Two*, a tranquil, seductive pop classic. . . . **THE NEATS** *The Monkey's Head in the Corner of the Room* 12-inch EP. Timeless electric folk/rock. Open, ringing chords. Gruff vocals, no harmonies; the Byrds meet Creedence. Beautiful.

► **EAT RECORDS** (400 Essex St., Salem, MA 01970) Eclectic, often eccentric pop label. Upcoming releases include a *Rubber Rodeo* dance EP plus LPs by Men And Volts, Vinny. . . . **RUBBER RODEO** *Eatum* 12-inch EP. "Modern cowboys find a home on the radar range." Despite a colorful package and an interesting premise — C&W plus electronics — this record fails to deliver. Glossy production is the villain. . . . **THE INCREDIBLE CASUALS/DUPLEX PLAYERS** *Picnic Ape* 45. Totally rockin' # features weird lyrics, radical reverb production. Great drum sound. Flipside is a dub/soundtext experiment showcasing various members of the Duplex Nursing Home. Double A-side, for sure.

► **MODERN METHOD** (268 Newbury St., Boston, MA 02116) Affiliated with Newbury Comics/ Record Store and *Boston Rock* magazine. These guys have a *lot* of political muscle. Have released two major Boston compilations, *A Wicked Good Time Vol. 1* and *2*. . . . **THIS IS BOSTON NOT L.A.** LP. Best document available of Boston's thriving hardcore scene. Includes the Proletariat, Gang Green, the Freeze, the F.U.'s plus more. Recommended. . . . **NOVEMBER GROUP** 12-inch EP. Boston's "next big thing," the November Group is a synth/dance quartet. "We dance . . . one body, one mind." No substance, totally artificial, very pretentious. Any band that has named themselves after an "early 20th century German art collective" has got to have some brains somewhere. I sincerely hope they start using them.

► **PROPELLER** (Box 658, Allston Station, Boston, MA 02134) Propeller is run as a cooperative and is a good resource for some of the more "alternative" pop bands. The group Christmas should be releasing something soon. . . . **PROPELLER PRODUCT** 4-song 7-inch compilation.

Features the forgettable Wild Stares, CCCP TV, and People in Stores. However, the Neats' "Six" is a modern, psychedelic masterpiece. Sounds totally different from their equally excellent EP. . . . **DANGER-OUS BIRDS** *Alpha Romeo/Smile On Your Face* 45. The A-side is nothing special. The flip is a very tough girl-group anthem, complete with chain gang vocals and claves. Excellent.

► **X-CLAIM!** (8 Longwood Rd., Lynn, MA 01904) Boston's "hardcore" label, run by and for the bands. Initiated by scenemakers S.S. Decontrol. Other releases include F.U.'s "Kill For Christ" 12" EP and an upcoming S.S. Decontrol 12-inch EP. . . . **S.S. DECONTROL** LP. Boston's most talked about thrash band, these guys ultimately don't stand out of the herd. They condemn conformity but are not original; they condemn violence but sing lines like "People who think we're pussies and afraid to fight/just come in our pit and feel our might." As an extra bonus, this band has also adopted Minor Threat's anti-drug "straight edge" philosophy. . . . Apparently, their new release has more dirge and metal influences.

Publication(s)

BOSTON ROCK (268 Newbury St., Boston, MA 02116) Boston's uninspired answer to the sorely missed N.Y. Rocker. . . . **TAKE IT!** (39 Union St. #2, Brighton, MA 02135) Diverse new music mag; last issue featured a flexi w/ the Flesheaters, Meat Puppets and Tex and the Horseheads. . . . **FORCED EXPOSURE** (76 Bromfield St., Watertown, MA 02172) Highly recommended hardcore publication. Provocative national interviews; sharp, accessible layout. Bi-monthly. . . . **CONFLICT** (c/o 9 Jefferey Rd., Wayland, MA 01778) Teenager Gerard Cosley is one of the most interesting critics in the country. Get *Conflict*. . . .

Please send records and tapes to:
SUB/POP U.S.A. c/o The Rocket
2322 Second Avenue / Seattle, WA 98121

New Bands

BLACKOUTS, CHRISTMAS, BEANBAG, D.Y.S., SORRY, CHILDREN OF PARADISE, IMPACT UNIT.

Store(s)

NEWBURY COMICS (c/o 268 Newbury St., Boston, MA 02116) Boston's only alternative record store.

Club(s)

Although Spit, the Rat and Storyville all book bands that play original material, out of town bands are advised to check out the following: **MAVERICK'S**: 112 Broad St., Boston, MA. Call Heidi at (617) 247-1774. . . . **THE CHANNEL**: 25 Necco St., Boston, MA. Call Warren Scott at (617) 451-1050. . . . An excellent booking agent named Julien can be reached at (617) 445-9329.

Sub/Pop U.S.A. Radio
► ► EVERY TUESDAY 6-7 PM • KCMU 90.5 FM ◄ ◄

Station(s)

I would recommend Seattle bands to flood the following stations with promos.

WMBR "Late Risers Club" 3 Ames St., Cambridge, MA 02142
WLYN 25 Exchange St., Lynn, MA 01903
WERS Emerson College, 130 Beacon St., Boston, MA 02116
WCOZ "Party Out Of Bounds" 441 Stuart St., Boston, MA 02116
WZBC Boston College Box K151, Newton, MA 02167
WMFO Tufts Univ., Box 65, Medford, MA 02153
WBRS Brandeis Univ., 415 South St., Waltham, MA 02154
WICN 75 Grove St., Worcester, MA 01605
WMWM Salem State College, 362 LaFayette St., Salem, MA 01970
WTBU Boston Univ., 30 Bay State Rd., Boston, MA 02215
WZLY Wellesley College, Wellesley, MA 02181
WHRB Harvard Radio, 45 Quincy St., Cambridge, MA 02138

SUB TEN National Hits

► **MINOR THREAT** *Out of Step* 12" EP. (Dischords) No doomsday nihilism here, just intimate, personal, powerful statements from this great American thrash band. (D.C.)
► **THE THREE O'CLOCK** *Baroque Hoedown* 12" EP. (Frontier) Pop surrealism. Vocalist Michael Quercio owns over 100 paisley shirts! "With A Cantaloupe Girlfriend" is classic. (L.A.)
► **100 FLOWERS** LP. (Happy Squid) Rock surrealism. "Presence Of Mind" is still the hit. Includes nude photo. (L.A.)
► **MINUTEMEN** *What Makes A Man Start Fires?* LP. (SST) Less jazzy, less atonal, less political. But they've still got style. (L.A.)
► **DUPLEX PLAYERS/INCREDIBLE CASUALS** *Picnic Ape* (DUB) 45. (Eat) Who needs Whitehouse or Cabaret

Voltaire when you can listen to members of the Duplex Nursing Home? (Boston)
► **TRECHEROUS 3** *Action* 12" single. (Sugarhill) Sensual, upbeat rap. Party, party, party. (NYC)
► **EMILY XYZ** *Who Shot Sadat?* 45. (Vinyl Repellant) Bang. Evocative, rapid-fire poetry with sheet metal percussion. Art school cool. (NYC)
► **WILD DOGS** *Wild Dogs* LP. (Shrapnel) Commercial yet headbangin' release from this country's top metal label. (Portland)
► **THE EMBARRASSMENT** *Dead Men Travel West* LP. (Fresh) They're from Wichita and they sing about Lewis and Clark. How much more American can you get?
► **THE START** *Look Around* LP. (Fresh) Honest, innocent pop gem from Kansas. Surprise guest appearance by Allen Ginsberg. (Lawrence)

By Bruce Pavitt

"Like the Blackouts, Ministry decided it was better to move to Boston than to stay in their home town, Chicago. Work on developing a local scene, and you won't have to feel the urge to move on."

should be releasing something soon. *Propeller Product* 4-song 7-inch compilation features the forgettable **WILD STARES**, **CCCP TV**, and **PEOPLE IN STORES**. However, the **NEATS'** "Six" is a modern, psychedelic masterpiece that sounds totally different from their equally excellent EP. **DANGEROUS BIRDS** "Alpha Romeo" b/w "Smile On Your Face" 45; the A-side is nothing special. The flip is a very tough girl-group anthem, complete with chain gang vocals and calves. Excellent.

X-CLAIM! (Lynn, MA) Boston's "hardcore" label, run by and for the bands. Initiated by scenemakers **S.S. DECONTROL**. Other releases include **F.U.'S** "Kill For Christ" 12" EP and an upcoming S.S. Decontrol 12-inch EP. Boston's most talked about thrash band, these guys ultimately don't stand out of the herd. They condemn conformity but are not original; they condemn violence but sing lines like "People who think we're pussies and afraid to fight/just come in our pit and feel our might." As an extra bonus, this band has also adopted **MINOR THREAT**'s anti-drug "straight edge" philosophy. Apparently, their new release has more dirge and metal influences.

PUBLICATIONS

Boston Rock (Boston, MA) Boston's uninspired answer to the sorely missed *New York Rocker*. *Take It!* (Brighton, MA) is a diverse new music mag; the most recent issue featured a flexi w/**THE FLESHEATERS**, **MEAT PUPPETS**, and **TEX AND THE HORSEHEADS**. *Forced Exposure* (Watertown, MA) is a highly recommended hardcore publication. Provocative national interviews; sharp, accessible layout. Bi-monthly. *Conflict* (Wayland, MA) Teenager Gerard Cosloy is one of the most interesting critics in the country. Get *Conflict*.

NEW BANDS

BLACKOUTS; **CHRISTMAS**; **BEANBAG**; **D.Y.S.**; **SORRY**; **CHILDREN OF PARADISE**; **IMPACT UNIT**

STORE

NEWBURY COMICS (Boston, MA) Boston's only alternative record store.

CLUBS

Although **SPIT**, **THE RAT**, and **STORYVILLE** all book bands that play original material, out-of-town bands are advised to check out the following: **MAVERICK'S** 112 Broad St., Boston. **THE CHANNEL** 25 Necco St., Boston.

STATIONS

I would recommend Seattle bands to flood the following stations with promos: **WMBR** "Late Risers Club" Cambridge, MA; **WLYN** Lynn, MA; **WERS** Boston, MA; **WCOZ** "Party out of Bounds" Boston, MA; **WZBC** Newton MA; **WMFO** Medford, MA; **WBRS** Waltham, MA; **WICN** Worcester, MA; **WMWM** Salem, MA; **WTBU** Boston, MA; **WZLY** Wellesley, MA; **WHRB** Cambridge, MA

SUB TEN

MINOR THREAT *Out of Step* 12" EP (Dischord) No doomsday nihilism here, just intimate, personal, powerful statements from this great American thrash band. (D. C.)

THE THREE O'CLOCK *Baroque Hoedown* 12" EP. (Frontier) Pop surrealism. Vocalist Michael Quercio owns over 100 paisley shirts! "With A Cantaloupe Girlfriend" is classic. (Los Angeles)

100 FLOWERS (Los Angeles) LP. (Happy Squid) Rock surrealism. "Presence Of Mind" is still the hit. Includes nude photo.

MINUTEMEN *What Makes A Man Start Fires?* LP. (SST) Less jazzy, less atonal, less political. But they've still got style. (Los Angeles)

DUPLEX PLAYERS/INCREDIBLE CASUALS *Picnic Ape* (DUB) 45. (Eat) Who needs **WHITEHOUSE** or **CABARET VOLTAIRE** when you can listen to members of the Duplex Nursing Home? (Boston)

TREACHEROUS THREE *Action* 12" single (Sugar Hill) Sensual, upbeat rap. Party, party, party. (New York)

EMILY XYZ *Who Shot Sadat?* 45. (Vinyl Repellant) Bang. Evocative, rapid-fire poetry with sheet metal percussion. Art school cool. (New York)

WILD DOGS *Wild Dogs* LP. (Shrapnel) Commercial yet head-bangin' release from this country's top metal label. (Portland, OR)

THE EMBARRASSMENT *Dead Men Travel West* LP. (Fresh) They're from Wichita and they sing about Lewis and Clark. How much more American can you get?

THE START *Look Around* LP. (Fresh) Honest, innocent pop gem from Kansas. Surprise guest appearance by Allen Ginsberg. (Lawrence, KS)

D.C. Seems to Have Everything

D.C.—great fucking scene. Maybe I'm losing it, but this place seems to have everything. Supportive media; a great all-ages club; record stores that couldn't give a fuck about **MEN AT WORK**; the list goes on and on. You want *art*? **1/2 JAPANESE** will change your life. Funk? The "go-go funk" sounds of **TROUBLE FUNK, MASS EXTINCTION**, and **EXPERIENCE UNLIMITED** will keep you jammin' without a break. Pop smash hits? **THE VELVET MONKEYS** and **UNDERHEAVEN**. Rockabilly? Scene veteran **BILLY HANCOCK** just toured France and showed 'em how to comb their hair. Ten-foot stage dives? Let **MINOR THREAT** turn up the volume. Wow. Find out more about Reagan's front lawn from the hefty fanzines listed below. And order these records.

LABELS/ARTISTS

DISCHORD (D.C.) The most consistently creative hardcore label in America. Surreal snippets of conversation, radical dub remixes—you can always expect a surprise or two from these guys. Earlier plastic includes the *Flex Your Head* compilation, **BRIGADE** and **GOVERNMENT ISSUE** EPs. On the **VOID/FAITH** split LP., the **FAITH** side is okay hardcore. **VOID** is one of the most intense records I've ever heard. Feedback, chaos—these people are held together by a thread. Ordering this record could be one of the most important decisions of your life. The **SCREAM** *Still Screaming* LP is thrash with occasional light funk and reggae references. More political than most D.C. bands. Songs include "U. Suck A.," "Solidarity," and "Your Wars." They also sing about girls. **MINOR THREAT** *Out of Step* 12-inch EP; honest, introspective, this release focuses on pride, honor, and friendship. It's also fast, loud and melodic. Get it.

D.E.T.T. RECORDS (Landover, MD) Standing for "Determination, Entertainment, Tolerance and Trust," D.E.T.T. is a great funk label. Started by **TROUBLE FUNK**, their catalogue includes dance records by **HOT, COLD, SWEAT**, and **TILT** (a techno-funk outfit that dresses up in Star Wars gear). They've also released a *Best of D.E.T.T.* cassette. Their **TROUBLE FUNK** *Let's Get Small* 12-inch single is one of the best records I've heard all year. This earthy, steamin' funk track features a harmonica hook that will stay with you for days. A ten-piece that pumps it out. "Live At The Paragon Too," should be out any day.

FOUNTAIN OF YOUTH (Bethesda, MD) This hardcore label has also released 7-inches with **ARTIFICIAL PEACE** and **EXILED**. The **GOVERNMENT ISSUE** *Boycott Staab* 9-song 12-inch offers radical mixing from producer Ian MacKaye. "Sheer Terror" is great experimental dub/hardcore. Very impressive record.

TOUCH AND GO (Maumee, Ohio) Covers Detroit and Ohio hardcore, plus D.C.'s **MEATMEN**. On the Meatmen's *We're the Meatmen and You Suck* LP, side one is a reissue of the *Blood Sausage* EP. Newer, live stuff on the flipside. Gnarly mix of humor and total decadence.

OUTSIDE RECORDS (Arlington, VA) the *Mixed Nuts Don't Crack* compilation LP is a diverse, abrasive collection including Chalk Circle, Social Suicide, Nuclear Crayons, and Hate From Ignorance.

WASP RECORDS (Arlington, VA) has released records by the **INSECT SURFERS**, **TRU FAX**, and the **INSANIACS**.

S›U›B/P›O›P

DC

Great fucking scene. Maybe I'm losing it, but this place seems to have everything. Supportive media, a great all ages club, record stores that could give a fuck about Men At Work, the list goes on and on. You want ART? ½ Japanese will change your life. Funk? The "Go-Go Funk" sounds of Trouble Funk, Mass Extinction and Experience Unlimited will keep you jammin' without a break. Pop smash hits? The Velvet Monkeys and Underheaven. Rockabilly? Scene veteran Billy Hancock just toured France and showed 'em how to comb their hair. 10 foot stage dives? Let Minor Threat turn up the volume. Wow. Find out more about Reagan's front lawn from the hefty fanzines listed below. And order these records.

Labels/Artists

►**DISCHORDS** (3819 Beecher St. NW, Washington, D.C. 20007) The most consistently creative hardcore label in America. Surreal snippets of conversation, radical dub remixes; you can always expect a surprise or two from these guys. Earlier plastic includes *The Flex Your Head Compilation, Brigade* and *Government Issue* 9-inch EPs. . . . **VOID/FAITH** LP. The Faith side is O.K. hardcore. Void is one of the most intense records I've ever heard. Feedback, chaos, these people are held together by a thread. Ordering this record could be one of the most important decisions of your life. . . . **SCREAM** *Still Screaming* LP. Thrash with occasional light funk and reggae references. More political than most D.C. bands. Songs include "U. Suck A.," "Solidarity," "Your Wars." They also sing about girls. . . . **MINOR THREAT** *Out of Step* 12-inch EP. Honest, introspective, this release focuses on pride, honor and friendship. It's also fast, loud and melodic. Get it.

►**D.E.T.T.** (3834 Ironwood Place, Landover, MD 20785) Standing for Determination, Entertainment, Tolerance and Trust, D.E.T.T. is a great funk label. Started by Trouble Funk, their catalogue includes dance records by **HOT, COLD, SWEAT** and **TILT** (a techno-funk outfit that dresses up in Star Wars gear). They've also released a *Best of D.E.T.T.* cassette. . . . **TROUBLE FUNK** *Let's Get Small* 12-inch single. One of the best records I've heard all year. This earthy, steamin' funk track features a harmonica hook that will stay with you for days. A ten-piece that pumps it out. "Live At The Paragon Too" should be out any day.

►**FOUNTAIN OF YOUTH** (5710 Durbin Rd., Bethesda, MD 20817) Hardcore label; have also released a 7-inch with *Artificial Peace* and *Exiled*. . . . **GOVERNMENT ISSUE** *Boycott Staab* 9-song 12-inch. Some radical mixing from producer Ian MacKaye. "Sheer Terror" is great experimental dub/hardcore. Very impressive record.

►**TOUCH AND GO** (Box 716, Maumee, Ohio 43537) Covers Detroit, Ohio hardcore plus D.C.'s Meatmen. . . . **THE MEATMEN** *We're the Meatmen and You Suck* LP. Side one is a reissue of the *Blood Sausage* EP. Newer, live stuff on the flipside. Gnarly mix of humor and total decadence.

►**OUTSIDE** (3111 1st St. N., Arlington, VA 22201) **MIXED NUTS DON'T CRACK** LP. Diverse, abrasive collection includes "Chalk Circle," "Social Suicide," "Nuclear Crayons," "Hate From Ignorance."

►**WASP** (821 N. Taylor St., Arlington, VA 22203) Have released records by the Insect Surfers, Tru Fax and the Insaniacs.

►**PRESS** (432 Moreland Ave. N.E., Atlanta, GA 30307) Affiliated with DB records. Have released the classic *Zombies of Mora-Tau* EP by Jad Fair plus Jad's new LP *Everyone Knew But Me* which I'm dying to hear. . . . **½ JAPANESE** *Horrible* 12-inch EP. Poignant, caustic stories of love and terror. "Walk Through Walls" is unreal.

Imports

The **SLICKEE BOYS** will be releasing a new LP on the German based LINE label. Rockabilly artist **BILLY HANCOCK** has just released an album on **BIG BEAT** records, a French label.

New Bands

BLOODY MANNEQUIN ORCHESTRA, NO TREND, MARGINAL MAN, (D.C.) MEATMEN, SPORT TURNED SPETACLE, FRENCH ARE FROM HELL, UNDERHEAVEN, WE ARE THEY THAT ACHE WITH AMOROUS LOVE.

Station(s)

WMUC-FM (Box 99, University of Maryland, College Park, MD 20742) Excellent college station. Minor Threat, Dangerous Birds, The Fall have recently received heavy airplay. . . . **WHFS-FM** (Attn: Music Director, 4853 Cordell, Bethesda, MD 20814) The country's last remaining no-format, progressive rock station. X, Joy Division, reggae, funk, local releases, etc. Will switch over to AM (WEAM 1390) this summer. Great commercial radio.

Stores

YESTERDAY AND TODAY RECORDS (1327 J Rockville Pike, Rockville, MD 20852) Affiliated with the Limp record label. **RTX** (821 N Taylor St., Arlington, VA 22203) Affiliated with the Wasp record label.

Clubs

9:30 (930 F St. N.W., The Atlantic Building, Washington, D.C. 202/393-0930) All ages. One of the best "new music" clubs in the country.

Sub/Pop U.S.A. Radio
►►EVERY TUESDAY 6-7 PM • KCMU 90.5 FM◄◄

Publications

TRULY NEEDY (Box 2271, Rockville, MD 20852) Diverse, open-minded. 60 pages. . . . **THRILLSEEKER** (12515 Brewster Lane, Bowie, MD 20715) Hardcore; open to other forms of music. . . . **TOUCH AND GO** (Box 32313, Washington, D.C. 20007) Hardcore mag edited by Meatmen vocalist Tescoe Vee. Chuckles, insults, etc. **WASHINGTON POST** (c/o Howard Wuelfing, 1912 S St. #6, Washington, D.C. 20009) Reviews independents.

Please send records and tapes to: SUB/POP U.S.A. c/o The Rocket 2322 Second Avenue / Seattle, WA 98121

National Hits

►**SHOCKABILLY** *The Dawn of Shockabilly* 12-inch EP (Rough Trade) Frenetic, staccato guitar, "cheap organ," tapes and percussion. Totally damaged rock 'n' roll covers from madman Eugene Chadbourne. (Greensboro, NC)

►**PYLON** *Chomp* LP (DB) Includes the "M-Train" and "Beep" 45s. Excellent disc from America's most unpretentious dance band. (Athens)

►**GRANDMASTER FLASH AND THE FURIOUS FIVE** *New York, New York* 12-inch single (Sugarhill) More urban realism from these masters of rap/commentary. But where's the "wheels of steel"? (NYC)

►**AFRICA BAMBAATA AND SOUL SONIC FORCE** *Looking for the Perfect Beat* 12-inch single (Tommy Boy) After months on the charts it still kicks. Techno-funk monster of the year. (NYC)

►**FIRST EDITION** *Candy Girl* 12-inch single (Streetwise) Young band with a sweet, soulful hit. Jackson 5 plus electronics. (NYC)

►**WHARF RAT** compilation LP (Wharf Rat) Good collection. Includes pop/psychedelic hits from the Rain Parade, 100 Flowers plus more. (L.A.)

►**BANGLES** 12-inch EP (Faulty) Girl group, formerly the Bangs. Fun, '60s revivalists. "Mary Street" sounds better than the Association.

►**FANG** *Land Shark!* 12-inch EP (Boner) Sleazy, powerful biker/hardcore crossover. Play loud, spray beer. (S.F.)

►**BOYS LIFE** 12-inch EP (SECO) Young boys dig the Jam, come up with a wailing pop classic. (Boston)

►**½ JAPANESE** *Horrible* 12-inch EP (Press) "There's a thing with a hook / tearing the heads off boyfriends / down on Lover's Lane." (Westminster, MD)

SUB TEN

Sub/Pop 9 Cassette

Box 85136, Seattle WA 98105) Includes smash pop hits from D.C. bands the Velvet Monkeys, Underheaven, Egoslavia, Sit! Boy, Girl, Boy, Girl. Plus disco, folk, Nursing Home Exploitation, bootlegged Swedish radio, Eastern Bloc hardcore, psychedelia etc., etc. $5.00 ppd. .

By Bruce Pavitt

Calvin Johnson spent time in D.C., networking with Dischord Records and the punk scene, and he came back with a Trouble Funk 12". That D.C. gogo music sounded like nothing I'd ever heard, and I started reviewing those. I wanted to hear and support anything being released independently on regional labels. It got to a point where there was no genre that I wouldn't review.

PRESS RECORDS (Atlanta, GA), affiliated with DB Records, has released the classic *Zombies of Mora-Tau* EP by **JAD FAIR** plus Jad's new LP *Everyone Knew But Me,* which I'm dying to hear. The **1/2 JAPANESE** *Horrible* 12-inch EP is poignant, caustic stories of love and terror. "Walk Through Walls" is unreal.

IMPORTS

The **SLICKEE BOYS** will be releasing a new LP on the Germany-based Line label. Rockabilly artist **BILLY HANCOCK** has just released an album on Big Beat records, a French label.

NEW BANDS

BLOODY MANNEQUIN ORCHESTRA; **NO TREND**; **MARGINAL MAN** (D.C.); **MEATMEN**; **SPORT TURNED SPECTACLE**; **FRENCH ARE FROM HELL**; **UNDERHEAVEN**; **WE ARE THEY THAT ACHE WITH AMOROUS LOVE**

STATION(S)

WMUC-FM (University of Maryland, College Park, MD) Excellent college station. **MINOR THREAT**, **DANGEROUS BIRDS**, **THE FALL** have recently received heavy airplay. **WHFS-FM** (Bethesda, MD) The country's last remaining no-format, progressive rock station. **X**, **JOY DIVISION**, reggae, funk, local releases, etc. Will switch over to AM (**WEAM** 1390) this summer. Great commercial radio.

STORES

YESTERDAY AND TODAY (Rockville, MD) Affiliated with the Limp record label. **RTX** (Arlington, VA) Affiliated with the Wasp record label.

CLUBS

9:30 CLUB (The Atlantic Building, Washington, D.C.) All ages. One of the best "new music" clubs in the country.

PUBLICATIONS

Truly Needy (Rockville, MD) Diverse, open-minded. 60 pages; *Thrillseeker* (Bowie, MD). Hardcore; open to other forms of music; *Touch and Go* (Washington, D.C.) Hardcore mag edited by **MEATMEN** vocalist Tesco Vee. Chuckles, insults, etc.; *Washington Post* (Washington, D.C.) Reviews independents.

SUB TEN

SHOCKABILLY *The Dawn of Shockabilly* 12-inch EP (Rough Trade) Frenetic, staccato guitar, "cheap organ," tapes and percussion. Totally damaged rock 'n roll covers from madman Eugene Chadbourne. (Greensboro, NC)

PYLON *Chomp* LP (DB) Includes the "M-Train" and "Beep" 45s. Excellent disc from America's most unpretentious dance band. (Athens, GA)

GRANDMASTER FLASH AND THE FURIOUS FIVE *New York, New York* 12-inch single (Sugar Hill) More urban realism from these masters of rap/commentary. But where's the"wheels of steel"? (NYC)

AFRIKA BAMBAATAA AND SOULSONIC FORCE *Looking for the Perfect Beat* 12-inch single (Tommy Boy) After months on the charts, it still kicks. Techno-funk monster of the year. (NYC)

FIRST EDITION *Candy Girl* 12-inch single (Streetwise) Young band with a sweet, soulful hit. **JACKSON 5** plus electronics. (NYC)

VARIOUS *Wharf Rat* compilation LP (Wharf Rat) Good collection. Includes pop/psychedelic hits from the **RAIN PARADE**, **100 FLOWERS** plus more. (L.A.)

BANGLES 12-inch EP (Faulty) Girl group, formerly the **BANGS**. Fun, '60s revivalists. "Mary Street" sounds better than the **ASSOCIATION**.

FANG *Land Shark* 12-inch EP (Boner) Sleazy, powerful biker/hardcore crossover. Play loud, spray beer. (SF)

BOYS LIFE 12-inch EP (SECO) Young boys dig the **JAM**, come up with a wailing pop classic. (Boston)

1/2 JAPANESE *Horrible* 12-inch EP (Press) "There's a thing with a hook /tearing the heads off boyfriends/ down on Lover's Lane." (Westminster, MD)

Fanzines Document U.S. Cult Bands

There are thousands of unusual, local artists in this country, expanding the concept of "pop" music. Ideas and trends come and go, evolve and splinter into more ideas, more change. How does one gain access to this elusive, "underground" information?

"Fanzines," publications put together with enthusiasm by fans, manage to document the most provocative local artists. Consequently, bands like the **MEAT PUPPETS** from Phoenix or **MR. EPP** from Seattle have developed cult followings in other cities. Through a network of independent distributors, noncommercial radio, and the aforementioned fanzines, avant-garde pop music is being heard and talked about in cities across the US and around the globe. All this without the visibility of major label record contracts. For people truly interested in the future of popular culture, these local, independent artists and publications can't be ignored.

Local and regional record labels took off primarily in the rural south, during the late '40s and early '50s. "Race" and "hillbilly" artists enjoyed popular support in some regions, receiving heavy airplay and local hero status, while remaining unheard of in other parts of the States. The integration of these two sounds, R&B and country, developed into the rock 'n roll mania that would eventually give youth a vote in a world dominated by adults.

As the world turned and the '60s became the '70s, a handful of large, multinational corporations—Warner Bros., CBS, RCA, MCA, EMI, Polydor—bought out local indies and exchanged creative decision-making for profiteering. A backlash formed: the punk/new wave rebellion of '76–'78. While most of these artists (**SEX PISTOLS**, **TALKING HEADS**) worked within the corporate mega-structure, their political posturing and/or arty rhetoric somehow forced a number of the world's youth to take charge of their own culture. Of course, small labels had never completely died out, but when the punk explosion hit, everything was up for grabs; hundreds of independent labels started happening. Unfortunately, because the US is so big, it's taken a few years for American labels to get off the ground. A tiny rock in the ocean called England has been kicking our ass for too long now, with a very organized independent music scene, supportive of unusual local talent. The key to a healthy culture is communication, and with a country the size of England, the flow of information has been rapid.

Not so with the United States. That's why the exchange and proliferation of printed media has been so important to the development of a growing grass-roots new music scene. With popular music in a corporate chokehold (witness MTV, *Solid Gold*, *Rolling Stone*, and 90 percent of the airwaves), the battle in the United States. has been uphill. College and community radio has been a blessing for those lucky enough to live within broadcasting range, but for the hipster in Arkansas who digs **PYLON**, **MINOR THREAT**, and the **MINUTEMEN**, well, fanzines are just about his/her only way of keeping up with the constantly changing local scenes across the country.

New pop music in America, however, is just as vital now, in 1983, as any other time in American history. As for the future, public access-able television and home computers will help in both preserving local

S›U›B/P›O›P

There are thousands of unusual, local artists in this country expanding the concept of "pop" music. Ideas and trends come and go, evolve and splinter into more ideas, more change. How does one gain access to this elusive, "underground" information? ► "Fanzines," publications put together with enthusiasm by fans, manage to document the most provocative local artists. Consequently, bands like the *Meat Puppets* from Phoenix or *Mr.*

Fanzines Document U.S. Cult Bands

Epp from Seattle, have developed cult followings in other cities. Through a network of independent distributors, non-commercial radio and the aforementioned fanzines, avant-garde pop music is being heard, talked about and debated in cities

across the U.S. and around the globe. All this without the visibility of a major label record contract. For people truly interested in the future of popular culture, these local, independent artists and publications can't be ignored. ► Local and regional record labels took off, primarily in the rural south, during the late '40s and early '50s. "Race" and "hillbilly" artists enjoyed popular support in some regions, receiving heavy airplay and local hero status, while remaining unheard of in other parts of the States. The integration of these two sounds, R&B and country, developed into the rock 'n' roll mania that would eventually give youth a vote in a world dominated by adults. ► As the world turned and the '60s became the '70s, a handful of large, multi-national corporations — Warner Bros., CBS, RCA, MCA, EMI, Polydor — bought out local indies and exchanged creative decision-making for profiteering. A backlash formed: the punk/new wave rebellion of '76-'78. While most of these artists (Sex Pistols, Talking Heads) worked within the corporate mega-structure, their political posturing and/or arty rhetoric somehow forced a number of the world's youth to take charge of their own culture. Of course small labels had never completely died out, but when the punk explosion hit, everything was up for grabs; hundreds of independent labels started happening. ► Unfortunately, because the U.S. is so big, it's taken a few years for American labels to get off the ground. A tiny rock in the ocean called England has been kicking our ass for too long now, with a very organized independent music scene, supportive of unusual, local talent. The key to a healthy culture is communication, and with a country the size of England, the flow of information has been rapid. Not so with the U.S. ► That's why the exchange and proliferation of printed media has been so important to the development of a growing grass roots new music scene. With popular music in a corporate chokehold (witness: MTV, *Solid Gold*, *Rolling Stone*, and 90 percent of the airwaves), the battle in the U.S. has been uphill. College and community radio has been a blessing for those lucky enough to live within broadcasting range, but for the hipster in Arkansas who digs *Pylon*, *Minor Threat*, and the *Minutemen*, well, fanzines are just about his/her only way of keeping up with the constantly changing local scenes across the country. ► New pop music in American however, is just as vital now, in 1983, as any other time in American history. As for the future, public access cable television and home computers will help in both preserving local culture and exchanging new ideas to other cultures. The network is growing.

> "New pop music in America, however, is just as vital now, in 1983, as any other time in American history. As for the future, public access-able television and home computers will help in both preserving local culture and exchanging new ideas to other cultures. The network is growing."

► **ALTERNATIVE AMERICA** (Blake Gumprecht, 814 ½ Massachusetts, Lawrence, KS 66044 $1.00) The only fanzine of its kind, *Alternative American* contains nothing but interviews with American bands. Their premier issue features a very stimulating group of artists who defy easy catagorization: *Mission of Burma* (Boston), *Gun Club* (L.A.), *Wipers* (Portland), *Rank and File* (Austin), *Martin Rev* (N.Y.) *R.E.M.* (Athens), *Husker Du* (Minneapolis), *the Embarrassment* (Wichita) plus more. These interviews were originally broadcast on KJHK in Lawrence, KS. Very well done.
► **OP** (John Foster, Lost Music Network, P.O. Box 2391, Olympia, WA 98507. $8.00/yr.) The best available resource for independent music. Small labels from around the world. Reggae, electronic, punk, jazz, bluegrass; no boundaries here. Each issue focuses on a different letter of the alphabet, featuring artists, labels and styles whose names begin with that letter. The "R" issue features rap, reggae, the *Raincoats* and *Jonathan Richman*. It also contains the usual awesome collection of current record reviews. They're already working on the "S" issue, and by "Z" they say it'll be all over. Subscribe while it lasts.
► **INDEPENDENT AMERICA** (Independent Label Project, 415 Layfayette St., NY, NY 10003. $1.00) More of a catalogue than a fanzine or magazine, this "guide to independent record releases" is a tremendous resource. Their first issue is a coalition of 18 different independent labels, covering new rock to avant-garde "New Music." Each label is given one to two pages to give a discography, talk about their releases and occasionally comment on the state of the industry. Highly recommended to both record collectors and to small labels trying to achieve more visibility.
► **MAXIMUM ROCK 'N' ROLL** (P.O. Box 288, Berkeley, CA 94701. $1.00) By far the most "political" of the hardcore-punk fanzines. Each issue includes extensive scene reports from around the country, as well as record reviews. Tim Yohannon, Jeff Bale and other involved with this organization put out a weekly, syndicated radio show; they've also released a double LP compilation of bands from the Bay area and Reno. *MRNR* is definitely a unifying force.
► **FORCED EXPOSURE** (Jimmy Johnson, 76 Bromfield St., Watertown, PA 02172. $1.50)

Excellent Boston hardcore 'zine. Well laid out, discriminating record reviews. One of the best resources available for hardcore-punk interviews. Issue #5 featured the *Effigies* (Chicago), *Misfits* (NY), *D.O.A.* (Vancouver) plus more.
► **FLIPSIDE** (Box 363, Whittier, CA 90608. $1.50) L.A.'s Flipside documents the best of the most vital rock scene in the country. Read: the unending aggro of *Black Flag* and *CH3*; the uncompromising dexterity of the *Minutemen*; the pop revivalism of the *3 O'clock*, and the *Bangles*; it's all there. Interviews with touring out of town bands, record reviews, comics. Get it.

THE MINUTEMEN

► **THE ATTACK!** (Jeff Smith, 1623 104th Ave SE, Bellevue, WA 98004. $1.00) The only "hardcore" fanzine in the country that will review harmolodic funk and the improvisational avant-garde, as well as loud, fast protest music.
► **THRILLSEEKER** and **TRULY NEEDY** (Steve Kiviat, 12515 Brewster Lane, Bowie, MD 20715. $1.50 / Barbaraanne Rice, P.O. Box 2271, Rockville, MD 20852. $1.00) Two outstanding fanzines from D.C. Both are very extensive (60 pages each). *Truly Needy* reviews more imports and *Thrillseeker* covers more hardcore, but they're both more open-minded than 90 percent of the competition. Read about great local bands like *Minor Threat*, *Trouble Funk*, *½ Japanese*, the *Velvet Monkeys* and lots more.
► **THE OFFENSE NEWSLETTER** (T.K.A., Box 12614, Columbus, OH 43212. $.50) *The Offense* has been around for some time. Now a weekly newsletter, it still remains one of the best tip sheets available for

modern rock and pop imports. Noteworthy American bands are also featured, as well as an infamous letters section.

Sub/Pop U.S.A.
►► Radio ◄◄
EVERY TUESDAY 6-7 PM • KCMU 90.5 FM

► **TESTUBE** (Box 8421, Columbus, OH 43201. $1.00) *Testube*, a distributor of independent publications and music, puts out an interesting catalogue/fanzine. Aside from reviewing their stock, they discuss independent culture in the context of home telecommunications. Thus, we get to read about art and video, music and computers. Their April issue included a fascinating article called "Fanzine Futures: Computer Bulletin Boards as Fanzines." Lots of obscure, relevant information here.
► **VOLUME** (One Ten Records/Volume, 110 Chambers St./NY, NY 10007. $12.95) Mammoth directory of "new wave" small labels, alternative clubs, radio stations, publications, etc. Due to the ever-changing nature of small business, however, some of this information is no longer valid. Good resource for rare, international contacts.
► **RE/SEARCH #6/7 (Industrial Culture Handbook)** (20 Romolo #B, San Francisco, CA 94133. $9.00) *Re/Search* has maintained a level of quality and integrity ever since it's original inception as *Search and Destroy* magazine. This handsome, softbound book is a special report of "industrial" noisemakers and performance artists. Interviews with conceptual heavyweights *SPK*, *Throbbing Gristle*, *Cabaret Voltaire*; plus local, Bay Area philosophers *Z'ev*, *Boyd Rice*, *Mark Pauline*, *Monte Cazazza* and *Johanna Went*. Morbid, intellectual commentary on dreams, explosives, sex art, sound poetry, organic robots, tape experiments, defacing billboards, zip guns, the Statue of Liberty, mass hypnotism. Absolutely essential reading for anyone interested in the darker side of noise and music. ■

Please send records and tapes to:
SUB/POP U.S.A. c/o The Rocket
2322 Second Avenue / Seattle, WA 98121

Sub/Pop 9 Cassette

21 groups from 14 countries plus cover by Charles Burns. Includes Velvet Monkeys, Underheaven, Egoslavia, Limp Richerds, Supershaft and more smash pop hits, disco, folk, Eastern Bloc hardcore and psychedelia. $5.00 ppd. from Box 85136, Seattle, WA 98105. ■

By Bruce Pavitt

culture and exchanging new ideas to other cultures. The network is growing.

Alternative American (Blake Gumprecht, Lawrence, KS, $1.00) The only fanzine of its kind, *Alternative American* contains nothing but interviews with American bands. Their premier issue features a very stimulating group of artists who defy easy cataqorization: **MISSION OF BURMA** (Boston), **GUN CLUB** (L.A.), **WIPERS** (Portland, OR), **RANK AND FILE** (Austin, TX), **MARTIN REV** (NY), **R.E.M.** (Athens, GA), **HÜSKER DÜ** (Minneapolis), the **EMBARRASSMENT** (Wichita, KS) plus more. These interviews were originally broadcast on KJHK in Lawrence, KS. Very well done.

OP (John Foster, Lost Music Network, Olympia, WA, $8.00/year) The best available resource for independent music. Small labels from around the world. Reggae, electronic, punk, jazz, bluegrass; no boundaries here. Each issue focuses on a different letter of the alphabet, featuring artists, labels, and styles whose names begin with that letter. The "R" issue features rap, reggae, the **RAIN-COATS**, and **JONATHAN RICHMAN**. It also contains the usual awesome collection of current record reviews. They're already working on the "S" issue, and by "Z" they say it'll be all over. Subscribe while it lasts.

Independent America (Independent Label Project, NYC, $1.00) More of a catalogue than a fanzine or magazine, this "guide to independent record releases" is a tremendous resource. Their first issue is a coalition of 18 different independent labels, covering new rock to avant-garde "new music." Each label is given one to two pages to give a discography, talk about their releases and occasionally comment on the state of the industry. Highly recommended to both record collectors and to small labels trying to achieve more visibility.

Maximum Rocknroll (Berkeley, CA, $1.00) By far the most "political" of the hardcore punk fanzines. Each issue includes extensive scene reports from around the country, as well as record reviews. Tim Yohannon, Jeff Bale, and others involved with this organization put out a weekly, syndicated radio show; they've also released a double LP compilation of bands from the Bay Area and Reno, NV. *MRR* is definitely a unifying force.

Forced Exposure (Jimmy Johnson, Watertown, MA, $1.50) Excellent Boston hardcore zine. Well laid out, discriminating record reviews. One of the best resources available for hardcore punk interviews. Issue #5 featured the **EFFIGIES** (Chicago), **MISFITS** (NY), **D.O.A.** (Vancouver) plus more.

Flipside (Whittier, CA. $1.50) L.A. 's *Flipside* documents the best of the most vital rock scene in the country. Read: the unending

aggro of **BLACK FLAG** and **CH3**; the uncompromising dexterity of the **MINUTEMEN**; the pop revivalism of the **3 O'CLOCK**, and the **BANGLES**; it's all there. Interviews with touring out-of-town bands, record reviews, comics. Get it.

The Attack! (Jeff Smith, Bellevue, WA, $1.00) The only "hardcore" fanzine in the country that will review harmolodic funk and the improvisational avant garde, as well as loud, fast protest music.

Thrillseeker and *Truly Needy* (Steve Kiviat, Bowie, MD, $1.50/Barbaraanne Rice, Rockville, MD, $1.00) Two outstanding fanzines from D.C. Both are very extensive at 60 pages each. *Truly Needy* reviews more imports and *Thrillseeker* covers more hardcore, but they're both more open-minded than 90 percent of the competition. Read about great local bands like **MINOR THREAT**, **TROUBLE FUNK**, **1/2 JAPANESE**, the **VELVET MONKEYS** and lots more.

The Offense Newsletter (T.K.A., Columbus, OH. $.50) *The Offense* has been around for some time. Now a weekly newsletter, it still remains one of the best tip sheets available for modern rock and pop imports. Noteworthy American bands are also featured, as well as an infamous letters section.

Testube (Columbus, OH. $1.00) *Testube*, a distributor of independent publications and music, puts out an interesting catalogue/fanzine. Aside from reviewing their stock, they discuss independent culture in the context of home telecommunications. Thus, we get to read about art and video, music, and computers. Their April issue included a fascinating article called "Fanzine Futures: Computer Bulletin Boards as Fanzines." Lots of obscure, relevant information here.

Volume (One Ten Records/Volume, NY, $12.95) Mammoth directory of new wave small labels, alternative clubs, radio stations, publications, etc. Due to the ever-changing nature of small business, however, some of this information is no longer valid. Good resource for rare, international contacts.

Re/Search #6/7: Industrial Culture Handbook (SF, CA. $9.00) *Re/Search* has maintained a level of quality and integrity ever since its original inception as *Search and Destroy* magazine. This handsome, softbound book is a special report of "industrial" noisemakers and performance artists. Interviews with conceptual heavyweights **SPK**, **THROBBING GRISTLE**, **CABARET VOLTAIRE**; plus local Bay Area philosophers **Z'EV**, **BOYD RICE**, **MARK PAULINE**, **MONTE CAZAZZA**, and **JOHANNA WENT**. Morbid, intellectual commentary on dreams, explosives, sex art, sound poetry, organic robots, tape experiments, defacing billboards, zip guns, the Statue of Liberty, and mass hypnotism. Absolutely essential reading for anyone interested in the darker side of noise and music.

West Coast Secedes From Nation

What the hell, let's talk about West Coast independents. Listed below are five pick hits for August '83, plus an interview with Joe Carducci. Joe originally worked with Systematic Record Distributors in Berkeley, and now helps manage L.A. hardcore band **BLACK FLAG**. He's also part of the brain trust at SST Records, one of the strongest independent rock labels on the West Coast.

BLACK FLAG: BEYOND THE MOHAWK

*How did the **BLACK FLAG**/**MINUTEMEN** European tour go?*

Joe: The audiences, in general, are really conservative over there. A lot more leather jackets. People were yelling at **BLACK FLAG**, calling 'em hippies. They played two shows in London, eight in Germany; they played in Austria, Geneva, Milan, Amsterdam. It seems like everyone watches what their friends do, and if their friends are not into it then neither are they; it inhibits the whole audience response.

That almost sounds like L.A.

I don't think so anymore. L.A.'s really fragmented at this point. There's a lot of different little scenes, and when **BLACK FLAG** plays, there aren't a lot of people who are identifiably new wave or punk.

So, Joe, is psychedelia the new big thing in L.A.?

Bands get tied together and they get marketed. Places like Wong's or the Roxy won't book the **MINUTEMEN** or the **CIRCLE JERKS**, but they will book things like the **RAIN PARADE**. It's irritating, because they're just retreads in most cases. The **DREAM SYNDICATE** has gotten somewhere, and so they've

fostered other bands. There's a real safe little scene developing. **GREEN ON RED** is real good, but they date back a long time, they're a real thing. I don't know that these other bands are real at all.

What are some future projects for SST Records?

New **MEAT PUPPETS** album (Phoenix); **MINUTEMEN** 12"; **HÜSKER DÜ** 12" (Minneapolis); and an album by the **STAINS. SACCHARINE TRUST** is about to start recording. There's also an **OVERKILL** album and a **ST. VITUS** album.

Overkill is kind of a metal/hardcore crossover?

Yeah. A lot of it is very fast, so they're more into the **MOTÖRHEAD** thing. Most of the **ST. VITUS** stuff is slower, more along the lines of early **BLACK SABBATH**. Real heavy metal. Real heavy.

What do you think of the San Francisco scene compared to L.A.?

It's more nebulous down here in L.A., and not as political. It's just as small-minded, I guess, but San Francisco, of course, is really colored by the politics of *Maximum Rocknroll* (fanzine/radio show). There's talk of boycotting the Eastern Front (a hardcore punk, etc., festival) because it's being booked by SST.

Why is there this animosity towards SST?

Well, people were phoning in to *Maximum Rocknroll* and complaining that we were ignoring San Francisco talent, which goes back to what I was saying. If people are in a band and they're not really playing music, they're just being "in the scene." I think **ANGST** is the best band in San Francisco right now.

CLEAR LIGHT SYSTEMS
CONCERT STAGE LIGHTING
RENTALS & SALES

Ask our satisfied customers:
Elvin Bishop, Queensryche, Shock, Rail, Kashmir
and Chuck Berry.

SEATTLE • 608 19th E • CAPITOL HILL • 322-88??

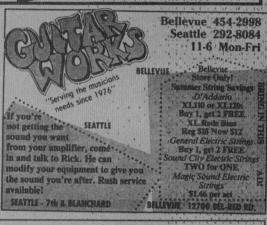

GUITAR WORKS

Bellevue 454-2998
Seattle 292-8084
11-6 Mon-Fri

"Serving the musicians
needs since 1976"

BELLEVUE

If you're
not getting the
sound you want
from your amplifier, come
in and talk to Rick. He can
modify your equipment to give you
the sound you're after. Rush service
available!

SEATTLE

SEATTLE - 7th & BLANCHARD

BRING IN THIS AD!

Bellevue
Store Only!
Summer String Savings
D'Addario
XL110 or XL120:
Buy 1, get 2 FREE.
XL Reds Blue
Reg $18 Now $12
General Electric Strings
Buy 1, get 2 FREE
Sound City Electric Strings
TWO for ONE
Magic Sound Electric
Strings
$1.66 per set

BELLEVUE 12700 BEL-RED RD.

MORNINGTOWN

4110 ROOSEVELT WY NE ; ORDER TO GO
632-6317

LATER.

OPEN AT 7:00 FOR PASTRY, CREPES, AND ESPRESSO
PIZZA, SUBS, SALADS, ETC. FROM 11:30 TO MIDNIGHT.

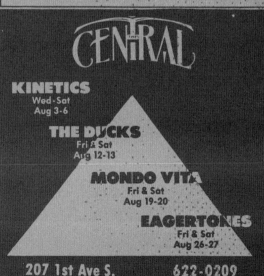

CENTRAL

KINETICS
Wed - Sat
Aug 3-6

THE DUCKS
Fri & Sat
Aug 12-13

MONDO VITA
Fri & Sat
Aug 19-20

EAGERTONES
Fri & Sat
Aug 26-27

207 1st Ave S.   622-0209

S›U›B / P›O›P

West Coast Secedes From Nation

What the hell, let's talk about West Coast independents. Listed below are five pick hits for August '83, plus an interview with Joe Carducci. Joe originally worked with Systematic Record Distributors in Berkeley and now helps manage L.A. ''hardcore'' band Black Flag. He's also part of the brain-trust at SST Records, one of the strongest independent rock labels on the West Coast.

Black Flag: Beyond the Mohawk

GLEN E. FRIEDMAN

How did the Black Flag/Minutemen European tour go?

Joe: The audiences, in general, are really conservative over there. A lot more leather jackets. People were yelling at Black Flag, calling 'em hippies. They played two shows in London, eight in Germany; they played in Austria, Geneva, Milan, Amsterdam. . . . It seems like everyone watches what their friends do and if their friends are not into it then neither are they; it inhibits the whole audience response.

That almost sounds like L.A.

I don't think so anymore. L.A.'s really fragmented at this point. There's a lot of different little scenes, and when Black Flag plays, there aren't a lot of people who are identifiably new wave or punk.

So Joe, is psychedelia the new big thing in L.A.?

Bands get tied together and they get marketed. Places like Wong's or the Roxy won't book the Minutemen or the Circle Jerks but they will book things like the Rain Parade. It's irritating because they're just retreads in most cases. The Dream Syndicate has gotten somewhere and so they've fostered other bands. There's a real safe little scene developing. Green on Red is real good, but they date back a long time; they're a real thing. I don't know that these other bands are real at all.

What are some future projects for SST records?

New Meat Puppets album (Phoenix), Minutemen 12'', Husker Du 12'' (Minneapolis), and an album by the Stains. Saccharine Trust is about to start recording. There's also an Overkill album and a St. Vitus album.

Overkill is kind of a metal/hardcore cross-over?

Yeah. A lot of it is very fast so they're more into the Motorhead thing. Most of the St. Vitus stuff is slower, more along the lines of early Black Sabbath. Real heavy metal. Real heavy.

What do you think of the San Francisco scene compared to L.A.?

It's more nebulous down here in L.A. and not as political. It's just as small minded I guess but San Francisco, of course, is really colored by the politics of Maximum Rock 'N' Roll (fanzine/radio show). There's talk of boycotting the Eastern Front (hardcore-punk, etc. festival) because it's being booked by SST.

Why is there this animosity towards SST?

Well, people were phoning in to Maximum Rock 'N' Roll and complaining that we were ignoring San Francisco talent, which goes back to what I was saying, there isn't any. . . . If people are in a band they're not really playing music, they're just being ''in the scene.'' . . . I think Angst is the best band in San Francisco right now.

Does anybody ever talk about the Northwest down there?

People talk about bands that they know, like D.O.A. and the Fartz, the Wipers. The Fartz are thought of highly in the Frisco scene because of the anarchy thing.

Do any of the kids in L.A. listen to funk or black music?

That's more in line with the arty Hollywood scene. There's people in L.A. trying to do the New York thing. . . . There was a funk club, one of the members of the Screamers was a DJ. They had a lot of problems with it because it started out as all white Hollywood people and then black people came. I don't know what New York's like, but Los Angeles is a real segregated city.

- Black Flag will be in Seattle at the Eagles Nest, 710 Union, on Sunday, Aug. 7 at 8 p.m. Appearing with them will be the mighty Meat Puppets from Phoenix, and locals Ellis Dee (a.k.a. 10 Minute Warning). SST Records can be contacted at P.O. Box 1, Lawndale, CA 90260.

Sub / Pop U.S.A.
› Radio ‹
EVERY TUESDAY 6-7 PM KCMU 90.5 FM

Please send records and tapes to:
SUB/POP U.S.A. c/o The Rocket
2322 Second Avenue / Seattle, WA 98121

LOS ANGELES

THE FLESHEATERS: A Hard Road to Follow, LP. (Upsetter Records, Box 48 1144, L.A., CA 90048) Rarely does a vocalist creep under your skin like Chris D. Yecchh. He's got character I guess, straining for the right note, then smothering it, the microphone halfway down his throat. But wait, **A Hard Road to Follow**, the Flesheaters' 4th LP, reaffirms that Chris D. is the most evocative rock lyricist on the West Coast, possibly the U.S.A. Romance and pain, a creepy world. Rusty nails, tattered dresses and beds of cold concrete. Wow. Read it.

SAN FRANCISCO

PELL MELL: The Bumper Crop, 5-song 12'' (Sixth Street International, c/o Rough Trade, 326 Sixth Street, San Francisco, CA 94103) Round hole, square peg. Instrumentalists Pell Mell remain the most original band on the West Coast. Yes folks, that's right — trying to package these guys as the latest blah-blah whatever is fucking impossible. The minimal, hypno-surf sound of their first record is over with. Now it's bass, drums and guitar plus new addition, Steve Fisk on synthesizer. It's a busier sound; rich, ornate and rational as hell. Like **Duane Eddy** and **A Certain Ratio**, whom they've cited as influences, Pell Mell is in love with tone and atmosphere; modern mood music. Good for at least 50 listens!

SACRAMENTO

REBEL TRUTH: 9-song 7'' (Version Sound Independent Communications, P.O. Box 429, Yellow Springs, OH 45387. $2.00) Hardcore/thrash. Some bands want to drink beer and show off their new mohawk, others, like Rebel Truth, are more concerned with protest and social change. Rebel Truth definitely RISE ABOVE. They attack war and middle class values, not with cheap slogans, but with incisive criticism and intelligence. They are strict vegetarians and are committed to ''honor, honesty and compassion.'' This band plays very tight thrash with effective chant/chorus counterpart. Their music is physical, sincere, and, just possibly, more important than a new skateboard or a studded wrist band.

PORTLAND

WIPERS: Over The Edge LP. (Trap Records, Box 42465, Portland, OR 97242) This record is great. This record makes me cry. The Wipers are God. There is so much beauty, so much soul and so much power in this recording that I cannot recommend it enough. No quirky trends or gimmicks here — just three people who believe in what they're doing. No, it's not scratch-dub-hardcore, it's TOTAL CLASSIC ROCK. Frustration, loneliness, alienation, rebellion. Conviction. A few psychedelic flourishes held over from their last LP, **Youth of America**; subtle use of feedback; tremolo bar. Greg Sage's guitar playing, like his voice, is stylish, powerful yet understated. A simple glance across the room and the house caves in. The Wipers are the best Northwest rock band since the Sonics and ''Over the Edge'' is a total American classic.

VANCOUVER

CULTURE SHOCK: Forever and Ever/Thought You Were a Friend, 45 (c/o Brian Maitland, 4204 Boxer St., Burnaby, B.C. V5J 2V9 Canada. $2.00.) Unassuming yet ''utterly charming'' garage-pop 45. Warm, sincere, CATCHY. They dig the Buzzcocks and it shows. It's a drag that 45s like this one are going out of style, they're so fun, and who needs LP filler anyway? ''Thought You Were a Friend'' is pure pop.

By Bruce Pavitt

Does anybody ever talk about the Northwest down there?

People talk about bands that they know, like **D.O.A.** and the **FARTZ**, the **WIPERS**. The Fartz are thought of highly in the Frisco scene because of the anarchy thing.

Do any of the kids in L.A. listen to funk or black music?

That's more in line with the arty Hollywood scene. There's people in L.A. trying to do the New York thing. There was a funk club, one of the members of the **SCREAMERS** was a DJ. They had a lot of problems with it, because it started out as all-white Hollywood people, and then black people came. I don't know what New York's like, but Los Angeles is a real segregated city.

BLACK FLAG *will be in Seattle at the Eagles Nest, 710 Union, on Sunday, Aug. 7, at 8 p.m. Appearing with them will be the mighty* **MEAT PUPPETS** *from Phoenix, and locals* **ELLIS DEE** *(a.k.a.* **10 MINUTE WARNING***).*

LOS ANGELES

THE FLESHEATERS *A Hard Road to Follow* LP. (Upsetter Records: L.A.) Rarely does a vocalist creep under your skin like Chris D. Yecch. He's got character, I guess, straining for the right note, then smothering it, the microphone halfway down his throat. But wait; *A Hard Road to Follow*, **THE FLESHEATERS'** 4th LP, reaffirms that Chris D. is the most evocative rock lyricist on the West Coast, possibly the USA Romance and pain, a creepy world. Rusty nails, tattered dresses and beds of cold concrete. Wow. Read it.

SAN FRANCISCO

PELL MELL *The Bumper Crop* 5-song 12" (Sixth Street International, c/o Rough Trade: San Francisco) Round hole, square peg. Instrumentalists **PELL MELL** remain the most original band on the West Coast. Yes folks, that's right—trying to package these guys as the latest blah-blah whatever is fucking impossible. The minimal, hypno-surf sound of their first record is over with. Now its bass, drums, and guitar, plus new addition Steve Fisk on synthesizer. It's a busier sound; rich, ornate, and rational as hell. Like **DUANE EDDY** and **A CERTAIN RATIO**, whom they've cited as influences, **PELL MELL** is in love with tone and atmosphere; modern mood music. Good for at least 50 listens!

SACRAMENTO

REBEL TRUTH 9-song 7" (Version Sound Independent Communications, Yellow Springs, OH) Hardcore/thrash. Some bands want to drink beer and show off their new mohawk, others, like Rebel Truth, are more concerned with protest and social change. Rebel Truth definitely rise above. They attack war and middle class values, not with cheap slogans, but with incisive criticism and intelligence. They are strict vegetarians, and are committed to "honor, honesty, and compassion." This band plays very tight thrash with effective chant/chorus counterpart. Their music is physical, sincere, and, just possibly, more important than a new skateboard or a studded wrist band.

PORTLAND

THE WIPERS *Over the Edge* LP. (Trap Records, Portland, OR) This record is great. This record makes me cry. The Wipers are God. There is so much beauty, so much soul, and so much power in this recording that I cannot recommend it enough. No quirky trends or gimmicks here—just three people who believe in what they're doing. No, it's not scratch-dub-hardcore, it's *total classic rock*. Frustration, loneliness, alienation, rebellion. Conviction. A few psychedelic flourishes held over from their last LP, *Youth of America*; subtle use of feedback, tremolo bar. Greg Sage's guitar playing, like his voice, is stylish, powerful yet understated. A simple glance across the room and the house caves in. The Wipers are the best Northwest rock band since the **SONICS**, and *Over the Edge* is a total American classic.

VANCOUVER

CULTURE SHOCK "Forever and Ever" b/w "Thought You Were a Friend" single (c/o Brian Maitland, Burnaby, B.C.) Unassuming yet "utterly charming" garage-pop 45. Warm, sincere, *catchy*. They dig the **BUZZCOCKS** and it shows. It's a drag that 45s like this one are going out of style; they're so fun, and who needs LP filler anyway? "Thought You Were a Friend" is pure pop.

All the Trends You Can Eat

No matter how trendy things get, there will always be the outcasts, the uncool dorks who will continue to pursue their own bent visions. As always, the trends are strong, the sheep are fat—but some folks just can't squeeze into the right uniform. Below are nine artists who refuse to bend over.

DAVID THOMAS *Variations On A Theme* LP (Sixth International) David Thomas is eccentric. His vocals flutter and stretch, refusing to remain in captivity. Formerly with **PERE UBU**, David Thomas continues the introspective style of Ubu's last few LPs. The spontaneous clouds of noise, the physical drive, and the tense, spooky atmosphere of Pere Ubu's earlier material is not present, unfortunately. But let's not dwell on the past. The musicianship here is clever, self-indulgent, and boring, featuring the talents of Anton Fier, Richard Thompson, Lindsay Cooper, and Chris Cutler. In short, this is "progressive" rock. This LP features Mr. Thomas as a mumbling fuddy-duddy, about as exciting as my ninth grade biology professor. Nature is a popular subject, one song even being called "A Day at the Botanical Gardens." How exciting. At its best, this record is arty yet accessible, interesting. A great museum piece, it definitely belongs behind glass.

JAD FAIR *Everyone Knew... But Me* LP (Press) Visionaries and nonconformists will always meet frowns and "what is this shit?" every time they turn a corner. Needless to say, Jad Fair isn't for everybody. After I played "Amy" and "Walking with Cindy" on KCMU, somebody actually phoned in and asked, in all sincerity, "Hey, that guy from D.C., is he retarded?" Jad Fair is a member of **1/2 JAPANESE**. This, his second record, contains 29 songs about love and monsters.

Some are electronic, some are acoustic. Jad's songs are always awkward, always sincere, sometimes to the point of total embarrassment. Jad works in a daycare center and occasionally performs at the Duplex Nursing Home. You can't dance to this record.

SONIC YOUTH *Confusion is Sex* (Neutral) LP An extremely dark post-**VELVETS** trip. A black candle in a black room, this clanging, intense, moody statement starts to penetrate your consciousness around 3 a.m. "...the memory drained/the life from a doll/an ocean of insects/worked like a sheet/the immovable fact/buried my mind/in a horsehair coat/in a pile on the floor." Bonus track includes a live, burning vision of **IGGY**'s "I Wanna Be Your Dog," recorded live in Raleigh, North Carolina. Other cuts include "Shaking Hell," "Freezer Burn," and "Making the Nature Scene." Total ghetto beatnik city.

SHOCKABILLY *Earth vs. Shockabilly* LP (Rough Trade) **EUGENE CHADBOURNE** is a total nut. Live, Shockabilly is the wackiest cartoon around. Sporting an elastic face and a Perma Press paisley business suit, Eugene spits out spazz freeform guitar solos on top of '60s classics like "Are You Experienced" and "People Are Strange." Tapes, organs, drums. The rest of Shockabilly sport facial hair and dress appropriately. Unfortunately, there's no way this madness could ever be translated to vinyl. So see them at the Metropolis on 9/25 or at the Rainbow 9/30-10/1.

BAD BRAINS *Rock For Light* LP (PVC) A few years back these bad boys broke in on the underground rock scene with their thrash and burn classic "Pay to Cum." Then, in midstep, they turned Rastafarian, splitting their set into a mix of hardcore punk and dub reggae.

Half Japanese was a huge favorite during my time at KAOS-FM in Olympia. I was very interested in the surreal thinking of young children as an influence for punk art, and Jad Fair was channeling his inner three-year-old. He displayed a unique form of genius; he could create a musical backdrop and then improvise a storyline on top of that. He was an inspired amateur to the *max*. The punk underground was just a network of inspired amateurs, and he was more inspired than most.

S›U›B/P›O›P

All the Trends You Can Eat

No matter how trendy things get, there will always be the outcasts, the uncool dorks who will continue to pursue their own bent visions. As always, the trends are strong, the sheep are fat but some folks just can't squeeze into the right uniform. Below are nine artists who refuse to bend over.

● **DAVID THOMAS** Variations On A Theme (Sixth International) LP ★ David Thomas is eccentric. His vocals flutter and stretch, refusing to remain in captivity. Formerly with Pere Ubu, David Thomas continues the introspective style of Ubu's last few LPs. The spontaneous clouds of noise, the physical drive and the tense, spooky atmosphere of Pere Ubu's earlier material is not present, unfortunately. But let's not dwell on the past. The musicianship here is clever, self-indulgent and boring, featuring the talents of Anton Fier, Richard Thompson, Lindsay Cooper and Chris Cutler. In short, "progressive" rock. This LP features Mr. Thomas as a mumbling fuddy-duddy, about as exciting as my ninth grade biology professor. Nature is a popular subject, one song even being called "A Day at the Botanical Gardens." How exciting. At its best, this record is arty yet accessible, interesting. A great museum piece, it definitely belongs behind glass.

● **JAD FAIR** Everyone Knew . . . But Me (Press) LP ★ Visionaries and nonconformists will always meet frowns and "What is this shit?" every time they turn a corner. Needless to say, Jad Fair isn't for everybody. After I played "Amy" and "Walking with Cindy" on KCMU, somebody actually phoned in and asked, in all sincerity, "Hey, that guy from D.C., is he retarded?!" Jad Fair is a member of ½ Japanese. This, his second record, contains 29 songs about love and monsters. Some are electronic, some are acoustic. Jad's songs are always awkward, always sincere, sometimes to the point of total embarrassment. Jad works in a daycare center and occasionally performs at the Duplex Nursing Home. You can't dance to this record.

● **SONIC YOUTH** Confusion is Sex (Neutral) LP ★ An extremely dark post-Velvets TRIP. A black candle in a black room, this clanging, intense, moody statement starts to penetrate your consciousness around 3 a.m. ". . . the memory drained/the life from a doll/an ocean of insects/worked like a sheet/in the immovable fact/buried my mind/in a horsehair coat/in a pile/on the floor." Bonus track includes a live, burning vision of Iggy's "I Wanna Be Your Dog," recorded live in Raleigh, North Carolina. Other cuts include "Shaking Hell," "Freezer Burn," and "Making the Nature Scene." Total ghetto beatnik city.

● **SHOCKABILLY** Earth vs. Shockabilly (Rough Trade) LP ★ Eugene Chadbourne is a total nut. Live, Shockabilly is the wackiest cartoon around. Sporting an elastic face and a perma-press paisley business suit, Eugene spits out spazz free-form guitar solos on top of '60s classics like "Are You Experienced" and "People Are Strange." Tapes, organ, drums. The rest of Shockabilly sport facial hair and dress appropriately. Unfortunately there's no way this madness could ever be translated to vinyl. So see them at the Metropolis on 9/25 or at the Rainbow 9/30-10/1.

● **BAD BRAINS** Rock For Light (PVC) LP ★ A few years back these bad boys broke in on the underground rock scene with their thrash 'n' burn classic *Pay to Cum*. Then, in midstep, they turned Rastafarian, splitting their set into a mix of hardcore punk and dub reggae. This LP shows no surprises — expect to hear the usual squeals of vocalist H. R. plus radical changes in tempo as we go from tumbling stage dives to lazy puffs on *ganja*. "I and I Survive," "Destroy Babylon," and "Right Brigade" may already be familiar to some readers as these prophets have toured a lot. The only band of its kind, the Bad Brains have alienated people because of their unusual mixing of styles and their self-righteous attitude, the most infamous example being the "blood-clot faggots" rap they laid on the Big Boys down in Texas. Speaking of which. . . .

● **BIG BOYS** Lullabies Help the Brain Grow (Moment) LP ★ Hey, these big white boys from Texas do it. A weird, punchy mix of thrash and funk. Raspy, shredded vocals and the occasional horn section put these guys out in left field. Songs like "Gator Fuckin'," "White Nigger" and "Baby Let's Play God" obviously define some sort of contemporary Texas lifestyle. The real hit though is "We Got Your Money," a fun, fun party song about ripping off "frat boys." This record is an unusual, brash, urban mix of skateboards and ghetto blasters. FUN!

● **JANDEK** Six and Six (Corwood) LP ★ Mr. Jandek is an obscure neurotic, content to play guitar in his bedroom on a cassette deck and pump out album after album. **Six and Six**, his second release, came out in 1981 and I'm still trying to figure it out. Featuring an out of tune guitar and a lonely man possessed with a vision, Jandek remains an uncommercial artist, a man without a market. Ironically, you can only purchase this record in units of 25, for a mere fifty bucks! A sample of his genius: "the tree gave up its fruit at once/Ahh my hand burns/the scars of a prince/they will leave when I die/it is a fact/the blood will drain/infection will mix/ with a blue corpse." Bob Dylan or Charlie Manson? The real high point on this disc is when the microphone falls over on "Delinquent Words." Believe me, it's worth the fifty bucks.

● **REPLACEMENTS** Hootenanny (Twin Tone) LP ★ Homegrown garage rock 'n' roll "mostly recorded . . . at a warehouse in some godawful suburb north of Mpls." Although these guys have energy and a raw sound, they're pretty much laughed at by all the new recruits in big black boots. It's not thrash, but it is unpretentious and they seem to have a lot of fun. Aside from the chaotic, bluesy riffing that predominate their sound these guys experiment with dub echo on "Willpower" and come up with a radical folk thing called "Treatment Bound." If the Replacements had really followed through with their folknik "Hootenanny" hype, they would have come up with more gems like this last one.

● **HI SHERIFFS OF BLUE** (Jimboco) 12-inch single ★ Mark Dagley used to perform with the Girls, one of the weirdest new wave bands of the late '70s. Mr. Dagley has since moved from Boston to N.Y., starting the HSOB, a group that originally emphasized "hardcore R&B." The band's latest 12-inch on Jimboco digs even deeper into the American psyche and comes up with a C&W classic called "War Between the States" as well as a brutal blues number called "19-80 NOW!" The various instruments on this release include 12-string guitar, harmonica, steel guitar and "sax-o-bone." An interesting, eclectic release. Oh yeah, Dagley is also a Rastafarian.

Jandek: Obscure neurotic.

► **BAD BRAINS:** PVC c/o Jem Records, South Plainfield, NJ 07080
► **BIG BOYS:** Moment, Box 12424, Austin, TX 78711
► **SONIC YOUTH:** Neutral, 325 Spring St., N.Y., N.Y. 10013. 10013
► **HIGH SHERIFFS OF BLUE:** Jimboco Records, Box 203 Ansonia Station, N.Y., N.Y. 10023
► **JAD FAIR:** Press Records, 432 Moreland Ave. NE, Atlanta, GA 30307
► **JANDEK:** Corwood Industries, Box 15375, Houston, TX 77020. Mail order, 25 count box: $50.
► **REPLACEMENTS:** Twin Tone, 445 Oliver Ave. S., Minneapolis, MN 55405
► **SHOCKABILLY:** Rough Trade U.K., c/o Rough Trade, 326 Sixth St., San Francisco, CA 94103
► **DAVID THOMAS AND THE PEDESTRIANS:** Sixth International Records/ Rough Trade, 326 Sixth St., San Francisco, CA 94103

Please send records and tapes to:
SUB/POP U.S.A. c/o The Rocket
2322 Second Avenue / Seattle, WA 98121

Sub/Pop U.S.A.
► ► Radio ◄ ◄
EVERY TUESDAY 6-7 PM • KCMU 90.5 FM

By Bruce Pavitt

This LP shows no surprises—expect to hear the usual squeals of vocalist H. R. plus radical changes in tempo as we go from tumbling stage dives to lazy puffs on ganja. "I and I Survive," "Destroy Babylon," and "Right Brigade" may already be familiar to some readers as these prophets have toured a lot. The only band of its kind, the Bad Brains have alienated people because of their unusual mixing of styles and their self-righteous attitude; the most infamous example being the "blood-clot faggots" rap they laid on the **BIG BOYS** down in Texas. Speaking of which....

BIG BOYS *Lullabies Help the Brain Grow* LP (Moment) Hey, these big white boys from Texas do it. A weird, punchy mix of thrash and funk. Raspy, shredded vocals and the occasional horn section put these guys out in left field. Songs like "Gator Fuckin'," "White Nigger," and "Baby Let's Play God" obviously define some sort of contemporary Texas lifestyle. The real hit though is "We Got Your Money," a fun, fun party song about ripping off frat boys. This record is an unusual, brash, urban mix of skateboards and ghetto blasters. FUN!

JANDEK *Six and Six* LP (Corwood) Mr. Jandek is an obscure neurotic, content to play guitar in his bed-room on a cassette deck and pump out album after album. *Six and Six*, his second release, came out in 1981 and I'm still trying to figure it out. Featuring an out-of-tune guitar and a lonely man possessed with a vision, Jandek remains an uncommercial artist, a man without a market. Ironically, you can only purchase this record in units of 25, for a mere fifty bucks! A sample of his genius: "the tree gave up its fruit at once/Ahh my hand burns/the scars of a prince/they will leave when I die/it is a fact/the blood will drain/infection will mix/with a blue corpse." **BOB DYLAN** or **CHARLIE MANSON**? The real high point on this disc is when the microphone falls over on "Delinquent Words." Believe me, it's worth the fifty bucks.

REPLACEMENTS *Hootenanny* LP (Twin Tone, Minneapolis, MN) Homegrown garage rock 'n roll "mostly recorded... at a warehouse in some godawful suburb north of Mpls." Although these guys have energy and

a raw sound, they're pretty much laughed at by all the new recruits in big black boots. It's not thrash, but it is unpretentious and they seem to have a lot of fun. Aside from the chaotic, bluesy riffing that dominates their sound, these guys experiment with dub echo on "Willpower" and come up with a radical folk thing called "Treatment Bound." If the **REPLACEMENTS** had really followed through with their folknik *Hootenanny* hype, they would have come up with more gems like this last one.

HI SHERIFFS OF BLUE 12-inch single (Jimboco, NYC) Mark Dagley used to perform with the **GIRLS**, one of the weirdest new wave bands of the late '70s. Mr. Dagley has since moved from Boston to N. Y., starting the HSOB, a group that originally emphasized "hardcore R&B." The band's latest 12-inch on Jimboco digs even deeper into the American psyche, and comes up with a C&W classic called "War Between the States," as well as a brutal blues number called "19-80 NOW!" The various instruments on this release include 12-string guitar, harmonica, steel guitar, and "sax-o-bone" An interesting, eclectic release. Oh yeah, Dagley is also a Rastafarian.

NYC: Black/Funk/Rap

SURPRISE. Up to 20 percent of all top-selling black singles are on small, independently-run record labels. Compare that to zero-to-one percent for *Billboard*'s Pop 100. It's no joke that black radio and dance clubs are offering some of the most innovative sounds in town. Expect the latest in synthesizer and computer tech, "scratching" (turntables as instruments), and break mixing (mixing different discs, emphasizing the most exciting breaks while maintaining a seamless beat). Producers, of course, are the new gods, mixing and remixing, turning knobs and offering dub, a cappella, vocoder versions, and more. Below I've listed some of the, most exciting black/funk/rap labels currently releasing records.

SUGAR HILL (Englewood, NJ) New York's most widely distributed rap/funk label. At lease two of their releases have changed history: the harsh urban rap of *The Message* by **GRANDMASTER FLASH AND THE FURIOUS FIVE**, and the surreal scratch/mix masterpiece *Adventures on the Wheels of Steel*, a solo effort by Grandmaster Flash. My major complaint with this label is that there's just too much filler. If you want powerful funk, be sure to avoid lame acts like **JOCKO** and the **MOMENTS**. The only consistent bets on Sugar Hill are G. Flash and the Furious Five and the marvelous **TREACHEROUS THREE**, whose "Action" 12-inch is Sugar Hill's strongest release in 1983. (It should also be mentioned that Sugar Hill is doing everyone a favor with their Chess Records blues/R&B reissue series!)

TOMMY BOY (NYC) Run by Tom Silverman, the man who publishes *Dance Music Report*, Tommy Boy has been the leader in futuristic techno-funk. Using modern computer and synth technology, house producers Arthur Baker and John Robie are mapping out the dance-floor avant garde. Their first hit, **AFRIKA BAMBAATAA AND SOULSONIC FORCE**'s "Planet Rock" (inspired by the German electronics of **KRAFTWERK**'s "Trans-Europe Express") was a huge hit and opened the door for more electronic innovation in "urban/contemporary" music. The high point of this sound is "Looking for the Perfect Beat," a brilliant, polyrhythmic *tour de force* released this year by Soulsonic Force. Of course, some of this gadgetry can sound cold and calculated, my main gripe with gimmicky outfits like the popular **JONZUN CREW**. Real soul will always endure, which is why **PLANET PATROL**, featuring five-part Tempt-style harmonies will undoubtedly sound great 10 years from now; check out their first monster, "Play At Your Own Risk," as well as "Cheap Thrills," their latest .

STREETWISE (NYC) Arthur Baker, demi-god producer from Tommy Boy, decided to start his own label, so now we have Streetwise. Their biggest seller has been **FIRST EDITION**, some Boston kids ("**JACKSON FIVE** of the '80s") whose "Candy Girl" single went straight to # 1 on the black charts. Other notable releases have been "Walking on Sunshine" by **ROCKERS REVENGE** and the amazing "I.O.U." by **FREEZE**. Using an E-mu Emulator, house keyboard whiz John Robie performs a solo featuring pre-recorded syllables: "A, E, I, O, U, Y." Digitally manipulated into several octaves, these six basic sounds become an entire choir; a great example of the new technology. Also of interest is the "Confusion" 12-inch, just released by Britain's hip white supergroup **NEW ORDER**. Baker and Robie, like Leiber and Stoller, are classic examples of savvy young white producers work-

S>U>B/P>O>P

Surprise. Up to 20 percent of all top-selling black singles are on small, independently-run record labels. Compare that to 0-1 percent for *Billboard*'s Pop

NYC: Black/Funk/Rap

100. It's no joke that black radio and dance clubs are offering some of the most innovative sounds in town. Expect the latest in synthesizer and computer tech, "scratching" (turntables as instruments) and break mixing (mixing different discs, emphasizing the most exciting breaks while maintaining a seamless beat). Producers, of course, are the new gods, mixing and remixing, turning knobs and offering dub, a cappella, vocoder versions and more. Below I've listed some of the most exciting black/funk/rap labels currently releasing records.

"Surprise! Up to 20 percent of all top-selling black singles are on small, independently-run record labels. Compare that to 0-1 percent for Billboard's Pop 100. It's no joke that black radio and dance clubs are offering some of the most innovative sounds in town. Expect the latest in synthesizer and computer tech, 'scratching' and break mixing."

Grandmaster Flash (2nd from left) and Three of the Five.

► **SUGARHILL** (96 West St., Englewood, N.J. 07631) New York's most widely distributed rap/funk label. At lease two of their releases have changed history: the harsh urban rap of "The Message" by **Grandmaster Flash and the Furious Five**, and the surreal scratch/mix masterpiece "Adventures on the Wheels of Steel," a solo effort by Grandmaster Flash. My major complaint with this label is that there's just too much filler. If you want powerful funk, be sure to

avoid lame acts like **Jocko** and **The Moments**. The only consistent bets on Sugarhill are G. Flash and the Furious Five and the marvelous **Treacherous Three**, whose "Action" 12-inch is Sugarhill's strongest release in 1983. (It should also be mentioned that Sugarhill is doing everyone a favor with their Chess blues/R&B reissue series!)

► **TOMMY BOY** (223 E. 85th St., N.Y.C. 10028) Run by Tom Silverman, the man who publishes *Dance Music Report*, Tommy Boy has been the leader in futuristic techno-funk. Using

modern computer and synth technology, house producers Arthur Baker and John Robie are mapping out the dance floor *avant-garde*. Their first hit, **Afrika Bambaataa and Soul Sonic Force**'s "Planet Rock" (inspired by the German electronics of Kraftwerk's "Trans-Europe Express") was a huge hit and opened the door for more electronic innovation in "urban/contemporary" music. The high point of this sound is "Looking For the Perfect Beat," a brilliant, polyrhythmic tour de force released this year by Soul Sonic Force. Of course, some of this gadgetry can sound cold and calculated, my main gripe with gimmicky outfits like the popular **Jon-zun Crew**. Real soul will always endure, which is why **Planet Patrol**, featuring five-part Tempt-style harmonies will undoubtedly sound great 10 years from now; check out their first monster, "Play At Your Own Risk" as well as "Cheap Thrills," their latest.

► **STREETWISE** (25 W. 43rd St., Suite 1202, N.Y.C. 10036) Arthur Baker, demi-god producer from Tommy Boy, decided to start his own label, so now we have Streetwise. Their biggest seller has been **First Edition**, some Boston kids ("Jackson Five of the '80s") whose "Candy Girl" single went straight to #1 on the black charts. Other notable releases have been "Walking on Sunshine" by **Rockers Revenge** and the amazing "I.O.U." by **Freeze**. Using an EMu Emulator, house keyboard whiz John Robie performs a solo featuring pre-recorded syllables: A, E, I, O, U, Y. Digitally manipulated into several octaves, these six basic sounds become an entire choir; a great example of the new technology. Also of interest is the "Confusion" 12-inch, just released by Britain's hip white supergroup **New Order**. Baker and Robie, like Leiber and Stoller, are classic examples of savvy young white

producers working with streetwise black performers. Look for more hits from this diverse label.

► **ENJOY** (611 W. 125th St., N.Y.C. 10027) A groundbreaking rap label. This is where **Grandmaster Flash and the Furious Five, Funky Four + 1, The Fearless 4** and **Disco 4** all made their start. At one time a leader in the rap market, Enjoy has slowed down its releases and has had little luck with distribution outside of N.Y. Their last big hit, "Rockin' It" by the Fearless 4, received critical attention but failed to make its way out West. However, a great compilation of early Enjoy singles is available in Seattle as an import, *Enjoy* on New York Connexion records.

► **PRELUDE** (200 W. 57th St., N.Y.C. 10019) Basically a disco label, Prelude features more female artists than the average; check out disco queens like **Sharon Redd** and **Jeanette "Lady" Day**. Their big act, though, is **D-Train**. Gospel/soul singer James Williams and former jazz pianist Hubert Eaves create soulful pop like "You're The One For Me" and "Keep On." Frankly, these guys would sound better if they stripped down the production and simply unleashed the awesome Mr. Williams. D-Train's dub tracks come closest to real power, especially on "Keep On."

► **PROFILE** (250 W. 57th St., N.Y.C. 10107) **Run D.M.C.** is God. "It's Like That" boomed from every blaster in town, an anthem for '83. Rappers Run and D.M.C. came up with *the* hit of the summer, a lean 'n' mean rap that challenged "The Message" as docu-drama of the decade. More urban realism. Profile is a very strong New York label; **Disco 4, Dr. Jeckyl and Mr. Hyde** and even **The Rake** of! stand as heavyweights. Profile has the beat. ■

RECOMMENDED INDIES ON THE BILLBOARD BLACK SINGLES CHART (FOR WEEK ENDING 10/1/83)

New Edition Is This The End? (Streetwise) #13
Freeeze I.O.U. (Streetwise) #15
Newcleus Jam On Revenge (Sunnyview) #26
Planet Patrol Cheap Thrills (Tommy Boy) #30
West Street Mob Break Dance–Electric Boogie (Sugarhill) #48
Sugarhill Gang Kick It Live From 9 to 5 (Sugarhill) #50
Run–D.M.C. It's Like That (Profile) #99

A FEW OBSCURE HITS
Time Zone Wildstyle (Celluloid)
Spyder-D Smerphies Dance (Telestar Cassettes)
Crash Crew On The Radio (Bay City)
Love Bug Starski You've Gotta Believe (Fever)

Please send records and tapes to:
SUB/POP U.S.A. c/o The Rocket
2322 Second Avenue / Seattle, WA 98121

Sub/Pop U.S.A.
► Radio ◄
EVERY TUESDAY 6-7 PM • KCMU 90.5 FM

By Bruce Pavitt

ing with streetwise black performers. Look for more hits from this diverse label.

ENJOY (NYC) A groundbreaking rap label. This is where **GRANDMASTER FLASH AND THE FURIOUS FIVE, FUNKY FOUR + 1, THE FEARLESS 4**, and **DISCO 4** all made their start. At one time a leader in the rap market, Enjoy has slowed down its releases and has had little luck with distribution outside of New York. Their last big hit, "Rockin' It," by the Fearless 4, received critical attention but failed to make its way out West. However, a great compilation of early Enjoy singles is available in Seattle as an import, *Enjoy!*, on New York Connexion records.

PRELUDE (NYC) Basically a disco label, Prelude features more female artists than the average; check out disco queens like **SHARON REDD** and **JEANETTE "LADY" DAY**. Their big act, though, is **D-TRAIN**. Gospel/soul singer James Williams and former jazz pianist Hubert Eaves create soulful pop like "You're The One For Me" and "Keep On." Frankly, these guys would sound better if they stripped down the production and simply unleashed the awesome Mr. Williams. D-Train's dub tracks come closest to real power, especially on "Keep On."

PROFILE RECORDS (NYC) **RUN-D.M.C.** is God. "It's Like That" boomed from every blaster in town, an anthem for '83. Rappers Run and D.M.C. came up with the hit of the summer, a lean and mean rap that challenged "The Message" as docudrama of the decade. More urban realism. Profile is a very strong New York label; **DISCO 4, DR. JECKYL AND MR. HYDE**, and even **THE RAKE** all stand as heavyweights. Profile has the beat.

RECOMMENDED INDIES ON THE BILLBOARD BLACK SINGLES CHART (FOR WEEK ENDING IN 10/1/83)

NEW EDITION "Is This The End?" (Streetwise) #10

FREEZE "I.O.U." (Streetwise) #15

NEWCLEUS "Jam On Revenge" (Sunnyview) #26

PLANET CONTROL "Cheap Thrills" (Tommy Boy) #30

WEST STREET MOB "Break Dance - Electric Boogie" (Sugar Hill) #48

SUGAR HILL GANG "Kick it Live From 9 to 5" (Sugar Hill) #50

RUN-D.M.C. "It's Like That" (Profile) #99

A FEW OBSCURE HITS

TIME ZONE "The Wildstyle" (Celluolid)

SPYDER-D "Smerphies Dance" (Telestar Cassettes)

CRASH CREW "On the Radio" (Bay City)

LOVE BUG STARSKI "You've Gotta Believe" (Fever)

Ten Records

GOLDEN PALOMINOS LP (O.A.C./Celluloid). If you've been bored with noisy, pretentious "art," try the Golden Palominos. Their debut LP is a free-for-all, guts-and-rhythm blast; a dynamic, articulate effort by some of the most gifted musicians in the new-noise New York underground. The transient personnel here include Fred Frith, Arto Lindsay, Anton Fier, Bill Laswel, Jamaaladeen Tacuma, John Zorn, David Moss, and more. A landmark, the Palominos mix funk, scratch, John Cage, and the kitchen sink into the most invigorating album of the year. Eat or be eaten.

THE SMITHEREENS *Beauty and Sadness* 5-song 12" (Little Ricky). Northern New Jersey has been ground zero for the best contemporary pop in America; **THE FEELIES, INDIVIDUALS, BONGOS.** The Smithereens aren't quite in that league—they lack spirited melodies and unusual conceptual hooks—but they're still a healthy, wholesome outfit that steals convincingly from R&B and the British Invasion. Produced by Alan Betrock, this EP includes a bonus instrumental mix of the title cut.

NEATS LP (Ace of Hearts). One of Boston's best continues the classic American sound they established on their first EP. Hints of the **BYRDS, CREEDENCE,** and **R.E.M.** surface from the electrified folk chords and tough, soulful wailings of Eric Martin. Timeless and transcendent, this record should receive heavy college airplay.

BLACK MARKET BABY *Senseless Offerings* LP (Fountain of Youth). As entertainment, Black Market Baby kicks ass. Anthems filled with punch and power. Green Beret chanting completes the muscle of this surprisingly forceful record. Unfortunately, these guys are reactionary, sexist pigs. "Strike First" and "Gunpoint Affection" are violent and degrading without a trace of irony. I'm not sure which is better—stupid, powerful music like this, or lame "politically correct" rantings (like the latest dud from **MDC**). You decide.

NO TREND 3-song 7" (No Trend). A big bomb in your brain, this visionary piece of plastic is so far out that it automatically goes to the head of the class. "Teen Love" is a lecture with feedback; it includes big words and will force you to think. "Mass Sterilization Caused by Venereal Disease" is composed of one sentence, repeated, repeated, repeated, with mass use of mass dub echo. Fringe hardcore for the intellectually impoverished, No Trend should inspire fans of **FLIPPER** and **MR. EPP.**

SLICKEE BOYS "When I Go To The Beach"/ "Invisible People" 45 (Dacoit/Twin Tone). This unfashionable hippie/wave pop band has released a series of local hits in the D.C. area. (A collection of these singles is available as a German import on Line Records.) The Slickee Boys mix surf, psychedelia, and other fun artifacts from the '60s with great success. This 45 is a double A-side.

SAFETY LAST *Struck By Love* LP (Twin Tone). Rockabilly occasionally laced with sweet country harmonies. Stylish guitar playing, male/female vocals. Production consists of light, airy reverb all over the place. Cross-generational appeal.

JEFF WARYAN *Figures* LP (Twin Tone). Commercially-produced singer/songwriter. Possibly the next **MARSHALL CRENSHAW** or **BRUCE SPRINGSTEEN.** A strong mainstream release from this increasingly middle-of-the-road Minneapolis label.

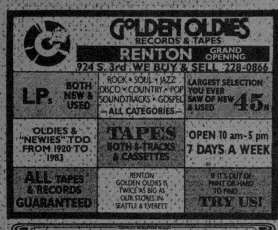

GOLDEN OLDIES
RECORDS & TAPES
RENTON GRAND OPENING
924 S. 3rd WE BUY & SELL 228-0866

LPs	BOTH NEW & USED	ROCK • SOUL • JAZZ DISCO • COUNTRY • POP SOUNDTRACKS • GOSPEL — ALL CATEGORIES —	LARGEST SELECTION YOU EVER SAW OF NEW & USED 45s
OLDIES & "NEWIES" TOO FROM 1920 TO 1983		TAPES BOTH 8-TRACKS & CASSETTES	OPEN 10 am-5 pm 7 DAYS A WEEK
ALL TAPES & RECORDS GUARANTEED		RENTON GOLDEN OLDIES IS TWICE AS BIG AS OUR STORES IN SEATTLE & EVERETT	IF IT'S OUT OF PRINT OR HARD TO FIND... TRY US!

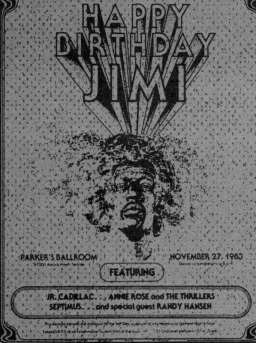

HAPPY BIRTHDAY JIMI

PARKER'S BALLROOM   NOVEMBER 27, 1983

FEATURING

JR. CADILLAC... ANNIE ROSE and THE THRILLERS
SEPTIMUS... and special guest RANDY HANSEN

JR. CADILLAC

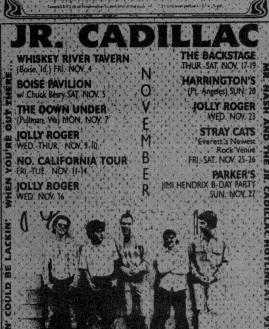

NOTHIN' COULD BE LACKIN' WHEN YOU'RE OUT THERE...

MR. NASH AND THE JR. CADILLAC HOTLINE AT... 937-4325

NOVEMBER

WHISKEY RIVER TAVERN
(Boise, Id.) FRI. NOV. 4

BOISE PAVILION
w/ Chuck Berry SAT. NOV. 5

THE DOWN UNDER
(Pullman, Wa) MON. NOV. 7

JOLLY ROGER
WED.-THUR. NOV. 9,10

NO. CALIFORNIA TOUR
FRI.-TUE. NOV. 11-14

JOLLY ROGER
WED. NOV. 16

THE BACKSTAGE
THUR.-SAT. NOV. 17-19

HARRINGTON'S
(Pt. Angeles) SUN. 20

JOLLY ROGER
WED. NOV. 23

STRAY CATS
Everett's Newest Rock Venue
FRI.-SAT. NOV. 25-26

PARKER'S
JIMI HENDRIX B-DAY PARTY
SUN. NOV. 27

P.O. BOX 16305 SEATTLE, WA. 98116

S>U>B/P>O>P

► **GOLDEN PALOMINOS** LP (O.A.C./ Celluloid). If you've been bored with noisy, pretentious "art," try the **Golden Palominos**. Their debut LP is a free-for-all guts and rhythm blast; a dynamic, articulate effort between some of the most gifted musicians in the new-noise N.Y. underground. The transient personnel here includes **Fred Frith, Arto Lindsay, Anton Fier, Bill Laswell, Jamaaladen Tacuma, John Zorn, David Moss** and more. A landmark, the Palominos mix funk, scratch, John Cage and the kitchen sink into the most invigorating album of the year. Eat or be eaten.

► **THE SMITHEREENS** *Beauty and Sadness* 5-song 12" (Little Ricky). Northern New Jersey has been ground zero for the best contemporary pop in America: the **Feelies, Individuals, Bongos**. The **Smithereens** aren't quite in that league—they lack spirited melodies and unusual conceptual hooks—but they're still a healthy, wholesome outfit that steals convincingly from R&B and British Invasion. Produced by Alan Betrock, this EP includes a bonus instrumental mix of the title cut.

► **NEATS** LP (Ace of Hearts). One of Boston's best continues the classic American sound they established on their first EP. Hints of the **Byrds, Creedence** and **R.E.M.** surface from the electrified folk chords and tough, soulful wailings of Eric Martin. Timeless, transcendent, this record should receive heavy college airplay. (The Neats will be at the Metropolis on 11/18.)

► **BLACK MARKET BABY** *Senseless Offerings* LP (Fountain of Youth). As entertainment, **Black Market Baby** kicks ass. Anthems filled with punch and power. Green Beret chanting completes the muscle of this surprisingly forceful record. Unfortunately, these guys are reactionary, sexist pigs. "Strike First" and "Gunpoint Affection" are violent and degrading without a trace of irony. I'm not sure which is better, stupid, powerful music like this or lame, "politically correct" rantings (like the latest dud from **MDC**). You decide.

► **NO TREND** 3-song 7" (No Trend). A big bomb in your brain, this visionary piece of plastic is so far out that it automatically goes to the

Sub/Pop U.S.A.
► Radio ◄
EVERY TUESDAY 6-7 PM • KCMU 90.5 FM

head of the class. "Teen Love" is a lecture with feedback; it includes big words and will force you to think. "Mass Sterilization Caused By Veneral Disease" is composed of one sentence, repeated, repeated, repeated with mass use of mass dub echo. Fringe hardcore for the intellectually impoverished, **No Trend** should inspire fans of **Flipper** and **Mr. Epp**.

► **SLICKEE BOYS** *When I Go To The Beach/Invisible People* 45. (Dacoit/ Twin Tone). Unfashionable hippie/ wave pop band that has released a series of local hits in the D.C. area. (A collection of these singles is available as a German import on Line records.) The **Slickee Boys** mix surf, psychedelia and other fun artifacts from the '60s with great success. This 45 is a double A-side.

► **SAFETY LAST** *Struck By Love* LP (Twin Tone). Rockabilly occasionally laced with sweet country harmonies. Stylish guitar playing, male/female vocals. Production consists of light, airy reverb all over the place. Cross-generational appeal.

► **JEFF WARYAN** *Figures* LP (Twin Tone). Commercially produced singer/songwriter. Possibly the next Marshall Crenshaw or Bruce Springsteen. A strong mainstream release from this increasingly middle-of-the-road Minneapolis label.

► **THE SLEEPING DOGS** *Beware* 5-song 7" (Crass). **The Sleeping Dogs** are the first American band to be signed to London's "anarchist" **Crass** record label. The sound here is experimental, a little weird, and consequently uneven, not unlike Seattle's **Audio Letter**. Heavy

Ten Records

words, propaganda confront war, affluence, prejudice, torture and shopping malls. The fold-out cover includes newspaper clippings on Central America. If the Sleeping Dogs are occasionally excessive, they are also provocative and worth investigating.

► **ANGST** 7-song 12" (Happy Squid). A California collaboration between S.F. and L.A., this is a major West Coast release. Because **Angst** is a rock 'n' roll band that doesn't fit the "hardcore" straightjacket,

Angst: major West Coast release.

they've had trouble developing a strong following in San Francisco. Maybe that's why they're on **Happy Squid**, one of the more open-minded labels in L.A. Bruce Licher, from L.A.'s **Independent Project** records, also gave a hand by manufacturing the cover art with his letter press. Needless to say, the packaging

and sound quality are excellent. As for the music, it's up and down. "Another Day" is an immediate classic; an earthy strung-out tale of drug addiction that clocks in at 90 seconds; a great song. At the low end we've got a few quirky, silly statements like "Neil Armstrong" and "Pig." Overall, though, it's a 60/40 bet with the good outshining the bad. ∎

- **O.A.O./Celluloid:** 260 W. 39th St., NYC, NY. 10018.
- **Little Ricky:** 1133 Broadway, Suite 1107, NYC, NY 10010.
- **Ace of Hearts:** Box 579, Kenmore Station, Boston, MA 02215.
- **Fountain of Youth:** 5710 Durbin Rd., Bethesda, MD 20817.
- **No Trend:** 1014 Ashton Rd., Ashton, MD 20861.
- **Twin Tone:** 445 Oliver Ave. S., Mpls, MN 55405.
- **Crass:** import.
- **Happy Squid:** Box 64184, LA, CA 90064.

By Bruce Pavitt

Please send records and tapes to: SUB/POP U.S.A. c/o The Rocket 2322 Second Avenue / Seattle, WA 98121

THE SLEEPING DOGS *Beware* 5-song 7" (Crass). The Sleeping Dogs are the first American band to be signed to London's "anarchist" **CRASS** record label. The sound here is experimental, a little weird, and consequently uneven, not unlike Seattle's **AUDIO LETTER**. Heavy words and propaganda confront war, affluence, prejudice, torture, and shopping malls. The fold-out cover includes newspaper clippings on Central America. If the Sleeping Dogs are occasionally excessive, they are also provocative and worth investigating.

ANGST 7-song 12" (Happy Squid/Los Angeles). A California collaboration between SF and L.A., this is a major West Coast release. Because Angst is a rock 'n roll band that doesn't fit the "hardcore" straightjacket, they've had trouble developing a strong following in San Francisco. Maybe that's why they're on Happy Squid, one of the more open-minded labels in L.A. Bruce Licher, from L.A.'s Independent Project records, also, gave a hand by manufacturing the cover art with his letter press machine. Needless to say, the packaging and sound quality are excellent. As for the music, it's up and down. "Another Day" is an immediate classic; an earthy strung-out tale of drug addiction that clocks in at 90 seconds; a great song. At the low end we've got a few quirky, silly statements like "Neil Armstrong" and "Pig." Overall, though, it's a 60/40 bet with the good outshining the bad.

Awesome, Face Melting, Bone Crushing

WARDS *The World Ain't Pretty and Neither Are We* 10-song 7" (No Thanks) The first hardcore disc I've ever heard from Vermont. Side two is just what you'd expect, too—faceless, generic thrash about Reagan. But wait, there is one great song here, "Weapon Factory." It's raw, it's not 100 m.p.h., and it features some spooky industrial percussion. Is this just one more obscure hit that will never make it outside of Nowheres-ville?! Check it out. On blue vinyl.

Z'EV *Elemental Music* LP (Subterranean) Bald man with earring, knee pads, metal cans, modern dance, karate, homemade percussion fury and rhythm. San Francisco performance artist Z'ev (alias Stefan Weisser) has an international reputation. He's an original. He's taken the game of kick the can and paid the rent with it. While I expected lots of sharp, metallic bangs and chaos, I was surprised to hear a low, relentless rumbling like rolling thunder. Performed live, this is a great mood piece, capturing the ambience and acoustics of the room and the crowd. (A fascinating interview with Z'ev can be found in *Re/Search #6/7: Industrial Culture Handbook*).

BRUCE LOSE "What's Your Name"/ "Waking to Sleep" 45 (Subterranean) Former vocalist with **FLIPPER** goes solo with a rhythm box, some tapes, and electronic processing. Artsy damaged psychedelia.

GREAT PLAINS *The Mark, Don and Mel* EP (New Age) Intellectual/nurd pop classics about abstract love; Great Plains is a great new Midwest band that should fill the void left by **THE EMBARRASS-MENT**. Vocalist Ron House is sincere and sounds lonely and awkward one minute, carefree and awkward the next. "The Way She Runs A Fever" is brilliant word play; bookworm with a beat.

BAD RELIGION *Into the Unknown* LP (Epitaph) Weird. Real schlock sell-out bad gross commercial disc from (formerly) one of L.A.'s best hardcore bands. The hardcore scene certainly needs to mature into new directions, but not at the expense of the emotional intensity that makes it great in the first place. Frontman Greg Graffin has always had a great voice—too bad he discovered Valium and **STYX**.

METALLICA *Kill 'Em All* LP (Megaforce) There's been a dramatic increase in small-label metal releases lately, and this LP by San Francisco's Metallica is the best I've heard. Packaged within you'll find A.) Four guys dressed in long hair, denim, and spandex. B.) Razor-edged logo dripping with blood. C.) Comic book lyrics about demons, repentance, and hell. In short, your basic ingredients for your basic heavy metal band. Except this stuff punches so hard you'll forget where you left your face. Songs like "Whiplash" are an ultra-fast blur, ranking along with UK hardcore/metal crossovers like **MOTÖRHEAD** and **DISCHARGE**. For once, phrases like "face melting" and "bone crushing" start to sound appropriate. Awesome.

AVENGERS LP (CD) The Avengers were a great band, and this is a classic, must-have collection. First-wave Bay Area punk rock reached its zenith with "We Are The One," a garage protest anthem that assaulted political and religious ideology. For the Avengers, rules didn't count; rebellion and individuality were inseparable. Like most of the '77–'79 punk bands, this band rejected peer pressure and the status quo not only with aggression, but with style and originality as well. Vital.

S›U›B/P›O›P

▶ **WARDS** *The World Ain't Pretty and Neither Are We* 10-song 7" (No Thanks) The first "hardcore" disc I've ever heard from Vermont. Side two is just what you'd expect, too — faceless, generic thrash about Reagan. But wait, there is one great song here, "Weapon Factory." It's raw, it's not 100 m.p.h. and it features some spooky industrial percussion. Is this just one more obscure hit that will never make it outside of Nowheres-ville?! Check it out. On blue vinyl.

▶ **Z'EV** *Elemental Music* LP (Subterranean) Bald man with earring, knee pads, metal cans, modern dance, karate, homemade percussion; fury and rhythm. San

Metallica: Awesome, face melting, bone crushing

Francisco performance artist **Z'ev** (alias Stefan Weisser) has an international reputation. He's an original. He's taken the game of kick the can and paid the rent with it. While I expected lots of sharp, metallic bangs and chaos, I was surprised to hear a low, relentless rumbling like rolling thunder. Performed live, this is a great mood piece, capturing the ambience and acoustics of the room and the crowd. (A fascinating interview with Z'ev can be found in *RE/SEARCH #6/7: Industrial Culture Handbook*).

▶ **BRUCE LOSE** *What's Your Name/Waking to Sleep* 45 (Subterranean) Former vocalist with **Flipper** goes solo with a rhythm box, some tapes and electronic processing. Arty, damaged psychedelia.

Penelope of The Avengers

Sub/Pop U.S.A.
▶▶ **Radio** ◀◀
EVERY TUESDAY 6-7 PM • KCMU 90.5 FM

▶ **GREAT PLAINS** *The Mark, Don and Mel* EP (New Age) Intellectual/nurd pop classics about abstract love; **Great Plains** is a great new Midwest band that should fill the void left by the Embarrassment. Vocalist Ron House is sincere and sounds lonely and awkward one minute, carefree and awkward the next. "The Way She Runs A Fever" is brilliant word play; bookworm with a beat.

▶ **BAD RELIGION** *Into the Unknown* LP (Epitaph) Weird. Real schlock sell-out bad gross commercial disc from (formerly) one of L.A.'s best hardcore bands. The "hardcore" scene certainly needs to mature into new directions, but not at the expense of the emotional intensity that makes it great in the first place. Frontman Greg Graffin has always had a great voice — too bad he discovered valium and Styx.

▶ **METALLICA** *Kill 'em All* LP (Megaforce) There's been a dramatic increase in small-label metal releases lately, and this LP by San Francisco's **Metallica** is the best I've heard. Packaged within you'll find A.) Four guys dressed in long hair, denim and spandex. B.) Razor-edged logo driping with blood. C.) Comic book lyrics about demons, repentance, and hell. In short, your basic ingredients for your basic heavy metal band. Except — this stuff punches so hard you'll forget where you left your face. Songs like "Whiplash" are an ultra fast blur, ranking along with U.K. hardcore/metal crossovers like **Motorhead** and **Discharge**. For once, phrases like "facemelting" and "bonecrushing" start to sound appropriate. Awesome.

▶ **AVENGERS** LP (CD) The **Avengers** were a great band and this is a classic, must-have collection. First-wave Bay Area punk rock reached its zenith with "We Are The One"; a garage protest anthem that assaulted political and religious ideology. For the **Avengers**, rules didn't count; rebellion and individuality were inseparable. Like most of the '77-'79 punk bands, this band rejected peer pressure and the status quo not only with aggression, but with style and originality as well. Vital.

▶ **RADIO TOKYO TAPES** Compilation LP (Ear Movie) Consistent L.A.

By Bruce Pavitt

compilation; a good introduction to the healthiest pop scene in the country. Tough, rockin' numbers by **The Last** and **The Long Ryders**. Paisley-wave action from mind-benders like **The Three O'clock** and **The Rain Parade**. L.A.'s two most creative bands, **Savage Republic** and **The Minutemen** duke it out on the beginning of side two. While I'm hard pressed to name one really *great* song, few of the performances are disappointing. Buy this first, then check out the amazing torrent of new releases that these individual artists have been pumping out.

▶ **DANGER IS THEIR BUSINESS** Compilation cassette (K) Speakin' of fun, there's a great *acapella* cassette from the **K** label in Olympia, WA. A real kick, we get to hear, among others, John Foster (*OP* mag) sing some blue-eyed soul in the shower, Lorraine Tong read minimalist poetry and get this — the Singer Family, some cute black kids, fool around in the studio and do the funniest version of "Jingle Bells" I've ever heard. This is the kind of off-beat novelty item that rarely makes it to vinyl. The beauty of low cost cassettes can be found in *Danger is Their Business*.

▶ **DISCO 3** *Reality* 12" single (Sutra) Ever since the urban realism of "The Message" by Grandmaster Flash, rappin' about crime is as popular as braggin' about break dancing. "It's Like That" by **Run D.M.C.** blew everybody away last summer, now it's "Reality" by **Disco 3**. How to get out of the ghetto? "Don't smoke no reefer, don't drink no beer . . . get yourself a J.O.B." The A-side is stripped down with a rhythm box and turntables, the flip adds keyboards for a tense, full-blown drama.

Z'ev: Bald man

NO THANKS ($5.00 c/o Box 3408, Burlington, VT 05402)
SUBTERRANEAN (577 Valencia, S.F., CA 984110)
NEW AGE ($4.00 c/o 1585 N. High St., Columbus, OH 43201)
EPITAPH (22458 Ventura Blvd., W.H., CA 91367)
MEGAFORCE (60 York St., Old Bridge, NJ 08857)
CD (1230 Grant Ave 531, S.F., CA 94133)
EAR MOVIE (Box 5040, Santa Monica, CA 90405)
K (Box 7154, Olympia, WA 98507)
SUTRA (1790 Broadway, NYC 10019)

Please send records and tapes to:
SUB/POP U.S.A. c/o The Rocket
2322 Second Avenue / Seattle, WA 98121

I was not into metal. Sabbath was only part of a wide variety of music I listened to before I got into punk and new wave. Bob Newman, the editor of the *Rocket*, said: "Look—on the East side of Seattle, over in Bellevue, there is a metal scene. Some of these bands, like Queensrÿche, are indie bands. I want you to consider covering some of this music." I was not really into it. Then he invited me into his office and played me "Whiplash," by Metallica." That was fucking amazing. From that point, I started broadening the palate and covering the indie metal stuff. "Whiplash" was the gateway drug for me, definitely.

VARIOUS *Radio Tokyo Tapes* compilation LP (Ear Movie) Consistent L.A. compilation; a good introduction to the healthiest pop scene in the country. Tough, rocking numbers by the **LAST** and the **LONG RYDERS**. Paisley-wave action from mindbenders like the **THREE O'CLOCK** and the **RAIN PARADE**. L.A.'s two most creative bands, **SAVAGE REPUBLIC** and the **MINUTEMEN**, duke it out on the beginning of side two. While I'm hard pressed to name one really great song, few of the performances are disappointing. Buy this first, then check out the amazing torrent of new releases that these individual artists have been pumping out.

VARIOUS *Danger Is Their Business* compilation cassette (K) Speaking of fun, there's a great a cappella cassette from the K label in Olympia, WA. A real kick. We get to hear, among others, John Foster (*OP* mag) sing some blue-eyed soul in the shower; Lorraine Tong read minimalist poetry; and get this—the Singer Family, some cute black kids, fool around in the studio and do the funniest version of "Jingle Bells" I've ever heard. This is the kind of off-beat novelty item that rarely makes it to vinyl. The beauty of low-cost cassettes can be found in *Danger Is Their Business*.

DISCO 3 *Reality* 12" single (Sutra) Ever since the urban realism of "The Message" by **GRANDMASTER FLASH**, rapping about crime is as popular as bragging about break dancing. "It's Like That" by **RUN-D.M.C.** blew everybody away last summer, now it's "Reality" by Disco 3. How to get out of the ghetto? "Don't smoke no reefer, don't drink no beer...get yourself a J.O.B." The A-side is stripped down with a rhythm box and turntables, the flip adds keyboards for tense, full-blown drama.

A Legacy of Stupidity

RAIN PARADE *Emergency Third Rail Power Trip* LP (Enigma). Light some incense and sit on a pillow. This is pop! Mellow LSD from L.A.'s now exploding paisley underground. Dreamy, kaleidoscopic textures. Jangling guitars, the occasional sitar and violin. Beautiful, surreal compositions like "What She's Done to Your Mind" and "Talking in My Sleep" make the floor melt and the head spin. A surprisingly mature LP.

THE LONG RYDERS *10-5-60* 5-song 12" (JEM). Still more retro '60s action! This one's more rockin' than the Rain Parade, but they still wear paisleys. Refreshing appearances by banjo and steel guitar give the thing a little country twang every so often. Good disc. L.A. is putting out the best pop smash hits in America.

THE THREE O'CLOCK *Sixteen Tambourines* LP (Frontier). Ever since their first incarnation as the **SALVATION ARMY**, Michael Quercio and friends have been impressing the US underground with intricate melodies. They've always been catchy. Initially part of the "paisley wave" whatever, they're now avoiding surreal lyrics about drugs, backward-guitar tapes, etc., and simply creating delicate ornate little pop songs that are about as lightweight as **SUPERTRAMP**. I'm sure they'll be sipping cocktails with **BARRY MANILOW** within the year. You might want to skip this and pick up the **THREE O'CLOCK**'s *Baroque Hoedown* EP.

LYRES "I Want to Help You Anne" b/w "I Really Want You Right Now" 45 (Ace of Hearts). Okay, okay. More retro-revival. This time it's from Boston. The Lyres have been sweating out their '60s style garage punk for three releases now, and this is the wildest thing they've done. Recorded in '81, this single has just been released on Boston's excellent Ace of Hearts label. Frantic, mind bending acid punk—the '60s do live on.

CH3 "I'll Take My Chances" b/w "How Come?" 45 (Posh Boy). Another great anthem from L.A.'s CH3. Life or death hooks and chants, these guys scream all the way home. Instant classic.

ESG *Come Away With ESG* LP (99). Sparse, minimal funk from these four sisters from the Bronx. Tito on congas. Hypno-groove, a good party record. "Dance," "Moody," and "The Beat" are dance hits that have been previously released.

DIMPLES D. "Sucker D.J.'s (I Will Survive)" 12" single (Party Time). Krista "Dimples D." is a wonderful young rapper who rhymes street crimes and party times with equal finesse. Plenty of turntable scratchin' on this disc; flip it over for dub and a cappella mixes. Favorite record of the past two months.

, 12" EP (Alternative Tentacles). Outrageous. Obnoxious. Intimidating. Abrasive. Hilarious. Bizarre. Noisy experimental hardcore. "Behind the foil-covered windows of a trailer home in San Antonio, Texas, the Surfers began a legacy of stupidity that has left in its wake ruined careers, broken bones, shattered relationships and loss of family ties." Listening to this record could be hazardous to your health. Proceed with caution.

IGGY POP *I Got A Right* LP (Invasion). Killer reissue of obscure, intense, early Iggy Pop, godfather of punk. Side one was recorded in Detroit between '73–'74, and includes (alternate versions of) the awesome "I Got A Right" b/w "Gimme Some Skin" 45 that was released on Siamese Records. Side two features tracks from the out-of-print *Kill City* LP released on Bomp. Iggy could

S>U>B/P>O>P

ESG: Sparse, minimal funk.

KRISTINE LARSEN

► **RAIN PARADE** *Emergency Third Rail Power Trip* **LP** (Enigma). Light some incense and sit on a pillow. This is pop! Mellow LSD from L.A.'s now exploding paisley underground. Dreamy, kaleidoscopic textures. Jangling guitars, the occasional sitar and violin. Beautiful, surreal compositions like "What She's Done to Your Mind" and "Talking in My Sleep" make the floor melt and the head spin. A surprisingly mature LP.

► **THE LONG RYDERS** *10-5-60* **5-song 12" LP** (JEM). Still more retro '60s action! This one's more rockin' than the Rain Parade, but they still wear paisleys. Refreshing appearances by banjo and steel guitar give the thing a little country twang every so often. Good disc. L.A. is putting out the best pop smash hits in America.

► **THE THREE O'CLOCK** *Sixteen Tambourines* **LP** (Frontier). Ever since their first incarnation as the Salvation Army, Michael Quercio and friends have been impressing the U.S. underground with intricate melodies, they've always been catchy. Initially part of the "paisley wave" whatever — they're now avoiding surreal lyrics about drugs, backward guitar tapes, etc. and simply creating delicate ornate little pop songs that are about as lightweight as Supertramp. I'm sure they'll be sipping cocktails with Barry Manilow within the year. You might want to skip this and pick up the Three O'clock's *Baroque Hoedown* EP.

► **LYRES** *I Want to Help You Anne/I Really Want You Right Now* **45** (Ace of Hearts). Okay, okay. *More* retro-revival. This time it's from Boston. The Lyres have been sweating out their '60s style garage punk for three releases now; this is the wildest thing they've done. Recorded in '81, this single has just been released on Boston's excellent Ace of Hearts label. Frantic, mindbending acid punk — the '60s *do* live on.

► **CH3** *I'll Take My Chances/How Come?* **45** (Poshboy). Another great anthem from L.A.'s CH3. Life or death hooks and chants, these guys scream all the way home. Instant classic.

► **ESG** *Come Away With ESG* **LP** (99). Sparse, minimal funk from these four sisters from the Bronx. Tito on congas. Hypno-groove, a good party record. "Dance," "Moody" and "The Beat" are dance hits that have been previously released.

► **DIMPLES D.** *Sucker D.J.'s (I Will Survive)* **12" single** (Party Time). Krista "Dimples D." is a wonderful young rapper who rhymes street crimes and party times with equal finesse. Plenty of turntable scratchin' on this disc; flip it over for dub and acappella mixes. Favorite record of the past two months.

► **BUTTHOLE SURFERS** **12" EP** (Alternative Tentacles). Outrageous. Obnoxious. Intimidating. Abrasive. Hilarious. Bizarre. Noisy, experimental hardcore. "Behind the foil-covered windows of a trailer home in San Antonio, Texas, the Surfers began a legacy of stupidity that has left in its wake ruined careers, broken bones, shattered relationships and loss of family ties." Listening to this record could be hazardous to your health. Proceed with caution.

BUTTHOLE SURFERS

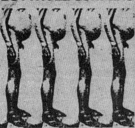

► **IGGY POP** *I Got A Right* **LP** (Invasion). Killer re-issue of obscure, intense, early Iggy Pop, godfather of punk. Side one was recorded in Detroit between '73-74 and includes (alternative versions of) the awesome "I Got A Right"/ "Gimme Some Skin" 45 that was released on Siamese Records. Side two features tracks from the out-of-print *Kill City* LP released on

---

Bomp. Iggy could be a slave, a dog and a monster, he *defined* rock 'n' roll — don't pass up this crucial document.

► **NO TREND** *Too Many Humans* **LP** (No Trend). Nobody denounces status quo lifestyles as harshly as No Trend, a bitter, intelligent dirge-hardcore outfit from D.C. Songs include "Do As You're Told," "Mindless Little Insects" and "Kiss Ass To Your Peer Group." The overall sound has a wind tunnel effect, lots of dense, natural reverb that will literally blow you away. Recorded at Inner Ear Studios by Don Zientara (same guy who did Void, early Minor Threat), this record successfully avoids artificial studio sound, my main complaint with the last Minor Threat EP. This record has atmosphere, intensity, intelligence. Best "hardcore" record I've heard since the No Trend 45.

NO TREND

TOO MANY HUMANS....

► **THE SOUND OF HOLLYWOOD GIRLS** **Compilation LP** (Mystic). America's sleaziest label brings you girl groups like "Bitch," "Butch" and "I.U.D." I guess there's a thin line between hardcore, heavy metal and white trash — and these people seem to have found it. Song titles include "S & M Blvd. Boy," "Baby Junky" and my personal favorite "Ugly and Slouchy." I guess you could call this urban folk music.

- **ENIGMA:** Box 2896, Torrance, CA 90509.
- **JEM:** Reseda, CA 91335.
- **FRONTIER:** Box 22, Sun Valley, CA 91352.
- **ACE OF HEARTS:** Box 579, Kenmore Station, Boston, MA 02215.
- **POSH BOY:** Box 38861, L.A., CA 90038.
- **99:** 99 MacDougal St., N.Y.C. 10012.
- **PARTY TIME:** c/o Streetwise, 25 W. 43 St., Suite 1202, N.Y.C. 10036.
- **ALTERNATIVE TENTACLES:** Box 11458, S.F., CA 94101.
- **INVASION:** see Enigma.
- **NO TREND:** c/o 1014 Ashton Rd., Ashton, MD 20861.

Please send records and tapes to:
SUB/POP U.S.A. c/o The Rocket
2322 Second Avenue / Seattle, WA 98121

Sub/Pop U.S.A.
► **Radio** ◄
EVERY TUESDAY 6-7 PM / KCMU 90.5 FM

By Bruce Pavitt

20% Off Entire Stock Until Dec. 24th

nick knacks
furniture
clothes

Christmas Trees-Lights & Cut Poinsettias

CLOSET•FANTASIES
2018 WESTLAKE AVE.
SEATTLE, WA. 98121
Visa/Mastercharge 206 682-1159
Welcome as of 12-14

NEW HOURS
Monday thru Friday 11:30 - 7:00
Sat. 2:00 - 6:00 THRU DEC

WALDOS
ROCKS THE EASTSIDE
KIRKLAND, WA.

ROCK WED thru SAT

Wed-Sat Dec 14-17	Tuesday Jan 3	Tuesday Jan 17
THE HEATS	BRAT	LEGACY

Wed-Sat Dec 21-24	Wed-Sat Jan 4-7	Wed-Sat Jan 18-21
LIGHT YEARS	BOIBS	COVER GIRLS

Wed-Sat Dec 28-31	Wed-Sat Jan 11-14	Wed-Sat Jan 25-28
SHYANNE	MACHINE	METRO

Heavy Metal Night Every other Tuesday
FREE COVER ON SUNDAYS

Rose Hill Shopping Center • 12655 NE 85th • 827-9292

Thousands of LP's for only

Pop Disco
Soul Vocal

10¢
Many factory sealed
Limit 10 per customer

Sony Super Walkman
WM-10 $89
Gift Wrapped

Broadway Record Centre
112 Broadway Ave. E. In the Broadway Arcade
325-9806

RECORDS Specializing in
New & Used Imports and Independents.
Open 12pm-8pm Seven Days a Week.
In the Broadway Arcade/Second Floor.
325-9805

BOMB SHELTER

be a slave, a dog, and a monster; he defined rock 'n roll—don't pass up this crucial document.

NO TREND *Too Many Humans* LP (No Trend). Nobody denounces status quo lifestyles as harshly as No Trend, a bitter, intelligent dirge-hardcore outfit from D. C. Songs include "Do as You're Told," "Mindless Little Insects," and "Kiss Ass to Your Peer Group." The overall sound has a wind tunnel effect, lots of dense, natural reverb that will literally blow you away. Recorded at Inner Ear Studios by Don Zientara (same guy who did **VOID** and early **MINOR THREAT**), this record successfully avoids artificial studio sound, which was my main complaint with the last Minor Threat EP. This record has atmosphere, intensity, intelligence. Best hardcore record I've heard since the No Trend 45.

VARIOUS *The Sound of Hollywood Girls* compilation LP (Mystic). America's sleaziest label brings you girl groups like **BITCH**, **BUTCH**, and **I.U.D.** I guess there's a thin line between hardcore, heavy metal and white trash—and these people seem to have found it. Song titles include "S & M Blvd. Boy," "Baby Junky," and my personal favorite, "Ugly and Slouchy." I guess you could call this urban folk music.

Creative + Unusual / Excessive + Obnoxious

NIHILISTICS LP (Braineater) Unrelenting hostility, brutality, and hatred from these four lads from NYC. Ultra-fast thrash, just enough changes to make it interesting. Lyrics are simple: "Hypocrite pigs call themselves the human race." Their press release brags about how their real fans are "a cross section of misfits and outcasts; the poor, the physically handicapped, and the unwanted. Musical and verbal statements this extreme are too funny to be taken seriously.

BEASTIE BOYS: *Cooky Puss* 12" (Rat Cage) The Beastie Boys turn the tables, literally. Formerly a thrash band, the Beastie Boys are the first hardcore kids to steal cut-and-scratch techniques from the South Bronx. The result is a fascinating hybrid. Their attempt at using the turntable-as-instrument is crazy, sloppy, and funny. Apparently they cut up their first thrash 7" plus (tell me if I'm wrong) an old **STEVE MARTIN** comedy LP. On top of all this is a grungy guitar riff, a cheap drum set, and a prank phone call. The Beasties plunder black culture even deeper on the flip, a dub reggae thing called "Beastie Revolution." The whole record is (a) creative and unusual; (b) excessive and obnoxious; or (c) all of the above.

ONO *Machines That Kill People* LP (Thermidor) Chicago's weirdest band, Ono defies easy explanation. Frontman/poet Dobbs wears dreadlocks and has been known to perform in women's undergarments. This is a man who likes to express himself. Combine the deep, resonant voice of Dobbs with the tones and textures of the rest of Ono, and you have what borders on religious ceremony. This is ambient, moody and slightly industrial; but is this a church or a warehouse? *Machines That Kill People* is a very strange record.

VARIOUS *English as a Second Language* compilation double LP (Freeway) Spoken word, mostly. Eighty-four intimate "statements" from various underground L.A. celebrities. Poetry (often obscene), voice on voice experiments, prose readings (often obscene), various miniature songs, or chunks of noise with words. Embarrassingly phony one minute, sincere and provocative the next. Pick hits: **HENRY ROLLINS, EXENE CERVENKA, STEVE WYNN**, and the crew from *Flipside* fanzine. If you can take it, "dirty old man" poet **SHARLES BUKOWSKI** is also here, and it's quite a party.

SWANS: *Filth* LP (Neutral) Plodding, bass-heavy art-ghetto garbage. Talentless loudmouths give everyone a stomachache and think they're God. Industrial percussion. "Strong Boss," "Weakling," and "Power" show how oppressive life can be. Great for clearing parties. What's mildly interesting for a few minutes becomes a nightmare after twenty. More depression from NYC—maybe these hipsters could do a double bill with the **NIHILISTICS**?

MALCOLM X *No Sell Out* 12" (Tommy Boy) An electro-beat cut-up of '60s black militant Malcolm X? I was hoping for greatness, but—sorry, wrong number. What a disappointment. The instrumental track (by **KEITH LEBLANC**) is limp and lifeless. The beatbox lacks punch and the keyboards are lazy and uninventive. And Malcolm? He's hardly there. Simple phrases like "no sell out" are okay, but sound superficial without any substance. Tommy Boy really should have stolen more of the speech. As an exploitation novelty record, it's pretty hip, but drags short of its potential.

The Beastie Boys were one of the most creative and culturally influential groups to come out of the '80s indie underground. They were consistently humorous, imaginative, and always evolving. Because they become extremely popular, they were sometimes ignored in hipster social circles. Not so in Seattle. I remember attending an after-hours party in Seattle at the Room Nine rehearsal space, a few weeks after *Licensed to Ill* came out. I popped the cassette in a blaster and the room went off. It was probably my best DJ gig ever—I simply played the whole tape 3 times in a row.

S›U›B·P›O›P
U ———— S ———— A
A GUIDE TO U.S. INDEPENDENTS

► **NIHILISTICS LP (Braineater)** Unrelenting hostility, brutality and hatred from these four lads from NYC. Ultra-fast thrash, just enough changes to make it interesting. Lyrics are simple: "Hypocrite pigs call themselves the human race." Their press release brags about how their *real* fans are "a cross section of misfits and outcasts . . . the poor, the physically handicapped and the unwanted." Musical and verbal statements this extreme are too funny to be taken seriously.

► **THE BEASTIE BOYS: COOKY PUSS** 12" (Rat Cage) The Beastie Boys turn the tables, literally. Formerly a thrash band, the Beastie Boys are the first "hardcore" kids to steal *cut* and *scratch* techniques from the South Bronx. The result is a fascinating hybrid. Their attempt at using the turntable-as-instrument is crazy, sloppy and funny. Apparently they cut up their first thrash 7" plus (tell me if I'm wrong) an old Steve Martin comedy LP. On top of all this is a grungy guitar riff, a cheap drum set and a prank phone call. The Beasties plunder black culture even deeper on the flip, a dub/reggae thing called "Beastie Revolution." The whole record is (a) creative and unusual (b) excessive and obnoxious or (c) all of the above.

► **ONO: MACHINES THAT KILL PEOPLE** LP (Thermidor) Chicago's weirdest band, Ono defies easy explanation. Frontman/poet Dobbs wears dreadlocks and has been known to perform in women's undergarments. This is a man who likes to express himself. Combine the deep, resonant voice of Dobbs with the tones and textures of the rest of Ono and you have what borders on religious ceremony. This is ambient, moody and slightly industrial; is this a church or a warehouse? *Machines That Kill People* is a very strange rcord.

By Bruce Pavitt

Please send records and tapes to: SUB/POP U.S.A c/o The Rocket 2322 Second Avenue / Seattle, WA 98121

Sub/Pop U.S.A.
► **Radio** ◄
EVERY TUESDAY 6-7 PM • KCMU 90.5 FM

► **ENGLISH AS A SECOND LANGUAGE** compilation double LP (Freeway Records) Spoken word, mostly. 84 intimate "statements" from various underground L.A. celebrities. Poetry, often obscene, voice on voice experiments, prose readings, often obscene, various miniature songs or chunks of noise with words. Embarrassingly phony one minute, sincere and provocative the next. Pick hits: Henry Rollins, Exene Cervenka, Steve Wynn, and the crew from *Flipside* fanzine. If you can take it, "dirty old man" poet Sharles Bukowski is also here, and it's quite a party.

► **SWANS: FILTH LP (Neutral)** Plodding, bass heavy art ghetto garbage. Talentless loudmouths give everyone a stomach ache and think they're God. Industrial percussion. "Strong Boss," "Weakling" and "Power" show how oppressive life can be. Great for clearing parties. What's mildly interesting for a few minutes becomes a nightmare after 20. More depression from NYC — maybe these hipsters could do a double bill with the Nihilistics?

► **MALCOLM X: NO SELL OUT** 12" (Tommy Boy) An electrobeat cut-up of '60s black militant Malcolm X? I was hoping for greatness, but sorry, wrong number. What a disappointment. The instrumental track (by Keith Leblanc) is limp and lifeless — the beatbox lacks punch and the keyboards are lazy, uninventive. And Malcolm? He's hardly there. Simple phrases like "no sell out" are okay but sound superficial without any substance. Tommy Boy really should have stolen more of the speech. As an exploitation novelty record, it's pretty hip, but drags short of its potential.

► **NAKED RAYGUN: BASEMENT SCREAMS** 12" (Ruthless) Hardcore sex. Having once opened for the Fall totally naked, Naked Raygun has often fueled its energy with perversion and sexual frustration. Remember "Libido" from the *Busted At Oz* compilation? Well this record has a song called "Potential Rapist." It's not surprising that this otherwise magnificent release is marred by callous sexism. If you like your music *politically correct*, then please skip this decadent trash. If you're looking for a distinctive hardcore band that writes real songs, go for it, you'll be whistling for days.

► **MINUTEMEN: BUZZ OR HOWL UNDER THE INFLUENCE OF HEAT** 12" EP (SST) The Minutemen are so prolific it's becoming a chore just keeping up with them. The ultimate beatnik/hardcore crossover, these cats record raw but their sound often leans toward a twisted interest in jazz. This record's even got horns. Minutemen lyrics are also becoming increasingly more abstract — can you imagine beat poet Ferlingetti writing a book called *Buzz or Howl Under the Influence of Heat*? I can. Yet another interesting record from that artcore outfit, the Minutemen.

► **TWILIGHT 22: ELECTRIC KINGDOM** 12" (Vanguard) The techno-funk, electrobeat style pioneeered by Tommy Boy is not dead or even dying, not as long as Electric Kingdom is turned up late and loud in dance clubs across the country. Ripping off the T-Boy sound of producers Baker and Robie, Twilight 22 have outdone their competitors. The song, through changes in style, sends us to African, Persian and European kingdoms. Recycled rhythms with a novel twist.

• **TOMMY BOY:** 210 E. 90th St., N.Y.C. 10028. • **FREEWAY:** P.O. Box 67930, L.A., CA 90067. • **BRAINEATER:** Box J, Island Park, NY 11558. • **NEUTRAL:** 325 Spring St., Rm. 331, N.Y.C. 10013. • **RAT CAGE:** Important Distrbutors, 149-03 New York Boulevard, Jamaica, NY 11434. • **SST:** P.O. Box 1, Lawndale, CA 90260. • **THERMIDOR:** 5618 Central Ave., Richmond, CA 94804. • **VANGUARD:** 71 W. 23rd St., N.Y.C. 10010. • **RUTHLESS:** c/o Naked Raygun, P.O. Box 578382, Chicago, IL 60657-8382.

NAKED RAYGUN *Basement Screams* 12" (Ruthless) Hardcore sex. Having once opened for **THE FALL** totally naked, Naked Raygun has often fueled its energy with perversion and sexual frustration. Remember "Libido" from the *Busted at Oz* compilation? Well, this record has a song called "Potential Rapist." It's not surprising that this otherwise magnificent release is marred by callous sexism. If you like your music politically correct, then please skip this decadent trash. If you're looking for a distinctive hardcore band that writes real songs, go for it, you'll be whistling for days.

MINUTEMEN *Buzz or Howl Under the Influence of Heat* 12" EP (SST) The Minutemen are so prolific it's becoming a chore just keeping up with them. The ultimate beatnik/hardcore crossover, these cats record raw but their sound often leans toward a twisted interest in jazz. This record's even got horns. Minutemen lyrics are also becoming increasingly more abstract— can you imagine beat poet Ferlinghetti writing a book called *Buzz or Howl Under the Influence of Heat*? I can. Yet another interesting record from that artcore outfit, the Minutemen.

TWILIGHT 22 *Electric Kingdom* 12" (Vanguard) The techno-funk electro-beat style pioneeered by Tommy Boy is not dead or even dying, not as long as "Electric Kingdom" is turned up late and loud in dance clubs across the country. Ripping off the T-Boy sound of producers Baker and Robie, Twilight 22 has outdone its competitors. The song, through changes in style, sends us to African, Persian, and European kingdoms. Recycled rhythms with a novel twist.

The Loudest vs. the Noisiest

EPP R.I.P.

Local punk/noise outfit Mr. Epp has called it quits. Starting out in Oct. '81, Epp has played approximately 20 shows around town, opening for such bands as the **DEAD KENNEDYS**, **REALLY RED**, and **NINA HAGEN**. They've appeared on several compilations, including *The Public Doesn't Exist* and *What Syndrome* cassettes; the *Mighty Feeble* collection on L.A.'s New Alliance label; and *Seattle Syndrome II* (Engram). Their five-song seven-inch, "Of Course I'm Happy, Why?" (Pravda), included the hit "Mohawk Man," which reached up to #1 on *Rodney on the ROQ* (KROQ), the most influential alternative rock show in L.A. Mr. Epp has recently released a 90-minute cassette entitled *Live As All Get Out!* which can be purchased for $4. Quotes frontman Jo Smitty: "When we were voted 'loudest band' in the *Rocket*, I said to Becky, 'Actually, it should have been the noisiest!'"

•

VIOLENT FEMMES "Gimme The Car" b/w "Ugly" 45 (Rough Trade import) The latest by the Femmes is all electric. The acoustic "folk-punk" trip was last year, now it's no more marimbas, violin, or acoustic guitar. Well, it's obvious that this band from Milwaukee is not going to stick with a formula, they're gonna do whatever the fuck they want—despite their fans. I can only say that I'm disappointed. Frontman Gordon Gano is still a talented songwriter; "Gimme the Car" is a sly piece of adolescent sex, but songs like "Gone Daddy Gone" from their debut LP still sound fresh, vibrant by comparison. Let's hear it for acoustic music.

DREAM SYNDICATE *Live* 12" (Rough Trade import) Extensive liner notes by Byron Coley. Exquisite packaging courtesy of Blue Note. But the music? The live side features "Some Kinda Itch" and "Sure Thing" from their first EP, plus a version of "Mr. Soul" by **BUFFALO SPRINGFIELD** Aside from some desperate last minute rave-up on "Sure Thing," this material does nothing but take up space. The exciting, sonic feedback of Karl Precoda is on vacation, the rest of the band is either asleep or stoned on pot. Turn the record over and you've got the hit, "Tell Me When It's Over," already available on their LP. If you like the **VELVET UNDERGROUND**, don't miss the first two releases by this band.

EARTHA KITT *Where Is My Man?* 12" single (Streetwise) Eartha Kitt. Born in 1928, this lady's been around. A friend and contemporary of Marilyn Monroe, James Dean, and Marlon Brando, Eartha's sexy, sensual performance made her an international cabaret star, selling millions of records. Never failing to speak her mind, Eartha's career slid to a halt when she was blacklisted in 1968, after speaking out against the Vietnam War at a White House luncheon. After a long unproductive stay in Europe, she is now back in the States and planning an LP for April. Needless to say, "Where is My Man?" is a sizzling, seductive dance track that avoids cold technology in favor of warmer R&B disco. Party record of the month!

TRUE WEST *Hollywood Holiday* mini LP (New Rose import) Become one with God. Get your nervous system out of neutral and blow your mind with the best of the whole neopaisley thing. Floating out from Davis, California, True West originally released this masterpiece on Bring Out Your Dead records, and it's now out of print domestically. Thank the Almighty for this superb French pressing—the vinyl is better and

RECORDS
BUY TRADE SELL
skateboards too!
In the Broadway Arcade · Second Floor
325-9805   MON-SAT 12-8 pm
BOMB SHELTER

CLEAR LIGHT SYSTEMS
CONCERT STAGE LIGHTING
RENTALS & SALES
HAVE LIGHTS, WILL TRAVEL
'DESIGNERS / OPERATORS
ONE NIGHTERS, WEEKENDS,
OUT OF TOWN & TOURS
PACKAGED SYSTEM RATES —VERY REASONABLE
SEATTLE • 608 19th E   • CAPITOL HILL • 322-85

Shades
in March

323-8397
For
Booking

The MINT
ZOO
Hall of Fame
Talk of the Town
Matzoh Momma's
SCARLET TREE
OWL CAFE
Talk Of The Town

S›U›B P›O›P

A GUIDE TO U.S. INDEPENDENTS

► **VIOLENT FEMMES: GIMME THE CAR/ UGLY 45 (Rough Trade import)** The latest by the **Femmes** is all electric. The acoustic "folk-punk" trip was last year, now it's *no more* marimbas, violin or acoustic guitar. Well, it's obvious that this band from Milwaukee is not going to stick with a formula, they're gonna do whatever the fuck they want — despite their fans. I can only say that I'm disappointed. Frontman **Gordon Gano** is still a talented songwriter; "Gimme the Car" is a sly piece of adolescent sex, but songs like "Gone Daddy Gone" from their debut LP still sound fresh, vibrant by comparison. Let's hear it for acoustic music.

► **DREAM SYNDICATE: LIVE** 12" **(Rough Trade import)** Extensive liner notes by Byron Coley. Exquisite packaging courtesy of Blue Note. But the music? The live side features "Some Kinda Itch" and "Sure Thing" from their first EP, plus a version of "Mr. Soul" by the Buffalo Springfield. Aside from some desperate last minute rave-up on "Sure Thing" this material does nothing but take up space. The exciting, sonic feedback of Karl Precoda is on vacation, the rest of the band is either asleep or stoned on pot. Turn the record over and you've got the hit, "Tell Me When It's Over," already available on their LP. If you like the Velvet Underground, don't miss the first two releases by this band.

► **EARTHA KITT: WHERE IS MY MAN?** 12" **Single (Streetwise)** Eartha Kitt. Born in 1928, this lady's been around. A friend and contemporary of Marilyn Monroe, James Dean and Marlon Brando, Eartha's sexy, sensual performance made her an international cabaret star, selling millions of records. Never failing to speak her mind, Eartha's career slid to a halt when she was blacklisted in 1968, after speaking out against the Viet Nam war at a White House luncheon. After a long unproductive stay in Europe, she is now back in the States and planning an LP for April. Needless to say, "Where is My Man?" is a sizzling, seductive dance track that avoids cold technology in favor of warmer R&B disco. Party record of the month!

► **TRUE WEST: HOLLYWOOD HOLIDAY** mini-LP **(New Rose import)** *Become one with God.* Get your nervous system out of neutral and blow your mind with the best of the whole Neo-paisley thing. Floating out from Davis, California, **True West** originally released this masterpiece on Bring Out Your Dead records, and it's now out of print domestically. Thank the Almighty for this superb French pressing — the vinyl is better and it comes with three extra tracks! What we've got here is ringing octaves, metalic percussion, feedback, *real songs.* The production is bright, biting, intense. For fans of early Pink Floyd, there's a killer version of "Lucifer Sam" which opens up side one. Keep going,

► **EPP R.I.P.** ◄

Local punk/noise outfit **Mr. Epp** has called it quits. Starting out in Oct. '81, Epp has played approximately 20 shows around town, opening for such bands as the Dead Kennedys, Really Red and Nina Hagen. They've appeared on several compilations including **The Public Doesn't Exist** and **What Syndrome** cassettes, the **Mighty Feeble** collection on L.A.'s New Alliance label, and **Seattle Syndrome II** (Engram). Their five-song seven-inch "Of Course I'm Happy, Why?" (Pravda) included the hit "Mohawk Man" which reached up to #1 on **Rodney on the ROQ** (KROQ), the most influential alternative rock show in L.A. Mr. Epp has recently released a 90-minute cassette entitled "Live As All Get Out!" which can be purchased for $4 ppd. c/o **P.O. Box 9609, Seattle, WA 98109.** Quotes frontman Jo Smitty, "When we were voted 'loudest band' in **The Rocket**, I said to Becky, 'Actually, it should have been the *noisiest.'"*

SUB/TEN INTERNATIONAL

TEST DEPT. Compulsion 12"12Some Bizarre) U.K.

TRUE WEST Hollywood Holiday LP (New Rose) U.S.A.

RUN D.M.C. Hard Times 12" (Profile) U.S.A.

EINSTURZENDE NEUBAUTEN 80-83 Strategies Against Architecture (Mute) W. Germany

ROCHEREAU Femme D'Autrui (Genidia) Zaire

EARTHA KITT Where Is My Man 12" (Streetwise) U.S.A.

SUPER MAZEMBE Shauri Yako 12" (Earthworks/Rough Trade) Kenya

SMITHS What Difference Does It Make (Rough Trade) U.K.

BELFEGORE Belfegore 12" (Pure Freude) W. Germany

ROTTERDAM SPUNK Compilation (Plastic Cheese) Netherlands

PULSE: Box 36075, L.A., CA 90036

STREETWISE: 25 W. 43rd St., N.Y., N.Y. 10107

DISCHORD: 3819 Beecher St. N.W., Wash., D.C. 20007

SELMA: 6657 Yucca St., Hollywood, CA 90028

MO DA MU: 374-810 W. Broadway, Vancouver, B.C. V5Z 1Jh CANADA

By Bruce Pavitt

Please send records and tapes to:
SUB/POP U.S.A., c/o The Rocket
2322 Second Avenue
Seattle, WA 98121

things are great, but you won't ha a religious experience til you flip and listen to "Steps to the Door "I'm Not Here," "And Then T Rain" and "Hollywood Holiday" one lump sum. Excellent.

► **54/40: SET THE FIRE 12" EP (M Da-Mu)** The second release by th Vancouver pop band is no disappointment. Although the coffee tab sophistication might seem too tas ful for those who eat live chicker there is tension here for those wh want it. "One Place Set" is rivetin ominous, a real creeper. And whi the collaboration between banjo ar trumpet may have its roots in Dixi land jazz, with **54/40** the result is melancholy strain of pop called "T Sound of Truth." At their best, 54/ create new pop territory, successful avoiding the *New Wavisms* so prev lent in the Seattle pop scene. A honorable release.

► **RUN D.M.C.: HARD TIMES / JA MASTER JAY 12"** single **(Profile)** An other master jam from NYC rappe **Run** and **D.M.C.** Heavy breathin and beat box rhythms on Kurt Blow's "Hard Times." Rhyming to gether, trading off, then rapping to gether again. Scratching and toug horns on "Jam Master Jay." Lik their last double shot hit "It's Lik That/Sucker M.C.'s" the arrange ments are lean, restrained. Th groove has me hooked.

► **TUPELO CHAIN SEX: JA-JAZZ** L.P **(Selma)** Well, it's *different*. Mixin jazz, blues, rockabilly and dub **Tupelo Chain Sex** come across as slightly demented Dan Hicks and Hi Hot Licks. Remember "Sugarcane" Harris? He's here playing fiddle other instruments include standin bass, marimba, piano and harmon ica. It's all pretty off-the-wall, bu what's *wow* and spontaneous to som is sure to be directionless to others Released on the Hollywood base Selma label, this record has bee issued in a limited edition of 100 copies.

► **DEAD HIPPIE: LIVING DEAD** LF **(Pulse)** Despite an anti-groovy name this record is neither "groovy" no "anti." This could have been a unique '60s meets '80s hybrid, a new monster to unleash on the faceles legion of U.S. hardcore bands. In stead, we get a few Hendrix licks and some no talent vocals. Forgettable.

► **FAITH: SUBJECT TO CHANGE** LF **(Dischord)** Powerful yet ultimately generic thrash from D.C. When you're up against legends like Void, Minor Threat and No Trend, I guess it's pretty hard to compete. What I really like about this record is the way it's put together — there's a picture of the drummer on one of the inner labels, a laughing track on one of the inner grooves, it's on blue vinyl. These are the kinds of gimmicks that make a record fun. All in all, worth picking up.

it comes with three extra tracks! What we've got here is ringing octaves, metalic percussion, feedback, real songs. The production is bright, biting, intense. For fans of early **PINK FLOYD**, there's a killer version of "Lucifer Sam" which opens up side one. Keep going, things are great, but you won't have a religious experience til you flip it and listen to "Steps to the Door," "I'm Not Here," "And Then The Rain," and "Hollywood Holiday" in one lump sum. Excellent.

54/40 *Set The Fire* 12" EP (Mo-Da-Mu) The second release by this Vancouver pop band is no disappointment. Although the coffee-table sophistication might seem too tasteful for those who eat live chickens, there is tension here for those who want it. "One Place Set" is riveting, ominous, a real creeper. And while the collaboration between banjo and trumpet may have roots in Dixieland jazz, with 54/40 the result is a melancholy strain of pop called the "Sound of Truth." At their best, 54/40 creates new pop territory, successfully avoiding the new wave-isms so prevalent in the Seattle pop scene. An honorable release.

RUN-D.M.C. "Hard Times" b/w "Jam Master Jay" 12" single (Profile). Another master jam from NYC rappers Run and D.M.C. Heavy breathing and beat box rhythms on **KURTIS BLOW**'s "Hard Times." Rhyming together, trading off, then rapping together again. Scratching and tough horns on "Jam Master Jay." Like their last double-shot hit, "It's Like That" b/w "Sucker M.C.'s," the arrangements are lean, restrained. This groove has me hooked.

TUPELO CHAIN SEX *Ja-Jazz* LP (Selma). Well, it's different. Mixing jazz, blues, rockabilly, and dub, Tupelo Chain Sex come across as a slightly demented **DAN HICKS AND HIS HOT LICKS**. Remember "Sugarcane" Harris? He's here playing fiddle; other instruments include standing bass, marimba, piano, and harmonica. It's all pretty off-the-wall, but what's wow and spontaneous to some is sure to be directionless to others. Released on the Hollywood based Selma label, this record has been issued in a limited edition of 1000 copies.

DEAD HIPPIE *Living Dead* LP (Pulse) Despite an anti-groovy name, this record is neither "groovy" nor ""anti." This could have been a unique '60s-meets-'80s hybrid, a new monster to unleash on the faceless legion of US hardcore bands. Instead, we get a few **HENDRIX** licks and some no-talent vocals. Forgettable.

FAITH: *Subject to Change* LP (Dischord) Powerful yet ultimately generic thrash from D.C. When you're up against legends like **VOID, MINOR THREAT**, and **NO TREND**, I guess it's pretty hard to compete. What I really like about this record is the way it's put together—there's a picture of the drummer on one of the inner labels; a laugh track on one of the inner grooves; it's on blue vinyl. These are the kinds of gimmicks that make a record fun. All in all, worth picking up.

SUB TEN INTERNATIONAL

TEST DEPT. (UK) *Compulsion* 12" (Some Bizarre)

TRUE WEST (USA) *Hollywood Holiday* LP (New Rose)

RUN-D.M.C. (USA) *Hard Times* 12" (Profile)

EINSTÜRZENDE NEUBAUTEN (West Germany) *Strategies Agains Architecture 80-83* (Mute)

ROCHEREAU (Zaire) *Femme D'Autruni* (Genidia)

EARTHA KITT (USA) "Where Is My Man?" 12" (Streetwise)

SUPER MAZEMBE (Kenya) *Shauri Yako* 12" (Earthworks/Rough Trade)

SMITHS (UK) *What Difference Does It Make* (Rough Trade)

BELFEGORE (West Germany) *Belfegore* 12" (Pure Freude)

VARIOUS (The Netherlands) *Rotterdam Spunk* compilation (Plastic Cheese)

Where Does Vitamix Get His Records?

VITAMIX

From out of Sunset High School in Portland comes 17-year-old **VITAMIX**, a break-mixer who's currently cutting the only alternative rap/funk radio show in Portland. *The King Crewsade* can be heard from 3 to 7 a.m. every Sunday night on KBOO-FM (90.7). The show features guest rappers from around the Portland area, as well as unusual mixes of the latest.

Where does "Vitamix," aka Chris Blanchard, get his records? "From friends in NY and the House of Sound, the best store in Portland for 12-inch dance records."

Although he used to, Chris rarely break-dances anymore—too many other people are doing it. "Anyone who's athletic can spin around on their head. I'd rather watch the body poppers doing their mechanical thing, that takes a little more skill. Right now people are breaking all over, at the Blazers games, downtown; the best crew in town is the Cleveland High School Breakers."

But while Chris dabbles with various facets of Wild Style culture like graffiti art and breakdancing and rapping, what he does best is working the turntables. If you'd like to check out just what this guy is doing, then write away for one of his tapes. The latest one's called *Break Dance* and features a mix of "Rock It" as well as some more obscure hits. Send $3 to: Vitamix, Portland, OR. The tapes are also available at Park Ave. and Singles Going Steady record stores in Portland.

•

JOHN TRUBEE AND THE UGLY JANITORS OF AMERICA *The Communists Are Coming to Kill Us* LP (Enigma). This is a sick record. This is a bad record. This is the worst record I've ever heard. Obscene phone calls and lyrics, lightweight jazz and self indulgent synthesizer noodling. If songs like "Dumping Buckets of Phlegm on Bitchy Old Ladies" is your idea of art or entertainment, I suggest you see a psychiatrist. Enigma Records has put out a lot of trash, but I never thought they could get this low.

GUADALCANAL DIARY *Watusi Rodeo* 12" EP (Entertainment on Disc). Strong pop debut. Using cowboy and Third World references, we get to hear about Michael Rockefeller's unfortunate trip to Papua, New Guinea, as well as bravado concerning the death of John Wayne (with a tip o' the hat to **MORRICONE** and *The Good, the Bad, and the Ugly*). Remember "Indian Reservation" by **MARK LINDSAY**? Well, it would sound AOK next to "Liwa Wechi" with its simple maracas and coyote crooning. Produced by Bruce Baxter of Georgia's DB Records, this anthemic, minimal pop sound will probably appeal to fans of the late, great **PYLON**.

YOUR FOOD *Poke it With a Stick* LP (Screaming Whoredog Records). Fairly interesting release from the Louisville, KY underground. Simple, primitive riffing provides the background the offbeat yet personal lyrics. Should be of interest to fans of **THE FALL**.

MEAT PUPPETS *II* LP (SST). Okay, these guys from Phoenix have always beeen a little odd. Despite publicly stating an interest in pot and the **GRATEFUL DEAD**, the Meat Puppets still uncork chaos—their last LP was pure sonic sandpaper. Now it's Meat Puppets *II* and everything's starting to make sense.

"America's most awesome machine [Black Flag] is currently touring the States; can't wait to see 'em again. Of course they'll be pushing *My War*...it's a radical direction which will excite some and turn off just as many, so flip a coin."

S›U›B›P›O›P

U — S — A

A GUIDE TO U.S. INDEPENDENTS

JOHN TRUBEE AND THE UGLY JANITORS OF AMERICA **The Communists Are Coming to Kill Us** LP (Enigma). This is a sick record. This is a bad record. This is the worst record I've ever heard. Obscene phone calls and lyrics, lightweight jazz and self indulgent synthesizer noodling. If songs like "Dumping Buckets of Phlegm on Bitchy Old Ladies" is your idea of art or entertainment, I suggest you see a psychiatrist. Enigma Records has put out a lot of trash, but I never thought they could get this low.

GUADALCANAL DIARY **Watusi Rodeo** 12" EP (Entertainment on Disc). Strong pop debut. Using cowboy and Third World references, we get to hear about Michael Rockefeller's unfortunate trip to Papua, New Guinea, as well as bravado concerning the death of John Wayne (with a tip o' the hat to Moriccone and "The Good, the Bad and the Ugly"). Remember "Indian Reservation" by Mark Lindsay? Well, it would sound A-OK next to "Liwi Wechi" with its simple maracas and coyote crooning. Produced by Bruce Baxter of Georgia's DB Records, this anthemic, minimal pop sound will probably appeal to fans of the late, great Pylon.

YOUR FOOD **Poke It With A Stick** LP (Screaming Whoredog Records). Fairly interesting release from the Louisville, KY underground. Simple, primitive riffing provides the background the offbeat yet personal lyrics. Should be of interest to fans of **The Fall**.

MEAT PUPPETS II LP (SST). O.K. These guys from Phoenix have always been a little odd. Despite publicly stating an interest in pot and the Grateful Dead, the Meat Puppets still uncork chaos — their last LP was pure sonic sandpaper. Now it's Meat Puppets II and everything's starting to make sense. "Plateau" and "Climbing" are folksy country songs that could have come off *Workingman's Dead*. In fact, some girl from Tacoma went so far as to call this "Ozark Mountain shit." So much for the general public. My guess is that true Meat Puppets fans will go for it, because it's their eccentricity and willingness to take risks that earned the Meat Puppets a cult following in the first place.

VITAMIX

From out of Sunset High School in Portland comes 17-year-old "Vitamix," a break-mixer who's currently cutting the only alternative rap/funk radio show in Portland. "The King Crewsade" can be heard from 3-7 a.m. every Saturday night on KBOO-FM (90.7). The show features guest rappers from around the Portland area as well as unusual mixes of the latest.

Where does "Vitamix" (aka Chris Blanchard) get his records? "From friends in N.Y. and The House of Sound, the best store in Portland for 12-inch dance records."

Although he used to, Chris rarely break-dances anymore — too many other people are doing it. "Anyone who's athletic can spin around on their head. I'd rather watch the body poppers doing their mechanical thing, that takes a little more skill. Right now people are breaking all over, at the Blazers' games, downtown . . . the *best* crew in town is the Cleveland High School Breakers."

But while Chris dabbles with various facets of Wild Style culture like graffitti art and breakdancing and rapping, what he does best is working the turntables. If you'd like to check out just what this guy is doing, then write away for one of his tapes. The latest one's called **Break Dance** and features a mix of "Rock It" as well as some more obscure hits. Send $3 to: Vitamix, 2005 NE 22nd, Portland, OR 97212. The tapes are also available at Park Ave. and Singles Going Steady record stores in Portland.

SCREAMING WHOREDOG: 2425 Bardstown Rd. Apt. 2F, Louisville, KY 40205.
RELATIVITY: 149-03 Brewar Blvd., Jamaica, N.Y. 11434.
FUNK DUNGEON: 1704 N. 5th St., Philadelphia, PA 19122.
ENIGMA: Box 2896, Torrance, CA 90509.
SST: Box 1, Lawndale, CA 90260.
FAKE DOOM: GPO Box 1698, NYC 10116.
FATAL MARBLE: 1792 Shattuck Ave., Berkeley, CA 94709.
RESISTANCE: Box 11563, Marina Del Rey, CA 90291.
ENTERTAINMENT ON DISC: 100 Hansell St., Marietta, GA 30060.
C.I.A.: 1231 Ashland, Houston, TX 77008.

By Bruce Pavitt

Sub/Pop U.S.A.
▶▶ Radio ◀◀
every Tuesday 6-7 PM • KCMU 90.5 FM

BUNNYDRUMS P.K.D. 12" EP (Funk Dungeon). A compilation of previously released material. **Bunnydrums** and their friends **Executive Slacks** are putting Philadelphia on the map with a taut, sometimes abrasive mix of pop and technology. Synthesizers don't have to sound sterile. Recommended.

BLACK FLAG My War LP (SST). America's most awesome machine is currently touring the States; can't wait to see 'em again. Of course they'll be pushing *My War*, their first in a series of four LPs to be released this year on SST. So the album . . . well, it's pretty good. Thrash on side one and *ultra* slow dirge on side two. Continuing in the vein of "Damaged" these slow tunes are raw, with coarse vocals by Henry ("I'm gonna blow my cool all over the place") and off-kilter metallic solos by Gregg Gihn. It's a radical direction which will excite some and turn off just as many, so flip a coin.

Black Flag, the Meat Puppets and Nig Heist will be at the Norway Center in Seattle on April 27 at 9 p.m.

THE CUCUMBERS 4-song 12" (Fake Doom). Fun pop record from N.Y. Melodic counterpoint between bass and guitar; female vocals. Songs celebrate day to day routines, friendship. For the most part a real success, **Individuals** fans take note.

THE DARK Don't Feed the Fashion Sharks 12" EP (Relativity). Superficial synth-pop from Boston. Vocalist sounds like David Bowie with a cold. Could be a hit at the Vogue.

17 PYGMIES Hatikva 12" EP (Resistance). For those who enjoy the ethnic and industrial mix of L.A.'s **Savage Republic**, **17 Pygmies** is a record to pick up. "Lawrence of Arabia" is powerful and exotic, a camel driven caravan; heavy drums, guitar, organ. "To No Avail" is another middle-eastern instrumental. The packaging here is similar to Independent Project recordings; the cover is hand printed and numbered. Grab it!

MYDOLLS Speak Softly and Carry a Big Stick 12" EP (C.I.A.). Houston girl-group the Mydolls have come up with a follow up to their Siouxsie-inspired 45, "Imposter," released two years ago. The *Speak Softly* side and *Carry a Big Stick* side are fairly self explanatory. Introverted vs. Aggressive. The Mydolls will appear in German filmmaker Wim Wenders' next production, *Paris, Texas*. Check it out.

PARIS WORKING 12" EP (Fatal Marble). Talented "new music" pop group from San Francisco. Danceable, mainstream fare that I can't get too excited about. Should fit the MTV/Rock of the '80s format quite nicely.

"Plateau" and "Climbing" are folksy country songs that could have come off *Workingman's Dead*. In fact, some girl from Tacoma went so far as to call this "Ozark Mountain shit." So much for the general public. My guess is that true Meat Puppets fans will go for it, because it's their eccentricity and willingness to take risks that earned the Meat Puppets a cult following in the first place.

BUNNYDRUMS *P.K.D.* 12" EP (Funk Dungeon). A compilation of previously released material. Bunny-drums and their friends **EXECUTIVE SLACKS** are putting Philadelphia on the map with a taut, some-times abrasive mix of pop and technology. Synthesiz-ers don't have to sound sterile. Recommended.

BLACK FLAG *My War* LP (SST). America's most awesome machine is currently touring the States; can't wait to see 'em again. Of course they'll be pushing *My War*, their first in a series of four LPs to be released this year on SST. So the album; well, it's pretty good. Thrash on side one, and ultra-slow dirge on side two. Continuing in the vein of *Damaged*, these slow tunes are raw, with coarse vocals by Henry ("I'm gonna blow my cool all over the place") and off-kilter metallic solos by Greg Ginn. It's a radical direction which will excite some and turn off just as many, so flip a coin.

THE CUCUMBERS 4-song 12" (Fake Doom). Fun pop record from New York. Melodic counterpoint be-tween bass and guitar; female vocals. Songs celebrate day-to-day routines, friendship. For the most part a real success. **INDIVIDUALS** fans take note.

THE DARK *Don't Feed the Fashion Sharks* 12" EP (Relativity). Superficial synth pop from Boston. Vocal-ist sounds like **DAVID BOWIE** with a cold. Could be a hit at the Vogue.

17 PYGMIES *Hatikva* 12" EP (Resistance). For those who enjoy the ethnic and industrial mix of L.A.'s **SAVAGE REPUBLIC**, 17 Pygmies is a record to pick up. "Lawrence of Arabia" is powerful and exotic, a camel-driven caravan; heavy drums, guitar, organ. "To No Avail" is another middle-eastern instrumental. The packaging here is similar to Independent Project Records; the cover is hand-printed and numbered. Grab it!

MYDOLLS *Speak Softly and Carry a Big Stick* 12" EP (C.I.A.). Houston girl group the Mydolls have come up with a followup to their **SIOUXSIE**- inspired 45, "Imposter," released two years ago. The "Speak Softly" side and "Carry a Big Stick" side are fairly self-explanatory. Introverted vs. aggressive. The Mydolls will appear in German filmmaker Wim Wenders' next production, *Paris, Texas*. Check it out.

PARIS WORKING 12" EP (Fatal Marble). Talented "new music" pop group from San Francisco. Dance-able, mainstream fare that I can't get too excited about. Should fit the MTV rock of the ' 80s format quite nicely.

I'm Glad I Didn't Live in Vancouver During the '60s!

THE TROPICANA

The Tropicana is a new all ages club that's recently opened in Olympia, Washington. Although it's a one-hour drive from Seattle, they've been bringing in some good bands at good prices. For example, the **THREE O'CLOCK** recently played there for only $4, compared to $8 in Seattle. Aside from the decent prices, it's also a fun place to go. Audiences are more starved for entertainment than their jaded Seattle counterparts. Quotes Bradley Sweek, "It's small, and when things are happening, everyone's into it. It's an intimate environment no matter who's playing."

Although the pay isn't great, Northwest bands might want to call Larry for a booking. This guy is honest and won't rip you off. The remodeled storefront also doubles as an art gallery. Visual artists should also give Larry a call.

To obtain a free monthly calendar and newsletter, write: The Tropicana, Olympia, WA.

VARIOUS *Afterthought*: *History of Vancouver Rock 'n Roll* LP (VRCA). A collection of 45s from '66 to '72, this recently-released disc apparently documents Vancouver's drug influenced "psychedelic era." Well, I'm glad I didn't live in Vancouver during the '60s! Avoiding the intense, surrealistic frenzy of acid punks like the **13TH FLOOR ELEVATORS** from Texas, Vancouver bands opted for diluted versions of Haight-Ashbury groups like the **DEAD**, the **CHARLATANS** and the **AIRPLANE**. Don't be misled by the title, this is not rock 'n roll.

SEPTIC DEATH LP (Pusmort). Who would have thought a band from Boise, Idaho, would help put Northwest hardcore on the map? Septic Death (featuring infamous gore illustrator "Pushead" on vocals) has come up with a decent high-speed thrash disc. Some time and commitment have obviously gone into the packaging and production of this record, both are first rate. And although the band uses speed to disguise their inability to write real songs, there's enough style here to make it stand out of the heap. Boise, I salute you.

ANIMAL SLAVES 12" EP (Mo-Da-Mu). I'm sure a lot of people are going to like this. First of all, it's released on Mo-Da-Mu, the most consistent alternative pop label in the Pacific Northwest, noted for its taste and maturity. The cover art here is bold and well executed. And the musicians are top-notch, too; Rachel Melas is an awesome, fluid bass player who must be seen live to be truly appreciated. Personally, though, I just can't get next to it. The thing is just too damn arty. With whining vocals, offbeat time signatures, and pretentious lyrics ("Let's hear it for the easy solutions that present themselves effortlessly as whispered platitudes insidiously convincing, carefully blanketing self-conceived madness") this outfit is daring to be different—but I'm simply not in the mood.

CURTISS A *Damage Is Done* LP (Twin Tone). This is the second LP by Minneapolis veteran Curtiss A. Although highly respected in some circles, I find this sub-Springsteen material stale and dated.

MINOR THREAT 12" EP (Dischord). Long-awaited reissue of the first two Minor Threat singles! Side one

KIDNEY ROCK
A Benefit for the Northwest Kidney Foundation

with **THE ALLIES**
MOVING PARTS
THE RANGE HOODS
Plus a Special Appearance By
TINY TONY

SUN MAY 27
PARKER'S
17001 AURORA N.
8:30 p.m.-1:30 a.m. $5
For more information
call 323-6896

TOP CASH PAID!!
FOR
RECORDS
& TAPES
STEREOS
GUITARS
TV's

2ND TIME AROUND
SEATTLE   TACOMA
4444 UNIV. WY. NE   2913 S. 38th
632-1698   472-0623

TATTOO YOU
Custom Tattooing
Body Piercing

THE FRONT ROOM
Gifts, Accessories, Leather
goods & Cosmetics for the
bizarre at heart.
Open Tues-Sat. 2-8
1017 E. Pike St.
324-6443

MICK'S
VINTAGE GUITARS

CLIP & MAIL

FREE CATALOG

NAME _____
ADDRESS _____
CITY, STATE, ZIP _____
_____

OPEN 11-6 MON-SAT

**3922 California Ave. S.W.
Seattle, WA 98116
(206) 937-0690**

S>U>B >P>O>P

U — S — A

A GUIDE TO U.S. INDEPENDENTS

AFTERTHOUGHT: *History of Vancouver Rock 'n' Roll* LP (VRCA). A collection of 45s from '66-'72, this recently released disc apparently documents Vancouver's drug influenced "psychedelic era." Well, I'm glad I didn't live in Vancouver during the '60s! Avoiding the intense, surrealistic frenzy of acid punks like the **13th Floor Elevators** (Texas), Vancouver bands opted for diluted versions of Haight-Ashbury groups like the **Dead**, the **Charlatans** and the **Airplane**. Don't be mislead by the title, this is *not* rock 'n' roll.

SEPTIC DEATH LP (Pusmort). Who would have thought a band from Boise, Idaho would help put Northwest hardcore on the map? **Septic Death** (featuring infamous gore illustrator "Pushead" on vocals) has come up with a decent high speed thrash disc. Some time and commitment have obviously gone into the packaging and production of this record, both are first rate. And although the band uses speed to disguise their inability to write real songs, there's enough style here to make it stand out of the heap. Boise, I salute you.

ANIMAL SLAVES 12" EP (Mo-Da-Mu). I'm sure a lot of people are going to like this. First of all, it's released on Mo-Da-Mu, the most consistent alternative pop label in the Pacific Northwest, noted for its taste and maturity. The cover art here is bold and well executed. And the musicians are top notch too; Rachel Melas is an awesome, fluid bass player who must be seen live to be truly appreciated.
Personally though, I just can't get next to it. The thing is just too damn arty. With whining vocals, offbeat time signatures and pretentious lyrics ("Let's hear it for the easy solutions that present themselves effortlessly as whispered platitudes insidiously convincing, carefully blanketing self conceived madness") this outfit *is* daring to be different but I'm simply not in the mood.

CURTISS A *Damage is Done* LP (Twin Tone). This is the second LP by Minneapolis veteran **Curtiss A.** Although highly respected in some circles, I find this sub-Springsteen material stale and dated.

MINOR THREAT 12" EP (Dischord). Long awaited re-issue of the first two **Minor Threat** singles! Side one of this 12-inch features early anthems like "Filler" and "Seeing Red"; flip it over for the truly great "In My Eyes." Now defunct, this legendary D.C. band was most famous for their "straight-edge" anti-drug philosophy. They also helped start Dischord, one of the most successful independent "hardcore" labels in America. **Minor Threat** was a

Photo by Mike Lavine

THE TROPICANA IS A NEW all ages club that's recently opened in Olympia, WA. Although it's an hour drive from Seattle, they've been bringing in some good bands at good prices. For example, The Three O'Clock recently played there for only $4 compared to $8 in Seattle. Aside from the decent prices, it's also a fun place to go. Audiences are more starved for entertainment and usually exhibit a lot more enthusiasm than their jaded Seattle counterparts. Quotes Bradley Sweek, "It's small, and when things are happening everyone's into it. It's an intimate environment no matter who's playing."
Although the pay isn't great, Northwest bands might want to call Larry (home phone 754-JAVA) for a booking. This guy is honest and won't rip you off.
The remodeled storefront also doubles as an art gallery. Visual artists should also give Larry a call.
To obtain a free monthly calendar and newsletter, write: The Tropicana, P.O. Box 1033, Olympia, WA 98507.
Selected highlights for May:
May 5: **New Music Festival** with various local avant-garde.
May 12: **54/40** (Vancouver), and **Life in General** (Seattle).
May 18: **Volume Three, Immoral Roberts** (Oly High School hardcore).

By Bruce Pavitt

group that had something to say and did it with skill and creativity, proving that there's more to life than panhandling for beer money.

STEVE FISK *Kiss This Day Goodbye* cassette (ARPH). Steve Fisk chews up America and spits out pop art. This tape is a witty mix of disco tape loops and obscure TV and radio blips. Steve augments this found footage with an occasional twisted vocal, keyboard overlay and/or octagon solo. Serious work with a rare sense of humor. Highly recommended.

BIG BLACK 12" EP (Ruthless/Fever). Spectacular second release by Chicago's hardcore/industrial **Big Black.** Writer/critic Steve Albini is the main man here, playing "klang guitar" and vocals; the rest of the artillery is on loan from various local bands. **Big Black** spent big bucks on production and they used it to their advantage — the clarity and separation of bangs, riffs and tapes is excellent. Lyrics are all-American too, with songs about Texas, Montana and Indiana. More!!

AWESOME FOURSOME *Funky Breakdown* 12" single (Party Time). Everybody's gonna crawl on the cardboard to this one — break tune of the month.

ADDRESSES:

PUSMORT: c/o Pushead 2713 Kerr, Boise, ID 83705.

THERMIDOR: 912 Bancroft Way, Berkeley, CA 94710.

PARTY TIME: c/o Streetwise, 25 West 43rd St., N.Y.C. 10036.

RUTHLESS: P.O. Box 1458, Evanston, IL 60204.

VRCA: c/o Neptune Records, 5766 Fraser St., Vancouver, B.C., Canada.

MO-DA-MU: Box 810 W. Broadway, Vancouver, B.C., Canada.

DISCHORD: 3819 Beecher St. NW, Washington, D.C. 20007.

ARPH Tapes: 1640 18th St., Oakland, CA 94607.

TWIN TONE: 445 Oliver Ave. S., Minneapolis, MN 55405.

Sub/Pop U.S.A.
► ► Radio ◄ ◄
every Tuesday 6-7 PM • KCMU 90.5 FM

Two million sharp rhythms all over the place. Sure it's goofy with Tarzan yells and Curly from the Three Stooges and maybe I *won't* be listening to this two years from now but who cares? The sun's coming out and the blaster's on *full volume.*

XX COMMITTEE *Network* LP (Thermidor). Fans of industrial "music" might want to check out this minimal, rigidly rhythmic project from Allentown, PA. Brutal machine arrangements that go on forever might just be what the doctor ordered. That, or maybe a pleasant hike in the mountains.

HIGHS IN THE MID SIXTIES Vol. 7: The *Northwest* LP (A.I.P.). From the collectors who brought you the **Pebbles** compilations comes another series of manic sixties garage punk. Earlier volumes have included LA, Michigan and Chicago; this, their seventh volume, takes aim on the Pacific Northwest. Ignoring classic bands like the **Sonics**, the **Raiders** and the **Kingsmen**, this LP digs deep for some extremely obscure one-shots; bands from Longview and Spokane, Newport and Eugene. Wild, rockin' young teen bands like **The Bootmen** and the **Jolly Green Giants.** Tiny record labels like **Redcoat, Tripp** and **Bang.** A collection of hopelessly obscure records, this (mostly) pre-psychedelic package is a must for fanatics of roots rock 'n' roll.

of this 12-inch features early anthems like "Filler" and "Seeing Red"; flip it over for the truly great "In My Eyes." Now defunct, this legendary D.C. band was most famous for their "straight-edge" anti-drug philosophy. They also helped start Dischord, one of the most successful independent hardcore labels in America. Minor Threat was a group that had something to say and did it with skill and creativity, proving that there's more to life than panhandling for beer money.

STEVE FISK *Kiss This Day Goodbye* cassette (ARPH). Steve Fisk chews up America and spits out pop art. This tape is a witty mix of disco tape loops and obscure TV and radio blips. Steve augments this found footage with an occasional twisted vocal, keyboard overlay, and/or octagon solo. Serious work with a rare sense of humor. Highly recommended.

BIG BLACK 12" EP (Ruthless/Fever). Spectacular second release by Chicago's hardcore/industrial Big Black. Writer/critic Steve Albini is the main man here, playing "klang guitar" and vocals; the rest of the artillery is on loan from various local bands. Big Black spent big bucks on production and they used it to their advantage—the clarity and separation of bangs, riffs, and tapes is excellent. Lyrics are all-American too, with songs about Texas, Montana, and Indiana. More!!

AWESOME FOURSOME *Funky Breakdown* 12" single (Party Time). Everybody's gonna crawl on the cardboard to this one—break tune of the month. Two million sharp rhythms all over the place. Sure it's goofy, with Tarzan yells and Curly from the Three Stooges, and maybe I won't be listening to this two years from now, but who cares? The sun's coming out and the blaster's on full volume.

XX COMMITTEE *Network* LP (Thermidor). Fans of industrial "music" might want to check out this minimal, rigidly rhythmic project from Allentown, PA. Brutal machine arrangements that go on forever might just be what the doctor ordered. That or maybe a pleasant hike in the mountains.

VARIOUS *Highs in the Mid Sixties Vol. 7: The Northwest* LP (A.I.P.). From the collectors who brought you the *Pebbles* compilations comes another series of manic sixties garage punk. Earlier volumes have included L.A., Michigan. and Chicago. This, their seventh volume, takes aim at the Pacific Northwest. Ignoring classic bands like the **SONICS**, the **RAIDERS** and the **KINGSMEN**, this LP digs deep for some extremely obscure one-shots; bands from Longview, Spokane, Newport, and Eugene. Wild, rockin' young teen bands like the **BOOTMEN** and the **JOLLY GREEN GIANTS** on tiny record labels like Redcoat, Tripp, and Bang. A collection of hopelessly obscure records, this (mostly) pre-psychedelic package is a must for fanatics of roots rock 'n roll.

Every Metal Band These Days Is Praising Satan

FANZINES

Seattle bands releasing tapes or records will want to send their promo copies effectively. There are hundreds of local and regional fanzines around the country that would be happy to review your work; however, sending hundreds of promos can get expensive. I have listed below three independent publications that I consider to be extremely influential; although they are quite different, all three have pretty much "cornered the market" as far as the musical genres they represent.

MAXIMUM ROCKNROLL

Maximum Rocknroll magazine, in two years, has become a global, unifying force for the "hardcore punk" movement. They've even released a couple of LP compilation. Coming out bi-monthly, *MRR* includes many scene reports and dedicates a lot of space to reviews. This includes demos. The hardcore scene's number 2 contender, *Flipside*, is currently more involved with video compilation. Write to MRR, Berkeley, CA. I recommend sending two copies, one for the magazine, the other for their syndicated radio show.

UNSOUND

For those noise makers whose interest leans toward the avant garde, *Unsound* is quickly becoming an organized media meeting place. Their latest issue features write-ups on **SONIC YOUTH**, **EINSTÜRZENDE NEUBAUTEN**, **HUNTING LODGE**, **ADRIAN SHERWOOD**, and Seattle's own **EPP**. Plenty of the experimental music covered here is in cassette form, so don't be afraid to send in a tape. Write *Unsound*, San Francisco, CA.

MATTER

This Chicago (Evanston, IL) publication is emerging as a strong voice for new pop. The staff here is open and covers all sorts of territory, but the focus is not rooted in any one extreme fashion. Issue #8 featured the **GO-BETWEENS**, **TROUBLE FUNK**, **LOVE TRACTOR**, **SPORT OF KINGS** and the **SMITHS**. Some good journalism here, too, from Blake Gumprecht and Steve Albini.

•

VARIOUS *Cottage Cheese From The Lips Of Death* Compilation LP (Ward 9). Redneck-rage hardcore compilation from Texas. All the big names are here: **BIG BOYS**, **BUTTHOLE SURFERS**, **D.R.I.**, **REALLY RED**, the **DICKS**, and the **MYDOLLS**. Some of this material has been previously released, so this disc works best as an introductory sampler. Even if you've got some of this already, though, you'll have to check out the surprise hit from **WATCHTOWER**!

ART IN THE DARK 12" EP (Somethin' Else). Layers of rich, haunting harmonies are the key to this outstanding New York pop EP. The lush, full sound comes courtesy of Mitch Easter, producer of **R.E.M.** and others. Pick hit: "Calling Anyone."

SHANGHAI DOG *Clanging Bells* 12" EP (SDEP). Pure torture. Dumb Vancouver rock band with quirky lyrics and arrangements. Sitting through records like

I trashed Hüsker Dü's Byrds cover. I also really thought that *Zen Arcade* was radically overrated. Everybody was so into the record. I thought it was pretty self-indulgent of them to release a double album. Previously, I thought they were pretty much one of the best bands in the country. Personally, I would never go out of my way at this point in my life to trash somebody's creative wok. I just don't have the capacity to endure people hating me for the rest of their lives—but at the time, I was up for it!

S·U·B·P·O·P
U — S — A
A GUIDE TO U.S. INDEPENDENTS

COTTAGE CHEESE FROM THE LIPS OF DEATH Compilation LP (Ward 9). Redneck rage hardcore compilation from Texas. All the big names are here — Big Boys, Butthole Surfers, D.R.I., Really Red, The Dicks, The Mydolls. Some of this material has been previously released, so this disc works best as an introductory sampler. Even if you've got some of this already though, you'll have to check out the surprise hit from Watchtower!

ART IN THE DARK 12" EP (Somethin' Else). Layers of rich, haunting harmonies are the key to this outstanding New York pop EP. The lush, full sound comes courtesy of Mitch Easter, producer of R.E.M. and others. Pick hit: "Calling Anyone."

SHANGHAI DOG *Clanging Bells* 12" EP (SDEP). Pure torture. Dumb Vancouver rock band with quirky lyrics and arrangements. Sitting through records like this can ruin your day. I'm going for a walk.

MINUTEMEN *Politics of Time* LP (New Alliance). A collection of obscure Minutemen cuts abducted from various sources. Side one shows the driving, angular hardcore/beat poetry of this outfit in top form. The production on side two is simply substandard. Stay tuned for a double LP currently in the works.

TROUBLE LP (Metal Blade). Seems like every metal band these days is praising Satan. But not Trouble. This Chicago band is spreading the name of the Lord with songs like "Psalm 9" and "The Fall of Lucifer." These prophets are so virtuous their record even comes on white vinyl. File next to Spinal Tap under "Novelty."

TOXIC REASONS *Kill by Remote Control* LP (Sixth International). The second LP by this San Francisco hardcore band shows some real maturity. While maintaining the essential frayed edge, there's actually a melody or two buried beneath the ranting and raving; and despite some sloganeering, the lyrics transcend the "beer and anarchy" approach in favor of higher ideals. Like all other releases on Sixth International, the packaging and production are excellent. Recommended.

By Bruce Pavitt
FANZINES

SEATTLE BANDS RELEASING tapes or records will want to send their promo copies effectively. There are hundreds of local and regional fanzines around the country that would be happy to review your work; however, sending hundreds of promos can get expensive. I have listed below three independent publications that I consider to be extremely influential; although they are quite different, all three have pretty much "cornered the market" as far as the musical genres they represent.

MAXIMUM ROCKNROLL

DOES PUNK SUCK ???

MAXIMUM ROCK N ROLL
Maximum Rock N Roll magazine, in two years, has become a global, unifying force for the "hardcore punk" movement. They've even released a couple of LP compilations. Coming out bi-monthly, MRR includes many scene reports and dedicates a lot of space to reviews. This includes demos. The hardcore scene's number 2 contender, Flipside, is currently more involved with video compilations. Write to MRR, Box 288, Berkeley, CA 94701. I recommend sending two copies, one for the magazine, the other for their syndicated radio show.

UNSOUND
For noise makers whose interest leans toward the avant-garde, *Unsound* is quickly becoming an organized media meeting place. Their latest issue features write-ups on Sonic Youth, Einstürzende Neubauten, Hunting Lodge, Adrian Sherwood and Seattle's own Epp. Plenty of the experimental music covered here is in cassette form, so don't be afraid to send in a tape. Write: Unsound, 801 22nd St., San Francisco, CA 94107.

MATTER
This Chicago publication is emerging as a strong voice for new pop. The staff here is open and covers all sorts of territory, but the focus is not rooted in any one extreme fashion. Issue #8 featured The Go-Betweens, Trouble Funk, Love Tractor, Sport of Kings and The Smiths. Some good journalism here too, from Blake Gumprecht and Steve Albini. Write: Matter, 624 Davis St. Evanston, IL 60201.

HASHIM *Al-Naafiysh (The Soul)* 12" single (Cutting). Push-button break hit from NYC. The rhythms are everywhere and the sound is modern, but what's here today is gone tomorrow. Fun for a month.

HUSKER DU *Eight Miles High* 45 (SST). Relentless slop. Husker Du digs deep and buries the beauty of this American folk/rock classic. I can hear The Byrds crying now. No definition, no intricacy, just plain mud. Go back to Minneapolis and send us The Replacements — you charlatans.

THE EMBARRASSMENT *Retrospective* Cassette (Fresh). Excellent! Live, unreleased and out-of-print songs from those crazy guys from Wichita. These "pop primitives" played it raw, with absurd lyrical twists and shifting, awkward one-word harmonies. Original rock 'n' roll — they will be missed.

MINIMAL MAN *Safari* LP (CD). The second LP by this S.F. artist makes for adequate entertainment but will hardly stand as a classic. Slick production and a big beat mixed with corrosive electronics falls somewhere between punk and disco. The moodier pieces, such as "Stop Running," are a lot more effective. If you played this loud enough it would be fun at a party, but I sure miss the visuals that accompany Minimal Man's live performances.

ADDRESSES
NEW ALLIANCE: P.O. Box 21, San Pedro, CA 90733.

FRESH SOUNDS, INC.: P.O. Box 36, Lawrence, KS 66044

CUTTING: 111 Dyckman Street, New York, NY 10040

SOMETHIN' ELSE RECORDS: P.O. Box 3287, New York, NY 10185.

WARD 9 RECORDS: 3014 Broadway, San Antonio, Texas 78209.

METAL BLADE: 22458 Ventura Blvd., Suite E., Woodland Hills, CA 91364.

SIXTH INTERNATIONAL: 326 Sixth St., San Francisco, CA 94103.

SST: P.O. Box 1, Lawndale, CA 90260.

CD: Suite 531, 1230 Grant Ave., San Francisco, CA 94133.

SDEP: 550 W. 6th Ave., Vancouver, B.C., Canada.

Sub/Pop U.S.A.
►► Radio ◄◄
every Tuesday 6-7 PM • KCMU 90.5 FM

this can ruin your day. I'm going for a walk.

MINUTEMEN *Politics of Time* LP (New Alliance). A collection of obscure Minutemen cuts abducted from various sources. Side one shows the driving, angular hardcore/beat poetry of this outfit in top form. The production on side two is simply substandard. Stay tuned for a double LP, currently in the works.

TROUBLE LP (Metal Blade). Seems like every metal band these days is praising Satan. But not Trouble. This Chicago band is spreading the name of the Lord with songs like "Psalm 9" and "The Fall of Lucifer." These prophets are so virtuous their record even comes on white vinyl. File next to **SPINAL TAP** in "Novelty."

TOXIC REASONS *Kill by Remote Control* LP (Sixth International). The second LP by this San Francisco hardcore band shows some real maturity. While maintaining the essential frayed edge, there's actually a melody or two buried beneath the ranting and raving; and despite some sloganeering, the lyrics transcend the "beer and anarchy" approach in favor of higher ideals. Like all other releases on Sixth International, the packaging and production are excellent. Recommended.

HASHIM *Al-Naafiysh* (The Soul) 12" single (Cutting). Push-button break hit from NYC. The rhythms are everywhere and the sound is modern, but what's here today is gone tomorrow. Fun for a month.

HÜSKER DÜ *Eight Miles High* 45 (SST). Relentless slop. Hüsker Dü digs deep and buries the beauty of this American folk/rock classic. I can hear the **BYRDS** crying now. No definition, no intricacy, just plain mud. Go back to Minneapolis and send us the **REPLACE-MENTS**—you charlatans.

THE EMBARRASSMENT *Retrospective* cassette (Fresh). Excellent! Live, unreleased, and out-of-print songs from those crazy guys from Wichita, Kansas. These "pop primitives" played it raw, with absurd lyrical twists and shifting, awkward one-word harmonies. Original rock 'n roll—they will be missed.

MINIMAL MAN *Safari* LP (CD). The second LP by this San Francisco artist makes for adequate entertainment, but will hardly stand as a classic. Slick production and a big beat mixed with corrosive electronies falls somewhere between punk and disco. The moodier pieces, such as "Stop Running," are a lot more effective. If you played this loud enough, it would be fun at a party, but I sure miss the visuals that accompany Minimal Man's live performances.

What's the Buzz?

Scooter clubs, heavily influenced by '60s "mod" culture, are zooming their way across the country. The mod/scooter scene is also developing a network of fanzines, bands, and clubs. I recently talked with Jeff Long, member of Seattle's **BUZZ SCOOTER CLUB** and co-editor of the fanzine *Let's Scoot* (currently undergoing a name change).

Jeff Says that members of Buzz ride Italian scooters only (Vespa, Lambretta), most of which are vintage models from the '60s. Despite the fact that the US stopped importing these brands a few years ago (making parts difficult to obtain), Buzz members feel that the '60s Italian models are much cooler than the current Japanese models from Honda and Yamaha. "The Japanese engines are good, but we don't like the body work," says Jeff. "We like the two-wheel sports car look of the Italian scooters."

Although Jeff denied that the Buzz gang was strictly a mod scooter group, he admitted that there was "a strong mod backbone. Several of my friends enjoy music from that period." The British mods were notorious for dressing sharp, and listening to British Invasion, ska, and soul.

The mod/scooter scene is growing in popularity around the world and around the US. Currently, L.A. is the real center, with scooter clubs like Pow, the 100 Club and Separate Identity. There are also mod nightclubs like Bullet and the On Club. L.A.'s top mod bands is the **UNTOUCHABLES**, although the **3 O'CLOCK** is also popular. An L.A. fanzine, *Twist*, will feature an article on Buzz in an upcoming issue.

There are 10–15 members in the Buzz Scooter Club. Group drives of 40–50 miles are driven most Sundays with a mechanic usually on hand. Jeff says that it would be impractical to have any more members in Buzz, although he encourages other scooter enthusiasts to get together—it's a lot of fun.

•

LYRES *On Fyre* LP (Ace of Hearts). Fans of '60s garage punk and pop will surely go for this fine rockin' LP. Although some of the songs drag a little, the Lyres love what they're doing and it shows. Also, producer Rick Harte has done a good job of capturing the atmosphere and vitality of this music. Once again, Harte's Ace of Hearts label proves itself to be Boston's strongest indie label.

RANCID VAT *Profiles in Pain* 7" EP (Pigface). Portland's notoriously sick, negative, cynical, bitter, and suicidal Pigface label has put out a variety of releases, mostly strange. Few surprises here, however, as the music is mid-tempo hardcore punk. The lyrics are the outstanding feature on this record; they are fully understandable (a rarity) and often quite funny, usually at other people's expense. On translucent pink vinyl.

THE REVERBS *The Happy Forest* LP (Enigma). The Reverbs play it pure—this is innocent, timeless pop. Acoustic and electric guitars, tambourine, and vocal trade-offs are all beautifully performed. This charming Chicago duo has put out a memorable release, the perfect antidote to all that relentless "wave" disco you keep hearing on TV commercials (and rock-of-the-'80s radio stations).

JAMES BROWN *The Federal Years Part I* and *Part II* LP (Solid Smoke). James Brown, the "godfather of soul," the "hardest working man in show business," and one of the coolest people who ever lived, is young and wailing on these two compilations chronicling his

Sonic Youth added intellectual depth to the scene. They were very inspiring people. I loved their early EP *Kill Yr Idols*. In early 1986 I came very close to attending the School of Visual Arts in New York. However, while I was visiting there, I had an epiphany that I could put out a vinyl counterpart to the *Sub Pop* cassettes. I asked Kim Gordon and Thurston Moore for permission to license the song "Kill Yr Idols." I knew by having a good Sonic Youth track, it would be a lot easier to get other bands to jump on board my compilation. That was the root of *Sub Pop 100*, the first Sub Pop record. Back in Seattle, I got so excited about doing the record, I decided to stay in Seattle and get a record label off the ground.

S›U›B›P›O›P
U — S — A
A GUIDE TO U.S. INDEPENDENTS

LYRES On Fyre
LP (Ace of Hearts). Fans of '60s garage punk and pop will surely go for this fine, rockin' LP. Although some of the songs drag a little, the Lyres love what they're doing and it shows. Also, producer Rick Harte has done a good job of capturing the atmosphere and vitality of this music. Once again, Harte's *Ace of Hearts* label proves itself to be Boston's strongest indie label.

RANCID VAT Profiles in Pain
7" EP (Pigface). Portland's notoriously sick, negative, cynical, bitter and suicidal Pigface label has put out a variety of releases, mostly strange. Few surprises here, however, as the music is mid-tempo hardcore punk. The lyrics are the outstanding feature on this record; they are fully understandable (a rarity) and often quite funny, usually at other people's expense. On translucent pink vinyl.

THE REVERBS The Happy Forest
LP (Enigma). The Reverbs play it pure — this is innocent, timeless pop. Acoustic and electric guitars, tambourine and vocal trade-offs, all are beautifully performed. This charming Chicago duo has put out a memorable release and the perfect antidote to all that relentless "wave" disco you keep hearing on TV commercials (and Rock of the '80s radio stations).

JAMES BROWN The Federal Years Part I and Part II
LP (Solid Smoke). James Brown, the "godfather of soul," the "hardest working man in show business" and one of the coolest people who ever lived, is young and wailing on these two compilations, chronicling his earliest recordings with the Famous Flames on the King/Federal label from '56 to '60. These earlier recordings featured slower, gospel-style group harmonies; many of these songs were impassioned ballads, although a few, like "That Dood It," are jumpin' R&B classics that still tear the house down. It's impossible to recommend one over the other, so get 'em both.

SONIC YOUTH Kill Yr Idols
12" EP (Zensor import). Unbridled hipness from one of NYC's most creative bands. They've taken the best from the *Confusion is Sex* LP, added three intense new tracks, and put it all on a kick-ass 12" at 45 rpm. This art/punk outfit from the Lower East Side literally redefines bass, drums and guitar — everything's wobbling and off the edge. The production is excellent too, lots of clarity but very raw. Seek and consume.

POP DEFECT Playing For Time
12" EP (Heart Murmur). Pop Defect has come up with some real hits. A talented, inspired pop trio, they blew me away live, coming across like early

By Bruce Pavitt

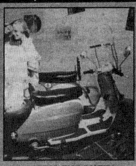

WHAT'S THE BUZZ?
Scooter clubs, heavily influenced by '60s "mod" culture, are zooming their way across the country. The mod/scooter scene is also developing a network of fanzines, bands and clubs. I recently talked with **Jeff Long**, member of Seattle's **Buzz Scooter Club** and co-editor of the fanzine *Let's Scoot* (currently undergoing a name change).

Jeff says that members of Buzz ride Italian scooters only (**Vespa, Lambretto**), most of which are vintage models from the '60s. Despite the fact that the U.S. stopped importing these brands a few years ago (making parts difficult to obtain), Buzz members feel that the '60s Italian models are much cooler than current Japanese models from Honda and Yamaha. "The Japanese engines are good but we don't like the body work," says Jeff. "We like the two-wheel sports car look of the Italian scooters."

Although Jeff denied that the Buzz gang was strictly a mod scooter group, he admitted that there was "a strong mod backbone; several of my friends enjoy music from that period." The British mods were notorious for dressing sharp and listening to British Invasion, ska and soul.

The mod/scooter scene is growing in popularity around the world and around the U.S. Currently, L.A. is the real center, with scooter clubs like **Pow, The 100 Club** and **Separate Identity**. There are also mod nightclubs like **Bullet** and the **On Club**. L.A.'s top mod band is the **Untouchables**, although **The 3 O'Clock** is also popular. An L.A. fanzine, **Twist**, will feature an article on Buzz in an upcoming issue.

There are 10-15 members in the Buzz Scooter Club. Group drives of 40-50 miles are driven most Sundays with a mechanic usually on hand. Jeff says that it would be impractical to have any more members in Buzz, although he encourages other scooter enthusiasts to get together — it's a lot of fun. ■

Sub/Pop U.S.A.
►► Radio ◄◄
every Tuesday 6-7 PM • KCMU 90.5 FM

Jam. Although the arrangements could sound fuller (more background vocals would add punch) I'm sure this record will appeal to many. Formerly from Seattle, I hope they make it big in L.A.

TRUE SOUNDS OF LIBERTY Change Today?
LP (Enigma). T.S.O.L. is a different band with every record. Aside from changes in personnel, their sound has gone from ultra-political thrash to horror rock to punk pop. The only thing T.S.O.L. seems committed to is change. Although I personally lost interest after their first, classic release, I find myself liking this record, despite their recent lame appearance in *Suburbia*. This is an aggressive, "mature" rock sound; singer Joe Wood is technically a proficient singer who owes much to Jim Morrison. The songs are tight, not abandoned. This is a good commercial record which will probably receive heavy college airplay.

EFFIGIES Forever Grounded
LP (Enigma). Chicago's Effigies are another punk band that's decided to really grow up. Sadly, the result is boring, and a disappointment after their first three releases. They've traded all their power for some flowery lyrics and cardboard vocals that lack depth or emotion. The production is claustrophobic and sterile; the energy is laying on the living room floor, staring at the ceiling.

LIVE SKULL
12" EP (Massive). Another hot record from the Lower East Side. Like Sonic Youth, Live Skull experiments with roasting, slower tempos and atonality, featuring both male and female vocalists. Both bands are also capable of stepping on the accelerator — "Boil" is a scorching vocal assault that leaves me flying. More.

MANIFEST DESTINY
LP (Mystic). There are a lot of ignorant, sleazy people in this world who have nothing to do but beat off and tell us how we're "dumbfucks." My advice to Manifest Destiny: pick up a book, learn to spell and do something with your life.

ADDRESSES
MYSTIC: 6277 Selma, Hollywood, CA 90028.
ACE OF HEARTS: Box 579, Kenmore Station, Boston, MA 02215.
MASSIVE: 231 W. 29th St., Suite 602, NYC, NY 10001.
HEART MURMUR: P.O. Box 42602, L.A., CA 90042.
SOLID SMOKE: Box 22372, S.F., CA 90509.
ENIGMA: Box 2896, Torrance, CA 90509.
PIGFACE: c/o P.O. Box 40832, Portland, OR 97240.

earliest recordings with the **FAMOUS FLAMES** on the King/Federal label from '56 to '60. These earlier recordings featured slower, gospel-style group harmonies; many of these songs were impassioned ballads, although a few, like "That Dood It," are jumpin' R&B classics that still tear the house down. It's impossible to recommend one over the other, so get 'em both.

SONIC YOUTH *Kill Yr Idols* 12" EP (Zensor import). Unbridled hipness from one of NYC's most creative bands. They've taken the best from the *Confusion is Sex* LP, added three intense new tracks, and put it all on a kick-ass 12" at 45 rpm. This art/punk outfit from the Lower East Side literally redefines bass, drums and guitar—everything's wobbling and off the edge. The production is excellent, too, lots of clarity but very raw. Seek and consume.

POP DEFECT *Playing for Time* 12" EP (Heart Murmur). Pop Defect has come up with some real hits. A talented, inspired pop trio, they blew me away live, coming across like early **JAM**. Although the arrangements could sound fuller (more background vocals would add punch) I'm sure this record will appeal to many. Formerly from Seattle, I hope they make it big in L.A.

TRUE SOUNDS OF LIBERTY *Change Today?* LP (Enigma). T.S.O.L. is a different band with every record. Aside from changes in personnel, their sound has gone from ultra-political thrash to horror rock to punk pop. The only thing T.S.O.L. seems committed to is change. Although I personally lost interest after their classic first release, I find myself liking this record; despite their recent lame appearance in *Suburbia*. This is an aggressive, "mature" rock sound; singer Joe Wood is technically a proficient singer who owes much to **JIM MORRISON**. The songs are tight, not abandoned. This is a good commercial record which will probably receive heavy college airplay.

EFFIGIES *Forever Grounded* LP (Enigma). Chicago's Effigies are another punk band that's decided to really grow up. Sadly, the result is boring, and a disappoint-ment after their first three releases. They've traded all their power for some flowery lyrics and cardboard vocals that lack depth or emotion. The production is claustrophobic and sterile; the energy is laying on the living room floor, staring at the ceiling.

LIVE SKULL 12" EP (Massive). Another hot record from the Lower East Side. Like **SONIC YOUTH**, Live Skull experiments with roasting, slower tempos and atonality, featuring both male and female vocalists. Both bands are also capable of stepping on the accelerator—"Boil" is a scorching vocal assault that leaves me flying. More.

MANIFEST DESTINY LP (Mystic). There are a lot of ignorant, sleazy people in this world who have nothing to do but beat off and tell us how we're "dumb-fucks." My advice to Manifest Destiny: pick up a book, learn to spell, and do something with your life.

The End of OP?

The Lost Music Network, the cooperative organization that publishes *OP*, the independent music magazine, held a conference in mid-July to discover the fate of the publication. People involved in the international independent music network met for a weekend of seminars, elbow rubbing, and original music. *OP* is headquartered, and the conference was held, in Olympia, Washington.

"After the 'Z' issue it's all over, at least for me," stated *OP* editor John Foster. "There is a burn-out factor. If some kind of publication is to be continued, things will have to be organized soon." Foster and art director Dana Leigh Squires are planning on joining the Peace Corps next year, and will hopefully work in Africa.

The conference was a great chance to meet other people involved with small record labels. Seminars covered various facets of the underground music business, including college and community radio, distribution, cassette networking, recording techniques, and magazine publishing. Most of the music occurred at Olympia's Tropicana, an all-ages club that recently opened. Members got to check out everything from experimental electronics to jazz to hardcore punk. Personal favorites were **BEAT HAPPENING, POP PHILOSOPHERS, YOUNG PIONEERS, WIMPS** and wild man **GEOFF KIRK**.

OP Magazine, starting in 1979 with the "A" issue, is considered the bible of the independent music scene. Covering every possible form of music, *OP* focuses on a different letter of the alphabet with each issue, featuring artists whose name begin with that letter (i.e. the "W" issue featured **WHIZ KID, WIPERS, MAL WALDRON**, etc.) All artists whose work appears on small record labels get a few lines in the awesome review section. Addresses are given.

Fortunately, by the end of the conference, a group of folks from L.A. had offered to pick up the pieces after the "Z" issue and start a new magazine using the networking information collected by *OP*. To the staff of *OP*—John, Dana, and Dave—I salute you for your tireless efforts and a job well done. *OP* is available from Lost Music Network, Olympia, WA.

•

VELVET MONKEYS *Future* LP (Fountain of Youth). Long awaited vinyl debut from D.C. area garage pop band. Their demo of "Everything Is Right" had me floored—classic *Pebbles* material. I've also heard raves about their live shows. So what's the problem? They've traded in their soul for a geek synthesizer. Very cold. The Velvet Monkeys have a good vocalist and decent material, but they're lost in a time warp. They're caught between the sixties and the eighties and they can't make it work.

SACCHARINE TRUST *Surviving You, Always* LP (SST). The second release by Saccharine Trust is denser and more frenetic than their last. Like labelmates **THE MINUTEMEN**, these art punks spew forth poetry instead of politics, abstractions instead of slogans. Frontman Joaquin Brewer is distinguished by his obsession with religion; words like faith, sin, and devotion constantly creep in. The credits also list them as providing "vocals and sermons." As for the music, there are references to jazz fusion and free jazz. The intro to "The House, the System, the Concrete" is minimal and extremely effective, with nothing but random footsteps to create a mood. Basically interesting.

OP was a visionary publication that stressed indie music of all genres. This core indie philosophy was initiated by John Foster, who I considered to be my mentor at Evergreen College. I was lucky to have access to John's record collection, full of really rare records from the middle of nowhere. At that time, the phrase "indie rock" did not exist. John Foster is the visionary that really promoted the idea of cultural self-empowerment, and the importance of community support for local artists who put out their own music. That was a revolutionary idea, and extremely punk in its own way. Sub Pop would not exist without OP magazine, period.

S‣U‣B‣P‣O‣P

U — S — A

A GUIDE TO U.S. INDEPENDENTS

By Bruce Pavitt

End of OP?

VELVET MONKEYS *Future* LP (Fountain of Youth). Long awaited vinyl debut from D.C. area garage pop band. Their demo of "Everything Is Right" had me floored — classic **Pebbles** material. I've also heard raves about their live shows. So what's the problem? They've traded in their soul for a geek synthesizer. Very cold. The **Velvet Monkeys** have a good vocalist and decent material, but they're lost in a time warp. They're caught between the sixties and the eighties and they can't make it work.

SACCHARINE TRUST *Surviving You, Always* LP (SST). The second release by **Saccharine Trust** is denser and more frenetic than their last. Like labelmates **The Minutemen**, these art punks spew forth poetry instead politics, abstractions instead of slogans. Frontman Joaquin Brewer is distinguished by his obsession with religion; words like faith, sin and devotion constantly creep in. The credits also list them as providing "vocals and *sermons*." As for the music, there are references to jazz fusion and free jazz. The intro to "The House, The System, The Concrete" is minimal and extremely effective, with nothing but random footsteps to create a mood. Basically interesting.

OH OK *Furthermore What* 12" EP (DB). Pop hit of the month is this big and beautiful EP from Athens. And look here — it's another Mitch Easter production. Rich harmonies from Lynda and Linda; twisting, soaring melodies. They've beefed up their sound by adding electric and acoustic guitars; their classic first 45 was simpler, using only vocal, bass and drums. Though they don't always hit home-runs (side *one* clicks) there's nothing wrong with a cool .500.

BANDS THAT COULD BE GOD *The Conflict Compilation* LP (Conflict). This is a local Boston compilation released by Gerard Cosley of *Conflict* fanzine. Music moves from hardcore (Deep Wound, Outpatients) to mid-tempo garage pop (Salem 66, Christmas, Busted Statues). If you're really interested in whatever's underground in Boston, however premature or forgettable, check this out. Technically, the packaging and overall production are good, but it takes more than a glossy cover to make an outstanding record.

BATTLE OF THE GARAGES *Volume II* LP (VOXX). As much as I generally dislike bands that do nothing but revive music from another era, I can't help but enjoy

THE LOST MUSIC NETWORK, a cooperative organization that published OP (independent music) magazine, held a conference in mid July to discover the fate of its publication. People involved in the international independent music network met for a weekend of seminars, elbow rubbing and original music. OP is headquartered and the conference was held in Olympia, Washington.

"After the 'Z' issue it's all over, at least for me," stated OP editor John Foster. "There *is* a burn out factor. If some kind of publication is to be continued things will have to be organized soon." Foster and art director Dana Leigh Squires are planning on joining the Peace Corps next year and will hopefully work in Africa.

The conference was a great chance to meet other people involved with small record labels. Seminars covered various facets of the underground music business, including college and community radio, distribution, cassette networking, recording techniques and magazine publishing. Most of the music occurred at Olympia's **Tropicana**, an all ages club that's recently opened. Members got to check out everything from experimental electronics to jazz to hardcore punk. Personal favorites were Beat Happening, Pop Philosophers, Young Pioneers, Wimps and wild man Geoff Kirk.

OP magazine, starting in 1979 with the "A" issue, is considered the bible of the independent music scene. Covering every possible form of music, OP focuses on a different letter of the alphabet with each issue, featuring artists whose names begin with that letter (i.e., the "W" issue featured Whiz Kid, Wipers, Mal Waldron, etc.). All artists whose work appears on small record labels get a few lines in the awesome review section. Addresses are given.

Fortunately, by the end of the conference, a group of folks from L.A. had offered to pick up the pieces after the "Z" issue and start a new magazine using the networking information collected by OP. To the staff of OP — John, Dana, and Dave — I salute you for your tireless efforts and a job well done. *OP is available from Lost Music Network, P.O. Box 2391, Olympia, WA 98507.* ■

Sub/Pop U.S.A.
►► Radio ◄◄
every Tuesday 6-7 PM • KCMU 90.5 FM

this rockin' compilation of trashy garage psychedelia. This is better than Volume I. Greg Shaw, godfather of the fanzine underworld, should be commended for both his work in releasing original tracks from the '60s, as well as these swell *Battle* compilations. It's hard to pick favorites on this one so I won't bother, just skip the one lame track by **The Impossible Years** and trip out.

MAGNIFICENT THREE AND FEARLESS MASTER *Crush* 12" Single (C.C.L.) This month's rap/break thing has all the ingredients — robot vocoder vocals, funny turntable scratching, beat boxes booming electronic rhythms for easy breaking, **Fearless Master and the Magnificent Three** rapping and rhyming. Every trite formula in the book, I love it though 'cause it's physical and it feels good. For you intellectual types there's a strange industrial instrumental mix on the second half of side one.

PARIAH *Youth of Age* LP (Posh Boy). Posh Boy is one of L.A.'s oldest and most consistent labels. Although they've had their share of duds as well as classics, Posh Boy has always come across with both a big studio sound and bands that write real songs. Most of this label's hardcore releases (Agent Orange, Channel 3) have been successful, and Pariah is no exception. Although this may be too slick for some, this record isn't just another blur of high energy — these songs will stick for days. Fave cut: "White Line."

J.F.A. LP (Placebo). The second LP by this Phoenix skate band. I say LP because there are 11 songs on this 12", although it spins at 45 rpm and lasts only 10 minutes a side. More and more thrash bands (i.e. Septic Death, Fang) are using this format as it's cheaper to produce and, due to the brevity and volume of the songs, comes across looking like an LP. Definitely a new trend in marketing. **J.F.A.**? They *shred*.

ADDRESSES

Conflict: 9 Jeffrey Rd., Wayland, MA 01778

Voxx: Box 7112, Burbank, CA 91510

Placebo: Box 23316, Phoenix, AZ 85063

C.C.L.: 3261 Broadway Suite 119, New York, NY 10027

DB: 432 Moreland Ave. N.E., Atlanta, GA 30307

Fountain of Youth: c/o 45 Alabama Ave., Island Park, NY 11558

SST: P.O. Box 1, Lawndale, CA 90260

Posh Boy: Box 38861, Los Angeles, CA 90038

OH OK *Furthermore What* 12" EP (DB). Pop hit of the month is this big and beautiful EP from Athens. And look here—it's another Mitch Easter production. Rich harmonies from Lynda and Linda; twisting, soaring melodies. They've beefed up their sound by adding electric and acoustic guitars; their classic first 45 was simpler, using only vocal, bass, and drums. Though they don't always hit home runs, side one clicks, and there's nothing wrong with a cool .500 average.

VARIOUS *Bands That Could Be God: The Conflict Compilation* LP (Conflict). This is a local Boston compilation released by Gerard Cosloy of *Conflict* fanzine. Music moves from hardcore (**DEEP WOUND, OUTPATIENTS**) to mid-tempo garage pop (**SALEM 66, CHRISTMAS, BUSTED STATUES**). If you're really interested in whatever's underground in Boston, however premature or forgettable, check this out. Technically, the packaging and overall production are good, but it takes more than a glossy cover to make an outstanding record.

VARIOUS *Battle of the Garages, Vol. II* LP (Voxx). As much as I generally dislike bands that do nothing but revive music from another era, I can't help but enjoy this rockin' compilation of trashy garage psychedelia. This is better than *Volume I*. Greg Shaw, godfather of the fanzine underworld, should be commended for both his work in releasing original tracks from the '60s, as well as these swell *Battle* compilations. It's hard to pick favorites on this one so I won't bother, just skip the one lame track by **THE IMPOSSIBLE YEARS** and trip out.

MAGNIFICENT THREE AND FEARLESS MASTER *Crush* 12" single (C.C.L.) This month's rap/break thing has all the ingredients—robot vocoder vocals, funny turntable scratching, beat boxes booming electronic rhythms for easy breaking, Fearless Master and the Magnificent Three rapping and rhyming. Every trite formula in the book. I love it, though, 'cause it's physical and it feels good. For you intellectual types, there's a strange industrial instrumental mix on the second half of side one.

PARIAH *Youth of Age* LP (Posh Boy). Posh Boy is one of L.A.'s oldest and most consistent labels. Although they've had their share of duds as well as classics,

Posh Boy has always come across with both a big studio sound and bands that write real songs. Most of this label's hardcore releases (**AGENT ORANGE, CHANNEL 3**) have been successful, and Pariah is no exception. Although this may be too slick for some, this record isn't just another blur of high energy—these songs will stick for days. Fave cut: "White Line."

J.F.A. LP (Placebo). The second LP by this Phoenix skate band. I say LP because there are 11 songs on this 12", although it spins at 45 rpm and lasts only 10 minutes a side. More and more thrash bands (i.e. **SEPTIC DEATH, FANG**) are using this format as it's cheaper to produce, and, due to the brevity and volume of the songs, comes across looking like an LP. Definitely a new trend in marketing. J.F.A.? They shred.

Mob Action at Graven Image!

FRIDAY, AUGUST 11, 1984

Mass people, and an over-capacity mob at Graven Image. **J.F.A.**, **YOUTH BRIGADE**, and **SUN CITY GIRLS**, ready to tear the house down. Another sweaty rock 'n roll hardcore night in the basement pit of Graven Image, an alternative art gallery and all-ages club.

The Sun City Girls, from Phoenix, play free-form noise and wear bags over their heads. I go out for a beer. Arriving later, psyched and wired for Youth Brigade, there it is. Mob action. Third and Washington on a hot August night. The street is spilling with local youth, leather and skateboards, make-up and studs. Younger kids in Bermuda shorts and **SUICIDAL** caps. And they all want their five dollars back. The fire marshall and his blue buddies have closed the doors for good. No show.

Authorities leave. Someone torches paper, throws on a few boxes. Daredevils skate downhill fast and spit fire from their boards, sparks fly. The crowd grows restless; where's my five? The bands want cash and so does the crowd. Meanwhile, owner Larry Reid attempts to give away a skate, a bone to the beast.

"Number 00184"!!" he screams above the rumble. The catcalls and chatter drown his words. After the tenth ticket is called out, some young punk scrambles and wins. Larry announces a free show for the next day, but nobody hears. "JFA and Youth Brigade, one o'clock, Ground Zero!" The bonfire grows.

Graven Image has thrown some great shows and parties this summer—the Bat Show, the Mod bash, **45 GRAVE, PELL MELL, THE U-MEN** bar-b-q au go go, **D.R.I.** quarter pipe action with **THE FACTION**. Although art shows will continue, the basement is now off limits to performance. Now that the Grey Door has also closed, all-ages shows will be limited to Ground Zero Gallery (also Third and Washington), Top of the Court on 15th W., and the Tropicana down in Olympia. Things look slim as the summer closes.

SUB TEN PICK HITS FOR SEPTEMBER

MINUTEMEN (L.A.) *Double Nickels on the Dime* LP (SST)

SALEM 66 (Boston) 12" EP (Homestead)

U-MEN (Seattle) 12" EP (Bomb Shelter)

HÜSKER DÜ (Minneapolis) *Zen Arcade* LP (SST)

SECOND WIND (Washington, D.C.) 12" EP (R&B)

BIG BLACK (Chicago) *Bulldozer* 12" EP (Ruthless)

SONIC YOUTH (NYC) *Kill Yr. Idols* 12" EP (Zensor)

VARIOUS (Olympia, WA) *Let's Together* compilation cassette (K)

BUNNYDRUMS "On the Surface" 12" EP (Red)

EXECUTIVE SLACKS (Philadelphia) *Our Lady* 12" single (Red)

BUNNYDRUMS *On the Surface* 12" EP (Red). Philadelphia's Red label has been releasing some outstanding records lately. On the Surface, their fourth release, has a lot more edge than I expected. Like some of their progressive NY counterparts (**SONIC YOUTH, LIVE SKULL**), the new BD disc stretches the boundaries of conventional instruments; the slippery, plummeting guitar chords are beyond way out or way cool. If you

S>U>B>P>O>P

U — — S — — A

A GUIDE TO U.S. INDEPENDENTS

By Bruce Pavitt

MOB ACTION AT GRAVEN IMAGE!!!

PHOTOGRAPHY BY ROBERT UBUNGEN

SUB TEN   Pick Hits for September

MINUTEMEN *Double Nickels on the Dime* LP (SST) / L.A.

SALEM 66 12" EP (Homestead) / Boston

U-MEN 12" EP (Bombshelter) / Seattle

HUSKER DU *Zen Arcade* LP (SST) / Minneapolis

SECOND WIND 12" EP (R&B) / D.C.

BIG BLACK *Bulldozer* 12" EP (Ruthless) / Chicago

SONIC YOUTH *Kill Yr. Idols* 12" EP (Zensor) / NYC

LET'S TOGETHER Compilation cassette (K) / Olympia

BUNNYDRUMS *On the Surface* 12" EP (Red) / Philadelphia

EXECUTIVE SLACKS *Our Lady* 12" single (Red) / Philadelphia

BUNNYDRUMS *On the Surface* 12" EP (Red). Philadelphia's **Red** label has been releasing some outstanding records lately. *On the Surface,* their fourth release, has a lot more edge than I expected. Like some of their progressive NY counterparts (Sonic Youth, Live Skull), the new BD disc stretches the boundaries of conventional instruments; the slippery, plummeting guitar chords are beyond way out or way cool. If you can get past a ridiculous name like **Bunnydrums,** nail this plastic to your turntable.

HUSKER DU *Zen Arcade* double LP (SST). Alright, I'm willing to throw in the towel and admit, finally, that we are in the presence of something awesome. This Minneapolis trio have taken their energy and gritty texture, thrown it like a fastball and meshed it with sleigh bells, acoustic guitar, piano and mass tapes running inside out. "Reoccuring Dreams" runs 14 minutes and sustains interest as well as feedback. As with almost any double LP, half the material is filler, but what's good is *good,* so listen up. *(P.O. Box 1, Lawndale, CA 90260.)*

MINUTEMEN *Nickels on the Dime* double LP (SST). If the Husker Du LP was half filler, this double meat patty from L.A.'s most prolific band is pure protein. No real surprises — they still mix poetry and politics, punk, funk and jazz — but they do it creatively, consistently, without being arty or embarrassing. The **Minutemen** have vision, integrity and endurance; their live show was one of the highlights of '84 as is *Double Nickels on the Dime. (P.O. Box 1, Lawndale, CA 90260.)*

BLOOD ON THE SADDLE LP (New Alliance). **New Alliance** does it again. This is pure spurs and barbed wire — rippin' cowpunk. And yes, vocalist Annette does give a credible (modern) treatment of the C&W classic "(I Wish I Was) A Single Girl Again." The whole LP is tough stuff, fast and grizzled, scorching. Much more than a gimmick or novelty. *(P.O. Box 21, San Pedro, CA 90733.)*

F RIDAY, AUGUST 11, 1984. MASS people, an over capacity mob at **Graven Image.** JFA, Youth Brigade and Sun City Girls. Ready to tear the house down. Another sweaty rock 'n' roll hardcore night in the basement pit of Graven Image, alternative art gallery and all-ages club.

The Sun City Girls, from Phoenix, play free-form noise and wear bags over their heads. I go out for a beer. Arriving later, psyched and wired for Youth Brigade, there it is. Mob action. Third and Washington on a hot August night. The street is spilling with local youth, leather and skateboards, make-up and studs. Younger kids in burmuda shorts and Suicidal caps. And they all want their five dollars back. The fire marshall and his blue buddies have closed the doors for good. No show.

Authorities leave. Someone torches paper, throws on a few boxes. Daredevils skate downhill fast and spit fire from their boards, sparks fly. The crowd grows restless; where's my five? The bands want cash and so does the crowd. Meanwhile, owner Larry Reid attempts to give away a skate, a bone to the beast.

"Number 00184!!" he screams above the rumble. The catcalls and chatter drown his words. After the tenth ticket is called out, some young punk scrambles and wins. Larry announces a free show for the next day but nobody hears. "JFA and Youth Brigade, one o'clock, Ground Zero!" The bonfire grows.

Graven Image has thrown some great shows and parties this summer — the Bat Show, the Mod bash, 45 Grave, Pell Mell, the U-Men bar-b-q au go go, D.R.I., quarter pipe action with the Faction. Although art shows will continue, the basement is now off limits to performance. Now that the Grey Door has also closed, all-ages shows will be limited to Ground Zero Gallery (also at Third and Washington), Top of the Court on 15th W., and the Tropicana down in Olympia. Things look slim as the summer closes. ■

Sub/Pop U.S.A.
►► Radio ◄◄
every Tuesday 6-7 PM • KCMU 90.5 FM

EXECUTIVE SLACKS *Our Lady* 12" single (Red). Another trip to the Twilight Zone, courtesy of **Red** records. Scary, ambient disco co-starring Youth from Killing Joke on bass. This deserves heavy club airplay because it throws you into the depths of hell and brings you back for another cocktail. Monster vocals let us chill out to the bone. You want this one. *(810 Longfield Rd., Philadelphia, PA 19118.)*

MILLIONS OF DEAD CHILDREN *Chicken Squawk* 45 (R Radical). Reflecting the political climate of the Bay Area, MDC is an aggressive, provocative group that plays intense, dogmatic hardcore thrash. Like the British group Crass, MDC is more interested in propaganda than writing a good song. *Chicken Squawk* is a country/thrash novelty promoting vegetarianism; the flipside is tuneless hardcore at its most forgettable. The 45 comes with eye-opening graphics and literature condemning world hunger. Very effective. Bands like **MDC** and **Crass** would be better off publishing magazines than recording "music." *(2440 16th #103, San Francisco, CA 94103.)*

SAVAGE REPUBLIC *Tragic Futures* 45 (Independent Project). **Independent Project** puts out another hand-made package, limited edition, 2000. This *thing* is one of my favorite American bands was recorded the same time the LP was, so technically this is not a new release. Partially recorded on a cassette deck in an empty parking garage, we get to hear six octave drone guitar and an industrial size oil drum. While the last single, *Film Noir,* complete with vocals, was an underground pop hit of sorts, this is a primitive groove. Score this for mood and atmosphere. *(P.O. Box 60357, Los Angeles, CA 90060.)*

THE ZANY GUYS *Party Hits Vol. II* 7" EP (Placebo). JFA's **Placebo** label is puttin' some bread on the table: wholesome, reckless fun from Phoenix. Some local authority figure, "Mr. Ackers," gets the heave ho and the big slag. Rock 'n' roll wins again. *(P.O. Box 23316, Phoenix, AZ 85063.)*

GRANDMASTER FUNK PERCUSSION ALL-STARS *Don't Stop* 12" single (Black Market). **Black Market** is a new label started by Bob George, the man responsible for Laurie Anderson's *O Superman* 45 on 110 Records. As such, I had high expectations. "Don't Stop" is a plodding groove that lacks the verbal wit of good rap or the physical kick of good funk or electronic hip hop. The record *is* distinguished by obscure and spacey organic percussion, but don't expect Trouble Funk. The B side comes across with the obligatory dub and scratch effects. Listenable. *(110 Chambers St., New York, NY 10007.)*

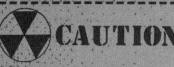

VISTA SOUND & LIGHT
743-6811

WE'VE MOVED TO SERVE YOU BETTER

8229 44th Ave. W., Suite C
Mukilteo, WA 98275
337-1420

☢ **CAUTION** ☢

THAT'S ATOMIC
THE BEST & WORST OF THE 50'S & 60'S
1504 E OLIVE WAY 325-4994

FALLOUT
RECORDS, SKATEBOARDS, VIDEOS
1506 E OLIVE WAY 323-BOMB

BROADWAY 201 BROADWAY E 323-1085

Please Call Theater for Showtimes

"A FEROCIOUSLY ORIGINAL COMEDY....
the funniest, most deliriously deranged movie I've seen all year."
—Jim Emerson, The Seattle Times

"The film is very, very funny..."
—William Arnold, Seattle P-I

"Fresh, virulently funny with an eye on life that's as offbeat as the early Beatles movies...a real discovery."
—Sheila Benson, LA Times

"REPO MAN is the real thing. It's a sneakily rude, truly zany farce that treats its lunatic characters with a solemnity that perfectly matches the way in which they see themselves."
—Vincent Canby, New York Times

REPO MAN

A MICHAEL NESMITH Presentation EDGE CITY Production "REPO MAN"
HARRY DEAN STANTON • EMILIO ESTEVEZ Written and Directed by ALEX COX
REPO MAN Theme Music by IGGY POP
A Universal Picture

can get past a ridiculous name like Bunnydrums, nail this plastic to your turntable.

HÜSKER DÜ *Zen Arcade* double LP (SST). Alright, I'm willing to throw in the towel and admit, finally, that we are in the presence of something awesome. This Minneapolis trio have taken their energy and gritty texture, thrown it like a fastball, and meshed it with sleigh bells, acoustic guitar, piano, and mass tapes running inside out. "Reoccuring Dreams" runs 14 minutes and sustains interest as well as feedback. As with almost any double LP, half the material is filler, but what's good is good, so listen up. (Lawndale, CA)

MINUTEMEN *Nickels on the Dime* double LP (SST). If the **HÜSKER DÜ** LP was half filler, this double meat patty from L.A.'s most prolific band is pure protein. No real surprises—they still mix poetry and politics, punk, funk, and jazz—but they do it creatively, consistently, without being arty or embarrassing. The Minutemen have vision, integrity, and endurance; their live show was one of the highlights of '84 as is *Double Nickels on the Dime*. (Lawndale, CA)

BLOOD ON THE SADDLE LP (New Alliance). New Alliance does it again. This is pure spurs and barbed wire-rippin' cowpunk. And yes, vocalist Annette does give a credible (modern) treatment of the C&W-classic "(I Wish I Was) a Single Girl Again." The whole LP is tough stuff, fast and grizzled, scorching. Much more than a gimmick or novelty. (San Pedro, CA)

EXECUTIVE SLACKS *Our Lady* 12" single (Red). Another trip to the twilight zone, courtesy of Red records. Scary, ambient disco costarring Youth from **KILLING JOKE** on bass. This deserves heavy club airplay, because it throws you into the depths of hell and brings you back for another cocktail. Monster vocals let us chill out to the bone. You want this one. (Philadelphia, PA)

MILLIONS OF DEAD CHILDREN *Chicken Squawk* 45 (R Radical). Reflecting the political climate of the Bay Area, MDC is an aggressive, provocative group that plays intense, dogmatic hardcore thrash. Like the British group **CRASS**, MDC is more interested in propaganda than writing a good song. *Chicken Squawk* is a country/thrash novelty promoting vegetarianism; the flipside is tuneless hardcore at its most forgettable. The 45 comes with eye-opening graphics and literature condemning world hunger. Very effective. Bands like MDC and Crass would be better off publishing magazines than recording "music." (San Francisco, CA)

SAVAGE REPUBLIC *Tragic Futures* 45 (Independent Project). Independent Project puts out another hand-made package, limited edition of 2000. This thing by one of my favorite American bands was recorded at the same time as the LP, so technically this is not a new release. Partially recorded on a cassette deck in an empty parking garage, we get to hear six-octave drone guitar and an industrial size oil drum. While the last single, "Film Noir," complete with vocals, was an underground pop hit of sorts, this is a primitive groove. Score this for mood and atmosphere. (Los Angeles, CA)

THE ZANY GUYS *Party Hits Vol. II* 7" EP (Placebo). JFA's Placebo label is puttin' some bread on the table: wholesome, reckless fun from Phoenix. Some local authority figure, "Mr. Ackers," gets the heave-ho and the big slag. Rock 'n roll wins again. (Phoenix, AZ)

GRANDMASTER FUNK PERCUSSION ALL-STARS *Don't Stop* 12" single (Black Market). Black Market is a new label started by Bob George, the man responsible for **LAURIE ANDERSON**'s "O Superman" 45 on 110 Records. As such, I had high expectations. "Don't Stop" is a plodding groove that lacks the verbal wit of good rap or the physical kick of good funk or electronic hip hop. The record is distinguished by some organic percussion, but don't expect **TROUBLE FUNK**. The B-side comes across with the obligatory dub and scratch effects. Listenable. (New York, NY.)

God, It's Out...

SUB TEN—PICK HITS FOR OCTOBER

NO TREND (Washington, D.C.) 12" EP (No Trend)

KONK (NYC) *Your Life* 12" single (Sleeping Bag)

U-MEN (Seattle) 12" EP (Bomb Shelter)

DIE KREUZEN (Milwaukee) LP (Touch and Go)

MINUTEMEN (L.A.) *Double Nickels on the Dime* 2 LP (SST)

SALEM 66 (Boston) 12" EP (Homestead/Dutch East India)

BLACK FLAG (L.A.) *Slip It In* LP (SST)

MOD FUN (New Jersey) *Happy Feeling* 45" (New)

DISCO 3 (NYC) *Human Beat Box* 12" EP (Sutra)

HÜSKER DÜ (Minneapolis) *Zen Arcade* 2LP (SST)

.

DIE KREUZEN LP (Touch & Go). God, it's out. Out of its cage, out of its mind. This band has broken the chains and destroyed the prison. Scary, unbridled thrash at its most extreme. Short of a silver bullet, nothing's gonna stop these guys.

SALEM 66 12" EP (Dutch East India). A few issues back, in my hurry to slag Boston's *Bands Who Could Be God* compilation, I failed to mention its one truly outstanding cut, "Sleep On Flowers" by Salem 66. This female trio has come up with an excellent pop record —beautiful harmonies, electric folk chords. Salem 66 is less cute than **OH OK** and just as sensual as **CLAY ALLISON**. "Sleep On Flowers" is included on this highly recommended EP.

MOD FUN "Happy Feeling" b/w "I Am With You" 45 (New). Single of the month goes to this mod trio from New Jersey. Catchy, exuberant rock 'n roll that owes plenty to classic British Beat groups like the **THE ACTION** and early **WHO**. Lyrics are shallow, but these anthems are sure to wake the jaded and/or the dead. "Happy Feeling" is the hit; Batman footage on the flip!

METALLICA *Ride the Lightning* LP (Megaforce). Last year's bone-scorching debut by metal monsters Metallica definitely out-thrashed the competition, hardcore or metal. This second release is more commercial, with **ZEPPELIN**-like forays into pot smoking, druid instrumentals. For those of you hard up for a fix, "Fight Fire with Fire" and "Creeping Death" should do the trick.

SECOND WIND *Security* LP (R&B). Took me a while to get past the dreadful cover art, but here it is. This D.C. band sounds a lot like **MINOR THREAT**. Give 'em an "F" for originality, an "A" for hook-filled raw power.

DISCO 3 "Fat Boys" b/w "Human Beat Box" 12" EP (Sutra). "Human Beat Box" is an a cappella rap novelty; turntables and beat box are created with grunts and slaps. Don't know about "classic" status, but it sure is fun, a deep throwdown. Cashing in on their awesome physical presence, the Disco 3 will be calling themselves **FAT BOYS** from now on.

VARIOUS *Flipside Vinyl Fanzine Vol. I* LP (Gasatanka). Starting out as a publication, *Flipside* has been expanding to other areas like video and vinyl. This is truly an audio fanzine; snippets of interviews make this compilation stand up. Bands include **G.I.**, **FU'S**, **BLACK MARKET BABY**, the **FREEZE**, **GBH**, **DICKIES**, and **GAY COWBOYS IN BONDAGE**. Catchier than *Rat Music II*, less "politically correct" than *Maximum Rocknroll*.

A GUIDE TO U.S. INDEPENDENTS

By Bruce Pavitt

> "'Human Beat Box' is an a cappella rap novelty; turntables and beat box are created with grunts and slaps. Don't know about 'classic' status but it sure is fun, a deep throwdown. Cashing in on their awesome physical presence, the Disco 3 will be calling themselves the 'Fat Boys' from now on."

DIE KREUZEN LP (Touch & Go). God, it's out. Out of its cage, out of its mind. This band has broken the chains and destroyed the prison. Scary, unbridled thrash at its most extreme. Short of a silver bullet, nothin's gonna stop these guys. *(P.O. Box 716, Maumee, OH 43537.)*

SALEM 66 12" EP (Dutch East India). A few issues back, in my hurry to slag Boston's *Bands Who Could Be God* compilation, I failed to mention its one truly outstanding cut, "Sleep On Flowers" by Salem 66. This female trio has come up with an excellent pop record — beautiful harmonies, electric folk chords. Salem 66 is less cute than Oh OK and just as sensual as Clay Allison. "Sleep On Flowers" is included on this highly recommended EP. *(45 Alabama Ave., Island Park, NY 11558.)*

MOD FUN *Happy Feeling/I Am With You* '45 (New). Single of the month goes to this mod trio from New Jersey. Catchy, exuberant rock 'n' roll that owes plenty to classic British Beat groups like The Action and early Who. Lyrics are shallow but these anthems are sure to wake the jaded and/or the dead. "Happy Feeling" is the hit; Batman footage on the flip! *(131 W. Passaic St., Maywood, NJ 07607.)*

James Hetfield of Metallica.

PHOTOGRAPH BY KEVIN HODAPP

METALLICA *Ride the Lightning* LP (Megaforce). Last year's bone scorching debut by metal monsters Metallica definitely out-thrashed the competition, hardcore or metal. This second release is more commercial, with Zeppelin like forays into pot smoking, Druid instrumentals. For those of you hard up for a fix, "Fight Fire with Fire" and "Creeping Death" should do the trick. *(60 York St., Old Bridge, NJ 08857.)*

SECOND WIND *Security* LP (R&B). Took me a while to get past the dreadful cover art but here it is. This D.C. band sounds a *lot* like **Minor Threat**. Give 'em an F for originality, an A for hook filled raw power. *(P.O. Box 25054, Washington, D.C. 20007.)*

DISCO 3 *Fat Boys/Human Beat Box* 12" EP (Sutra). Human Beat Box is an acappella rap novelty; turntables and beat box are created with grunts and slaps. Don't know about "classic" status but it sure is fun, a deep throwdown. Cashing in on their awesome physical presence, the Disco 3 will be calling themselves **Fat Boys** from now on. *(1790 Broadway, NYC 10019.)*

SUB TEN
Pick Hits for October

NO TREND, 12" EP (No Trend) D.C.

KONK, Your Life, 12" single (Sleeping Bag) NYC

U-MEN, 12" EP (Bombshelter) Seattle

DIE KREUZEN, LP (Touch and Go)

MINUTEMEN, Double Nickels on the Dime, 2 LP (SST) L.A.

SALEM 66, 12" EP (Homestead/Dutch East India) Boston

BLACK FLAG, Slip It In, LP (SST) L.A.

MOD FUN, Happy Feeling, 45 (New) upstate New Jersey

DISCO 3, Human Beat Box, 12" EP (Sutra) NYC

HUSKER DU, Zen Arcade, 2 LP (SST) Minneapolis

FLIPSIDE VINYL FANZINE *Vol. I* LP (Gasatanka). Starting out as a publication, *Flipside* has been expanding to other areas like video and vinyl. This is truly an audio fanzine; snippets of interviews make this compilation stand up. Bands include **G.I., FU's, Black Market Baby, The Freeze, GBH, Dickies** and **Gay Cowboys in Bondage.** Catchier than *Rat Music II*, less "politically correct" than *Maximum Rock N Roll*. *(1241 N. Harper, Suite 6, Hollywood, CA 90046.)*

KONK *Your Life* 12" single (Sleeping Bag). Wow! Great party record!!! Latin percussion! Horns! Three groove diving dance mixes, and for all you "whiz kids," one sound effects cut up that lets you mix it fresh! Go for it!!! *(1974 Broadway, NYC 10023.)*

NO TREND 12" EP. More intense than Die Kreuzen?! "Mass Sterilization Caused by Venereal Disease" has already proved to be a classic, an insane hybrid of hardcore and dub. On the quieter side, "Teen Love" is an intellectual rant in league with the Fall. This is a 12" reissue of last year's out-of-print 7". Remixed, remastered and repressed for maximum physical pleasure; there's a couple of bonus cuts as well. As with all great D.C. area recordings, this was recorded at Inner Ear Studios by Don Zientara. *(c/o 1014 Ashton Rd., Ashton, MD 20861.)*

Sub/Pop U.S.A.
▶▶ **Radio** ◀◀
every Tuesday 6-7 PM · KCMU 90.5 FM ·

LOVE TRACTOR *Til the Cows Come Home* 12" EP (DB). The third release by this Athens band; until now, strictly instrumentals. The music here is haunting, melancholy and might be too distant for some. Arrangements include a variety of instruments: acoustic guitar, piano, synthesizer, plus the occasional tabla, clarinet and dog bark. *(432 Moreland Ave. N.E., Atlanta, GA 30307.)*

MY SIN *Chains* 7" single (no label). A one-man Frankie Goes To Hollywood. Minimal bass, drums and synth. Sex is the main topic here. According to the press release, "Blind executives will become incredibly hip; lame conglomerates will be made to profit, for My Sin is the resurrection and the light." *(c/o 370 Turk St. #22, SF, CA 94102.)*

TRYPES *The Explorers Hold* 12" EP (Coyote). Featuring some former members of the Feelies, this group does experiment with layers of rhythms, a Feelies trademark. The Trypes are a seven piece outfit that features percussion, woodwinds, keyboards, and acoustic guitar. Overall, much too subdued, although "The Undertow" almost hits home. If you like discreet background music, pick up this and **Love Tractor**. *(P.O. Box 112, Uptown Hoboken, NJ.)*

BACK FROM THE GRAVE *Vol. II* LP. Totally rockin'.'60s punk compilation. Good sound quality, tough tunes. Aside from the homophobic liner notes, a real find. Includes the original version of "The Crusher" by the Novas. *(Address not available.)*

HIPSVILLE #29 B.C.

HIPSVILLE *29 B.C.* LP. Yet another release in the current '60s garage-punk sweepstakes. Includes: **The Guys Who Came Up From Downstairs, Fantastic D.J.'s,** pre-mom **Cowsills,** and the clincher, **Beaver and the Trappers** featuring **Theodore Cleaver!** Not quite as tough as the **Back From The Grave** series, but every bit as obscure. *(Address not available.)*

"I'm willing to throw in the towel, finally, and admit that we are in the presence of something awesome." Hüsker Dü at Fallout Records. **BRUCE PAVITT**

KONK *Your Life* 12" single (Sleeping Bag). Wow! Great party record!!! Latin percussion! Horns! Three groove-diving dance mixes, and for all you "whiz kids," one sound effects cut-up that lets you mix it fresh! Go for it!!!

NO TREND 12" EP. More intense than **DIE KREUZEN**?! "Mass Sterilization Caused by Venereal Disease" has already proved to be a classic, an insane hybrid of hardcore and dub. On the quieter side, "Teen Love" is an intellectual rant in league with **THE FALL**. This is a 12" reissue of last year's out-of-print 7". Remixed, remastered, and repressed for maximum physical pleasure; there's a couple of bonus cuts as well. As with all great D.C. area recordings, this was recorded at Inner Ear Studios by Don Zientara.

LOVE TRACTOR *Til the Cows Come Home* 12" EP (DB). The third release by this Athens band; until now strictly instrumentals. The music here is haunting, melancholy and might be too distant for some. Arrangements include a variety of instruments: acoustic guitar, piano, and synthesizer—plus the occasional tabla, clarinet, and dog bark.

MY SIN *Chains* 7" single (no label). A one-man **FRANKIE GOES TO HOLLYWOOD**. Minimal bass, drums, and synth. Sex is the main topic here. According to the press release: "Blind executives will become

incredibly hip; lame conglomerates will be made to profit; for My Sin is the resurrection and the light."

TRYPES *The Explorers Hold* 12" EP (Coyote). Featuring some former members of the **FEELIES**, this group does experiment with layers of rhythms, a Feelies trademark. The Trypes are a seven-piece outfit that features percussion, woodwinds, keyboards, and acoustic guitar. Overall, much too subdued, although "The Undertow" almost hits home. If you like discreet background music, pick up this and **LOVE TRACTOR**.

VARIOUS *Back From the Grave, Volume Two* LP (Crypt). Totally rockin' '60s punk compilation. Good sound quality, tough tunes. Aside from the homophobic liner notes, a real find. Includes the original version of "The Crusher" by the **NOVAS**.

VARIOUS *Hipsville 29 B.C.* LP (Kramden). Yet another release in the current '60s garage-punk sweepstakes. Includes: **THE GUYS WHO CAME UP FROM DOWNSTAIRS, FANTASTIC D.J.'S**, pre-mom **COWSILLS**, and the clincher, **BEAVER AND THE TRAPPERS** featuring Theodore Cleaver! Not quite as tough as the *Back From the Grave* series, but every bit as obscure.

November 1984

Live, Black Flag Is the Most Intense Band in the World

DECRY *Falling* LP (Toxic Shock). After releasing some low-fi multi-song seven-inchers, Toxic Shock gets back in the groove with this kick-ass party LP by San Gabriel's Decry. It won't change your life, but this obscure suburban thrash band is too good to get buried beneath the rubble. Play loud.

BLACK FLAG *Slip It In* LP (SST). Live, Black Flag is the most intense band in the world. Henry Rollins is a monster performer—spilling sweat, swaying, bending, thrusting, with hippie hair and tattoos, combining the raw sex of **ELVIS** or **JAMES BROWN** with the psychotic edge of **CHARLIE MANSON**. Back this guy with the hardest-working band in show business and you've got a religious experience. I just wish to hell that their records came across. Since *Damaged*, Black Flag have put out decent records, but not great ones. Recorded in a cardboard box, they lack crispness and life. But even a pale imitation of their live sound is worth a spin. Pick hit: "Black Coffee."

RAIN PARADE *Explosions in the Glass Palace* LP (Enigma). *Explosions...* is the latest from this sleepy flower power outfit from L.A. Sadly, the stinging Verlaine-like leads of their LP, *Emergency Third Rail Power Trip*, are gone. The production here is watered down and the lyrics are as sappy as ever. A disappointing follow-up to their **BYRDS**/**TELEVISION**-inspired debut.

RAPOLOGISTS *Hip Hop Beat* 12" single (Telstar Cassettes). Telstar Cassettes, a record label that has never released a cassette, specializes in black dance music. The notorious DJ Whiz Kid cuts up on this one, which is good enough reason to check this out. "Kid's

Rap" features Flakey C and Early Daze alternating between their real voices and cartoonish, electronic smurf sounds à la **NEWCLEUS**. Kinda silly. The "Party Rap" mix on the flip side is pretty cool, though.

SSD *How We Rock* LP (Modern Method). Third release by this hard 'n' heavy Boston battalion. Like the new **BLACK FLAG**, these guys slow down the thrash tempo, mix up the bass, and throw in some bursting leads for a truly h-e-a-v-y sound. The production is good, with clarity and muscle. The best gnarly/head-banging crossover I've heard all year. K.J. Doughton is gonna go for this one.

NIGHEIST *If You Love Me, Snort My Load* LP (Thermidor). **BLOWFLY**, **GENERAL ECHO**, and even **TESCO VEE** will have to move over for the **NIGHEIST**. Many acts throughout history have based their performance on obscenity and shock appeal. For those lacking in talent, it's a quick way to make a buck.

SAMHAIN *Initium* LP (Plan 9). Featuring former members of NY's horror/thrash **MISFITS**, *Initium* could well be considered the third Misfits LP, as Glenn Danzig is still on vocals. The music here is slower and moodier than previous efforts, helping to emphasize the spooky subject matter. Lyle Preslar, former guitarist with **MINOR THREAT**, steps in on some lead guitar; his presence is not outstanding. *Initium* is worth picking up, although I don't find it nearly as enjoyable as the Misfits' classic *Walk Among Us* LP.

YOUTH BRIGADE *What Price Happiness* 7" (Better Youth Organization). The BYO label has been releasing some fist clenching anthems, with L.A.'s Youth Brigade at the top of the hill. *What Price* is a good

ILLUSTRATION BY RAYMOND PETTIBON

S›U›B›P›O›P
U — S — A

A GUIDE TO U.S. INDEPENDENTS

By Bruce Pavitt

DECRY *Falling* LP (Toxic Shock). After releasing some low-fi multi-song seven-inchers, Toxic Shock gets back in the groove with this kick ass party LP by San Gabriel's **Decry**. It won't change your life, but this obscure suburban thrash band is too good to get buried beneath the rubble. Play loud. *(Box 242, Pomona, CA 91769.)*

BLACK FLAG *Slip It In* LP (SST). Live, **Black Flag** is the most intense band in the world. Henry Rollins is a monster performer—spilling sweat, swaying, bending, thrusting, with hippie hair and tattoos, combining the raw sex of Elvis or James Brown with the psychotic edge of Charlie Manson. Back this guy up with the hardest working band in show business and you've got a religious experience. I just wish to hell that their records came across. Since *Damaged*, Black Flag have put out decent records, but not great ones. Recorded in a cardboard box, they lack crispness and life. But even a pale imitation of their live sound is worth a spin. Pick hit: "Black Coffee." *(Box 1, Lawndale, CA 90260.)*

RAIN PARADE *Explosions in the Glass Palace* LP (Enigma). "Explosions..." is the latest from this sleepy flower power outfit from L.A. Sadly, the stinging Verlaine-like leads of their LP *Emergency Third Rail Power Trip*, are gone. The production here is watered down and the lyrics are as sappy as ever. A disappointing follow up to their Byrds/Television inspired debut. *(Box 2896, Torrance, CA 90509.)*

RAPOLOGISTS *Hip Hop Beat* 12" single (Telstar Cassettes). **Telstar Cassettes,** a record label that has never released a cassette, specializes in black dance music. The notorious DJ Whiz Kid cuts up on this one, which is good enough reason to check this out. The "Kid's Rap" features Flakey C and Early Daze alternating between their real voices and cartoonish, electronic smurf sounds ala **Newcleus.** Kinda silly. The "Party Rap" mix on the flip side is pretty cool, though. *(150 W. 58th St. NYC 10019.)*

SSD *How We Rock* LP (Modern Method). Third release by this hard 'n' heavy Boston batallion. Like the new **Black Flag,** these guys slow down the thrash tempo, mix up the bass and throw in some bursting leads for a truly h-e-a-v-y sound. The production is good, clarity and muscle. The best gnarly/headbanging crossover I've heard all year. I just know K.J. Doughton is gonna go for this one. *(332 Newbury St., Boston, MA 02115.)*

HIGHEIST *If You Love Me, Snort My Load* LP (Thermidor). **Blowfly, General Echo** and even **Tesco Vee** will have to move over for the Nigheist. Many acts throughout history have based their performance on obscenity and shock appeal. For those lacking in talent, it's a quick way to make a buck. *(912 Bancroft Way, Berkeley, CA 94710.)*

SUB TEN Pick Hits for November

KONK, Your Life, 12" single (Sleeping Bag) NYC

SALEM 66, 12" EP (Homestead) Boston

DIE KREUZEN, LP (Touch and Go) Milwaukee

SSD, How We Rock (Modern Method) Boston

YOUTH BRIGADE, What Price Happiness, (BYO) L.A.

BLACK FLAG, Slip It In, (SST) L.A.

JAMES BROWN/ AFRIKA BAMBAATA, Unity, 12" EP (Tommy Boy) N.Y.C.

BIRDSONGS OF THE MESOZOIC, Magnetic Flip, LP (Ace of Hearts) Boston

JOHN FOSTER'S POP PHILOSOPHERS, cassette (K) Olympia

BO DIDDLEY, singles compilation LP (Vogue reissue) Chicago '55-'58

SAMHAIN *Initium* LP (Plan 9). Featuring former members of NY's horror/thrash **Misfits,** *Initium* could well be considered the Misfits' third LP, as Glenn Danzig is still on vocals. The music here is slower and moodier than previous efforts, helping to emphasize the spooky subject matter. Lyle Preslar, former guitarist with **Minor Threat,** steps in on some lead guitar; his presence is not outstanding. *Initium* is worth picking up, although I don't find it nearly as enjoyable as the Misfits classic *Walk Among Us* LP. *(Box 41200, Lodi, NJ, 07644.)*

YOUTH BRIGADE *What Price Happiness* 7" (Better Youth Organization). The BYO label has been releasing some fist clenching anthems, with L.A.'s **Youth Brigade** at the top of the hill. "What Price..." is a good single, with sing-along vocals and aggressive bass and drums. A good example of the pop-edged, melodic hardcore that is becoming an L.A. trademark (see also: **Social Distortion,** early **Bad Religion, Posh Boy** material.) *(Box 67A54, L.A., CA 90067)*

Sub/Pop U.S.A.
▶▶ Radio ◀◀
every Tuesday 6-7 PM / KCMU 90.5 FM

BOLERO LAVA *Inevitable/Click of the Clock* 12" single (Mo-Da-Mu). Wave/pop/disco girl group from Vancouver. Keyboards, some exotic percussion. I guess they're a big deal across the border but I can't get too excited about their sound. The lyrics are pretty radical, though, with references to rape, war, the "police state" etc. *(347-810 W. Broadway, Vancouver, B.C. Canada V5Z 1J8.)*

DEJA VOODOO *Cemetary* LP (no label). "Sludgeabilly" duo from Montreal. Should appeal to Cramps fans. Unfortunately, there's no high end: no treble on the guitar or cymbals on the drums, making the whole thing sound like sludge. But I guess that's the point. Sample lyrics: "Big Scary Daddy is big and mean. Cover you in margarine." *(P.O. Box 182, Station F, Montreal, Quebec H3J 2L1 Canada.)*

BLAZING WHEELS AND BARKING TRUCKS Compilation LP (Thrasher). 20 years ago, surfers in California sang about the joys of catching a wave. Now, it's 1984 and skateboarding has become the number one trend for West Coast youth; and of course there are skate rock bands to sing about the joys of catching some air. This compilation, released by *Thrasher* skate mag, is a modest collection of garage punk-rock 'n' roll. For many consumers, the music here is secondary to the skating ability of the bands. Includes: **The Faction, J.F.A., McRad, Los Olvidados, Big Boys** and more. *(Box 24592, SF, CA 94124.)*

BIRDSONGS OF THE MESOZOIC *Magnetic Flip* LP (Ace of Hearts). Ex-members of Boston's art/punk **Mission of Burma** have thrown a serious party. Classically trained, wearing white gloves, these men compose, improvise, and occasionally shred. They cover Stravinsky's lynch mob classic "Rites of Spring" as well as the theme from Rocky and Bullwinkle. The majority of this record is rhythmically hypnotic, with a piano that moves from serenity to dissonance. *Magnetic Flip* may take a few spins, but the payoff's worth it. *(P.O. Box 579, Kenmore Station, Boston, MA 02215.)*

LONE RAGER *Metal Rap* 12" single (Megaforce). This year, rap artists **Run D.M.C.** released "Rock Box," featuring heavy metal lead guitar. Now the tables are turned, as the metal scene releases its first "rap" anthem. And it's bad. Outlining the history of guitar hero/heavy metal, **Lone Rager** name drops everyone from **Blue Cheer** to **Metallica.** Of course, this novelty schlock comes nowhere near the power of either. Be sure to flip it over for the "Special Air-Guitar Headbanging Dub." *(Megaforce, 60 York St., Old Bridge, NY 08857.)*

In 1984, circa *My War*, Black Flag with Henry Rollins was the most intense live band I had ever experienced, and possibly have ever experienced yet. My cohort doing the *Sub Pop* zine, Calvin Johnson, felt the same. I never thought their recordings really captured the rawness of their live show. They were a phenomenon, and had a huge influence on the Seattle grunge bands— that *My War* tour was seen by Mark Arm of Mudhoney, Kurt Cobain of Nirvana, Buzz from the Melvins, and a whole lot of others.

single, with sing-along vocals and aggressive bass and drums. A good example of the pop-edged, melodic hardcore that is becoming an L.A. trademark (see also: **SOCIAL DISTORTION**, early **BAD RELIGION**, Posh Boy material.)

BOLERO LAVA "Inevitable" b/w "Click of the Clock" 12" single (Mo-Da-Mu). Wave/pop/disco girl group from Vancouver, Canada. Keyboard, some exotic percussion. I guess they're a big deal across the border, but I can't get too excited about their sound. The lyrics are pretty radical, though, with references to rape, war, the "police state," etc.

DEJA VOODOO *Cemetery* LP (OG Music) "Sludgea-billy" duo from Montreal. Should appeal to **CRAMPS** fans. Unfortunately, there's no high end; no treble on the guitar, nor cymbals on the drums, making the whole thing sounds like sludge. But I guess that's the point. Sample lyrics: "Big scary daddy is big and mean. Cover you in margar-ine."

VARIOUS *Blazing Wheels and Barking Trucks* compilation LP (Thrasher). Twenty years ago, surfers in California sang about the joys of catching a wave. Now, it's 1984 and skateboarding has become the number one trend for the West Coast youth. Of course, there are skate rock bands to sing about the joys of catching some air. This compilation, released by *Thrasher* skate mag, is a modest collection of garage-punk rock 'n roll. For many consumers, the music here is secondary to the skating ability of the bands. Includes: **THE FACTION, J.F.A., MCRAD, LOS OLVIDADOS, BIG BOYS**, and more.

BIRDSONGS OF THE MESOZOIC *Magnetic Flip* LP (Ace of Hearts). Ex-members of Boston's art/punk **MISSION OF BURMA** have thrown a serious party. Classically trained, wearing white gloves, these men compose, improvise, and occasionally shred. They cover **STRAVINSKY**'s lynch mob classic "Rites of Spring" as well as the theme from *Rocky and Bullwinkle*. The majority of this record is rhythmically hypnotic, with a piano that moves from serenity to dissonance. *Magnetic Flip* may take a few spins, but the payoff's worth it.

LONE RAGER *Metal Rap* 12" single (Megaforce). This year, rap artist **RUN-D.M.C.** released "Rock Box," featuring heavy metal lead guitar. Now the tables are turned, as the metal scene releases its first "rap" anthem. And it's bad. Outlining the history of guitar hero heavy metal, Lone Rager name drops everyone from **BLUE CHEER** to **METALLICA**. Of course, this novelty schlock comes nowhere near the power of either. Be sure to flip it over for the "Special Air-Guitar Headbanging Dub."

SUB TEN—PICK HITS FOR NOVEMBER

KONK (NYC) *Your Life* 12" single (Sleeping Bag)

SALEM 66 (Boston) 12" EP (Homestead)

DIE KREUZEN (Milwaukee) LP (Touch and Go)

SSD (Boston) How We Rock (Modern Method)

YOUTH BRIGADE (L.A.) *What Price Happiness* (BYO)

BLACK FLAG (L.A.) *Slip It In* (SST)

JAMES BROWN/AFRIKA BAMBAATA (NYC) *Unity*, 12" EP (Tommy Boy)

BIRDSONGS OF THE MESOZOIC (Boston) *Magnetic Flip* LP (Ace of Hearts)

JOHN FOSTER'S POP PHILOSOPHERS (Olympia) cassette (K)

BO DIDDLEY (Chicago) *singles compilation* LP (Vogue reissue)

The Replacements Have Scored Big

BARRENCE WHITFIELD AND THE SAVAGES LP (Mamou). Boston's favorite party band has gotta be the Savages. Basically a cover band, Barrence Whitfield and friends unearth obscure R&B classics and snap 'em back to life. Featuring Peter Greenberg (ex-**LYRES**) on guitar and Mr. Whitfield on burnin' baritone vocals, the Savages are ready to tear off the roof and blow the house down.

VOIVOD *War and Pain* LP (Metal Blade). Blitzkreig metal/thrash with Snake on throat, insults, screaming, and mike torture. The leads are fairly spontaneous, avoiding the pompous choreography we've come to expect from most heavy metal rock stars. In '84, metal bands are meeting head on with hardcore. The result, as in this case, can be deadly.

JOHN FOSTER'S POP PHILOSOPHERS cassette (K). Foster is a soulful vocalist who has been recording with various Olympia line-ups for the past four years. When he's on target, John exposes sharp fragments— he's a personal, intimate, expressive performer who never fails to move an audience. The **POP PHILOSO-PHERS**, an ever-changing ensemble that has included a diversity of musicians (includinng Steve Fisk, Steve Peters, and Dana Leigh Squires) have always experimented with arrangements. White soul meets avant garde. Although "Candy Store" is my favorite cut, the heart of this tape is a 20-minute slice of America called the "Kennedy Saga." In a music scene where business and marketing concerns are increasingly shutting out original material, it's nice to hear something a little different.

THE REPLACEMENTS *Let It Be* LP (Twin Tone). The Replacements, that hard rockin' foursome from Minneapolis, have scored big with their latest LP. This is mature, diverse rock that could well shoot these regional boys into the national mainstream. Today's Replacements play with a rich assortment of textures, instruments and styles, all the time keeping the loose, brash approach that won them an underground following. Vocalist Paul Westerburg sings from the heart and he knows how to break it. Although this doesn't come across with the fuck-you excitement of "Kids Won't Follow," the Replacements have been able to keep the edge while opening up to commercial airplay.

GET SMART! *Action Reaction* LP (Fever). It's finally out. Get Smart!, a midwest garage trio that plays pop with punch, has been shopping this demo around for two years. Now it's been picked up by Fever and will be marketed and distributed through Enigma. It's a real break for this transplanted Kansas group. With good male and female vocals, this gritty pop-edged material should stand up for years to come.

VARIOUS *Middle of America* compilation LP (Highly In Debt). One of the better aggressive compilations to come out lately; this should help put Chicago on the map. Two of my favorite US bands, **NAKED RAY-GUN** and **BIG BLACK**, don't come off quite as great as their 12" releases, but hey, they're both on one LP. Other bands include the **EFFIGIES, SAVAGE BELIEFS**(!), **ARTICLES OF FAITH, NADSAT REBEL**, and more.

RJ'S CUSTOM STAGE LIGHTING

RENTALS SALES LEASES OF QUALITY NEW & USED EQUIPMENT
CLUB TO CONCERT PRODUCTIONS . . . FEATURING

A.E.I. - TOP QUALITY DIMMING AND CONTROL
WestStar - COMPUTERIZED CONTROL, APPLE, IBM
R & R - WORLD'S TOUGHEST ROAD CASES
L & E - PARS AND OTHER FIXTURES
Genie - TOWERS AND TREES
AirCraftLandinglites - RACKS OF FOUR

DOWNTOWN OFFICE - 622·PARS

MICK'S
VINTAGE GUITARS

Christmas Sale

• 1966 Gibson Firebird	$275.00
• 1952 Gibson Les Paul	$699.00
• 1980 Gibson Les Paul Special	$299.00
• 1965 Gibson Melody Maker	$199.00
• 1971 Fender Mustang	$150.00
• 1982 Fender Stratocaster	$399.00
• Fender Jazz Bass	$350.00
• Gibson EB1 Bass	$299.00
• Gretsch Project-O-Sonic	$450.00
• Gretsch Corvette	$125.00
• Rickenbacker 365	$399.00
• Hamer Special	$275.00
• Guild Starfire IV	$275.00
• 1962 Martin 00028C	$399.00

10-6 M-F   10-5 SAT

**3922 California Ave. S.W.
Seattle, WA 98116
(206) 937-0690**

METRIX
Recording Studios

The best 8 track studio . . . period!

December Special!

Free — 20 duplicated cassettes of your song(s)
with boxes & labels with 6 or more hours booked

**8 track tape — 25% off
½ track master tape — 50% off
Special Rates**

• Control
room • Main studio
rooms • 2 isolation rooms
• full record & demo production
• Video production • Tape duplicating
• Mobile recording van
OTARI, LEXICON, TEAC, ORBAN, TAPCO,
NEUMANN, SENNHEISER, SYMETRIX, ROLAND,
JBL, HAFFLER, TECHNICS, AKG,
SHURE, ASHLEY, CALREC
AND MORE!!!

**CALL FOR RATES (206)347-3824
10830 1st Dr. S.E., Everett, WA 98204**

S‣U‣B / P‣O‣P
U — S — A
A GUIDE TO U.S. INDEPENDENTS

By Bruce Pavitt

BARRANCE WHITFIELD AND THE SAVAGES LP (Mamou). Boston's favorite party band has gotta be the **Savages**. Basically a cover band, Barrance Whitfield and friends unearth obscure R&B classics and snap 'em back to life. Featuring Peter Greenberg (ex-Lyres) on guitar and Mr. Whitfield on burnin' baritone vocals, the Savages are ready to tear off the roof and blow the house down. *(Box 56, Hanover Street Station, Boston, MA 02113.)*

VOIVOD *War and Pain* LP (Metal Blade). Blitzkreig metal/thrash with **Snake** on throat, insults, screaming and mike torture. The leads are fairly spontaneous, avoiding the pompous choreography we've come to expect from most heavy metal rock stars. In '84, metal bands are meeting head on with hardcore. The result, as in this case, can be deadly. *(22458 Ventura Blvd, Suite E, Woodland Hills, CA 91364.)*

JOHN FOSTER'S POP PHILOSOPHERS cassette (K). **Foster** is a soulful vocalist who has been recording with various Olympia line-ups for the past four years. When he's on target, John exposes sharp fragments — he's a personal, intimate, expressive performer who never fails to move an audience. The **Pop Philosophers**, an ever-changing ensemble that has included a diversity of musicians (Steve Fisk, Steve Peters, Dana Leigh Squires...) have always experimented with arrangements. White soul meets *avant-garde*. Although "Candy Store" is my favorite cut, the heart of this tape is a 20-minute slice of America called the "Kennedy Saga." In a music scene where business and marketing concerns are increasingly shutting out original material, it's nice to hear something a little different. *(Box 7154, Olympia, WA 98507.)*

THE REPLACEMENTS *Let It Be* LP (Twin Tone). **The Replacements**, that hard rockin' foursome from Minneapolis, have scored big with their latest LP. This is mature, diverse rock that could well shoot these regional boys into the national mainstream. Today's Replacements play with a rich assortment of textures, instruments and styles, all the time keeping the loose, brash approach that won them an underground following. Vocalist Paul Westerburg sings from the heart and he knows how to break it. Although this doesn't come across with the *fuck you* excitement of "Kids Won't Follow," the Replacements have been able to keep the edge while opening up to commercial airplay. *(c/o 445 Oliver Ave S., Minneapolis, MN 55405.)*

The Replacements

SUB TEN
PICK HITS FOR DECEMBER

DIE KREUZEN, LP (Touch and Go) Milwaukee

REPLACEMENTS, Let It Be, LP (Twin Tone) Minneapolis

TRUE WEST, Drifters, LP, (PVC) L.A.

BARRANCE WHITFIELD /SAVAGES, LP (Mamou) Boston

HUSKER DU, Metal Circus, EP (SST) Minneapolis

REPLACEMENTS, The Replacements Stink, EP (Twin Tone) Minneapolis

BLACK FLAG, Family Man, LP (SST) L.A.

BLACK FLAG, Slip it in, LP (SST) L.A.

JOHNNY CASH, Hot and Blue Guitar, LP (Sun) Memphis '56

GET SMART, Action Reaction, LP (Fever/Enigma) Chicago

GET SMART! *Action Reaction* LP (Fever). It's finally out. **Get Smart!**, a midwest garage trio that plays pop with punch, has been shopping this demo around for two years. Now it's been picked up by Fever and will be marketed and distributed through Enigma. It's a real break for this transplanted Kansas group. With good male and female vocals, this gritty pop-edged material should stand up for years to come. *(c/o Box 3800 Merchandise Mart, Chicago, IL 60654.)*

MIDDLE OF AMERICA compilation LP (Highly In Debt). One of the better aggressive compilations to come out lately; this should help put Chicago on the map. Two of my favorite U.S. bands, **Naked Raygun** and **Big Black**, don't come off quite as great as their 12" releases, but hey, they're both on one LP. Other bands include the **Effigies**, **Savage Beliefs(!)**, **Articles of Faith**, **Nadsat Rebel** and more. *(Box 25, Evanston, IL 60204.)*

TRUE WEST *Drifters* LP (PVC). **True West**, one of the best pop bands in America, has shifted gears on their second release. Like many L.A. bands, these guys have gone for a country feel, leaving their psychedelic roots behind. Acoustic and slide guitar, the occasional twangy lead and three-part male harmonies make a real change in scenery. But whether they're milking a cow or a trend, it doesn't matter; **True West** writes good songs and they know how to sing. Members of other L.A. bands — **Green on Red** and the Long Ryders — step in for some extra harmonies. Expect heavy college airplay.

TEEN IDLES/S.O.A./G.I./YOUTH BRIGADE LP (Dischord). The long awaited re-pressing of four classic D.C. thrash 45s, all on one LP at a low price. Teen Idles, the first release on the legendary Dischord label, features Ian Mackaye and Jeff Nelson, who later formed **Minor Threat**. S.O.A. comes across with the first words of Henry Rollins, now with **Black Flag**. Favorite cut on the whole LP is "Barbed Wire" by Youth Brigade (*not* the L.A. Youth Brigade), an intense mix of hardcore and dub — possibly the first band to experiment with that hybrid. Most of the songs here are anti-drug and anti-fashion. By today's standards, many of the songs sound generic and dated; however, this record does serve as an important historical document, outlining the roots of one of the most influential and successful independent hardcore/punk labels.

JANDEK *Interstellar Discussion* LP (Corwood). Insane cult figure Jandek has just released his *ninth* LP. His, um, naive approach to music could well appeal to fans of **Jad Fair**. Until recently, his atonal mutterings were accompanied by acoustic guitar (check out the classic *Staring at the Cellophane*) but this time around he's bangin' away at some drums like a fourth grader after school. Most people would call this junk — I say it's scary. By the by, SST will be releasing an acoustic Charlie Manson LP in the near future, recorded behind bars. *(c/o Box 15375, Houston, TX 77020. Still "$55.00 for a 25 count box, any mix.")*

WORK PARTY *Work Song* 12" single (Mo Da Mu). First **Bolero Lava**, and now this. Lightweight dance music from Vancouver's once respectable Mo Da Mu label. The vocalist on "Work Song" does a pretty good Joan Armatrading rip-off, but it's not enough to save the pedestrian arrangement. Frisbee of the month. *(374-810 W. Broadway, Vancouver, B.C. Canada V5Z 1J8.)*

Sub/Pop U.S.A.
▶ ▶ Radio ◀ ◀

every Tuesday 6-7 PM • KCMU 90.5 FM

TRUE WEST DRIFTERS LP (PVC). True West, one of the best pop bands in America, has shifted gears on their second release. Like many L.A. bands, these guys have gone for a country feel, leaving their psychedelic roots behind. Acoustic and slide guitar, the occasional twangy lead, and three-part male harmonies make a real change in scenery. But whether they're milking a cow or a trend, it doesn't matter; True West writes good songs and they know how to sing. Members of other L.A. bands—**GREEN ON RED** and the **LONG RYDERS**—step in for some extra harmonies. Expect heavy college airplay.

TEEN IDLES/S.O.A./G.I./YOUTH BRIGADE LP (Dischord). The long-awaited repressing of four classic D.C. thrash 45s, all on one LP at a low price. Teen Idles, the first release on the legendary Dischord label, features Ian Mackaye and Jeff Nelson, who later formed **MINOR THREAT**. S.O.A. comes across with the first words of Henry Rollins, now with **BLACK FLAG**. Favorite cut on the whole LP is "Barbed Wire" by Youth Brigade (not the L.A. Youth Brigade), an intense mix of hardcore and dub—possibly the first band to experiment with that hybrid. Most of the songs here are anti-drug and anti-fashion. By today's standards, many of the songs sound generic and dated; however, this record does serve as an important historical document, outlining the roots of one of the most influential and successful independent hardcore/ punk labels.

JANDEK *Interstellar Discussion* LP (Corwood). Insane cult figure Jandek has just released his ninth LP. His, um, naive approach to music could well appeal to fans of **JAD FAIR**. Until recently, his atonal mutterings were accompanied by acoustic guitar (check out the classic "Staring at the Cellophane") but this time around he's bangin' away at some drums like a fourth grader after school. Most people would call this junk— I say it's scary. (And still "$55.00 for a 25 count box, any mix.") By the by, SST will be releasing an acoustic **CHARLIE MANSON** LP in the near future, recorded behind bars.

WORK PARTY *Work Song* 12" single (Mo Da Mu). First **BOLERO LAVA**, and now this. Lightweight dance music from Vancouver's once respectable Mo Da Mu label. The vocalist on "Work Song" does a pretty good **JOAN ARMATRADING** rip-off, but it's not enough to save the pedestrian arrangement. Frisbee of the month.

SUB TEN—PICK HITS FOR DECEMBER

DIE KREUZEN (Milwaukee) LP (Touch and Go)

REPLACEMENTS (Minneapolis) *Let It Be* LP (Twin Tone)

TRUE WEST (L.A.) *Drifters* LP (PVC)

BARRENCE WHITFIELD/SAVAGES (Boston) LP (Mamou)

HÜSKER DÜ (Minneapolis) *Metal Circus* EP (SST)

REPLACEMENTS (Minneapolis) *The Replacements Stink* EP (Twin Tone)

BLACK FLAG (L.A.) *Family Man* LP (SST)

BLACK FLAG (L.A.) *Slip It In* LP (SST)

JOHNNY CASH (Memphis '56) *Hot and Blue Guitar* LP (Sun)

GET SMART! (Chicago) *Action Reaction* LP (Fever/ Enigma)

Yo! 1984!

LABELS

Indie labels had been revived in the mid/late '70s as part of the punk/wave backlash, but these organizations were financially impoverished, usually dying after a few releases. Only a handful of people were buying these records, and most of these people were starving artists in their early '20s. The market was small, investment was small. Around '80 or '81, most bands were still struggling to put out 45s. Then two things happened. First, punk rock expanded into the suburbs. This was a start of the whole young, suburban "hardcore" thing. As younger people outside of urban areas became involved in alternative rock 'n roll, the market for independents became much larger. Secondly, labels like Slash and Posh Boy in L.A., and Twin Tone in Minneapolis, got some real cash together. These labels were serious, releasing four-color LPs that could compete in Tower Records if given the chance.

Today, there are real labels. Labels with healthy back catalogues. Labels with effective methods of promotion and distribution. Labels that will sign bands, not just from their home town, but from anywhere, and give royalties. Independent rock 'n roll labels are a real business. Four years ago, for a relatively obscure regional band to release a 12" record was rare. Now they're coming out every day.

Because independent releases are taking off as a business, however, a lot of the spontaneity and sheer zaniness of the early 45s, those primitive one-shots, is missing. Although an indie label will give an artist a maximum amount of creative control, the question "Will it sell?" is more predominant now than eight years ago. Of course, if you do everything yourself, you don't have to worry about compromises. Right now, the most flexible offbeat labels are often on cassette

only. Why? The investment is a lot smaller. Nationally, here are some "alternative" rock 'n roll indie labels with muscle, many of whom are now doing trans-regional signings. So listen up, Seattle bands! PVC/Jem, Enigma, Homestead, CD, Twin Tone, BYO, Posh Boy, 7th Street International, Frontier, Mo Da Mu, Fever, Toxic Shock, Ace of Hearts, R Radical, Dischord, Neutral, New Alliance, Modern Method, DB, Touch and Go, Mystic, SST, Fresh Sounds, and Thermidor.

FILM

1984 was the year underground bands made a dent in the film industry. The black rap/graffiti/breakdance scene peaked with intense popularity, breaking out of the Bronx and entering theaters via *Wild Style, Style Wars, Beat Street,* and *Breakin'.* White suburban punks from the L.A. area showed their ugly mugs in *Suburbia* and the outrageous *Repo Man.* I want to see more teen exploitation films with gratuitous rock 'n roll.

CLUBS

Video bars continued to proliferate among the over-21 alcohol crowd. All-ages shows started to decline in NY and SF due to reported skinhead/gang intimidation. A preview of things to come? Locally, spring of '84 saw the closure of the Metropolis; although only open for nine months, it remained a stable, indestructible hangout for rebellious youth. It also put on some great shows. Grave Image art gallery closed its doors to performance this summer due to a fire marshal clampdown during the **YOUTH BRIGADE/JFA** show. A riot ensued.

PUBLICATIONS

Olympia's *OP* magazine, that heavyweight bible of independent music, published its "Z" issue this fall,

S>U>B P>O>P

A GUIDE TO U.S. INDEPENDENTS

By Bruce Pavitt

YO! 1984!

• LABELS: Indie labels had been revived in the mid/late '70s as part of the punk/wave backlash, but these organizations were financially impoverished, usually dying after a few releases. Only a handful of people were buying these records, and most of these people were starving artists in their early 20s. The market was small, investment was small. Around '80-'81, most bands were still struggling to put out 45s, when two things happened. First, punk rock expanded into the suburbs. This was the start of the whole young, suburban "hardcore" thing. As younger people outside of urban areas became involved in alternative rock 'n' roll, the market for independents became much larger. Secondly, labels like Slash and Posh Boy in L.A. and Twin Tone in Minneapolis got some real cash together. These labels were serious, releasing four color LPs that could compete in Tower if given the chance.

Today there are real labels. Labels with healthy back catalogues. Labels with effective methods of promotion and distribution. Labels that will sign bands, not just from their home town, but from anywhere, and give royalties. Independent rock 'n' roll labels are a real business. Four years ago, for a rel-

"Institutionalized" by Suicidal Tendencies was one of the biggest indie hits of the year.

atively obscure regional band to release a 12" record was rare. Now they're coming out every day.

Because independent releases are taking off as a business, however, a lot of the spontaneity and sheer zaniness of the early 45s, those primitive one-shots, is missing. Although an indie label will give an artist a maximum amount of creative control, the question "Will it sell?" is more predominant now than eight years ago. Of course, if you do everything yourself, you don't have to worry about compromises. Right now, the most flexible, offbeat labels are often on cassette only. Why? The investment is a lot smaller. . . . Nationally, here are some "alternative" rock 'n' roll indie labels with muscle, many of whom are now doing transregional signings. So listen up, Seattle bands. *PVC/Jem, Enigma,*

Homestead, CD, Twin Tone, BYO, Posh Boy, 7th Street International, Frontier, Mo Da Mu, Fever, Toxic Shock, Ace of Hearts, R Radical, Dischord, Neutral, New Alliance, Modern Method, DB, Touch and Go, Mystic, SST, Fresh Sounds, Thermidor.

• FILM: '84 was the year underground bands made a dent in the film industry. The black rap/graffiti/break dance scene peaked out with intense popularity, breaking out of the Bronx and entering theaters via *Wild Style, Style Wars, Beat Street* and *Breakin'.* White suburban punks from the L.A. area showed their ugly mugs in *Suburbia* and the outrageous *Repo Man.* I want to see more teen exploitation films with gratuitous rock 'n' roll.

• CLUBS: Video bars continued to proliferate among the over-21 alcohol

In '84, skateboarding was as integral to hardcore punk as break-dancing was to hip hop.

crowd. All ages shows started to decline in NY and SF due to reported skinhead/gang intimidation. A preview of things to come? Locally, spring of '84 saw the closure of the *Metropolis*; although only open for nine months, it remained a stable, indestructible hang out for rebellious youth. It also put on some great shows. *Graven Image* art gallery closed its doors to performance this summer due to a fire marshal clampdown during the Youth Brigade/JFA show; a riot ensued.

• PUBLICATIONS: Olympia's *OP* magazine, that heavyweight bible of independent music, published its "Z" issue this fall, thus ending a five year career. Two magazines inspired by OP will be making their debut in '85, *Options* and *Sound Choice*; expect wide, unbiased coverage of independent music. As for independent "rock" and "pop," *Matter* magazine stepped forward as the most comprehensive, featuring reviews and features from top notch fanzine editors and writers from across the country. *Beano* continued to do an excellent job covering rootsy American music. *Maximum Rock N Roll* was the most visible hardcore punk fanzine, pushing generic thrash and left wing politics; columnist Mykel Board is a must read. *Unsound* continued covering noise and the avant-garde. Also, lots of '60s garage punk 'zines out this year, with *Breakthrough* being one of the best.

• TRENDS: Skate Rock. Skateboarding became increasingly popular with the underground bands cashing in. The *Big Boys, Agent Orange* and *Black Flag* all introduced their own skate model. *Thrasher* skate mag released an LP compilation of bands that either sang about skating or lived to skate. Tales of Terror sang "Make skates, not war, drop acid, not

bombs." As a musical trend, ska rock is ambiguous; just be sure to po with a skateboard.

• Hardcore/Metal Crossover. Band like *Black Flag, SSD* and *Corrosion* Conformity met head on with *Metallica, Slayer* and *Voivod.* The music wa raw and lead and rhythm guitaris were on an equal footing. The primar difference between punk and metal re mained in the lyrics: "hardcore" song reflect both everyday life and the ex treme dynamics of the world in whic we live; "metal" songs have little bas in reality, emphasizing satanism, fan tasy and mythology. But it's all rock 'n roll.

• Country? A variety of bands, mostl from L.A., have adopted a rootsie country feel. Aside from the wel known *Rank and File* and *Jason an the Scorchers,* we heard from *Blood o the Saddle, Tex and the Horseheads, Green on Red, True West, Long Ryders, Meat Puppets. The Last Roundup* from Hoboken, N.J. are rumoured to sing authentic blue-eyed soul and are headed for hillbilly heaven.

• '60s Revival. Despite all the press about a "psychedelic" resurgence, the strongest '60s revival this year was straight ahead garage/punk. Along with a tremendous output of bootleg re-issues, bands like *Yard Trauma, The Chesterfield Kings, The Pandoras, The Vipers, The Cheepskates* and move revived the '65-'66 punk sound: garage rock 'n' roll before the Summer of Love. A revived interest in Mod culture also produced some British Beat groups, such as *Mod Fun.*

• Electro-beat. As breakdancing swept the country and the world (i.e. Russia, China, Greenland) the polyrhythmic techno/break sound pioneered by Baker and Robie's Tommy Boy discs became the dominant sound in indie dance 12", replacing the warmer funk/rap style made popular by Sugarhill. Despite the exciting, dynamic rhythmic possibilities, most of these formula hits had all the soul of a computer in orbit.

• Meanwhile, a handful of bands continue to break new ground. Making that rare bridge between intellect, emotion and style, expect to hear more about *Sonic Youth, Live Skull, Big Black, Husker Du, Run-DMC, The Minutemen* and Seattle's own *U-Men.* ∎

Sub/Pop U.S.A.
►► Radio ◄◄
every Tuesday 6-7 PM • KCMU 90.5 FM

PHOTOGRAPH BY PETE KUHNS

"Today there are real labels. Labels with healthy back catalogues. Labels with effective methods of promotion and distribution. Labels that will sign bands, not just from their home town, but from anywhere, and give royalties. Independent rock 'n roll labels are a real business. Four years ago, for a relatively obscure regional band to release a 12" record was rare. Now they're coming out every day."

thus ending a five-year career. Two magazines inspired by *OP* will be making their debut in '85, *Options* and *Sound Choice*; expect a wide, unbiased coverage of independent music. As for independent "rock" and "pop," *Matter* magazine stepped forward as the most comprehensive, featuring reviews and features from top-notch fanzine editors from across the country. *Beano* continued to do an excellent job covering rootsy American music. *Maximum Rocknroll* was the most visible hardcore punk fanzine pushing generic thrash and left-wing politics; columnist Mykel Board is a must read. *Unsound* continued covering noise and the avant garde. Also, lots of '60s garage punk zines out this year, with *Breakthrough* being one of the best.

•

TRENDS: SKATE ROCK

Skateboarding became increasingly popular, with the underground bands cashing in. **THE BIG BOYS**, **AGENT ORANGE**, and **BLACK FLAG** all introduced their own skateboard models. *Thrasher* skate mag released an LP compilation of bands that either sang about skating or lived to skate. **TALES OF TERROR** sang "Make skates, not war, drop acid, not bombs." As a musical trend, skate rock is ambiguous; just be sure to pose with a skateboard.

HARDCORE/METAL CROSSOVER

Bands like **BLACK FLAG**, **SSD**, and **CORROSION OF CONFORMITY** met head on with **METALLICA**, **SLAYER**, and **VOIVOD**. The music was raw and lead and rhythm guitarists were on an equal footing. The primary difference between punk and metal remained in the lyrics: hardcore songs reflect both everyday life and the extreme dynamics of the world in which we live; "metal" songs have little basis in reality, emphasizing satanism, fantasy, and mythology. But it's all rock 'n roll.

COUNTRY?

A variety of bands, mostly from L.A., have adopted a rootsier, country feel. Aside from the well known **RANK AND FILE** and **JASON AND THE SCORCHERS**, we heard from **BLOOD ON THE SADDLE, TEX AND THE HORSEHEADS, GREEN ON RED, TRUE WEST, LONG RYDERS,** and **MEAT PUPPETS. THE LAST ROUNDUP** from Hoboken, New Jersey, are rumored to sing authentic blue-eyes soul, and are headed for hillbilly heaven.

'60S REVIVAL

Despite the press about a "psychedelic" resurgence, the strongest '60s revival this year was straight ahead garage/punk. Along with a tremendous output of bootleg reissues, bands like **YARD TRAUMA**, the **CHESTERFIELD KINGS**, the **PANDORAS**, the **VIPERS**, the **CHEEPSKATES** and more revived the '65–'66 punk sound: garage rock 'n roll before the Summer of Love. A revived interest in mod culture also produced some British Beat groups, such as **MOD FUN**.

ELECTRO-BEAT

As breakdancing swept the country and the world (i.e. Russia, China, Greenland) the polyrhythmic techno break sound pioneered by Baker and Robie's Tommy Boy discs became the dominant sound in indie dance, replacing the warmer funk/rap style made popular by **SUGAR HILL**. Despite the exciting, dynamic rhythmic possibilities, most of these formula hits had all the soul of a computer in orbit.

Meanwhile, a handful of bands continue to break new ground. Making that rare bridge between intellect, emotion, and style, expect to hear more about **SONIC YOUTH, LIVE SKULL, BIG BLACK, HÜSKER DÜ, RUN-D.M.C.**, the **MINUTEMEN** and Seattle's own **U-MEN**.

U.S. Game Plan for '85

Live at the Meatlockers on New Year's Eve, Henry Rollins, vocalist for **BLACK FLAG**, was good. Skipping most of his poetry, he read forceful, penetrating accounts of his personal life. His redneck father. His hyperactivity. His psychoanalysis. Plenty of references to job frustration, lonely apartments, suicide, the endless American network of fast food establishments, and life on the road. With Black Flag, while stopping to perform at a small town in the midwest, he was told a woman had recently put a gun to her head at the Kmart next door. A Black Flag fan had managed to find a few brain fragments in the parking lot; and, cradling the pieces in a McDonald's cheeseburger wrapper, had walked over to the club and shown them to Henry. Yes! The performance was angry, vivid and honest; his occasional poems (Roaches are your gods/They are a superior species!) worked well. Which is more than I can say for Black Flag's *Family Man* spoken word/ instrumental LP (SST, Lawndale, CA). Two readings, "Family Man" and "Rattus Norvegicus" would have made an intriguing novelty 45. Instead, we get two highlights and a lot of filler. The flip, the instrumental side, has Greg Ginn playing rock star. Now for the good news. Black Flag *Live '84* (cassette, SST) is awesome. Black Flag has consistently failed to translate their emotional intensity through studio recordings. Recording them live was the answer. Definitive.

There've been some great licensing deals lately, with US indie labels signing good bands from overseas. French pop group **CALAMITIES** came up with a real sleeper; now we've got the **NOMADS** from Sweden. Classic rock 'n roll, lots of '60s punk covers, excellent production. Rockin' from start to finish, this is one of the few albums I've heard lately that deserves to be an entire LP. Next month we'll talk **MILKSHAKES**.

Drinking tea, swimming in a lake, having dinner with her family. What's this all about? **BEAT HAPPENING** finds beauty in the mundane. Everyday life is yet another adventure for this trio. Maybe that's why I'm crazy about their cheap little low-budget 45 "Our Secret"/ "What's Important" (K, Olympia, WA, $2.00). Innocent and sincere, this is a quiet escape from the brutality of most "modern" music. Minimal electric folk (drums, maracas, electric guitar), this owes a big debt to two underrated bands, the **MODERN LOVERS** and the **MARINE GIRLS**. Calvin sings baritone on side one, Heather sings the flip. Simple, effective four-track production by Greg Sage (**WIPERS**). Send a copy to your family.

On the cassette scene: **TIM BROCK** has released an outrageously offbeat tape called *Hot-Cha-Cha* (Burgerland, Seattle, WA). An eccentric young composer, Tim has embellished a small string orchestra with industrial noises and powerful drumming. Add to this a few pop, martini music novelty numbers, and yer talkin' creative project. This is a perfect example of something so unmarketable, that financially the cassette medium was the only justifiable way to go. The real underground is upon us.

100 FLOWERS is not dead. They live on, post mortem, with *Drawing Fire*, a newly released 12" EP on Happy Squid (Los Angeles). The music is stiff, intellectual and anguished. Brainy young rockers sandwiched between a cardboard sleeve. For fans of early **FALL, MEKONS**, and **GANG OF FOUR**.

Women are certainly making a dent in the underground American pop scene. **SALEM 66**, following through on their excellent debut 12" EP, continue to produce rich, electric folk music. Their new 45 *Across the Sea* (Homestead Records, Island Park, NY)

S›U›B›P›O›P
U — S — A

A GUIDE TO U.S. INDEPENDENTS

Shultz Cripples Moscow: U.S. Game Plan For '85

By Bruce Pavitt

► Live at the Meatlockers on New Year's Eve, **Henry Rollins**, vocalist for Black Flag, was good. Skipping most of his poetry, he read forceful, penetrating accounts of his personal life. *His redneck father. His hyperactivity. His psychoanalysis.* Plenty of references to job frustration, lonely apartments, suicide, the endless American network of fast food establishments and life on the road. With Black Flag, while stopping to perform at a small town in the midwest, he was told a woman had recently put a gun to her head at the K-mart next door. A Black Flag fan had managed to find a few brain fragments in the parking lot; and, cradling the pieces in a Mc-Donald's cheeseburger wrapper, had walked over to the club and shown them to Henry. Yes! The performance was angry, vivid and honest; his occasional poems (Roaches are your Gods/They are a superior species!) worked well. Which is more than I can say for **Black Flag**'s *Family Man* spoken word/instrumental LP (SST, Box 1, Lawndale, Ca 90260). Two readings, "Family Man" and "Rattus Norvegicus" would have made an intriguing novelty 45. Instead, we get two highlights and a lot of filler. The flip, the instrumental side, has Greg Ginn playing rock star. Now for the good news. **Black Flag** *Live '84* (cassette, SST) is awesome. Black Flag has consistently failed to translate their emotional intensity through studio recordings. Recording them live was the answer. Definitive.

► There've been some great licensing deals lately, with U.S. indie labels signing good bands from overseas. French pop group **Calamities** came up with a real sleeper; now we've got the **Nomads** from Sweden. Classic rock 'n' roll, lots of '60s punk covers, excellent production. Rockin' from start to finish, this is one of the few albums I've heard lately that deserves to be an entire LP. Next month we'll talk **Milkshakes**. (Nomads c/o What Goes On, 45 Alabama Ave., Island Park, NY 11558).

► Drinking tea, swimming in a lake, having dinner with *her* family. What's this all about? **Beat Happening** finds beauty in the mundane. Everyday life is yet another adventure for this trio. Maybe *that's* why I'm crazy about their cheap little low-budget 45 *Our Secret/What's Important* (K, Box 7154, Olympia, WA 98507, $2.00). Innocent and sincere, this is a quiet escape from the brutality of most "modern" music. Minimal electric folk (drums, maracas, electric guitar), this owes a big debt to two underrated bands, **The Modern Lovers** and **The Marine Girls**. Calvin sings baritone on side one, Heather sings the flip. Simple, effective four-track production by Greg Sage (Wipers). Send a copy to your family.

► On the cassette scene: **Tim Brock** has released an outrageously offbeat tape called *Hot-Cha-Cha* (Burgerland c/o 4216 S.W. Myrtle, Seattle, WA 98136). An eccentric young composer, Tim has embellished a small string orchestra with industrial noises and powerful drumming. Add to this a few pop, martini-music novelty numbers

and yer talkin' creative project. This is a perfect example of something so unmarketable, that financially the *cassette* medium was the only justifiable way to go. The real underground is upon us.

► **100 Flowers** is not dead. They live on, post mortem, with *Drawing Fire*, a newly released 12" EP on Happy Squid (Box 64184, L.A., CA 90064). The music is stiff, intellectual and anguished. Brainy young rockers sandwiched between a cardboard sleeve. For fans of early Fall, Mekons, Gang of Four.

► Women are certainly making a dent in the underground American pop scene. **Salem 66**, following through on their excellent debut 12" EP, continue to produce rich, electric folk music. Their new 45 *Across the Sea* is softer than previous, but the music remains first rate with beautiful harmonies. If the lyrics weren't so uninspired this record would rule. **Kendra Smith**, former bass player with the Dream Syndicate, has put together an exquisite EP of lush, sensual folk music. *Fell From The Sun* is slow, long and luxurious. I love it, especially the title track; stay tuned for an import version with one extra song. Fans of Nico would do well to give this a chance. (Salem 66 c/q Homestead, 45 Alabama Dr., Island Park, NY 11558. Kendra Smith c/o Serpent, Box 2896, Torrance, CA 90509).

► **Rednecks**. Some of Boston's top hardcore bands (**Gang Green**, **SSD**) are known for their reverence for beer and Van Halen. While these bands are simply decadent, irresponsible and fun-loving, the **FU'S** are intolerant right-wing scum. Why? Here are some lyrics from their latest LP, *Do We Really Want To Hurt You?* (Gasatanka, c/o Enigma, Box 2896, Torrance, CA 90509). "Join us or we'll blow you away... Don't need to justify it, don't need a reason... Time to lick my shiny boots... I'm standing tall and you're on your knees... I've known some total slime, well buddy, you top everything."

► As I type this, only eight more days till **Sonic Youth**! Guitarists **Thurston Moore** and **Lee Ranaldo** are *radical* experimenting with dissonant tunings, static; minimal rhythms and slippery chord changes. **Sonic Youth**'s latest release, *Death Valley 69/Brave Men Run (in My Family)* 45 (Irridescence, address unknown) features the overrated Lydia Lunch on the title track but is worth a listen. If you're just starting out on this innovative NY noise band, I'd suggest their *Burning Spear* 12" EP (Neutral) or the truly awesome *Kill Yr Idols* 12" EP (Zensor import) as the fidelity is ten times better. **Lydia Lunch** has a new 12" EP out, *In Limbo* (Double Vision). It's slow, ponderous, moody and dull. Lydia remains an untalented celebrity whose only gift is to be at the right place/right time. As such, she's a good indicator of what's hip. Like Sonic Youth.

► As the market for independent rock music gets bigger, goals of fame, fortune and MTV become increasingly prominent. Lately, there's been a whole slew of mainstream rock releases on indie labels. **Kraut**'s new LP *Whetting the Scythe* is a passable record, a few catchy hard rock tunes with just the right amount of thrash and speed-metal to give it street credibility. As product, I'm sure it will do well. (Cabbage c/o Enigma, Box 2896, Torrance, CA 90509.)

MEAL CONSUMED, LIGHT CONVERSATION, MORE BAD JOKES, OCCASIONAL SEXUAL INNUENDO

CONTROLLED BOASTING

POLITE QUESTIONING

► **Matt Groening** is God. His new independent publication, *Love Is Hell* (Box 36E64, L.A., CA 90036) is so funny it's dangerous. This guy breaks apart relationships just to look inside; who cares if he can only draw rabbits? Seattle cartoonist Lynda Barry is the only one who can compete with his insight. Nab it, folks.

S · U · B · T · E · N

SUB POP USA RADIO Every Tuesday 6-7pm KCMU 90.5 FM

"Matt Groening is God. His new independent publication, *Love Is Hell* is so funny it's dangerous. This guy breaks apart relationships just to look inside; who cares if he can only draw rabbits? Seattle cartoonist Lynda Barry is the only one who can compete with his insight. Nab it, folks."

is softer than previous, but the music remains first-rate, with beautiful harmonies. If the lyrics weren't so uninspired this record would rule. Kendra Smith, former bass player with the **DREAM SYNDICATE**, has put together an exquisite EP of lush, sensual folk music. *Fell From the Sun* (Serpent Records, Torrance, CA) is slow, long and luxurious. I love it, especially the title track; stay tuned for an import version with one extra song. Fans of **NICO** would do well to give this a chance.

Rednecks. Some of Boston's top hardcore bands (**GANG GREEN, SSD**) are known for their reverence for beer and **VAN HALEN**. While these bands are simply decadent, irresponsible, and fun-loving, the **F.U.'S** are intolerant right-wing scum. Why? Here are some lyrics from their latest LP, *Do We Really Want to Hurt You?* (Gasatanka Records, Torrance, CA). "Join us or we'll blow you away/Don't need to justify it, don't need a reason/Time to lick my shiny boots/I'm standing tall and you're on your knees/I've known some total slime, well buddy, you top everything."

As I type this, only eight more days 'til **SONIC YOUTH**! Guitarists Thurston Moore and Lee Ranaldo are radical; experimenting with dissonant tunings, static, minimal rhythms, and slippery chord changes. Sonic Youth's latest release, "Death Valley '69" b/w "Brave Men Run (in My Family)" 45 (Iridescence) features the overrated **LYDIA LUNCH** on the title track, but is worth a listen. If you're just starting out on this innovative NY noise band, I'd suggest their *Burning Spear* 12" EP (Neutral) or the truly awesome *Kill Yr Idols* 12" EP (Zensor import) as the fidelity is ten times better. Lydia Lunch has a new 12" EP out, *In Limbo* (Double Vision). It's slow, ponderous, moody, and dull. Lydia remains an untalented celebrity whose only gift is to be at the right place/right time. As such, she's a good indicator of what's hip. Like Sonic Youth.

As the market for independent rock music gets bigger, goals of fame, fortune and MTV become increasingly prominent. Lately, there's been a whole slew of mainstream rock releases on indie labels. **KRAUT**'s new LP *Whetting the Scythe* (Cabbage) is a passable record, a few catchy hard rock tunes with just the right amount of thrash and speed metal to give it street credibility. As product, I'm sure it will do well.

MATT GROENING is God. His new independent publication, *Love Is Hell* is so funny it's dangerous. This guy breaks apart relationships just to look inside; who cares if he can only draw rabbits? Seattle cartoonist Lynda Barry is the only one who can compete with his insight. Nab it, folks.

SUB TEN

HENRY ROLLINS Live at the Meatlockers, New Year's, Seattle

BLACK FLAG (L.A.) *Live '84* cassette (SST)

BEAT HAPPENING (Olympia) "Our Secret" b/w "What's Important" 45 (K)

KENDRA SMITH (L.A.) *Fell From The Sun* 12" EP (Serpent/Enigma)

NOMADS (Sweden/USA) LP (What Goes On/Homestead)

SALEM 66 (Boston) *Across The Sea* 45 (Homestead)

SONIC YOUTH (New York) *Death Valley '69* 45 (Irridescence)

MATT GROENING (L.A.) *Love Is Hell* book (Life In Hell)

100 FLOWERS (L.A.) *Drawing Fire* 12" EP (Happy Squid)

TIM BROCK (Seattle) *Hot-Cha-Cha* cassette (Burgerland)

The Untouchable Force

SAN FRANCISCO has a rep for alternative media. *Search and Destroy* and its offspring *Re/Search* come to mind, as well as *Another Room* and *Maximum Rock-nroll*. Through these publications, San Francisco has helped organize underground culture. In addition to the printed word, the Bay Area also has Target Video, an organization that has documented the punk scene from the start. Two newly released tapes are highly recommended. **THE CRAMPS**' *Live at Napa State Mental Hospital* speaks for itself. Recorded in 1978, this is pure voodoo trashabilly with Bryan Gregory on guitar and the ever-insane Lux on vocals. Also, there's some wild dancing and vocal participation from the audience. The tape is short, too short, but worth seeing once a day, every day. **SURVIVAL RESEARCH LABORATORIES**' *A Scenic Harvest from the Kingdom of Pain* is pretty damn bizarre. Mark Pauline and crew create industrial performance art that features robots, projectiles and explosives. Metal creatures crawl, spin, chew, and lunge in an orgy of destruction and mayhem. An indictment of our current, unstoppable military-industrial complex? Perhaps. My guess is that it's just three boys who like to play with guns and matches. Whatever their motive, there is an immense creativity here that simply must be seen.

UTFO

Although the rap and hip hop scene has taken a sharp dive, a few gems still pop up. UTFO are fine, funky and fresh with two earthy raps called "Hanging Out" and "Roxanne, Roxanne" (Select Records) The cardboard box production gives this 12" a real underground feel—this is not high-tech disco. "Roxanne" is such a hit that it's already inspired three records in response.

New Day Rising LP. **HÜSKER DÜ** delivers and saves us, again. Mammoth, uniquely textured guitar, scorching vocals, screaming harmonies. Side one brings us to the temple, serving hit after bone-crushing hit: "Heaven Hill," "I Apologize," "Celebrated Summer." Seeking meaning in a barren desert, Hüsker Dü show us the way—original style, aching emotion, lyrical content. Commandment of the decade: "There's more to life than being right or wrong/there's something in between called getting along." (SST, Lawndale, CA)

With a name like the **,** you can expect a few moments of rude behavior. But aside from the bathroom humor, there is a mega new sound here. Alien, otherworldly, like their forefathers the **13TH FLOOR ELEVATORS**, these hardcore Texas locos plunder the subconscious, their sun-baked minds spewing whimsy and weirdness. Side two of *Another Man's Sac*, beginning with "Cherub," is the most demented, most original music I've heard yet in '85. (Touch and Go, Dearborn, MI)

Historic Recordings 1952-1953. Blues legend **LIGHTNING HOPKINS** plays raw electric guitar on these rediscovered 78s. A tap dancer occasionally steps in and flails away on foot percussion. Totally cool. (Arhoolie, El Cerrito, CA)

CHRIS D. is a brilliant writer. Formerly with *Slash* mag and the **FLESHEATERS**, Chris has a solo LP out, *Divine Horseman*, which draws from country, western, and folk. A deep, dark look at sin and salvation, *Divine Horseman* is a strong, American roots record which could just make you cry if you give it the chance. Chris is backed by John and Exene of **X**, Jeffrey Lee Pierce, and an L.A. cast of thousands. (Upsetter/Enigma, Torrance, CA)

"Survival Research Laboratory's *A Scenic Harvest from the Kingdom of Pain* is pretty damn bizarre. Mark Pauline and crew create industrial performance art that features robots, projectiles, and explosives. Metal creatures crawl, spin, chew and lunge in an orgy of destruction and mayhem. An indictment of our current, unstoppable military-industrial complex? Perhaps. My guess is that it's just three boys who like to play with guns and matches."

S›U›B›P›O›P

By Bruce Pavitt

A GUIDE TO U.S. INDEPE[NDENT]

● **New Day Rising** L.P. **HUSKER DU** deliver and save us, again. Mammoth, uniquely textured guitar, scorching vocals, screaming harmonies. Side One brings us to the temple, serving hit after bone crushing hit: **Heaven Hill, I Apologize, Celebrated Summer.** Seeking meaning in a barren desert, Husker Du show us the way — original style, aching emotion, lyrical content. Commandment of the decade: "There's more to life than being right or wrong / there's something in between called getting along." (SST, P.O. Box 1, Lawndale, CA 90260)

Although the rap 'n' hip hop scene has taken a sharp dive, a few gems still pop up. **U.T.F.O.** are fun, funky and fresh with two earthy raps called **Hanging Out** and **Roxanne, Roxanne.** The cardboard box production gives this 12" a real underground feel — this is not high tech disco. **Roxanne** is such a hit that it's already inspired three records in response. (Select, 175 5th Ave., NYC NY 10010)

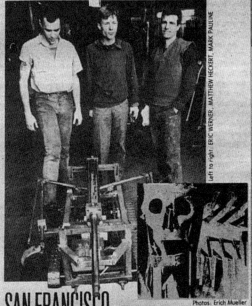

Left to right: ERIC WERNER, MATTHEW HECKERT, MARK PAULINE

Photos: Erich Mueller

SAN FRANCISCO HAS A REP FOR ALTERNATIVE MEDIA.

SEARCH AND DESTROY and its offspring **RE/SEARCH** come to mind, as well as **ANOTHER ROOM** and **MAXIMUM ROCKNROLL**. Through these publications, S.F. has helped organize underground culture. In addition to the printed word, the Bay Area also has **TARGET VIDEO**, an organization that has documented the punk scene from the start. Two newly released tapes are highly recommended. **THE CRAMPS'** Live at NAPA State Mental Hospital speaks for itself. Recorded in 1978, this is pure voodoo trashabilly with Bryan Gregory on guitar and the ever insane Lux on vocals. Also, there's some wild dancing and vocal participation from the audience. The tape is short, too short, but worth seeing once a day, every day. **SURVIVAL RESEARCH LABORATORY'S A Scenic Harvest from the Kingdom of Pain** is pretty damn bizarre. **MARK PAULINE** and crew create industrial performance art that features robots, projectiles and explosives. Metal creatures crawl, spin, chew and lunge in an orgy of destruction and mayhem. An indictment of our current, unstoppable military-industrial complex? Perhaps. My guess is that it's just three boys who like to play with guns and matches. Whatever their motive, there is an immense creativity here that simply must be seen.

the chance. Chris is backed by John and Exene of X, Jeffrey Lee Pierce, and a L.A. cast of thousands. (Upsetter/Enigma, Box 2896, Torrance, CA 90509)

● By the late '50s, public interest had declined in gospel music. Thus, many of the hard-edged, streamlined gospel quartets that flourished in America's post-war economy were compelled to enter the secular pop market. This is where we find **Stand Up and Testify** by the **PILGRIM TRAVELERS** (featuring Lou Rawls). Recorded in '57-'58, these recordings document the end of both The Pilgrim Travelers and the "Golden Age of Gospel." Some instruments have been added — bass, guitar, drums — to flesh out the sound and give it more of an R&B feel. One song, "Why," mirrored the doo-wop vocal group style that was coming into prominence and was the closest the Travelers came to a pop hit. Despite its leanings toward pop, **Testify** is a soulful gospel LP and a worthwhile re-issue. Gospel quartets of the '40s and '50s came across with plenty of raw power; expect more on this roots American style in upcoming columns. (Solid Smoke, P.O. Box 22372, S.F., CA 94122)

● **BILLY BRAGG**, a modern folk troubadour with an electric guitar, sings about love and politics with wit, sincerity and a cockney accent. His first record, **Spy Vs. Spy**, was a huge independent hit in the U.K., and rightly so — he was the perfect antidote to the fashion plate pretensions of most trendy British groups. CD records, from S.F., has just licensed Billy's second record, an LP, **Brewing Up with Billy Bragg**. This time Mr. Bragg has occasionally embellished his naked guitar work with trumpet or organ — experimenting without losing the essence of his live sound. However, the physical immediacy, the *presence* of his first record is missing. He's no longer in your living room, he's in the next county. **Brewing** has good material, but is not as immediately appealing as his classic first EP. (CD, 1230 Grant Ave., Suite 531, S.F., CA 94133)

● With a name like the **BUTTHOLE SURFERS** you can expect a few moments of rude behavior. But aside from the bathroom humor, there is a mega new sound here. Alien, otherworldly, like their forefathers the **13TH FLOOR ELEVATORS**, these hardcore Texas locos plunder the subconscious, their sun baked minds spewing whimsy and weirdness. Side Two of **Another Man's Sac**, beginning with "Cherub," is the most demented, most original music I've heard yet in '85. (Touch and Go, Box 433, Dearborn, MI 48121)

● **Historic Recordings 1952-1953.** Blues legend **LIGHTNING HOPKINS** plays raw electric guitar on these rediscovered 78s. A tap dancer occasionally steps in and flails away on foot percussion. Totally cool. (Arhoolie, 10341 San Pablo Ave., El Cerrito, CA 94530)

● **CHRIS D.** is a brilliant writer. Formerly with **Slash** mag and **The Flesheaters**, Chris has a solo LP out, **Divine Horseman**, which draws from country, western and folk. A deep, dark look at sin and salvation, **Divine Horseman** is a strong, roots American record which could just make you cry if you give it

SUB / TE[M]

HUSKER DU New Day Rising LP (SST) Minneapolis
BUTTHOLE SURFERS Another Man's Sac LP (Touch and Go) San Antonio
CRAMPS Live at the NAPA State Mental Hospital video (Target) S.F.
S.R.L. A Scenic Harvest from the Kingdom of Pain video (Target) S.F.
LIGHTNING HOPKINS Historic Recordings 1952-1953 LP (Arhoolie) Houston
ACID SCRATCH EP (Rabid) Austin
U.T.F.O. Roxanne, Roxanne 12" EP (Select) N.Y.C.
BILLY BRAGG Brewing Up With Billy Bragg LP (CD) U.K./U.S. release
CHRIS D. Divine Horseman LP (Upsetter/Enigma) L.A.
PILGRIM TRAVELERS Stand Up and Testify! LP (Annex/Solid Smoke) L.A.

SUB POP USA RADIO Every Tuesday 6-7pm KCMU 90.5 FM

By the late '50s, public interest had declined in gospel music. Thus, many of the hard-edged, streamlined gospel quartets that flourished in America's post-war economy were compelled to enter the secular pop market. This is where we find *Stand Up and Testify* (Solid Smoke) by **THE PILGRIM TRAVELERS** (featuring **LOU RAWLS**). Recorded in '57–'58, these recordings document the end of both the Pilgrim Travelers and the "golden age of gospel." Some instruments have been added—bass, guitar, drums—to flesh out the sound and give it more of an R&B feel. One song, "Why," mirrored the doo-wop vocal group style that was coming into prominence, and was the closest the Travelers came to a pop hit. Despite its leanings toward pop, *Testify* is a soulful gospel LP and a worthwhile re-issue. Gospel quartets of the '40s and '50s came across with plenty of raw power; expect more on this roots American style in upcoming columns.

BILLY BRAGG, a modern folk troubadour with an electric guitar, sings about love and politics with wit, sincerity, and a Cockney accent. His first record, *Spy Vs. Spy*, was a huge independent hit in the UK, and rightly so—he was the perfect antidote to the fashion-plate pretensions of most trendy British groups. CD records, from San Francisco, has just licensed Billy's second record, an LP, *Brewing Up with Billy Bragg*. This time Mr. Bragg has occasionally embellished his naked guitar work with trumpet or organ—experimenting without losing the essence of his live sound. However, the physical immediacy, the presence of his first record is missing. He's no longer in your living room, he's in the next county. *Brewing* has good material, but is not as immediately appealing as his classic first EP.

SUB TEN

HÜSKER DÜ (Minneapolis) *New Day Rising* LP (SST)

BUTTHOLE SURFERS, (Texas) *Another Man's Sac* LP (Touch and Go)

CRAMPS (SF) *Live at the Napa State Mental Hospital* video (Target)

S.R.L. (SF) *A Scenic Harvest from the Kingdom of Pain* video (Target)

LIGHTNING HOPKINS (Houston, TX) *Historic Recordings 1952–1953* LP (Arhoolie)

ACID SCRATCH (Austin, TX) EP (Rabid)

UTFO (NYC) *Roxanne, Roxanne* 12" EP (Select)

BILLY BRAGG (UK/USA) *Brewing Up With Billy Bragg* LP (CD)

CHRIS D. (L.A.) *Divine Horseman* LP (Upsetter/Enigma)

PILGRIM TRAVELERS (LA) *Stand Up and Testify!* LP (Annex/Solid Smoke)

Something Fresher Than AC/DC Guitar Lines

ROIR tapes from NY continues their extensive catalogue of cassette-only releases. Their latest promo package includes *R.I.P.*, a fans-only history of unreleased **RICHARD HELL** tracks. A punk poet who was involved in such seminal underground NY bands as the **HEARTBREAKERS**, **NEON BOYS**, **TELEVISION** and the **VOIDOIDS**, Mr. Hell was a major scenemaker in late '70s NY. Frankly, I'd pass on this collection of shoddy filler and grab the archival "Neon Boys" b/w "Voidoids" 45 on Shake Records, if you can find it. *Garage Sale* is possibly the best compilation available of paisley/Voxx/fuzztone revival groups. Although the bands (**PANDORAS**, **VIPERS**, etc.) are carbon copies of '60s garage punk/psych, there are some catchy hooks that make for fun, if mindless, entertainment. *World Class Punk* is an international collection of 27 modern punk bands from 25 different countries, including Hungary, Iceland, and Yugoslavia. Awesome in scope, diverse in approach, this collection is an impressive achievement. ROIR, despite its ups and downs, continues to release significant material. It's a shame that, due to marketing strategy and financial restrictions, this material has to be released on cassettes that have been duplicated on high speed machines—some of this deserves the longevity and sound quality of good vinyl. (ROIR, New York)

•

RUN-D.M.C. and the **BEASTIE BOYS** are both creating a rock/rap fusion featuring raps and rhythms overlaid with hard rock guitar. Although I'm glad these groups are integrating black and white audiences, I think '85 needs something fresher than **AC/DC** guitar lines. Which is one reason why I think Run-D.M.C.'s pre-"Rock Box" material ("It's Like That," "Sucker M.C.'s," "Hard Times") remains their strongest. Their new LP, *King of Rock*, features wimpy, underproduced rhythms, a tired delivery, and trite guitar shit. There's also a miserable attempt at rap/reggae fusion featuring talentless guest toaster **YELLOWMAN**. On the other hand, the Beastie Boys come on like gang warfare with ultra-tight, machine-gun raps and *booming* beatbox rhythms. Tough. This NY ex-thrash group gone hip hop is truly powerful on "Beastie Groove." While last year's "Cooky Puss" single was interesting—street punks adopting black culture—it was so sloppy that it couldn't be taken seriously; it remains a novelty record. However, "Beastie Groove" is so good, so tight, that it demands heavy crossover airplay. And yes, the flip, "Rock Hard" features hard rock guitar. And somehow the Beasties make it sound fresh.

•

Last year, Minneapolis hit the jackpot with triple gold from **HÜSKER DÜ**, the **REPLACEMENTS** and **PRINCE**. In '85 there will be at least one more group to add to that list. **SOUL ASYLUM** has an excellent debut LP out called *Say What You Will* (produced by Bob Mould of Hüsker Dü). Soul Asylum shares the eclecticism and diversity of the Replacements, as well as a great lead vocalist, but comes across with more edge. If you think the Replacements are too mainstream, check out Soul Asylum. Pick hits: "Long Day," "Religiavision." (Twin Tone, Mnpls, MN)

D.O.A. are one of the few political punk bands to survive the '80s. But although they've retained their political integrity, playing benefits and promoting labor and anti-war causes, their latest record is their most commercial sounding to date. *Don't Turn Yer Back on*

ROUND THE SOUND STUDIO'S

24HR
Practice Rooms
Rentals Nightly, Weekly or Monthly.

- Electronic Repair Service
- Easy Access/Free Parking
- Quality Acoustic Sound
- Security Building
- Showers/Restrooms
- Loading Docks
- Creative/Supportive Atmosphere
- Promo Kits

1454 N.W. 45
(under the Ballard Bridge)

783-7371

A PROFESSIONAL FACILITY

RJ's CUSTOM STAGE LIGHTING

- **RENTALS, SALES & LEASES OF QUALITY NEW & USED EQUIPMENT**
- **FROM CLUBS TO CONCERT TOURS**
- **CALL US FOR A BID**

206·622·PARS

FALLOUT

best hardcore · radical skates
1506 e olive wy & MORE! 323-bomb

METRIX
Recording Studios

8 Tracks
that sound like more!

- Top professional equipment
- Hot engineer
- Creative Atmosphere
- Control Room, Main Room, Two Iso Rooms
- **EXCELLENT RATES/EXCELLENT RESULTS!**

Just five minutes from Lynnwood & I-5

Add **YOUR** name to our list!

CALL FOR RATES (206) 347-3824
10830 1st Dr. S.E., Everett, WA 98204

24 THE ROCKET April 1985

S·U·B·P·O·P

A GUIDE TO U.S.

By Bruce Pavitt

● Last year, Minneapolis hit the jackpot with triple gold from Husker Du, the Replacements and Prince. In '85 there will be at least one more group to add to that list. **SOUL ASYLUM** has an excellent debut LP out called **SAY WHAT YOU WILL** (produced by Bob Mould of Husker Du). Soul Asylum shares the eclecticism and diversity of the Replacements, as well as a great lead vocalist, but comes across with more edge. If you think the Replacements are too mainstream, check out Soul Asylum. Pick hits: "Long Day," "Religiavision." (Twin Tone, 445 Oliver Ave., S., Mnpls, MN 55405)

● **D.O.A.** are one of the few political punk bands to survive the '80s. But although they've retained their political integrity, playing benefits and promoting labor and anti-war causes, their latest record is their most commercial sounding to date. **DON'T TURN YER BACK ON DESPERATE TIMES** was recorded last spring in London and broadcast on BBC 1 as a John Peel "session." Perhaps this influential British DJ will help D.O.A. receive the radio airplay they deserve. This 12" EP contains two old songs rerecorded — **GENERAL STRIKE, RACE RIOT** — and two new anthems, A

RICHARD HELL ... **TAPES FROM NY CONTINUES THEIR EXTENSIVE** catalogue of cassette-only releases. Their latest promo package includes R.I.P., a fans-only history of unreleased **RICHARD HELL** tracks. A punk poet who was involved in such seminal underground NY bands as the Heartbreakers, Neon Boys, Television and the Voidoids, Mr. Hell was a major scene maker in late '70s NY. Frankly, I'd pass on this collection of shoddy filler and grab the archival Neon Boys/Voidoids 45 on Shake records, if you can find it. Garage Sale is possibly the best compilation available of paisley/Voxx/fuzztone revival groups. Although the bands (Pandoras, Vipers etc.) are carbon copies of '60s garage punk/psych, there are some catchy hooks that make for fun, if mindless, entertainment. World Class Punk is an international collection of 27 modern punk bands from 25 different countries, including Hungary, Iceland and Yugoslavia. Awesome in scope, diverse in approach, this collection is an impressive achievement. ROIR, despite its ups and downs, continues to release significant material. It's a shame that, due to marketing strategy and financial restrictions, this material has to be released on cassettes that have been duplicated on high speed machines — some of this deserves the longevity and sound quality of good vinyl. (ROIR, 611 Broadway, NYC, NY 10012)

Amos Milburn

RUN D.M.C. and **THE BEASTIE BOYS** are both creating a rock/rap fusion featuring raps and rhythms overlaid with hard rock guitar. Although I'm glad these groups are integrating black and white audiences, I think '85 needs something fresher than AC/DC guitar lines. Which is one reason why I think Run D.M.C.'s pre-**ROCK BOX** material (It's Like That, Sucker M.C.'s, Hard Times) remains their strongest. Their new LP, **KING OF ROCK**, features wimpy, underproduced rhythms, a tired delivery and trite guitar shit. There's also a miserable attempt at rap/reggae fusion featuring talentless guest toaster Yellow Man. On the other hand, **THE BEASTIE BOYS** come on like gang warfare with ultra tight, machine gun raps and BOOMING beatbox rhythms. Tough. This NY ex-thrash group gone hip hop is truly powerful on **BEASTIE GROOVE**. While last year's Cooky Puss single was interesting — street punks adopting black culture — it was so sloppy that it couldn't be taken seriously; it remains a novelty record. However, Beastie Groove is so good, so tight, that it demands heavy cross-over airplay. And yes, the flip, Rock Hard features hard rock guitar. And somehow the Beasties make it sound fresh. (Run D.M.C./Profile: 1775 Broadway, NYC, NY 10019. Beastie Boys/Def Jam: 5 University Place, NYC, NY 10003)

SEASON IN HELL and BURN IT DOWN. (Alternative Tentacles, Box 11458, SF, CA 94101)

● Surprise hit of the spring goes to **SCRATCH ACID** from Austin, TX. Their debut EP on Rabid Records is a psychotic slab of rock 'n' roll that calls for an immediate straight jacket. Cramps/Birthday Party fans will go crazy. Cannibals, monsters, insanity, it's all here, buried alive and waitin' to be discovered. (Rabid, P.O. Box 49263, Austin, TX 78765)

● **THE SWANS** are part of a current NY scene of dirgy, dissonant rock bands that includes Sonic Youth, Live Skull and Rat at Rat R. The Swans are totally devoid of melodic hooks, relying instead on a dense, heavy, abrasive texture that can be numbing if consumed in large doses (more than one song). The tempo is slow, the bass rules, there's guitar feedback and junkyard percussion. Lyrics are simply stated (I give you money/you are superior) and are fascinating in their bluntness. The production on their latest LP, **COP**, is much fuller than their previous, **FILTH**; consequently it's more effective. Swans are an interesting group who will be appreciated if given the chance. (Kelvin import)

● The new **BLACKOUTS** EP is quite good and should be a mega-hit with the current gothic, moody, postBauhaus, nose-ring, crucifix earring, black lace, death rock club scene. The Blackouts are now residing in San Francisco. (Wax Trax! Records, 2449 N. Lincoln Ave. Chicago, IL 60614)

● Boogie woogie, blues and jumpin' R&B are all here on **LET'S HAVE A PARTY**, a super fine re-issue of **AMOS MILBURN** material (originally released from '45 to '56 on the Aladdin label, a pioneering indie based in L.A.). Amos loved to play the piano and drink hard; **GOOD, GOOD WHISKEY** and **BAD, BAD WHISKEY** were both hits. For rollickin' roots rock 'n' roll, check out **CHICKEN SHACK BOOGIE**, recorded way back in '47! Amos was hep! (Pathe Marconi import)

SUBSYSTEM

SCRATCH ACID	12" LP (Rabid) Austin
BEASTIE BOYS	Beastie Groove/Rock Hard 12" (Def Jam) N.Y.C.
BLACKOUTS	Idiot 12" EP (Wax Trax!) S.F.
SOUL ASYLUM	Say What You Will LP (Twin Tone) Minneapolis
SWANS	Cop LP (Kelvin import) N.Y.C.
AMOS MILBURN	Let's Have A Party re-issue LP (Aladdin) L.A. '45 '56
RAUNCH HANDS	Stomp It 45 (GOON) N.Y.C.
D.O.A.	Don't Turn Yer Back 12" EP (Alternative Tentacles) Vancouver, B.C.
U-MEN	demo tape, Seattle
GREEN RIVER	demo tape, Seattle

SUB POP USA RADIO Every Tuesday 6-7pm KCMU 90.5 FM

Desperate Times was recorded last spring in London, and broadcast on BBC 1 as a John Peel session. Perhaps this influential British DJ will help D.O.A. receive the radio airplay they deserve. This 12" EP contains two old songs rerecorded—"General Strike" and "Race Riot"—and two new anthems, "A Season In Hell" and "Burn It Down." (Alternative Tentacles, SF, CA)

Surprise hit of the spring goes to **SCRATCH ACID** from Austin, TX. Their debut EP on Rabid Records is a psychotic slab of rock 'n roll that calls for an immediate straightjacket. **CRAMPS/BIRTHDAY PARTY** fans will go crazy. Cannibals, monsters, insanity, it's all here, buried alive and waitin' to be discovered. (Rabid, Austin, TX)

THE SWANS are part of a current NY scene of dirgy, dissonant rock bands that includes **SONIC YOUTH**, **LIVE SKULL**, and **RAT AT RAT R**. The Swans are totally devoid of melodic hooks, relying instead on a dense, heavy, abrasive texture that can be numbing if consumed in large doses (more than one song). The tempo is slow, the bass rules, there's guitar feedback and junkyard percussion. Lyrics are simply stated ("I give you money/You are superior") and are fascinating in their bluntness. The production on their latest LP, *Cop*, is much fuller than their previous, *Filth*; consequently it's more effective. Swans are an extreme group who will be appreciated if given the chance. (Kelvin import)

The new **BLACKOUTS** EP is quite good and should be a mega-hit with the current gothic, moody, post-**BAUHAUS**, nose-ring, crucifix earring, black lace, death rock club scene. The Blackouts are now residing in San Francisco. (Wax Trax! Records, Chicago, IL)

Boogie woogie, blues and jumpin' R&B are all here on *Let's Have A Party*, a super fine reissue of **AMOS MILBURN** material (originally released from '45 to '56 on the Aladdin label, a pioneering indie based in L.A.) Amos loved to play the piano and drink hard; "Good, Good Whiskey" and "Bad, Bad Whiskey" were both hits. For rollickin' roots rock 'n roll, check out "Chicken Shack Boogie," recorded way back in '47! Amos was hep! (Pathe Marconi import)

SUB TEN

SCRATCH ACID (Austin) 12" EP (Rabid)

BEASTIE BOYS (NYC) "Beastie Groove" b/w "Rock Hard" 12" (Def Jam)

BLACKOUTS (SF) "Idiot" 12" track (Wax Trax!)

SOUL ASYLUM (Minneapolis) *Say What You Will* (Twin Tone)

SWANS (NYC) *Cop* LP (Kelvin import)

AMOS MILBURN (L.A. '45–'46) *Let's Have a Party* reissue LP (Aladdin)

RAUNCH HANDS (NYC) "Stomp It" 45" (Egon)

D.O.A. (Vancouver, B.C.) "Don't Turn Yer Back" 12" (Alternative Tentacles)

U-MEN (Seattle) demo tape

GREEN RIVER (Seattle) demo tape

Speed Trials

At last count there were almost 450 art galleries in New York City. Being the center of America's art world, it's not surprising that NYC has had a history of art rebels involved with music. The **VELVET UNDERGROUND**, who originally worked with Warhol, come to mind, as well as the "No New York" crowd of the late '70s. So it comes as no surprise that many of the NY "noise" bands were captured live at an art gallery. The *Speed Trials* compilation was taped at White Columns, an alternative space similar to Seattle's legendary Rosco Louie Gallery. Although the recording quality is spotty, the best of NY's avant garde is represented—**SONIC YOUTH, SWANS**—as well as **LIVE SKULL**, the **BEASTIE BOYS**, and **LYDIA LUNCH**. There's also a special guest appearance by **THE FALL**, long one of Britain's most controversial bands. Although the "art" tag often implies self-indulgent posing of the most vile sort, the best of these groups come across with deeply felt style—not the latest cosmetic "concept." They are also deeply rooted in the soul, guts and behavior of rock 'n roll, as opposed to the polite, formalistic boundaries of modern rock composition. Homestead, currently the most adventurous independent rock label in America, has cornered the market on New York noise. Aside from releasing the *Speed Trials* compilation, they've just put out the *Bad Moon Rising* LP by Sonic Youth and the *Raping a Slave* 12" by Swans. When Sonic Youth came to town last February, they carried eight guitars, all with different tunings. They also rammed screwdrivers and drumsticks behind the strings. With experimental guitars, the plaintive, **NICO**-ish vocals of Kim Gordon, and rock-hard rhythms, Sonic Youth proved to be the '80s answer to the Velvet Underground. Their new LP, while not their best release to date, justifies the comparison. Last month, I mentioned how the dense, bass heavy sounds of Swans was starting to mature on their new LP, *Cop*. Due to the increasingly sensual, physical possibilities of this band, it was inevitable that they would release a 12" EP—a record with wide grooves, meaning higher highs and lower lows. *Raping a Slave*, aside from being the most provocative title of the year, is one of the most awesome things ever put on vinyl; by far their best to date. Stay tuned for more info on this very vibrant NY scene.

•

NAKED RAYGUN sing about sex and war. Their new LP, *Throb Throb* (Homestead) proves this underrated Chicago band to be one of the best sing-along punk bands in America; "Rat Patrol" is a total anthem. Whether singing about his libido or Managua, singer Jeff Pezzati knows that sex plus war equals aggression.

I guess the **BIG BOYS** decided to stick it out. Rumored to have broken up, their imminent success seems to have persuaded them to stay together. Their second album, *No Matter How Long the Line Is at the Cafeteria, There's Always a Seat* (Enigma), is as good as their first; a mix of straight punk and straight funk with a few true gems in between. Highlights include the **BLACK FLAG**-ish "No" and the excellent "I Do Care," an aggressive punk/funk hybrid that, like "We Want Your Money" from the first album, shows the Big Boys in their most creative form. Chalk up another one for Texas.

One of the greatest rock 'n roll records of all time!! The **SONICS** were the most intense garage band of the '60s—raw, screaming, lungs out of control. Seattle's proudest moment is captured on *Full Force* (Etiquette), the ultimate Sonics compilation. All the

FALLOUT

323- BOMB

records & skateboards
the best gets better!

RAD SKATE EVENT MAY 19

!!PACIFIC NORTHWEST ROCK COLLECTION SERIES!!

THEE 'LOUIE LOUIE' 45 RECORD

NEW RELEASES

!!FULL FORCE!!

ROCKIN ROBIN ROBERTS

WAILERS AT THE CASTLE

WRITE FOR MORE INFO 1985 CATALOG

FROM Etiquette

DOWNBEAT TO VINYL

★ Superior Acoustics
★ Professional Staff
★ State of the Art Equipment
★ RECORDING CLASSES
(starting May 18th)

CROW RECORDING STUDIO

634-3088

READYMADE FAMILY

THE READYMADE FAMILY, WHO RECENTLY CAMPAIGNED AND DONA-ted a large sum of money to Red Cross Ethiopia Famine Relief Fund, is at it again. The group plans to soon release their single "To CARE With Love," a percentage will be donated to CARE. For more information on CARE to the Earth, call 382-8289.

S>U>B>P>O>P

U — S — A

By Bruce Pavitt

A GUIDE TO U.S. INDEPENDENTS

At last count there were almost 450 art galleries in NYC. Being the center of America's art world, it's not surprising that NYC has had a history of art rebels involved with music; The Velvet Underground, who originally worked with Warhol, come to mind, as well as the No New York crowd of the late '70s. So it comes as no surprise that many of the new NY "noise" bands were captured live at an art gallery. **The Speed Trials** compilation was taped at White Columns, an alternative space similar to Seattle's legendary Roscoe Louie gallery. Although the recording quality is spotty, the best of NY's avant-garde is represented — **SONIC YOUTH, SWANS** — as well as **LIVE SKULL, THE BEASTIE BOYS** and **LYDIA LUNCH**. There's also a special guest appearance by **THE FALL**, long one of Britain's most controversial bands. Although the "art" tag often implies self-indulgent posing of the most vile sort, the best of these groups come across with deeply felt style — not the latest cosmetic "concept." They are also deeply rooted in the soul, guts and behavior of rock 'n' roll, as opposed to the polite, formalistic boundaries of modern composition. **Homestead**, currently the most adventurous independent rock label in America, has cornered the market on NY noise. Aside from releasing the Speed Trials compilation, they've just put out the **Bad Moon Rising** LP by **SONIC YOUTH** and the **Raping a Slave** 12" by **SWANS**. When Sonic Youth came to town last February, they carried eight guitars, all with different tunings. They also rammed screwdrivers and drumsticks between the strings. With experimental guitar, the plaintive, Nico-ish vocals of Kim Gordon and rock hard rhythms, SONIC YOUTH proved to be the '80s answer to the Velvet Underground. Their new LP, while not their best release to date, justifies the comparison. Last month, I mentioned how the dense, bass heavy sounds of SWANS was starting to mature on their new LP, **Cop**. Due to the incredibly sensual, physical possibilities of this band, it was inevitable that they would release a 12" EP — a record with wide grooves, meaning higher highs and lower lows. **Raping a Slave**, aside from being the most provocative title of the year, is one of the most awesome things ever put on vinyl; by far their best to date. Stay tuned for more info on this very vibrant NY scene. (Homestead, 45 Alabama Avenue, Island Park, NY)

NY NOISE

• **NAKED RAYGUN** sing about sex and war. Their new LP, **THROB, THROB** proves this underrated Chicago band to be one of the best sing-along punk bands in America; **RAT PATROL** is a total anthem. Whether singing about his libido or Managua, singer Jeff Pezzati knows that sex plus war equals aggression. (Homestead, 45 Alabama Ave., Island Park, NY 11558)

• I guess the **BIG BOYS** decided to stick it out. Rumoured to have broken up, their imminent success seems to have persuaded them to stay together. Their second album, **NO MATTER HOW LONG THE LINE IS AT THE CAFETERIA, THERE'S ALWAYS A SEAT**, is as good as their first; a mix of straight punk and straight funk with a few true gems in between. Highlights include the Black Flagish **NO** and the excellent **I DO CARE**, an aggressive punk/funk hybrid that, like **WE WANT YOUR MONEY** from the first album, shows the Big Boys in their most creative form. Chalk up another one for Texas. (Enigma, Box 2896, Torrance, CA 90509)

the SONICS

• One of the greatest rock 'n' roll records of all time!! The **SONICS** were the most intense garage band of the '60s — raw, screaming, lungs out of control. Seattle's proudest moment is captured on **FULL FORCE**, the ultimate Sonics compilation. All the hits from their two albums: **THE WITCH, BOSS HOSS, PSYCHO, CINDERELLA**, and of course, the definitive **LOUIE, LOUIE**. Recorded in '65/'66 this is maximum teenage entertainment before drugs turned our children into zombies!!! (Etiquette, 2442 NW Market St., Suite 273, Seattle, WA 98107)

• This dirty roots rockin' 45 from Hoboken really kicks. The **RAUNCH HANDS** play a tune called **Stomp It** that's got Bo Diddley rhythms 'n' a singer who drinks black whiskey for breakfast. Flip it over for a mean Ray Charles cover (**I Got A Woman**) and a cool guitar instrumental. Slap yer big paws on this one, daddy. (EGON, 719 Garden St., Hoboken, NJ 07030)

BIG BOYS

SUB POP USA RADIO
Every Tuesday
5-7pm KCMU 90.5 FM

SONICS	Full Force	LP	(Etiquette) Seattle/Tacoma
SWANS	Raping a Slave	12"	(Homestead) NYC
SONIC YOUTH	Bad Moon Rising	LP	(Homestead) NYC
NAKED RAYGUN	Throb, Throb	LP	(Homestead) Chicago
HUSKER DU	New Day Rising	LP	(SST) Mpls.
VARIOUS	Speed Trials	LP	(Homestead) NYC
BIG BOYS	No Matter How Long The Line	LP	(Enigma) Austin
RAUNCH HANDS	Stomp It	45	(EGON) Hoboken
SALEM 66		12"	(Homestead) Boston
MODERN LOVERS		LP	(Beserkley) Boston '76

hits from their two albums: "The Witch," "Boss Hoss," "Psycho," "Cinderella," and, of course, the definitive "Louie, Louie." Recorded in '65/'66 this is maximum teenage entertainment before drugs turned our children into zombies!!!

his dirty roots rockin' 45 from Hoboken really kicks. The **RAUNCH HANDS** play a tune called "Stomp It" that's got **BO DIDDLEY** rhythms and a singer who drinks black whiskey for breakfast. Flip it over for a mean **RAY CHARLES** cover ("I Got A Woman") and a cool guitar instrumental. Slap yer big paws on this one, daddy. (Egon Records, Hoboken, NJ)

SUB TEN

SONICS (Seattle/Tacoma) *Full Force* LP (Etiquette)

SWANS (NYC) *Raping a Slave* 12" EP (Homestead)

SONIC YOUTH (NYC) *Bad Moon Rising* LP (Homestead)

NAKED RAYGUN (Chicago) *Throb Throb* LP (Homestead)

HÜSKER DÜ (Mnpls) *New Day Rising* LP (SST)

VARIOUS *Speed Trials* compilation LP (Homestead)

BIG BOYS (Austin, TX) *No Matter How Long the Line* LP (Enigma)

RAUNCH HANDS "Stomp It" 45 (Egon)

SALEM 66 (Boston) 12" EP (Homestead)

MODERN LOVERS (Boston) LP (Beserkley)

Tutti Frutti English Style

From some odd reason, the best reissues of vital American rock 'n roll, R&B, blues, and hillbilly recordings have been coming out of England. Labels like Ace, Edsel, Charly, Cascade, and Detour have done an outstanding job of preserving American culture. Ace, arguably the best of the lot, has just put out three excellent releases. **GEORGE JONES** *The Lone Star Legend* (covers '57–'64) features devastating tear jerkers about love, heartache, and loneliness from this veteran country singer. "Mr. Fool" shows what blue-eyed soul is all about. **JACKIE WILSON** *Reet Petite* (covers '57–'63) displays the full glory of this acrobatic soul stylist. The upbeat title track is a total classic. Suberb fidelity on this one. And in the corner we have **LITTLE RICHARD** *His Greatest Recordings* (covers '55–'58). This is the definitive compilation. Digitally mastered from the originally Specialty recordings, this Ace reissue breathes life into the most flamboyant and outrageous rock 'n roll star of the '50s. Mr. Richard is now serving in the ministry. Meanwhile, over on Edsel, we've got *Frenzy* by **SCREAMIN' JAY HAWKINS**. This is a lounge lizard novelty record that would sound equally at home in both Las Vegas and underground teen clubs. For the most part, it's schmaltzy arrangements laced with seriously demented vocals. "I Put a Spell on You" is the undeniable classic here. Although most of the best reissues come from overseas, there are exceptions. The prolific Rhino label (Santa Monica, CA), despite its reputation for tasteless trash, will occasionally come up with a gem. *All They Had To Do Was Dream* by the **EVERLY BROTHERS** ('57–'60) is a series of intimately recorded studio outtakes; there's between-song chatter and a raw, unpolished sound. The Everlys were noted for their introduction of country-based harmonies into rock 'n roll, as well as emphasizing acoustic guitar. "Leave My Woman Alone" is beauty in its purest form. On a final note, *Back From The Grave, Vol. 5* is out, and it's every bit as rocking as previous issues. The Crypt label (Morristown, NJ) has put out the best collection of '60s garage bands since the early *Pebbles* series; the sound quality has lots of punch, too. Okay, now that we've done our homework, let's get on the wild young sounds of today's confused and tormented youth.

•

From San Francisco comes a noisy, **FLIPPER**-esque group of women called **FRIGHTWIG**. Lots of screams and guitar feedback, plus ironic lines like "There are times when I just want to be your trophy" and "Yes, I base my worth on who I get to fuck me." It's rare to hear about sexual relationships with such insight and frankness, especially from a female perspective. Finally, an American response to **AU PAIRS**.

Vancouver, B.C., has a new label called Nettwerk which has released some 12" EPs. **SKINNY PUPPY** experiments with abrasive electronics and should appeal to fans of early **CABARET VOLTAIRE**. Their live show is rumored to be insanity personified. Let's hope they make it to Seattle. The **GRAPES OF WRATH** have released some beautifully constructed pop songs— they definitely give fellow scene makers a hard act to follow. Unfortunately, production on both discs is a bit austere; kinda like walking through a museum.

Chicago's **BIG BLACK** comes across with a decent follow-up to last year's numbing *Bulldozer* EP. The new EP, *Racer X* (Homestead), continues their post-punk bridge of noise and rhythm. Although I'd rather hear real drums than the push button variety, there's enough radical "knife guitar" here to overcome the

I covered indie music, and occasionally I would cover a good reissue as well. I've always loved a lot of soul and funk music. I remember getting some of the early Sugar Hill releases, and my friends looking at me funny, like, "Why are you listening to this? I don't get it, aren't we punk?" To me, just about any indie record has some personality, and that's what appealed to me. One of my favorite records of all time is "Super Rappin'," by Grandmaster Flash and the Furious Five on Enjoy!

S>U>B / P>O>P

By Bruce Pavitt

A GUIDE TO U.S. INDEPENDENTS

TUTTI FRUTTI ENGLISH STYLE

For some odd reason, the best re-issues of vital American rock 'n' roll, R&B, blues and hillbilly recordings have been coming out of England. Labels like **Ace**, **Edsel**, **Charly**, **Cascade**, and **Detour** have done an outstanding job preserving American culture. Ace, arguably the best of the lot, has just put out three excellent releases. **GEORGE JONES The Lone Star Legend** ('57-'64) features devastating tear jerkers about love, heartache & loneliness from this veteran country singer. **Mr. Fool** shows what blue eyed soul is all about. **JACKIE WILSON Reet Petite** ('57-'63) displays the full glory of this acrobatic soul stylist. The upbeat title track is a total classic. Superb fidelity on this one. And in this corner we have **LITTLE RICHARD His Greatest Recordings** ('55-'58). This is the definitive compilation. Digitally mastered from the original Specialty recordings, this Ace re-issue breathes life into the most flamboyant and outrageous rock 'n' roll star of the '50s. Mr. Richard is now serving in the ministry. Meanwhile, over on Edsel, we've got **Frenzy** by **SCREAMIN' JAY HAWKINS**. This is a lounge lizard novelty record that would sound equally at home in both Las Vegas and underground teen clubs. For the most part, it's schmaltzy arrangements laced with seriously demented vocals. **I Put a Spell on You** is the undeniable classic here. Although most of the best re-issues come from overseas, there are exceptions. The prolific **Rhino** label, despite its reputation for tasteless trash, will occasionally come up with a gem. **All They Had to Do Was Dream** by the **EVERLY BROTHERS** ('57-'60) is a series of intimately recorded studio outtakes; there's between-song chatter and a raw, unpolished sound. The Everlys were noted for their introduction of country-based harmonies into rock 'n' roll, as well as emphasizing acoustic guitar. **Leave My Woman Alone** is beauty in its purest form. On a final note, **BACK FROM THE GRAVE VOL. 5** is out and it's every bit as rockin' as previous issues. The Crypt label has put out the best collection of '60s garage bands since the early **Pebbles** series; the sound quality has lots of punch, too. Okay, now that we've done our homework, let's get on to the wild young sounds of today's confused and tormented youth. (Rhino, 1201 Olympic Blvd., Santa Monica, CA 90404. Crypt, Box 9151, Morristown, NJ 07960) ●

● From San Francisco comes a noisy, Flipperesque group of women called **FRIGHTWIG**. Lots of screams and guitar feedback, plus ironic lines like *There are times when I just want to be your trophy* and *Yes, I base my worth on who I get to fuck me*. It's rare to hear about sexual relationships with such insight and frankness, especially from a female perspective. Finally, an American response to Au Pairs. (Subterranean, 577 Valencia St., SF, CA 94110)

● Vancouver, B.C. has a new label called **Netwerk** which has released some 12" EPs. **SKINNY PUPPY** experiments with abrasive electronics and should appeal to fans of early Cabaret Voltaire. Their live show is rumoured to be insanity personified. Let's hope they make it to Seattle. **THE GRAPES OF WRATH** have released some beautifully constructed pop songs — they definitely give fellow scene makers a hard act to follow. Unfortunately, production on both discs is a bit austere; kinda like walking through a museum. (Netwerk, Box 330, 1755 Robson St., Vancouver, B.C. Canada V6G 1C9)

● Chicago's **BIG BLACK** comes across with a decent follow-up to last year's numbing **Bulldozer** EP. The new EP, **Racer X**, continues their post-punk bridge of noise and rhythm. Although I'd rather hear real drums than the push button variety, there's enough radical "knife guitar" here to overcome the complaint. Except for the monotonous title track, this is a strong disc, with at least one song (**Sleep!**) being an all-out monster hit. '85 continues to see many bands (B-hole Surfers, Sonic Youth, Swans, Husker Du) retain emotional intensity while coming up with fresh ideas. Oh yeah, *great* liner notes by madman Albini. (Homestead, 45 Alabama Ave., Island Park, NY 11558)

LITTLE RICHARD

FRIGHTWIG

MINOR THREAT

● **MINOR THREAT**, legendary hardcore/thrash unit from D.C., has pulled some material out of the vault. **Salad Days** is the A-side and features ringing church bells, adding majesty and power. The flipside of this 45 includes a cover of the Standells' **Sometimes Good Guys Don't Wear White**. A sure shot, this one. (Dischord, 3819 Beecher St NW, Washington D.C. 20007)

● I don't know if it's art, but it sure is entertaining. **HENRY ROLLINS**, vocalist with Black Flag, has a new book out, **Two Thirteen Sixty One**, filled with concise memoirs and brutal stabs at poetry. Lotta pain here. Day jobs and the unifying force of 7-11's are covered, as well as existential despair and suicide as therapy. (SST, Box 1, Lawndale, CA 90260)

● Like the unrelenting tension of a good gore movie, today's young metal merchants seek to wreak havoc and overload the nervous system. If you can close your eyes to mindless violence and sexism, bands like **EXODUS** might give you just the cheap thrill you're looking for. **Bonded by Blood**, the debut LP by Exodus, is a total rush. (Torrid/Combat, Box 183-8, Scarsdale, NY 10583)

S U B / T E N

SUB POP USA RADIO
Every Tuesday
6-7pm KCMU 90.5 FM

● **GEORGE JONES** The Lone Star Legend LP (Ace) UK
● **EVERLY BROTHERS** All They Had To Do Was Dream LP (Rhino) LA
● **BIG BLACK** Racer X EP (Homestead) Chicago
● **SWANS** Raping A Slave EP (Homestead) NYC
● **MINOR THREAT** Salad Days 45 (Dischord) DC
● **VARIOUS** Back From The Grave Vol. 5 LP (Crypt) NJ
● **SCREAMIN' JAY HAWKINS** Frenzy LP (Edsel) UK
● **LITTLE RICHARD** His Greatest Recordings LP (Ace) UK
● **HENRY ROLLINS** Two Thirteen Sixty One Book (SST)
● **GRAPES OF WRATH** EP (Netwerk) Vancouver, B.C.

complaint. Except for the monotonous title track, this is a strong disc, with at least one song ("Sleep!") being an all-out monster hit. 1985 continues to see many bands (**B-HOLE SURFERS**, **SONIC YOUTH**, **SWANS**, **HÜSKER DÜ**) retain emotional intensity while coming up with fresh ideas. Oh yeah, great liner notes by madman Albini.

MINOR THREAT, legendary hardcore/thrash unit from D.C., has pulled some material out of the vault. "Salad Days" (Dischord) is the A-side, and features ringing church bells, adding majesty and power. The flip side of this 45 includes a cover of the **STAND-ELLS**' "Sometimes Good Guys Don't Wear White." A sure shot, this one.

I don't know if it's art, but it sure is entertaining. **HENRY ROLLINS**, vocalist with **BLACK FLAG**, has a new book out, *Two Thirteen Sixty One*, filled with concise memoirs and brutal stabs at poetry. Lotta pain here. Day jobs and the unifying force of 7-11s are covered, as well as existential despair and suicide as therapy.

Like the unrelenting tension of a good gore movie, today's young metal merchants seek to wreak havoc and overload the nervous system. If you can close your eyes to mindless violence and sexism, bands like **EXODUS** might give you just the cheap thrill you're looking for. *Bonded by Blood* (Torrid/Combat), the debut LP by Exodus, is a total rush.

SUB TEN

GEORGE JONES *The Lone Star Legend* LP (Ace)

EVERLY BROTHERS *All They Had To Do Was Dream* LP (Rhino)

BIG BLACK *Racer X* EP (Homestead)

SWANS *Raping a Slave* EP (Dischord)

MINOR THREAT "Salad Days" 45 (Dischord)

VARIOUS *Back From The Grave, Vol. 5* LP (Crypt)

SCREAMIN' JAY HAWKINS *Frenzy* LP (Edsel)

LITTLE RICHARD *His Greatest Recordings* (Ace)

HENRY ROLLINS *Two Thirteen Sixty One* book

GRAPES OF WRATH EP (Nettwork)

Poon-Tang and Bald Head

"Poon-Tang" and "Bald Head" are only two crazy reasons to check out **THE TRENIERS** *Rockin' Is Our Bizness* (covering '51–'55). These swingin' hepcats built a bridge between big band rock and rock 'n roll, then set up camp just left of Las Vegas. Feverish lounge entertainment. Their jump 'n jive is short on soul, but big on laughs (Edsel import)

Gas Food Lodging LP. As the sun comes up, **GREEN ON RED** kick off their shoes and go hillbilly. Twang and thunder. Nashville skyline. Poundin' those ivory keys and slidin' that guitar. Conventional but honest. A fresh alternative to Top 40 new-wave disco. (Enigma)

New York's **GOLDEN PALOMINOS** feature a revolving door of guest musicians, spinning around drummer Anton Fier. Their debut LP, released in '83, was an exhilarating mix of atonal funk and whatever was laying around the studio. For those interested in hearing a piece of that rare LP, the B-side of this 45 features a re-mix of "I.D.", a noise hurricane featuring Arto Lindsay, Fred Frith, Bill Laswell , John Zorn, and more. For the A-side, little Tony Fier has allied both noise and pop for a modern attack on **MOBY GRAPE**'s "Omaha." This one stars Michael Stipe (**R.E.M.**) and Chris Stamey (**DB'S**) from the pop sector, with some serious artillery from improv guitarist **HENRY KAISER**. Although I'd much rather hear Arto sing than the wimpy Mr. Stipe, "Omaha" is still a challenge for most radio stations. (Celluloid)

Pop hit department, chapter one. *Terminal* by the **WINDBREAKERS**. Two guys from down South. The package and production are strictly commercial, but the weaving melodies and rich tonality make it big. Fuzz and acoustic guitar, sitar, piano. **R.E.M.**, the **BYRDS** and the **BEATLES**' *Revolver* LP show up at

the door. Members of **RAIN PARADE** come in for a version of **TELEVISION**'s "Glory". Glossy but good. Yet another pop-fly-from-nowhere is *Why Are All the Good People Going Crazy* by the **OUTNUMBERED** from Champaign, IL. Rockin' electric folk with a garage feel. Love, love, love. Byrds meet **MODERN LOVERS**. Cool. cool. cool. (Homestead)

Too Cool To Live, Too Smart To Die is the latest filth from Montreal's **DEJA VOODOO**. Two underworld hit men who take their orders from the **CRAMPS** and the ghost of **BO DIDDLEY**. Sludgeabilly. Guitar and foot stompin' 'n mumblin' 'n chokin'. They put out a contract on Midnight Records, that infinitely rockin' label from NYC. Mission accomplished. (Midnight)

GREG SAGE, flannel-shirted guru of Portland, Oregon's, classic, legendary and timeless **WIPERS**, has released a solo LP which you should nab immediately. Never mind that side two is pure '60s death wish, with trancendental brain damage like "Astro Cloud" and "Lost in Space," because side one is great! Laced with acoustic guitar, the title hit "Straight Ahead" is the best anthem I've heard all year—shattered optimism with a will to survive. Pure rock 'n roll, no drugs. And the whole LP features the warm, intimate production Sage is famous for. Also of interest is the Wipers *Live* LP, a fierce account of their lengthy history. Lots of raw power here, though the tempo drags a bit. The official fan club bootleg. (Enigma)

With a name like **GOD AND THE STATE** you know it's gonna be serious. One of those highbrow art bands that talk and pretend to sing, making references to doctrines, testaments, and manifestos. And they pull it off. The lyrics show depth, and the arrangements are dissonant and compelling. For those who care, the LP

ROCK CUTS
BY
Thomas

THOMAS MEYER
FAROUCHE HAIR DESIGN
11105 N.E. 2ND · BELLEVUE
464-6534

SEATTLE
RECORD
CONVENTION!!

JULY 21st 1985
SEATTLE CENTER
SNOQUALMIE ROOM
10am to 6pm
ADMISSION $1
EARLY ENTRY ADMISSION — $5 — 9am

For more information call John: 206 / 244-9537
or Carol: 206 / 324-1381

DEALER INFORMATION
8 ft Table — $30   Set Up Time — 8am
Send Checks to PO Box 58772, Seattle, WA 98188
Made Payable to JOHN DEBLAISO

*It usually sells out — tables will be
first check, first served

TIGERFOOT
Sight & Sound

EIGHT TRACK RECORDING
FOR YOUR BUSINESS & PLEASURE

•relaxed, country atmosphere
•RIA trained engineers
•low hourly or project rates
•digital & analog 2 track mastering
•video capability
•the latest LEXICON digital reverb
 & delay
•TASCAM, APHEX, SYMETRIX
 and more

Issaquah, Wa.
(206) 451-8116

S›U›B›P›O›P

U.S.A

By Bruce Pavitt — A GUIDE TO U.S. INDEPENDENTS

★ GAS FOOD LODGING LP. As the sun comes up, GREEN ON RED kick off their shoes and go hillbilly. Twang and thunder. Nashville skyline. Poundin' those ivory keys and slidin that guitar. Conventional but honest. A fresh alternative to Top 40 new wave disco. (Enigma, Box 2896, Torrance, CA 90509).

★ NY's GOLDEN PALOMINOS. A revolving door of guest musicians, spinning around drummer Anton Fier. Their debut LP, released in '83, was an exhilirating mix of atonal funk and whatever was laying around the studio. For those interested in hearing a piece of that rare LP, the B-side of this 45 features a re-mix of ID, a noise hurricane featuring Arto Lindsay, Fred Frith, Bill Laswell, John Zorn and more. For the A-side, little Tony Fier has allied both noise and pop for a modern attack on Moby Grape's OMAHA. This one stars Michael Stipe (R.E.M.) and Chris Stamey (Db's) from the pop sector, with some serious artillery from improv guitarist Henry Kaiser. Although I'd much rather hear Arto sing than the wimpy Mr. Stipe, OMAHA is still a challenge for most radio stations. (Celluloid, 155 W. 29th St., NYC 10001).

★ Pop hit department, chapter one. TERMINAL by the WINDBREAKERS. Two guys from down south. The package and production are strictly commercial, but the weaving melodies and rich tonality make it big. Fuzz and acoustic guitar, sitar, piano. R.E.M., the Byrds and the Beatles' REVOLVER LP show up at the door. Members of Rain Parade come in for a version of Television's GLORY. Glossy but good. Yet another pop fly from nowhere is WHY ARE ALL THE GOOD PEOPLE GOING CRAZY by the OUTNUMBERED from Champaign, IL. Rockin' electric folk with a garage feel. Love, love, love. Byrds meet Modern Lovers. Cool, cool, cool. (Homestead, 45 Alabama Ave, Island Park, NY 11558).

★ TOO COOL TO LIVE, TOO SMART TO DIE is the latest filth from Montreal's DEJA VOODOO. Two underworld hit men who take their orders from the Cramps and the ghost of Bo Diddley. Sludgeability. Guitar and foot stompin' 'n' mumblin' 'n' chokin'. They put out a contract on Midnight Records, that infinitely rockin' label from NYC. Mission accomplished. (Midnight, Box 390, Old Chelsea Station, NYC, 10011).

PoonTang

and BALD HEAD are only two crazy reasons to check out THE TRENIERS ROCKIN' IS OUR BIZNESS ('51-'55). These swingin' hep cats built a bridge between big band rock and rock 'n' roll, then set up camp just left of Las Vegas. Feverish lounge entertainment. Their jump 'n' jive is short on soul, but big on laughs. (Edsel import).

HALF TIME
BEST YET IN '85

HUSKER DU
NEW DAY RISING
LP (SST) Mnpls
• • •
SWANS
RAPING A SLAVE
EP (Homestead) NYC
• • •
SCRATCH ACID
EP (Rabid) Austin
• • •
SONIC YOUTH
BAD MOON RISING
LP (Homestead) NYC
• • •
BUTTHOLE SURFERS
ANOTHER MAN'S SAC
LP (Touch and Go) San Antonio
• • •

★ GREG SAGE, flannel shirted guru of Portland's classic, legendary and timeless WIPERS, has released a solo LP which you should nab immediately. Never mind that side two is pure '60s death wish, with trancendental brain damage like ASTRO CLOUD and LOST IN SPACE, 'cause side one is great! Laced with acoustic guitar, the title hit STRAIGHT AHEAD is the best anthem I've heard all year — shattered optimism with a will to survive. Pure rock 'n' roll, no drugs. And the whole LP features the warm, intimate production Sage is famous for. Also of interest is the WIPERS LIVE LP, a fierce account of their lengthy history. Lots of raw power here, though the tempo drags a bit. The official fan club bootleg. (Enigma, Box 2986, Torrance, CA 90509).

★ With a name like GOD AND THE STATE you know it's gonna be serious. One of those high-brow art bands that talk and pretend to sing, making references to doctrines, testaments and manifestos. And they pull it off. The lyrics show depth and the arrangements are dissonant and compelling. For those who care, the LP itself, RUINS, is packaged in the infamous shirt-cardboard of the Independent Project Press. Sounds good next to 100 Flowers (especially their last EP, also out on Happy Squid), early Gang of Four, The Fall, even Little Bears From Bangkok. (Happy Squid, Box 64184, L.A., CA 90064).

★ Vancouver, B.C. has been pumping vinyl. Lots of local indie releases, one of which is DOG EAT DOG by ANIMAL SLAVES. The Slaves still play moody funk, overlaid with spacey electronics. The rhythm section is excellent, but I gag on the tortured melodrama of the vocalist. Sure they're trying to do something a little different, but at the expense of sincerity and gut emotion. Arty and pretentious. (MO DA MU, Box 374-810 W. Broadway, Vancouver, B.C. Canada V5Z 1J8).

SUB TEN

SUB POP USA RADIO
Every Tuesday
6-7pm KCMU 90.5 FM

GREG SAGE STRAIGHT AHEAD LP (Enigma) Portland
DEJA VOODOO TOO COOL TO LIVE... LP (Midnight) Montreal
GOLDEN PALOMINOS OMAHA 45 (Celluloid) NYC
WIPERS LIVE LP (Enigma) Portland
OUTNUMBERED... GOING CRAZY LP (Homestead) Champaign, IL
WINDBREAKERS TERMINAL LP (Homestead) Jackson, MI
TRENIERS Rockin is our Bizness LP (Edsel) '51-'55
GOD AND THE STATE RUINS LP (Happy Squid) L.A.
SCRATCH ACID EP (Rabid) Austin
U-MEN STOP SPINNING EP (Homestead) Seattle

itself, *Ruins*, is packaged in the infamous shirt-cardboard of the Independent Project Press. Sounds good next to **100 FLOWERS** (especially their last EP, also out on Happy Squid), early **GANG OF FOUR, THE FALL**, even **LITTLE BEARS FROM BANGKOK**. (Happy Squid)

Vancouver, B.C. has been pumping out vinyl. Lots of local indie releases, one of which is *Dog Eat Dog* by **ANIMAL SLAVES**. The Slaves still play moody funk, overlaid with spacey electronics. The rhythm section is excellent, but I gag on the tortured melodrama of the vocalist. Sure they're trying to do something a little different, but at the expense of sincerity and gut emotion. Arty and pretentious. (Mo Da Mu)

HALF TIME— BEST YET IN '85

HÜSKER DÜ (Mnpls.) *New Day Rising* LP (SST)

SWANS (NYC) *Raping a Slave* EP (Homestead)

SCRATCH ACID (Austin, TX) EP (Rabid)

SONIC YOUTH (NYC) *Bad Moon Rising* LP (Homestead)

, (San Antonio, TX) *Another Man's Sac* LP (Touch And Go)

SUB TEN

GREG SAGE (Portland, OR) *Straight Ahead* LP (Enigma)

DEJA VOODOO (NYC) *Too Cool To Live* LP (Celluloid)

GOLDEN PALOMINOS (NYC) "Omaha" 45 (Celluloid)

WIPERS (Portland, OR) *Live* Lp (Enigma)

OUTNUMBERED (Champaign, IL) *Going Crazy* LP (Homestead)

WINDBREAKERS (Jackson, MI) *Terminal* LP (Homestead)

TRENIERS *Rockin Is Our Bizness* LP (Edsel)

GOD AND THE STATE (L.A.) *Ruins* (Happy Squid)

SCRATCH ACID (Austin, TX) EP (Rabid)

U-MEN (Seattle) *Stop Spinning* EP (Homestead)

Lounge Act

The only band to play both CBGB and the Berlin Jazz Festival, the **LOUNGE LIZARDS** inspire with their fractured tales of bop and cool. *Live 79–81* (ROIR) is a crisply recorded cassette, chronicling their evolution through three different guitar players. The early CBGB tracks feature Arto Lindsay choking his six-string, and is the crudest part of the journey; by the time they get to Berlin in '81, the group swings with much more precision and control. Handsome alto player John Lurie is the essence of hip, currently cutting across cultures to perform in both music and film. I predict more soundtracks from this gentleman, as he pursues his acting career. And, for those of you who were enchanted with the stark minimalism of *Stranger Than Paradise*, director Jim Jarmusch has written some very cinematic liner notes. Recommended.

Unlike New York's Homestead label, which has been signing every obscure regional band they can get their mitts on, L.A.'s SST Records has stuck with a small core of heavyweights—**HÜSKER DÜ, BLACK FLAG, MEAT PUPPETS,** and **THE MINUTEMEN**. Finally, however, they've signed some fresh blood. Sort of. **DC3** and **OCTOBERFACTION** contain friends, roadies and relatives of Black Flag; it's obvious that SST has looked no further than its own living room for new talent. The sad result is a stunned, retarded L.A. in-breeding. *This Is the Dream* by DC3 is an LP full of spacey, bluesy jam-rock (complete with "progressive" keyboard fills) made popular by glue sniffers in the early '70s. If you can remember **DEEP PURPLE, CAPTAIN BEYOND, HUMBLE PIE,** and **MOUNTAIN,** you just may want to swallow this. And now for the good news. The *October Faction* LP is the world's lightest frisbee. Standing on the roof of my apartment, I was able to fling this fucker all the way to Broad-way and Madison. This lame live recording of sub-**HENDRIX** jamming gives new meaning to the word onanism. Sample titles: "Bad Acid" and "Gimme a Quarter, Twenty Five Cents for the Bus." Worst record of '85. And in addition to these insults, SST (who I do respect for giving their artists 100% creative control) have had to release grossly commercial records by their big boys—Black Flag's *Loose Nut*, Minutemen's *Project: Mersh*, and the Meat Puppets' *Up on the Sun*. A big three strikes and you're out. Aside from the magnificent *New Day Rising*, Hüsker Dü's best record to date, SST has pumped out nothing but garbage in '85, despite their reputation as one of the largest and most progressive indie labels in America.

Groove Jumping (Detour import) is worth selling the wife, kids, and house for. Totally awesome, frenetic, furious R&B certified to slice, dice, shred, and maim any modest social gathering. Released on Britain's Detour label, this compilation of old RCA/Groove tracks from '53–'56 is a screaming gold bullet punching hit after hit. Although I'd never heard of **TINY KENNEDY, "BIG" JOHN GREER,** or **THE DU-DROPPERS,** I was delighted to see the flames burst from my turntable. From **MICKEY BAKER** we hear feverish, blistering guitar; manic, intense, raunchy, and raw. This LP is an absolute must!!

Rick Lewis, singer from Olympia's **IMMORAL ROBERTS,** wasted himself by flying from a pickup truck. The insurance money paid for some studio time, and the result is *No Accident*, a shockingly good cassette from the ever busy K label. Tumbling car crash rock with descendlng background vocals. Gripping the mike, our man barks, "I'm turning green and so Is the light!"

"Unlike New York's Homestead label, which has been signing every obscure regioal band they can get their mitts on, L.A.'s SST has stuck with a small core of heavyweights—Hüsker Dü, Black Flag, Meat Puppets and the Minutemen. Finally, however, they've signed some fresh blood. Sort of. DC3 and Octoberfaction contain friends, roadies and relatives of Black Flag; it's obvious that SST has looked no further than their own living room for new talent. The sad result is a stunned, retarded L.A. in-breeding.

S>U>B>P>O>P

Lounge Act

A GUIDE TO U.S. INDEPENDENTS

By Bruce Pavitt

• The only _____ band to play both CBGB's and the Berlin Jazz Festival, the **LOUNGE LIZARDS** inspire with their fractured tales of bop and cool. *LIVE 79/81* is a crisply recorded cassette, chronicling their evolution through three different guitar players. The early CBGB tracks feature Arto Lindsay choking his six-string and is the crudest part of the journey; by the time they get to Berlin in '81, the group swings with much more precision and control. Handsome alto player John Lurie is the essence of hip, currently cutting across cultures to perform in both music and film. I predict more soundtracks from this gentleman, as he pursues his acting career. And, for those of you who were enchanted with the stark minimalism of *Stranger Than Paradise*, director Jim Jarmusch has written some very cinematic liner notes. Recommended. *(ROIR, 611 Broadway, Suite 725, NYC, 10012.)*

• Unlike NY's Homestead label, which has been signing every obscure regional band they can get their mitts on, L.A.'s SST has stuck with a small core of heavyweights — Husker Du, Black Flag, Meat Puppets and the Minutemen. Finally, however, they've signed some fresh blood. Sort of. DC3 and OCTOBERFAC-TION contain friends, roadies and relatives of Black Flag; it's obvious that SST has looked no further than their own living room for new talent. The sad result is a stunned, retarded L.A. in-breeding. *THIS IS THE DREAM* by DC3 is an LP full of spacey, bluesy jam rock (complete with "progressive" keyboard fills) made popular by glue sniffers in the early '70s. If you can remember Deep Purple, Captain Beyond, Humble Pie and Mountain, you just may want to swallow this. And now for the good news. The OCTOBERFAC-TION LP is the world's lightest frisbee. Standing on the roof of my apartment, I was able to fling this fucker all the way to Broadway and Madison. This lame live recording of sub-Hendrix jamming gives new meaning to the word onanism. Sample titles: *Bad Acid* and *Gimme a Quarter, Twenty Five Cents For the Bus*. Worst record of '85. And in addition to these insults, SST (who I *do* respect for giving their artists 100% creative control) have had to release grossly commercial records by their big boys — BLACK FLAG's *LOOSE NUT*, MINUTEMEN's *Project: MERSH*, and the MEAT PUPPETS' *UP ON THE SUN*. A big three strikes and you're out. Aside from the magnificent *NEW DAY RISING*, HUSKER DU's best record to date, SST has pumped nothing but garbage in '85, despite their reputation as one of the largest and most progressive indie labels in America. *(SST, P.O. Box 1, Lawndale, CA 90260.)*

• GROOVE JUMPING is worth selling the wife, kids and house for. Totally awesome, frenetic, furious R&B certified to slice, dice, shred and maim any modest social gathering. Released on Britain's Detour label, this compilation of old RCA/Groove tracks from '53-'56 is a screaming gold bullet punching hit after hit. Although I'd never heard of Tiny Kennedy, "Big" John Greer or The Du-Droppers, I was delighted to see the flames burst from my turntable. From Mickey Baker we hear feverish, blistering guitar; manic, intense, raunchy and raw. This LP is an absolute must! ! *(Detour Import.)*

• RICK LEWIS, singer from Olympia's IMMORAL ROBERTS, wasted himself by flying from a pickup truck. The insurance money paid for some studio time, and the result is *NO ACCIDENT*, a shockingly good cassette from the ever busy K label. Tumbling car crash rock with descending background vocals. Gripping the mike, our man barks, "I'm turning green and so is the light"! *(K, Box 7154, Olympia, WA 98507.)*

• Although I've become increasingly bored with "modern" music these days, as evidenced by the increasing amount of re-issues covered in this column, there have been a handful of discs released this year that are worth stealing, killing or nuking third world countries for. It's too bad nothing this month falls into that category. *VERY LONG FUSE* by BREAK-ING CIRCUS is a damn good record, though. For starters, it's not 1) satanic speed metal 2) generic hardcore thrash or 3) uninspired paisley revival. Like most good music, it can't be pigeonholed easily. It's got guts, it's got hooks. Hard-edged modern pop — angry vocals, programmed drums, occasional sax. Breaking Circus are from Chicago — a happening spot these days — and has the fat production Iain Burgess (the Chi-town producer) is famous for. Anthemic without being thrashy. *(Homestead, Box 570, Rockville Center, NY 11571.)*

• NERVOUS NORVUS was the weirdest, wildest hunk o' white trash ever to hit the *Billboard* charts. Originally released in '56, all three of his Dot 45s — *Transfusion, Ape Call, The Fang* — have been re-issued as an EP on Britain's Ace/Big Beat label. The ultimate hayseed novelty records, these tunes are full of slang, sound effects and twisted backwoods drama. "Get in cat, let's get earthbound, I'm the FANG!" *(Ace/Big Beat import available through City Hall Distribution.)*

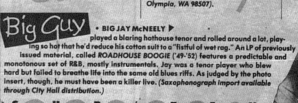

Big Guy

• BIG JAY McNEELY ▶ played a blaring hothouse tenor and rolled around a lot, playing so hot that he'd reduce his cotton suit to a "fistful of wet rag." An LP of previously issued material, called *ROADHOUSE BOOGIE* ('49-'52) features a predictable and monotonous set of R&B, mostly instrumentals. Jay was a tenor player who blew hard but failed to breathe life into the same old blues riffs. As judged by the photo insert, though, he must have been a killer live. *(Saxophonograph Import available through City Hall distribution.)*

S U B T E N

SUB POP USA RADIO
Every Tuesday
6-7pm KCMU 90.5 FM

Although I've become increasingly bored with "modern" music these days, as evidenced by the increasing amount of reissues covered In this column, there have been a handful of discs released this year that are worth stealing, killing, or nuking third-world countries for. It's too bad nothing this month falls into that category. *Very Long Fuse* (Homestead Records) by **BREAKING CIRCUS** is a damn good record, though. For starters, It's not 1) satanic speed metal; 2) generic hardcore thrash; or 3) uninspired paisley revival. Like most good music, It can't be pigeon-holed easily. It's got guts, it's got hooks. Hard-edged modern pop—angry vocals, programmed drums, occasional sax. Breaking Circus are from Chicago—a happening spot these days—and their record has the fat production Iain Burgess (the Chi-town producer) is famous for. Anthemic without being thrashy.

NERVOUS NORVUS was the weirdest, wildest hunk o' white trash ever to hit the *Billboard* charts. Originally released in '56, all three of his Dot 45s— "Transfusion," "Ape Call," and "The Fang"—have been reissued as an EP on Britain's Ace Big Beat label. The ultimate hayseed novelty records, these tunes are full of slang, sound effects, and twisted backwoods drama. "Get in cat, let's get earthbound, I'm the *fang*!" (available through City Hall Distribution.)

BIG JAY MCNEELY played a blaring hothouse tenor sax and rolled around a lot, playing so hot that he'd reduce his cotton suit to a "fistful of wet rag." An LP of previously issued materlal, called *Roadhouse Boogie* (ranging from '49–'52), features a predictable and monotonous set of R&B, mostly instrumentals. Jay was a tenor player who blew hard but failed to breathe life into the same old blues riffs. As judged by the photo insert, though, he must have been a killer live. (Saxophonograph import)

SUB TEN

VARIOUS *Groove Jumping* LP (Detour)

LOUNGE LIZARDS *Live 79-81* cassette (ROIR)

NERVOUS NORVUS *Transfusion* EP (Ace/Big Beat)

BREAKING CIRCUS *Very Long Fuse* EP (Homestead)

FEELIES *Crazy Rhythms* LP (Stiff)

IMMORAL ROBERTS *No Accident* cassette (K)

Wig Out fanzine (Tacoma)

SONIC YOUTH absolutely anything

JOHNNY CASH early Sun recordings

DANGER BUNNY (Seattle) *Highland Drive* demo

Both Boots Walking on American Soil

What Surf II (What Records) is a collection of surf guitar instrumentals. A style made popular in the early '60s by blonde boys with biceps, the staccato guitar riffing of surf and sand was originally mastered by such Southern California hipsters as **DICK DALE**, the **CHANTAYS**, and the **PYRAMIDS** (and, of course, the **VENTURES** from Tacoma). The LP in question here features one reissued song, the great "Penetration" by the Pyramids, plus a lot of filler recorded in modern, sterile studios by contemporary artists— **AGENT ORANGE**, the **HALIBUTS**, etc.—and has-beens like drummer Sandy Nelson. Better to skip this one and pick up *The History of Surf Music Vol. 1* on Rhino, the definite collection.

A $10.00 acoustic guitar, late-night bedroom ramblings. Put out ten albums and never tune the guitar. *9:30* LP (Corwood Industries). Think about all those years at the asylum, the job, the paycheck that will allow you to put out your eleventh album. You are **JANDEK**. You are God. "Put your mind in a paper bag."

The Firstborn Is Dead (Homestead Records), the second LP by **NICK CAVE AND THE BAD SEEDS**, has been released by the domestic indie label Homestead. Nick still pushes literature, but his latest seems less inspired by the flowery prose of Melville and more concerned with the starkness of American blues and cowboy mythology. Certainly, the awesome talents of **JOHN LEE HOOKER** and **JOHNNY CASH** are given their due. This former Australian has both boots walkin' on American soil. And going far beyond a dry lesson in history, "Train Long-Suffering," "Tupelo," and "Black Crow King" swell with life, featuring heroic call-and-response chain gang vocals. This is a brilliant tribute to American roots culture and one of the most refreshing records heard this year.

The **TAILGATORS** come on like a New Orleans version of the **BLASTERS**, recycled rock 'n roll with a shot of Cajun zydeco. Their LP *Swamp Rock* (Wrestler Records) is pleasant enough, and would sound just fine piped through a Pizza Hut. For the real thing, try throwing a party with **CLIFTON CHENIER** and **JOHNNY BURNETTE**!!!

Recorded behind iron bars in '59, *Angola Prisoner's Blues* (Arhoolie) documents three different inmates playing acoustic country blues. Inviting the men into a small tool room downstairs, the Arhoolie label taped intimate performances by **ROBERT PETE WILLIAMS**, **MATTHEW "HOGMAN" MAXEY**, and **ROBERT "GUITAR" WELCH**. Living (or, rather, existing) in Angola, Louisiana, these guys are said to have heard a lot of Houston-based **LIGHTNIN' HOPKINS** on the radio, and it shows. "Mm, sheets and pillow cases torn all to pieces, baby, and blood stains all over the wall..."

Forced Exposure, issue #7/8, defines a literary circle whose impacts may well be as influential as the Burroughs/Ginsberg/Kerouac connection of the Beat Generation. This fanzine from Boston has released a landmark issue, a document that will serve as a reference point for years to come. There have been an increasing number of poets, playwrights, and authors involved in the new music scene. This mag, under the editor Jimmy Johnson, has put together the most

"A $10.00 acoustic guitar, late night bedroom ramblings. Put out ten albums and never tune the guitar. *9:30 LP*. Think about all those years at the asylum, the job, the paycheck that will allow you to put out your eleventh album. You are Jandek. You are God."

controversial of their new writers, unified by a shared fascination with extreme sex/violence and the other limits of human behavior. Included are collaborations between **NICK CAVE** and **LYDIA LUNCH** (one-page plays) excerpts from Jeffery Lee Pierce's **GUN CLUB** travel diary, new fiction by Chris D. of the **FLESHEATERS**, photo and book review of emerging poet **HENRY ROLLINS**, the philosophical ravings of Chicago's **STEVE ALBINI** (brash loudmouth, critic, and vocalist for **BIG BLACK**) and remembrances of things past by the truly sick **TESCO VEE** of the **MEATMEN**. Explosive, these radical celebrities, pen in hand, will make themselves known either through style or pure shock value; some are good writers, others are merely fascinating personalities. Saving the best for last, I must insist that **MICHAEL GIRA**, vocalist with NYC's powerful **SWANS** is a major talent. His collection of 14 brief, simply stated scenarios are brutal, beautiful in their stylistic restraint and conciseness. Gira is the '80s response to Beat novelist **WILLIAM BURROUGHS** (who endured an obscenity trial for *Naked Lunch* in '62) and is every bit as provocative. Both authors are obsessed with power, control, and the degradation of those who are powerless; the major difference being the way they express themselves. Gira is an absolute minimalist. Every word, pause, and period contains force and weight; relentless, extreme visions that are suffocating in their intensity. "A Whore," "A Coward," "Impotent," and "Punishment" are a few titles. Burroughs, consumed by heroin addiction, threw up whatever was willed by his subconscious. The result was scrambled and hallucinatory, a flip of the coin to Gira's compact precision. But find out for yourself. The new nihilism is here, on paper—you like it, it likes you. (*Forced Exposure*, Newtonville, MA)

SUB/TEN

Forced Exposure #7/#8 fanzine (Boston)

NICK CAVE *The Firstborn is Dead* LP (Homestead)

U-MEN (Seattle) *Stop Spinning* EP (Homestead)

VARIOUS *Angola Prisoner's Blues* LP (Arhoolie)

BO DIDDLEY Bo Diddley, Bo Diddley!!!

RAW #7 mag w/**CHARLES BURNS**

TREECLIMBERS (Seattle) "Greener Pastures" song

SHONEN KNIFE *Burning Farm* cassette (K Records)

JANDEK *9:30* LP (Corwood)

October 1985

Buy...Borrow..Burn.

SMACK *On You* LP (Pink Dust). Sleaze hit for sure. Domestic release from seedy, wasted Finnish rockers who plunder forth with warm beer, stringy hair, bad complexions, and sweaty leather pants. Their rock 'n roll unburies **ALICE COOPER**, **MC5**, **STOOGES**, **DOLLS**, etc. Yet another slab of mindless all-out entertainment. Be sure to open the bottle with your teeth.

MEATMEN *War of the Superbikes* LP (Homestead). The offensive, infamous Mr. Tesco Vee, former editor of *Touch and Go* fanzine, continues his Meatmen saga. Now based in D.C., the new Meatmen play warmed over heavy metal, a step sideways from their lame thrash attempts. If you want to punish yourself, you'll get this for the outrageous lyrics. "Kisses in the Sunset" is the one true hit here—a flamenco novelty number that squeezes every sexual metaphor known to humanity into one song.

G.I. *The Fun Just Never Ends* LP (Fountain of Youth). Despite their long standing rep in D.C., this is drained, generic hardcore on its death bed. If these are the leaders of tomorrow, I'll push the button today.

ALGEBRA SUICIDE *Explanation for That Flock of Crows* 45. Four miniature pieces from this Chicago husband/wife team. She's a poet, evocative, and less pretentious than, let's say, **LYDIA LUNCH**; he's the music man who ' needs to find a beat box with more muscle. Worth a spin.

COPERNICUS *Nothing Exists* LP (Ski Records). Fifty-year old beatnik thinks he's **BARRY WHITE**, complete with 13-piece orchestra. "I Won't Hurt You" is subdued, intense white soul; after that, it gets noisy. Weird and wonderful.

THE DEAD MILKMEN *Big Lizard in My Backyard* LP (Fever Records). Wacky punk band from Philadelphia attacks with witty, biting sarcasm. Vacant suburban lifestyles get torched, especially on their hit "Bitchin' Camero." My only question: Who is Electric Love Muffin?

CAMPER VAN BEETHOVEN *Telephone Free Landslide Victory* LP. Coolest pop record of '85? On paper, a mix of ska, country, and Greek party music sounds too absurd to work, but this is a seamless, flawless pop masterpiece!! Funny as hell, too. Independent Project is a label that dares to take a risk, and this time it worked.

SONIC YOUTH *Death Valley '69* EP (Homestead). If you haven't checked out this innovative, atonal New York guitar band, this is the place to start. This 12" includes one strong cut from each of their four records plus an extra track, "Satan Is Boring," which is, uh (cough) hmmm, kind of interesting, I guess. Aside from the "intro to SY" angle, though, "Death Valley '69" sounds like thunder in a 12" format.

ROCKMASTER SCOTT AND THE DYNAMIC THREE *Roof Is on Fire* (scratch remix) 12" (Reality). Totally cool remix of one of the tougher street raps to hit the box. "We don't need no water let the mutha fucka burn." Count em: three different versions.

HÜSKER DÜ *Makes No Sense at All* 45 (SST Records). More raw pop from the Hüskers. Sounds weak, though, compared to the explosive one-two punch of "Heaven Hill" and "I Apologize" from *New Day Rising*. Flip it over for the theme to the *Mary Tyler Moore Show*.

In the early 1980s I was really taken with the energy of hardcore, and how young these bands were; 17-year-olds putting out their own singles. In 1984, I helped open up the first indie record shop on Capitol Hill in Seattle, Fallout Records. I had worked at a shop on Broadway called Bomb Shelter that only existed for six months. I first met Mark Arm there; he was a customer, as was Duff McKagan. At that time, young people who were living at home and could afford to buy records were buying hardcore and punk. From 1980 to 1984, I really appreciated the energy of hardcore. And as a record store owner, I could sell a lot of this stuff! But things got too generic and I became disinterested around the same time that Hüsker Dü and Sonic Youth started putting out good records.

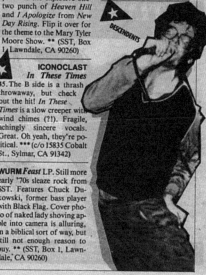

ICONOCLAST *In These Times* 45 (Flipside). The B side is a thrash throwaway, but check out the hit! "In These Times" is a slow creeper with wind chimes (?!). Fragile, achingly sincere vocals. Great. Oh yeah, they're political.

WÜRM *Feast* LP (SST Records). Still more early '70s sleaze rock from SST. Features Chuck Dukowski, former bass player with **BLACK FLAG**. Cover photo of naked lady shoving apple into camera is alluring, in a biblical sort of way, but still not enough reason to buy.

SKATE DEATH *You Break It, You Buy It* LP. Hardcore thrash from Alaska. Numbingly predictable and conservative: a few offbeat lyrics though: "There was a man and he was mad/He jumped into a pudding bag/ The pudding bag it was so thick/ He jumped into a walking stick." But it's still not enough to save this from total extinction.

VOLCANO SUNS *The Bright Orange Years* LP (Homestead). The latest hot thing from Boston. Features the former drummer whats-his-name from **MISSION OF BURMA**. The Suns have the same cryptic intelligence of Burma, but more hooks and more real songs. Intellectual without being stiff or phony.

DESCENDENTS *I Don't Want to Grow Up* LP (New Alliance). Not as good as the classic *Milo* LP, but hey, these guys can't fail. Catchy tunes, raspy vocals from Milo and more rad songs about love and sex. One of L.A.'s best. Pick hit: side two.

Before I close the door on my cell, I'd like to say how much fun I had at the **DANGER BUNNY**/**VITAMIX** loft party on 9/13. I didn't even get frisked at the door. Also, a hearty congratulations to the **U-MEN**, whose mighty **CRAMPS/B-PARTY/SONICS** sound is pushed to extremes on their excellent new EP *Stop Spinning* on NY's Homestead label. We're proud of ya. Seattle's **GREEN RIVER** will also uplift the hope and integrity of a nation with their early **STOOGES** (i.e. *Funhouse*) heaviness; also due out on Homestead.

SUB TEN

U-MEN *Stop Spinning* EP (Homestead)

COPERNICUS *Nothing Exists* LP (Ski)

SONIC YOUTH *Death Valley '69* 12" EP (Homestead)

CAMPER VAN BEETHOVEN *Telephone Free Landslide Victory* LP (Independent Project)

VOLCANO SUNS *The Bright Orange Years* LP (Homestead)

ROCKMASTER SCOTT AND THE DYNAMIC THREE "Roof Is on Fire" 12" (Reality)

HÜSKER DÜ "Makes No Sense at All" 45 (SST)

DESCENDENTS *I Don't Want to Grow Up* LP (New Alliance)

ICONOCLAST "In These Times" 45 (Flipside)

YOUNG FRESH FELLOWS *3 Sides* 45 (PopLlama)

Provoke, Amuse, and Drive Your Neighbors Batty

FALL DOWN GET DOWN BROWN

JAMES BROWN AND HIS FAMOUS FLAMES
Live at the Apollo Volume II: Parts 1 and 2 LPs. When
James Brown released *Live at the Apollo Volume I*,
recorded in '62, it became the first million-selling LP
marketed specifically for black youth—it was raw,
tight upbeat soul that was to project a sound and an
identity for millions of young blacks. In fact, it was
so popular that many stations played it in its entirety,
daily. It remains the ultimate fall-down soul party
experience. Which brings us to to two new records
recently reissued by the Rhino label: James Brown *Live
at the Apollo, Volume II*—*Part 1* and *Part 2*. Recorded
a solid five years later, these LPs capture the godfather
of soul while still in top form. Both LPs cover much of
the same territory as his '62 performance, but are less
raw and more refined (for example, there are strings
on some of the cuts.) And both records include some
of his later hits: *Part 1* has "Cold Sweat" ('67) and *Part
2* has a gripping version of "It's a Man's Man's World"
('66). Of the two records, *Part 2* is superior, and is
possibly the most mature live recording of Brown's
career. The intensity is still there, but there are more
extremes—he's both ferocious and subdued. And of
course the whole thing is pure sex: by side two you'll
be rolling on the carpet. So get it and get down and get
with it.

FLIPPED OUT

HÜSKER DÜ *Flip Your Wig* LP (SST). Hooks,
harmonies and total abrasive power, the Hüskers have
proven to be the ultimate masters of raw pop. Aside

from one novelty—"The Baby Song" is 0:46 of vibraphone and slide whistle—and a few instrumentals at
the end of side two, *Flip Your Wig* buries the competition. Yet another amazing LP by America's most copious power trio.

Tellus #10: All Guitars! cassette compilation. Tellus is
a New York-based cassette series that is sponsored in
part by the New York State Council on the Arts. Their
latest, focusing on experimental guitar works, is excellent, and reads like a who's who of the avant-guitar
underworld: **LEE RANALDO** and **THURSTON
MOORE** of **SONIC YOUTH, ARTO LINDSAY,
GLENN BRANCA, BOB MOULD** of **HÜSKER
DÜ**, the **BUTTHOLE SURFERS, STEVE ALBINI** of
BIG BLACK, BLIXA BARGELD of **NEUBAUTEN,
WHARTON TIERS, ELLIOT SHARP,** and more,
more, more big weird stuff that will provoke, amuse
and drive your neighbors batty.

PHRANC *Folksinger* LP (Rhino). Former vocalist
with avant/noise unit **NERVOUS GENDER**, Phranc
has been an L.A. scene maker for years. *Folksinger*, her
first LP, is basically *Blue*-era **JONI MITCHELL** with
a butch haircut. Musically, this doesn't push folk Into
the '80s, like **BILLY BRAGG** or **SUZANNE VEGA**,
and the lyrics are surprisingly lightweight. But there
is an intimacy, honesty and vulnerability here that is
desperately missing from most of the big-hair poseur
spew coming out these days. A refreshing break in the
routine.

DOUG E. FRESH AND THE GET FRESH CREW
"The Show" b/w "La Di Da Di" 12" single (Reality).

SUB ▲ POP

U S A

A GUIDE TO U.S. INDEPENDENTS
BY BRUCE PAVITT

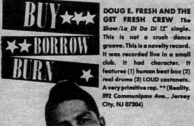

TELLUS #10 *All Guitars* cassette compilation. *Tellus* is a NY based cassette series that is sponsored in part by the NY State Council on the Arts. Their latest, focusing on experimental guitar works, is excellent and reads like a who's who of the avant-guitar underworld: Lee Ranaldo and Thurston Moore of Sonic Youth, Arto Lindsay, Glenn Branca, Bob Mould of Husker Du, The Butthole Surfers, Steve Albini of Big Black, Blixa Bargeld of Neubauten, Wharton Tiers, Elliot Sharp and more, more, more big weird stuff that will provoke, amuse and drive your neighbors batty. *** (Tellus, 143 Ludlow St. #14, NY, NY 10002)

PHRANC *Folksinger* LP. Former vocalist with avant/noise unit Nervous Gender, Phranc has been an L.A. scene maker for years. *Folksinger*, her first LP, is basically *Blue* Joni Mitchell with a butch haircut. Musically, this doesn't push folk into the '80s, like Billy Bragg or Suzanne Vega, and the lyrics are surprisingly lightweight. But there is an intimacy, honesty and vulnerability here that is desperately missing from most of the big hair poseur spew coming out these days. A refreshing break in the routine. *** (Rhino, 1201 Olympic Blvd, Santa Monica, CA 90404)

DOUG E. FRESH AND THE GET FRESH CREW *The Show/La Di Da Di* 12" single. This is not a crush dance groove. It was recorded live in a small club. It had character. It features (1) human beat box (2) real drums (3) LOUD castanets. A very primitive rap. ** (Reality, 592 Communipaw Ave., Jersey City, NJ 07304)

JAMES BROWN AND HIS FAMOUS FLAMES *Live at the Apollo Vol. II: Parts One and Two* LPs. When James Brown released *Live at the Apollo Vol I*, recorded in '62, it became the first million selling LP marketed specifically for black youth — it was raw, tight, upbeat soul that was to project a sound and an identity for millions of young blacks. In fact, it was so popular that many stations played it in its entirety, daily. It remains the ultimate falldown soul party experience. Which brings us to two new records recently re-issued by the Rhino label: *James Brown Live at the Apollo Vol II — Part One* and *Part Two*. Recorded a solid five years later, these LPs capture the godfather of soul while still in top form. Both LPs cover much of the same territory as his '62 performance, but are less raw and more refined (for example, there are strings on some of the cuts). And both records include some of his later hits: *Part One* has *Cold Sweat* ('67) and *Part Two* has a gripping version of *It's A Man's, Man's, Man's World* ('66). Of the two records, *Part Two* is superior, and is possibly the most mature live recording of Brown's career. The intensity is still there, but there are more extremes — he's both ferocious and subdued. And of course the whole thing is pure sex: by side two you'll be rolling on the carpet. So get up and get it and get down and get with it. Part One: ** / Part Two: ***

JUSTICE LEAGUE *Think or Sink* 7" EP. Like the promo sheet says, this is positive punk. *Time to Stop* is "dedicated to an end of the Gang and individual violence which is destroying everything we're working for." Cool. I just wish that generic thrash bands like this would drop the "unity" pose and just be themselves. Expressing any kind of individuality is probably the most radical thing these guys could do. * (Fartbottom Enterprises, P.O. Box 818, Pomona, CA 91769)

MISSION OF BURMA *The Horrible Truth About Burma* LP. Boston's legendary art/punk band recorded live, featuring previously unreleased material. These men spill their blood on a Stooges cover (1970) then mystify with an early Pere Ubu head trip (*Heart of Darkness*). They got 'em both: guts 'n' brains. *** (Ace of Hearts, Box 579, Kenmore Station, Boston, MA 02215)

PENTAGRAM LP. I was passing out to Black Sabbath over 12 years ago, and this *Pentagram* record is bringing back all those beautiful memories: blacklight posters, cheap incense and gallons of Mad Dog. Wow, 12 years go by real fast. ** (Pentagram, 2000 S. Eads St. Suite 127, Arlington, VA 22202)

THE CLINTONS *Girl Next Door* 45. These guys seem to be a hip item with the NY roots rock 'n' roll scene. But if I want Chuck Berry I'll listen to Chuck Berry. Item: cover photo of topless '60s girl group should boost sales. * (Coyote, Box 112, Uptown, Hoboken, NJ 07030)

HUSKER DU *Flip Your Wig* LP. Hooks, harmonies and total abrasive power, the Huskers have proven to be the ultimate masters of raw pop. Aside from one novelty — *The Baby Song* is 0:46 of vibraphone and slide whistle — and a few instrumentals at the end of side two, *Flip Your Wig* buries the competition: yet another amazing LP by America's most copious power trio. *** (SST, P.O. Box 1, Lawndale, CA 90260)

SUB TEN

- JAMES BROWN *Live at the Apollo Vol II — Part 2* (Rhino)
- HUSKER DU *Flip Your Wig* LP (SST) Mnpls
- TELLUS #10 *All Guitars* cassette (Tellus) NYC
- PHRANC *Folksinger* LP (Rhino) L.A.
- MISSION OF BURMA *The Horrible Truth* LP (Ace of Hearts) Boston
- DOUG E. FRESH/GET FRESH CREW *The Show* 12" (Reality) NYC
- U-MEN *Step Spinning* EP (Homestead) Seattle
- PENTAGRAM LP (Pentagram) Arlington
- WIPERS *Better Off Dead* 45 (Trap) Portland '78
- GREEN RIVER *whatever*

SUB POP U.S.A. RADIO Every Tuesday 6-7pm KCMU 90.5 FM

THE SQUEEGEES
Custom
- T-Shirts • Jackets • Posters • Banners
- Signs • Hats • Buttons • Decals

Quantity Pricing
STATE OF THE ART QUALITY
Complete
• Modern Colors and Techniques • Artwork • Camera • Volume Production

SilverScreen GRAPHICS

"We've forgotten more about screenprinting than 'the other guys' will ever know."

2926 Western Ave. Seattle WA 98121   441-1555

Retro Viva
MORE DASH! LESS CASH!
Pike Place Market
1511 1st Avenue
Seattle, WA • 624-2529

SCOTT LINDENMUTH GUITAR INSTRUCTION
ROCK   JAZZ   CLASSICAL   FUSION

776-6362

EMERALD CITY AUCTION
TRY THE TITUS TOUCH
CHUCK TITUS
OWNER • AUCTIONEER
909 SW 151ST • BURIEN
LICENSE #376
Consignments Welcome!

HANGER TAVERN
LIQUIDATION, TUES.
OCTOBER 29, 10 AM
PREVIEW 8 AM

MUSICIAN'S EQUIPMENT
Monday Nov 18th, 1985 7:00pm
Preview 4:00pm

- YAMAHA, PEAVEY, KUSTOM
- ROLAND, FENDER, TASCAM
- SONY, TAPCO, SHURE, TAMA
- CANNON, SOUNDCRAFT & MORE!

GUITARS, KEYBOARDS, DRUMS, DIG. SYNTH., GUITAR SYNTH., MIXERS, AMPS, SPEAKERS, CASSETTE, 8tr, 4tr RECORDERS, TAPE ECHO, DIG. DELAY & MORE!

ITEMS TOO NUMEROUS TO MENTION!
over 70K inventory
CALL FOR DETAILS

151 ST & AMBAUM 244-7794

This is not a crush dance groove. This is a novelty record. It was recorded live in a small club. It had character. It features 1. human beat box; 2. real drums; 3. *loud* castanets. A very primitive rap.

JUSTICE LEAGUE *Think or Sing* 7" EP (Fartblossom Enterprizes). Like the promo sheet says, this is positive punk. "Time To Stop" is "dedicated to an end of the gang and individual violence which is destroying everything we're working for." Cool. I just wish that generic thrash bands like this would drop the "unity" pose and just be themselves. Expressing any kind of individuality is probably the most radical thing these guys could do.

MISSION OF BURMA *The Horrible Truth About Burma* LP (Ace of Hearts). Boston's legendary art/punk band recorded live, featuring previously unreleased material. These men spill their blood on a **STOOGES** cover ("1970") then mystify with an early **PERE UBU** head trip ("Heart of Darkness"). They got 'em both: guts 'n brains.

PENTAGRAM LP. I was passing out to **BLACK SABBATH** over 12 years ago, and this Pentagram record is bringing back all those beautiful memories: black light posters, cheap incense, and gallons of Mad Dog. Wow, 12 years go by real fast.

The **CLINTONS** "Girl Next Door" 45 (Coyote). These guys seem to be a hip item with the NY roots rock 'n roll scene. But if I want **CHUCK BERRY** I'll listen to Chuck Berry. Item: cover photo of topless '60s girl group should boost sales.

SUB TEN

JAMES BROWN *Live at the Apollo, Volume II —Part 2* (Rhino)

HÜSKER DÜ *Flip Your Wig* LP (SST)

VARIOUS *Tellus #10 All Guitars!* cassette (Tellus)

PHRANC *Folksinger* LP (Rhino)

MISSION OF BURMA *The Horrible Truth* LP (Ace of Hearts)

DOUG E. FRESH/GET FRESH CREW "The Show" 12" (Reality)

U-MEN *Stop Spinning* EP (Homestead)

PENTAGRAM LP (Pentagram)

WIPERS *Better off Dead* 45 (Trap)

GREEN RIVER whatever

Incredibly Rockin' Roots R&B Rave Up!

PONTIAC BROTHERS *Doll Hut* LP (Frontier). YES!!!! *Incredibly rockin' roots R&B rave-up!!! Wailin' slide guitar from Ward Dotson, formerly of the* **GUN CLUB**!! Although these guys are a carbon copy of the early **ROLLING STONES**, there's not a dud on here. This is gutsy, with great songs, great playing. Frontier Records continues to be extremely selective; a quality label.

THE ARMS OF SOMEONE NEW *Susan Sleepwalking* LP (Office Records). In this modern world of speed, stress, and turbulence, there comes an aching need for relaxation. Tranquilizers, television, biofeedback, even tantric sex may provide momentary shelter. However, nothing approached the tranquility of *Susan Sleepwalking*. This is beautiful music. Reference points: early **DURUTTI COLUMN**, *Faith*-period **CURE**.

THIN WHITE ROPE *Exploring the Axis* LP (Frontier). This Southern Cal band lists **JOHNNY CASH** and gore director **GEORGE ROMERO** as primary influences. What we've got here is a desert-parched psychedelic/country mutation with creepy lines like "3 sixes on your head, 3 eyes and one is red." The whole thing gets stronger as we flip it over; keep ridin' the bronco and you'll go over the top for sure.

RAGING FIRE *A Family Thing* EP (Pristine). Great white thrash country/blues from Nashville. "A Family Thing," the song of the month, starts out with back porch acoustic guitar. Then it stands up and splinters that old rockin' chair. For fans of **X**, **GUN CLUB**.

DWIGHT YOAKUM *Guitars, Cadillacs, Etc., Etc.* EP (Oak). Heard good things about this straight-ahead country EP by upstart Yoakum. And, yeah, this is the real thing. It's no wonder kids in rural areas listen to metal instead of country—the music coming out of Nashville sucks! It's all rhinestone schlock, and the lyrics don't cut deep enough. But Yoakum plays it raw and his authentic nasal twang goes straight to the heart. He's got roots. While Yoakum's revivalism is refreshing, I think he'd be more on target if he hit on more contemporary themes. Heartaches, drinkin', and prison is classic material, but there are other, more intense topics that concern today's small-town working class, like the paranoia of the survivalist movement or the emerging poverty of displaced farm and factory workers. Yoakum has the power to unite the vitality of roots-style country with the social problems of the '80s. I'm waiting for the next record.

GUITAR SLIM *The Things I Used To Do* LP. (Ace import) R&B artist Guitar Slim recorded out of New Orleans in the late '40s and early '50s. He was a contemporary of other early electric guitar players such as **CLARENCE "GATEMOUTH" BROWN** and **T-BONE WALKER**. One of the first players to experiment with fuzztone distortion, Slim could be a wild-man on stage. At one show, he appeared wearing blue hair, a blue suit, blue shoes, and 350 feet of mic wire. His valet then carried him out on his shoulders into the crowd, out the door, and into oncoming traffic. This LP is an excellent collection of lazy, creeping blues anthems, "I Done Got Over It" being my personal favorite. In 1959, after living and drinking hard on the Southern R&B circuit, Guitar Slim died of bronchial pneumonia. End of the book report.

SUB ▲ POP
U.S.A.

A GUIDE TO U.S. INDEPENDENTS
By Bruce Pavitt

PONTIAC BROTHERS *Doll Hut* LP. YES!!!! INCREDIBLY ROCKIN' ROOTS R&B RAVE UP!!! WAILIN' SLIDE GUITAR FROM WARD DOTSON, FORMERLY OF THE GUN CLUB!! Although these guys are a carbon copy of early Rolling Stones, there's not a dud on here. This is gutsy, with great songs, great playing. Frontier Records continues to be extremely selective; a quality label. *** (Frontier, Box 22, Sun Valley, CA 91353)

THE ARMS OF SOMEONE NEW *Susan Sleepwalking* LP. In this modern world of speed, stress and turbulence, there comes an aching need for relaxation. Tranquilizers, television, biofeedback, even tantric sex may provide momentary shelter. However, nothing approaches the tranquility of *Susan Sleepwalking*. This is beautiful music. Reference points: early Durrutti Column, *Faith*-period Cure. *** (Office Records, Box 2081, Station A, Champaign, IL 61820)

RAGING FIRE *A Family Thing* EP. Great white trash country/blues from Nashville. "A Family Thing," the song of the month, starts out with back porch acoustic guitar. Then it stands up and splinters that old rockin' chair. For fans of X, Gun Club. *** (Pristine, 10-C Hickory Village, Hendersonville, TN 37075)

THIN WHITE ROPE *Exploring the Axis* LP. This Southern Cal band lists Johnny Cash and gore director George Romero as primary influences. What we've got here is a desert parched psychedelic / country mutation with creepy lines like "3 sixes on your head, 3 eyes and one is red." The whole thing gets stronger as we flip it over: keep ridin' this bronco and you'll go over the top for sure. *** (Frontier, Box 22, Sun Valley, CA 91353)

BUY ★★★
BORROW ★★
BURN ★

DWIGHT YOAKUM *Guitars, Cadillacs, etc., etc.* EP. Heard good things about this straight-ahead country EP by upstart Yoakum. And yeah, this is the real thing. It's no wonder kids in rural areas listen to metal instead of country — the music coming out of Nashville sucks! It's all rhinestone schlock and the lyrics don't cut deep enough. But Yoakum plays it raw and his authentic nasal twang goes straight for the heart. He's got roots. While Yoakum's revivalism is refreshing, I think he'd be more on target if he hit on more contemporary themes. Heartaches, drinkin' and prison is classic material, but there are other, more intense topics that concern today's small town working class, like the paranoia of the Survivalist movement or the emerging poverty of displaced farm and factory workers. Yoakum has the power to unite the vitality of roots-style country with the social problems of the 80's. I'm waiting for the next record. ** (AK, 6201 Santa Monica Blvd., Hollywood, CA 90038)

GUITAR SLIM *The Things I Used to Do* LP. R&B artist Guitar Slim recorded out of New Orleans in the late '40s and early '50s. He was a contemporary of other early electric guitar players such as Clarence "Gatemouth" Brown and T-Bone Walker. One of the first players to experiment with fuzztone distortion, Slim could be a wildman on stage. At one show, he came on stage wearing blue hair, a blue suit, blue shoes and 350 feet of mic wire. His valet then carried him out on his shoulders into the crowd, out the door and into oncoming traffic. This LP is an excellent collection of lazy, creeping blues anthems, "I Done Got Over It" being my personal favorite. In 1959, after living and drinking hard on the Southern R&B circuit, Guitar Slim died of bronchial pneumonia, End of book report. *** (Ace import, available through City Hall Distribution)

SONICS / WAILERS / GALAXIES *Merry Christmas* LP. One of the most rockin' Christmas LPs ever. Three of the Pacific Northwest's all-time great garage bands wail on holiday classics plus their own originals. Previously an out-of-print collector's item, this has just been reissued by Etiquette. Buy it for the Sonics' *Santa Claus*. *** (Etiquette, 2442 NW Market, Suite 273, Seattle WA 98107)

Notes From the Pop Underground
edited by Peter Belsito

Book. It takes a creative mind to synthesize information in new ways to find abstract relationships. Peter Belsito (editor of *Street Art, Hardcore California*) has brought together, in one book, a diverse mix of some of the most provocative minds of this decade. Peter has pulled together and defined his own underground country club. And what a party! We get interviews with: Survival Research Laboratories (industrial performance art from SF), Jim Jarmusch (director of US indie film *Stranger than Paradise*), Diamanda Galas (uninhibited new music demon vocalist), Keith Haring (NY graffiti artist and painter), Francoise Mouly and Art Spiegelman (publishers of RAW graphics magazine), Church of the SubGenius members (bizarre conceptual cult) plus interviews with Jello Biafra, Spalding Grey, Robert Anton Wilson and Michael Peppe. The list speaks for itself: buy this book. *** (Last Gasp)

LIVE SKULL *Bringing Home the Bait* LP. Live Skull is a NY "noise" band who are concerned more with mood, atmosphere and texture than pop hooks or vocal harmonies. Their second release continues the dirgy ambience of prior material, but seems less focused and mature than NY counterparts SONIC YOUTH and SWANS. *** (Homestead, PO Box 570, Rockville Centre, NY 11571)

BLACK FLAG *In My Head* LP. I can remember when Black Flag put everything they had into putting out one great 45 a year, like *Wasted* or *Six-Pack*. Now we're talking filler with four LPs a year. *In Your Head* sounds like it was pumped out in an afternoon, in between photo sessions. There's some power here, but the songs just don't go anywhere. Best Pettibon cover yet though. ** (SST, Box 1, Lawndale, CA 90260)

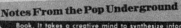

SUB/TEM

■ **Notes from the Pop Underground** Book (Last Gasp) SF
■ **Pontiac Brothers** Doll Hut LP (Frontier) LA
■ **Raging Fire** A Family Thing EP (Pristine) Nashville
■ **The Arms of Someone New** Susan Sleepwalking LP (Office) Champaign
■ **Thin White Rope** Exploring the Axis LP (Frontier) LA
■ **Guitar Slim** The Things I Used to Do LP (Ace Import) New Orleans
■ **Sonics/Wailers/Galaxies** Merry Christmas LP (Etiquette) Tacoma
■ **Pere Ubu** Heaven 45 (Hearthan) Cleveland
■ **Dwight Yoakum** Guitars, Cadillacs LP (AK) Bakersfield
■ **Live Skull** Bringing Home the Bait LP (Homestead) NY

SUB
POP
U.S.A.
RADIO
Every Tuesday
6-7pm KCMU 90.5 FM

DIAMANDA GALAS
AND CHARLES BURNS:
NOTES FROM
THE POP UNDERGROUND

Play It Your Way

Sure, you can buy a guitar that sounds like everyone else's. But when you're ready, we can build a guitar that looks and sounds like you!

EXPERT REPAIR
• Fast, economical
• 15 years experience
• Complete warranty service
• Custom bodies, necks & finishes

Stephens
STRINGED INSTRUMENTS
702 Blanchard 10-5:30 Mon.-Sat.
340-0966

TIME TRAVELERS
1511 Second Avenue   Seattle, WA 98101   206/624-7806

Records
Comics
T-Shirts
Video
Tapes
Vans
Robots
Jimmy-Z
Magazines
Skateboards

& other stuff

Raw Power Productions presents
PACIFIC METAL EXPLOSION
A Benefit for Northwest Harvest Featuring

SENTENCE (Formerly Juvenile)

with C.O.M.A. Recording Artists

MISTRUST

Giveaways Galore

Friday, Dec. 6, 1985 - 8 P.M.
Ballard High School
1618 NW 65th
$5.00 ($4.00 with Can of Food)

Tickets Available at Budget Tapes and Records, 847 N.E. Northgate Way or Ballard High, Night of Show

MISTRUST and LOOK OUT can be heard on the newly released PACIFIC METAL PROJECT LP. SENTENCE info: 3202 36th W. Seattle 98199

COMA
Coca-Cola   Centre Stage   The Rocket   Budget Tapes and Records
AMERICAN MUSIC   Silverscreen

SONICS/WAILERS/GALAXIES *Merry Christmas* LP (Etiquette). One of the most rockin' Christmas LPs ever. Three of the Pacific Northwest's all-time great garage bands wail on holiday classics plus their own originals. Previously an out-of-print collector's item, this has just been reissued by Etiquette. Buy it for the Sonics' "Santa Claus."

Notes From the Pop Underground, edited by Peter Belsito book (Last Gasp). It takes a creative mind to synthesize information in new ways to find abstract relationships. Peter Belsito (editor of *Street Art, Hardcore California*) has brought together, in one book, a diverse mix of some of the most provocative minds of this decade. Peter has pulled together and defined his own underground country club. And what a party! We get interviews with: **SURVIVAL RESEARCH LABORATORIES** (industrial performance art from SF); Jim Jarmusch (director of US indie film *Stranger than Paradise*); **DIAMANDA GALAS** (uninhibited new music demon vocalist); Keith Haring (NY graffiti artist and painter); Francoise Mouly and Art Spiegelman (publishers of *RAW* graphics magazine); members of **CHURCH OF THE SUBGENIUS** (bizarre conceptual cult); plus interviews with **JELLO BIAFRA, SPALDING GREY, ROBERT ANTON WILSON,** and **MICHAEL PEPPE**. The list speaks for itself; buy this book.

LIVE SKULL *Bringing Home the Bait* LP (Homestead). Live Skull is a NY "noise" band who are concerned more with mood, atmosphere, and texture than pop hooks or vocal harmonies. Their second release continues the dirgy ambience of prior material, but seems less focused and mature than NY counterparts **SONIC YOUTH** and **SWANS**.

BLACK FLAG *In My Head* LP (SST Records). I can remember when Black Flag put everything they had into putting out one great 45 a year, like "Wasted" or "Six Pack." Now we're talking filler, with four LPs a year. *In Your Head* sounds like it was pumped out in an afternoon, in between photo sessions. There's some power here, but the songs just don't go anywhere. Best Pettibon cover yet though.

SUB TEN

Notes from the Pop Underground book (Last Gasp)

PONTIAC BROTHERS *Doll Hut* LP (Frontier)

RAGING FIRE *A Family Thing* EP (Pristine)

THE ARMS OF SOMEONE NEW *Susan Sleepwalking* LP (Office)

THIN WHITE ROPE *Exploring the Axis* LP (Frontier)

GUITAR SLIM *The Things I Used To Do* LP (Ace import)

SONICS/WAILERS/GALAXIES *Merry Christmas* LP (Etiquette)

PERE UBU "Heaven" 45 (Hearpen)

DWIGHT YOAKUM *Guitars, Cadillacs, Etc., Etc.* EP (Oak)

LIVE SKULL *Bringing Home the Bait* LP (Homestead)

1985 How Def Was It?

Was 1985 a good year for independent American music? Yes and no. Labels continued to explode and expand, releasing endless amounts of product; 45s and EPs were replaced by full length LPs, dramatizing the amount of music that's flooding the marketplace. But, although the "scene" is bigger than ever, it's also a lot less interesting. Few bands or labels took risks, opting instead to cash in on generic, marketable movements like hardcore skate thrash, speed metal, hip hop and '60s punk/paisley revival. In short, there was an awful lot of uninspired music, packaged in full-length LPs stuffed with filler. However, although the ratio of bad to good was top heavy to the extreme, the sheer volume of releases guaranteed at least a few stunning originals.

In '85, the two most vital forces in the indie music scene came from reactionary revivalists and radical progressives. In the reactionary camp we had music like straight-ahead C&W of **DWIGHT YOAKUM** and the R&B rave-up of the **PONTIAC BROTHERS**. These and other artists tried to rediscover the roots of rock 'n roll, coming across with passion and sincerity: a welcome relief from jaded, artificial poseurs. In the radical sector we heard from bands like **SWANS** and **SONIC YOUTH**, who, while still using that American staple—the electric guitar—managed to reinvent rock 'n roll through texture and atonality.

Potentially the most exciting trend to emerge in the mid-'80s is the cultural diversification of artists involved in the independent music scene. Truly motivated and creative individuals are crossing over into small press publication, film, video, etc. This year we saw emerging writer/poet **HENRY ROLLINS** (vocalist with **BLACK FLAG**) release three volumes of writing. **MICHAEL GIRA** of **SWANS** will also be releas-

ing a book. **JIM JARMUSCH**'s award winning indie film, *Stranger Than Paradise*, featured actors who were involved with East Village bands like the **LOUNGE LIZARDS** and **KONK**. L.A. director **PENELOPE SPHEERIS**, who directed the punk documentary *The Decline of Western Civilization*, has continued to create independent films, with her *Boys Next Door* being released this year. Independent record labels like SST are also aggressively pursuing the production of rock videos, challenging the preconceptions of MTV. Overall, this integration and crossing is setting us up for a big new cultural explosion.

Listed below are some of the most vital events and consumer items of 1985.

BAND OF THE YEAR

HÜSKER DÜ America's most consistently great guitar band. Two awesome LPs this year—*New Day Rising* and *Flip Your Wig*. This raw pop trio was the only band in the country who could spew out this much material and not have it sound like filler.

RECORD OF THE YEAR

SWANS *Raping a Slave* EP. Aside from having the most provocative song title of the year, this record displayed maximum style. The graphics, the lyrics, and the music all pushed minimalism to new extremes. Love it, hate it; this was the most unique, most distinctive record of '85.

NATIONAL LABEL

Homestead. This adventurous New York label signed unknown regional bands from all over the country as well as New York heavyweights **SONIC YOUTH** and **SWANS**. Head honcho Gerard Cosloy took risks and

SUB ▲ POP
U.S.A.

A GUIDE TO U.S. INDEPENDENTS — *By Bruce Pavitt*

ILLUSTRATION BY CHARLES BURNS

Was 1985 a good year for independent American music? Yes and no. Labels continued to explode and expand, releasing endless amounts of product; 45s and EPs were replaced by full length LPs, dramatizing the amount of music that's flooded the marketplace. But, although the "scene" is bigger than ever, it's also a lot less interesting. Few bands or labels took risks, opting instead to cash in on generic, marketable movements like hardcore skate thrash, speed metal, hip hop and '60s punk/paisley revival. In short, there was an awful lot of uninspired music, packaged in full length LPs, stuffed with filler. However, although the ratio of bad to good was top heavy to the extreme, the sheer volume of releases guaranteed at least a few stunning originals.

In '85, the two most vital forces in the indie music scene came from reactionary revivalists and radical progressives. In the reactionary camp we had

1985

HOW
DEF
WAS
IT?

music like the straight-ahead C&W of Dwight Yoakum and the R&B rave-up of the Pontiac Brothers. These and other artists tried to rediscover the roots of rock 'n' roll, coming across with passion and sincerity; a welcome relief from jaded, artificial poseurs. In the radical sector we heard from bands like Swans and Sonic Youth, who, while still using that American staple — the electric guitar — managed to reinvent rock 'n' roll through texture and atonality.

Potentially the most exciting trend to emerge in the mid-'80s is the cultural diversification of artists involved in the independent music scene. Truly motivated and creative individuals are crossing over into small press publication, film, video, etc. This year we saw emerging writer/poet Henry Rollins (vocalist with Black Flag) release three volumes of writing. Michael Gira of Swans will also be releasing a book. Jim Jarmusch's award winning indie film, Stranger Than Paradise, featured actors who were involved with East Village bands like the Lounge Lizards and Konk. L.A. director Penelope Spheeris, who directed the punk documentary The Decline of Western Civilization, has continued to create independent films, with her Boys Next Door being released this year. Independent record labels like SST are also aggressively pursuing the production of rock video, challenging the preconceptions of MTV. Overall, this integration and crossing over is setting us up for a big new cultural explosion.

Listed below are some of the most vital events and consumer items of 1985.

Band of the Year
Husker Du. America's most consistently great guitar band. Two awesome LPs this year — New Day Rising and Flip Your Wig. This raw pop trio was the only band in the country who could spew out this much material and not have it sound like filler.

Record of the Year
Swans Raping a Slave EP. Aside from having the most provocative song title of the year, this record displayed maximum style. The graphics, the lyrics and the music all pushed minimalism to new extremes. Love it, hate it: this was the most unique, most distinctive record of '85.

National Label
Homestead. This adventurous NY label signed unknown regional bands from all over the country as well as NY heavyweights Sonic Youth and Swans. Head honcho Gerard Cosley took risks and usually won; for example, Seattle's relatively unknown U-Men were signed and came up with one of the best selling indie releases of November.

Personality of the Year
Henry Rollins. As vocalist for Black Flag, Rollins has proved to be the most intense frontman in rock 'n' roll, lurching with as much raw sex as Iggy or Elvis. In addition to being America's top savage, Rollins has also released three volumes of short, sharp, brutally honest writings and poems. His spoken word performances are sure to influence an entire generation of potential punk poets.

FUTURE FORECASTS
● European "industrial" bands will finally connect with an American audience. Expect more American bands to put down their guitars and experiment with tape manipulation, high-tech digital electronics and low-tech industrial machinery. Noise and rhythm on the dance floor.
● As culture recycles itself, expect a mega Barry White revival.

Regional Label
K. Olympia's K label released some heavyweight stuff this year, including a tape of girl/pop group Shonen Knife from Japan and a great compilation tape of (primarily) regional material called Let's Kiss. This tape featured national league material from the Melvins, Danger Bunny and The Young Pioneers, among others. Expect a Beat Happening EP soon. Runner up: Vancouver B.C.'s Nettwork label.

Show of the Year
Jonathan Richman & the Modern Lovers at the Backstage. America's most sincere performer finally made it to Seattle.

TOP 10 RECORDS
(alphabetical order)

BIG BLACK Racer-X EP (Homestead) Chicago
BUTTHOLE SURFERS Another Man's Sac LP (Touch and Go) nomadic lifestyle
CAMPER VAN BEETHOVEN LP (Independent Project) L.A.
GREG SAGE Straight Ahead LP (Enigma) Portland
HUSKER DU New Day Rising LP (SST) Minneapolis
SCRATCH ACID EP (Rabid) Atlanta
SONIC YOUTH Bad Moon Rising LP (Homestead) NYC
SWANS Raping a Slave EP (Homestead) NYC
U-MEN Stop Spinning EP (Homestead) Seattle
UTFO Hangin' Out/Roxanne, Roxanne EP (Select) NYC

TOP 5 RE-ISSUES
GEORGE JONES Lonestar Legend LP (Ace) import
SONICS Full Force LP (Etiquette)
EVERLY BROS. All They Had to Do Was Dream LP (Rhino)
JAMES BROWN Live at the Apollo Vol. 2 Part 2 (Rhino)
BACK FROM THE GRAVE LP series (Crypt)

TOP DOMESTIC RELEASES BY OVERSEAS ARTISTS
BILLY BRAGG Spy Vs Spy/ Between the Wars LP (CD/Go!)
NICK CAVE First Born is Dead LP (Homestead/Mute)
SHONEN KNIFE Burning Farm cassette (K/Zero)

OTHER STUFF WORTH GRABBING:
Anything by Copernicus, Green River, Salem 66, Windbreakers, Doug E. Fresh, Pontiac Bros., Dwight Yoakum, Soul Asylum, Naked Raygun, Volcano Suns, Modern Lovers, Young Fresh Fellows, Beat Happening, Phranc, Ambitious Lovers, Steve Fisk, No Trend, Executive Slacks, Crippled Pilgrims, Skinny Puppy, Beastie Boys.

> "Was 1985 a good year for independent American music? Yes and no. Labels continued to explode and expand, releasing endless amounts of product; 45s and EPs were replaced by full-length LPs, dramatizing the amount of music that's flooded the marketplace. But, although the 'scene' is bigger than ever, it's also a lot less interesting. Few bands or labels took risks, opting instead to cash in on generic, marketable movements like hardcore skate thrash, speed metal, hip hop and '60s punk/paisley revival."

usually won: for example, Seattle's relatively unknown **U-MEN** were signed and came up with one of the bestselling indie releases of November.

PERSONALITY OF THE YEAR

HENRY ROLLINS. As vocalist for **BLACK FLAG**, Rollins has proved to be the most intense frontman in rock 'n roll, lurching with as much raw sex as **IGGY** or **ELVIS**. In addition to being America's top savage, Rollins has also released three volumes of short, sharp, brutally honest writings and poems. His spoken-word performances are sure to influence an entire generation of potential punk poets.

REGIONAL LABEL

K Records. Olympia's K label released some heavyweight stuff this year, including a tape of girl/pop group **SHONEN KNIFE** from Japan, and a great compilation tape of (primarily) regional material called *Let's Kiss*. This tape featured national-league material from the **MELVINS**, **DANGER BUNNY**, and the **YOUNG PIONEERS**, among others. Expect a **BEAT HAPPENING** EP soon. Runner up: Vancouver B.C.'s Nettwerk label.

SHOW OF THE YEAR

JONATHAN RICHMAN & THE MODERN LOVERS at the Backstage. America's most sincere performer finally made it to Seattle.

TOP DOMESTIC RELEASES BY OVERSEAS ARTISTS

BILLY BRAGG *Spy Vs. Spy/Between the Wars* LP (CD/Go!)

NICK CAVE AND THE BAD SEEDS *First Born is Dead* LP (Homestead/Mute)

SHONEN KNIFE *Burning Farm* cassette (K/Zero)

FUTURE FORECASTS

European "industrial" bands will finally connect with an American audience. Expect more American bands to put down their guitars and experiment with tape manipulation, high-tech digital electronics, and low-tech industrial machinery. Noise and rhythm on the dance floor. And as culture recycles itself, expect a mega **BARRY WHITE** revival.

TOP 10 RECORDS

BIG BLACK *Racer-X* EP (Homestead) Chicago , *Another Man's Sac* LP (Touch and Go)

CAMPER VAN BEETHOVEN LP (Independent Project)

GREG SAGE *Straight Ahead* LP (Enigma)

HÜSKER DÜ *New Day Rising* LP (SST)

SCRATCH ACID EP (Rabid)

SONIC YOUTH *Bad Moon Rising* LP (Homestead)

SWANS *Raping a Slave* EP (Homestead)

U-MEN *Stop Spinning* EP (Homestead)

UTFO Hangin' Out/Roxanne, Roxanne EP (Select)

TOP 5 REISSUES

GEORGE JONES *Lonestar Legend* LP (Ace import)

SONICS *Full Force* LP (Etiquette)

EVERLY BROTHERS *All They Had to Do Was Dream* LP (Rhino)

JAMES BROWN *Live at the Apollo, Volume II —Part 2* (Rhino)

VARIOUS *Back From The Grave* LP series (Crypt)

OTHER STUFF WORTH GRABBING

Anything by **COPERNICUS, GREEN RIVER, SALEM 66, WINDBREAKERS, DOUG E. FRESH, PONTIAC BROTHERS, DWIGHT YOAKUM, SOUL ASYLUM, NAKED RAYGUN, VOLCANO SUNS, MODERN LOVERS, YOUNG FRESH FELLOWS, BEAT HAPPENING, PHRANC, AMBITIOUS LOVERS, STEVE FISK, NO TREND, EXECUTIVE SLACKS, CRIPPLED PILGRIMS, SKINNY PUPPY,** and **BEASTIE BOYS.**

God Is Alive and Living in Ellensburg

In the heart of America's rust belt lies one of the most radical record labels in the world. Detroit's Touch and Go Records, originally started as a fanzine, has just released two of the most menacing packages of '86: *Snakeboy* by **KILLDOZER** (LP) and *Movin' to Florida* by the , (EP). Madison, Wisconsin's Killdozer is plodding, intense, and frayed to pieces. "We're going to the lake! Mom made some chocolate cake!" Such happy lyrics, such creepy music. "King of Sex" and "Going to the Beach" would've made a killer single, instead we get a decent LP. The B-Hole Surfers, originally from San Antonio, live in a van, travel the country, and put on one of the wildest, weirdest live rock 'n roll shows this side of **SCREAMIN' JAY HAWKINS**. "Moving to Florida" maintains their rep as one of the most demented groups ever to crawl out of the mud. I'm not even gonna attempt to describe this noisy loudness; in fact, I think I just blew the bass out of my speaker. So much for art.

With rich assholes pushing all the cool people out of New York City, it's no wonder all the best pop bonds are living across the water in Hoboken, New Jersey. *Luxury Condos Coming to Your Neighborhood Soon* (Coyote Records) is a good collection of pop hits, quite a bit of it with a folk or country feel; and the stuff sounds sincere—no poseurs, gimmicks, or stupid haircuts. In it you'll find old-timers like Janet and Doug Wygal, formerly of the **INDIVIDUALS**, now starring in their own production, the **WYGALS**. Glenn Mercer and Bill Million used to be in the legendary **FEELIES**, they're now hangin' out with the **TRYPES**. My favorite cut is a shimmering acoustic country ballad by the promising **LAST ROUNDUP** ("produced in Michael's bathroom"). Roots rockers the **RAUNCH HANDS** also burn up the floor, as do **RAGE TO LIVE** and yes, even **SCRUFFY THE CAT**. This is a strong document of a very vital regional scene. Let's just hope those luxury condos stay in Manhattan.

BEAT HAPPENING sings about KGB agents and teen rebellion. They also sing about love, affection, and intimacy without sounding like wimps. Produced by Greg Sage of **WIPERS** fame, this totally rockin' acoustic folk LP (K Records) has more character, more genuine personality, than anything I've heard all month. Calvin swings his hips with an awkward deep baritone, and trades off on vocals with Heather. Bongos and maracas are also in the mix. Like the **MODERN LOVERS** and the late **MARINE GIRLS**, Beat Happening is a positive force; sincere and willing to take risks, they show that it's just as radical to openly like someone as it is to brutalize and degrade through cheap sensationalism. Great record!

Snowball fights and dead car batteries. Minneapolis is cold, but look out for **SOUL ASYLUM**. Now that the **REPLACEMENTS** and **HÜSKER DÜ** have been signed to the majors, Soul Asylum will have to prove, once again, that Minneapolis is the city in the Midwest for rough-edged melodic pop. Their new 45, "Tied to the Tracks" (Twin/Tone), is as great as last year's LP. If you're a Replacements fan, go for it.

What I really like about these black hip hop/ghetto rap 12-inchers is the language. These kids rip English apart and slap it back up, with style. They'll step on words

SUB POP USA

A GUIDE TO U.S. INDEPENDENTS

By Bruce Pavitt

BEAT HAPPENING

> **"With rich assholes pushing all the cool people out of New York City, it's no wonder all the best pop bonds are living across the water in Hoboken, New Jersey...Let's just hope those luxury condos stay in Manhattan."**

► With rich assholes pushing all the cool people out of New York City, it's no wonder all the best pop bonds are living across the water in Hoboken, New Jersey. LUXURY CONDOS COMING TO YOUR NEIGHBORHOOD SOON is a good collection of pop hits, quite a bit of it with a folk or country feel; and the stuff sounds sincere — no poseurs, gimmicks or stupid haircuts. In it you'll find old timers like Janet and Doug Wygal, formerly of the Individuals, now starring in their own production: the Wygals. Glenn Mercer and Bill Million used to be in the legendary Feelies, they're now hangin' out with the Trypes. My favorite cut is a shimmering acoustic-country ballad by the promising Last Roundup ("produced in Michael's bathroom"). Roots rockers the Raunch Hands also burn up the floor, as do Rage to Live and yes, even Scruffy the Cat. This is a strong document of a very vital regional scene. Let's just hope those luxury condos stay in Manhattan. (Coyote, Box 112 uptown, Hoboken, NJ 07030).

► Beat Happening sings about KGB agents and teen rebellion. They also sing about love, affection and intimacy without sounding like wimps. Produced by **Greg Sage** of Wipers fame, this totally rockin' acoustic folk LP has more character, more genuine personality than anything I've heard all month. Calvin swings his hips with an awkward, deep baritone and trades off on vocals with Heather. Bongos and maracas are also in the mix.

Like the Modern Lovers and the late Marine Girls, Beat Happening is a positive force: sincere and willing to take risks, they show that it's just as radical to openly like someone as it is to brutalize and degrade through cheap sensationalism. Great record! (K, Box 7154, Olympia, WA 98507).

► Snowball fights and dead car batteries. Minneapolis is cold but look out for **Soul Asylum**. Now that the Replacements and Husker Du have been signed to the majors, Soul Asylum will have to prove, once again, that Minneapolis is the city in the Midwest for rough-edged, melodic pop. Their new 45, *Tied to the Tracks*, is as great as last year's LP. If you're a Replacements fan, go for it. (Twin/Tone, 2541 Nicollet Ave. S., Minneapolis, MN 65404).

► What I really like about those black hip hop/ghetto rap 12-inchers is the *language*. These kids rip English apart and slap it back up, with style.

They'll step on words like *fly* and *juice* and spit out their own vocabulary. Fuck the dictionary! Slang is the poetry of the streets. One *def* and *mighty* jam is *No Show/We're Treacherous* by female rappers the Symbolic 3, a clever response record to *The Show* by Doug E. Fresh. Open it up for some minimal, powerful scratching and a few human beat box tricks. The rhymes are streetwise, and the dialect and grammar will not be found on network television. This record has character. And really, how much whitebread mall culture can you stand? Snap out of bland McRecord Muzak nothingness and grab this plastic. It's on the Reality label so you know it's gonna be raw. (Reality, 592 Communipaw Ave., Jersey City, NJ 07304).

► If anybody out there cares about life and love and flowery beautiful things and the total power of rock 'n' roll, then run out and steal your neighbor's copy of *Under Water* by D.C.'s **Crippled Pilgrims**. And while you're rifling through the jewelry chest, go ahead and nab *A Ripping Spin* by Boston girl-rockers Salem 66. Both LPs are great sensitive folk/rock things that will make you feel more alive and more human than that Twisted Sister your brother keeps playing. (Homestead, Box 570, Rockville Center, NY 11571-0570).

► God is alive and living in Ellensburg, Washington. I know it's hard to believe, but Steve Fisk *is* God. His new cassette, *'til the Night Closes In*, is an ingenious, twisted recycling of trash pop culture: cult church

STEVE FISK

services, *Dallas*, Japanese sci-fi, *The Monkees*. Simultaneous tape loops as well as lengthy narrative are meshed to create a truly melted psychedelic mind spurt. Steve, also noted for his work with Pell Mell, is backed up on some cuts by the funky drums, bass, and guitar of this classic outfit. Fisk also plays synthesizers and an *Optigon* (a prehistoric keyboard thing with rubbery flexi-discs, which he plays both forwards and backwards). PLEASE: do not attempt to operate heavy machinery while under the influence. Stay tuned for an upcoming double LP on Thermidor. (ARPH/K co-release, K, Box 7154, Olympia, WA 98507).

► By the way, Seattle's **Green River** flames like hell on their mighty *Come On Down* slab. A fat nod to the Stooges' *Funhouse*. HEAVY. On Homestead.

PUBLIC NOTICE

On New Year's Eve some of my buddies were attacked in a random act of senseless gang violence. **Rick Lewis**: if you're out of your coma by the time this issue comes out, I just want to say: I love you, you're a way cool dude and I want to buy your next painting.

In the heart of America's rust belt lies one of the most radical record labels in the world. Detroit's **Touch and Go***, originally started as a fanzine, has just released two of the most menacing packages of '86: Snakeboy by* **Killdozer** *(LP) and Movin' to Florida by the* **Butthole Surfers** *(EP). Madison's Killdozer is plodding, intense and frayed to pieces.* We're going to the lake! Mom made some chocolate cake! *Such happy lyrics, such creepy music. "King of Sex" and "Going to the Beach" would've made a killer single, instead we get a decent LP. The B-Hole Surfers, originally from San Antonio, live in a van, travel the country and put on one of the wildest, weirdest live rock 'n' roll shows this side of Screamin' Jay Hawkins. Movin' to Florida maintains their rep as one of the most demented groups ever to crawl out of the mud. I'm not even gonna attempt to describe this noisy loudness; in fact, I think I just blew the bass out of my speaker. So much for art. (Touch and Go, Box 433, Dearborn, MI 48121).*

like "fly" and "juice" and spit out their own vocabulary. Fuck the dictionary! Slang is the poetry of the streets. One def and mighty jam is "No Show"/"We're Treacherous" (Reality) by female rappers **THE SYMBOLIC 3**, a clever response record to "The Show" by **DOUG E. FRESH**. Open it up for some minimal, powerful scratching, and a few human beat box tricks. The rhymes are streetwise, and the dialect and grammar will not be found on network television. This record has character. And really, how much white-bread mall culture can you stand? Snap out of bland McRecord Muzak nothingness and grab this plastic. It's on the Reality label, so you know it's gonna be raw.

If anybody out there cares about life and love and flowery beautiful things, and the total power of rock 'n roll, then run out and steal your neighbor's copy of *Under Water* (Fountain of Youth) by D.C.'s **CRIPPLED PILGRIMS**. And while you're rifling through the jewelry chest, go ahead and nab *A Ripping Spin* (Homestead) by Boston girl-rockers **SALEM 66**. Both LPs are great sensitive folk/rock things that will make you feel more alive and more human than that **TWISTED SISTER** your brother keeps playing.

God is alive and living in Ellensburg, Washington. I know it's hard to believe, but **STEVE FISK** is God. His new cassette, *'Til the Night Closes In* (A.R.P.H./K) is an ingenious, twisted recycling of trash pop culture: cult church services, Dallas, Japanese sci-fi, the **MONKEES**. Simultaneous tape loops as well as lengthy narrative are meshed to create a truly melted psychedelic mind spurt. Steve, also noted for his work with **PELL MELL**, is backed up on some cuts by the funky drums, bass, and guitar of this classic outfit. Fisk also plays synthesizers and an Optigan (a prehistoric keyboard thing with rubbery flexi-discs, which he plays both forwards and backwards). *Please*: do not attempt to operate heavy machinery while under the influence. Stay tuned for an upcoming double LP on Thermidor.

By the way, Seattle's **GREEN RIVER** flames like hell on their mighty *Come on Down* slab. A fat nod to the **STOOGES**' *Funhouse. Heavy*. On Homestead.

PUBLIC NOTICE

On New Year's Eve, some of my buddies were attacked in a random act of senseless gang violence. Rick Lewis: if you're out of your coma by the time this issue comes out, I just want to say: I love you, you're a way cool dude, and I want to buy your next painting.

SUB TEN

BEAT HAPPENING LP (K)

CRIPPLED PILGRIMS *Under Water* LP (Fountain of Youth/Homestead)

STEVE FISK *'Til the Night Closes In* cassette (A.R.P.H./K)

GREEN RIVER *Come on Down* LP (Homestead)

SOUL ASYLUM "Tied to the Tracks" 45 (Twin/Tone)

SYMBOLIC 3 "We're Treacherous" 12" (Reality)

, *Moving to Florida* EP (Touch and Go)

KILLDOZER *Snake Boy* LP (Touch and Go)

SALEM 66 *A Ripping Spin* LP (Homestead)

VARIOUS *Luxury Condos Coming to Your Neighborhood Soon* compilation LP (Coyote)

I Hate Ugly Records

BIG BABY CURSE OF THE MOLEMEN

Nobody can twist romance like **CHARLES BURNS**. America's coolest and coldest illustrator has just released a children's book—for adults only—that rips open the heart of love. Rampaging jealousy and scary "lady monsters" show us kids that people aren't property. All executed in classic style. *Another great one-shot from RAW Publications.* ($8.00 ppd. RAW Books and Graphics)

New York's **RAUNCH HANDS** play real roots rock 'n roll. The production is dirty, cheap, and raunchy. The vocalist sounds black, and the whole band is drunk and fucked up. "Spit It on the Floor" is a sordid tale of sleazy sex laced with alcohol and blood. These guys make the **BLASTERS** sound like *Star Search* material. *El Rauncho Grande* (Relativity) is a killer 6-song EP that you want to buy. Unless you're a wimp. And you don't like **BO DIDDLEY**.

I hate ugly records. Which is why I like Independent Project. This Los Angeles label, organized by designer Bruce Licher of **SAVAGE REPUBLIC**, puts out some of the best-looking records in the country. And considering that 90 percent of US independents look like they came out of a junior high art class, Licher knows there's little competition. **TEN FOOT FACES** is the latest release, a 3-song 45 hand-screened on shirt cardboard in a limited edition of 1500. From the cover to the label to the insert, this thing kills. And the music inside is just as fun—surf garage/pop hits like "Sand Fuck"! Cool record and a great label.

"Confessions of a Congressional Page" gets the *Sub Pop* song-title-of-the month award. This prestigious trophy will be sent to **TOASTERHEAD**, a teen-age thrash band from Raleigh, North Carolina. Their new LP, *A Number of Things* (Fartblossom), while not particularly daring, is still an honest attempt to force parents into submission. Other anthems include "Barrel of Shit" and "Justice for All." On the critically acclaimed Fartblossom label.

A Diamond Hidden in the Mouth of a Corpse (Giorno Poetry Systems) is a bold package of innovative music and spoken word. Put together by poet **JOHN GIORNO** on his own label, this collection features a lot of in-crowd New York art scene-makers, plus raw pop from **HÜSKER DÜ**, plus industrial workouts from England's **CABARET VOLTAIRE** and **COIL**. However, due to the unique characters of the artists involved, the record lacks cohesion. All we can do is vote for the hits: **SONIC YOUTH** has a beautifully sensual, dissonant piece called "Halloween," with Kim on vocals; Michael Gira of **SWANS** performs a powerful, minimal spoken-word thing that will prove his status as American rock's most intense writer. Stuff that made me cringe include the John Giorno Band's "Scum and Slime," heavily contrived rock posturing that shows Giorno is better off publishing books or doing straight spoken word. Other jizz you'll want to investigate: **WILLIAM S. BURROUGHS, DIAMAN-DA GALLAS, DAVID VAN TIEGHEM, JESSICA HAGERDORN & THE GANGSTER CHOIR, DAVID JOHANSEN**. Cover art by **KEITH HARING**, the Peter Max of the '80s.

SUB ▲ POP

A GUIDE TO U.S. INDEPENDENTS

By Bruce Pavitt

O.K., I'VE GOT MY FLASHLIGHT, SWISS ARMY KNIFE, A PILLOWCASE FOR THE TREASURE AND MY SCREAMING SKULL RING FOR GOOD LUCK...

BIG BABY

CURSE OF THE MOLEMEN (book). Nobody can twist romance like Charles Burns. America's coolest and coldest illustrator has just released a children's book — for adults only — that rips open the heart of love. Rampaging jealousy and scary "lady monsters" show us kids that people aren't property. All executed in classic style. **ANOTHER GREAT ONE-SHOT FROM RAW PUBLICATIONS.** ($8.00 ppd. RAW Books and Graphics, 27 Greene St., NYC 10013, or Art in Form bookstore, 2237 2nd Ave.)

New York's Raunch Hands play *real roots rock 'n' roll.* The production is dirty, cheap and raunchy. The vocalist sounds black and the whole band is drunk and fucked up. *Spit it on the Floor* is a sordid tale of sleazy sex laced with alcohol and blood. These guys make the Blasters sound like Star Search material. *El Rauncho Grande* is a killer 6-song EP that you want to buy. Unless you're a wimp. And you don't like Bo Diddley. (Relativity. Fan Club: Box 1588, Madison Sq. Station, NYC, NY 10159)

I hate ugly records. Which is why I like **Independent Project.** This L.A. label, organized by designer **BRUCE LICHER** (Savage Republic), puts out some of the best-looking records in the country. And considering that 90 percent of U.S. independents look like they came out of a jr. high art class, Licher knows there's little competition. **Ten Foot Faces** is the latest release, a 3-song 45 hand-screened on shirt cardboard (limited edition 1500). From the cover to the label to the insert, this thing kills. And the music inside is just as fun — surf garage/pop hits like SAND FUCK! Cool record and a great label. (Independent Project: Box 60357, L.A., CA 90060)

Confessions of a Congressional Page
gets the Sub Pop song-title-of-the-month award. This prestigious trophy will be sent to **Toasterhead,** a teen-age thrash band from Raleigh, North Carolina. Their new LP, **A Number of Things,** while not particularly daring, is still an honest attempt to force parents into submission. Other anthems include **Barrel of Shit** and **Justice For All.** On the critically acclaimed **Fartblossom** label. [Fartblossom: Box 818, Pomona, CA 91769]

A Diamond Hidden in the Mouth of a Corpse
is a bold package of innovative music and spoken word. Put together by poet John Giorno on his own label, this collection features a lot of in-crowd NY art scene-makers *plus* raw pop from **Husker Du** *plus* industrial workouts from England's **Cabaret Voltaire** and **Coil.** However, due to the unique character of the artists involved, the record lacks cohesion. All we can do is vote for the hits:
(1) **Sonic Youth** has a beautifully sensual, dissonant piece called *Halloween*, with Kim on vocals.
(2) **Michael Gira** of Swans performs a powerful, minimal spoken word thing that will prove his status as American rock's most intense writer. Stuff that made me cringe include the **John Giorno Band's** *Scum and Slime:* heavily contrived rock posturing that shows Giorno is better off publishing books or doing straight spoken word. Other jiz you'll want to investigate: **William S. Burroughs, Diamanda Galas, David Van Tigham, Jessica Hagedorn & The Gangster Choir, David Johansen.** Cover art by **Keith Haring,** the Peter Max of the 80's. (Giorno Poetry Systems Institute, Inc., 222 Bowery, New York, N.Y. 10012)

Big, Big Country
If anybody out there gets a kick out of listening to white trash sing about real things that really matter — sex and booze and trucks and pickin' cotton — then check out **Twenty Great Country Recordings of the 50's and 60's Vol. One and Vol. Two.** They're available as imports on the Cascade label. *Excellent.* (Available through City Hall Distributors.)

Yamaha, Kawasaki, Honda. **Freestyle** are from Miami and they ride Japanese motorbikes only. They also play robotic electro-funk with hot latin percussion. Their latest 12-inch DON'T STOP THE ROCK is a disposable, synthetic KRUSH GROOVE that you will play over and over and over till you drop and crawl . . . leather skirts and see-thru jeans . . . FREAK-A-THON!!! (Music Specialists Fan Club: 67 N.W. 71st, Miami, FL 33150)

Gimmick of the month: paisley vinyl. That's right, a 5-song EP dressed in lime and strawberry paisley. And dig: **The Seeing Eye Gods** play perfect psychedelia. No thirty minute jams, no hysteria, no trips to the hospital. This is pure, uncut pop. Perfectly trendy. And if you'd like the floor to stop breathing, just turn away from the spinning the spinning the spinning paisley. (Epitaph Records. Fan Club: 3355 W. El Segundo Bl., Hawthorne, CA 90250)

CHARLES BURNS *Big Baby: Molemen* book (RAW) Italian exile
A DIAMOND HIDDEN IN THE MOUTH OF A CORPSE *LP* (Giorno) NYC
TEN FOOT FACES *Sand Fuck 45* (Ind. Project) LA
RAUNCH HANDS *El Rauncho Grande EP* (Relativity) NYC
FREESTYLE *Don't Stop The Rock 12-inch single* (Music Specialist) Miami
GREEN RIVER *Come On Down LP* (Homestead) Seattle
BEAT HAPPENING *anything* (Olympia)
WALKABOUTS *Cyclone demo* (Seattle)
WIG OUT *fanzine* (Tacoma)
SCRAPING FOETUS OFF THE WHEEL *Nail LP* (Homestead) NYC

The late Dale Yarger was the gentleman who designed the Sub Pop column until the last year or so. I loved his work. The look of the column was a little different from your typical cut-and-paste zine like what Sub Pop had been previously. He introduced a more dynamic presentation that complemented the rest of the publication. The design sensibility was strong throughout the rest of *the Rocket*, too, and many well-known designers came out of that publication including Art Chantry, Wes Anderson, and Helene Silverman.

BIG BIG COUNTRY

If anybody out there gets a kick out of listening to white trash sing about real things that really matter—sex and booze and trucks and picking cotton—then check out *Twenty Great Country Recordings of the '50s and '60s Vols. One and Two*. They are available as imports on the Cascade label. Excellent.

Yamaha, Kawasaki, Honda; **FREESTYLE** are from Miami and they ride Japanese motorbikes only. They also play robotic electro-funk with hot Latin percussion. Their latest 12-inch, "Don't Stop the Rock" (Music Specialists) is a disposable, synthetic krush groove that you will play over and over and over till you drop and crawl. Leather skirts, and see-thru jeans—*freak-a-thon*!!!

GIMMICK OF THE MONTH

Paisley vinyl. That's right, a five-song EP (from Epitaph Records) dressed in lime and strawberry paisley. And dig: the **SEEING EYE GODS** play perfect psychedelia. No thirty-minute jams, no hysteria, no trips to the hospital. This is pure, uncut pop. Perfectly trendy. And if you'd like the floor to stop breathing, just turn away from the spinning the spinning the spinning paisley.

SUB TEN

CHARLES BURNS *Big Baby: Curse of the Molemen* book (RAW)

VARIOUS *A Diamond Hidden in the Mouth of a Corpse* LP (Giorno Poetry Systems)

TEN FOOT FACES "Sand Fuck" 45 (Ind. Project)

RAUNCH HANDS *El Rauncho Grande* EP (Relativity)

FREESTYLE "Don't Stop The Rock" 12-inch single (Music Specialists)

GREEN RIVER *Come on Down* LP (Homestead)

BEAT HAPPENING anything (Olympia)

WALKABOUTS "Cyclone" demo (Seattle)

Wig Out fanzine (Tacoma)

SCRAPING FOETUS OFF THE WHEEL *Nail* LP (Homestead)

If You Want to Sell Art, Package it as Pornography

DEEP SIX LP

You got it. It's slow **SLOW** and heavy **HEAVY** and it's *the* predominant sound of underground Seattle in '86. **GREEN RIVER**, **SOUND GARDEN**, the **MELVINS**, **MALFUNKSHUN**, and even **SKIN YARD** prove that you don't have to live in the suburbs and have a low I.Q. to do some *serious* headbanging. As an extra bonus, you also get one cut by local sex gods the **U-MEN**; "They" is one of their mega-hits, but sounds quirky and out of context. (A fat slab from the skull thumpers **MY EYE** would've made more sense). But enough slack. *This record rocks.*

Pit Hits:

GREEN RIVER "10,000 Things"

MALFUNKSHUN "With Yo' Heart (Not Yo' Hand)"

SOUND GARDEN "Tears to Forget"

BUY THIS RECORD. OR MOVE (*Deep Six* compilation LP c/o C/Z Records, Seattle, WA)

Okay. Skip the introductions. You wanna *rock out*?! You wanna blow your gourd? Well, so do I, man. That's why whenever I get up in the morning, I put on *Made To Be Broken* (Twin/Tone), by **SOUL ASYLUM**. Intense post-thrash pop from Minneapolis that's gonna shrink-wrap the egos of **HÜSKER DÜ** and **THE REPLACEMENTS**. You want it.

Is sex is the essence of pop culture, then **HENRY ROLLINS** must the most popular guy on the block. "Slip It In" from the new live **BLACK FLAG** LP *Who's Got the 10 1/2?* (SST Records) shows Rollins and

Black Flag in their purest form, proving themselves to be America's most physical live act. Recorded at the Starry Night in Portland, this record documents the power of Black Flag more than *any* studio LP. Fucking awesome.

DEATH OF SAMANTHA are from Cleveland and play jagged, extremely articulate pop; **DYLAN** fucks **THE FALL**. Their debut LP is called *Strung Out on Jargon* (Homestead) and it's very, very cool.

MATT GROENING, the most interesting person alive today, has a new book out called *Work Is Hell* (Life In Hell). Matt is *so* perceptive and *so* funny that one wonders why this man does not rule the world. Beyond genius.

We Won't Play Nature to Your Culture by **BARBARA KRUGER** (book). Barbara Kruger manipulates the language of advertising to create art that functions as propaganda. Barbara Kruger is God. A. Advertising is art; B. Art is propaganda; C. Propaganda is advertising. A=B=C. Buy the book and pretend the pages are billboards.

The Right Side of My Brain (video). A 30-minute erotic nightmare starring **LYDIA LUNCH**. Co-starring **HENRY ROLLINS** and **JIM FOETUS**. If you want to sell art, distribute it as pornography. ($22.50 to R. Kern)

SONIC YOUTH America's top noise/guitar band has a new 12" single out on Homestead featuring an extremely sensual "Halloween," plus another sex/power of love anthem called "Flower" on the flip. Bass player Kim Gordon sings and seduces both sides.

SUB▲POP

U S A

A GUIDE TO U.S. INDEPENDENTS
By Bruce Pavitt

GREEN RIVER

PHOTOGRAPHS BY CHARLES PETERSON

SOUND GARDEN

DEEP SIX LP. You got it. It's slow SLOW and heavy HEAVY and it's *THE* predominant sound of underground Seattle in '86. **Green River, Sound Garden, The Melvins, Malfunkshun** and even **Skin Yard** prove that you don't have to live in the suburbs and have a low I.Q. to do some SERIOUS head-banging. As an extra bonus you also get one cut by local sex gods the **U-Men**. *They* is one of their mega-hits but sounds quirky and out of context (a fat slab from skull thumpers **My Eye** would've made more sense). But enough slack. THIS RECORD ROCKS.

Pick hits:
1/ GREEN RIVER 10,000 Things
2/ MALFUNKSHUN With Yo' Heart (Not Yo' Hand)
3/ SOUND GARDEN Tears To Forget.
<u>BUY THIS RECORD. OR MOVE.</u>
(C/Z Records, 1407 E. Madison, Seattle, WA 98122).

O.K. Skip the introductions. You wanna ROCK OUT?! You wanna blow your gourd? Well, so do I, man. That's why whenever I get up in the morning, I put on MADE TO BE BROKEN, by **Soul Asylum**. Intense post-thrash pop from Minneapolis that's gonna shrink-wrap the egos of Husker Du and The Replacements. You want it. (Twin Tone, 445 Oliver Ave. S., Mnpls, MN 55405.)

If sex is the essence of pop culture, then Henry Rollins must be the most popular guy on the block. SLIP IT IN from the new live **Black Flag** LP **Who's Got The 10½?** shows Rollins and Black Flag in their purest form, proving themselves to be America's most physical live act. Recorded at the Starry Night in Portland, this record documents the power of Black Flag more than ANY studio LP. Fucking awesome. (SST, P.O. Box 1, Lawndale, CA 90260.)

Death of Samantha are from Cleveland and play jagged, extremely articulate pop; **Dylan** fucks **The Fall**; their debut LP is called STRUNG OUT ON JARGON and it's very, very, cool. (Homestead label.)

Matt Groening, the most interesting person alive today, has a new book out called **Work Is Hell**. Matt is SO perceptive and SO funny that

one wonders why this man does not **rule the world**. Beyond genius. (Life In Hell P.O. Box 36E64, Los Angeles, CA 90036.)

WORK IS HELL!

BAD JOB CHECKLIST
PLACE AN "X" IN EACH APPROPRIATE BOX. USE YOUR OWN PENCIL. PLEASE DO NOT CRUMPLE THIS CHECKLIST. IT IS ONLY A CARTOON!

1. HEALTH
☐ WORK WITH DANGEROUS, NOXIOUS CHEMICALS
☐ WORK WITH DANGEROUS, NOXIOUS CO-WORKERS

2. WORK OVERLOAD
☐ LAUGHABLY UNREALISTIC DEADLINES
☐ WORK IS PILED ON UNTIL YOUR HEAD EXPLODES

3. WORK UNDERLOAD
☐ REQUIRED TO LOOK BUSY WHEN THERE'S NOTHING TO DO
☐ BRAIN IS ATROPHYING FROM IDLENESS

4. TIME PRESSURES
☐ HAVE TO WORK TOO FAST
☐ HAVE TO WORK TOO SLOW
☐ HAVE TO WORK LIKE A MACHINE
☐ DON'T HAVE TIME TO FINISH THIS CHECKLIST

We won't play nature to your culture by Barbara Kruger (book). Barbara Kruger manipulates the language of advertising to create art that functions as propaganda. Barbara Kruger is God. 1) Advertising is art. 2) Art is propaganda. 3) Propaganda is advertising A=B=C. Buy the book and pretend the pages are billboards. (Available from Art in Form bookstore, 2237 2nd Ave., Seattle, WA 98121.)

The Right Side of My Brain VIDEO. A 30-minute erotic nightmare starring **Lydia Lunch**. Co-starring **Henry Rollins** and **Jim Footus**. If you want to sell art, distribute it as pornography. ($22.50 to R. Kern, P.O. Box 1322, NYC, 10009.)

SONIC YOUTH. America's top noise/guitar band has a new 12" single out featuring an extremely sensual HALLOWEEN plus another slow sex/power of love anthem called FLOWER on the flip. Bass player Kim Gordon

sings and seduces both sides. (Homestead, P.O. Box 570, Rockville Centre, NY 11571-0570.)

Before you think about buying food for the week, I'd suggest you track down TERMINAL TOWER by **Pere Ubu**. This collection of previously out-of-print Hearthan singles (plus a few surprises) shows this legendary Cleveland experiment at their most inspired. Insanity never felt so good. (Twin Tone, 445 Oliver Ave. S. Mnpls, MN 55405.)

Ex-Pere Ubu lead singer **David Thomas** will perform with his band **The Wooden Birds** which includes Ubu alumni Allen Ravenstine and Tony Maimone) in Seattle on April 5th at 1516 2nd Ave. at 8pm.

Because bands from the U.K. receive so much international press, I've made it a policy not to review imports. Which means I can't tell you how great those **HULA** albums are.

DEEP SIX compilation LP (C/Z) Seattle
PERE UBU Terminal Tower LP (Twin Tone) Cleveland
RIGHT SIDE OF MY BRAIN video (Kern) NYC
BLACK FLAG Who's Got The 10½? LP (SST) L.A.
SOUL ASYLUM Made To Be Broken LP (Twin Tone) Mnpls
MY EYE demo Seattle
SONIC YOUTH Halloween 12" single (Homestead) NYC
SOUNDGARDEN live Seattle
PYRHIC VICTORY cassette compilation Seattle
64 SPIDERS live guitar solos with feedback Seattle

"*Deep Six* compilation LP. You got it. It's slow *slow* and heavy *heavy* and it's *the* predominant sound of underground Seattle in '86. Green River, Sound Garden, the Melvins, Malfunkshun and even Skin Yard prove that you don't have to live in the suburbs and have a low I.Q, to do some *serious* headbanging."

The local scene had a mixed reaction to Soundgarden singer Chris Cornell, as he didn't sound like an inspired amateur. He sounded professional, which felt out of place in the divey Seattle club system. Of course, I was a bit prejudiced because I grew up with guitarist Kim Thayil and bass player Hiro Yamamoto in Illinois.

Before you think about buying food for the week, I'd suggest you track down *Terminal Tower* (Twin/Tone) by **PERE UBU**. This collection of previously out-of-print Hearthan singles (plus a few surprises) shows this legendary experiment at their most inspired. Insanity never felt so good.

Ex-Pere Ubu lead singer David Thomas will perform with his band the **WOODEN BIRDS** (which includes Ubu alumni Allen Ravenstine and Tony Maimone) in Seattle on April 5th at 1516 2nd Ave. at 8pm.

Because bands from the United Kingdom receive so much international press, I've made it a policy not to review imports. Which means I can't tell you how great those **HULA** albums are.

SUB TEN

VARIOUS *Deep Six* compilation LP (C/Z)

PERE UBU *Terminal Tower* LP (Twin Tone)

Right Side of My Brain video (Kern)

BLACK FLAG *Who's Got the 10 1/2?* LP (SST)

SOUL ASYLUM *Made To Be Broken* LP (Twin/Tone)

MY EYE demo (Seattle)

SONIC YOUTH "Halloween" 12" single (Homestead)

SOUNDGARDEN live (Seattle)

VARIOUS *Pyrrhic Victory* cassette compilation

64 SPIDERS live guitar solos with feedback (Seattle)

Yet More Fat Evidence That Seattle Is Pumpin' Hot

The guys in **SLOW** aren't cut out of some magazine. They're just five awesome dudes with the courage to be normal jerks. Their live set at the Rainbow was rockin' and *fun* and sloppy. No cigarettes, no props, no fog machine. It's easy to see why they's the most popular teen band in Vancouver. Unfortunately, their debut EP *Against the Glass* on Zulu Records is a lot slicker than their live show. Put anybody in a studio long enough, and they'll sound stiff and contrived. See 'em live.

NEO BEATNIK DEPT

New York's **COPERNICUS** and L.A.'s **SACCHARINE TRUST** both play live, improvised music avec poetry. *Victim Of The Sky* (Sky Records) by Copernicus continues the large orchestration and holy ramblings established on his *Nothing Exists* LP. But slogans like "Bruce Springsteen is descended from bacteria!" have me convinced that this guy should go back to doing Barry White imitations. But hey, what about Saccharine Trust!!! Jazzy guitar/bass/drums and dense lyrics, not unlike the **MINUTEMEN**. Their best effort yet, *Worldbroken* (SST Records) shows us a band that's intense, intelligent, and strong enough not to snap under peer pressure. Crank the applause meter.

Monkey Business (Green Monkey Records) is yet more fat evidence that Seattle is pumpin' it out. A quick snapshot of the local pop scene, this compilation LP easily competes with its predecessors, the *Seattle Syndrome* series. Local hit-makers to watch include **DANGER BUNNY**, the **WALKABOUTS**, and **GREEN PAJAMAS**. And of course veteran rockers the **FASTBACKS** wail on the Geritol and kick out a garage anthem, "Time Passes." Despite the lame cover art, you'll want to crush and maim your way to the checkout line and *purchase*.

Meanwhile, Chicago's **NAKED RAYGUN** are afraid to try anything different. Their flag-waving thrash anthems of the past—"Bomb Shelter" and "Rat Patrol"—were pretty cool, but it's 1986 and their formula just sounds tired. Their new LP, *All Rise* (Homestead), would almost be listenable if the tall vocals of Jeff Pezzati were mixed in-yer-face where they belong. A bad mix does little to help weak material. At least one song—"Peacemaker"—shows possible signs of maturity. So who knows, maybe the next disc will blow yer face off. Meanwhile, I'll just listen to old **ALICE COOPER** and **BARRY WHITE** records. At least *they* knew how to mix up the vocals.

CAMPER VAN BEETHOVEN is *different*. America's most eccentric pop band is back for more abuse with their second LP, oddly titled *II & III* (Pitch-a-Tent). These guys throw the whole world in a blender: How about **ZZ TOP** *goes to Egypt* or a honky tonk cut-up of **SONIC YOUTH**'s "I Love Her All the Time"? Fun, wacky adventurous, uncompromising. *Cool.*

DARBY CRASH

Trendsetter, cult leader, dead punk rocker. Singer for the **GERMS**. And despite the gnarly vocal spew, a visionary poet in league with other L.A. heavies like Chris Desjardins (**FLESHEATERS**) and John and Exene Doe (**X**). *Rock n' Rule* (XES Records) is a newly issued recording of the Germs (one of the first L.A. punk bands) recorded live at the Masque Reunion, Christmas 1979. It sounds like shit. I'd recommend tracking down the out-of-print *G.I.* LP and reading the lyrics sheet. Now THAT'S cool.

wed	thur	fri F25 RHYTHM MISSION	sat S26 RHYTHM MISSION
	APRIL		
NEW FOLK MUSIC W30	MAY T.1 LOST ARCHITECTS	TBA F2	NO NEWS S3
SYMPATHY CARDS W7	FATAL CHARM T8	NO MEANS NO DIVE F9	GREEN RIVER S10
	VOLUME III T.15	MAGIC IF w/ TREY GUNN F16	BLACKWOOD LAIRD S17

ditto Tavern 5th & Bell ADDRESS 682-1080

FALLOUT PRESENTS
THE SECOND ANNUAL
WAKE UP
AND SMELL THE
PAVEMENT
STREET STYLE FREESTYLE
CONTEST

WHERE: o WASHINGTON MIDDLE o SCHOOL 20th JACKSON
WHEN: o MAY 25th o (RAIN DAY JUNE 1st)
HOW: o $2. ENTRY FEE o SIGN UP 10:00AM

LET'S HEAD TO FALLOUT!
SORRY, GOTTA PRACTICE

RJ's CUSTOM STAGE LIGHTING

RENTALS & SALES OF QUALITY EQUIPMENT AND ACCESSORIES
COMPUTERIZED LIGHTING AND CONTROL
COMPLETE PRODUCTIONS FROM CLUBS TO TOURS
ALSO, DANCES, FAIRS, FASHION, THEATRE, VIDEOS

206·622·PARS

Portnow Productions Presents

BLACK FLAG,
PAINTED WILLIE, GONE

Two Shows — 5:30 & 9:45 PM
Serbian Hall (4352 15th Ave. S.)

SAT MAY 31st
All ages welcome.

Tickets at Fallout,
Time Travelers, Cellophane Sq.
$10.50 advance

SUB ▲ POP U.S.A.

A GUIDE TO U.S. INDEPENDENTS   By Bruce Pavitt

The guys in **SLOW** aren't cut out of some magazine. They're just five awesome dudes with the courage to be normal jerks. Their live set at the Rainbow was rockin' and FUN and sloppy. No cigarettes, no props, no fog machine. It's easy to see why they're the most popular teen band in Vancouver. Unfortunately, their debut EP **Against The Glass** on Zulu Records is a lot slicker than their live show. Put anybody in a studio long enough and they'll sound stiff and contrived. See 'em live. (Zulu, 1869 W. 4th Ave., Vancouver, B.C. Canada V6J 1M4.) ◄

PHOTOGRAPH BY CAM GARRETT

NEO BEATNIK DEPT: NYC's **COPERNICUS** and LA's **SACCHARINE TRUST** both play live, improvised music avec poetry. 1) VICTIM OF THE SKY by **COPERNICUS** continues the large orchestration and holy ramblings established on his NOTHING EXISTS LP. But slogans like BRUCE SPRINGSTEEN IS DESCENDED FROM BACTERIA! have me convinced that this guy should go back to doing Barry White imitations. 2) But hey, what about **SACCHARINE TRUST!!!** Jazzy guitar/bass/drums and dense lyrics, not unlike the Minutemen. Their best effort yet, WORLD-BROKEN, shows us a band that's intense, intelligent, and strong enough not to snap under peer pressure. Crank the applause meter. (Copernicus: Sky, Box 150, Brooklyn, N.Y. 11217. See SST for Saccharine Trust.)
MONKEY BUSINESS is yet more fat evidence that Seattle is pumpin' it out. A quick snapshot of the local pop scene, this compilation LP easily competes with its predecessors, the SEATTLE SYNDROME series. Local hit-makers to watch include **DANGER BUNNY, THE WALKABOUTS,** and **GREEN PAJAMAS.** And of course veteran rockers **THE FASTBACKS** wail on the Genitol and kick out a garage anthem, TIME PASSES. Despite the lame cover art, you'll want to crush and maim your way to the checkout line and PURCHASE. (Green Monkey Records, Box 31983, Seattle, WA 98103.)

Meanwhile, Chicago's **NAKED RAYGUN** are afraid to try anything different. Their flag-waving thrash anthems of the

past — BOMBSHELTER and RAT PATROL — were pretty cool, but it's 1986 and their formula just sounds tired. Their new LP, ALL RISE, would almost be listenable if the tall vocals of Jeff Pezzati were mixed in-yer-face where they belong: a bad mix does little to help weak material. At least one song — PEACEMAKER — shows possible signs of maturity. So who knows, maybe the next disc will blow yer-face-off. Meanwhile, I'll just listen to old Alice Cooper and Barry White records. At least THEY knew how to mix up the vocals. (Homestead, P.O. Box 570, Rockville Centre, N.Y. 11571.)

CAMPER VAN BEETHOVEN is DIFFERENT. America's most eccentric pop band is back for more abuse with their second LP, oddly titled II AND III. These guys throw the whole world in a blender. How about ZZ TOP GOES TO EGYPT or a honky tonk cut-up of **SONIC YOUTH**'s I LOVE HER ALL THE TIME? Fun, wacky, adventurous, uncompromising. COOL. (Pitch-a-Tent, 1025 Broadway, Santa Cruz, CA 95062.)

DARBY CRASH: trend setter, cult leader, dead

punk rocker. Singer for the Germs. And despite the gnarly vocal spew, a visionary poet in league with other L.A. heavies like Chris Desjardins (Flesheaters) and John and Exene Doe (X). ROCK 'N' RULE is a newly issued recording of **THE GERMS** (one of the first L.A. punk bands) recorded live at the Masque Reunion, Christmas 1979. It sounds like shit. I'd recommend tracking down the out-of-print G.I. LP and reading the lyric sheet. Now THAT'S cool. (XES Records, no address.)

TOKEN SYNTH BAND REVIEW: **SHOCK THERAPY** (EP) are some hick band from Nashville that play rock 'n' roll with synthesizers. Maybe if they squeezed some PAIN and ECSTASY out of their cold machines, they could justify mixing **Korg** synthesizers with **Les Paul** guitars. But they don't. And I believe people still get lynched in Tennessee. (Metro American, Box 37044, Detroit, MI 48237.)

SST: Now that HUSKER DU has gone to the majors and The MINUTEMEN have disbanded (due to the heartbreaking death of D. Boon) L.A.'s mighty SST label is looking

for a few good bands. 1) **GONE** LET'S GET REAL, REAL GONE (LP) is the latest project from Black Flag guitarist Greg Ginn. The band is a bone-crunching instrumental combo featuring Ginn at his most restrained. Decent. 2) **DC3** THE GOOD HEX (LP) is back again, starring ex-Black Flag bass player/vocalist Dez. Their PCP induced recycling of Captain Beyond sounds slightly better the second time around. But I still don't get the joke. 3) **PAINTED WILLIE** (LP) is the latest entry in the EARLY '70s HARD ROCK sweepstakes. Blunt lyrics but the vocalist lacks power. Side two goes pop, diving into the '60s with a cover of **Love's** LITTLE RED BOOK. They coulda been a contender. But not now. 4) **ANGST** LITE LIFE (LP) is the first Bay Area signing for SST. Their disc is worth grabbing for their monster hit, NEVER GOING TO APOLOGIZE. Too many herky, jerky, quirky arrangements, though. STAY TUNED TO SST FOR THE NEXT LP BY NY's **SONIC YOUTH.** (SST, P.O. Box 1, Lawndale, CA.) **GONE** and **PAINTED WILLIE** will open for **BLACK FLAG** on May 31 at the Serbian Hall.

SUB ▲ TEN

GREEN RIVER *10,000 Things* song (C/Z) Seattle
SONIC YOUTH *Halloween* 12" single (Homestead) NYC
BLACK FLAG *Who's Got The 10½?* LP (SST) LA
CAMPER VAN BEETHOVEN *II and III* LP (Pitch-a-Tent) LA
SACCHARINE TRUST *Worldbroken* (SST) LA
MONKEY BUSINESS *compilation* LP (Green Monkey) Seattle
CRAMPS *A Date With Elvis* LP (Big Beat import) LA
BOYS NEXT DOOR *film by director Penelope Spheeris* / LA
BUTTHOLE SURFERS *video* Touch and Go
SLOW *Against The Glass* EP (Zulu) Vancouver, BC

TOKEN SYNTH BAND REVIEW

SHOCK THERAPY (EP on Metro America) are some hick band from Nashville that play rock 'n roll with synthesizers. Maybe if they squeezed some *pain* and *ecstasy* out of their cold machines, they could justify mixing Korg synthesizers with Les Paul guitars. But they don't. And I believe people still get lynched in Tennessee.

SST RECORDS

Now that **HÜSKER DÜ** has gone to the majors and the **MINUTEMEN** have disbanded due to the heartbreaking death of D. Boon, L.A.'s mighty SST label is looking for a few good bands. 1. **GONE** *Let's Get Real, Real Gone* LP is the latest project from **BLACK FLAG** guitarist Greg Ginn. The band is a bone-crushing instrumental combo featuring Ginn at his most restrained. Decent. 2. **DC3** *The Good Hex* LP is back again, starring ex-Black Flag bass player/vocalist Dez. Their PCP-induced recycling of **CAPTAIN BEYOND** sounds slightly better the second time around. But I still don't get the joke. 3. **PAINTED WILLIE** is the latest entry in the early '70s hard rock sweepstakes. Blunt lyrics, but the vocalist lacks power. Side two of *Mind Bowling* goes pop, diving into the '60s with a cover of **LOVE**'s "Little Red Book." They coulda been a contender. But not now. 4. **ANGST** *Like Life* LP is the first Bay Area signing for SST. Their disc is worth grabbing for their monster hit, "Never Going to Apologize." Too many herky, jerky, quirky arrangements, though. Stay tuned to SST for the next LP by New York's **SONIC YOUTH**.

Gone and Painted Willie will open for Black Flag on May 31 at the Serbian Hall.

SUB TEN

GREEN RIVER "10,000 Things" (C/Z)

SONIC YOUTH "Halloween" 12" single (Homestead)

BLACK FLAG *Who's Got The 10 1/2?* LP (SST)

CAMPER VAN BEETHOVEN *II & III* LP (Pitch-a-Tent)

SACCHARINE TRUST *Worldbroken* (SST)

VARIOUS *Monkey Business* compilation LP (Green Monkey)

CRAMPS *A Date With Elvis* LP (Big Bear import)

BOYS NEXT DOOR film directed by Penelope Spheeris

, home video (Touch and Go)

SLOW *Against the Glass* EP (Zulu)

Stop the World, I Want To Get Off!

FILMED IN TERRORAMA

Even from its original inception as *Search and Destroy* (San Francisco's intellectual "punk" fanzine), *Re/Search* has always focused on anti-authoritarian themes. Their latest project, *Re/Search #10*, is a large paperback titled *Incredibly Strange Films*. An excellent guide to obscure, low-budget, anti-establishment cult films, this book features interviews with various directors as well as a detailed analysis of different genres: sexploitation, biker, LSD, women in prison, mondo, and *more*. If you want to expose yourself to uninhibited creativity, unbound by the restraints of "good taste," then throw away your homework, buy this book, and get a real education.

BIG BLACK "Il Duce" b/w "Big Money" 45 (Homestead). Big Black are from Chicago. They play "vertical" and "horizontal" guitars. They are troublemakers. They will shove noise in yer face and then force you to dance to their drum machine. They are the new thing. The big thing. The God thing. They are fascists and they want big money. So give it to them.

Atoms will not split and the universe will not collide. **GET SMART!** does not threaten, provoke, or challenge. They do come up with consistently memorable pop/rock songs that are fun to hum while you're doing the dishes. Mark, Frank, and Lisa all sing. The second album by this ex-Kansas, now-Chicago, group, *Swimming With Sharks* (Fever Records), should become big and popular on college radio.

STOP THE WORLD! I WANT TO GET OFF!

Life just shouldn't be this cool. I just heard the official "Live" **SONIC YOUTH** bootleg import and I'm thinkin' "yeah, life has *meaning*." All the usual tricks are here: twisted guitar tunings and **MADONNA** records stuffed in between songs; intense dissonance; raw white soul all over the place. Half of this double LP features former drummer Bob Bert, the other half includes new boy Steve Shelley. Great package, great sound, great this, great that. Leap now or *buy*. Limited edition of 2000.

REDNECK RAVEUP

Two bluesy 'n brawlin 'n rockin' 'n ravin' LPs out now. Originating from Tucson, we've got *Under The Blue Marlin* (Frontier Records) by **NAKED PREY**. From deep down Florida way we're rockin' to *Route 33* (Twin Tone Records) by **CHARLIE PICKETT**. Both bands *blaze* with slide guitar and an American sound. Although neither band cuts as deep as the **GUN CLUB**, they're still decent, hard workin' guys who deserve your support.

HIT PARADE

In Winston/Salem, North Carolina, there exists a studio called the Drive-In. In this studio live two men. These two men—let's call them Mitch Easter and Don Dixon—have produced some of America's great pop bands: the **DB'S, R.E.M., LET'S ACTIVE, PYLON**, and the **WINDBREAKERS**. The sound here is always warm, never cold and sterile. Case in point: the *Positively Dumptruck* LP (Big Time) features guitars that chime and ring. It is beautiful. Under the direction of Don Dixon. *Positively* has to be the best-sounding pop album of '86. (This is a "rave" review.) *Rave*.

SUB ▲ POP

A GUIDE TO U.S. INDEPENDENTS
By Bruce Pavitt

■ **BIG BLACK** *IL DUCE/BIG MONEY* 45. Big Black are from Chicago. They play "ver-[b]al" and "especial" ble makers as they shove noise, interference and their force into a dance in their machine. They are one thing. The one thing God thinks they are fascists and they [don't] need money. So give it to them. (Homestead, Box 570, Rockville Center, NY 11570)

■ Atoms will not split and the Universe will not collide. **GET SMART!** does not threaten, provoke or challenge. They *do* come up with consistently memorable pop/ rock songs that are fun to hum to while you're doing the dishes. Mark, Frank and Lisa all sing. The second album by this ex-Kansas now-Chicago group, *Swimming With Sharks*, should become big 'n popular on college radio. (Fever Records, 621 S. Fourth, Philadelphia, PA 19147)

■ **STOP THE WORLD! I WANT TO GET OFF!** Life just shouldn't *be* this cool. I just heard the official "*LIVE*" **SONIC YOUTH** bootleg import and I'm thinkin' "yeah, life has MEANING." All the usual tricks are here: twisted guitar tunings and Madonna records stuffed in between songs: intense dissonance: raw white soul all over the place. Half of this double LP features former drummer Bob Bert, the other half includes new boy Steve Shelley. Great package, great sound, great this, great that. Leap now or BUY. Limited edition 2000. (Available at Time Travelers and Fallout)

■ **REDNECK RAVE-UP:** Two bluesy 'n brawlin 'n rockin' 'n ravin' LP's out NOW. Originating from Tucson, we've got *UNDER THE BLUE MARLIN* by **NAKED PREY**. From deep down Florida way we're rockin' to *ROUTE 33* by **CHARLIE PICKETT**. Both bands BLAZE with slide guitar and an American sound. Although neither band cuts as deep as The Gun Club, they're still decent, hard workin' guys who deserve your support. (NP c/o Frontier, Box 22, Sun Valley, CA 91353. CP c/o Twin Tone, 445 Oliver Ave. S., Mpls., MN 55405)

■ **HIT PARADE:** In Winston/Salem, North Carolina there exists a studio called The Drive-In. In this studio live two men. These two men — let's

call them Mitch Easter and Don Dixon — have produced some of America's great pop bands: The D.B.'s, R.E.M., Let's Active, Pylon, The Windbreakers. The sound here is always warm, never cold and sterile. CASE IN POINT: *POSITIVELY DUMPTRUCK* (LP) features guitars that chime and ring. It is beautiful. Under the direction of Don Dixon, *Positively* has to be the best sounding pop album of '86. (This is a "rave" review.) RAVE. (Big Time, 6410 Santa Monica Blvd., L.A., CA 90038)

■ Cassette compilations are a cheap and easy way for local bands to get their demos heard. *PYRRHIC VICTORY* is a great example. This ten song tape documents vital material from the Seattle underground ('80-'85) that, for economic reasons, might never have made it to vinyl. Music ranges from HEAVY (10 Minute Warning, Soundgarden) to busy "progressive rock" (Mental Mannequin). Other cult bands include: The Fags, Vexed, Colour Twigs and Skin Yard. Sharp graphics, good sound quality. (922 15th Ave., Seattle, WA 98122 $5.00 ppd.)

■ **TOTALLY WIRED:** dense, frenetic spasms from the latest in New York noise. **RAT AT RAT R** shred and bludgeon the average listener with poetic excess: *I'm senseless greed on sun-baked tar monoliths where garbage falls onto filth amongst germs stagnating hookworm ringworm syphilis . . .* Instruments include slide guitar, bowed guitar, bowed bass and violin. This band *could* be great if they took a cue from local scenemakers Sonic Youth and learned to be more dynamic: soft *and* hard, slow *and* fast, vulnerable *and* aggressive: there's *more* to life than straight black coffee. But go ahead, punish yourself and ask for it by name: *ROCK AND ROLL IS DEAD*. Long live Rat At Rat R. (Neutral, 415 Lafayette St., NYC 10003)

SUB ▲ TEN

RE/SEARCH #10 *Incredibly Strange Films* book SF
SONIC YOUTH "*LIVE*" LP (bootleg) NYC
BIG BLACK *Il Duce* 45 (Homestead) Chicago
DUMPTRUCK *Positively* LP (Big Time) Boston
PYRRHIC VICTORY *compilation* cassette Seattle
NAKED PREY *Under the Blue Marlin* LP (Frontier) LA/Tucson
CHARLIE PICKETT *Route 33* LP (Twin Tone) Miami
GET SMART! *Swimming with Sharks* LP (Fever) Chicago
RAT AT RAT R *Rock and Roll is Dead* LP (Neutral) NYC
STEVE FISK *Go at Full Throttle* demo Ellensburg, WA

FALLOUT RECORDS + SKATEBOARDS
1506 E. OLIVE WAY SEATTLE • 323-2662

The gob $hoppe

Hot June Record & Tape Sale

Nu Shooz and Moody Blues, just to name a few

Hours: Mon.-Sat. 10-9
Sunday 12-6

If You Could Call the Guys Who Have Recorded:

Blue Sky • Walt Wagner • David Peterson • Wayne Shorter
George Cables • Dave Valentin • Diane Schuur • Bochinche

YOU'D CALL US!

blue charles productions

Specializing in Contemporary Digital Recording

In Seattle: **783-6797**
In Tacoma: **272-5507**

Cassette compilations are a cheap and easy way for local bands to get their demos heard. *Pyrrhic Victory* ($5.00 ppd) is a great example. This ten-song tape documents vital material from the Seattle underground ('80–'85) that, for economic reasons, might never nave made it to vinyl. Music ranges from *heavy* (**10 MINUTE WARNING**, **SOUNDGARDEN**) to busy progressive rock (**MENTAL MANNEQUIN**). Other cult bands include: the **FAGS**, **VEXED**, **COLOUR TWIGS**, and **SKIN YARD**. Sharp graphics, good sound quality.

TOTALLY WIRED

Dense, frenetic spasms from the latest in New York noise. **RAT AT RAT R** shred and bludgeon the average listener with poetic excess: "I'm senseless greed on sunbaked tar monoliths where garbage falls onto filth amongst germs stagnating hookworm ringworm syphilis..." Instruments include slide guitar, bowed guitar, bowed bass, and violin. This band could be great if they took a cue from local scene makers **SONIC YOUTH** and learned to be more dynamic; soft and hard, slow and fast, vulnerable and aggressive. There's more to life than straight black coffee. But go ahead, punish yourself and ask for it by name: *Rock and Roll Is Dead. Long Live Rat at Rat R.* (Neutral)

SUB TEN

Re/Search #10 Incredibly Strange Films book

SONIC YOUTH *"Live"* LP (bootleg)

BIG BLACK "II Duce" 45 (Homestead)

DUMPTRUCK *Positively* LP (Big Time)

VARIOUS *Pyrrhic Victory* compilation cassette

NAKED PREY *Under the Blue Marlin* LP (Frontier)

CHARLIE PICKETT *Route 33* LP (Twin/Tone)

GET SMART! *Swimming with Sharks* LP (Fever)

RAT AT RAT R *Rock and Roll Is Dead* LP (Neutral)

STEVE FISK "Go at Full Throttle" demo

The Summer of '86

The summer of '86. More than groovy, more than awesome or radical, it's the best summer since the **RAMONES** and **TELEVISION** and **PERE UBU** and **DEVO** blew out the speakers at a neighborhood barbecue almost ten years ago. Check it out: In the past few months we've seen new releases by artists as diverse as **SONIC YOUTH**, **BIG BLACK**, **SCRATCH ACID**, the **WIPERS**, **SWANS**, and **CAMPER VAN BEETHOVEN**. 1986 is turning out to be a *great* period for new American music, a time when people are actively disowning themselves from trends, cults, movements, or other forms of mass group identity. The message is clear: It's *alright* to be totally uninhibited; to love people for who they really are; to naturally express oneself honestly and sincerely, without being a slave to peer pressure. All of which leads me up to *Rembrandt Pussyhorse* (Touch and Go) by the **BUTT-HOLE SURFERS**. The coolest record ever made, this unbridled, surreal burst of imagination is enough to erase years of indoctrination by schools and television viewing. It's finally okay to do whatever the fuck you want. We can only go up from here.

BIG BLACK come roaring out of Chicago with their first feature length monster: *Atomizer* (Homestead). With a relentless rhythm machine and noisy twin guitars that riff and riff until they're finally tossed across the room, this whirring tower of destruction leaves little room for life. Big Black stars controversial guitarist/vocalist/rock critic Steve Albini, who is a master manipulator, often giving outrageous quotes and writing even more outrageous liner notes. (I trust the man is neither a racist or a pedophile.) Albini's brash personality is a large reason for this band's cult status: so please bear that in mind when you listen to

this, an awesome though one-dimensional record that could have been stripped down to an EP. Big Black is a distinctive, important hit squad that needs to learn more about dynamics before releasing another full length album. Hit: "Kerosene".

"Hank Johnson, an old bachelor of bad axe, cut off the heads of all his chickens recently, made a bonfire of his best clothes, and killed himself with arsenic." All sorts of backwoods atrocities are noted on the inner sleeve of *Goin' to Hell in a Handbasket* (Monster) by **COUNTRY BOB AND THE BLOOD FARMERS**. From the packaging to the lyrics to the music, these boys exploit the gruesome edge of hillbilly mythology. It's all very funny, considering this band is from the suburbs of Detroit.

Independent black music from Los Angeles is noted for dense electronic dance rhythms, like the rapid-fire knob twisting of **EGYPTIAN LOVER**. For hard aggressive street raps, New York City is the scene. **RUN-D.M.C.** and **LL COOL J** rule. But there are exceptions. From L.A. comes **ICE-T**, with an iron-hard anthem called "Ya Don't Quit" (Techno Hop). The B-side of this twelve-inch has a raw, naked vocal mix, occasionally punctuated by a brutal one-chord guitar attack. "Like a pit bull rockin' on a Doberman's neck/I'm Ice-T and I'm due for respect."

ANTI-SCRUNTI FACTION Although the tedious thrash of this Midwestern group is nothing special, the fact that they're all female gives the lyrics a fresh twist: check out "Slave to My Estrogen." The album is called *Damsel in Distress* (Flipside/Unclean).

For all you young adults who want to re-live the martini and bongo lifestyle established in the late '40s

SUB ▲ POP
U S A

A GUIDE TO U.S. INDEPENDENTS
By Bruce Pavitt

THE SUMMER OF '86: MORE THAN GROOVY: MORE THAN AWESOME OR RADICAL: IT'S THE BEST SUMMER SINCE THE RAMONES AND TELEVISION AND PERE UBU AND DEVO BLEW OUT THE SPEAKERS AT A NEIGHBORHOOD BAR-B-Q ALMOST TEN YEARS AGO. CHECK IT OUT: IN THE PAST FEW MONTHS WE'VE SEEN NEW RELEASES BY ARTISTS AS DIVERSE AS SONIC YOUTH, BIG BLACK, SCRATCH ACID, THE WIPERS, SWANS AND CAMPER VAN BEETHOVEN. 1986 IS TURNING OUT TO BE A GREAT PERIOD FOR NEW AMERICAN MUSIC, A TIME WHEN PEOPLE ARE ACTIVELY DISOWNING THEMSELVES FROM TRENDS, CULTS, MOVEMENTS OR OTHER FORMS OF MASS GROUP IDENTITY. THE MESSAGE IS CLEAR: IT'S ALL RIGHT TO BE TOTALLY UNINHIBITED: TO LOVE PEOPLE FOR WHO THEY REALLY ARE: TO NATURALLY EXPRESS ONESELF HONESTLY AND SINCERELY, WITHOUT BEING A SLAVE TO PEER PRESSURE. ALL OF WHICH LEADS ME UP TO *REMBRANDT PUSSYHORSE* BY THE **BUTTHOLE SURFERS**. THE COOLEST RECORD EVER MADE, THIS UNBRIDLED, SURREAL BURST OF IMAGINATION IS ENOUGH TO ERASE YEARS OF INDOCTRINATION BY SCHOOLS AND TELEVI-

PHOTOGRAPH BY JOHN WITHERSPOON MELLENCAMP

SION VIEWING. IT'S FINALLY OK TO DO WHATEVER THE FUCK YOU WANT. WE CAN ONLY GO UP FROM HERE. (Touch and Go: Box 322, Dearborn, MI 48121)

BIG BLACK come roaring out of Chicago with their first feature length monster: ATOMIZER. With a relentless rhythm machine and noisy twin guitars that riff and riff until they're finally tossed across the room, this whirring tower of destruction leaves little room for life. **BIG BLACK** stars controversial guitarist/vocalist/rock critic Steve Albini, who is a master manipulator, often giving outrageous quotes and writing even more outrageous liner notes (I trust the man is neither a racist nor a pedophile). Albini's brash personality is a large reason for this band's cult status; so please bear that in mind when you listen to this, an awesome though one-dimensional record that could have been stripped down to an EP. **BIG BLACK** is a distinctive, important hit squad that needs to learn more about dynamics before releasing another full length album. Hit: KEROSENE. (Homestead: Box 570, Rockville Ctr, NY 11570)

HANK JOHNSON, AN OLD BACHELOR OF BAD AXE, CUT OFF THE HEADS OF ALL HIS CHICKENS RECENTLY, MADE A BONFIRE OF HIS BEST CLOTHES AND KILLED HIMSELF WITH ARSENIC. All sorts of backwoods atrocities are noted on the inner sleeve of GOIN' TO HELL IN A HANDBASKET by **Country Bob and the Blood Farmers**. From the packaging to the lyrics to the music, these boys exploit the gruesome edge of hillbilly mythology. It's all very funny, considering this band is from the suburbs of Detroit. (Manster: Box 1394, Royal Oak, MI 48067)

DRAWING BY GREGORY MOORE

ANTI SCRUNTI FACTION: although the tedious thrash of this midwestern group is nothing special, the fact that they're all female gives the lyrics a fresh twist: check out SLAVE TO MY ESTROGEN. The album is called DAMSEL IN DISTRESS. (Flipside/Unclean: Box 725, Sand Springs, OK 74063)

For all you young adults who want to re-live the martini and bongo lifestyle established in the late '40s and '50s, finish your olive now, and pick up HE'S FUNNY THAT WAY, an intimate, swingin' four-song cassette by Ms. **Jan Brock**. Like Doris Day, side one plays it sweet and straight. Flip it over for a sultry, smoke-filled nightclub scene from some trashy FILM NOIR. Excellent package and production. (K: Box 7154, Olympia, WA 98507)

The **Wipers**, a band, who, in the right social circles, is considered to be God, have just released their fourth studio LP, LAND OF THE LOST. Recording since '78, the **Wipers** have released a series of records (including three singles and one live LP) that stand up, ultimately, as the most powerfully heartfelt, honest tegrity and refusal to compromise, the **Wipers** have yet to filter their way into mainstream popularity. I can only hope that one day, perhaps even today, the **Wipers** will be recognized as a great American rock 'n' roll band, paralleled by heavyweights such as Creedence, the Stooges.

> "i can only hope that one day the WIPERS will be recognized as a great American rock 'n' roll band

and true collection of rock 'n' roll ever released from the Pacific Northwest. Because of their staunch in and early Ramones. As for the record, Land of the Lost has some great material, like THE SEARCH and DIFFERENT WAYS, but is not a great album. The intimate vocal presence that made OVER THE EDGE an instant classic is missing from far too many songs. Land of the Lost is simply more evidence that the **Wipers**, once they finally put out a greatest hits album, will prove, once and for all, that God is NOT dead. (Restless: P.O. Box 2428, El Segundo, CA 90245-1528)

PHOTOGRAPH BY CAM GARRETT

Independent black music from LA is noted for dense electronic dance rhythms like the rapid fire knob twisting of Egyptian Lover. For hard, aggressive street raps, NYC is the scene: Run DMC and LL Cool J rule. But there are exceptions. From LA comes **Ice T** with an iron hard anthem called YA DON'T QUIT. The B-side of this twelve-inch has a raw, naked vocal mix, occasionally punctuated by a brutal one-chord guitar attack. LIKE A PIT BULL ROCKIN ON A DOBERMAN'S NECK / I'M ICE T / AND I'M DUE FOR RESPECT (Techno Hop: 6209 Santa Monica Blvd. Hollywood. CA 90038)

SUMMER OF LOVE: EVOL is the latest testament from New York's Sonic Youth. With an entire arsenal of raggedly tuned guitars, this group creates infinite beauty out of the most abrasive guitar textures available. EVOL, a great record, is more subdued, but ultimately more varied than any previous release: there's even a few attempts at real singing. This is a slow, sparkling "pop" record by one of the most consistently challenging and innovative bands in the world. Hit: Expressway To Yr. Skull. (SST: Box 1, Lawndale, CA 90260)

SUB ▲ TEN

BUTTHOLE SURFERS *Rembrandt Pussyhorse* LP (Touch and Go) nomadic lifestyle
SONIC YOUTH *EVOL* LP (SST) NYC
BEAT HAPPENING *New Girl* demo Olympia
BIG BLACK *Atomizer* LP (Homestead) Chicago
WIPERS *Land of the Lost* LP (Restless) Portland
ICE T *Ya Don't Quit* 12" single (Techno Hop) LA
FEAST live and like totally heavy Seattle
MANTRONIX *Needle to the Groove* 12" single (Sleeping Bag) NYC
JAN BROCK *He's Funny That Way* cassette (K) Olympia
SIR MIX-A-LOT live and like totally computerized Seattle

July Special
16 Track Recording
8 hours for $150.00

mention this ad, book during July

STUDIO
9620 16th S.W.
SEATTLE, WA 98106

ONE RECORDERS
206/763-4560

CasCioppo Brothers
ITALIAN MEAT MARKET

"Number One Italian Sausage In Town"
John Owen Seattle P-I

Cascioppo Brothers Meats is barbecue headquarters. Located at 2364 NW 80th en route to Golden Gardens, we feature homemade smoked beef jerky, salami, pepperoni, marinated flank steak and of course our famous Italian Sausage. Cool down with our ice cold beer prices (weekly specials!)

206-784-6121

SALE

Rock Fashion Definitely Bitchin'!

JHAD EXPERIENCE
912 ALASKAN WAY SEATTLE WA 98104 624-0960

and '50s, finish your olive now, and pick up *He's Funny That Way* (K Records), an intimate, swingin' four-song cassette by Ms. **JAN BROCK**. Like **DORIS DAY**, side one plays it sweet and straight. Flip it over for a sultry, smoke-filled nightclub scene from some trashy film noir. Excellent package and production.

The **WIPERS**, a band, which, in the right social circles, is considered to be God, has just released its fourth studio LP, *Land of the Lost* (Restless). Recording since '78, the Wipers have released a series of records (including three singles and one live LP) that stand up, ultimately, as the most powerfully heartfelt, honest, and true collection of rock 'n roll ever released from the Pacific Northwest. Because of their staunch integrity and refusal to compromise, the Wipers have yet to filter their way into mainstream popularity. I can only hope that one day, perhaps even today, the Wipers will be recognized as a great American rock 'n roll band, paralleled by heavyweights such as **CREEDENCE**, the **STOOGES**, and early **RAMONES**. As for the record, *Land of the Lost* has some great material, like "The Search" and "Different Ways," but is not a great album. The intimate vocal presence that made "Over the Edge" an instant classic is missing from far too many songs. *Land of The Lost* is simply more evidence that the Wipers, once they finally put out a greatest hits album, will prove, once and for all, that God is *not* dead.

SUB TEN

BUTTHOLE SURFERS, *Rembrandt Pussyhorse* LP (Touch and Go)

SONIC YOUTH *Evol* LP (SST) NYC

BEAT HAPPENING "New Girl" demo

BIG BLACK *Atomizer* LP (Homestead)

WIPERS *Land of the Lost* LP (Restless)

ICE-T "Ya Don't Quit" 12" single (Techno Hop)

FEAST live and, like, totally heavy (Seattle)

MANTRONIX "Needle to the Groove" 12" single (Sleeping Bag)

JAN BROCK *He's Funny That Way* cassette (K)

SIR MIX-A-LOT live and, like, totally computerized (Seattle)

Pass the Espresso

MEAT PUPPETS *Out My Way* EP (SST Records). From Phoenix, the Meat Puppets continue their journey into Southwestern country/rock 'n roll/psychedelia. Of course you could just as easily skip this, chew on some peyote and listen to old **GRATEFUL DEAD** records. This is their most commercial effort to date.

SACCHARINE TRUST We Became Snakes LP (SST Records). And Saccharine Trust continues to redefine what it means to be beat in the '80s. Jazzy free-flowing arrangements fronted by poet/preacher Joaquin Brewer. Pass the espresso.

YO LA TENGO *Ride the Tiger* LP (Coyote). There's been quite the buzz on this East Coast pop quartet and, yeah, I can see it. No rave or anything, but these college kids in cowboy hats have something goin' on.

SCRATCH ACID: *Just Keep Eating* LP (Rabid Cat). Disappointing followup to the mighty *Scratch Acid* EP, easily the most rockin' record of '85. On this, the songs and performances are good, but no time was spent at the mixing board. The sound is very flat, very dry, and lacks any kind of depth or vitality. I think they spent more time on the limited edition package (way cool) than they did on the music itself.

UTFO "We Work Hard) 12" single (Select Records). This is the sing/dance/rap trio that brought you last year's biggest dance bust: "Hangin' Out." Well, they're back in full force with a relentless percussive workout, inspired by D.C.-area go-go bands like **TROUBLE FUNK**. Tighten up and *go* for it.

DIE KREUZEN *October File* LP (Touch and Go). Spooky production this time around from Milwaukee's heaviest. A bog boot above most of the thrash/metal army they've successfully escaped from. Cool package. Yet another supreme Touch and Go product.

BIG STICK "Drag Racing" 45 (Recess Records). Two mop tops cut it up on this ultra-hip and essential 45. Disorienting, yes; random tapes and weird guitar. He goes crazy when she talks about her tube top. Expect a 4-song EP out on Rough Trade UK.

LEAVING TRAINS *Kill Tunes* LP (SST). Totally great, teetering, slobbering rock 'n roll anthems that will quickly define your summer. Act now. Roots rave-up stuff like the **PONTIAC BROTHERS** and **NAKED PREY**, only better. Totally rocks, man, totally.

MOJO NIXON AND SKID ROPER *Frenzy* LP (Restless). I don't know a damn thing about these guys. I do know that everybody in town seems to be bootlegging cassette copies of this thing, and it's quickly turning into the cult hit of the summer. Briefly, Mojo Nixon is an extremely demented, totally rockin' street musician who, along with sidekick Skid Roper, plays furiously funny, on-the-spot anthems about feeling existential/standing outside of Winchell's, etc. Hey, dig me, Mojo Nixon rules.

MY DAD IS DEAD *...And He's Not Gonna Take it Any More* LP (St. Valentine Records). Cleveland scene maker Mark Edwards takes the one-man band approach. A diverse mix of introspective pop/rock; most effective when accompanied by real drums. This is the ultimate do-it-yourself project.

THE REAL ROXANNE WITH HITMAN HOWIE TEE "Bang Zoom (Let's Go Go)" 12" single (Select). For my money, this is the first hip hop/go-go/industrial/dub fusion yet. Although the whole thing falls apart when they try and cut Bugs Bunny cartoons into the mix, this is still a fascinating hybrid, and a good indicator of where the underground black music scene is going.

SUB▲POP USA

A GUIDE TO U.S. INDEPENDENTS

By Bruce Pavitt

> "Run and D.M.C. are the two hardest rappers in New York City which means the world. [*Raising Hell*] has to be the heaviest, toughest and believe it or not most intelligent album of the summer and if you don't think 'It's Tricky' is the toughest jam of the year you might as well go back to your Talking Heads collection."

MEAT PUPPETS: Out My Way EP. From Phoenix, the MEAT PUPPETS continue their journey into southwestern country/rock 'n' roll/psychedelia. Of course you could just as easily skip this, chew on some peyote and listen to old Grateful Dead records. This is their most commercial effort to date. (SST: Box 1, Lawndale, CA 90260)

[The Meat Puppets will be at the Central Tavern on August 9 at 9pm.]

Cris Kirkwood
Derrick Bostrom
Curt Kirkwood
(bottom to top)

DIE KREUZEN: October File LP. Spooky production this time around from Milwaukee's heaviest. A big boot above most of the thrash/metal army they've successfully escaped from. Cool package. Yet another supreme Touch and Go product. (Touch and Go: Box 433, Dearborn, MI 48121)

SACCHARINE TRUST: We Became Snakes LP. And SACCHARINE TRUST continues to redefine what it means to be *beat* in the '80s. Jazzy free-flowing arrangements fronted by poet/preacher Joaquin Brewer. Pass the espresso. (SST)

YO LA TENGO: Ride the Tiger LP. There's been quite the buzz on this East Coast pop quartet and yeah, I can see it, no rave or anything but these college kids in cowboy hats have something goin' on. (Coyote: Box 112, uptown Hoboken, NJ 07030)

SCRATCH ACID: Just Keep Eating LP. Disappointing follow-up to the mighty SCRATCH ACID EP, easily the most rockin' record of '85. On this, the songs and performances are good, but no time was spent at the mixing board. The sound is very flat, very dry and lacks any kind of depth or vitality. I think they spent more time on the limited edition package (way cool) than they did on the music itself. (Rabid Cat: Box 49263, Austin, TX 78765)

UTFO: We Work Hard 12" single. This is the sing/dance/rap trio that brought you last year's biggest dance bust: *Hangin' Out.* Well, they're back in full force with a relentless percussive workout, inspired by D.C. area *go-go* bands like Trouble Funk. Tighten up and GO for it. (Select: 175 5th Ave., NYC 10010)

BIG STICK: Drag Racing 45. Two mop tops cut it up on this ultra-hip and essential 45. Disorienting, yes: random tapes and weird guitar. *He* goes crazy when *she* talks about her tube top. Expect a 4-song EP out on Rough Trade U.K. (Recess: 26-10 18th St., Astoria, NY 11102)

THE LEAVING TRAINS: Kill Tunes LP. Totally great, teetering, slobbering rock 'n' roll anthems that will quickly define your summer if you act *now.* Roots rave-up stuff like the Pontiac Bros. and Naked Prey only better. Totally man, rocks, man, *totally.*

[Leaving Trains will be at the Central Tavern on Aug. 1 with Room 9.]

MOJO NIXON AND SKID ROPER: Frenzy LP. I don't know a damn thing about these guys. I do know that everybody in town seems to be bootlegging cassette copies of this thing and it's quickly turning into the cult hit of the summer. Briefly, Mojo Nixon is an extremely demented, totally rockin' street musician who, along with sidekick Skid Roper, plays furiously funny, on-the-spot anthems about *feeling existential / standing out-* side of Winchell's, etc. Hey, dig me, MOJO NIXON rules. (Restless: 1750 East Holly Ave., P.O. Box 2428, El Segundo, CA 90245)

MY DAD IS DEAD: and he's not gonna take it any more LP. Cleveland scene maker Mark Edwards takes the one-man-band approach. A diverse mix of introspective pop/rock: most effective when accompanied by real drums. This is the ultimate Do It Yourself project. (St. Valentine: Box 79116, Cleveland, OH 44107)

THE REAL ROXANNE (WITH HITMAN HOWIE TEE): Bang Zoom (Let's Go Go) 12" single. For my money, this is the first hip hop/go-go/industrial/dub fusion yet. Although the whole thing falls apart when they try and cut *Bugs Bunny* cartoons into the mix, this is still a fascinating hybrid and a good indicator of where the underground black music scene is going. (Select)

RUN-DMC Raising Hell LP. Along with the awesome L.L. Cool J, Run and DMC are the two hardest rappers in New York City which means *the world.* Along with Jam Master Jay doing abnormal and surreal things with two turntables they've got all sorts of ROCK guitar stuff all over this record and they even do a bitchin' cover of *Walk This Way* featuring those two white guys from Aerosmith. And this record rocks way harder than their last one and it has to be the heaviest, toughest and believe it or not most *intelligent* album of the summer and if you don't think *It's Tricky* is the toughest jam of the year you might as well go back to your Talking Heads collection. (Profile: 1775 Broadway, NYC 10019)

SUB TEN

RUN-D.M.C. *Raising Hell* LP (Profile). Along with the awesome **LL COOL J**, Run and D.M.C. are the two hardest rappers in New York City, which means the world. Along with Jam Master Jay doing abnormal and surreal things with two turntables, they've got all sorts of *rock* guitar stuff all over this record; they even do a bitchin' cover of "Walk This Way" featuring those two white guys from **AEROSMITH.** This record rocks way harder than their last one, and has to be the heaviest, toughest, and, believe it or not, most intelligent album of the summer. If you don't think "It's Tricky" is the toughest jam of the year, you might as well go back to your **TALKING HEADS** collection.

SUB TEN

RUN-D.M.C. *Raising Hell* LP (Profile)

MOJO NIXON AND SKID ROPER (please come to Seattle)

LEAVING TRAINS *Kill Tunes* LP (SST)

BIG STICK "Drag Racing" 45 (Recess)

DIE KREUZEN *October File* LP (Touch and Go)

UTFO "We Work Hard" 12" single (Select)

GIRL TROUBLE live sex on stage (Tacoma)

GREEN RIVER "Together We'll Never" demo (Seattle)

MY DAD IS DEAD *..And He's Not Gonna Take it Any More* (St. Valentine)

YO LA TENGO *Ride the Tiger* LP (Coyote)

Hey Lois, Is This White Trash or What?

At first listen, **DINOSAUR** sounds like a mess. **NEIL YOUNG** on top of **LED ZEPPELIN** on top of arty lyrics like: "The world/It melts like gravy." But the sloppiness and awkwardness is what ultimately makes this such a cool disc. Their 45 (Homestead) features two hits: "Repulsion" (from their LP) and "Bulbs of Passion." This is one of those off-kilter, creeper records that sounds good today but great tomorrow. Awesome pic sleeve, too.

No brakes, cement truck, downhill. **URGE OVER-KILL** crushes the crowd with *Strange, I...*, a 5-song EP out on Chicago's Ruthless label. This is smart, loud, thrashy, live, raw, and nobody's got a driver's license.

From the fertile hills of West Virginia comes a man who is weird and crude and scary as hell. *Out to Hunch* (Norton) documents bedroom rockabilly recordings created by **HASIL ADKINS** between 1955 and 1965. Hail is fond of singing about girls, their heads, and how he would like to hang those heads on his wall. A tragic product of too much inbreeding. Hey Lois, is this white trash or what?

Baby...You're Bummin' My Life Out in a Supreme Fashion (Epitaph) Hey, with a title like that, you gotta take notice. Hollywood's **THELONIOUS MONSTER** play guitars: four guitars, free jazz, blues, Hendrix wah-wah, whatever. They've also got millions of friends who like to play horns. This is jazz. This is rock. This is crazy shit about heroin and gin and not paying your rent.

Detroit's Touch and Go label has released a record by

THE VIRGIN PRUNES, a Scottish band. The B-side of this 12" single is an elaborate, bizarre mix that will certainly clear the dance floor. The A-side, "Lovelornalimbo," features a lot of embarrassing vocals by some guy who thinks he's David Bowie.

NICK CAVE, former wildman with Australia's legendary **BIRTHDAY PARTY**, continues his fascination with roots American music. **CASH**, **LEADBELLY**, and **ORBISON** are covered on his latest 12" single on Homestead. "The Singer" is a haunting country/pop lament, while "Black Betty" is a stark and raving interpretation of the Leadbelly blues classic. Great production and sound on this must-have disc.

Totally electronic groove disco is now the underground black sound in both Miami and L.A. For a real hit, try the latest 12-inch from the Southern California axis; an abrasive cruiser called "It's Time to Rock" (Jam City Records) by **MATRIX**. It's totally disposable and devoid of soul, but it's still the purest physical rush of the month. And that's entertainment.

LIVE SKULL couldn't write a real song if they wanted to. Which is okay by me; this modern New York City guitar band is more concerned with texture, mood, and atmosphere. But their latest LP, *Cloud One* (Homestead), falls short of their tremendous promise by producing everything to sound one-dimensional. By being more creative in the studio, this band could emphasize the rich sensuality of their music. Be sure to check out the brilliantly thrashy cover sleeve.

SAVAGE REPUBLIC has a mini LP out, *Trudge*. Although the band is from L.A., this beautifully packaged record is available only as a Belgian import.

SUB POP U.S.A.

A GUIDE TO U.S. INDEPENDENTS

By Bruce Pavitt

From the fertile hills of West Virginia comes a man who is weird and crude and scary as hell. OUT TO HUNCH documents bedroom rockabilly recordings created by HASIL ADKINS between 1955 and 1965. Hasil is fond of singing about girls, their heads, and how he likes to hang those heads on his wall. A tragic product of too much inbreeding.

Hey Lois, is this white trash or what? (Norton: Box 646, Cooper Station, NYC, NY 10003.)

BABY...YOU'RE BUMMIN' MY LIFE OUT IN A SUPREME FASHION: Hey, with a title like that, you gotta take notice. Hollywood's THELONIUS MONSTER play guitars: *four guitars*: free jazz, blues, Hendrix wah-wah, whatever. They've also got millions of friends who like to play *horns*. This is

NO brakes, cement truck, downhill. URGE OVERKILL crushes the crowd with *Strange, I....*, a 5-song EP out on Chicago's Ruthless label. This is smart, loud, trashy, live, raw and nobody's got a driver's license. (Ruthless: Box 1458, Evanston, IL 60204.)

jazz. This is rock. This is crazy shit about heroin and gin and not paying your rent. (Epitaph: 3355 W. El Segundo Blvd., Hawthorne, CA 90250.)

Detroit's Touch and Go label has released a record by the VIRGIN PRUNES, a Scottish band. The b-side of this 12" single is an elaborate, bizarre mix that will certainly clear the dance floor. The a-side, *Lovelornalimbo*, features a lot of embarrassing vocals by some guy who thinks he's David Bowie. (Touch and Go: Box 433, Dearborn, MI 48121)

NICK CAVE, former wildman with Australia's legendary Birthday Party, continues his fascination with roots American music. Cash, Leadbelly and Orbison are covered on his latest 12" single on Homestead. *The Singer* is a haunting country/pop lament, while Black Betty is a stark and raving interpretation of the Leadbelly blues classic. Great production and sound on this must-have disc. (Home-

stead: Box 570, Rockville Centre, NY 11571-0570.)

Totally electronic groove-disco is now *the* underground black sound in both Miami and L.A. For a real hit, try the latest 12-inch from the Southern California axis: an abrasive cruiser called *It's Time to Rock* by MATRIX. It's totally disposable and devoid of soul, but it's still the purest physical rush of the month. And that's entertainment. (Jam City: 6209 Santa Monica Blvd., Hollywood, CA 90038.)

LIVE SKULL couldn't write a real song if they wanted to. Which is OK by me: this modern NYC guitar band is more concerned with *texture*, *mood* and *atmosphere*. But their latest LP, *Cloud One*, falls short of their tremendous promise by producing everything to sound one-dimensional. By being more creative in the studio, this band could emphasize the rich sensuality of their music . . . Be sure to check out the brilliantly trashy cover sleeve. (Homestead.)

SAVAGE REPUBLIC has a mini LP out: *Trudge*. Although the band is from L.A., this beautifully packaged record is available only as a Belgian import. Recorded between the mighty tribal/industrial *Tragic Figures* LP and the subdued *Ceremony*

LP, this record reaches a compromise fans of both sounds can live with. Marching drums, chants, hypnotically tuned guitars. A worldly, exotic travelogue. (Import.)

Every so often a band from the "middle of nowhere" saves up their pennies and puts out a few hundred copies of a 45 hoping that maybe a handful of friends will buy their record. Such is the case: FOR/AGAINST from Lincoln, Nebraska, have an excellent *droning* guitar pop single: *Autocrat/It's a Lie*. The inner label is silk screened by hand, limited edition of 250. Seriously worth ordering (also: look for upcoming LP on L.A.'s Independent Project label). (Republic: Box 5794, Lincoln, NE 68505.)

At first listen, DINOSAUR sounds like a mess. Neil Young on top of Led Zeppelin on top of arty lyrics like: *the world /it melts like gravy.* But the sloppiness and awkwardness is what ultimately makes this such a cool disc. Their 45 features two hits: *Repulsion* (from their LP) and *Bulbs of Passion*. This is one of those off-kilter, creeper records that sounds good today but great tomorrow. Awesome pic sleeve, too. (Homestead.)

SUB TEN

DINOSAUR *Repulsion 45 (Homestead) Boston*
SAVAGE REPUBLIC *Trudge EP (Bias) L.A.*
NICK CAVE *The Singer 12" single (Homestead)*
FOR/AGAINST *It's a Lie 45 (Republic) Lincoln*
MATRIX *It's Time to Rock 12" single (Jam City) L.A.*
HASIL ADKINS *Out to Hunch LP (Norton) W. Virginia*
ROOM 9 *various studio demos Seattle*
THELONIOUS MONSTER *Baby . . . You're Bummin' My Life Out In a Supreme Fashion LP (Epitaph) Hollywood*
URGE OVERKILL *Strange, I.... EP (Ruthless) Chicago*

"At first listen, Dinosaur sounds like a mess. Neil Young on top of Led Zeppelin on top of arty lyrics like: "the world/ it melts like gravy." But the sloppiness and awkwardness is what ultimately makes this such a cool disc. Their 45 features two hits: "Repulsion" (from their LP) and "Bulbs of Passion." This is one of those off-kilter, creeper records that sounds good today but great tomorrow."

Recorded between the mighty tribal/industrial *Tragic Figures* LP and the subdued *Ceremony* LP, this record reaches a compromise fans of both sounds can live with. Marching drums, chants, hypnotically tuned guitars; a worldly, exotic travelogue.

Every so often a band from the "middle of nowhere" saves up their pennies and puts out a few hundred copies of a 45, hoping that maybe a handful of friends will buy their record. Such is the case here. **FOR/AGAINST**, from Lincoln, Nebraska, have an excellent droning guitar pop single: "Autocrat" b/w "It's a Lie." The inner label is silk-screened by hand in a limited edition of 250. Seriously worth ordering. Also look for an upcoming LP on L.A.'s Independent Project label.

SUB TEN

DINOSAUR "Repulsion" 45 (Homestead)

SAVAGE REPUBLIC *Trudge* EP (Bias)

NICK CAVE "The Singer" 12" single (Homestead)

FOR/AGAINST "It's a Lie" 45 (Republic)

MATRIX "It's Time to Rock" 12" single (Jam City)

HASIL ADKINS *Out to Hunch* LP (Norton)

ROOM 9 various studio demos (Seattle)

THELONIOUS MONSTER *Baby...You're Bummin' My Life Out In a Supreme Fashion* LP (Epitaph)

URGE OVERKLLL *Strange, I...* EP (Ruthless)

I Hear You Want Something Really Twisted

GOD

The new **GREEN RIVER** 45 ($2.00) rocks like holy hell. "Together We'll Never" is a heavy **STOOGES** rip-off. "Ain't Nothin' To Do" is an obscure **DEAD BOYS** cover. Although it suffers from a lack of originality, the intensity of the band comes through with atomic force. The production, with the vocals shoved up front, has more presence than anything on their *Come on Down* LP, and the package, exhibiting the full glory of singer Mark Arm's manliness, is a bold, clever, low-budget design. On green vinyl.

Just when you hoped that thrash was dead, out comes Seattle's **ACCUSED**, wielding various weapons and rushing at 1,000,000,000,000 an hour. Vocalist Blaine, formerly with the **FARTZ**, is a very sick man and should either be locked up or given a recording contract. I double if you'll find a more manic record this year. The name of the LP is *The Return of Martha Splatterhead* (Subcore).

BURN

Some people believe that personal growth and maturity involves becoming more conservative, more predictable, and, ultimately, more bland. Well, those people can fucking die. Like the **DREAM SYNDICATE**. Their new LP, *Out of the Grey,* has about as much character as a junior salesman for the Wonder Bread corporation. Although the early Syndicate material was a **VELVET UNDERGROUND** rip-off, at least it rocked. Songs like "Halloween" showed real emotion, real intensity. *Out of the Grey* is dull; stuffed with trite lyrics and predictable guitar wanking. The production is bland and commercial. Highly recommended to those people who are divorced from sensations or life.

WHY THE DEAD MILKMEN ARE SO COOL

1. They don't wear black. 2. They're from Philadelphia. 3. They're just regular guys having *fun.* 4. They write the funniest lyrics of anyone around except for maybe **CAMPER VAN BEETHOVEN.** 5. Their new album, *Eat Your Paisley* (Fever/Restless), doesn't have any throwaway novelty silliness like their last record. And you can sing along. 6. So get it.

BUT THE NEW FEELIES ALBUM

Six years ago, four gawky nerds from New Jersey released a transcendent, original pop classic called *Crazy Rhythms.* It was distinguished by layered, spinning guitar and percussion. Now, after hiding out and occasionally playing with other Hoboken bands, the **FEELIES** are back with a beautifully hypnotic LP, *The Good Earth* (Coyote/Twin Tone). Although the sound has mellowed, it's still driving and propulsive to the point of dizziness and blackout. So buy ten of 'em.

Oh yeah, the new **SQUIRREL BAIT** 45 rocks almost as hard as Green River. It's called "Slake Train Coming" and it's out on Homestead.

Now that all of the art/punk bands like **BIG BLACK, SWANS,** and **SONIC YOUTH** have left Homestead, it seams that Homestead is focusing its attention on flannel-shirt garage rock. Unpretentious stuff from normal guys. The most promising of these normal bands has to be **OUTNUMBERED,** an underrated group from Champaign, Illinois. Their second LP, *Holding the Grenade Too Long,* is as good as their debut, and cuts through with intelligent, melodic rockers, not unlike early **JAM** (minus the British accents). The

SUB POP USA

A GUIDE TO U.S. INDEPENDENTS

By Bruce Pavitt

GOD: the new **GREEN RIVER** 45 rocks like holy hell. **Together We'll Never** is a heavy Stooges rip-off, **Ain't Nothin' To Do** is an obscure Dead Boys cover. Although it suffers from a lack of originality, the intensity of the band comes through with atomic force. The production, with the vocals shoved up front, has more presence than anything on their **Come On Down** LP, and the package, exhibiting the full glory of singer Mark Arm's manliness, is a bold, clever, low-budget design. On green vinyl. ($2 c/o Box 85396, Seattle, WA 98145.)

Just when you hoped that THRASH was dead, out comes Seattle's **ACCUSED** wielding various weapons and rushing at 1,000,000,000,000 miles an hour. Vocalist Blaine, formerly with the Fartz, is a very sick man and should either be locked up or given a recording contract. I doubt if you'll find a more manic record this year. The name of the LP is **The return of Martha Splatterhead**. (Subcore: 2006 35th Ave. W., Seattle, WA 98199.)

BURN: some people believe that personal growth and maturity involves becoming more conserva- tive, more predictable, and, ulti- mately, more bland. Well, those people can fucking die. Like **THE DREAM SYNDICATE**. Their new LP **Out of the Grey** has about as much character as a junior sales- man for the Wonder Bread cor- poration. Although the early Syn- dicate material was a Velvet Un- derground rip off, at least it rock- ed. Songs like Halloween show- ed real emotion, real intensity. **Out of the Grey** is dull, stuffed with inane lyrics and predictable guitar wanking. The production

is bland and commercial. Highly recommended to those people who are divorced from sensation or life. (Big Time.)

WHY THE DEAD MILKMEN ARE SO COOL: 1/ they don't wear black. 2/ they're from Philadel- phia. 3/ they're just regular guys having FUN. 4/ they write the funniest lyrics of anyone around except for maybe Camper Van Beethoven. 5/ their new al- bum, **Eat Your Paisley**, doesn't have any throw-away novelty sil- liness like their last record. And you can sing along. 6/ so get it. (Fever/Restless.)

BUY THE NEW FEELIES AL- BUM: six years ago, four gawky nerds from New Jersey released a transcendent, original pop classic called **Crazy Rhythms**. It was distinguished by layered, spinning guitar and percussion. Now, after hiding out and occa- sionally playing with other Hobo- ken bands, the **FEELIES** are back with a beautifully hypnotic LP, **The Good Earth**. Although the sound has mellowed, it's still driving and propulsive to the point of dizziness and blackout. So buy ten of 'em. (Coyote/Twin Tone.)

Oh yeah, the new **SQUIRREL BAIT** 45 rocks almost as hard as **GREEN RIVER**. It's called **Slake Train Coming** and it's out on Homestead.

Now that all of the art/punk bands like Big Black, Swans and Sonic Youth have left Home- stead, it seems that Homestead is focusing its attention on flan- nel-shirt garage rock. Unpreten- tious stuff from normal guys. The most promising of these normal

bands has to be the **OUTNUM- BERED**, an underrated group from Champaign, IL. Their sec- ond LP, **Holding the Grenade Too Long**, is as good as their debut and cuts through with intelli- gent, melodic rockers, not unlike early **Jam** (minus the British ac- cents). The Outnumbered look normal and sound normal. They're worth getting to know. (Homestead.)

NOISE: O.K. so I hear you want something really twisted. Something that will get you fired from your job. Something that will make your parents lock the door for- ever. Well, I'd recommend the **Groovy Hate Fuck** EP by **PUSSY GALORE**. It's nasty, it's gnarly, and it's totally twisted. This would result in the immediate loss of my posi- tion at The Rocket. Sorry, really can't tell you more. [ABOVE 901 O.S. NW. Washington, D.C. 20001]

SUBTEN

SUB POP 100 *various god like shit LP Seattle (SUB POP)*
GREEN RIVER *Together We'll Never 45 Seattle (Green River)*
PUSSY GALORE *Groovy Hate Fuck EP D.C. (Shove)*
FEELIES *The Good Earth LP Hoboken (Coyote)*
ACCUSED *Return of Martha Splatterhead LP Seattle (Subcore)*
SQUIRREL BAIT *Slake Train Coming 45 Louisville (Homestead)*
DEAD MILKMEN *Eat Your Paisley LP Philadelphia (Fever)*
OUTNUMBERED *Holding the Grenade Too Long - LP Champaign (Homestead)*
SOUNDGARDEN *total fucking Godhead live Seattle*
451 *Seattle's coolest mag =2*

WARNING: Hey everybody I've been working on this SUB POP compilation for a whole year now and it's finally out and you know what? It really sucks. So what if it's got every great band in the world, huh? Cause it really sucks. And who cares if it's got hit after hit, anyway? Right? Cause I know we're all bored with Sonic Youth and the Wipers and Scratch Acid and Steve Albini and those darned U-Men and Skinny Puppy and Savage Republic and Steve Fisk and ya know that Japanese girl group Shonen Knife al- ways did kinda suck. Right? So don't buy this record. Because just between you and me, it really sucks. (LP or chrome cassette shipped to anywhere in the world for only 8 bucks. SUB POP: Box 20645, Seattle, WA 98102.

Sub Pop 100 was the first record released on the Sub Pop record label. The compilation came out in 1986, and was meant to compliment the earlier *Sub Pop* mix tapes. I think it holds up well; it features one of my favorite Sonic Youth tracks of all time, "Kill Yr Idols", as well as "Gila" by the U-Men— Seattle's greatest band in the mid '80s. The record sold 5000 copies, which at the time, in the indie world, was like having a gold record.

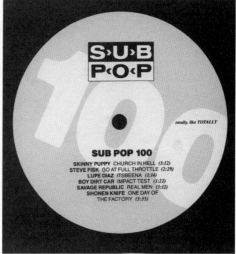

Outnumbered look normal and sound normal. They're worth getting to know.

NOISE

Okay, so I hear you want something really twisted. Something that will get you fired from your job. Something that will make your parents lock the door forever. Well, I'd recommend the *Groovy Hate Fuck* LP (Shove) by **PUSSY GALORE**. It's noisy, it's gnarly, and it's totally twisted. it's the coolest rock 'n roll record you'll ever hear. Reprinting the song titles would result in the immediate loss of my position at *the Rocket*. Sorry, really can't tell you more.

SUB TEN

VARIOUS *Sub Pop 100* various god shit LP (Sub Pop Records)

GREEN RIVER "Together We'll Never" 45 (Green River)

PUSSY GALORE *Groovy Hate Fuck* EP (Shove)

FEELIES *The Good Earth* LP (Coyote)

ACCUSED *The Return of Martha Splatterhead* LP (Subcore)

SQUIRREL BAIT "Slake Train Coming" 45 (Homestead)

DEAD MILKMEN *Eat Your Paisley* LP (Fever)

OUTNUMBERED *Holding the Grenade Too Long* LP (Homestead)

SOUNDGARDEN total fucking godhead live in Seattle

451 Seattle's coolest mag #2

WARNING

Hey everybody, I've been working on this *Sub Pop 100* compilation for a whole year now, and it's finally out. You know what? It really sucks. So what if it's got every great band in the world, huh? Cause it really sucks. And who cares if it's got hit after hit, anyway? Right? Cause I know we're all bored with **SONIC YOUTH** and the **WIPERS** and **SCRATCH ACID** and **STEVE ALBINI** and those darned **U-MEN** and **SKINNY PUPPY** and **SAVAGE REPUBLIC** and **STEVE FISK**...and, you know, that japanese girl group **SHONEN KNIFE** always did kinda suck. Right? So don't buy this record. Because just between you and me, it really sucks. (LP or chrome cassette shipped to anywhere in the world for just 8 bucks. Sub Pop Records, Seattle, WA)

Lo-Fi Can Be Cool

Of course most people hate the **SWANS**. What I refer to as "ultra-bold minimalism" is generally referred to, by the peasant masses, as "really boring and repetitious." Never mind that *Greed* (Jem) is the most mature work yet by the New York band. The frontman Michael Gira is a total original, whose pursuit of power, truth, and total heaviness is unequaled by anyone else living or dead. If you want to challenge yourself, then check out *Greed* by Swans. If you're afraid if might be "really boring and repetitious," then go back to your daily routine.

Local boys the **MELVINS** finally put out their own record on C/Z. They are a good band. They practice a lot. They are slow and heavy, but sometimes they thrash. They are great live. But the sound on their six-song seven-inch record is weak and thin and lame. The Melvins need to put out a good recording before they put out a good record.

Most original pop album of the month has to be from Boston's **CHRISTMAS**. *In Excelsior Dayglo* (Big Time) is an eccentric mix of pop art and pop hooks that rarely gets too cute or pretentious. I can't even give it the usual, "you know, sounds like blah blah." Creative whatever from Michael, Liz, and Dan.

Olympia's K Records continues its quest for world domination in the indie cassette market. First off, the **FEW** (from Guemes Island, WA) have a charming lo-fi electric folk-rock collection out. It's thirty minutes long, and was recorded on a ghetto blaster in someone's bedroom. The **CANNANES** are the Australian counterpart to the Few. Lo-fi electric folk recorded in someone's living room, distinguished by the occasional piano and trombone. Their six-song tape is called *Happy Swing* (K). Folks, lo-fi can be cool.

Montreal's **GRUESOMES** have bangs that hang over their eyes, They also play a fairly wild set of '60s-style garage punk. Though I'd rather listen to original '60s bands like the **SONICS** any day, these teen tyrants do have a totally creepy classic here called "Dementia 13." They're also cool enough to cover "My Broken Heart Will Never Mend (Unless You Come Back With the Glue)", a trashy number that originally appeared on *The Flintstones* costume party episode. The name of the album is *Tyrants of Teen Trash* (Og Music).

JAD FAIR paints pictures like a four-year-old. Jad Fair plays music like a four-year-old. If this appeals to you, then pick up *Best Wishes* (Iridescence), his newest LP. Myself, I like Jad best when he sings about monsters and girls. It's too bad he doesn't sing on his new album. He just makes noise.

"Have you ever seen your sister naked? Have you ever had sex while doing acid?" Thurston Moore (**SONIC YOUTH**) probes the intricate mind of Steve Albini (**BIG BLACK**) in issue #7 of Thurston's *Killer* fanzine. Questions worth answering. ($3. Ltd. edition of 700.)

SENSITIVE, GENTLE AND CARING
The new **ZOOGZ RIFT** album is entitled *Island of Living Puke* (SST). It's crazy and obscene and offensive. It's a novelty record. It's got songs like "The MoFo's Are After Me" and "A Very Pretty Song for a Very Special Young Lady." If you'll buy this, you'll buy anything.

The San Francisco-based independent label Strange Weekend has been kind enough to license a beautiful collection of pop songs from New Zealand entitled *Tuatura*. This is a great record—a highly recommended assortment of raw guitar hits previously available on the excellent Flying Nun label. Big hit: "Pink Frost" by the **CHILLS**.

SUBPOP

U S A

A GUIDE TO U.S. INDEPENDENTS

By Bruce Pavitt

SWANS

OF COURSE MOST PEOPLE HATE THE SWANS. WHAT I REFER TO AS "ULTRA BOLD MINIMALISM" IS GENERALLY REFERRED TO, BY THE PEASANT MASSES, AS "REALLY BORING AND REPETITIOUS." NEVER MIND THAT GREED IS THE MOST MATURE WORK YET BY NY'S SWANS. THAT FRONTMAN MICHAEL GIRA IS A TOTAL ORIGINAL, WHOSE PURSUIT OF POWER, TRUTH AND TOTAL HEAVINESS IS UNEQUALED BY ANYONE ELSE LIVING OR DEAD. IF YOU WANT TO CHALLENGE YOURSELF, THEN CHECK OUT GREED BY SWANS. IF YOU'RE AFRAID IT MIGHT BE "REALLY BORING AND REPETITIOUS," THEN GO BACK TO YOUR DAILY ROUTINE. (JEM)

Local boys the Melvins finally put out their own record. They are a good band. They practice a lot. They are slow and heavy, but sometimes they thrash. They are great live. But the sound on their six song seven-inch record is weak and thin and lame. The Melvins need to put out a good recording before they put out a good record. (CZ: 1407 E. Madison, Seattle, WA 98122)

Most original pop album of the month has to be from Boston's Christmas. *In Excelsior Dayglo* is an eccentric mix of pop art and pop hooks that rarely gets too cute or pretentious. I can't even give it the usual "you know, sounds like blah blah." Creative whatever from Michael, Liz and Dan (Bigtime: 6777 Hollywood Blvd., Seventh floor, Hollywood, CA 90028)

Olympia's K label continues its quest for world domination in the indie cassette market. First off, The Few (from Guemes Island, WA) have a charming lo-fi electric folk-rock collection out. It's 30 minutes long and was recorded on a ghetto blaster in someone's bedroom.   The Cannanes are the Australian counterpart to The Few. Lo-fi electric folk recorded in someone's living room, distinguished by the occasional piano and trombone. Their six-song tape is called Happy Swing. Folks, lo-fi can be cool. (K: Box 7144, Olympia, WA 98507)

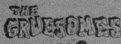

Montreal's Gruesomes have bangs that hang over their eyes. They also play a fairly wild set of '60s-style garage punk. Though I'd rather listen to original '60s bands like The Sonics any day, these teen tyrants *do* have a totally creepy classic here called *Dementio 13*. They're also cool enough to cover *My Broken Heart Will Never Mend (Unless You Come Back With the Glue)*, a trashy number that originally appeared on The Flintstones (costume party episode). The name of the album is *Tyrants of Teen Trash*. (OG: Box 162, Station F, Montreal, Quebec H3J 2L1)

Jad Fair paints pictures like a four-year-old. Jad Fair plays music like a four-year-old. If this appeals to you, then pick up *Best Wishes*, his newest LP. Myself, I like Jad best when he sings about monsters and girls. It's too bad he doesn't sing on his new album. He just makes noise. (Iridescence: Box 3556, Culver City, CA 90230)

Have you ever seen your sister naked? Have you ever had sex while doing acid? Thurston Moore (Sonic Youth) probes the intricate mind of Steve Albini (Big Black) in issue #7 of Thurston's KILLER fanzine. Questions worth answering. (Limited edition 700. KILLER: 84 Eldridge St. #5, NYC, NY 10002. $3)

SENSITIVE, GENTLE AND CARING: The new Zoogz Rift album is entitled *Island of Living Puke*. It's crazy and obscene and offensive. It's a novelty record. It's got songs like *The Mo-Fo's Are After Me* and *A Very Pretty Song For A Very Special Young Lady*. If you'll buy this you'll buy anything. (SST: P.O. Box 1, Lawndale, CA 90260)

The San Francisco based independent label Strange Weekend has been kind enough to license a beautiful collection of pop songs from New Zealand, entitled *Tuatara*. This is a great record — a highly recommended assortment of raw guitar bits previously available on the excellent Flying Nun label. Big hit: *Pink Frost* by The Chills. (Strange Weekend, 396 'A' Frederick St., SF, CA 94117)

Long Island's Phantom Tollbooth come spewing forth with a jazzy, chaotic mess that some people might call rock 'n' roll. Busy chord changes laced with noisy guitar feedback. *More Paranoia* is uncontrolled, manic, wild: they should lock this song up before it destroys New York City. For fans of Minutemen, Vold. (Homestead: Box 570, Rockville Centre, NY 11571-0570)

WOODSHOCK '85: A double LP recorded live at the Hurlbut ranch outside of Austin. Mass bands, mass beer, hot sun, naked bodies, dancing, lewd gestures, etc. It's a real party and all sorts of scum are totally rocking out to Austin legends like Poison 13, Cargo Cult and The Hickoids. And out of town guests the U-Men are doing their *Shoot 'Em Down* routine with Bigley probably on his knees with a beer in each hand looking for the goddamn milke. And I heard that the audience started pelting 'em with rocks and garbage 'cause the U-Men were fags but then the U-boys stood up and rocked so hard that the whole crazy mob decided not to lynch 'em. And I heard that by the end of the show the drunk Texas people thought the U-Men were like, total fucking god. So get the record. (El Jefe Records: 225 Congress, Suite #203, Austin, TX 78701)

SUB TEN

SUB POP 100 *buy it I'll destroy myself LP (SUB POP) Seattle*
TUATURA *compilation LP (Strange Weekend/Flying Nun) S.F./New Zealand*
SWANS *Greed LP (Jem) NYC*
CHRISTMAS *In Excelsior Dayglo LP (Big Time) Boston*
WOODSHOCK '85 *compilation LP (El Jefe) Austin*
SEA HAGS/GREEN RIVER/GIRL TROUBLE *live (courtesy Lynch Smoke Productions)*
JAD FAIR *Best Wishes (cover art only) LP (Iridescence) D.C.*
THE FEW *cassette (K) Guemes Island*
CHEMISTRY SET *plays pure pop, live, Seattle*
PHANTOM TOLLBOOTH *LP (Homestead) Long Island*

"Of course most people hate the Swans. What I refer to as 'ultra-bold minimalism' is generally referred to, by the peasant masses, as 'really boring and repetitious.' Never mind that Greed is the most mature work yet by New Yorks's Swans. The frontman Michael Gira is a total original, whose pursuit of power, truth and total heaviness is unequaled by anyone else living or dead. If you want to challenge yourself, then check out Greed by Swans. If you're afraid if might be 'really boring and repetitious,' then go back to your daily routine."

Long Island's **PHANTOM TOLLBOOTH** (Homestead Records) come spewing forth with a jazzy, chaotic mess that some people might call rock 'n roll. Busy chord changes laced with noisy guitar feedback. "More Paranoia" is uncontrolled, manic, wild; they should lock this song up before it destroys New York City. For fans of **MINUTEMEN** and **VOID**.

Woodshock '85 (El Jefe Records) A double LP recorded live at the Hurlbut ranch outside of Austin, Texas. Mass bands, mass beer, hot sun, naked bodies, dancing, lewd gestures, etc. It's a real party, and all sorts of scum are totally rocking out to Austin legends like **POISON 13**, **CARGO CULT**, and the **HICKOIDS**. Out-of-town guests the **U-MEN** are doing their "Shoot 'Em Down" routine with Bigley probably on his knees with a beer in each hand, looking for the goddamn mike. I heard that the audience started pelting 'em with rocks and garbage, 'cause the U-Men "were fags," but then the U-boys stood up and rocked so hard that the whole crazy mob decided not to lynch 'em. And I heard that by the end of the show, the drunk Texas people thought the U-Men were like, total fucking god. So get the record.

SUB TEN

VARIOUS *Sub Pop 100* LP Buy it I'll destroy myself (Sub Pop Records)

VARIOUS *Tuatura* compilation LP (Strange Weekend/Flying Nun)

SWANS *Greed* LP (Jem)

CHRISTMAS *In Excelsior Dayglo* LP (Big Time)

Woodshock '85 compilation LP (El Jefe)

SEA HAGS/GREEN RIVER/GIRL TROUBLE live (courtesy 7-inch Snake Productions)

JAD FAIR *Best Wishes* (cover art only) LP (Iridescence)

THE FEW cassette (K Records)

CHEMISTRY SET play pure pop live (Seattle)

PHANTOM TOLLBOOTH EP (Homestead)

K Is Cool! Long Live K

K RECORDS is a tiny label doing big things. Based in Olympia, Washington, the K label is a shoestring operation that is networking small-town bands throughout Washington state. **CALVIN JOHNSON**, K president, feels that the more sophisticated Seattle bands are ultimately trendy, and that bands from small towns are cool because "they are so isolated they can't help but develop their own sound."

K is digging sounds from towns that nobody cares about. Dumb towns like Tacoma, Olympia, Ellensburg, Montesano, and Anacortes. Dumb towns with great bands who seemingly have little chance for success despite their talent. But regardless of commercial appeal, this is timeless music; "folk music, music made by peasants." And that's what counts.

K isn't interested in slick production. Calvin prefers to record in mono, on old tube equipment. The emphasis is on warmth, on a "live" sound that modern studios can't duplicate, no matter how much money one throws at them.

Despite the non-commercial small-town lo-fi sensibility, K is stirring things up. By being consistent and working hard, K is developing a network of real fans. And by working creatively with little cash, Calvin has been able to distribute nationally and internationally, a sizable collection of the most rocking music this state has to offer. In essence, Calvin Johnson is a cultural diplomat, trickling out cassettes and records to interested parties around the state and around the globe.

Thanks to K, the remote Eastern Washington village of Ellensburg has become known for more than beef and food processing. The **SCREAMING TREES** are a wild garage band whose existence might have been forever obscured without the release of their first cassette, *Other Worlds*. The tape is rooted in '60s psych/punk, but has a fresh punch. It's a great collection of songs, and there remains a strong possibility that L.A. bigwig **GREG SHAW** (of Bomp!/*Pebbles* fame) will release it in album format.

Ellensburg's mixmaster and avant-garde studio whiz **STEVE FISK** is also documented on K. His latex cassette, *'Til The Night Closes In*, features surreal tape manipulation and has received national applause. In part, due to his low-budget beginning with K, Fisk had been asked to release a double LP on San Francisco's Thermidor label.

GIRL TROUBLE, from Tacoma, are another torch in the K parade. Live, their rocking sound and supreme lack of inhibition make for an instant party. Inspired by rock 'n roll greats like **LINK WRAY**, the **SONICS**, and the **CRAMPS**, these trash tyrants rock the house with obscure covers plus original gems like "She No Rattle My Cage." They are currently working on both a live cassette and a 45.

Another big 7-inch from K will be released by the **FEW**, from Guernes Island. Ghostly harmonies, acoustic guitar, bones, and rattles make for haunting, rocking folk. Their previous cassette release was recorded on a ghetto blaster in somebody's bedroom, and keeps with the immediate "lo-fi" recording approach of most of the K peasant/artist types.

But wait—*there's more!*

The big story is **BEAT HAPPENING**. Fronted by K kingpin Calvin Johnson, these charming peasant-rockers have worked out a pact with big-time Rough Trade UK. This influential British label has agreed to release both the Beat Happening LP and 45 together,

"K is a tiny label doing big things…a shoe-string operation that is networking small-town bands throughout Washington State. K isn't interested in slick production. Calvin prefers to record in mono, on old tube equipment. The emphasis is on warmth, on a 'live' sound that modern studios can't duplicate no matter how much money one throws at them."

SUB POP
U S A
A GUIDE TO U.S. INDEPENDENTS
By Bruce Pavitt

K IS COOL!
Long Live K

K is a tiny label doing big things. Based in Olympia, WA, the K label is a shoe-string operation that is networking small town bands throughout Washington state. CALVIN JOHNSON, K president, feels that the more sophisticated Seattle bands are ultimately trendy and that bands from small towns are cool because "they are so isolated they can't help but develop their own sound."

K is digging sounds from towns that nobody cares about. Dumb towns like Tacoma, Olympia, Ellensburg, Montesano, Anacortes. Dumb towns with great bands who seemingly

have little chance for success, despite their talent. But regardless of commercial appeal, this is timeless music, "folk music, music made by peasants." And that's what counts.

K isn't interested in slick production. Calvin prefers to record in mono, on old tube equipment. The emphasis is on warmth, on a "live" sound that modern studios can't duplicate no matter how much money one throws at them.

Despite the non-commercial small-town lo-fi sensibility, K is stirring things up. By being consistent and working hard, K is developing a network of real fans. And by working creatively with little cash, Calvin has been able to distribute, nationally and internationally, a sizable collection of the most rockin' music this state has to offer. In essence, Calvin Johnson is a cultural diplomat, trickling out cassettes and records to interested parties around the state and around the globe.

Thanks to K, the remote eastern village of Ellensburg is known for more than beef and food processing. THE SCREAMING TREES are a wild garage band whose existence might have been forever obscured without the release of their first cassette, OTHER WORLDS. The tape is rooted in 60's psych/punk but has a fresh punch. It's a great collection of songs, and there remains a strong possibility that L.A. bigwig Greg Shaw (of Bomp/Pebbles fame) will release it in album format.

Ellensburg's mixmaster and avant-garde studio whiz STEVE FISK is also documented on K. His latest cassette, TIL THE NIGHT CLOSES IN, features surreal tape manipulation and has received national applause. In part, due to his low-budget beginnings with K, Fisk has been asked to release a double LP on San Francisco's Thermidor label.

GIRL TROUBLE, from Tacoma, are another torch in the K parade. Live, their rockin' sound and supreme lack of inhibition make for an instant party. Inspired by rock 'n' roll greats like Link Wray, the Sonics and the Cramps, these trash tyrants rock the house with obscure covers plus original gems like SHE NO RATTLE MY CAGE. They are currently working on both a "live" cassette and a 45.

Another big 7-inch from K will be released by the FEW from Guemes Island. Ghostly harmonies, acoustic guitar, bones and rattles make for haunting, rockin' folk. Their previous cassette release was recorded on a ghetto blaster in somebody's bedroom and keeps with the immediate "lo-fi" recording approach of most of the K peasant/artist types.

But wait: there's more! The big story is BEAT HAPPENING. Fronted by K kingpin Calvin Johnson, these charming peasant-rockers have worked out a pact with big time Rough Trade U.K. This influential British Label has agreed to release both the Beat Happening LP and 45 together, for mass distribution and consumption. At last count, both NME and Melody Maker were calling overseas for interviews. Stay tuned for a new 45 out on K.

But the best way to check out the shoe-string lo-fi folk-peasant K label, is to pick up one of their three cassette compilations. All of these feature small-town bands from around Washington state, complimented by guest appearances by bands from other states and other countries. LET'S SEA is their new comp and it's their best yet. For more information about K releases, write for a free subscription to their newsletter/catalogue. K: Box 7154, Olympia, WA 98507.

GIRL TROUBLE

STEVE FISK

SCREAMING TREES

Olympia K Wash. U.S.A.

SUBPOP DESIGN BY DALE YARGER

for mass distribution and consumption. At last count, both *NME* and *Melody Maker* were calling overseas for interviews. Stay tuned for a new 45 out on K.

But the best way to check out the shoestring lo-fi folk-peasant K label, is to pick up one of their three cassette compilations. All of these feature bands from around Washington State, complemented by guest appearances by bands from other states and other countries. *Let's Sea* is their new comp, and it's their best yet. For more information about K releases, write for a free subscription to their newsletter/catalogue. (K, Olympia, WA)

1986: Well, It Was Okay

STATE OF AFFAIRS

1986. Well, it was okay. I got to sell hundreds of bad records and eat Chinese food for lunch.That was cool.

THE GOOD STUFF

The following records are great ones, and do not suffer from weak production, embrrassing lyrics, or grossly immature art direction. If you wish to gain status among your peers, then buy them. They are listed randomly.

RUN-D.M.C. (NYC) *Raising Hell* LP (Profile) The ultimate rock and rap mega-mix

, (Austin) *Rembrandt Pussyhorse* LP (Touch and Go) Bizarre, surreal masters of the unpredictable

KILLDOZER (Milwaukee) *Burl* EP (Touch and Go) Raspy rednecks redefine the midwest.

BEAT HAPPENING (Olympia) LP (K/Rough Trade) Totally innocent, totally rockin'; hold hands and kiss

SWANS (NYC) *Holy Money* LP (PVC/K.422) Ultra-bold minimalism, boring and brutal

FEELIES (Hoboken, NJ) *The Good Earth* LP (Coyote/Rough Trade) Transcendent percussive pop

PANDORAS (L.A.) *Stop Pretending* LP (Rhino) Trashy sluts rock out.

DUMPTRUCK (Boston) *Positively* LP (Big Time) Wimpy pop—we need it.

BIG BLACK (Chicago) *Atomizer* LP (Homestead) Please hate them.

SONIC YOUTH (NYC) *Evol* LP (SST) Atonal guitar gods; the best

GREATEST SONG ON A SO-SO ALBUM

"Whoa!" by **SOUL ASYLUM**. From the *Made to Be Broken* LP (Twin/Tone). This song rocks.

SINGLE OF THE YEAR

"Halloween" (Homestead) by **SONIC YOUTH**. Kim Gordon, I am your love slave.

ALBUM TITLE OF THE YEAR

Fiesta en fa Biblioteca by **THE PONTIAC BROTHERS** (Frontier).

CASSETTE OF THE YEAR

For Years We Stood Clearly as One Thing (K Records) by **PELL MELL** (Portland, OR). Brilliant, obscure demo tapes finally released!

COOLEST PART OF THE COUNTRY

The Midwest: **BIG BLACK** (Chicago); **KILLDOZER** (Madison); **SOUL ASYLUM** (Mnpls.).

LABEL OF THE YEAR

TOUCH AND GO pushes really ugly bands that don't conform to trends. They've recently moved from Detroit to Chicago, and are consolidating artists from outside of New York or Los Angeles. Check this out: **BUTTHOLE SURFERS, KILLDOZER, DIE KREUZEN**, and **BIG BLACK**.

LOCAL GODLIKE STUFF

BEAT HAPPENING (Olympia, WA) LP (K)

SCREAMING TREES (Ellensburg, WA) *Clairvoyance* LP (Velvetone)

GREEN RIVER (Seattle, WA) "Together We'll

SUB POP USA

A GUIDE TO U.S. INDEPENDENTS
By Bruce Pavitt

STATE OF AFFAIRS

1986: Well, it was o.k. I got to sell hundreds of bad records and eat Chinese food for lunch. That was cool.

THE GOOD STUFF: The following records are great ones and do *not* suffer from weak production, embarrassing lyrics or grossly immature art direction. If you wish to gain status among your peers, then buy them. They are listed randomly.

(NYC) **RUN D.M.C.** *Raising Hell* LP (Profile) the ultimate rock and rap mega-mix.

(Austin) **BUTTHOLE SURFERS** *Rembrandt Pussyhorse* LP (Touch and Go) bizarre, surreal masters of the unpredictable.

(Milwaukee) **KILLDOZER** *Burl* EP (Touch and Go) raspy rednecks redefine the midwest.

(Olympia) **BEAT HAPPENING** LP (K/Rough Trade) totally innocent, totally rockin', hold hands and kiss.

(NYC) **SWANS** *Holy Money* LP (PVC/K.422) ultra-bold minimalism, boring and brutal.

(Hoboken) **FEELIES** *The Good Earth* LP (Coyote/Rough Trade) transcendent-percussive pop.

(L.A.) **PANDORAS** *Stop Pretending* LP (Rhino) trashy sluts rock out.

(Boston) **DUMPTRUCK** *Positively* LP (Big Time) wimpy pop, we need it.

(Chicago) **BIG BLACK** *Atomizer* LP (Homestead) please hate them.

(NYC) **SONIC YOUTH** *EVOL* LP (SST) atonal guitar gods, the best.

GREATEST SONG ON A SO SO ALBUM: *Whoa!* by **SOUL ASYLUM**. From the made to be broken LP (Twin Tone). This song rocks.

SINGLE OF THE YEAR: *Halloween* by **SONIC YOUTH** (Homestead). Kim Gordon I am your love slave.

ALBUM TITLE OF THE YEAR *Fiesta en la Biblioteca* by **THE PONTIAC BROTHERS** (Frontier). L.A.

CASSETTE OF THE YEAR: *For Years We Stood Clearly as One Thing* by **PELL MELL** (K) Portland. Brilliant, obscure demo tapes finally released!

COOLEST PART OF THE COUNTRY: **THE MIDWEST**. Big Black (Chicago), Killdozer (Madison), Soul Asylum (Mnpls).

LABEL OF THE YEAR: **TOUCH AND GO** pushes really ugly bands that don't conform to trends. They've recently moved from Detroit to Chicago, and are consolidating artists from outside of NY or LA. Check this out: Butthole Surfers, Killdozer, Die Kreuzen, Big Black.

LOCAL GOD-LIKE STUFF: **BEAT HAPPENING** LP (K) Olympia. **SCREAMING TREES** *Clairvoyance* LP (Velvetone) Ellensburg. **GREEN RIVER** *Together We'll Never* 45 (Green River) Seattle. **YOUNG FRESH FELLOWS** *Topsy Turvy* LP (Popllama) Seattle. **DEEP SIX** *Various* LP (C/Z) Seattle.

LOCAL BANDS TO WATCH: **SOUNDGARDEN** **FEAST** **GUT REACTION**

BEST LOCAL LIVE BAND: **GIRL TROUBLE** (Tacoma)

LOCAL READING MATTER: **451** (art) and **WIG OUT** (trash) both rule.

INCREDIBLE LOCAL DEMOS THAT WILL DESTROY IN '87: **GREEN RIVER** EP, **ROOM 9** LP.

FINAL NOTE: The Seattle scene is gearing up for a major explosion. Despite the desperate lack of a good club, Seattle has rarely seen so many bands. Expect great records to come out of this region in '87.

SONIC YOUTH · KILLDOZER · SWANS · GIRLTALK · SCREAMING TREES · SOUL ASYLUM · FOUR·FIVE·ONE · TOUCH and GO RECORDS · ACCESSORIES

SUBPOP DESIGN BY DALE YARGER

> **"The Seattle scene is gearing up for a major explosion. Despite the desperate lack of a good club, Seattle has rarely seen so many bands. Expect great records to come out of this region in '87."**

Never" 45 (Green River Records)

VARIOUS *Deep Six* LP (C/Z Records)

LOCAL BANDS TO WATCH

SOUNDGARDEN

FEAST

GUT REACTION

BEST LOCAL LIVE BAND

GIRL TROUBLE (Tacoma)

LOCAL READING MATTER

451 (art) and *Wig Out* (trash); both rule.

INCREDIBLE LOCAL DEMOS THAT WILL DESTROY IN '87

GREEN RIVER EP

ROOM 9 LP

FINAL NOTE

The Seattle scene is gearing up for a major explosion. Despite the desperate lack of a good club, Seattle has rarely seen so many bands. Expect great records to come out of this region in '87.

Rock Yer Bones

Occasionally, stuff collides to create something *really important*. Like here: *Burl* (Touch and Go) the new six-song EP by Madison, Wisconsin's **KILLDOZER**. This garage trio has been a "band to watch" ever since their initial *Intellectual Are the Shoeshine Boys of the Ruling Elite* LP. On this, they've matured and grown into a monster: *Burl* is *heavy* rootsy dirge with lyrics rooted in the populist mythology of country and blues. Somehow, a compilation tape featuring **HOWLING WOLF**, **JOHNNY CASH**, the avant bone-crushing **SWANS** and the new Killdozer make perfect sense. It sure made my day. Highly recommended.

Parker's Bark is a great fanzine out of Portland, Oregon. It's edited by a girl, so there's not a lot of *heavy boy rock*, but, hey, it's cool anyway. Some very creative minds here. (Send a 22¢ stamp)

To their credit, the **YOUNG FRESH FELLOWS** have written some very clever, catchy, beer-soaked rock 'n roll anthems; "How Much About Last Night Do You Remember?" from the *Topsy Turvy* LP being an excellent example. Sometimes, though, their *fun* sensibilities get to be too cute and wacky, a complaint I have with other "funny" bands like the **DEAD MILKMEN** and **CAMPER VAN BEETHOVEN**. Regardless, their latest single, "Beer Money," (PopLlama) doesn't stack up to the best material on either of the LPs. The "live" production sounds good, but the song itself is...uh...weak. A frat party throwaway?

Rumor has it that **SOUL ASYLUM** weren't too happy about their third album. *While You Were Out* (Twin/Tone). I dunno. Sounds damn good to me. Although their last LP *Made To Be Broken* produced their best song ever—the ultra heavy "Whoa!"—it also spewed forth a lot of country rock rambling. They didn't know whether they wanted to be **BLACK SABBATH** or the **ALLMAN BROTHERS**. The album was uneven and lacked integration. Not so with the new one. If you can forgive the overly clean recording, you'll find *While You Were Out* to be the most consistent record yet by one of America's greatest rock 'n roll bans. Minneapolis still kicks!

DEJA VOODOO These two mojo madmen from Montreal have come up with twenty-two low-budget recordings of "sludgeabilly," a ranchy, distorted mix of rockabilly and garage rock 'n roll. But although their new LP, *Swamp of Love* (Og Music), is rock rock rockin', one drummer and one guitar player for a whole album is a bit tedious. They need to add some *power* to their sound and diversify a bit or else get smart and release 45s. Fans of the **CRAMPS** and **GIRL TROUBLE** will want to at least send away for their favorite newsletter. Rock yer bones, people.

Every song on the new **SCREAMING TREES** album is a hit. These farm boys from tiny Ellensburg, Washington, have literally plowed the local competition!!! This is manic, '60s-inspired punk/psych with hooks and power and energy!!! The great thing about the *Clairvoyance* LP (Velvetone), though, is that it's not a museum piece. This record is not trying to mimic and recapture a lost decade. This recording was produced with *modern* technology and, as such, comes across with a *modern* sound. And folks, everything about this disc, from the packaging to the production to the songwriting to the performance, is excellent!!! And be sure to see these farm boys live, because they *totally rock*!!!

Boston has a lot of colleges. Boston has a lot of students. Boston has a lot of "smart" rock 'n roll bands

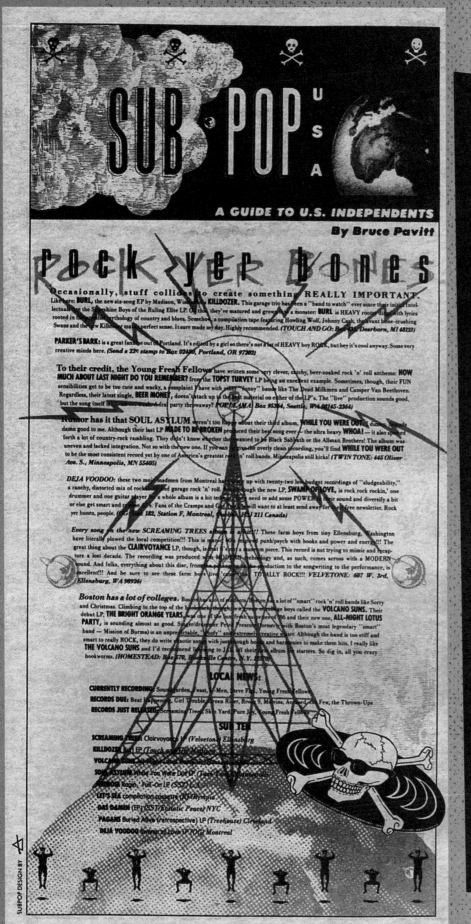

The February 1987 *Rocket* column stated that Soundgarden was recording; I predicted that C/Z or Slash would release the band's debut EP. In fact, guitar player Kim Thayil suggested that I and my fledgling Sub Pop label join forces to release the record with Jon Poneman, a DJ, local concert promoter, and bass player in the Tree Climbers. He had booked Green River's Sub Pop record release party at the popular club Scoundral's Lair. We released Soundgarden's *Screaming Life* in the fall of 1987, the start of a creative partnership that thrived throughout the infamous Sub Pop grunge era, 1987–94; since then, Jon has run things successfully on his own.

like **SORRY** and **CHRISTMAS**. Climbing to the top of the bookstack, though, is a group of college boys called **VOLCANO SUNS**. Their debut LP, *The Bright Orange Years*, was one of the fun, fresh surprises of '86, and their new one, *All-Night Lotus Party* (Homestead), is sounding almost as good. Singer/drummer Peter Prescott (formerly of Boston's most legendary "smart" band— **MISSION OF BURMA**) is an unpredictable, "goofy" and extremely creative writer. Although the band is too stiff and smart they totally *rock*, they do write chaotic songs with just enough hooks and harmonies to make them hits. I really like the Volcano Suns, and I'd recommend listening to "Jak" off their first album for starters. So dig in, all you crazy bookworms!

LOCAL NEWS

Currently recording: **SOUNDGARDEN, FEAST, U-MEN, STEVE FISK, YOUNG FRESH FELLOWS**

Records due: **BEAT HAPPENING, GIRL TROUBLE, GREEN RIVER, ROOM 9**, the **MELVINS**, the **ACCUSED**, the **FEW**, the **THROWN-UPS**

Records just released: **SCREAMING TREES, SKIN YARD, PURE JOY, YOUNG FRESH FELLOWS**

SUB TEN

SCREAMING TREES *Clairvoyance* LP (Velvetone)

KILLDOZER *Burl* EP (Touch and Go)

VOLCANO SUNS *All-Night Lotus Party* LP (Homestead)

SOUL ASYLUM *While You Were Out* LP (Twin/Tone)

FIREHOSE *Ragin', Full-On* LP (SST)

VARIOUS *Let's Sea* compilation cassette (K Records)

DAS DAMEN EP (SST/Ecstatic Peace)

PAGANS *Buried Alive* retrospective LP (Treehouse)

DEJA VOODOO *Swamp of Love* (Og Music)

This Year, the Topic is BEER

One of the best *party* records of '85 was *Doll Hut* by the **PONTIAC BROTHERS**. Featuring the slide guitar of Ward Dotson (ex-**GUN CLUB**), the whole thing rocked like early **STONES**. The latest from these rootsy rockers is an LP called *Fiesta en la Biblioteca* (Frontier). Here, the production and the guitar playing are commercial, which is disappointing. The whole thing just doesn't sound as dirty and uninhibited and dangerous and their first release. Singer Matt Simon is still a tearjerker, though, despite his infatuation with Jagger. So yeah, pick up *Doll Hut*, an underrated American classic.

BUDWEISER BANDWAGON

VERBAL ABUSE *Rocks Your Liver* LP (Boner Records) get this month's all-night-sleaze award. Five years ago, every "rad" kid in America was politically correct and sang about El Salvador. This year the topic is *beer*. Yo, it's the new style.

Well, there's this 10-year old singer from Elma, Washington. He's really cool. His mom calls him Travis, but his real name is **HUMAN SKAB.** He's also got this incredibly wild cassette out called *Thunder Hips and Saddlebags* (c/o Human Skab). Picture this: the Skab zips around the living room shooting toy guns. He hits the family piano with his fists. He tries real hard to play guitar. He makes up songs about terrorism and radiation and throwing rocks at windows. Cool! The whole family will wig on this noisy novelty! The tape is worth every penny of your $3.50! And yes, the cassette comes with a different backyard snapshot of Travis. Uh, I mean Human Skab.

Seattle is gearing up for world domination in '87. This city has never seen so many independent releases. The latest is the **SKIN YARD** LP (C/Z Records), a project that Skin Yard fans will not be disappointed with; the packaging and production are first rate. The band itself is rooted in early '70s "progressive rock," like **KING CRIMSON**, featuring busy, slightly "difficult" arrangements, which although interesting, often interfere with their ability to *rock the house*. But that's a minor point. Also, vocals tend to be inflated and melodramatic to the point of insincerity, but again, a minor point because the real reason to pick this up is for the twisted and often amazing guitar damage. The relentlessly advertised Skin Yard has permanently disfigured some brain cells in this city, and with this new album, they're sure to disfigure the world.

The American hardcore movement (the suburban teen backlash against urban art-school new wave) peaked between '82 and '84. During that time, **MINOR THREAT** from D.C. proved themselves to be the true leaders, initiating the anti-drug straightedge movement and creating music that was deeply personal, vulnerable even, yet physically powerful and anthemic in scope. But although Minor Treat has disbanded, members Ian MacKaye and Jeff Nelson have continued to release records on their successful Dischord label. The latest is a 45 recorded by themselves as a duo, and it's called **EGG HUNT** "Me and You" b/w "We All Fall Down" (Dischord). Although the record lacks the whiplash aggression and the strong melody of the Minor Threat material, both songs are monsters that creep up on you in a big way. Also, art director Jeff

A GUIDE TO U.S. INDEPENDENTS

By Bruce Pavitt

One of the best PARTY records of '85 was *Doll Hut* by *The Pontiac Brothers*. Featuring the slide guitar of Ward Dotson (ex-Gun Club) the whole thing rocked like early Stones. The latest from these rootsy rockers is an LP called *Fiesta En La Biblioteca*. Here, the production and the guitar playing are commercial, which is disappointing. The whole thing just doesn't sound as dirty and uninhibited and dangerous as their first release. Singer Matt Simon is still a tear-jerker though, despite his infatuation with Jagger. So yeah, pick up *Doll Hut*, an underrated American classic. (Frontier: P.O. Box 22, Sun Valley, CA 91353)

BUDWEISER BANDWAGON: *Verbal Abuse ROCKS YOUR LIVER (LP)* gets this month's all-night-sleaze award. Five years ago, every "rad" kid in America was politically correct and sang about El Salvador. This year the topic is BEER. Yo. It's the *new* style. (BONER: P.O. Box 2081, Berkley, CA 94702)

Well, there's this 10-year old singer from Elma, Washington. He's really cool. His mom calls him Travis but his real name is *Human Skab*. He's also got this incredibly wild cassette out called *Thunder Hips and Saddlebags*. Picture this: the Skab zips around the living room shooting toy guns. He hits the family piano with his fists. He tries real hard to play guitar. He makes up songs about terrorism and radiation and throwing rocks at windows. Cool! The whole family will wig on this noisy novelty! The tape is worth every penny of your $3.50! And yes, every cassette comes with a different backyard snapshot of Travis. Uh, I mean Human Skab. (HUMAN SKAB: P.O. Box 1130, Elma, WA 98451)

Seattle is gearing up for world denomination in '87: this city has never seen so many independent releases. The latest is the *SKIN YARD LP*, a project that *SKIN YARD* fans will not be disappointed with: the packaging and production are first rate. The band itself is rooted in early 70's "progressive rock" like King Crimson, featuring busy, slightly "difficult" arrangements, which although interesting, often interfere with their ability to ROCK THE HOUSE. But that's a minor point. Also, vocals tend to be inflated and melodramatic to the point of insincerity, but again, a minor point because the real reason to pick this up is for the twisted and often amazing guitar damage. The relentlessly advertised *SKIN YARD* has permanently disfigured some brain cells in this city, and with this new album, they're sure to disfigure the world. ($6.00 ppd. c/o C/Z: 1407 E. Madison, Seattle, WA 98122)

The American Hardcore movement (the suburban teen backlash against urban art-school *New Wave*) peaked between '82 and '84. During that time, *Minor Threat* (from Georgetown, a suburb of D.C.) proved themselves to be true leaders, initiating the anti-drug straight-edge movement and creating music that was deeply personal, vulnerable even, yet physically powerful and anthemic in scope. But although *Minor Threat* has disbanded, members Ian MacKaye and Jeff Nelson have continued to release records on their successful Dischord label; the latest of which is a 45 recorded by themselves as a duo, and it's called ... *Egg Hunt* (Me and You b/w We All Fall Down).

Although this record lacks the whiplash aggression, and the strong melody, of the *Minor Threat* material, both songs are monsters that creep up on you in a big way. Also, art director Jeff Nelson has come up with the coolest package of the year. ($2.50 ppd. c/o DISCHORD: 3819 Beecher St. NW, Washington D.C. 20007)

TOUCH AND GO, the most radical rock 'n' roll label in America, has a compilation out called *God's Favorite Dog*. Six bands with big brains and loud guns: Butthole Surfers, Big Black, Scratch Acid, Happy Flowers, Hose, Killdozer. Go ahead, invest. (TOUCH AND GO: P.O. Box 433, Dearborn, MI 48121)

Thousands of years ago, in Greece, the hip thing to do was to drink wine and frolic around in a toga playing pan pipes. Currently, a few artists are reviving this tradition. *Zamfir*, of course, is the world king of the pan flute, having recorded infamous covers of such hits as Chariots of Fire and Love Theme from Tchaikovsky. For those of you looking for an alternative, try checking out *ALWAYS AUGUST*. Their first LP, *Black Pyramid*, sounds like mellow Grateful Dead and, yes, includes pan pipes. Songs like Spacin Out and Pan's Lament are sensitive ballads that sound great in a toga. (SST: P.O. 1, Lawndale, CA 902650)

BIG BLACK, that noisy band from Chicago, have a retrospective LP out called *Hammer Party*. It includes both of their first two out-of-print EP's: *Lungs* and *Bulldozer*. *Lungs*, their first, was basicaly a solo project by frontman Steve Albini, featuring vocals, guitar and beat box. This was when Steve was lonely, disturbed and angry. By the time *Bulldozer* (best *Big Black* record ever) came out, Steve, who came to Chicago from Montana, had made a few friends, like Santiago Durango and Jeff Pezzati. Needless to say, Steve wasn't lonely any more. Just disturbed and angry. Buy this record. (HOMESTEAD: P.O. Box 570, Rockville Centre, NY 11571-0570)

SUB TEN

HUMAN SCAB Thunder Hips and Saddlebags cassette (Skab) Elma, Washington

GOD'S FAVORITE DOG Compilation LP (Touch and Go) various

BIG BLACK Hammer Party (Homestead) Chicago

EGG HUNT Me and You 45 (Dischord) D.C.

SEA HAGS demo San Francisco

SKIN YARD LP (C/Z) Seattle

LIVE SKULL Pusherman 12" single (Homestead) NYC

MELVINS heaviest band in the world, love Montesano, Washington

CONFLICT coolest fanzine in the world NYC

THE PONTIAC BROS. Fiesta En La Biblioteca LP (Frontier) L.A.

SUBPOP DESIGN BY

HIGH-QUALITY 8-TRACK RECORDING AND PRODUCTION SERVICES AT $17.00 PER HOUR

RECIPROCAL RECORDING
4230 LEARY WAY NW, SEATTLE, WA 98107 782-6411

"BOSS T-SHIRTS"

Exclusive new designs!

NEW! ST #2: Gorgeous grey sweat. 50/50. The most beautiful Bruce shirt! M, L, EX. **$18.**

NEW! TS #10: Live type shirt. Black with blue. 50/50. Back is song list. S, M, EX. **$11.**

NEW! TS #11: Collage shirt. White 50/50. Back says "Live/ 1975-1985." S, M, L, EX. **$11.**

NEW! TS #12: Live cover shirt. Black. 50/50. Back is song list. S, M, L, EX. **$11.**

TO ORDER: Send check or money order, list of styles and sizes (with alternates when possible) and add $1.99 per shirt in the US and Canada ($2.99 per shirt overseas, US funds) and send to T-Shirts, Backstreet Records, PO Box 51219, Seattle, WA 98115. All other styles are now sold out. We also accept Visa, Mastercard and Eurocard—send your number, expiration date, signature and phone number. Satisfaction guaranteed on all items—these are awesome shirts!

*** NEW WAVE *** 60'S ROCK *** BUTTONS *** POSTERS *** MAGAZINES *** IMPORTS ***

Seattle Record Convention

Seattle Center Snoqualmie Room Sunday, March 22, 1987 10 a.m. -6 p.m.

Admission $1
9 A.M. ADMISSION $5

† **DEALERS:** †
8 FT. TABLE $30
MAKE CHECKS PAYABLE TO:
JOHN DeBLAISO
P.O. BOX 58772
SEATTLE, WA 98188
YOUR CHECK OR MONEY ORDER RESERVES YOUR TABLE
SETUP TIME IS 7:30 A.M.
RESERVATION DEADLINE IS THURSDAY, MARCH 19

For more information, call John 228-3537 or Carol 324-1381

PICTURE DISCS *** PICTURE SLEEVES *** ROCK *** COLORED VINYL *** RADIO SHOWS

Nelson has come up with the coolest package of the year.

Touch and Go, the most radical rock 'n label in America, has a compilation out called *God's Favorite Dog*. Six bands with big brains and loud guns: **BUTT-HOLE SURFERS**, **BIG BLACK**, **SCRATCH ACID**, **HAPPY FLOWERS**, **HOSE**, and **KILLDOZER**. Go ahead, invest.

Thousands of years ago, in Greece, the hip thing to do was to drink wine and frolic around in a toga playing pan pipes. Currently, a few artists are reviving this tradition. **ZAMFIR**, of course, is the world king of the pan flute, having recorded infamous covers of such hits as "Chariots of Fire" and "Love Theme from Tchaikovsky." For those of you looking for an alternative, try checking out **ALWAYS AUGUST**. Their first LP, *Black Pyramid* (SST Records), sounds like mellow **GRATEFUL DEAD**, and, yes, includes pan pipes. Songs like "Spacin' Out" and "Pan's Lament" are sensitive ballads that sounds great in a toga.

BIG BLACK, that noisy band from Chicago, have a retrospective LP out called *Hammer Party* (Homestead Records). It includes both of their first two out-of-print EPs, *Lungs* and *Bulldozer*. *Lungs*, their first, was basically a solo project by frontman Steve Albini, featuring vocals, guitar, and beat box. By the time *Bulldozer* (best Big Black record ever) came out, Steve, who came to Chicago from Montana, had made a few friends, like Santiago Durango and Jeff Pezzati. Needless to say, Steve wasn't lonely any more. Just disturbed and angry. Buy this record.

SUB TEN

HUMAN SKAB *Thunder Hips and Saddlebags* cassette (Human Skab)

VARIOUS *God's Favorite Dog* compilation LP (Touch and Go)

BIG BLACK *Hammer Party* (Homestead)

EGG HUNT "Me and You" 45 (Dischord)

SEA HAGS demo (San Francisco)

SKIN YARD LP (C/Z Records)

LIVE SKULL "Pusherman" 12" single (Homestead)

MELVINS heaviest band in the world

Conflict coolest fanzine in the world (New York City)

PONTIAC BROTHERS *Fiesta en la Biblioteca* LP (Frontier)

This Is a Fake Column

La di da. Let me see. I went to the zoo yesterday. It was sunny. I bought a hot dog. I saw an elephant. It was big.

HO. **SCRATCH ACID** at the Central!! Do those guys rock or what? No wonder their new EP is called *Berserker*. Buy it or move to Russia.

Another good disc out this month is *Hot Animal Machine* by **HENRY ROLLINS**. Henry is the guy who shaved his head, and then grew his hair long, and then shaved his head again. There are a few all-out thrashers here, plus some arty poetry/rock things. The slow and screaming "No One" is the hit for me.

BIG NEWS

Ellensburg's **SCREAMING TREES** have just been signed to the big and powerful SST label down in Los Angeles. Knob-twister Steve Fisk will be producing.

JACK YR BODY PARTY

FROSTMASTER CHILL did some devastating cut-ups of **AC/DC**'s *Back in Black* while his fellow MC rocked the mike. These guys are interested in playing more rock shows, and can be reached in care of Cheri. Frostmaster plans on touring England this fall.

Favorite *fuck* band in town has to be the relentlessly goofy **WHITE BOYS**. "White Boys rule, Beastie Boys suck." And who could forget those go-go girls?

Soon to be Seattle's *cult single of the year*: "Felch" by the **THROWN UPS**. Pure noise, pure beauty. Uh, nobody can sing like Eddie. And nobody can play guitar like Steve. And nobody can play drums, especially Mark, but he's got long hair. It's pressed in a limited edition of 500, and is available on Tom Hazelmyer's Amphet-amine Reptile label. By the way, army dude Hazel-

meyer has been playing bass with the **U-MEN**. It's sure to be a short-lived romance, though, as Tom is always in flux between Seattle and Minneapolis, where he's released three singles by his group, **HALO OF FLIES**.

Hey, Philadelphia's **SCHOOLY D** has a new 12" out called "Saturday Night." He and his fellow DJ Code Money are toughest, rawest hip hop act around. A must buy. (Check out Music Menu on Rainier South for this one.)

Speaking of 12" singles: "Jack Yr Body" by **STEVE "SILK" HURLEY** is a dance hit of the month. Chicago "House" music (minimal, stripped-down disco, created by Chicago club DJs) has been hard to find in Seattle. I found "Jack" at Penny Lane on Broadway; they've got a whole section on House.

PUSSY GALORE has moved from D.C. to New York, and have picked up **BOB BERT**, former drummer with **SONIC YOUTH**. *Pussy Gold 5000*, their new EP, maintains their status as *band most likely to be hated by your parents*. These guys would make a great double bill with the Thrown Ups.

TACOMA

T-town funnyman Jimmy May has just opened a non-profit all ages space called Community World. Music, film, vaudeville, all sorts of unusual entertainment. Bands interested in booking shows should call. Mean-while, consumers can get on the mailing list.

Aside from a few notable exceptions, there are very few fun, catchy, intelligent pop bands putting out records in the US. Not so with the UK. Two excellent compilations of garage pop from overseas are: *I Love the Smell of Napalm*, a collection of songs from the

SUB/POP USA

A GUIDE TO U.S. INDEPENDENTS

By Bruce Pavitt

HI EVERYBODY.

THIS IS A FAKE COLUMN.

La di da. Let me see. I went to the zoo yesterday. It was sunny. I bought a hot dog. I saw an elephant. It was big.

HO. **Scratch Acid** at the Central!! Do those guys rock or what? No wonder their new EP is called **Berserker**. Buy it or move to Russia.

Another good disc out this month is **Hot Animal Machine** by **Henry Rollins**. Henry is the guy who shaved his head and then grew his hair long and then shaved his head again. There are a few all out thrashers here plus some arty poetry/rock things. The slow and screaming **No One** is the hit for me.

BIG NEWS: Ellensburg's **Screaming Trees** have just been signed to the big and powerful **SST** label down in L.A. Knob-twister Steve Fisk will be producing.

JACK YR BODY PARTY: **Frostmaster Chill** did some devastating cut-ups of AC/DC's **Back In Black** while his fellow MC rocked the mike. These guys are interested in playing more rocks shows and can be reached in care of Cheri at 634-3277. Frostmaster plans on touring England the Fall.

Favorite FUCK band in town has to be the relentlessly goofy **White Boys**. "White Boys rule, Beastie Boys suck." And who could forget those go-go girls?

Soon to be Seattle's CULT SINGLE OF THE YEAR: **Felch** by **The Thrown Ups**. Pure noise, pure beauty. Uh, nobody can sing like Eddie. And nobody can play guitar like Steve. and nobody can play drums, especially Mark, but he's got long hair. It's pressed in a limited edition of 500 and is available on Tom Hazelmeyer's **Amphetamine Reptile** label (4932 33rd Ave. S., Mnpls. MN 55417). By the way, army dude Hazelmeyer has been playing bass with the U-Men. It's sure to be a short lived romance though, as Tom is always in flux between Seattle and Minneapolis, where he's released three singles by his group, **Halo of Flies**.

Hey, Philadelphia's **Schoolly D** has a new 12" out called **Saturday Night**. He and his fellow d.j. Code Money are toughest, rawest hip hop act around. A must buy. Check out Music Menu on Rainier South for this one.

Speaking of 12" singles: **Jack Yr Body** by Steve "Silk" Hurley is dance hit of the month. Chicago "House" music (minimal, stripped down disco, created by Chicago club d.j.'s) has been hard to find in Seattle. I found **Jack . . .** at Penney Lane on Broadway; they've got a whole section on House.

Pussy Galore has moved from D.C. to New York and

have picked up Bob Bert, former drummer with Sonic Youth. **Pussy Gold 5000**, their new EP, maintains their status as BAND MOST LIKELY TO BE HATED BY YOUR PARENTS. These guys would make a great double bill with The Thrown Ups.

TACOMA: T-town funnyman **Jimmy May** has just opened a non-profit all ages space called **Community World.** Music, film, vaudeville, all sorts of unusual entertainment. Bands interested in booking shows should call 1-473-4299. Meanwhile, consumers can get on the mailing list: 5441 S. Main St., Tacoma, WA 98408.

Aside from a few notable exceptions, there's very few fun, catchy, intelligent pop bands putting out records in the U.S. Not so with the U.K. Two excellent compilations of garage pop from overseas are: (1) **I Love the Smell of Napalm**, a collection of songs from the **Creation** label released domestically on Rough Trade. (2) **Take The Subway to Your Suburb**, a collection from the **Suburb** label.

By the by, K kingpin **Calvin** will be licensing an EP by Subway artists **The Flatmates**. Calvin also says that he and fellow **Beat Happening** members are negotiating a multi-record offer from N.Y.'s **Homestead** label. Poverty Pop rules. Rumor has it that somebody from Slash records will be checking out the ultra-heavy Soundgarden, but their upcoming record will most likely be a six song EP on Seattle's **C/Z** label.

Looks like **Green River** is banned from both the Central and the Ditto. Yes, these bad boys rock as hard as The Stooges. Hopefully, scene-maker Jon Poneman will have an open door policy at his new club, as yet unnamed. The space will be above Scoundral's Lair Restaurant, located between the U-district and East Lake. Vancouver's industrial Skinny Puppy has a video on MTV. They'll be turning the Moore Theater upside down on Sat. April 10. On the more abrasive side, The Butthole Surfers, U-Men and Soundgarden will be playing the same night at the Crescent Ballroom in Tacoma.

Portland's **Wiper's** will be releasing their fifth studio LP this month. Their last one, **Land of The Lost**, was a real creeper and sounds better with every listen. Glad to see that local bands like **Skin Yard** and the **Walkabouts** are making it down to Portland to play at The Satyricon. This club has a great jukebox and rocks harder than any club in Seattle. Their Greek owner also serves great gyros.

LOUDEST CLOTHES IN TOWN: Pan Ams and A.D.R.D.

SUB TEN

SCRATCH ACID: *Destroys the Central Tavern, live*
SCHOOLY D: *Saturday Night 12" single* (Schooly D) Philadelphia
SCRATCH ACID: *Berserker EP* (Touch and Go) Austin
HENRY ROLLINS: *Hot Animal Machine LP* (Texas Hotel) Santa Monica
TAKE THE SUBWAY TO YOUR SUBURB: *Compilation LP* (Subway) U.K.

PUSSY GALORE: *Pussy Gold 5000 EP* (Buy Our Records) NYC
MINUTEMEN: *Ballot Result double LP* (SST) L.A.
BREAKING CIRCUS: *The Ice Machine LP* (Homestead) Mnpls.
MAGNOLIAS: *Concrete Pillbox LP* (Twin Tone) Mnpls.
SQUIRRELBAIT: *Skag Heaven LP* (Homestead) Louisville

SUBPOP DESIGN BY

FALLOUT RECORDS & SKATEBOARDS PRESENT

BUTTHOLE SURFERS

WITH

U·MEN

ST. VITUS

SOUND GARDEN

FRI. APRIL 10 7 PM

CRESCENT BALLROOM

1102 S. FAWCETT DOWNTOWN TACOMA

ALL AGES!

DEATH VALLEY '87

TICKETS $8 ADVANCE FROM FALLOUT RECORDS & SKATEBOARDS, TIME TRAVELLERS, CELLOPHANE SQUARE AND TICKETMASTER OUTLETS (PHONE 628-0888). $10 AT THE DOOR

FALLOUT RECORDS & SKATEBOARDS
1506 E. OLIVE WAY   323-BOMB

BUTTHOLE SURFERS

SEE 'EM LIVE . . . GET THEIR NEW LP. "LOCUST ABORTION TECHNICIAN"

ONLY $6.50 IN APRIL

NEW SCRATCH ACID BERSERKER OUT NOW!
NEW BIG BLACK HEADACHE OUT SOON!

KJET AND KCMU WELCOME

HÜSKER DÜ

**THELONIUS MONSTER
SCREAMING TREES**

SAT. MAY 2   8PM

ALL AGES

$11.50 ADV. $13.50 at DOOR
$10.50 WITH UW STUDENT ID AT HUB TICKET OFFICE

HUB BALLROOM

TICKETS AVAILABLE AT HUB TICKET OFFICE CELLOPHANE SQUARE
(SEATTLE & BELLEVUE) FALLOUT TIME TRAVELLERS SPINNERS

PRESENTED BY

717   ASUW   MONQUI PRESENTS

Pussy Galore in fall 1987, from the first photo session with guitarist Kurt Wolf (far right). In late February 1987, I was returning from Europe and stopped off in NYC to visit my friend Michael Lavine. I'll never forget how enthusiastic he was about Pussy Galore. They were playing a show at the Cat Club, and he insisted that I check them out. The band was mind-blowingly intense. Their unique industrial percussion/garage rock hybrid was one of the great creative forces of the '80s sub-popular underground. An astonishing detail in this picture is the barely visible copy of the first single-artist Sub Pop Records release, Green River's Dry as a Bone, released in July 1987, laying face-up here on a flat surface behind Jon Spencer at far left.
PHOTO BY MICHAEL LAVINE

Creation label released domestically on Rough Trade; and *Take the Subway to Your Suburb*, a collection from the Suburb label.

By the by, K Records kingpin Calvin will be licensing an EP by Subway artists the **FLATMATES**. Calvin also says that he and fellow **BEAT HAPPENING** members are negotiating a multi-record offer from New York's Homestead label. Poverty pop rules.

Rumor has it that somebody from Slash Records will be checking out the ultra-heavy **SOUNDGARDEN**, but their upcoming record will most likely be a six-song EP on Seattle's C/Z label.

Looks like **GREEN RIVER** is banned from both the Central and the Ditto. Yes, these bad boys rock as hard as the **STOOGES**. Hopefully, scene-maker **JON PONEMAN** will have an open-door policy at his new club, as yet unnamed. The space will be above Scoundrel's Lair Restaurant, located between the U-district and East Lake.

Vancouver's industrial **SKINNY PUPPY** has a video on MTV. They'll be turning the Moore Theatre upside down on Sat. April 10. On the more abrasive side, the **BUTTHOLE SURFERS**, **U-MEN**, and **SOUNDGARDEN** will be playing the same night at the Crescent Ballroom in Tacoma.

Portland's **WIPERS** will be releasing their fifth studio LP this month. Their last one, *Land of The Lost*, was

a real creeper and sounds better with every listen. Glad to see that local bands like **SKIN YARD** and the **WALKABOUTS** are making it down to Portland to play at the Satyricon. This club has a great jukebox and rocks harder than any club in Seattle. Their Greek owner also serves great gyros.

LOUDEST CLOTHES IN TOWN

Pan Ams and A.D.R.D.

SUB TEN

SCRATCH ACID destroy the Central Tavern (live)

SCHOOLY D: "Saturday Night" 12" single (Schooly D)

SCRATCH ACID *Berserker* EP (Touch and Go)

HENRY ROLLINS Hot Animal Machine LP (Texas Hotel)

VARIOUS *Take the Subway to Your Suburb* compilation LP (Subway)

PUSSY GALORE *Pussy Gold 5000* EP (Buy Our Records)

MINUTEMEN *Ballot Result* double LP (SST)

BREAKING CIRCUS *The Ice Machine* LP (Homestead)

MAGNOLIAS *Concrete Pillbox* LP (Twin/Tone)

SQUIRREL BAIT *Skag Heaven* LP (Homestead)

May 1987

Hi Everybody. Life Is Cool.

Hi everybody. Life is cool and it's springtime and I'm leaving for London and Amsterdam in two days! Hopefully I'll have some stories for next month. In the meantime, quit your day job and take off your clothes **BIG BLACK** at the Showbox was hallucinatory. Their revenge-of-the-nerds assault was one of the greatest rock shows this town has seen. I want more! Big Black will soon be releasing both a 12" EP (*Headache*) and a 45 ("Heartbeat") Be on the lookout for a special limited-edition package that will feature both records plus bizarre paraphernalia! And yes, their upcoming LP will be called *Songs About Fucking*. It seems that Big Black had fun while they were out here; activities included cheeseburgers at Dick's, rice candy, a visit to Bruce Lee's grave, and a quick stop at the Crypt on Capitol Hill for an x-tra large cock ring

ALBUM OF THE MONTH

Locust Abortion Technician by Austin's **BUTTHOLE SURFERS**. The most psychedelic band of the '80s keeps getting more disjointed and surreal with every release. *Lots* of odd tape manipulation on this one, plus a couple of all-out rockers like "Sweet Loaf" (a wild cover of **BLACK SABBATH**'s "Sweet Leaf"). There's also a blatant **U-MEN** parody on a song called "The O-Men." Coolest jacket of the year, too.

45 OF THE MONTH

"Look Around" b/w "That Girl" by **BEAT HAPPEN-ING**. This single has charm, personality, and character, and sounds great next to innocent lost songs by UK "shambling" bands like the **PASTELS**. (Send $2.50 to K Records.)

Some local demos that rock include the layered guitar pop of **CHEMISTRY SET**. They've got a song out called "Fields" that should be pressed immediately. There's also a demo floating around by some Olympia teens who go under the generic name of **METAL DEATH**. They play a complicated "progressive" thrash/metal that is unlike anything I've heard; they, like, totally destroy.

Congrats to Seattle's funny foursome the **YOUNG FRESH FELLOWS**. Their third LP, *The Men Who Love Music*, will be out on California's Frontier label. Another disc out on Frontier, *Moonhead*, by **THIN WHITE ROPE**, is a good one, and sounds bluesy heavy, raspy, and creepy. California's answer to **KILLDOZER**.

WEIRD PERFORMANCE

Composer/conductor **TIM BROCK** and conceptual humorist **JEFF BARTONE** will be giving an outdoor concert soon. On a yacht in Puget Sound, Brock will conduct the same music that was heard on the *Titanic* as it was sinking. Some of Brock's recent compositions, mostly experimental, will be available on cassette soon The new **GIRL TROUBLE** 45 (K Records) sure is different. I think it was recorded on an empty King-dome with one mic handing from the ceiling. "She No Rattle My Cage" and "River Bed" are swampy reverb-drenched tales that are sure to blow the fuck out of your speakers; in short, a rockin' cult hit.

Speaking of swampy, rootsy rock, grab *Weird Love* (Big Time) by Australia's **SCIENTISTS**. It's a re-recorded hits compilation, and it's cooler than you and me put together.

The latest **DAS DAMEN** LP, *Jupiter Eye* (SST) sounds like **HÜSKER DÜ**, only stoned. Layered, screaming anthems with trippy guitar. Worth a spin.

The Teen Dance Ordinance effectively put an end to all-ages punk shows in Seattle in 1985, just as the music scene was gaining international recognition; the law remained in effect until 2002. When I moved to Seattle in 1983, I started DJing at the Metropolis, an all-ages club in Pioneer Square. Although only in business for nine months, the impact of the venue was substantial. Many musicians that went on to represent Seattle, like Mark Arm of Mudhoney, spent time both on- and offstage there, figuring out their game. Sadly, Seattle's Teen Dance Ordinance effectively locked young people out of the scene for a very long time.

Sub Pop USA

A GUIDE TO U.S. INDEPENDENTS

By Bruce Pavitt

Hi everybody. Life is cool

and it's springtime and I'm leaving for London and Amsterdam in two days! Hopefully I'll have some stories for next month. In the meantime, quit your job and take off your clothes. . . BIG BLACK at the Showbox was hallucinatory. Their revenge-of-the-nerds assault was one of the greatest rock shows this town's seen. I want more! Big Black will soon be releasing both a 12" EP *(Headache)* and a 45 *(Heartbeat)*: be on the lookout for a special limited edition package that will feature both records plus bizarre paraphernalia! And yes, their upcoming LP *will* be called *Songs About Fucking*. It seems that Big Black had fun while they were out here: activities included cheese burgers at *Dick's*, rice candy, a visit to *Bruce Lee's* grave and a quick stop at *The Crypt* on Capitol Hill for an x-tra large cock ring. . . . ALBUM OF THE MONTH: *Locust Abortion Technician* by Austin's BUTTHOLE SURFERS. The most psychedelic band of the eighties keeps getting more disjointed and surreal with every release. LOTS of odd tape manipulation on this one plus a couple of all-out rockers like *Sweet Loaf* (a wild cover of Black Sabbath's *Sweat Leaf*). There's also a blatant U-Men parody on a song called *The O-Men*. Coolest jacket of the year, too. . . *45 OF THE MONTH: Look Around / That Girl* by BEAT HAPPENING. This single has charm, personality and character and sounds great next to innocent love songs by U.K. "shambling" bands like the Pastels. Send $2.50 to K, Box 7154, Olympia, WA 98507. . . Some local demos that rock include the layered-guitar pop of CHEMISTRY SET. They've got a song out called *Fields* that should be pressed immediately. There's also a demo floating around by some Olympia teens who go under the generic name of METAL DEATH. They play a complicated "progressive" thrash/metal that is unlike anything I've heard: they like, totally destroy. . . . Congrat's to Seattle's funny foursome the YOUNG FRESH FELLOWS: Their third LP, *The Men Who Love Music*, will be out on California's Frontier label. Another disc out on Frontier, *Moonhead* by Thin White Rope, is a good one and sounds bluesy, heavy, raspy and creepy. California's answer to Killdozer. . . . WEIRD PERFORMANCE: Composer/conductor Tim Brock and conceptual humorist Jeff Bartone will be giving an outdoor concert soon. On a yacht in Puget Sound, Brock will conduct the same music that was heard on the Titanic as it was sinking. Some of Brock's recent compositions, mostly experimental, will be available on cassette soon. . . . The new GIRL TROUBLE 45 sure is different. I think it was recorded in an empty King Dome with one mike hanging from the ceiling. *She No Rattle My Cage* and *River Bed* are swampy reverb-drenched tales that are sure to blow the fuck out of your speakers: in short, a rockin' cult hit. Available for $2.50 from K. . . .

. . . Speaking of swampy, rootsy rock, grab *Weird Love* by Australia's SCIENTISTS. It's a re-recorded hits compilation and it's cooler than you and me put together. Out on Big Time. . . . The latest DAS DAMEN LP, *Jupiter Eyes* (SST) sounds like Husker Du, only stoned. Layered, screaming anthems with trippy guitar. Worth a spin. . . . A five-song EP by Seattle's GREEN RIVER will be out soon. . . . THE SUB POP 100 LP has sold over 3000 copies. . . . REALLY BIG NEWS: a very cool new club called the OK HOTEL is opening up. During the day a cafe will be open. At night, the cafe will be complimented by a separate performance space with a capacity of 200 people. Due to the totally fucked Teen Dance Hall Ordinance, minors will not be allowed. (This ordinance calls for unreal insurance payments that can only be met by big business.) Anyhow, since alcohol won't be served, people as young as 18 will be allowed to come in off the street. The address is 212 Alaskan Way in the Pioneer Square area. More info on this space as things develop. . . . I'm still trying to figure out why Chris from Soundgarden is on the cover of the new "underground" Seattle compilation LOW LIFE. He's not even on the record. Despite the silly cover, there's some good hits by FEAST, BUNDLE OF HISS and ROOM 9. . . . Dave and Charly from CAT BUTT are currently trying to expand their wig collection. Give these lovely orphan boys a call at 323-3944. . . LANDREW The LOVE GOD, the beautiful and talented hermaphrodite singer for MALFUNKSHUN, tells me his band's first studio project will be a "tribute to Liberace". . . Last month's Sub Pop photo: Lead Singer of Scratch Acid at the Central Tavern, April 5. Photo by Cam Garrett. May Sub Pop photo: Big Black at the Showbox, March 28. Photo by Cam Garrett.

SUB TEN

BUTTHOLE SURFERS *Locust Abortion Technician* LP (Touch & Go), Austin, TX
SCIENTISTS *Weird Love* LP (Big Time) Australia
BEAT HAPPENING *Look Around* 45 (K) Olympia, WA
CREEPERS *Miserable Sinners* LP (In Tape/Last Time Around) U.K.
WISEBLOOD *Stumbo* 12" single (Relativity) NYC
THIN WHITE ROPE *Moonhead* LP (Frontier) Southern California
GIRL TROUBLE *She No Rattle My Cage* 45 (K) Tacoma, WA
LOW LIFE compilation LP Seattle, WA
DAS DAMEN *Jupiter Eye* LP (SST) NYC
HONOR ROLL *Jank* 45 (Eskimo) Richmond, VA

SUBPOP DESIGN BY

A five-song EP by Seattle's **GREEN RIVER** will be out soon.

The *Sub Pop 100* compilation LP has sold over 3000 copies.

REALLY BIG NEWS

A very cool new club called the **OK HOTEL** is opening up. During the day, a cafe will be open. At night, the cafe will be complemented by a separate performance space with capacity of 200 people. Due to the totally fucked Teen Dance Ordinance in Seattle, minors will not be allowed. (This ordinance calls for unreal insurance payments that can only be met by big business.) Anyhow, since alcohol won't be served, people as young as 18 will be allowed to come in off the street. The address is 212 Alaskan Way in the Pioneer Square area. More info on this space as things develop.

I'm still trying to figure out why **CHRIS CORNELL** from **SOUNDGARDEN** is on the cover of the new "underground" Seattle compilation *Low Life*. He's not even on the record. Despite the silly cover, there's some good hits by **FEAST**, **BUNDLE OF HISS**, and **ROOM 9**.

Dave and Charlie from **CAT BUTT** are currently trying to expand their wig collection. Give these lovely orphan boys a call.

LANDREW THE LOVE GOD, the beautiful and talented hermaphrodite singer for **MALFUNKSHUN**, tells me his band's first studio project will be a "tribute to Liberace."

SUB TEN

BUTTHOLE SURFERS, *Locust Abortion Technician* LP (Touch and Go)

SCIENTISTS *Weird Love* LP (Big Time)

BEAT HAPPENING "Look Around" 45 (K)

CREEPERS *Miserable Sinners* LP (In Tape/Last Time Around)

WISEBLOOD "Stumbo" 12" single (Relativity)

THIN WHITE ROPE *Moonhead* LP (Frontier)

GIRL TROUBLE "She No Rattle My Cage" 45 (K)

VARIOUS *Low Life* compilation LP

DAS DAMEN *Jupiter Eye* LP (SST)

HONOR ROLE "Purgatory" b/w "Jank" 45 (Eskimo)

June 1987

Please Buy This Record So I Can Pay My Dad Back

Motorcycles are fun if you don't fall off. Now, let's talk about the West Coast!...

LOS ANGELES

REDD KROSS are the coolest! Here's why: They started recording as young teens and grew up loving **KISS**, the **PARTRIDGE FAMILY** and Charlie Manson headlines. They were the first band to openly embrace the "awful" culture of the '70s. Also, they grew their hair to the hips when it was totally uncool. Plus, they've made a couple of thrashy cult super-8 films featuring the naughty **LOVEDOLLS** (currently available around town on video). So anyway, *now*, in addition to securing their status as trendsetters and scene makers, Redd Kross have come with their best disc yet! The *Neurotica* LP (Big Time) is a total rush of '60s pop harmonies and '70s hard rock. In short, a summer party hit. *Buy*....

SAN FRANCISCO

CAMPER VAN BEETHOVEN consistently mix country, psychedelic and ethnic world music into pop hits that makes sense. They are one of the most interesting bands of the decade. Although all three LPs are interesting, their first, *Telephone Landslide Victory*, remain their strongest. Currently, "Take The Skinheads Bowling" has been released as a 45 in England, where it's topping the indie charts. Camper Van Beethoven have just been signed to IRS.

PORTLAND

THE WIPERS have been around since 1977. Their first 45, "Better Off Dead" (1978) remains one of the great punk singles from that era. They have released five excellent studio albums, a rare accomplishment from any band. When I walked into the Milky Way in Amsterdam last month, the DJ was playing the Wipers. Unfortunately, they've remained more popular in Europe (especially Germany and Holland) than the US. Their new LP, *Follow Blind* (Restless) is a good compliment to last year's *Land of the Lost*. Both LPs are softer, more introspective, and more melancholy than previous, and seem influenced by seminal '60s psych like **LOVE** and **HENDRIX**. Greg Sage and the Wipers sing about loneliness and alienation better than any band I can think of.

SEATTLE

The next few years will see the ultra-heavy rock of Seattle rival the Motor City scene of the early '70s. I believe that bands like **GREEN RIVER** and **SOUND-GARDEN** are every bit as great as the **STOOGES** and the **MC5**. To prove my point, I've borrowed $2,000 from my Dad to help Green River put out their latest EP, *Dry as a Bone* (Sub Pop). For me, songs like "This Town" and "P.C.C." are as hard and heavy as anything I've ever heard. Please buy this record so I can pay my Dad back! The fun and exciting record release party will be on Friday, June 5, above Scoundrel's Lair!

VANCOUVER

NOMEANSNO are smart guys with plenty to say. Their Seattle shows have earned them a cult following and I'm sure their new LP, *Sex Mad* (Alternative Tentacles) will do well here. The production, packaging, and lyrics are excellent. The music itself, though, is stiff, herky-jerky, and completely unsexy. However, I'm sure fans of the band will not be disappointed.

FALLOUT RECORDS AND SKATEBOARDS PRESENT

U-MEN
SOLID ACTION
DIG IT A HOLE

NEW SINGLE ON

ONLY $2.50 AT FALLOUT

Black Label **RECORDS**

A SUBSIDIARY OF FALLOUT RECORDS & SKATEBOARDS
1506 E. OLIVE WAY SEATTLE WA 98122

Guitar Instruction
for music readers and non-music readers

College Credit Available
Gift Certificates

PRIVATE INSTRUCTION
OFFERED IN:
**ALL STYLES OF
ROCK GUITAR**
- Jazz Guitar
- Fusion Guitar
- Classical Guitar
- Improvisation
- Theory
- Transcription
- Ear Training
- Sight Reading

**SCOTT LINDENMUTH
776-6362**

WIPERS
KILLDOZER MELVINS GIRL TROUBLE
Sat. JUNE 20
8 pm ALL AGES
CRESCENT BALLROOM
13th and Fawcett   Downtown Tacoma
Tickets $7 in Advance From Fallout, Time Travelers,
Cellophane Square, Spinners & TicketMaster
(628-0888) $9 at the door.

ROCK FASHION
EXPERIENCE IT!

JEANS, DENIM
JACKETS, TUX, TAILS,
SPANDEX — WE HAVE
IT ALL TOGETHER
FOR YOU!

EXPERIENCE IT!
POWER COATS,
DISTRESSED LEATHER,
FRINGE, SHOES,
INCLUDING SNAKESKIN
HI-TOPS AND
OUTRAGEOUS
ACCESSORIES,

THE EXPERIENCE
(we've shortened the name)
912 Alaskan Way Seattle WA 98104
624.0960
Send $1 for Catplog. Refundable.
PHOTO: JIM HADLEY

SUBPOP USA

A GUIDE TO U.S. INDEPENDENTS

By Bruce Pavitt

Motorcycles are fun if you don't fall off. Now, let's talk about the West Coast!...

LOS ANGELES: Redd Kross are the coolest. Here's why: They started recording as young teens and grew up loving Kiss, *The Partridge Family* and Charlie Manson headlines. They were the first band to openly embrace the "awful" culture of the 70's. Also, they grew their hair to their hips when it was totally uncool. Plus, they've made a couple of trashy, cult super-8 films featuring the naughty *Love Dolls* (currently available around town on video). So anyway, NOW, in addition to securing their status as trend-setters and scene makers, Red Kross have come up with their best disc yet! Their *Neurotica LP* (Big Time) is a total rush of 60's pop harmonies and 70's hard rock. In short, a summer party hit. BUY...

SAN FRANCISCO: Camper Van Beethoven consistently mix country, psychedelic and ethnic world music into pop hits that make sense. They are one of the most interesting bands of the decade. Although all three LP's are interesting, their first, *Telephone Landslide Victory*, remains their strongest. Currently, *Take The Skinheads Bowling* has been released as a 45 in England where it's topping the indie charts. Camper Van Beethoven have just been signed to IRS...

PORTLAND: The Wipers have been around since 1977. Their first 45, *Better Off Dead* (1978) remains one of the great punk singles from that era. They have released five excellent studio albums, a rare accomplishment for any band. When I walked into *The Milky Way* in Amsterdam last month, the DJ was playing the Wipers. Unfortunately they've remained more popular in Europe (especially Germany and Holland) than the US. Their new LP, *Follow Blind* (Restless) is a good compliment to last year's *Land of the Lost*. Both LP's are softer, more introspective and more melancholy than previous, and seem influenced by seminal 60's psych like Love and Hendrix. Greg Sage and the Wipers sing about loneliness and alienation better than any band I can think of.

SEATTLE: The next few years will see the ultra-heavy rock of Seattle rival the Motor City scene of the early '70s. I believe that bands like Green River and Soundgarden are every bit as great as the Stooges and the MC5. To prove my point, I've borrowed $2,000 from my Dad to help Green River put out their latest EP, *Dry as a Bone* (Sub Pop). For me, songs like *This Town* and *PCC* are as hard and heavy as anything I've ever heard. Please buy this record so I can pay my Dad back! The fun and exciting record release party will be on Friday, June 5, right above Scoundrel's Lair!...

VANCOUVER: No Means No are smart guys with plenty to say. Their Seattle shows have earned them a cult following and I'm sure their new LP, *Sex Mad* (Alternative Tentacles) will do well here: the production, packaging and lyrics are excellent. The music itself, though, is stiff, herky-jerky and completely unsexy. However, I'm sure that fans of the band will not be disappointed.

As long as we're talking about Canadians, let's talk Cowboy Junkies. The group is from Ontario and plays a low-key, whispered blues that sounds great at three in the morning. Singer Margo is sensual, sultry and sexy. For those of you who missed their excellent Seattle show, check out their new LP *Whites Off Earth Now!!* (this one might be hard to find). Write: Latent Recordings 407 The Kingsway, Islington, Ontario, Canada M9A 3W1)....

By the way, Seattle's wildest thrash band, The Accused, have just been licensed through *Time Travelers* by New York's *Combatcore*. Combatcore is quoted as saying "these guys are gonna be bigger than Slayer"... . Next month we'll look into local recordings by The Melvins, Green Pajamas, Room 9 and The Walkabouts. And be on the look out for a limited edition promo 45 by Soundgarden!...

Oh, I almost forgot: *Richies Dog* by Halo of Flies ROCKS! Write away for this essential 45: Amphetamine Reptile, 4932 33rd Ave. S., Mnpls, MN 55417.

SUB TEN

GREEN RIVER *Dry As A Bone EP* (SUB POP) Seattle
REDD KROSS *Neurotica LP* (Big Time) L.A.
WIPERS *Follow Blind LP* (Restless) Portland
COWBOY JUNKIES *Whites Off Earth Now!!* (Latent) Ontario
SONGS WE TAUGHT THE CRAMPS compilation LP (Monster A Go Go)

HALO OF FLIES *Richies Dog 45* (Amphetamine Reptile) Mnpls.
BIG DIPPER *Boo Boo EP* (Homestead) Boston
NO MEANS NO *Sex Mad LP* (Alternative Tentacles) Vancouver
THE EASTERN DARK *Long Live The New Flesh EP* (What Goes On) Australia
THE FEW *Friends 45* (K) Guemes Island, WA

Bruce Fairweather of Green River with main squeeze Stephanie Barber

Photo by Cam Garrett.

SUBPOP DESIGN BY

As long as we're talking about Canadians, let's talk **COWBOY JUNKIES**. The group is from Ontario, and plays a low-key, whispered blues that sounds great at three in the morning. Singer Margo is sensual, sultry, and sexy. For those of you who missed their excellent Seattle show, check out their new LP *Whites Off Earth Now!!* This one might be hard to find. (Try Latent Recordings, Ontario, Canada)

By the way, Seattle's wildest thrash band, the **ACCÜSED**, have just been licensed through Time Travelers by New York's Combatcore. Combatcore is quoted saying, "these guys are going to be bigger than **SLAYER**"

Next month, we'll look into local recordings by the **MELVINS**, **GREEN PAJAMAS**, **ROOM 9**, and the **WALKABOUTS**. And be on the lookout for a limited edition promo 45 by **SOUNDGARDEN**!

Oh, I almost forgot: "Richies Dog" (Amphetamine Reptile) by **HALO OF FLIES** *rocks*! Write away for this essential 45.

SUB TEN

GREEN RIVER *Dry as a Bone* EP (Sub Pop)

REDD KROSS *Neurotica* LP (Big Time)

WIPERS *Follow Blind* LP (Restless)

COWBOY JUNKIES *Whites Off Earth Now!!* (Latent)

VARIOUS *Songs We Taught the Cramps* compilation LP (Monster A Go-Go)

HALO OF FLIES "Richies Dog" 45 (Amphetamine Reptile)

BIG DIPPER *Boo Boo* EP (Homestead)

NOMEANSNO *Sex Mad* LP (Alternative Tentacles)

THE EASTERN DARK *Long Live The New Flesh* EP (What Goes On)

THE FEW Friends 45 (K Records)

I Just Want To Lay in Bed and Stare at the Ceiling

I think I have sleeping sleepness. I'm tired. I just want to lay in bed and stare at the ceiling. I don't want to write this column but I *have* to because it's *due* tomorrow. Right now it's 10:00 p.m. Monday night, and I'm just going to fill up these pages. Okay? Ho hum. Well, I have this **FEAST** cassette here. They spent a million dollars on the packaging and it looks cool. It comes in a black cardboard box with **FEAST** printed in silver on top. When I open the box, a picture of Tom springs out like a jack-in-the-box. I unfold the cardboard sheet. Hmm. It says there that Feast "reside in a musical world of murky shadows alternating with powerful shrieks of light." Gosh. Whoever wrote that should be embarrassed. A bit pretentious. They should have said: "Feast rock like motherfuckers." Then people would get a good idea of what their music sounds like. It also says that Nils Bernstein is their manager. I'm glad to see that Nils has a new hobby.

Wait a minute—Feast has quoted me as saying: "Feast is the band to watch in 1987." I'm sorry, but I never said that. I do think "Feast rock like motherfuckers."

The Feast sound is heavy and sexy, and their grinding version of "Immigrant Song" could squeeze the life out of an entire nation. As for their original material, it's a bit long. And the recordings here, while powerful, are one-dimensional. Sure, people are going to say "Wow, great drum sound," but big deal. Feast needs a producer who can get them to experiment more in the studio. Bands shouldn't even bother going into a 24-track until they've gained experience and confidence. But, yes, I agree, it's a great drum sound. I should also mention the intense live pictures of Feast here, taken by Charles Peterson. By the way, Charles was going to buy a house

but his loan didn't come through. He's now looking for a house to rent though, so if anybody has a hot tip give him a call. Well, the weird thing about this Feast cassette is this: it's the most elaborately packaged cassette I've ever seen. (I haven't even discussed the nest of shredded black paper that the tape rests upon, inside the black box.) This band could possibly sell a trillion copies all over the world, but they only made 50 copies to send out to label magnate types who might want to sign them and treat them like royalty, which is fine—but what about all the people who want to *buy* one of these damn tapes! People like yourself, who have just invested five minutes of your time learning everything there is to know about Feast and their *really cool tape.* See, *you can't buy this tape because they only made 50. It comes in a cute cardboard box, it was recorded on a 24-track and features a great drum sound and includes the coolest version of "Immigrant Song" ever, plus it has great sexy pictures of Tom all over it, and you can't even buy it.* What a fucking drag. I think Feast should make more of these so their friends can have something to remember them by. A memento to remind them of all the hangovers of their youth. Something to commemorate all the noise and all the beer. Sexy rock music is for everyone to enjoy, not just 50 rock executive types. In two days Feast is playing at the Vogue. I'm going to march right down there and *demand* that they make more of these tapes. And if they ignore me, I'll get drunk and beg them. Fuck am I tired.

SPECIAL IMPORTANT ANNOUNCEMENT

Tacoma's Community World Theater, the coolest all-ages club ever, is throwing a *big* benefit show to help keep things going. People, this will be *fun* so you have

"You can't buy this tape because they only made 50. It comes in a cute cardboard box, it was recorded on a 24-track and features a great drum sound and includes the coolest version of 'Immigrant Song' ever plus it has great sexy pictures of tom all over it and y ou can't even buy it. What a fucking drag. Feast should make more of these so their friends can have something to remember them by. A memento to remind them of all the hangovers of their youth. Something to commemorate all the noise and all the beer. Sexy rock music is for everyone to enjoy, not just 50 rock executive types. In two days Feast is playing at the Vogue. I'm going to march right down there and DEMAND that they make more of these tapes. And if they ignore me, I'll get drunk and beg them."

CHEWING A FEAST

I think I have sleeping sleepness. I'm tired. I just want to lay in bed and stare at the ceiling. I don't want to write this column but I **HAVE** to because it's **DUE** tomorrow. Right now it's 10:00 pm Monday night and I'm just going to fill up these pages. OK?

Ho Hum. Well, I have this Feast cassette here. They spent a million dollars on the packaging and it looks cool. It comes in a black cardboard box with **FEAST** printed in silver on top. When I open the box, a picture of Tom springs out like a jack-in-the-box. I unfold the cardboard sheet. Hmm. It says here that *"Feast reside in a musical world of murky shadows alternating with powerful shrieks of light."* Gosh. Whoever wrote that should be embarrassed. A bit pretentious. They should have said: **"Feast rock like motherfuckers."** Then people would get a good idea of what their music sounds like. It also says that Nils Bernstein is their manager and can be reached at 547-7437. I'm glad to see that Nils has a new hobby.

Wait a minute. Feast has quoted me as saying "Feast is the band to watch in 1987." I'm sorry, but I never said that. I do think "Feast rock like motherfuckers."

The Feast sound is heavy and sexy and their grinding version of *Immigrant Song* could squeeze the life out of an entire nation. As for their original material, it's a bit long. And the recordings here, while powerful, are one-dimensional. Sure, people are going to say "Wow, great drum sound," but big deal. Feast needs a producer who can get them to **experiment** more in the studio. Bands shouldn't even **bother** going into a 24-track until they've gained experience and confidence. But, yes, I agree, it is a great drum sound. I should also mention the intense live pictures of Feast here, taken by Charles Peterson. By the way, Charles was going to buy a house but his loan didn't come through. He's now looking for a house to rent though, so if anybody has a hot tip give him a call at 324-0116. Well, the weird thing about this Feast cassette is this: it's the most elaborately packaged cassette I've ever seen (I haven't even discussed the nest of shredded black paper that the tape rests upon, inside the black box.) and this band could possibly sell a trillion copies all over the world, but they only made 50 copies to send out to label magnate types who might want to sign them and treat them like **royalty,** which is fine, but what about all the people who want to BUY one of these damn tapes! People like yourself, who have just invested five minutes of your time learning everything there is to know about Feast and their REALLY COOL TAPE. See, YOU CAN'T BUY THIS TAPE BECAUSE THEY ONLY MADE 50. IT COMES IN A CUTE CARDBOARD BOX, IT WAS RECORDED ON A 24-TRACK AND FEATURES A GREAT DRUM SOUND AND INCLUDES THE COOLEST VERSION OF IMMIGRANT SONG EVER PLUS IT HAS GREAT SEXY PICTURES OF TOM ALL OVER IT AND YOU CAN'T EVEN BUY IT. What a fucking drag. I think Feast should make more of these so their friends can have something to remember them by. A memento to remind them of all the hangovers of their youth. Something to commemorate all the noise and all the beer. Sexy rock music is for **everybody** to enjoy, not just 50 rock executive types. In two days **Feast** is playing at the Vogue. I'm going to march right down there and **DEMAND** that they make more of these tapes. And if they ignore me, I'll get drunk and beg them. Fuck am I tired.

SPECIAL IMPORTANT ANNOUNCEMENT: Tacoma's Community World Theater, the coolest all-ages club ever, is throwing a **BIG** benefit show to help keep things going. People, this will be **FUN** so you have no excuse not to come. Friday, July 3rd, will feature the mind-warp of **Room 9** plus the ultra heavy and sexy **Soundgarden.** In addition to these two, there will be special guest appearances by groovy and awesome types from all over the state, including **Greinke** and **Angus,** the primitive genius of **Spook, Gary Allen May,** cartoons, odd film shorts and more. Call Jimmy for more info at 473-4299. All bookings are tentative but nobody will be disappointed.

BY BRUCE PAVITT

SUB 10

G.G. ALLIN Hated in the Nation cassette (ROIR) **NY**
Ultra sick and totally offensive weirdo punk rock to the max.
FLESHEATERS Greatest Hits LP (SST) **L.A.**
Brilliant poetry from under-rated maniacs. R.I.P.
WHITE ZOMBIE Psycho-Head Blow Out EP (Silent Explosion) **NYC**
Sonic Youth with hair. Sexy. Soon to be great.
BIG BLACK Headache EP (Touch & Go) **Chicago**
Big noise! I guess they're playing their last show ever in Seattle! Limited edition violence.
GREEN PAJAMAS Book of Hours LP (Green Monkey) **Seattle**
These guys need to do more drugs. Too stiff.
PONTIAC BROS. Be Married Song EP (Frontier) **L.A.**
Commercial and twangy. o.k.
TIM BROCK Performed at the Hotel Olympian cassette (K) **Olympia**
Intellectual string quartet stuff from genius composer.
TEN FOOT FACES Daze of Corndogs & Yo Yo's LP (Pitch) **S.F.**
I tried my first corndog last year. It was good.
PARADISE Paradise A go-go 12'' single (Big City) **D.C.**
Party record of the month. Lots of D.C.-style percussion.
S.G.M. Strunk cassette (S.G.M.) **Seattle**
Young, loud and crazy. Better than Soundgarden and Green River put together. Better than Led Zep and the Stooges even.

Charles Peterson, 1985: "He's now looking for a house to rent, so if anybody has a hot tip give him a call."

no excuse not to come. Friday, July 3, will feature the mind warp of **ROOM 9**, plus the ultra-heavy and sexy **SOUNDGARDEN**. In addition to these two, there will be special guest appearances by groovy and awesome types from all over the state, including Greinke and Angus, the primitive genius of Spook, Gary Allen May, cartoons, odd film shorts, and more. Call Jimmy for more info. All bookings are tentative, but nobody will be disappointed.

SUB 10

G.G. ALLIN *Hated in the Nation* cassette (ROIR) Ultra-sick and totally offensive weirdo punk rock to the max

FLESHEATERS *Greatest Hits* LP (SST) Brilliant poetry from under-rated devil maniacs. R.I.P.

WHITE ZOMBIE *Psycho-Head Blow Out* EP (Silent Explosion)

SONIC YOUTH with hair. Sexy. Soon to be great.

BIG BLACK *Headache* EP (Touch and Go) Big noise! I guess they will be playing their last show ever in Seattle! Limited edition violence.

GREEN PAJAMAS *Book of Hours* LP (Green Monkey) These guys need to do more drugs. Too stiff.

PONTIAC BROTHERS *Be Married Song* EP (Frontier) Commercial and twangy. Okay.

TIM BROCK *Performed at the Hotel Olympian* cassette (K Records) Intellectual string stuff from genius composer

TEN FOOT FACES *Daze of Corndogs and Yo Yos* LP (Pitch) I tried my first corndog last year. It was good.

PARADISE "Paradise A Go-Go" 12" single (Big City) D.C. Party record of the month. Lots of D.C.-style percussion

S.G.M. *Strunk* cassette (S.G.M.) Young, loud and crazy. Better than Soundgarden and Green River put together. Better than Led Zep and the Stooges even.

Dear Mom and Dad

Hi. It's raining outside. It's cold. The weather this summer has not been fun. But I've been keeping busy having fun anyway.

Last night I went out to Squid Row. That's a bar where young people drink cheap beer and try to make eye contact with hopeful sexual partners. My friend Chris wanted to make out with an underage brunette with braces, but no such luck. I had fun dancing to a couple of old **JAMES BROWN** songs. Then Chris and I left on his motorcycle.

We headed for the Central Tavern to see a band from Boston called **DINOSAUR**. They have a new album coming out called *You're Living All Over Me*, which rocks heavily. The singer has a lot of emotional depth. It's rare to hear young male singers who can sound vulnerable as well as aggressive. I think even you might like it. Anyway, after Chris and I rode through the rain, we hung out in front of the Central and talked with the singer. He had long hair and was friendly. By now it was eleven, and only ten people had showed up. He said their whole trip across the US had been like that. He also said that he didn't like the people in Portland because they were "weird." I think he was bummed.

Then Chris and I drove down to Tugs to meed Cyd, Melissa, and Lisa. Cyd had a new hat. Melissa was wearing tie-dyed stretch pants. Lisa had blue hair. We drank bottles of Budweiser and danced.

It was so much fun we almost forgot about Dinosaur. Chris and I raced back to the Central just in time to catch a few songs. They were loud and great. My friend Mark from **GREEN RIVER** said it was the best show he'd seen since **SCRATCH ACID**. I could tell he was impressed. Steve and Eddie from the **THROWN UPS** were there, too, and everybody (all ten of them) were screaming for an encore at the top of their lungs. People just wanted to rock out and have a good time.

This morning I woke up with a screaming hangover and called in sick at Muzak. About all I could do was sit here and type this letter. In a few days, I'll be in New York checking out the New Music Seminar. This is a big convention where young music-biz types meet to drink expensive beer and make eye contact. Maybe I can even push the Green River record.

And Dad, thanks again for the loan. The Green River record is going into its third pressing, and I'm sure I'll be able to pay you back on time.

Love, Bruce

SUB 10

DINOSAUR *You're Living All Over Me* LP (SST) Way solid and cool disc. Lots of wah-wah. Singer sounds like a cross between **NEIL YOUNG** and Thurston from **SONIC YOUTH**.

SONIC YOUTH *Sister* LP (SST) Dissonant cheap guitars. Recorded this time on old tube equipment for a warmer sound. Peasant intellectuals rock the masses. *Great.*

DAVID THOMAS AND THE WOODEN BIRDS *Blame the Messenger* LP (Twin Tone) A modern interpretation of traditional folk music. Features almost all of the old members of **PERE UBU**.

MY DAD IS DEAD *Peace, Love and Murder* LP (Birth) Mark plays all the instruments. He's cynical and smart. Not as heavy as **BIG BLACK** but neither are you.

"This morning I woke up with a screaming hangover and called in sick at Muzak. About all I could do was sit here and type this letter. In a few days I'll be in New York checking out The New Music Seminar. This is a big convention where young music-biz types meet to drink expensive beer and make eye contact. Maybe I can even push the Green River record."

SUB POP

By Bruce Pavitt

Dear Mom & Dad, SUB 10

Hi. It's raining outside. It's cold. The weather this summer has not been fun. But I've been keeping busy having fun anyway.

Last night I went out to *Squid Row*. That's a bar where young people drink cheap beer and try to make eye contact with hopeful sexual partners. My friend Chris wanted to make out with an underage brunette with braces but no such luck. I had fun dancing to a couple of old James Brown songs. Then Chris and I left on his motorcycle.

We headed for the Central Tavern to see a band from Boston called **Dinosaur**. They have a new album out called *You're Living All Over Me*, which rocks heavily. The singer has a lot of emotional depth. It's rare to hear young male singers who can sound vulnerable as well as aggressive. I think even you might like it.

Anyway, after Chris and I rode through the rain, we hung out in front of the Central and talked with the singer. He had long hair and was friendly. By now it was eleven and only ten people had showed up. He said their whole trip across the U.S. had been like that. He also said that he didn't like the people in Portland because they were "weird." I think he was bummed.

Then Chris and I drove down to Tugs to meet Cyd, Melissa and Lisa. Cyd had a new hat. Melissa was wearing tye-dye stretch pants. Lisa had blue hair. We drank bottles of Budweiser and danced.

It was so much fun we almost forgot about **Dinosaur**. Chris and I raced back to the Central just in time to catch a few songs. They were loud and great. My friend Mark from Green River said it was the best show he'd seen since Scratch Acid. I could tell he was impressed. Steve and Eddie from **The Thrown Ups** were there too and everybody (all ten of them) were screaming for an encore at the top of their lungs. People just wanted to rock out and have a good time.

This morning I woke up with a screaming hangover and called in sick at Muzak. About all I could do was sit here and type this letter. In a few days I'll be in New York checking out the New Music Seminar. This is a big convention where young music-biz types meet to drink expensive beer and make eye contact. Maybe I can even push the **Green River** record.

And Dad, thanks again for the loan. The **Green River** record is going into its third pressing and I'm sure I'll be able to pay you back on time.

Love, Bruce

DINOSAUR *You're Living All Over Me LP* (SST) Boston
Way solid and cool disc. Lots of wah-wah. Singer sounds like a cross between Neil Young and Thurston from Sonic Youth.

SONIC YOUTH *Sister LP* (SST) NYC
Dissonant cheap guitars. Recorded this time on old tube equipment for a warmer sound. Peasant intellectuals rock the masses. GREAT.

DAVID THOMAS AND THE WOODEN BIRDS *Blame the Messenger LP* (Twin Tone) Cleveland
A modern interpretation of traditional folk music. Features almost all of the old members of Pere Ubu.

MY DAD IS DEAD *Peace, Love and Murder LP* (Birth) Cleveland
Mark plays all the instruments. He's cynical and smart. Not as heavy as Big Black but neither are you.

RU PAUL *Is Star Booty LP* (Fun Tone, USA) Atlanta
I hear this black transsexual has one of the wildest live shows around. The "Prince" of Atlanta.

VARIOUS ARTISTS *Wailing Ultimate LP* (Homestead) USA
Excellent compilation of contemporary garage rock 'n' roll. No phony middle-class haircuts. Features Dinosaurs' coolest: "Repulsion." Other Homestead bands include Big Dipper, Salem 66, Volcano Suns, Live Skull.

U-MEN *Dig It A Hole 45* (Black Label) Seattle
Avant R&B from the kings of black. Their best yet. Glad to see them getting closer to the Sonics and farther away from that poseur Birthday Party stuff. A stunning four-color silk screen jacket on this one.

THE WALKABOUTS *Cyclone 45* (Necessity) Seattle
Hippie outcasts come up with a hit. "Cyclone" is perfectly recorded folk-rock, featuring Chris, the stronger of the two vocalists. I can see why San Francisco thinks this gang is cool.

THE ACCUSED *More Fun Than An Open Casket Funeral LP* (Combat) Seattle
Big-League gnarly thrash stuff that's intense, even if it is predictable and generic. Surprisingly intelligent, socially aware lyrics.

SCREAMING TREES *Even If and Especially When LP* (SST) Ellensburg, Washington
These guys are fat, they sweat like pigs and they rock like hell. Note for note, record for record, this is the greatest band in Washington State. All the kids who threw rocks at the Conner brothers as they walked home from school can all go fucking die. Growing up as an outcast in a tiny redneck town in eastern Washington can force some people to transcend by fighting with everything they have. This record is yet more GREAT psyche/punk from people who totally believe in what they're doing.

PAGE DESIGN BY

RUPAUL *Is Star Booty* LP (Fun Tone USA) I hear this black drag queen has one of the wildest live shows around. The "prince" of Atlanta.

VARIOUS *Wailing Ultimate* LP (Homestead) Excellent compilation of contemporary garage rock 'n roll. No phony middle-class haircuts. Features Dinosaur's coolest, "Repulsion." Other Homestead bands include **BIG DIPPER, SALEM 66, VOLCANO SUNS**, and **LIVE SKULL.**

U-MEN "Dig It A Hole" 45 (Black Label) Avant R&B from the kings of black. Their best yet. Glad to see them getting closer to the **SONICS** and farther away from that poseur **BIRTHDAY PARTY** stuff. A stunning four-color silkscreen jacket on this one.

THE WALKABOUTS "Cyclone" 45 (Necessity) Hippie outcasts come up with a hit. "Cyclone" is perfectly recorded folk-rock featuring Chris, the stronger of the two vocalists. I can see why San Francisco thinks this gang is cool.

THE ACCUSED *More Fun Than an Open Casket Funeral* LP (Combat) Big-league gnarly thrash stuff that's intense, even if it is predictable and generic. Surprisingly intelligent, socially-aware lyrics.

SCREAMING TREES *Even If and Especially When* LP (SST) These guys are fat, they sweat like pigs, and they rock like hell. Note for note, record for record, this is the greatest band in Washington State. All the kids who threw rocks at the Conner brothers as they walked home from school can all go fucking die. Growing up as an outcast in a tiny redneck town in eastern Washington can force some people to transcend by fighting with everything they have. This record is yet more *great* psych/punk from people who totally believe in what they're doing.

Goodbye Big Black

NO TREND Tritonian Nash–Vegas Polyester Complex LP (Touch and Go). Touch and Go retains its status as America's strongest and most daring indie label. Their latest, by D.C.'s No Trend, is a frenzied zany mix of bells, bongos, and brass. A totally weird punk-Vegas schlock monster. It's campy, it's damaged, it's "out there." Possibly influenced by early **MOTHERS OF INVENTION**.

VARIOUS *A Texas Trip* compilation LP (Caroline). The , made enough money selling pot to school children that they were able to build their own recording studio. This is a seven-song collection featuring Austin's surreal Surfers plus three of their friends: **STEVE FITCH** (great!), **STICK MEN WITH RAY GUNS**, and **DANIEL JOHNSTON**. Daniel has long been an underground favorite with his neurotic Mr. Rogers imitation. Sadly, the tracks here are too overproduced for his mild-mannered, innocent little songs. Daniel has recently been institutionalized for clubbing his boss, a Burger King manager, into a coma.

JACK Starting this September, I'll be spinning records one Sunday a month at the Vogue. A local band, of the God variety, will also be featured. This month: **SWALLOW**. Admission one dollar.

RAGING SLAB *Assmaster* LP (Buy Our Records) This is the "biker" band from NYC that all the cool people have been talking about. They sound like a cross of **AEROSMITH** and **BLACK OAK ARKANSAS**. They have long hair and tight pants. They rock. Unfortunately, they are pure nostalgia. At least the ultra-hard rock bands in Seattle listen to modern stuff like **SWANS**, **BUTTHOLE SURFERS**, and **BIG BLACK**. Oh, I forgot—this record also comes with a really bad comic book.

1/2 JAPANESE and **VELVET MONKEYS** *Big Big Sun* cassette (K) Two of D.C.'s fave bands, captured live at the Vogue in Seattle. Half Jap, featuring the genius of **JAD FAIR**, is not your everyday "quirky art band." Jad has always created art and words from a child's perspective and probably has a lifetime supply of crayons on his desk. A unique man. The Velvet Monkeys play a thrashy, '60s-inspired punk/psych that sounds good even without the wigs. My favorite part of the show was when Don from the Velvets wrapped his cord around Julie and sang "Why Don't We Do it in the Road?"

SKIN *Blood, Women, and Roses* LP (Product Inc. import) Jarboe lives with Michael Gira. Michael is the brains and muscle behind the ultra-heavy, minimalist Swans. Jarboe wanted to make a record, so Michael helped her. Jim from Muzak calls this "easy listening Swans." Subtle yet heavy.

MELVINS *Gluey Porch Treatments* LP (Alchemy). Everybody knows that the Melvins are the heaviest band in the world. And *Gluey Porch Treatments* is the heaviest record in the world. Weighing in at over a million tons, this things will squish you like a tiny bug. Dan, the cool drummer from **KILLDOZER**, said, "These guys are a cross between **SWANS** and **BLUE CHEER**! They only do one thing but they do it perfectly! I think they're going to make us look pretty bad!" Thank you, Dan. Oh, I'd also like to mention that Montesano, Washington, is the *heaviest city in the world*.

MY FAVORITE SHOW EVER

I cut my hand. I cut my hand trying to grab a piece of broken guitar. The strings of the guitar cut into my hand and my hand bled on the stage. **BIG BLACK** is God. **BIG BLACK** destroyed everything. I wanted a piece of **BIG BLACK**. Now my hand hurts. Because somebody tugged and sliced a guitar string into my hand. Now they have a big piece of **BIG BLACK** and I don't. I have a Band-Aid on my palm. It's hard to write with a hole in your hand. Goodbye **BIG BLACK**.

The Music Bank
REHEARSAL STUDIOS

- OPEN 24 HOURS — EVERY DAY
- 45 ROOMS
- SECURITY BUILDING

783-8213
1451 NW 45th ST., SEATTLE 98107
(UNDER THE BALLARD BRIDGE)

BY GOVERNMENT ORDER

ALL MUTANTS MUST REGISTER AT:

FALLOUT
RECORDS & SKATEBOARDS
1506 E. OLIVE WAY
323-BOMB
YOUR OFFICIAL
MUTANT REGISTRATION CENTER

NAME: Karl Wagner alias Nightcrawler
POWER: agility; teleportation
STATUS: EXCALIBUR; former member—X-MEN

MARVEL COMICS

Scott Lindenmuth
Guitar Instruction
for music readers and non-music readers
Private Instruction Offered in:

All Styles of Rock Guitar
Jazz Guitar
Fusion Guitar
Classical Guitar
Improvisation
Theory
Transcription
Ear Training
Sight Reading
College Credit Available
Gift Certificates

776-6362

NOBODY'S BULLETPROOF...

...and in L.A. they're proving it

T-SHIRTS
sm., med., lg., x-lg.
$10 each
red & black
on white t-shirt

DARE TO BE TASTELESS!

Send $10 per shirt to:
Counter Productions
T.L.P.O. Box 8351
Kirkland, WA 98034

SubPop
By Bruce Pavitt

NO TREND Tritonian Nash-Vegas Polyester Complex LP (Touch and Go) Touch and Go retains its status as America's strongest and most daring indie label. Their latest, by D.C.'s **No Trend**, is a frenzied, zany mix of bells, bongos and brass. A totally weird punk-Vegas schlock monster. It's campy, it's damaged, it's "out there." Possibly influenced by early Mothers of Invention. (Touch and Go: P.O. Box 25520, Chicago, IL 60625)

½ JAPANESE and **VELVET MONKEYS** Big Big Sun cassette (K) Two of D.C.'s fave bands, captured live at The Vogue in Seattle. ½ Jap, featuring the genius of Jad Fair, is not your everyday "quirky art band." Jad has always created art and words from a child's perspective and probably has a lifetime supply of crayons on his desk. A unique man. The Velvet Monkeys play a trashy, 60's inspired punk/psych that sounds good even without the wigs. My favorite part of the show was when Don from the Velvets wrapped his cord around Julie and sang *Why Don't We Do it in the Road?* (K: Box 7154, Olympia, WA 98507)

SKIN Blood, Women, Roses LP (Product Inc) Jarboe lives with Michael Gira. Michael is the brains and muscle behind the ultra-heavy, minimalist Swans. Jarboe wanted to make a record so Michael helped her. Jim from Muzak calls this "easy listening Swans." Subtle yet heavy. (British import.)

A TEXAS TRIP compilation LP (Caroline). The Butthole Surfers made enough money selling pot to school children that they were able to build their own recording studio. This is a seven song collection featuring Austin's surreal Surfers plus three of their friends: **Steve Fitch** (great!), **Stickmen With Rayguns** and **Daniel Johnston**. Daniel has long been an underground favorite with his neurotic Mr. Rogers imitations. Sadly, the tracks here are too overproduced for his mild mannered, innocent little songs. Daniel has recently been institutionalized for clubbing his boss, a Burger King manager, into a coma. (Caroline: 5 Crosby St., NYC, NY 10013.)

JACK: Starting this September, I'll be spinning records one Sunday a month at the Vogue. A local band, of the God variety, will also be featured. This month, **SWALLOW:** Sept. 13: eleven o'clock: admission one dollar.

RAGING SLAB Assmaster LP (Buy Our Records) This is the "biker" band from NYC that all the cool people have been talking about. They sound like a cross between Aerosmith and Black Oak Arkansas. They have long hair and tight pants. They rock.. Unfortunately, they are pure nostalgia. At least the ultra-hard rock bands in Seattle listen to modern stuff like Swans, Butthole Surfers and Big Black. Oh, I forgot, this record also comes with a really bad comic book. (Buy Our Records: P.O. Box 363, Vauxhaul, N.J. 07088.)

MELVINS Gluey Porch Treatments LP (Alchemy). Everybody knows that the **Melvins** are the heaviest band in the world. And Gluey Porch Treatments is the heaviest record in the world. Weighing in at over a million tons, this thing will squish you like a tiny bug. Dan, the cool drummer from Killdozer, said, "These guys are a cross between Swans and Blue Cheer! They only do one thing, but they do it perfectly! I think they're going to make us look pretty bad!" Thank you Dan. Oh, I'd also like to mention that Montesano, Washington, is the HEAVIEST CITY IN THE WORLD. (Alchemy: P.O. Box 597004, S.F., CA 94159. MELVINS FAN CLUB: 341 S. Bank Rd. E., Montesano, WA 98563.)

my favorite show ever

I cut my hand. I cut my hand trying to grab a piece of broken guitar. The strings of the guitar cut into my hand and my hand bled on the stage. **BIG BLACK** was on the stage. **BIG BLACK** is God. **BIG BLACK** destroyed everything. I wanted a piece of **BIG BLACK**. Now my hand hurts. Because somebody tugged and sliced a guitar string into my hand. Now they have a big piece of **BIG BLACK** and I don't. I now have a band-aid on my palm. It's hard to write with a hole in your hand. Goodbye **BIG BLACK**.

PHOTOGRAPH BY CAM GARETT

SUBPOP DESIGN BY ASHLEIGH RAFFICER AND LINDA OWENS

Divinely Jacked

Rock 'n roll is dead. Today we talk about drugs. My favorite drug is a red powder known as "pure" or "cayenne." Although some people consider this drug a spice, they are wrong. Nothing will get you higher than hot, loud food led with red pepper. Where's the best drugs in town? Here's a Thai hot spot that will put you in a hot sweat.

LAO CHAREAN (South Seattle) Located between Pioneer Square and the International District, this is an inexpensive connection into an exotic underworld of Far Eastern spices. People, often seen here in trench coats, are shamelessly addicted to the Toom Kha Gai soup here; coconut milk, chicken, lemongrass, lots of cayenne, plus a really weird mysterious tree root. You can order it from one to four stars, depending on how many grams of red powder you want. Four stars will make most people sick. To prevent a possible overdose, dilute the soup with a few spoons of jasmine rice. Of course nobody is allowed to leave the place without an order of pad thai: rice noodles, dredged in red pepper, and topped with a few chopped peanuts and lime juice. A sauce containing vinegar and ground chilis is optional and available as a condiment. Another powerful menu item is the divinely jacked see da shower, (a.k.a. "bathing rama" or "swimming angel"). This is chicken and spinach on rice with a fiery peanut sauce. For dessert, an iced sweet Thai coffee should put you over the edge. I have seen fully grown, unshaven men laugh uncontrollably under the criss-cross effect of caffeine and cayenne. It's a rush.

DEAD KENNEDYS *Give Me Convenience or Give Me Death* LP (Alternative Tentacles). In '78 the Dead Kennedys hit the San Francisco scene, and helped set the tone for the "political punk" activism that the area is still famous for. Now that the band has been dead for a few years, Alternative Tentacles has decided to release *Convenience*, an excellent document of early singles, unreleased material, and compilation tracks. The early singles "California Über Alles" and "Holiday in Cambodia" show leader Jello Biafra's wit at its most refined and powerful. By the way, Jello, who has been fighting hard against censorship, was recently acquitted of charges claiming that he was involved in "distribution of harmful matter to minors." This was a landmark case, and, if lost, would have set serious limitations on freedom of speech. Frankly, this guy is a hero. I'd like to see Jello and Ollie North duke it out in the '88 election!!

BEEFEATER *House Burning Down* LP (Dischord). I like the new Beefeater album because it has white people and black people playing together on the same record. Ever since the legendary **MINOR THREAT/ TROUBLE FUNK** Show a few years back, Washington, D.C., has shown the potential for interracial cooperation within its music community. *House Burning Down* is a unique mix of aggressive rock and funk, punctuated by randomly recorded conversations in the studio between musicians. It's one thing to sing political slogans about racism, it's another to open up and make new friends from a different culture.

LEE RANALDO *From Here -> Infinity* LP (SST). Lee Ranaldo plays guitar with **SONIC YOUTH**. This is his solo project. Every "song" is a short slab of pure noise. Every "song" has a lock-groove at the end; so the end of every song repeats till infinity. So one has to get up out of their chair and walk across the room and lift up the needle and advance the needle after every "song." This is a unique novelty item. It's currently being

"My favorite drug is a red powder known as 'pure' or 'cayenne.' Although some people consider this drug a spice, they are wrong. Nothing will get you higher than hot, loud food led with red pepper... I have seen fully grown, unshaven men laugh uncontrollably under the criss-cross effect of caffeine and cayenne. It's a rush."

DIVINELY JACKED

Rock 'n' Roll is dead. Today we talk about drugs. My favorite drug is a red powder known as "pure" or "cayenne." Although some people consider this drug a spice, they are wrong. Nothing will get you higher than hot, loud food laced with red pepper. Where's the best drugs in town? Here's a Thai hot spot that will put you in a cold sweat.

LAO CHAREAN (121 Prefontaine Place South, Seattle) Located between Pioneer Square and the International District, this is an inexpensive connection into an exotic underworld of far eastern spices. People, often seen here in trench coats, are shamelessly addicted to the Toom Kha Gai soup here: coconut milk, chicken, lemon grass, lots of cayenne plus a really weird mysterious tree root. You can order it from one to four stars, depending on how many grams of red powder you want. Four stars will make most people sick. To prevent a possible overdose, dilute the soup with a few spoons of Jasmine rice. Of course nobody is allowed to leave the place without an order of Phad Thai: rice noodles dredged in red pepper and topped with a few chopped peanuts and lime juice. A sauce containing vinegar and ground chilis is optional and available as a condiment. Another powerful menu item is the divinely jacked See Da Shower (a.k.a. "Bathing Rama" or "Swimming Angel"). This is chicken and spinach on rice with a fiery peanut sauce. For dessert, an iced, sweet Thai coffee should put you over the edge. I have seen fully grown, unshaven men laugh uncontrollably under the criss-cross effect of caffeine and cayenne. It's a rush.

DEAD KENNEDYS

Give Me Convenience Or Give Me Death. LP. (Alternative Tentacles). In '78 THE DEAD KENNEDYS hit the San Francisco scene and helped set the tone for the "political punk" activism that the area is still famous for. Now that the band has been dead for a few years, Alternative Tentacles has decided to release *Convenience*, an excellent document of early singles, unreleased material and compilation tracks. The early singles; *California Uber Alles* and *Holiday in Cambodia*, show leader Jello Biafra's wit at its most refined and powerful. By the way, Jello, who has been fighting hard against censorship, was recently acquitted of charges claiming that he was involved in "distribution of harmful matter to minors." This was a landmark case, and, if lost, would have set serious limitations on freedom of speech. Frankly, the guy is a hero. I'd like to see Jello and Ollie North duke it out in the '88 elections!! (Alternative Tentacles: P.O. Box 11458, San Francisco, California 94101.)

BEEFEATER

House Burning Down. LP. (Dischord). I like the new BEEFEATER album because it has white people and black people playing together on the same record. Ever since the legendary Minor Threat/Trouble Funk Show a few years back, Washington, D.C. has shown the potential for inter-racial cooperation within its music community. *House Burning Down* is a unique mix of aggressive rock and funk, punctuated by randomly recorded conversations in the studio between musicians. It's one thing to sing political slogans about racism, it's another to open up and make new friends from a different culture. (Dischord: 3819 Beecher Street NW, Washington, D.C., 20007.)

LEE RANALDO

From Here ► Infinity. LP. (SST). Lee Ranaldo plays guitar with Sonic Youth. This is his solo project. Every "song" is a short slab of pure noise. Every "song" has a lock-groove at the end: so the end of every song repeats till infinity. So, one has to get up out of the chair and walk across the room and lift up the needle and advance the needle after every "song." This is a unique novelty item. It's currently being pressed on grey vinyl. It also comes with an embossed cover jacket featuring a sketch by Savage Pencil (a famous artist from England). If you're going to buy only one brilliantly conceptual record this year, buy *Infinity*. (SST: Box 1, Lawndale, California 90260.)

HAPPY FLOWERS:

My Skin Covers My Body. LP. (Homestead). This is the weird cult band that all the cool fanzine people have been talking about. There are two guys in the band: Mr. Anus and Mr. Horribly Charred Infant. The classics "Mom, I Gave the Cat Some Acid" and "The Vacuum Ate Timmy" are included, as well as some new noise, like "I Wet the Bed." I hear that Santa was very upset with this record, so please don't put it on your Christmas list. (Homestead: Box 570 Rockville Centre, New York 11571-0570).

LIVE SKULL

Don't Get Any On You. LP. (Homestead). LIVE SKULL hates it when they're lumped together with other NYC noise-guitar bands like Sonic Youth and Rat At Rat R. So I'll try and not imply any association. I like this band because they don't have tattoos or nose rings. Although some of their previous records were scarred by flat, sterile production, *Don't Get Any* was recorded live and is the best sounding LIVE SKULL I've heard since their first EP. (Homestead: Box 570, Rockville Centre, New York, 11571-0570.)

FOR/AGAINST

LP. (Independent Project). This is moody guitar pop from Lincoln, NE. The songs are very pretty. The band sounds like they're from England. I think that teenagers in Nebraska listen to a lot of Cocteau Twins, even though their parents like Willie Nelson. The stunning, limited letterpress edition is yet another collectable work of art from the Independent Project Label. (IPR: Box 60357, L.A., CA 90060.)

GIRL TROUBLE

Tarantula/Old Time Religion. 45. (K). Party record of the month comes from the eternally rockin' GIRL TROUBLE from Tacoma. *Tarantula* is a perfect Link Wray-style instrumental: it's raunchy, it's dumb and it rocks like hell. *Old Time Religion* features Kurt singing about a preacher man. It's a good song, but comes across with more fullness and intensity live. Anyhow, it's a decent B-side to a great guitar shake-out. (K: Box 7154, Olympia, WA 98507.)

PAGE DESIGN BY LINDA OWENS & ASHLEIGH RAFFLER

SUNDAY, OCT. 25 EXPECT THE POP-GUN ASSAULT OF CHEMISTRY SET / THE BAND BEGINS AT 11 / I'LL BE SPINNING PLEASANT ROCK RECORDS FROM 9 PM ON / ADMISSION IS ONLY $2.!!!

pressed on grey vinyl. It also comes with an embossed cover jacket featuring a sketch by Savage Pencil (a famous artist from England). If you're going to buy only one brilliantly conceptual record this year, buy *Infinity*.

HAPPY FLOWERS *My Skin Covers My Body* LP (Homestead). This is the weird cult band that all the cool fanzine people have been talking about. There are two guys in the band: Mr. Anus and Mr. Horribly Charred Infant. The classics "Mom, I gave the Cat Some Acid" and "The Vacuum Ate Timmy" are included, as well as some new noise, like "I Wet the Bed." I hear that Santa was very upset with this record, so please don't put it on your Christmas list.

LIVE SKULL *Don't Get Any On You* LP (Homestead). Live Skull hates it when they're lumped together with other New York City noise-guitar bands like **SONIC YOUTH** and **RAT AT RAT R**. So I'll try and not imply any association. I like this band because they don't have tattoos and nose rings. Although some of their previous records were scarred by flat, sterile production, *Don't Get Any* was recorded live and is the best sounding Live Skull I've heard since their first EP.

FOR/AGAINST LP (Independent Project). This is moody guitar pop from Lincoln, Nebraska. The songs are very pretty. The band sounds like they're from England. I think the teenagers in Nebraska listen to a lot of **COCTEAU TWINS**, even though their parents like **WILLIE NELSON**. The stunning, limited letterpress edition is yet another collectable work of art from the Independent Project label.

GIRL TROUBLE "Tarantula" b/w "Old Time Religion" 45 (K). Party record of the month comes from the eternally rockin' Girl Trouble from Tacoma, Washington. "Tarantula" is a perfect **LINK WRAY**-style instrumental: it's raunchy, it's dumb, and it rocks like hell. "Old Time Religion" features Kurt singing about a preacher man. It's a good song, but comes across with more fullness and intensity live. Anyhow, it's a decent B-side to a great guitar shake-out.

Bigger Than Elvis

Big Black's final show, "The Last Blast," Georgetown Steam Plant, Seattle, Aug 9, 1987. CHARLES PETERSON

BIG BLACK *Songs About Fucking* LP (Touch and Go). Big Black, featuring the three most intelligent people ever to play in a rock band, has broken up, leaving this last and final statement. Here, as always, Big Black sings about ugly things that nobody wants to think about. They confront. As I write this, I'm not sure whether this is the best Big Black record ever, or the worst. I refuse to speculate. The music this band creates is so intense that it takes me months to fully appreciate what they're doing. I will always own every Big Black record ever released. They have changed my life. They are bigger than Elvis, and louder than Bo Diddley. I encourage you to get this record, because if

you don't, all of your friends will secretly think you are lame.

THE CRAMPS *Rockinnreelininaucklandnewzealand* LP (Vengeance). This is the "official" Cramps bootleg recorded in New Zealand, released in an edition of 20,000 on their own Vengeance label. The sound quality is big and clear. The performance is manic. Most of the material is from their last studio album, *A Date With Elvis*. If you are one of the millions of people who were disappointed with the commercial sound of that record, then you will die when you hear this live thing. It's raw and unrestrained. The cover has a picture of

"Henry Rollins, former punk rock superstar with Black Flag, is a most complex personality. Is he a poet, a singer, or a stand-up comedian? Is he a philosopher, a storyteller, or a future presidential candidate? Henry, like other punk rock celebrities such as Lydia Lunch and Jello Biafra, is constantly redefining his attack on mainstream America. Whether it's through films, books, plays, speeches ,or even music, these artists are always exercising their first amendment rights, challenging power structures with creativity."

SUB POP

Pussy Galore

Right Now LP (Caroline). In the early '60s, parents were confronted with the challenge: Would you let your daughter marry a Rolling Stone? The Beatles, of course, were the good boys and the Stones were the bad boys. So who are today's bad boys? My vote goes to PUSSY GALORE. They've got an ATTITUDE. PUSSY GALORE is noisy, abrasive and relentless: they do not compromise. BUT they're thick and tight and they feel good. They ROCK. Like the early Stones, PUSSY GALORE plays rootsy, gritty R&B, but the drummer (Bob Bart, ex of Sonic Youth) likes to bang on sheet metal. *Right Now* is the best PUSSY GALORE record yet, and even includes a few hits, like "Alright." Other song titles include "Fuck You, Man" and "Biker Rock" and "Really Suck." And if that doesn't scare your parents, tell them to look closely at the naked silhouette superimposed over the band photo on the cover. You want attitude? (CAROLINE: 5 Crosby St., NYC NY 10013.) (Special Note: former Olympia scenemaker turned hot-shot East Village rock photographer Mike Lavine did the photography for this thing. Look for more of his work on the upcoming White Zombie and Honeymoon Killers LP's.)

Misfits

Legacy of Brutality LP (Caroline). I used to think the Misfits were stupid. Four grown men dressed in spooky outfits pretending every day was Halloween. Well, I still think they're stupid. But I don't care. This collection of early rarities ('78-'80) shows us that stupid, catchy punk rock songs are O.K., even great. I'm not sure how fame escaped these guys, 'cause songs like "Angelfuck" and "Where Eagles Dare" are masterpieces of our time. You want this. (Caroline: see above.)

Mad Daddys

Apes Go Wild LP (New Rose). THE MAD DADDYS are a Cramps rip-off from New Jersey. A caveman garage-band. Ten years ago, The Cramps integrated roots-rock with noise and it was a hit. Today, bands like Pussy Galore are doing the same thing, but with their own unique voice. So where does that leave the Mad Daddys? Well, I'll give 'em an F for ORIGINALITY but a big gold star for FUN. Rave Hits: "I Rock" and "Stoned For the Rest of My Life". (New Rose: French import.)

The Furies

Fun Around The World LP (Infrasonic). A group of girls from San Francisco sing about hanging out with their friends. Songs read like chapters in a diary: the lyrics are folksy, honest and uncontrived. Although their relaxed live show was charming, their music is really better appreciated played around the house. For fans of Raincoats, Shop Assistants, Talulah Gosh. (Infrasonic: 2835 Sacramento St., SF, CA 94115.)

Big Black

Songs About Fucking LP (Touch and Go). BIG BLACK, featuring the three most intelligent people ever to play in a rock band, has broken up, leaving this last and final statement. Here, as always, BIG BLACK sings about ugly things that nobody wants to think about. They confront. As I write this, I'm not sure whether this is the best BIG BLACK record ever, or the worst. I refuse to speculate. The music this band creates is so intense that it takes me months to fully appreciate what they're doing. I will always own every BIG BLACK record ever released. They have changed my life. They are bigger than Elvis and louder than Bo Diddley. I encourage you to get this record, because if you don't, all of your friends will secretly think you are lame. (Touch and Go: Box 25520, Chicago, IL 60625.)

Cramps

Rockinnreelininaucklandnewzealand LP (Vengeance). This is the "official" CRAMPS bootleg recorded in New Zealand, released in an edition of 20,000 on their own Vengeance label. The sound quality is big and clear. The performance is manic. Most of the material is from their last studio album, *A Date With Elvis*. If you were one of the millions of people who were disappointed with the commercial sound of that record then you will die when you hear this live thing. It's raw and unrestrained. The cover has a picture of Lux crawling half naked on the stage and of course, Poisen Ivy in her Las Vegas showgirl outfit playing her loud guitar. You want culture? (Vengeance: no address.)

Henrietta Collins & the Wifebeating Childhaters

(featuring Henry Rollins) EP (Texas Hotel). Henry Rollins, former punk rock superstar with Black Flag, is a most complex personality. Is he a poet, a singer or a stand-up comedian? Is he a philosopher, a story teller or a future presidential candidate? Henry, like other punk rock celebrities such as Lydia Lunch and Jello Biafra, are constantly redefining their attack on mainstream America. Whether it's through films, books, plays or speeches or even music, these artists are always exercising their first amendment rights, challenging power structures with creativity. With this record, Rollins brings together the poetry/storytelling of his books with the vocal intensity of his punk roots. Sometimes, as with "Hey Henrietta," he is extremely successful. However, because of its scattershot approach, this record comes off as more of a *sampler* of music, spoken word and comedy. I'm hoping that his next record will be more cohesive. This one is recommended to fans of Lenny Bruce. (Texas Hotel: 122 Broadway, Santa Monica, CA 90401.)

ILLUSTRATION BY

Photographer Michael Lavine at home in New York City, self-portrait taken in 1986. The milk-crate shelving, Jenny Holzer poster, and bed-on-the-floor reflect how many of us were living at the time.
MICHAEL LAVINE

Lux crawling half naked on the stage, and, of course, Poison Ivy in her Las Vegas showgirl outfit playing her loud guitar. You want culture?

HENRIETTA COLLINS AND THE WIFEBEATING CHILD HATERS (featuring **HENRY ROLLINS**) EP (Texas Hotel). Henry Rollins, former punk rock superstar with **BLACK FLAG**, is a most complex personality. Is he a poet, a singer, or a stand-up comedian? Is he a philosopher, a storyteller, or a future presidential candidate? Henry, like other punk rock celebrities such as **LYDIA LUNCH** and **JELLO BIAFRA**, is constantly redefining his attack on mainstream America. Whether it's through films books, plays, or speeches or even music, these artists are always exercising their First Amendment rights, challenging power structures with creativity. With this record, Rollins brings together the poetry/storytelling of his books with the vocal intensity of his punk roots. Sometimes, as with "Hey Henrietta," he is extremely successful. However, because of its scattershot approach, this record comes off as more of a sampler of music, spoken word, and comedy. I'm hoping that his next record will be more cohesive. This one is recommended to fans of Lenny Bruce.

PUSSY GALORE *Right Now* LP (Caroline). In the early '60s, parents were confronted with the challenge: Would you let your daughter marry a **ROLLING STONE**? The **BEATLES**, of course, were the good boys, and the Stones were the bad boys. So who are today's bad boys? My vote goes to Pussy Galore. They've got an *attitude*. Pussy Galore is noisy, abrasive, and relentless; they do not compromise. *But* they're thick and tight and they feel good. They *rock*. Like the early Stones, Pussy Galore plays rootsy, gritty R&B, but the drummer (Bob Bert, ex-**SONIC YOUTH**) likes to bang on sheet metal. *Right Now* is the best Pussy Galore

record yet, and even includes a few hits, like "Alright." Other song titles include "Fuck You, Man," "Biker Rock," and "Really Suck." And if that doesn't scare your parents, tell them to look closely at the naked silhouette superimposed over the band photo on the cover. You want attitude? (Special note: former Olympia scene-maker turned hot shot East Village rock photographer Mike Lavine did the photography for this thing. Look for more of his work on the upcoming **WHITE ZOMBIE** and **HONEYMOON KILLERS** LPs.)

MISFITS *Legacy of Brutality* LP (Caroline). I used to think the Misfits were stupid. Four grown men dressed in spooky outfits pretending every day was Halloween. Well, I still think they're stupid. But I don't care. This collection of early rarities ('78–'80) shows us that stupid, catchy punk rock songs are okay, even great. I'm not sure how fame escaped these guys, 'cause songs like "Angelfuck" and "Where Eagles Dare" are masterpieces of our time. You want this.

MAD DADDYS *Apes Go Wild* LP (New Rose). The Mad Daddys are a **CRAMPS** rip-off from New Jersey. A caveman garage band. Ten years ago, The Cramps integrated roots rock with noise and it was a hit. Today, bands like Pussy Galore are doing the same thing, but with their own unique voice. So where does that leave the Mad Daddys? Well, I'll give 'em an "F" for *originality* but a big gold star for *fun*. Rave hits: "I Rock" and "Stoned for the Rest of My Life".

THE FURIES *Fun Around the World* LP (Infrasonic). A group of girls from San Francisco sing about hanging out with their friends. Songs read like chapters in a diary. The lyrics are folksy, honest, and uncontrived. Although their relaxed live show was charming, their music is really better appreciated played around the house. For fans of **RAINCOATS**, **SHOP ASSISTANTS**, and **TALULAH GOSH**.

I've Never Heard Anybody Sing Like You Before

DEAR EDDIE: Thanks for the new **THROWN UPS** 45. I think you are wild. I've never seen anybody dress up like Spock. And I've never heard anybody sing like you before. Although many people think you and your band are a joke, I think that your new record is the most uninhibited, crazy, raw, maddening, absurd, creative noise I've heard in awhile. Eddie, you rule. You are God. Just because you're a painter and you're from Australia doesn't mean that people can laugh behind your back. Who else would have written a song called "My Cock is the Coin to the Baby Machine"? There is a certain divine madness here, and I'm hoping to cash in on it before you leave the United States.

DEAR SHAUN: Thanks for your new **P.S. O'NEILL** album (*Tomorrow's Waiting* LP, Velvetone Records, Ellensburg, WA). By the way, have you finished up that video you've been working on? I can't remember if it was a monster movie, a drug exploitation flick, or a biker saga. Considering that both **FISK** and the **SCREAMING TREES** are in it, I imagine all three. So Shaun, what's the story on this record? You've got all these famous musician types sitting in and yet it comes off like outtakes from a **NEIL DIAMOND** session! The arrangements are pure schlock and the lyrics are pure sap. Is this some kind of conceptual joke?

DEAR JEAN: Calvin from K sent me your new **MECCA NORMAL** 45 ("Oh Yes You Can!" 45, K Records, Olympia, WA). I like it. Your feminist/intellectual stance as filtered through backporch Appalachian phrasing is quite unique. The next time you and your guitar-friend David come south from Vancouver, you should stop by my apartment. We can drink papaya nectar and talk about why America has so many serial killers. By the way, I think it's a smart idea to work as a duo. That way you can pack up and tour anytime. Calvin tells me that Mecca Normal and a bunch of people from the K label are going to do a West Coast tour of record stores and radio stations, bypassing all those seedy nightclub owners. Sounds like a clever grass-roots strategy. I hope you have fun.

DEAR MIKE: Thanks for the new **HELLCOWS** 45 ("G Spot Crush," Pigface Records, Portland, OR). It makes a lovely gift. Is that you banging on all those tin cans and stuff? I thought so. Your singer has a raspy voice and reminds me of **CAPTAIN BEEFBEART** or this guy from Seattle called John Bigley who sings in the **U-MEN**. Maybe you should come up from Portland and play a double bill with the U-Men? That would be cool. Hey, **I REMEMBER** when you used to hate my guts because I rejected your **JUNGLE NAUSEA** demo for a *Sub Pop* cassette compilation. I guess I never told you that the day your tape came in the mail I had eaten some LSD, and, well, I had this vision that you were the pure embodiment of evil, and that I would be doing the world a disservice by distributing your music. Oh well. Are you still fat? Do you still have a poster of Fred Flintstone hanging over your couch? I'm bald now and I listen to **LED ZEPPELIN**. Life is weird.

DEAR DANIEL: Thanks for the new **SKIN YARD** 45 ("Gelatin Babies" 45, C/Z Records, Seattle, WA). It sure is round. How was your lengthy tour across America? I hope you got some rest and ate some vitamins. It's not easy being stuffed in a van for 30 days. So Dan,

JUST IN TIME FOR CHRISTMAS

CHRIST·ON·A·RAPE

A MIND IS A TERRIBLE THING

NEW Lp ON ROUGH TRADE

FALLOUT RECORDS & SKATEBOARDS
1506 E. OLIVE WAY   323-BOMB

Do you question your future?

PSYCHIC READINGS

- *Tarot Cards & Astrology Wheel*
- *Readings by phone*
- *Live — NO Recordings*

1-976-3699

$3 1st minute 99¢ each add'l minute
MC/VISA 303-750-3699
Free Callbacks 24 hours

SOUNDGARDEN
6 Songs 12 inches 5 Bucks

SUB POP

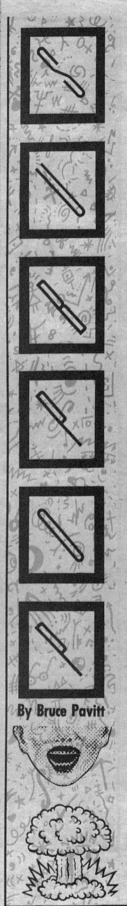

DEAR EDDIE: Thanks for the new **Thrown Ups** 45. I think you are wild. I've never seen anybody dress up like Spock. And I've never heard anybody sing like you before. Although many people think you and your band are a joke, I think that your new record is the most uninhibited, crazy, raw, maddening, absurd, creative noise I've heard in awhile. Eddie, you rule. You are God. Just because you're a painter and you're from Australia doesn't mean that people can laugh behind your back. Who else would have written a song called **"My Cock is the Coin to the Baby Machine"**? There is a certain divine madness here, and I'm hoping to cash in on it before you leave the United States. (**THE THROWN UPS Smiling Panties** 45 c/o Steve Turner: 3410 76th Pl. S.E., Mercer Island, WA 98040.)

DEAR SHAUN: Thanks for your new **P.S. O'Neil** album. By the way, have you finished up that video you've been working on? I can't remember if it was a monster movie, a drug exploitation flick or a biker saga. Considering that both **Fisk** and the **Screaming Trees** are in it, I imagine all three. So Shaun, what's the story on this record? You've got all these famous musician types sitting in and yet it comes off like outtakes from a Neil Diamond session! The arrangements are pure schlock and the lyrics are pure sap. Is this some kind of conceptual joke? (**P.S. O'NEIL Tomorrow's Waiting** LP c/o Velvetone Records: 607 W. 3rd, Ellensburg, WA 98926.)

DEAR JEAN: Calvin from **K** sent me your new **Mecca Normal** 45. I like it. Your feminist/intellectual stance as filtered through backporch Appalachian phrasing is quite unique. The next time you and your guitar-friend David come south from Vancouver, you should stop by my apartment. We can drink papaya nectar and talk about why America has so many serial killers. By the way, I think it's a smart idea to work as a duo. That way you can pack up and tour anytime. Calvin tells me that **Mecca Normal** and a bunch of people from the **K** label are going to do a West Coast tour of record stores and radio stations, bypassing all those seedy night-club owners. Sounds like a clever grassroots strategy. I hope you have fun. (**MECCA NORMAL: Oh Yes You Can!** 45 c/o K: Box 7154 Olympia, WA 98507.)

DEAR MIKE: Thanks for the new **Hellcows** 45. It makes a lovely gift. Is that you banging on all those tin cans and stuff? I thought so. Your singer has a raspy voice and reminds me of **Captain Beefheart** or this guy from Seattle called **John Bigley** who sings in the **U-Men**. Maybe you should come up from Portland and play a double bill with the U-Men. That would be cool. Hey, I remember when you used to hate my guts because I rejected your **Jungle Nausea** demo for a Sub Pop cassette compilation. I guess I never told you that the day your tape came in the mail I had eaten some LSD, and, well, I had this vision that you were the pure embodiment of evil and that I would be doing the world a disservice by distributing your music. Oh well. Are you still fat? Do you still have a poster of Fred Flintstone hanging over your couch? I'm bald now and I listen to Led Zeppelin. Life is weird. (**HELLCOWS G Spot Crush** 45: c/o Pigface Records: Box 8603, Portland, OR 97207.)

DEAR DANIEL: Thanks for the new **Skin Yard** 45. It sure is round. How was your lengthy tour across America? I hope you got some rest and ate some vitamins. It's not easy being stuffed in a van for 30 days. So Dan, about your record: I don't like it. In general, I don't like busy, melodramatic music that has roots in mid '70s "progressive rock." Maybe it's because the last time I heard King Crimson and Genesis at a party, somebody kicked bongwater all over the carpet. I hate bongwater. But I don't hate Skin Yard. I know you guys have the power to ROCK. I'm just hoping that I can feel it on your next record. (**SKIN YARD Gelatin Babies** 45 c/o C/Z: 1407 E. Madison #41, Seattle, WA 98122.)

DEAR RON: Thanks for the new **Room 9** LP. It looks nice on my coffee table. I'm listening to your record right now and I must say it's rather catchy. My favorite song is **"Red Dog."** Your voice really rocks out on that one. Is that the song about **Red Masque**? Why does your voice sound so angry? Anyway Ron, your surreal pop songs are going to get a lot of airplay. Maybe you guys can all move to England and live on the dole and hang out with **That Petrol Emotion** and have the time to pursue your craft. Because you write great hooks and deserve to be famous. Just one tip, though: get rid of those keyboards! That artificial "moody atmosphere" stuff sounds too much like **Siouxsie** and **The Cure**! Oh, and I think it's great that somebody all the way in Louisiana liked your music enough to pay for your record. Good luck! (**ROOM NINE Voices. . .Of a Summer Day** LP c/o C'est la Mort Records: Box 91, Baker, LA 70714.)

DEAR KURTISS: Thanks for the new **My Eye** 45. It's great. Your singer sounds like he used to be in Steppenwolf. Was he? And how come this rocks so hard? You guys always look like you're asleep when you're playing live. Are you now unleashed? And Kurtiss, bootlegging a few seconds off an old Johnny Cash record was a serious twist. A very noble and fine effort here. (**MY EYE So Much Going On** 45 c/o C/Z: 1407 E. Madison #41, Seattle, WA 98122.)

SUB POP SUNDAY

Hey everybody: I'll be spinning bad records before and after the Thrown Ups do their thing at The Vogue, Nov. 29. Only two bucks!

By Bruce Pavitt

about your record: I don't like it. In general, I don't like busy, melodramatic music that has roots in mid '70s "progressive rock." Maybe it's because the last time I heard **KING CRIMSON** and **GENESIS** at a party, somebody kicked bongwater all over the carpet. I hate bongwater. But I don't hate Skin Yard. I know you guys have the power to *rock*. I'm just hoping that I can feel it on your next record.

DEAR RON: Thanks for the new **ROOM 9** LP (*Voices Of a Summer Day* LP c/o C'est la Mort Records, Baker, LA). It looks nice on my coffee table. I'm listening to your record right now and I must say it's rather catchy. My favorite song is "Red Dog." Your voice really rocks out on that one. Is that the song about Red Masque? Why does your voice sound so angry? Anyway Ron, your surreal pop songs are going to get a lot of airplay. Maybe you guys can all move to England and live on the dole and hang out with **THAT PETROL EMOTION** and have the time to pursue your craft. Because you write great hooks and deserve to be famous. Just one tip, though: get rid of those keyboards! That artificial "moody atmosphere" stuff sounds too much like **SIOUXSIE** and **THE CURE**! Oh, and I think it's great that somebody all the way in Louisiana liked your music enough to pay for your record. Good luck!

DEAR KURTISS: Thanks for the new **MY EYE** 45 ("So Much Going On" 45, C/Z Records, Seattle, WA). It's great. Your singer sounds like he used to be in Steppenwolf. Was he? And how come this rocks so hard? You guys always look like you're asleep when you're playing live. Are you now unleashed? And Kurtiss, bootlegging a few seconds off an old **JOHNNY CASH** record was a serious twist. A very noble and fine effort here.

SUB POP SUNDAY

HEY EVERYBODY: I'll be spinning bad records before and after the **THROWN UPS** do their thing at the Vogue this November. Only two bucks!

27 Reasons Washington Is a Cool Place To Live

A.D.R.D. *Talk Is Cheap* demo

ACCUSED *More Fun Than an Open Casket Funeral* LP (Combat)

BEAT HAPPENING "Look Around" 45 (K)

BEERGARDEN "Swallow the Green Room" demo

BUNDLE OF HISS *Push* demo

CAT BUTT *Journey to the Center of Cat Butt* demo

CHEMISTRY SET *Fields* demo

THE FASTBACKS *...And his Orchestra* LP (Popllama)

FEAST cassette box set

GIRL TROUBLE "Tarantula" 45 (K)

The **GO TEAM** *Your Pretty Guitar* cassette

GREEN PAJAMAS *Book of Hours* LP (Green Monkey)

GREEN RIVER *Dry as a Bone* EP (Sub Pop)

H-HOUR production demo

MELVINS *Gluey Porch Treatments* LP (Alchemy)

MY EYE "So Much Going On" 45 (C/Z Records)

ROOM NINE *Voices... of a Summer's Day* LP (C'est La Mort)

S.G.M. *Strunk* cassette

SCREAMING TREES *Even If and Especially When* LP (SST)

64 SPIDERS cassette

SOUNDGARDEN *Screaming Life* EP (Sub Pop)

SWALLOW "Shooting Dope Gives Me a Boner" demo

TAD "Daisy" demo

THE THROWN UPS "Smiling Panties" 45 (Amphetamine Reptile)

The **U-MEN** "Solid Action" 45 (Black Label)

The **WALKABOUTS** "Psyclone" 45 (Necessity)

YOUNG FRESH FELLOWS *The Men Who Loved Music* LP (Frontier)

10 FAVORITE RECORDINGS OF 1987

1. **GREEN RIVER** *Dry as a Bone* EP (Sub Pop)
2. **DINOSAUR** *You're Living All Over Me* LP (SST)
3. **SONIC YOUTH** *Sister* LP (SST)
4. **REDD KROSS** *Neurotica* LP (Big Time)
5. **FEEDTIME** *Shovel* LP (Aberrant Records)
6. **BIG BLACK** *Songs About Fucking* LP (Touch + Go)
7. **PUSSY GALORE** *Right Now!* LP (Caroline)
8. **CRAZYHEAD** "What Gives You the Idea That You're So Amazing Baby?" 12" (Food)
9. **POP WILL EAT ITSELF** *Now for a Feast* LP (Rough Trade)
10. **SCREAMING TREES** *Even If & Especially When* LP (SST)

1987

Hey, did it suck or what? Maybe for the rest of the country, but not around here. This was easily the best year for local music since **BING CROSBY** rocked Tacoma. And that was back in '38. Despite the lack of a great club, there were *happening* shows almost every week of the year, with local bands often blowing away the national competition. Also, an unprecedented amount of recordings were released, with stars like the **SCREAMING TREES**, **YOUNG FRESH FELLOWS**, and the **ACCÜSED** getting signed to national labels and selling tons of records. And even though **GREEN RIVER**, the **MELVINS**, and **FEAST** broke up, there's still big momentum going with new bands like **MUDHONEY** and **DOLL SQUAD** ready to pick up the slack.

1988

In January alone, expect to see albums by Ellensburg's **STEVE FISK** and Olympia's **BEAT HAPPENING**. Tacoma's **GIRL TROUBLE** and Seattle's **U-MEN** are both recording albums. Also, the post-mortem **GREEN RIVER** LP is almost mixed down and ready to go. Hey, we even have our own TV show with Bombshelter Videos. And a new magazine called *Zero Hour* is about to hit. So why move? Life is cool.

"This was easily the best year for local music since Bing Crosby rocked Tacoma. And that was back in '38. Despite the lack of a great club, there were *happening* shows almost every week of the year, with local bands often blowing away the national competition. An unprecedented amount of recordings were released, with stars like Screaming Trees, the Young Fresh Fellows, and the Accüsed getting signed to national labels and selling tons of records. And even though Green River, the Melvins, and Feast broke up, there's still big momentum with new bands like Mudhoney and Doll Squad ready to pick up the slack."

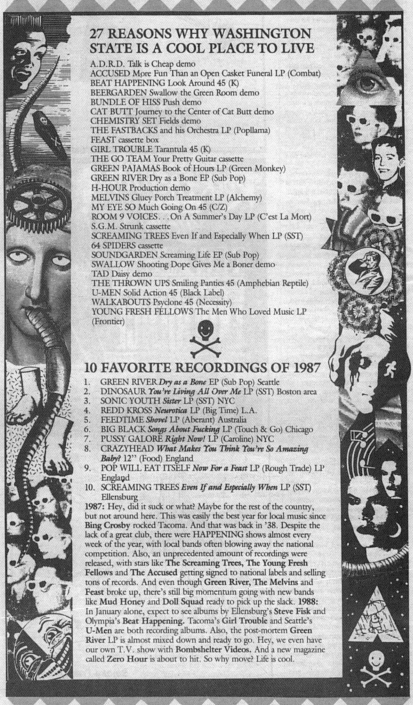

Ripping My Column Into Tiny Pieces

MALFUNKSHUN

In response to the public "roasting" I received from Malfunkshun during their last show at the Vogue: I think **MALFUNKSHUN** is great. Now, I'm not saying this because the singer insulted me by ripping my column into tiny pieces, I'm saying this because I recognize Malfunkshun as a unique and influential band in this area. In fact, many people credit them as the godfathers of the whole *heavy* glam scene (that was documented most successfully on the *Deep Six* compilation). Individually, and as a group, they have more personality than an entire evening's worth of most Seattle bands. The singer and bass player, Landrew the Love God, is flamboyant and outrageous, living the rock star fantasy to such an extreme as to make the fantasy real! He is hard rock's response to **LIBERACE**. Landrew's comic puffery is grounded by the loose and powerful drumming of Regan and the spacey, acid-damaged virtuosity of Kevin on guitar. When they are *on*, which is about half of the time, they are the weirdest, wildest freak show in town. I would recommend that Frank from Bombshelter Videos get together with Malfunkshun and make a video. With the right production, Malfunkshun might finally get the national attention they deserve.

AUSTRALIA

It's no secret that England dumped shitloads of convicts and crazies on this barren land of kangaroos and koala bears. The end result has been the most consistently intense *rock* to be heard around the world, from the **SAINTS** and **RADIO BIRDMAN** in the mid '70s to today's class: the **NEW CHRISTS, COSMIC PSYCHOS**, and the **PSYCHOTIC TURNBUCK-LES**. My favorite hit? I was recently turned on to a 6-song EP by the **PSYCHOTIC TURNBUCKLES** called *Destroy Dull City* that rocked with such uninhibited stupidity that I couldn't sleep til I found one. This record is it; the ancient scroll, the clay tablet, the bible of *dumb*. An entire civilization could spring forth from the wisdom of this record. Accept no substitute. This has been impossible to find in local stores, so here's the address: Rattlesnake Records, Rushcutters Bay, N.S.W., Australia.

CAR BOMB

Escape from Noise (SST Records), the new album by **NEGATIVLAND**, is funny. It's also disturbing and quite weird. Basically a collection of tape manipulation, it features rhythm loops, field recordings, radio bootlegs, and sound effects. There's also some synthesizer and singing. There's also a *lot* of celebrities, mostly from the Bay Area, who stop by for a minute of amusement. How's this for namedroppping: **JERRY GARCIA**, the **RESIDENTS, JELLO BIAFRA, MARK MOTHERSBAUGH**, and **HENRY KAISER**. Even our beloved **STEVE FISK** from Ellensberg, Washington, a master of tape manipulations himself, contributes some odd voice tapes that he dug up from some bizarre church group. Oh, there's a limited edition bumper sticker for your car, it reads **CAR BOMB**.

THE CHARLES BUKOWSKI OF ROCK

It's great to live in a society where people like **GG AL-LIN** can exist. I mean, the man has made a career out of challenging "normal" standards of decency, bluntly expressing fetishes, opinions and desires that are ugly

I have to say, I really upset a few people, especially local Seattle people, with some harsh reviews. Even though I was primarily a cheerleader of sorts, and very supportive of creative self-expression, I had to deliver harsh honesty when it was due. I took some of my cues from Steve Albini, then a critic for an indie publication called *Matter*, out of Chicago. His style of music reviews were just very well-written brutal candor.

BY COMMISSAR BRUCE PAVITT

MALFUNKSHUN:
In response to the public "roasting" I received from Malfunkshun during their last show at the Vogue: *I think Malfunkshun is great.* Now, I'm not saying this because the singer insulted me by ripping my column into tiny pieces. I'm saying this because I recognize Malfunkshun as a unique and influential band in this area; in fact, many people credit them as the godfathers of the whole HEAVY glam scene (that was documented most successfully on the *Deep Six* compilation). Individually, and as a group, they have more *personality* than an entire evening's worth of most Seattle bands. The singer and bass player, Landrew, the Love God, is flamboyant and outrageous, living the Rock Star fantasy to such an extreme as to make the fantasy real! He is hard rock's response to Liberace. Landrew's comic poofery is grounded by the loose and powerful drumming of Regan and the spacey, acid-damaged virtuosity of Kevin on guitar. When they are ON, which is about half the time, they are the weirdest, wildest freak show in town. I would recommend that Frank from Bombshelter Videos get together with Malfunkshun and make a *video*. With the right production, Malfunkshun might finally get the national attention they deserve.

AUSTRALIA
It's no secret that England dumped shiploads of convicts and crazies on this barren land of kangaroos and koala bears. The end result has been the most consistently intense ROCK to be heard round the world, from The Saints and Radio Birdman in the mid '70s to today's class: The New Christs, Cosmic Psychos and the Psychotic Turnbuckles. My favorite hit? I was recently turned on to a 6-song EP by THE PSYCHOTIC TURNBUCKLES called *Destroy Dull-City* that rocked with such uninhibited stupidity that I couldn't sleep til I found one. this record is *it*: the *ancient scroll*, the *clay tablet*, the *bible* of DUMB. An entire civilization could spring forth from the wisdom of this record. Accept no substitute. This has been impossible to find in local stores, so here's the address: Rattlesnake Records, P.O. Box 49, Rushcutters Bay, N.S.W. 2011, Australia.

CAR BOMB
Escape From Noise, the new album by *Negativeland*, is funny. It's also disturbing and quite weird. Basically a collection of tape manipulation, it features rhythm loops, field recordings, radio bootlegs and sound effects. There's also some synthesizer and singing. There's also a LOT of celebrities, mostly from the Bay Area, who stop by for a minute of amusement. How's this for name dropping: Jerry Garcia, The Residents, Jello Biafra, Mark Mothersbough, Henry Kaiser; even our beloved Steve Fisk from Ellensburg, a master of tape manipulation himself, contributes some odd voice tapes that he dug up from some bizarre church group. Oh, there's a limited edition bumper sticker for your car, it reads: CAR BOMB. On SST Records.

THE CHARLES BUKOWSKI OF ROCK:
It's great to live in a society where people like GG Allin can exist. I mean, the man has made a **career** out of challenging "normal" standards of decency, bluntly expressing fetishes, opinions and desires that are UGLY yet real. For many, his perversities and gross exhibitions established him as an outlaw; and until recently, he was denied any social status or critical attention, rejected by even the most liberal and open minded consumers of culture. But his outrage has endured. The man **defines** PUNK ROCK. He is an iconoclast. Ultimately, he is more confrontational than either Iggy Pop or Johnny Rotten. His early home-made recordings, once laughed at, are now rare collector's items, valued for their disregard for "taste" and convention. In my former life as a record retailer, I was once offered the opportunity to purchase one of GG's singles. It had a foldout sleeve which included photos of the artist jacking off and inserting a syringe into his arm. I was offended and refused to buy the record. Only in retrospect to I appreciate the deep care that GG has always taken in pushing the boundaries of civil liberty and self expression. There is a thin line between art and insanity. GG forces us to think about that line. We shouldn't be scared of people like GG. Our evolution as a species depends upon our willingness to investigate freaks of nature and to learn from them. . . The definitive collection of the man's work can be found on the **Hated In The Nation** cassette compilation on ROIR. His most recent release is the **You Give Love A Bad Name** LP on Homestead.

LIVE SEX
Back in '82, The Descendents released one of the true gems of the American "hardcore" scene, an album called ***Milo Goes To College***. Amazingly, it was a brilliant, sensitive record about love and sex by a bunch of gnarly teenage guys from Southern California. For those who care, a large selection of songs from the Milo LP are on a new LIVE collection of Descendents material called **LIVE-AGE**. Out on the SST label.
Mr. Pavitt will be DJing at the Vogue Sunday Jan. 31st with My Beer Drunk Soul is Sadder Than All the Dead Xmas Trees in the World — that's really their name.

KILL THE PAIN
more stuff to check out:

LAUGHING HYENAS Merry Go Round EP (Touch & Go)

SWANS Children of God double LP (Caroline)

NICE STRONG ARM Reality Bath LP (Homestead)

HALO OF FLIES Garbage Rock! EP (Twin Tone)

NEAT STUFF #9 COMIC by Peter Bagge

JELLO BIAFRA No More Cocoons double LP (Alternative Tentacles)

MARK STEWART & MAFFIA LP (Upside Up)

THE CURSE Scary movie I saw in Bellevue.

DISRUPTING ROUTINE
Creative pranks can be seen as conceptual art or symbolic warfare, disrupting routine and challenging people to reconsider their acceptance of the mundane. The latest RE/SEARCH publication (#11) is a large, strikingly designed paperback celebrating PRANKS: "devious deeds and mischievous mirth." It features almost 40 interviews with counterculture heroes as diverse as **Abbie Hoffman, Henry Rollins** and **John Waters**. There's also insightful essays and infamous quotations. As it stands, the entire RE/SEARCH catalogue is a unique and ominous resource, easily worth the price of a few weeks of college indoctrination. (RE/SEARCH: 20 Romolo #B, S.F., CA 94133)

yet real. For many, his perversities and gross exhibitions establishes him as an outlaw; and until recently, he was denied any social status or critical attention, rejected by even the most liberal and open-minded consumers of culture. But his outrage has endured. The man defines *punk rock*. He is an iconoclast. Ultimately, he is more confrontational than either **IGGY POP** or **JOHNNY ROTTEN**. His early homemade recordings, once laughed at, are now rare collector's items, valued for their disregard for "taste" and convention. In my former life as a record retailer, I was once offered the opportunity to purchase one of GG's singles. It had a foldout sleeve which included photos of the artist jacking off and inserting a syringe into his arm. I was offended and refused to buy the record. Only in retrospect do I appreciate the deep care that GG has always taken in pushing the boundaries of civil liberty and self expression. There is a thin line between art and insanity. GG forces us to think about that line. We shouldn't be scared of people like GG. Our evolution as a species depends upon our willingness to investigate freaks of nature and to learn from them. The definite collection of the man's work can be found on the *Hated in the Nation* cassette compilation on ROIR. His most recent release is the *You Give Love a Bad Name* LP on Homestead.

LIVE SEX

Back in '82, the **DESCENDENTS** released one of the true gems of the American hardcore scene, an album called *Milo Goes to College*. Amazingly, it was a brilliant, sensitive record about love and sex by a bunch of gnarly teenage guys from Southern California. For those who care, a large selection of songs from the *Milo* LP are on the new live collection of Descendents material called *Liveage*. Out on the SST label.

KILL THE PAIN

More stuff to check out:

LAUGHING HYENAS *Merry Go Round* EP (Touch and Go)

SWANS *Children of God* double LP (Caroline)

NICE STRONG ARM *Reality Bath* LP (Homestead)

HALO OF FLIES *Garbage Rock!* EP (Twin/Tone)

PETER BAGGE *Neat Stuff* #9 comic

JELLO BIAFRA *No More Cocoons* double LP (Alternative Tentacles)

MARK STEWART & THE MAFFIA LP (Upside)

The Curse a scary movie I saw in Bellevue

DISRUPTING ROUTINE

Creative pranks can be seen as conceptual art or symbolic warfare, disrupting routine and challenging people to reconsider their acceptance of the mundane. The latest *Re/Search* publication (#11) is a large, strikingly designed paperback celebrating *Pranks*: "devious deeds and mischievous mirth." It features almost 40 interviews with countercultural heroes as diverse as **ABBIE HOFFMAN**, **HENRY ROLLINS**, and **JOHN WATERS**. There's also insightful essays and infamous quotations. As it stands, the entire *Re/Search* catalogue is a unique and ominous resource, easily worth the price of a few weeks of college indoctrination.

Mr. Pavitt will be DJing at the Vogue on Sunday, January 31, with **MY BEER DRUNK SOUL IS SADDER THAN ALL THE DEAD XMAS TREES IN THE WORLD**—that's really their name.

Music for Baking Pies

BUY THE NEW KILLDOZER ALBUM

KILLDOZER, featuring the tiny frame and raspy throat of Michael Gerald, is an *All-American kind of band*. Despite their cult following amongst elite fans of "noise," Killdozer is populist, small-town, and working class. Michael sings songs about real men: meat packers, golden glove boxers, and grain elevator operators. His men play chords and pound beers and knock heads! On *Little Baby Buntin'* (Touch and Go), their fourth record, the noisy guitar band with the funny redneck anthems adds a different twist. Just as **ELVIS** went from humble trucker to rhinestone cowboy, Killdozer grows up and makes a nod to Las Vegas schlock; they cover **NEIL DIAMOND**'s "I Am, I Said"; they bootleg part of an **ENGELBERT HUMPERDINCK** record; they even quote a line from the lounge classic "Macarthur Park." "Someone left the cake out in the rain." It's good that Killdozer is retaining their style and sensibility as avant-working class; it's also good to hear them expand the limits of their rigid formula.

BUY THE NEW WALKABOUTS ALBUM

The **WALKABOUTS** have cornered the sensitive, liberal folk/rock market in Seattle, and are now ready for world domination. *See Beautiful Rattlesnake Gardens* (PopLlama Records) is an excellent record. The arrangements are carefully thought out and never overstated. The "warm" production also shows a good ear fro the natural acoustics of a room. Many recordings in the '80s are typically sterile and lifeless; this is not. And amazingly, the lyrics are often poetic, encouraging the listener to actually play the thing more than once. This is not a disposable piece of pop fluff. My only complaint is that the Celtic folk-maiden style of Carla Torgerson is too deeply rooted in the Irish peasant tradition to sound indigenous to this country. Frankly, that bugs me. In short, however, this record is "tasteful," which means mass airplay and heavy sales in sensitive, liberal college towns.

BUY THE NEW SWANS ALBUM

The **SWANS**, who stunned the world with songs like "Raping a Slave," have seen the light and gone new age. Yes, the heaviest band in the world, infamous for their crushing minimalism and lyrics about sexual and economic domination, have a double LP of religious propaganda called *Children of God* (Caroline Records). The music employs post-hippy, new age trademarks such as flutes, angelic choirs, and sound affects from nature, such as waterfalls. All of this serves to evoke some mystical, heavenly garden of Eden. The good news is that this is the richest, most texturally sophisticated Swans disc to date. The Swans have always been about one thing: power. They have not abandoned that premise. The Swans have simply integrated their brutality with tenderness. Their worldview is now fuller, more complex. *Children of God* is loud and soft, passive and aggressive. It's the heaviest record since *Jesus Christ Superstar*. Pick hits: "Beautiful Child" and "Sex, God, Sex."

BUY THE NEW BEAT HAPPENING RECORD

Okay. A lot of people I know think that Olympia's **BEAT HAPPENING** suck. I don't. I think they're unique, charming, and lyrically brilliant. Opponents usually slog their "cuteness" and Calvin's off-key baritone. Certainly, it's obvious that their pop is primitive, and that they don't practice a whole lot. But so what. For those who care, Beat Happening's latest LP, *Jamboree* (K/Rough Trade), deserves a PG rating, as it is wilder than the G-rated innocence of their last LP

SubPop

SUB POP SUNDAY:
SNOWBUD and *THE FLOWER People from Portland!* Also: debut of the *GIRL TROUBLE* video! At the Vogue on Feb. 28

BUY THE NEW KILLDOZER ALBUM: *Killdozer*, featuring the tiny frame and raspy throat of Michael Gerald, is an **ALL AMERICAN KIND OF BAND.** Despite their cult following amongst elite fans of "noise," Killdozer is populist, small town and working class. Michael sings songs about real men: *meat packers* and *golden glove boxers* and *grain elevator operators.* His men play cards and pound beers and knock heads. On *Little Baby Buntin',* their fourth record, the noisy guitar band with the funny redneck anthems add a different twist. Just as Elvis went from humble trucker to rhinestone cowboy, Killdozer grows up and takes a nod to Las Vegas schlock: they cover Neil Diamond's "I Am, I Said"; they bootleg part of an Engelbert Humperdinck record; they even quote a line from the lounge classic "Macarthur Park": 'someone left the cake out in the rain." It's good that Killdozer is retaining their style and sensibility as *avant* working class; it's also good to hear them expand the limits of their rigid formula. **(Touch and Go: Box 25520, Chicago, IL 60625.)**

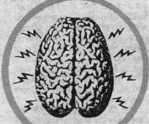

BUY THE NEW BEAT HAPPENING RECORD: O.K. A *lot* of people I know think that Olympia's **Beat Happening** suck. I don't. I think they're unique, charming and lyrically brilliant. Opponents usually slag their "cuteness" and Calvin's off-key baritone. Certainly, it's obvious that their pop is primitive and that they don't practice a whole lot. But so what. For those who care, **Beat Happening**'s latest LP, *Jamboree,* deserves a PG rating, as it is wilder than the G-rated innocence of their last LP and two

BUY THE NEW WALKABOUTS ALBUM: The *Walkabouts* have cornered the sensitive, liberal folk/rock market in Seattle and are now ready for world domination. *See Beautiful Rattlesnake Gardens* is an excellent record. The arrangements are carefully thought out and never over-stated. The "warm" production also shows a good ear for the natural acoustics of a room; many recordings in the '80s are typically sterile and lifeless: this is not. And, amazingly, the lyrics are often poetic, encouraging the listener to actually play the thing more than once. This is not a disposable piece of pop fluff. My only complaint is that the Celtic folk-maiden vocal style of Carla Torgerson is too deeply rooted in the Irish peasant tradition to sound indigenous to this country; and frankly, that bugs me. In short, however, this record is "tasteful," which means mass airplay and heavy sales in sensitive, liberal college towns. **(Popllama: Box 95364, Seattle, WA 98145-2364.)**

singles. Yes, surprise, *Jamboree* ROCKS: there's some noisy guitar feedback and even a guest/appearance by the awesome Lee Conner, guitarist with **The Screaming Trees**. But to people who listen to X-rated bands like **Big Black** and **the Swans**, **Beat Happening** will seem quaint and old fashioned: Nobody in this Donna Parker universe ever gets pregnant or smokes crack. The people in Calvin's songs *bake pies* and *play croquet* and go *swimming in the lake*. The songs are simple, but the simplicity is deceptive: Calvin reworks myth-

BUY THE NEW SWANS ALBUM: The Swans, who stunned the world with songs like "Raping a Slave," have seen the light and gone New Age. Yes, the heaviest band in the world, infamous for their crushing minimalism and lyrics about sexual and economic domination, have a double LP of religious propaganda called **Children of God**. The music employs post-hippy New Age trademarks such as flutes, angelic choirs and sound affects from nature, such as waterfalls. All of this serves to evoke some mystical, heavenly Garden of Eden. The good news is that this is the richest, most texturally sophisticated Swans disc to date. The Swans have always been about one thing: power. They have not abandoned that premise. The Swans have simply integrated their brutality with tenderness. Their world-view is now fuller, more dynamic and more complex. **Children of God** is loud and soft, passive and aggressive. It's the heaviest record since **Jesus Christ Superstar**. PICK HITS: "Beautiful Child" and "Sex, God, Sex." **(Caroline: 5 Crosby St., NYC, NY 10013.)**

ical pop images of the **AMERICAN TEEN** in abstract and symbolic ways that truly display genius. He captures the awkwardness of adolescence more incisively than any singer/songwriter since Jonathan Richman of the **Modern Lovers**. Beat Happening is an important band. They have a strong identity. They have received international media attention and with **Jamboree** they will continue to do so. The LP is available on 53rd & 3rd in the U.K. and Rough Trade/K in the U.S. **(Rough Trade, 326 6th St., S.F., CA 94103.)**

OTHER STUFF TO CHECK OUT:
AFRICAN HEAD CHARGE *Off the Beaten Track* LP *(ON-U)* **U.K.**
WHITE ZOMBIE *Soul Crusher* LP *(Silent Explosion)* **NYC**
FLESH AND BONES *fanzine* **NYC**

SWELLSVILLE *fanzine* **Seattle**
OPINION RAG *cool design and packaging from this* **Seattle** *mag*
LIVE SKULL *Dusted* LP *(Homestead)* **NYC**
JACK YR BODY PARTY *coming in March*
PELL MELL *Bumper Crop* LP *(SST)* **S.F.**

"Killdozer is populist, small-town, and working class. Michael Gerald sings songs about real men: meat packers and golden glove boxers and grain elevator operators. His men play chords and pound beers and knock heads! On *Little Baby Buntin'*, their fourth record, the noisy guitar band with the funny redneck anthems add a different twist. Just as Elvis went from humble trucker to rhinestone cowboy, Killdozer grows up and gives a nod to Las Vegas schlock."

and two singles. Yes, surprise, *Jamboree* rocks: there's some noisy guitar feedback, and even a guest appearance by the awesome Lee Conner, guitarist with the **SCREAMING TREES**. But to people who listen to X-rated bands like **BIG BLACK** and the **SWANS**, Beat Happening will seem quaint and old-fashioned. Nobody in this Donna Parker universe ever gets pregnant or smokes crack. The people in Calvin's songs bake pies and play croquet and go swimming in the lake. The songs are simple, but the simplicity is deceptive. Calvin reworks mythical pop images of the *American teen* in abstract and symbolic ways that truly display genius. He captures the awkwardness of adolescence more incisively than any singer/songwriter since Jonathan Richman of the **MODERN LOVERS**. Beat Happening is an important band. They have a strong identity. They have received international media attention and with *Jamboree* they will continue to do so.

SUB POP SUNDAY

SNOWBUD and the **FLOWER PEOPLE** from Portland! Also: debut of the **GIRL TROUBLE** video! At the Vogue on February 28.

OTHER STUFF TO CHECK OUT

AFRICAN HEAD CHARGE (U. K.) *Off the Beaten Track* LP (ON-U)

WHITE ZOMBIE (NYC) *Soul Crusher* LP (Silent Explosion)

Flesh and Bones (NYC) fanzine

Swellsville (Seattle) fanzine

Opinion Rag cool design and packaging from this Seattle mag

LIVE SKULL (NYC) *Dusted* LP (Homestead)

Jack Yr Body party (Seattle) coming in March

PELL MELL (SF) *Bumper Crop* LP (SST)

Seven Days With Me, Bruce Pavitt

SATURDAY

I spent Saturday in San Francisco. I was visiting my friend Anne and her roommate Angela. They had just moved away from Seattle, because they felt there were few opportunities for artistic development. Plus there are a lot more guys down here. After checking out *Hairspray* (the most subversive family film since *Pee-wee's Big Adventure*), we caught a bus and rode down to Filmore and Haight. In a two-block area, we visited four bars, including a new age "water bar" that served over forty brands of mineral water from around the world. We sat in beanbag chairs and watched cloud formations on TV. It was fun, until a cluster of young lawyers came in and changed the channel. After that, we walked down a few blocks and discovered a record store that only sold classic soul 45s. Upon entering, I noticed three young women, all with jet-black hair, debating over which **BARRY WHITE** single to buy. Myself, I was happy to find an original Volt copy of "Whatcha See is Whatcha Get" by the **DRAMATICS**. I left the neighborhood feeling very excited and impressed.

SUNDAY

Anne and I took the subway to Berkeley for a punk rock record convention. It was being sponsored by *Maximum Rocknroll* magazine, and was being held at the Gilman Street hangout/all-ages club that they started. Once there, I sold some old hardcore/punk rock singles—**LOCKJAW, RUDIMENTARY PENI, SUBHUMANS**—and picked up some cool bootleg 45s, like a live recording of **SONIC YOUTH** singing "I Wanna be Your Dog" with Iggy Pop barking like a dog at the end of the song. Civilization doesn't get any more exciting.

MONDAY

Angela and I took a ferry boat to Alcatraz Island. We toured the infamous prison and read about several brilliant escape attempts. I left convinced that our prisons contain some very creative people. Perhaps *Zero Hour*, the new local mag whose byline reads "Where Culture Meets Crime," can tap into some philosophers over at Washington State Penitentiary in Walla Walla.

TUESDAY

Today I'm back at Muzak, here in Seattle. They've hired a new guy named Phillip; he moved here from Jamaica six years ago. Right now, he's putting together a sound system so he can DJ some *heavy dub* parties. He went to high school with **EEK-A-MOUSE** so I guess he knows his stuff. I predict there will be heavy clouds of ganja this summer.

WEDNESDAY

I got a copy of the new **GIRL TROUBLE** demo in the mail today. It sounds great. They recorded it over in Ellensburg, Washington, using antique effects but recording the whole thing digitally—the best of two worlds. Also got a note from California. The **BEAT HAPPENING** tour is going well, except for a recent coffeehouse show. The band had to leave because they were "too loud." They finished the show in front of a laundromat, unamplified. Their new album was just named "Rock Record of the Week" by the *New York Times*.

S·U·B P·O·P

P.O. BOX 20645, Seattle, WA 98102

Limited edition color vinyl LP or chrome cassette with extra track available for 8 bucks ppd.

GREEN RIVER
Rehab Doll

ALSO OUT		COMING SOON
BLOOD CIRCUS TWO WAY STREET/SIX FOOT UNDER 45 on red vinyl **3 BUCKS**	**SWALLOW** GUTS/ TRAPPED 45 on yellow vinyl **3 BUCKS**	from Denver **THE FLUID** CLEAR BLACK PAPER LP **8 BUCKS**

ALSO AVAILABLE

SUB POP 100 compilation **LP/CASSETTE**
with U-MEN, WIPERS, STEVE FISK, SONIC YOUTH
and more
8 BUCKS
GREEN RIVER DRY AS A BONE **EP**
awesome STOOGES/AEROSMITH grunge
5 BUCKS

6 Songs 12 Inches 5 Bucks

SubPop

SEVEN DAYS WITH ME, BRUCE PAVITT

SATURDAY: I spent Saturday in San Francisco. I was visiting my friend Anne and her roommate Angela. They had just moved away from Seattle because they felt there were few opportunities for artistic development. Plus there are a lot more guys down here. After checking out *Hairspray* (the most subversive family film since *Pee Wee's Big Adventure*) we caught a bus and rode down to Filmore and Haight. In a two-block area, we visited four bars, including a New Age "water bar" that served over forty brands of mineral water from around the world. We sat in bean bag chairs and watched cloud formations on TV. It was fun until a cluster of young lawyers came in and changed the channel. After that, we walked down a few blocks and discovered a record store that only sold classic soul 45s. Upon entering, I noticed three young women, all with jet black hair, debating over which Barry White single to buy. Myself, I was happy to find an original Volt copy of "Watcha See is Watcha Get" by The Dramatics. I left the neighborhood feeling very excited and impressed.

SUNDAY: Anne and I took the subway to Berkeley for a Punk Rock record convention. It was being sponsored by *Maximum Rock N Roll* magazine and was being held at the Gilman Street hangout/all ages club that they started. Once there, I sold some old hardcore/ punk rock singles — *Lockjaw, Rudimentary Peni, Subhumans* — and picked up some cool bootleg 45s: like a live recording of **Sonic Youth** singing *I Wanna be Your Dog* with **Iggy Pop** barking like a dog at the end of the song. Civilization doesn't get any more exciting.

MONDAY: Angela and I took a ferry boat to Alcatraz Island. We toured the infamous prison and read about several brilliant escape attempts. I left convinced that our prisons contain some very creative people. Perhaps **Zero Hour**, the new local mag whose byline reads *Where Culture Meets Crime*, can tap into some philosophers over at Walla Walla.

TUESDAY: Today I'm back at Muzak, here in Seattle. They've hired a new guy named Phillip; he moved here from Jamaica six years ago. Right now, he's putting together a sound system so he can d.j. some HEAVY DUB parties. He went to high school with **Eek A Mouse** so I guess he knows his stuff. I predict there will be heavy clouds of ganja this summer.

WEDNESDAY: I got a copy of the new **Girl Trouble** demo in the mail today. It sounds great. They recorded it over in Ellensberg, using antique effects but recording the whole thing digitally — the best of both worlds. Also got a note from California. The **Beat Happening** tour is going well except for a recent coffee house show: the band had to leave because they were "too loud." They finished the show in front of a laundromat, unamplified. Their new album was just named **Rock Record of the Week** by *The New York Times*.

 THURSDAY: I don't remember what I did today.

FRIDAY: My last and final day at **Muzak** corporation. They threw a party, which was wild. All my co-workers were there: Tad from **H-Hour**, Chris from **Swallow**, Ron from **Room Nine**, Grant from **The Walkabouts**, Mark from **Mudhoney**. They all work at Muzak. Muzak serves as a think tank for alternative youth culture. Of course none of these guys have anything to do with the programming, but it's nice to know that the Muzak paycheck keeps them alive. There were snacks and Tequila. *I Wanna be Your Dog* was blasting at full volume and the president of Muzak shook my hand.

SUBTEN

1. **STEVE FISK** *448 Deathless Days* LP (SST)
2. **U-MEN** *Freeze Bomb* 45 (Amphetamine Reptile)
3. **RICH JENSON** *Two Million Years* cassette (K)
4. **BUNDLE OF HISS** *demo*
5. **PANDEMONIUM II** *book* (with John Waters, Charles Manson, John Hinckley, John Gacy)
6. **COVERT ACTION INFORMATION BULLETIN** *magazine*
7. early **AUGUSTUS PABLO** *recordings*
8. **ALCATRAZ FEDERAL PENITENTIARY** *brochure*
9. **THE HOME BREW PARTY** where The Walkabouts played in some professor's mansion and everybody tripped on liquid acid.
10. **THY KINGDOM COME** *Documentary*

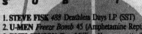

 SUB POP SUNDAY: March 27 at The Vogue. Featuring **Doll Squad**.

THURSDAY

I don't remember what I did today.

FRIDAY

My last and final day at Muzak corporation. They threw a party, which was wild. All my co-workers were there: Tad from **H-HOUR**, Chris from **SWALLOW**, Ron from **ROOM NINE**, Grant from the **WALK-ABOUTS**, Mark from **MUDHONEY**. They all work at Muzak. Muzak serves as a think tank for alternative youth culture. Of course none of these guys have anything to do with the programming, but it's nice to know that the Muzak paycheck keeps them alive. There were snacks and tequila. "I Wanna be Your Dog" was blasting at full volume and the president of Muzak shook my hand.

SUB TEN

1. **STEVE FISK** *488 Deathless Days* LP (SST)

2. **U-MEN** "Freeze Bomb" 45 (Amphetamine Reptile)

3. **RICH JENSON** *Two Million Years* cassette (K)

4. **BUNDLE OF HISS** demo

5. *Pandemonium II* book (with **JOHN WATERS**, **CHARLES MANSON**, **JOHN HINCKLEY**, **JOHN GACY**)

6. *Covert Action Information Bulletin* magazine

7. early **AUGUSTUS PABLO** recordings

8. *Alcatraz Federal Penitentiary* brochure

9. The home brew party where the **WALKABOUTS** played in some professor's mansion, and everybody tripped on liquid acid.

10. *Thy Kingdom Come* documentary

SUB POP SUNDAY

March 27 at The Vogue. Featuring **DOLL SQUAD**.

Everything You Heard Is True

Everything you heard is true. We rule. Per capita, Washington State is currently unleashing the thickest torrent of **ROCK** in the United States.

A. I just saw **CAT BUTT** at the Vogue the other night. This backwoods clan of losers and derelicts drink to insanity, and have to be considered heavyweights in the arena of *sweat*. Transcendence and ecstasy in hillbilly punk-rock heaven. Their new 45, out on some California label, is probably out *now*. And it's probably *real good*. If you don't have this record, at least ask David to show you the **BAY CITY ROLLERS** patch on his jean jacket.

B. Fans of the **U-MEN** would do well to check out a record from Australia called **LUBRICATED GOAT** *Plays the Devil's Music*. It rock in a gritty, R&B sorta way, but is full of weird twists. By the way, the most recent U-Men 45—"Freezebomb"—is a runaway hit and features Gnostic chanting, perhaps an indication of their new found spiritual commitment (i.e. sex, drugs, rock 'n roll). Their new LP is almost finished. Val says it's good.

C. TAD. Tad Doyle, former drummer for the disbanded **H-HOUR**, is a big man and has been working as my bodyguard ever since I started receiving death threats from various lame local bands (you know who you are). In addition to his bodyguard duties, Tad has been working on some demos over at Reciprocal Studios. The result is *amazing*. Tad plays all instruments and can even sing and write intelligent lyrics. Expect a 45 by June.

D. Karl "Wheat Paste" Krogstad had just produced the new **BOOM BOOM G.I.** video. I just hope it's better than their live show.

E. The **WALKABOUTS** will be touring the West Coast this Spring in promotion of their *See Beautiful Rattlesnake Garden* LP. Drummer Grant "Rainbow Assortment" Eckman will continue to pursue "marketing research" in the Bay Area.

F. So what if they smoke pot? **BLOOD CIRCUS** rocks as hard as **CREEDENCE** and **MOTÖRHEAD** in a head-on train wreck. Watch.

G. The **SCREAMING TREES** will be releasing their fourth LP, *Invisible Lantern*, on SST. Sounds like guitarist Gary Lee Conner has been listening to **HENDRIX** and **RON ASHETON**. Yet another rock 'n roll *hit* from this world-class act.

H. Brain booster **STEVE FISK** recently drove from Ellensburg to record a 12" for the ultra-"commercial" **SOUNDGARDEN**. expect some radical production.

I. Fans of **ROOM NINE** will want to check out an LP by the **SHAMEN** called *Drop*. The band is from Ireland, and they play moody psychedelic pop. It's available in the States through Georgia's Fundamental label. Room Nine will be back in the studio to record more material for the Louisiana label, C'est La Mort. However, the band will *not* be marketing a new designer drug called Space Base.

"Tad Doyle, former drummer for the disbanded H-Hour, is a big man and has been working as my bodyguard ever since I started receiving death threats from various lame local bands. (You know who you are.) In addition to his bodyguard duties, Tad has been working on some demos over at Reciprocal Studios. The result is *amazing*. Tad plays all instruments and can even sing and write intelligent lyrics. Expect a 45 by June."

SUBPOP

BY BRUCE PAVITT

IN YOUR FACE

EVERYTHING YOU HEARD IS TRUE. We rule. Per capita, Washington State is currently unleashing the thickest torrent of ROCK in the U.S.

A. I just saw **CAT BUTT** at the Vogue the other night. This backwoods clan of losers and derelicts drink to insanity, and have to be considered heavyweights in the arena of SWEAT. Transcendence and ecstasy in hillbilly punk-rock heaven. Their new 45, out on some California label, is probably out NOW. And it's probably REAL GOOD. If you don't buy this record, at least ask David to show you the Bay City Rollers patch on his jean jacket.

B. Fans of the **U-MEN** would do well to check out a record from Australia called *Lubricated Goat Plays the Devil's Music*. It rocks in a gritty, R&B sorta way, but is full of weird twists. By the way, the most recent U-Men 45 — *Freezebomb* — is a runaway hit and features Gnostic chanting, perhaps an indication of their new found spiritual commitment (i.e., sex, drugs, rock 'n' roll). Their new LP is almost finished. Val says it's good.

C. **TAD.** Tad Doyle, former drummer for the disbanded **H-Hour,** is a big man and has been working as my bodyguard ever since I started receiving death threats from various lame local bands (you know who you are). In addition to his bodyguard duties, Tad has been working on some demos over at Reciprocal Studios. The results are AMAZING. Tad plays all instruments and can even sing and write intelligent lyrics. Expect a 45 by June.

D. Karl "Wheat Paste" Krogstad has just produced the new **BOOM BOOM G.I.** video. I just hope it's better than their live show.

E. **THE WALKABOUTS** will be touring the West Coast this Spring in promotion of their *See Beautiful Rattlesnake Garden* LP. Drummer Grant "Rainbow Assortment" Eckman will continue to pursue "marketing research" in the Bay Area.

F. So what if they smoke pot? **BLOOD CIRCUS** rocks as hard as Creedence and Motorhead in a head-on train wreck. Watch.

G. **THE SCREAMING TREES** will be releasing their fourth LP, *Invisible Lantern*, on SST. Sounds like guitarist Gary Lee Conner has been listening to Hendrix and Rou Ashton. Yet another rock 'n' roll HIT from this world-class act.

H. Brain booster **STEVE FISK** recently drove in from Ellensburg to record a 12" for the ultra-"commercial" **SOUNDGARDEN**. expect some radical production.

I. Fans of **ROOM NINE** will want to check out an LP by **THE SHAMEN** called *Drop*. The band is from Ireland and they play moody, psychedelic pop. It's available in the States through Georgia's Fundamental label. **ROOM NINE** will be back in the studio to record more material for the Louisiana label, C'est La Mort. However, the band will NOT be marketing a new designer drug called *Space Base*.

THE THROWN UPS, those ugly guys in lime tuxedos you keep seeing all over town, have just recorded their third 45 and man does it SUCK. The band you love to hate.

LOUD THINGS YOU'LL WANT NOW:

BIRDCRASH cassette compilation

(K). Non-Seattle comp featuring sensitive vocal ramblings from primitive genius "Spook." Beyond trendy.

AWAY FROM THE PULSEBEAT fanzine. Includes godhead 45 featuring Red Kross (U.S.), Broken Jug (W. Germany), Nikki Sudden (U.K.), and feed-time (Australia).

BIG BLACK "Peel Session" bootleg 45. Impossible to find so don't bother.

TRAGIC MULATTO *Locos Por El Sexo* LP (Alternative Tentacles). Sure, I've heard the "fast lesbian" angle. So what? Totally under-rated disc for Butthole Surfers groupies. Cool.

DIDJITS *Hey Judester* LP (Touch & Go). Corn-cob rock from Illinois, without which your party will be DULL. Buy.

OFRA HAZA *Fifty Gates of Wisdom* LP (Shanachie). Enchanting Middle Eastern pop-disco via Israel.

DAVE KUSWORTH *The Bounty Hunters* LP (Texas Hotel). Whiny love songs from the U.K. Excellent.

AFRICAN RUBBER DUB LP (Revolver). Adrian "On-U" Sherwood goes dubwise in Jamaica. Heavy.

THE VASELINES *Teenage Superstar* EP (53rd & 3rd). Sweet girl/guy punk rock combo.

PIXIES *Surfer Rosa* LP (4AD/Rough Trade U.S.). Mild mannered "rock" from Boston. Produced by Steve Albini. Naked lady on cover.

SUB POP SUNDAY

THE DERELICTS
The Vogue
Sunday, May 29

THE THROWN UPS, those ugly guys in lime tuxedos you keep seeing all over town, have just recorded their third 45, and man does it *suck*. The band you love to hate.

LOUD THINGS YOU'LL WANT NOW

VARIOUS *Birdcrash* cassette compilation (K Records) Non-Seattle comp featuring sensitive vocal ramblings from primitive genius "Spook." Beyond trendy.

Away From the Pulsebeat fanzine. Includes godhead 45 featuring **REDD KROSS** (US), **BROKEN JUG** (West Germany), **NIKKI SUDDEN** (UK), and **FEEDTIME** (Australia).

BIG BLACK *Peel Sessions* bootleg 45. Impossible to find so don't bother.

TRAGIC MULATTO *Locos por el Sexo* LP (Alternative Tentacles) Sure, I've heard the "fat lesbian" angle. So what? Totally underrated disc for , groupies. Cool.

DIDJITS *Hey Judester* LP (Touch and Go) Corn-cob rock from Illinois, without which your party will be *dull*. Buy.

OFRA HAZA *Fifty Gates of Wisdom* LP (Shanachie) Enchanting Middle Eastern pop-disco via Israel.

DAVE KUSWORTH *The Bounty Hunters* LP (Texas Hotel). Whiny love songs from the UK. Excellent.

VARIOUS *African Rubber Dub* LP (Revolver) Adrian "On-U" Sherwood goes dubwise in Jamaica. Heavy.

THE VASELINES *Teenage Superstar* EP (53rd & 3rd) Sweet girl/guy punk rock combo.

PIXIES *Surfer Rosa* LP (4AD/Rough Trade) Mild-mannered "rock" from Boston. Produced by Steve Albini. Naked lady on cover.

NYC Memories

Hi, i just got off an airplane. this is what **I REMEMBER**.

I REMEMBER sitting in an airplane and reading a book about the CIA and LSD. "By the mid-1960s, nearly fifteen-hundred military personnel had served as guinea pigs in LSD experiments conducted by the US Army Chemical Corps." The book was fascinating.

I REMEMBER taking a subway into the East Village. Chris and I walked over to St. Mark's Pizza and bumped into **SONIC YOUTH**. "You just missed **GWAR**!" said Thurston. (Later I found out that Gwar dress like Conan the Barbarian and have big machines that spit blood.)

I REMEMBER meeting a DJ named Laurie. We had a "rock 'n roll rumble" on her radio show. New York vs. the Pacific Northwest. I started off with **SONICS** and she attacked with the **VELVET UNDERGROUND**. I played the **WIPERS** and she played the **RAMONES**. The rumble lasted two hours. It was a tie.

I REMEMBER my friend Mike was excited because the Frito-Lay company was going to pay him big bucks to take pictures of **LL COOL J** at Radio City Music Hall. The photos would be used as part of a "just say *no* to drugs" campaign. I don't think Frito-Lay would be happy if someone started a "just say *no* to junk food" campaign.

I REMEMBER laying down on a mound of grass in Central Park. I could feel my skin sunburn. A young man walked over to a young woman who was lying down. He tried to make friends with her by saying, "Hey babe, can I borrow your sunglasses?" After she said no, he yelled at her for playing her **MADONNA** tape too loud. He was a jerk.

I REMEMBER going to a hip hop record shop near Times Square. The soundtrack to *Colors* was playing on the turntable. I reached over to look at the new **ICE-T** record and a friendly but assertive black man told me: "You don't want that record." (Ice-T is an L.A. rap superstar who is not popular in New York.) In fact: "Ice-T is not popular anywhere East of Louisianna [sic]."

I REMEMBER buying some potent mushrooms from a guy in a tie-dyed T-shirt. Then Katy, Dave, Chris, Mike, and I went to The Rock and Roll Fag Bar and rocked until four in the morning. Listening to "The Age of Aquarius" on the awesome sound system made the **FIFTH DIMENSION** sound like God.

I REMEMBER meeting two people from **RAGING SLAB**. This is the band that sound like **AEROSMITH** but looks like **BLACK OAK ARKANSAS**. He wore a Jack Daniel's T-shirt and leather bell bottoms. She wore an Annie Green Springs T-shirt and a faded jean jacket. Raging Slab likes to party.

I REMEMBER seeing the **SWANS**. They were boring. Their music was heavy, but they were too cool for their audience. People stood around and acted uncomfortable. The air was thick and there was no ventilation.

I REMEMBER going to Maxwell's in Hoboken, New Jersey. People don't smoke in New Jersey so the air in the club was fresh. People were friendly. **DAS DAMEN** was on stage and they rocked. The DJ played "Le Freak" by **CHIC** and "La Grange" by **ZZ TOP**. Maxwell's and Hoboken are great.

LOUD THINGS THAT YOU WANT

MUDHONEY (Seattle) "In 'n' Out of Grace" demo

UNION CARBIDE PRODUCTIONS (Sweden) *In the Air Tonight* LP (Radium 226.05)

THE BROKEN JUG (Germany) "Sally" 45 (Glitterhouse)

TALL DWARFS *Hello Cruel World* LP (Flying Nun)

WORLD DOMINATION ENTERPRISES (UK) *Let's Play Domination* LP (Caroline)

THE BREAK BOYS (NYC) "And The Break Goes On" 12" (Fourth Floor)

ACID DREAMS: *The CIA, LSD and the Sixties Rebellion* book (Grove Press)

MORAL CRUX (Ellensburg) LP (Velvetone)

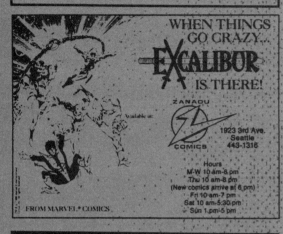

BINARY RECORDS

Featuring the Finest Music
Produced in the Northwest
RECORDS, CASSETTES,
VIDEO'S
Write for FREE Catalog.
P.O. Box 1520 • Bellingham, WA 98227

WHEN THINGS
GO CRAZY...

EXCALIBUR

IS THERE!

ZANADU
COMICS

Available at:
1923 3rd Ave.
Seattle
443-1316

Hours
M-W 10 am-8 pm
Thu 10 am-8 pm
(New comics arrive at 6 pm)
Fri 10 am-7 pm
Sat 10 am-5:30 pm
Sun 1 pm-5 pm

FROM MARVEL® COMICS

S·U·B P·O·P

GREEN RIVER
Rehab Doll

*Limited edition color vinyl LP or
chrome cassette with extra track
available for 8 bucks ppd.*

OUT NOW		COMING SOON
BLOOD CIRCUS	SWALLOW	SOUNDGARDEN
Two Way Street	*Guts/Trapped*	12"
Six Foot Under	45	FLUID
45	on yellow vinyl	LP
on red vinyl	3 bucks	MUDHONEY
3 bucks		45
		TAD
		45

ALSO AVAILABLE

SOUNDGARDEN *Screaming Life* EP 5 bucks
GREEN RIVER *Dry As A Bone* EP 5 bucks
SUB POP 100 compilation LP or cassette 8 bucks
(includes: U-Men, Wipers, Steve Fisk, Sonic Youth and more)

Stores! It's cheaper when you buy direct!
Call Bruce or Jon at (206) 441-8441.

P.O. BOX 20645, Seattle, WA 98102

28 THE ROCKET JUNE 1988

SUB POP

BY BRUCE PAVITT

hi. i just got off an airplane. this is what I REMEMBER.

I REMEMBER meeting a d.j. named Laurie. We had a "rock 'n' roll rumble" on her radio show. New York vs. the Pacific Northwest. I started off with the **Sonics** and she attacked with **The Velvet Underground.** I played the **Wipers** and she played the **Ramones.** The rumble lasted two hours. It was a tie.

I REMEMBER watching Kevin buy a magazine. The magazine had pictures of men with breasts. A homeless person was trying to sell it for five dollars. "We can use one of these pictures for our CD booklet," said Kevin. Kevin is from Austin. His band is called Nice Strong Arm.

I REMEMBER seeing The Swans. They were boring. Their music was heavy but they were too cool for the audience. People stood around and acted uncomfortable. The air was thick and there was no ventilation.

MUDHONEY In "n" Out of Grace *demo* Seattle
UNION CARBIDE PRODUCTIONS In the Air Tonight LP *(Radium 226.05)* Sweden
THE BROKEN JUG Sally 45 *(Glitterhouse)* W. Germany
TALL DWARFS Hello Cruel World LP *(Flying Nun)* New Zealand

I REMEMBER taking a subway into the East Village. Chris and I walked over to St. Mark's Pizza and bumped into Sonic Youth. "You just missed GWAR!" said Thurston. (Later I found out that **GWAR** dress like Conan the Barbarian and have big machines that spit blood.)

I REMEMBER laying down on a mound of grass in Central Park. I could feel my skin sunburn. A young man walked over to a young woman who was lying down. He tried to make friends with her by saying: "Hey babe, can I borrow your sunglasses?" After she said no, he yelled at her for playing her Madonna tape too loud. He was a jerk.

I REMEMBER buying some potent mushrooms from a guy in a tie die t-shirt. Then Katy, Dave, Chris, Mike and I went to **The Rock and Roll Fag Bar** and rocked until four in the morning. Listening to "The Age of Aquarius" on an awesome sound system made the **Fifth Dimension** sound like God.

I REMEMBER going to Maxwell's in Hoboken, New Jersey. People don't smoke in New Jersey so the air in the club was fresh. People were friendly. Das Damen was on stage and they rocked. The d.j. played "Le Freak" by Chic and "La Grange" by ZZ Top. Maxwell's and Hoboken are great.

LOUD THINGS THAT YOU WANT

I REMEMBER sitting in an airplane and reading a book about the CIA and **LSD.** "By the mid-1960s nearly fifteen hundred military personnel had served as guinea pigs in LSD experiments conducted by the US Army Chemical Corps." The book was fascinating.

I REMEMBER my friend Mike was excited because the Frito-Lay company was going to pay him big bucks to take pictures of **LL Cool J** at Radio City Music Hall. The photos would be used as part of a "just say no to drugs" campaign. I don't think Frito-Lay would be happy if somebody started a "just say no to junk food" campaign.

I REMEMBER going to a hip hop record shop near Times Square. The soundtrack to Colors was playing on the turntable. I reached over to look at the new **Ice T** record and a friendly but assertive black man told me: "You don't want that record." (Ice T is an L.A. rap superstar who is not popular in New York.) In fact: "Ice T is not popular anywhere east of Louisianna."

I REMEMBER meeting two people from Raging Slab. This is the band that sounds like Aerosmith but looks like Black Oak Arkansas. HE wore a Jack Daniels t-shirt and leather bell bottoms. SHE wore an Annie Green Springs t-shirt and a faded jean jacket. Raging Slab likes to party.

WORLD DOMINATION ENTERPRISES Let's Play Domination LP *(Caroline)* U.K.
THE BREAK BOYS And The Break Goes On 12" *(Fourth Floor)* NYC.
ACID DREAMS The CIA, LSD and the Sixties Rebellion book *(Grove Press)*
MORAL CRUX LP *(Velvetone)* Ellensburg.

DESIGN BY

What's Hot and What Sucks?

CELEBRITY POLL

Hey everybody. It's *hot* outside and I'm lazy. This month *you* write the column by answering basic marketing information. Namely: what's *hot* and what *sucks*?

TIM (the guy at Fallout Records store with the tattoo): *Hey Judester* by the **DIDJITS** is *hot*. The **ODD MAN OUT** LP totally *sucks*.

LORI (edits *Flaccid* mag in Eugene): *hot*? 1. *The Best of Roy Clark*. 2. **GORE** (Fundamental reissue) 3. **GALAXY 500** 7" called "Tugboat." *sucks*? 1. "classic rock" trend in radio. 2. **BITCH MAGNET**'s manager: "the epitome of suckation." 3. Running out of clean underwear.

SLAM (music fan often mistaken for a serial killer): "Freezebomb" by the **U-MEN** is *hot*. "Kerosene" by **BIG BLACK** is *hot*. **GREEN RIVER** broke up and that *sucks*. There's no regular all-ages clubs, and that *sucks*, too. Oh yeah, the **MELVINS** break-up *sucks*.

KURT (bass player from **BUNDLE OF HISS** who just started growing sideburns): **THE HEAD OF DAVID** *Dustbowl* LP is *hot*. What *sucks*? A broken chain saw *sucks*.

FAITH (music director at **KCMU**) *hot*: **MUDHONEY** and **GOSPEL AT COLONUS** reissue (Nonesuch). *sucks* —People who snort coke in the bathroom when you need to pee.

TOM (Green Monkey label czar): The Detroit Pistons and the Life are *hot*. George Bush *sucks*.

JON (sleazy record executive): *hot*? Madagascar cuisine. *sucks*? The *Sub Pop* column.

ART (editor of *Away from the Pulsebeat* mag, New York): The new **BEAT HAPPENING/SCREAMING TREES** collaboration on Homestead is *hot*. **ALWAYS AUGUST**; why do they have records? And who would want to buy a **PAINTED WILLIE** album? They *suck*.

STEVE (guitar player with the **THROWN UPS**, obsessive record collector, potential college drop-out): **BLUE CHEER** and **BILLY CHILDISH** and shows at the Alamo are *hot*. New **TAR BABIES** and **MEAT PUPPETS** *suck*.

MARK (guy who was booted out of **GREEN RIVER** for being a poseur): the **WIPERS** *Land of the Lost* has been on my turntable a lot. *Punch N Judy* by Denver's the **FLUID**. *Everybody Knows this is Nowhere* by **NEIL YOUNG**. Yes, these records are *hot*. *sucks*? Tony "7-inch Snake" and Promocide Productions because he has no respect for local bands. Sydney (a.k.a. worm-doll-baby): **TAD** is *totally hot*. This guy is going to be a star. *sucks*? The doorman at the Central who uses the electric shocker. And commercial art schools.

SUZY (glamorous retail clerk): Clothes that look like underwear are *hot*. **JAY WARD**, the genius behind *Rocky and Bullwinkle* is *hot*. Stubble is lame. And compact discs *totally suck*.

HEY!!! ALL AGES SUB POP PARTY!!!!

Featuring **MUDHONEY, BLOOD CIRCUS**, plus special guests. *Yes*, it's a psychedelic disco party with punk rock bands *all* packed into the ultra-sweaty Boxing Club next to the Comet Tavern right off of Broadway and Pike. Only five bucks. Oh yeah, it's on Friday, July 8. And remember: no blotter or naked table dancing, or else we'll have to close early.

By the end of the column, I felt that writing about Sub Pop Records was a conflict of interest. It was hard. I did review records that I had put out myself, but it became uncomfortable to promote records that I really believed in and that I thought were good. I could only pump up Green River, Mudhoney, and Soundgarden as much as I did so many times. *Sub Pop starting out as a mission to cover the scene, but it became the scene.*

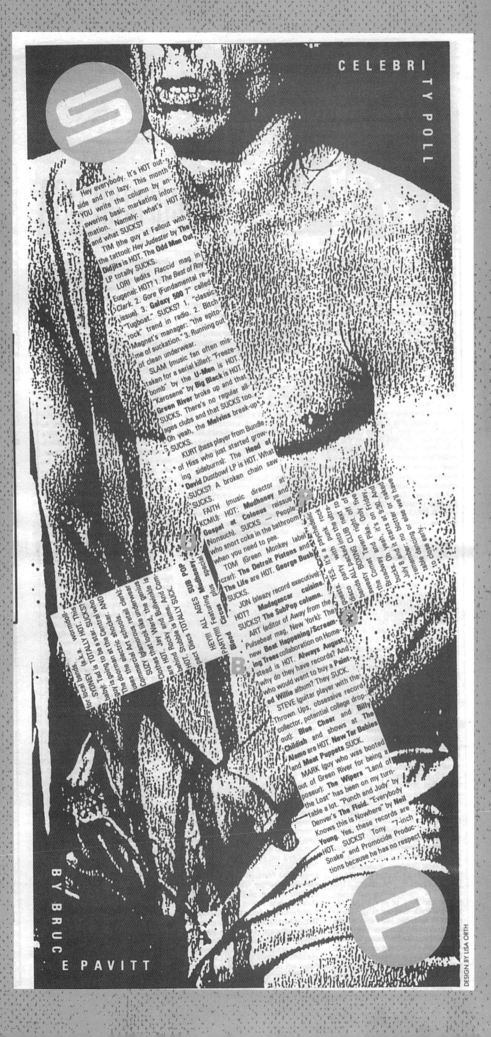

DESIGN BY LISA ORTH

From top: Sonic Youth, Daydream Nation *photo shoot, New York City, July 1988; Mudhoney, "Touch Me I'm Sick" photo shoot, Seattle, July 1988. Mudhoney is one of the greatest rock 'n roll bands I have ever seen. They were at peak form right out of the box, with the "Touch Me I'm Sick" 7" and* Superfuzz Bigmuff *E.P. Mark Arm and Steve Turner were both record scholars and turned me on to a lot of great music. With their irreverence, spontaneity, and charm, they quickly built a national buzz and helped put Seattle on the map. They are still rocking it, twenty-five years later.* **PHOTOS BY MICHAEL LAVINE**

It Was an Epic Time

I am still grateful for the opportunity to write for the *Rocket*. The *Rocket* was an amazing paper that never really got the respect that it deserved. Besides being an excellent free alternative music monthly with great writing, it had an art department that was very advanced and always staffed with talented designers. Since this paper was distributed throughout Washington State, my column was read by fans and musicians not just in Seattle but also in the many surrounding small towns. For example, Kurt Cobain was able to pick up copies in his home town of Aberdeen.

My Sub Pop column ended in July 1988, as I was becoming extremely busy with the Sub Pop label. Several legendary shows happened during that month. On July 2, Mudhoney, Soundgarden, and the Fluid played at the Central Tavern in Seattle's Pioneer Square. A fan from Brooklyn, Ed McGinley, heard about the event beforehand and embarked on a three-thousand-mile Greyhound bus trip just to see those bands. That was the moment I realized Seattle was going to be huge. Six days later, Mudhoney played at the Boxing Club on Capitol Hill and compounded my excitement. So the Sub Pop column really ended just as the Seattle scene really started to get some traction.

Later that July, Jon Poneman and I went to New York to check out the New Music Seminar. I got to spend time with my friend, the photographer Michael Lavine. He had just been in Seattle to shoot some Mudhoney photos for their upcoming "Touch Me I'm Sick" 45. He showed me some images he had just taken of Sonic Youth for their *Daydream Nation* LP. Both bands were destined to work together and to rise on a coming tide of wild American independent rock.

In November of 1988, Sub Pop released the debut single, "Love Buzz," by Aberdeen, Washington–based Nirvana. In December, Sonic Youth and Mudhoney released a split single on Sub Pop; the two bands toured Europe together, which set the stage for Mudhoney's breakthrough in popularity there. The fall 1989 conquest of Europe by three Sub Pop bands— Mudhoney, Tad, and Nirvana—is a separate story, explored in my book *Experiencing Nirvana: Grunge in Europe, 1989*.

During the sweep of a decade, *Sub Pop* had morphed from a radio show to a zine to a mixtape to a newspaper column to an internationally recognized record label closely identified with independent values and a previously sleepy but wild corner of the United States.

It was an epic time.

Band Index

Contributors

I first met **CHARLES R. CROSS** when he took over as editor at Seattle magazine the *Rocket* in 1986. Since then, Charles has chronicled the stories of Pacific Northwest music legends with his books *Heavier Than Heaven: A Biography of Kurt Cobain* and *Room Full of Mirrors: A Biography of Jimi Hendrix*. His most recent book is *Here We Are Now: The Lasting Impact of Kurt Cobain*.

CALVIN JOHNSON was already a legend when I first arrived at KAOS-FM in 1979. The only teenager in Olympia to have a punk rock radio show, Calvin eventually collaborated with me on *Subterranean Pop*. He then started the K Records empire and created a host of brilliant songs with Beat Happening. His most current music project is the Hive Dwellers.

While visiting Boston in 1982, I was told by the singer of the Neats, a local band, that I had to meet **GERARD COSLOY**. Acting on that tip, I made an effort to meet up with the only 17-year-old writer for the influential *New York Rocker*. As the '80s unfolded, Gerard went on to create *Conflict* fanzine. He worked with a number of indie acts as the head of Homestead Records. He is currently a partner in Matador Records.

ANN POWERS was one of my favorite colleagues at the *Rocket* in the mid-1980s. After her work in Seattle, she went on to write for the *New York Times* and the *Village Voice*. She coedited the book, *Rock She Wrote: Woman Write About Rock, Pop and Rap*. She currently writes for NPR Music, and is a contributor for the *Los Angeles Times*.

LARRY REID was the first person I met in Seattle (1980). One of the founders of the infamous Rosco Louie Gallery, Larry was an early supporter of visual artists Lynda Barry and Charles Burns. After the gallery closed in 1982, the always provocative Mr. Reid helped host shows performed by Big Black, the U-Men, and Nirvana. He founded the Graven Image Gallery and Seattle's Center on Contemporary Art (CoCA). He currently manages the Fantagraphics Bookstore and Gallery in Seattle's Georgetown district.

Every time I went to a show in 1980s Seattle, I would see photographer **CHARLES PETERSON** at the edge of the stage. I was first introduced to his images at a party at the infamous Room 9 house in the spring of '86 and was immediately captivated by his ability to intimately capture the energy of the local scene. His photos helped inspire the creation of the Sub Pop record label, and his books *Touch Me I'm Sick* and *Screaming Life* are essential documents of Seattle rock culture.

Although photographer **MICHAEL LAVINE** was a fellow student at the Evergreen State College in Olympia, I didn't really get to know him until he moved to New York City. Whenever I visited New York, I would crash at Michael's loft in the Bowery, situated just across from CBGB. By 1987, Michael had started photographing portraits of influential NYC art/punk bands like Sonic Youth and Pussy Galore. He also documented Seattle bands when they came through town. Track down his books *Noise From the Underground* and *Grunge*.

In 1981, as an intern at *OP* magazine in Olympia, Washington, I came across a copy of an Oakland, California, zine, *Another Room*, which featured illustrations by an artist named **CHARLES BURNS**. I showed the images to Dana Squires, the *OP* art director, who told me that Charles had been a student in Olympia at the Evergreen State College. With this in mind, I contacted Charles, and his brilliant artwork went on to grace the covers of all three *Sub Pop* mixtapes. Be sure to check out his classic graphic novel, *Black Hole*.

About the Author

Sub Pop founder **BRUCE PAVITT** is the man who made Seattle happen. Although the record label was established in 1986, the Chicago-bred Pavitt started out in 1980 with his *Subterranean Pop* magazine, a name he shortened to *Sub Pop* the following year. Inspired by Rough Trade's alternative approach in the UK, Pavitt began documenting the American alternative and punk rock scene, with a specific focus on smaller cities ignored by the majors and mainstream media. He started the US Indie Chart, and alternated his magazine with mixtapes—compilations of alternative rock, which Rough Trade distributed to record stores around America. Moving to Seattle in 1983, Pavitt helped set up Fallout Records and Skateboards in the bohemian neighborhood of Capitol Hill. In this popular store, records from labels like STT, 4AD, Factory, and Rough Trade were sold beside skateboards and streetwear clothing. Also writing Sub Pop articles for a local newspaper and hosting a Sub Pop radio show on FM radio, Pavitt was both documenting and influencing the local music scene. By 1988, Bruce Pavitt and his new business partner, Jon Poneman, were running a Sub Pop mail-order label out of a one-room office; their first batch of 45s included Green River, Soundgarden, Mudhoney, and Nirvana. And out of this Seattle happening, things began exploding in all directions.

—Gareth Murphy, author, *Cowboys and Indies*

Bruce Pavitt, Seattle, summer 1987

THANK YOU: Ian Christe and Bazillion Points, Dan Burke, John Foster, Calvin Johnson, Bob Newman, Dale Yarger, Charles R. Cross, Larry Reid, Ann Powers, Gerard Cosloy, Charles Peterson, Michael Lavine, Charles Burns, Lynda Barry, Mark Arm, KCMU-FM (KEXP), KAOS-FM, the *Rocket*, Sub Pop Records, Jacob McMurray, and the Experience Music Project.

For my daughter the archivist, **IRIS PARKER PAVITT**

To Whom It May Concern

TheRocket

Rocket Towers
2322 2nd Avenue
Seattle, WA 98121
206 / 728-7625

2/10/86

To Whom It May Concern:

I am writing to recommend Bruce Pavitt, who has worked as the editor of the Sub/Pop column in The Rocket magazine for the past three years. The Rocket is a monthly music and entertainment publication with a circulation of 65,000 in the Seattle/Puget Sound region.

In the time Bruce has produced the Sub/Pop column it has grown to be, in my opinion, one of the most authoritative and influential independent music columns in the country. When Bruce started his column it was the only independent music column in the country in a mass circulation publication. Currently there are a number of other columns, but none with the savvy and passion for the subject that Bruce brings to Sub/Pop.

Bruce brings considerable skill to the column in his ability to synthesize various information and data and still maintain a sense of pursuing a cohesive cultural theory. Bruce has strong opinions on both independent music and popular culture, and he makes sure that these opinions reach the reader. At the same time he covers an extremely broad range of material--certainly one of the broadest and most diverse of any music column I'm familiar with. At the same time, Bruce has managed to find the time to produce a local radio show--also titled Sub/Pop--in conjunction with his column. This weekly show has been literally an audio version of his column, and has been a valuable tool both in promoting his column in the paper and providing his audience with additional information and material.

In addition to his writing and editing skills, Bruce has done considerable work as the design director of the Sub/Pop column. The column's popularity in Seattle has attracted a number of talented designers to work on it....in fact, people practically fight to get the chance to design Sub/Pop. Bruce has set the design tone, recruited individual designers, and organized and collected graphics, drawings and photographs for the column. He has also given designers valuable feedback and direction. The Rocket has attracted a name for its editorial design. Pages from the magazine have been reprinted in Print magazine annuals, and have won numerous local and regional design awards. Past Rocket art directors have gone on to work at Mademoiselle, Vanity Fair, the Village Voice, Metropolis, the Seattle Times and many other publications. We believe that Bruce Pavitt's work--both graphically and editorially--fits into our high standards.

TheRocket

Rocket Towers
2322 2nd Avenue
Seattle, WA 98121
206 / 728-7625

Finally, I should mention Bruce's character points. In his role as Sub/Pop editor, Bruce has been extremely professional, both in manner and performance. He meets deadlines, accepts criticism, is dedicated and enthusiastic. He is always concerned with improved growth and quality in his work, and has always been eager to offer support and help to other areas of the paper.

I would receommend Bruce as a strong addition to any program. He's dedicated, open minded and intelligent--the type of qualities that would benefit any organization.

Please feel free to call me if you need further information.

Yours,

Robert Newman

Robert Newman
Editor, The Rocket

NOW LISTEN TO AN ONGOING ROTATION OF PLAYLISTS INCLUDING MUSIC FROM THE SUB POP ZINES, THE ROCKET COLUMN, AND OTHER INSPIRED SUBTERRANEAN SOURCES:

WWW.SUBPOPUSA.COM

Featuring Ex-members of
Mr. Epp, Deranged Diction + Spluii Numa

GREEN RIVER THE MELVINS

GREY DOOR LOCALS
"R" GANG
FALSE LIBERTY

AUG. 11
SATURDAY · 9PM
The GREY DOOR · $3.

GUN CLUB
U·MEN

†

207
METROPOLIS 2ND AVE. S.
9 PM
$7.50 FRI. JUNE 24

JULY 2nd

ALL PROCEEDS GO TO COVER THE COSTS OF THE July 2nd DEMONSTRATION
AGAINST RACISM, SEXISM, AND U.S. INTERVENTION IN LATIN AMERICA $3

IMP RICHERDS 9:30
MR EPP
U MEN Langston
Hughs
17th & Yesler

BOMBSHELTER VIDEO AND KCMU RADIO
WELCOME FROM N.Y.C.

SONIC YOUTH
WITH SCREAMING TREES
AND MUD HONEY

FRI.
NOV
11
8PM ALL AGES
UNION STATION
@ JACKSON
12.00 ADVANCE
CALL
TICKETMASTER
628-0888

THE CRAMPS
$9
U·MEN TUES JAN 24 8 pm
Any age/any one
Metropolis

Tickets on sale at: Cellophone Square,
Acme Records, and Metropolis
207 Second Avenue S. 382-9495

BLACK FLAG

$5 adv. SACCHARINE TRUST Tues.
Green River Tom Troccoli Sept. 25 MOUNTAINEERS
900 3rd ave. W
Tickets at: Cellophone, Time Travelers, Dreamland, Fallout, Urban Renewal, Rubato BUSES: 1,2,3,15,18,19,24,33

HARDCORE CALIFORNIA
A HISTORY OF PUNK ROCK THROUGH PICTURES AND POSTERS

CURATED BY PETER BELSITO

OPENING FRIDAY THE THIRTEENTH OF APRIL AT 9:00 PM $5
FROM LOS ANGELES
JOHANNA WENT · U-MEN · TARGET VIDEO
WITH TAPE MANIPULATIONS BY MARK WHEATON VIDEO TERMINAL COURTESY OF THE FABULOUS RAINBOW
CLOSING PARTY ON SATURDAY APRIL 21 AT 9:00 PM $5
FROM SAN FRANCISCO
MINIMAL MAN AND 10 MINUTE WARNING
WITH KRISTEN OPPENHEIM
APRIL 13-APRIL 21 GRAVEN IMAGE GALLERY 311 S. WASHINGTON ST.
SPONSORED BY THE ROCKET AND GRAVEN IMAGE

SOUNDGARDEN

MALFUNKSHUN
& MY EYE
Thursday, July 3
at the CENTRAL

SONIC YOUTH
U MEN
GREEN RIVER

JAN 19
saturday
gorilla gardens